INTERNATIONAL BANKING AND FINANCE

By the same author

FOREIGN INVESTMENT, CAPITAL CONTROLS,
AND THE BALANCE OF PAYMENTS (*co-author*)

International Banking and Finance

FRANCIS A. LEES

Director, Business Research Institute,
St John's University, New York

A HALSTED PRESS BOOK

JOHN WILEY & SONS
New York · Toronto

First published in the United Kingdom 1974 by

THE MACMILLAN PRESS LTD
Published in the U.S.A. and
Canada by Halsted Press, a
Division of John Wiley & Sons, Inc.,
New York.

Library of Congress Cataloging in Publication Data

Lees, Francis A
   International banking and finance.

   "A Halsted Press book."
    1. Banks and banking, International.   2. International finance.   I. Title.
   HG3881.L435   332.1'5   73–11884
   ISBN 0–470–52273–9

Printed in Great Britain

To my wife and parents

Contents

List of Tables

List of Illustrations

Preface

Business is one of the most prominent engines of social and economic change. In the past decade and a half the business of banking has itself become transformed into one of these catalysts of growth on a global basis. The multinationalisation of business and banking is but one phase in the many long cycles of economic growth and fluctuations that have gripped the world since the industrial revolution. In the current phase there is a strong likelihood that the socialist and capitalist ideologies will become welded together in a common market web. The Russians have a friend at Chase Manhattan – now located at No. 1 Karl Marx Square, Moscow; the British have the Moscow-Narodny Bank in London; and the Mainland Chinese have Mr Nixon's affirmations of peace and freer trade.

A single volume on international banking can do little more than survey the scene, outline the major elements, and provide a brief but critical analysis of the effectiveness and efficiency of existing institutions and operations. At present international banking is in the midst of a dramatic expansion phase, accompanied by an upheaval in its organisational forms and competitive relationships. It is effecting change, as well as being affected by these changes. As an essential ingredient in the growth of multinational business, development financing, and stabilisation of the world economy, international banking now appears destined to occupy a permanent 'seat on the exchange', after having been made virtually extinct during the excesses of deep depression and catastrophic wars.

This book may be used for several purposes. It is written for the banker and businessman who wishes to obtain a broad picture of what international banking is about, and to understand more clearly how the various aspects of international banking fit together. It is written for the teacher of courses in international finance and investment, international corporate finance, and international banking, who wishes to have a deeper understanding of the organisational approaches, the broad type of lending and investment operations conducted by international banks, and the many financial service areas into which banks have moved. Finally, it is written for the university and special programme student who wishes to dig deeply into an enormously interesting and significant aspect of banking and business.

International Banking and Finance is intended for college and university courses in international finance and international business, at the graduate and upper division undergraduate levels. It would also be appropriate for use in management institutes or executive development programmes in Europe, the United States, or in other countries. While previous background or course work in banking or international economics would be desirable, this volume has been written so that such background is not essential. In this connection this book might be used as a supplement or companion reader in introductory courses in banking and international economics.

Research and writing of this volume was initiated by the author in 1969, largely due to the wide information gap found after searching for specific facts and descriptions of overseas and international banking activities. In the course of researching and collecting information many widely dispersed sources of information had to be consulted. The following acknowledges the helpful assistance of those who provided information, or in other ways materially aided in the preparation of this volume.

A substantial debt is owed to those who generously supplied information concerning operational, regulatory, or other aspects of international banking. This includes Roger A. Hood and Robert E. Mitchell, both Assistant General Counsel, Federal Deposit Insurance Corp.; Paul Horvitz, Division of Research, FDIC; Frederick R. Dahl, Division of Supervision & Regulation, Board of Governors of the Federal Reserve System; Norman Klath, Economics Department, Morgan Guaranty

Trust Co.; Don Cameron, Chase Manhattan Bank; Robert Scully and Richard Capone, United California Bank International, New York; Frank Carlson and Robert F. Cassidy, New York State Banking Department; Zissimos A. Frangopoulos and Karl Bernd, Chemical Bank, New York; Y. C. Jao, Professor of Economics, University of Hong Kong; Bernard Norwood, Division of International Finance, Board of Governors of the Federal Reserve System; Walter Holland, Richard Lee, Joseph Vacca, and Walter Richter, First National City Bank of New York; R. N. Christiansen, International Banking Division, Seattle First National Bank; A. Blake Friscia, Chase Manhattan Bank; Donald E. Pearson, Superintendent of Banks, California; Bertwing C. Mah, Director of Research, California State Banking Department; Roland W. Blaha, Commissioner of Banks and Trust Cos., State of Illinois; John H. Sherman, Chief Deputy, California State Banking Department; Wallace R. Anker, Director of International Division, Comptroller of the Currency; William Boyd, Jr, Pittsburg National Bank, President of Bankers Association for Foreign Trade (1970–71); and Arthur L. Reisch, President of Bankers Association for Foreign Trade (1971–72).

A number of experts and specialists in the field of international finance and banking read various chapters of the book, and offered many helpful comments and suggestions for improvement. These include Fred H. Klopstock, Manager, International Research Department, Federal Reserve Bank of New York; Lee C. Nehrt, Professor of International Business, Indiana University; Charles N. Henning, Graduate School of Business Administration, University of Washington; Sipa Heller, St John's University; and Maximo Eng, St John's University. Residual errors accrue to the author.

Much of the work on data collection and digging into sources was undertaken by several capable graduate assistants, including Kenneth Heard, Joseph Schwartz, and William Marino. Herculean typing efforts were expended by Ethel Angeletti and Margaret Willaum. Finally, a deep debt of gratitude is due to the administration of St John's University and its president, Father Joseph Cahill, for the substantial resource support that was made available to me during my work on the manuscript.

May 1973 FRANCIS A. LEES

I
BACKGROUND
AND REGULATORY
ENVIRONMENT

1 Introduction

Each year the international operations of American banks account for a larger and increasingly important share of their total activities. At year-end 1972, 107 U.S. commercial banks operated 627 overseas branches. At the same time these overseas branches held $80 billion in assets, equivalent to 10 per cent of the domestic assets of all U.S. banks. At year-end 1972 close to 35 per cent of the deposits of New York Clearing House banks resided in their foreign branches. London branches account for approximately 54 per cent of foreign branch assets of American banks, indicating the importance of this financial centre to the international operations of American banks. Reciprocally, American banks hold close to 44 per cent of non-sterling liabilities in U.K. banks, most of which is centered in London, reflecting the dominant position held by American banks in this important financial entrepôt centre. London continues to challenge New York for the lead in international finance. However, New York houses a substantial and growing number of foreign bank branches, agencies and banking corporations. In addition, New York banks hold a major part of the $14 billion of foreign deposits in American banks.

U.S. leadership in international banking is of recent vintage. However, the awakening interest of American banks in international operations goes back to the nineteenth century. Seventy-five years ago, at the turn of the century, the United

States became a major world trader. Shortly later, during World War I, this country became a major international creditor nation. In the years since 1918 the United States has provided a major portion of international investment capital. Today the United States functions as a world banker.

Since World War I the role of world banker has accrued to the United States in a gradual and somewhat intermittent manner. During the 1920s, as a young and relatively inexperienced world banker, the United States committed a number of mistakes. A painful adjustment and amalgamation process took place for some fifteen years thereafter. At the close of the second World War the United States was in a far better position to assume the leadership responsibilities of an international banker than ever before. Until that time it could be said that the international banking activities of American banks had been little more than an appendage.[1] In large measure this volume describes and analyses how U.S. banking institutions have cooperated in the assumption of this leadership responsibility.

A. INTERNATIONAL BANKER AND WORLD BANKER

This volume examines the development of U.S. international banking, the regulatory aspects, methods of organisation for international banking, functions, and future prospects for international banking. International banking is given a relatively broad meaning in this book, and includes overseas banking by U.S. and foreign commercial banks, their branches and affiliates; the role of U.S. and foreign banking institutions in servicing international transactions, flows of funds, and credit needs of American and non-resident customers; and the commercial, investment, and central banking aspects of these operations.

While the United States probably accounts for a major share of the international banking activities in the world, it has also functioned as a world banker. As world banker, the United States assumes obligations that exceed those ordinarily taken on by private sector banks motivated by considerations of profit. The functions of world banker have devolved upon this country by a mixture of circumstances including the financial policies followed by the United States government and the gradual evolution of a certain type of international monetary system. More is said concerning the role and status of the

United States as world banker in Chapter 14, which deals with the benefits and costs for the United States from its world banker role.

International banking activities provide another avenue through which sovereign governments establish and develop unique linkages with one another. The desire on the part of a major U.S. bank to establish a foreign branch or purchase an interest in an overseas banking corporation brings into focus the relative advantages and costs to sovereign nations. American bankers are not unmindful of these considerations—witness the interest in international finance and banking of the American Bankers Association and the Bankers Association for Foreign Trade, and the prominent membership of bankers on the Business Council for International Understanding, the National Foreign Trade Council and similar organisations.

The growth and development of international banking can result in an extension of sovereignty on the part of the host or investing country. For example, in a recent case, the United States Court of Appeals rendered a finding requiring a United States bank with a German branch to reveal information regarding a German client of that branch. The case involved a question of possible price fixing by the German consignor, wherein the U.S. revenue authorities held that the Frankfurt branch of First National City Bank, New York, must produce loan documents that might yield supporting evidence. The New York bank held that compliance with this request would violate German bank secrecy law.[2] Doubtless, FNCB feared revocation of its license by the *Bundesbank*, as well as a possible adverse effect on relations between American banks and their European customers. Finally, other major U.S. banks that intervened on behalf of FNCB recognised the danger that American overseas customers would be disinclined to put their money in overseas branches of U.S. banks. It is reasonable to expect that in future there will be other situations of the type described above.

B.   NATURE OF INTERNATIONAL BANKING ROLE

1. IMPORTANCE OF UNITED STATES

The United States appears to be amply qualified to assume a leading position in international banking. As a creditor nation the United States is able to exchange financial assets with other countries on a basis that satisfies the liquidity and investment requirements of many nations. Moreover, until the foreign exchange crises of 1971 and 1973 this creditor status was supported by a relatively stable currency in which other nations of the world displayed a high degree of confidence.

The world-wide strength and prestige of U.S. international banking institutions is based upon a broad volume of international transactions including foreign trade, where the United States accounts for close to 15 per cent of the world's merchandise trade. In addition, U.S. international transactions for service and capital transfers are important. The United States remains the most important single source of international capital, in recent years providing close to 40 per cent of world development capital, and approximately 25 per cent of the funds invested in foreign and international bond issues.[3]

The magnitude of U.S. foreign investment and short-term lending overseas reflects the massiveness of the U.S. capital markets. The Joint Economic Committee study of U.S. and Western European capital markets published in 1964 provided a direct comparison between these markets, and indicated the importance of size and technical efficiency in facilitating an economic, low-cost allocation and transfer of funds.[4] The institutions and instruments of the money and capital markets, which in the United States focus on New York, permit this country to serve as a leading financial center and international banker for the world.

2. BRIEF OVERVIEW OF INTERNATIONAL BANKING OPERATIONS

American banks have organised themselves to conduct international banking operations along the following general lines. Several hundred of the largest U.S. banks have established international departments or international divisions. These units are located at the head offices of major American banks, and are responsible for carrying out day-to-day operations, and management and supervision of the international activities of the bank that may be conducted from foreign branches or other operating units. Day-to-day operations include purchase and sale of foreign exchange, provision of letter of credit financing for imports and exports, deposit and loan activities for international customers, and servicing transactions for account of foreign correspondent banks.

Over one hundred U.S. banks have established one or more foreign branches. Most of these banks have located a branch in London or Nassau. London has been preferred due to its central position in the international market for loans and deposits. Nassau branches generally afford nearly as good access to international business, with the further advantage of requiring a minimal investment in physical and operational facilities. The foreign branches of American banks conduct a broad range of regular banking transactions for corporate and individual customers of the bank in overseas areas. In addition, they are active in the Eurocurrency market, in which internationally mobile funds may be readily transferred from one country to another. In this capacity their activities resemble those of a money broker. The foreign branches operate in local currencies, U.S. dollars, and other foreign currencies.

Over seventy-five U.S. banks have established Edge Act or Agreement affiliates. These corporations engage in a wide variety of banking and financing functions including those performed at the international division of the parent bank at head office. American banks have established Edge Act affiliates in cities other than the headquarters city of the parent bank. In this way the bank can provide international banking services for customers in various principal centres around the United States. In addition, Edge Act affiliates undertake specialised financing at long-term, and make equity investments for the parent bank in foreign banks, finance companies, and investment companies.

C.   ENVIRONMENTAL ASPECTS

Environmental aspects play an important role in influencing the structure, growth and performance of international banking. In this section we examine two aspects of the international banking activities. In Chapter 2 we further extend our analysis of the regulatory environment by examining the framework of U.S. regulation of international banking.

Table 1.1

Key Statistics relating to the role of the
United States in International Banking

		$ billions		
	1960	*1967*	*1969*	*1972*
GENERAL:				
1. U.S. Merchandise Exports	19.5	30.7	36.5	49.2
2. Size of Eurodollar Market	–	24.8	58.3	131.8
BANK OPERATIONS:				
3. Short-term liabilities to foreigners reported by U.S. Banks	21.3	30.5	40.3	60.7
4. Short-term claims on foreigners reported by U.S. Banks	3.6	8.6	9.6	15.5
5. Dollar acceptances of U.S. Banks	2.0	4.3	5.5	6.9
6. Number of Edge Act Companies	10	46	63	87
OVERSEAS BRANCHES OF U.S. BANKS:				
7. Number of Overseas Branches of Member Banks	124	295	460	627
8. Number of Member Banks with Overseas Branches	8	15	53	107
9. Assets held by Overseas Branches of Member Banks	12.4	15.6	41.1	80.0
10. Liabilities of U.S. Banks to their Foreign Branches	–	4.2	13.0	2.2

Sources: Line 1, U.S. Department of Commerce. Line 2, Bank for International Settlements. Lines 3, 4 and 5, *Federal Reserve Bulletin*. Lines 6, 7, 8, 9, and 10, Board of Governors of the Federal Reserve System.

1. THE INTERNATIONAL MONETARY SYSTEM

Much of the postwar expansion of U.S. international banking has taken place in the short period 1964–71. During this span of years the international monetary system provided an environment conducive to the growth of international banking operations, and tended to be favourable toward U.S. banks operating from a dollar source of domestic funds. Until 1971 the Bretton Woods inspired system of relatively fixed exchange rates, supported by marginal doses of international liquidity available to members of the International Monetary Fund, operated as a major conditioning force. The U.S. dollar stood at the centre of this system, serving as an international monetary standard, source of liquidity, and means of international exchange. A stable relationship between the dollar and gold, and the dollar and other major currencies, provided a basis for rapid expansion of global trade and investment. Steady and persistent injections of dollars into the international flows of funds supported growth of international credit, deposits, and loans. Backed up by the universality of the dollar, American banks enjoyed an unprecedented expansion in their international activities.

The international financial crises of 1971 and 1973, and devaluation of the dollar in these same years, have generated some questions regarding the competitive status of American banks in the future. U.S. banks have attained a wider base of operation via their overseas branch and affiliate representation and we may expect that future development of their operations will be less dependent upon the domestic dollar base.

2. FOREIGN REGULATION

The regulatory environment in overseas areas may differ significantly from that experienced by banks at home. American banks have experienced such differences for the following reasons:

1. the balance between formal and informal regulation varies from country to country
2. the competitive situation

3. differences in attitude regarding the appropriate functions of commercial banks
4. the attitudes of countries toward foreign ownership of banking institutions.

While U.S. regulation of banking has been codified and formalised in written statute, elsewhere regulation is less formal, often consisting of gentlemen's agreements. For example, in Britain banking regulation is by suasion, and banks are generally free from comprehensive regulation and inspection of their activities.[5]

The competitive situation generally varies from one country to another. In some cases legally recognised cartel associations fix many of the terms under which deposits are received and loans are provided.[6] In Australia where foreign banks are not permitted to establish branches, the American banking system is regarded as overly geared toward marketing and the competitive hard sell.

American banks may encounter difficulties abroad simply because of differences in views regarding the proper functions performed by commercial banks. American banks are accustomed to extending medium-term loans, but are not permitted to make direct equity investments. Both of these 'practices' run contrary to banking activities prevalent in many other countries.

Countries differ in their attitudes toward foreign ownership of domestic business and banking institutions. A variety of motives underlie these attitudes. One such motive is the desire to protect culture and economic independence. The Scandinavian countries have long followed a policy of limiting entry of foreign business. For example, in Sweden bank directors and stockholders must be Swedish citizens. In Canada we find a country where the desire to protect a unique culture seems to be an important underlying reason for restricting foreign ownership of domestic banking.

Strategic considerations often enter into the determination of government policy toward foreign ownership. For example India and Japan have made a practice of singling out specific industry sectors as strategic, and therefore limited in the extent of permissible foreign influence. Banking holds an unusually sensitive status in this classification of strategic industries.

Foreign governments have also been motivated by the desire to protect existing institutions. In Australia the expense of operating extensive branch bank systems is one major reason why local bankers are opposed to allowing foreign banks to form branches. The four major trading banks in Australia each operate over one thousand branches, so that every part of the nation has access to banking services. While the Australian trading banks may experience losses on their small branches, the profits earned from foreign exchange business and other services helps support their extensive branch networks. Foreign exchange trading is an area in which the non-bank financial institutions are not allowed to participate.[7]

In the late 1960s a survey taken by the American Bankers Association indicated that there were at least nine countries which by legislation or discretionary policy were closed to further direct American branches or affiliates. Included among these countries were Mexico, Canada, Sweden, Australia, Denmark, Trucial States, Saudi-Arabia, Senegal and Taiwan.

D. A GLOBAL PERSPECTIVE OF INTERNATIONAL BANKING

In this section we examine the growth in number of banks engaged in international banking and their overseas offices, on the basis of country of origin and geographic distribution. In 1955 the Board of Governors of the Federal Reserve System published comprehensive statistics reflecting the number of banks with foreign offices, and the number and location of their foreign offices.[8] The results of this Federal Reserve study indicated that ninety-nine banks, representing approximately twenty nationalities maintained over 1,200 foreign offices in the form of branches, agencies, and representative offices.[9] The study reflected a concentration of foreign facilities in the hands of United Kingdom, Continental European, Canadian, United States, and Rest of Sterling Area banks, in that order. Only forty-six foreign offices or 4 per cent of the total number, were designated as belonging to banks in the 'Other' category (banks with Latin American, Asian, African, and Middle Eastern nationality). In 1954, the year covered by the study, approximately 40 per cent of the foreign facilities were offices of

U.K. banks, and over 30 per cent were offices of Continental European banks. U.S. and Canadian banks each held between 9 and 10 per cent of the foreign offices covered in the study.

An analysis of similar data reflecting the situation in 1968 indicates that in the fourteen year period 1954–68 international banking has enjoyed a considerable expansion. Table 1–2 summarises this growth with data on number of banks with an international orientation, and number of foreign offices by country of parent bank. Several points are highlighted by the statistics in this table.

First, the number of countries whose parent banks enjoy the advantages of foreign offices has increased to approximately forty, a doubling in the fourteen year period. Interest in international banking has become diffused to countries that fall in the less developed category. This is an interesting and highly significant phenomenon. Second, the number of banks with foreign offices has increased to 219. Third, the number of foreign facilities has increased to close to 2,800. These figures indicate a more than doubling of banks and foreign offices involved in international banking.

Fourth, the distribution of foreign banking offices by nationality of parent bank has shifted considerably. In 1968 U.K. banks accounted for 27 per cent of foreign office facilities, down from approximately 40 per cent in 1954. U.S. banks accounted for 18 per cent of foreign facilities, nearly a doubling in relative importance since 1954. Continental European banks experienced a relative decline in importance, with 21 per cent of foreign facilities in 1968. Canadian banks held 7 per cent of foreign facilities in 1968, while Japanese banks held 3 per cent.

Table 1.2

Major Banks with Foreign Offices, 1968
(by Country)

Country of Ownership	Number of Banks with Foreign Offices	Number of Foreign Branches, Agencies, and Representative Offices
United States	31	470
United Kingdom	20	723
Overseas British[a]	5	256
Continental Europe	69	582
France	18	218
Netherlands	3	55
Italy	10	62
Belgium	5	25
Switzerland	9	51
Germany	9	52
Other	15	119
Canada	5	184
Japan	13	88
Latin America	13	39
Middle East	19	123
Far East	26	136
Australia and New Zealand	5	13
Africa	4	9
Soviet Bloc	5	14
International Banks[b]	4	105
Totals	219	2,744

[a] The Overseas British category includes the Australia & New Zealand Bank Ltd, the English Scottish & Australian Bank Ltd, the National Bank of New Zealand, Barclays' Bank DCO, and the Standard Bank Ltd. Generally, these banks reflect U.K. ownership, and an extensive system of branches outside the U.K. The bulk of the branches located outside the U.K. are regarded as local banks. Hence only offices and branches of these banks in countries other than their principal branching areas are treated as foreign. The figures in this table exclude over 1800 offices of the first three banks in Australia and New Zealand, over 1300 offices in Africa of Barclays' Bank DCO, and close to 1100 offices of the Standard Bank in Africa.

[b] Banks are designated 'International' on the basis of ownership, geographic distribution of offices, and type of business carried out.

The 'Other' category, which includes the less developed countries of Africa, the Far East, Latin America, and the Middle East, accounted for 11 per cent of foreign banking offices, a sharp increase in relative importance.

The location of foreign banking offices of banks with such facilities is as important and interesting as the nationality of parent banks. Table 1–3 provides us with an overview of the location of the nearly 2,800 foreign banking offices in 1968. The major recipient areas in order of importance were Latin America, the Far East, Africa, Continental Europe, and the Middle East. U.K. bank offices in the Far East represent the largest single entry in Table 1–3, whereas U.S. bank offices in Latin America represent the second most important measure of affinity between regions of the globe. As might be expected, the less developed countries constituted the most important areas in which foreign banking offices were located, although Continental Europe served as an important area in attracting foreign banking offices. Similarly, the United Kingdom and the United States each enjoyed well in excess of a hundred foreign banking offices, indicating the growing importance of international connections between developed countries.

The four banks included in this category are Bank of London & Montreal, owned jointly by Bank of London and South America (Bolsa), Bank of Montreal, and Barclays' Bank DCO; French American Banking Corporation, affiliated with Banque de l'Indochine, Banque Nationale de Paris, and Compagnie Financie de Suez et de Commerciale Unione Parisienne; Hong Kong & Shanghai Banking Corp.; and Sassoon (E.D.) Banking Co. Ltd.

Source: Based on data in *Bankers Almanac and Yearbook*, 1968–69.

Table 1.3

Location of Foreign Branches, Agencies, or Offices of Major Banks, 1968

Country or area in which located	Nationality of Parent Bank													Total
	U.S.	U.K.	British Overseas[a]	Continental Europe	Canada	Japan	Latin America	Middle East	Far East	Australia and N.Z.	Africa	Soviet Bloc	International Banks[b]	
United States	—	13	4	29	20	24	6	6	7	—	1	2	5	119
United Kingdom	32	—	24	31	14	12	—	6	18	11	2	3	3	157
Continental Europe	92	38	8	95	7	9	9	16	4	—	3	3	2	288
Canada	9	—	—	4	—	2	—	1	—	—	—	—	—	16
Japan	7	5	1	5	—	—	—	—	3	—	—	—	4	28
Latin America	203	72	148	188	139	9	24	5	—	—	—	—	44	854
Middle East	14	73	71	36	1	2	—	75	4	—	1	3	—	286
Far East	92	366	—	43	3	28	—	2	81	2	—	3	46	675
Australia and New Zealand	4	—[b]	—[a]	1	—	—	—	—	—	—	—	—	1	6
Africa	17	156	—[a]	150	—	2	—	12	21	—	2	—	—	362
All Areas	470	723	256	582	184	88	39	123	138	13	9	14	105	2,744

[a] See footnote [a] in the preceding table.
[b] See footnote [b] in the preceding table.

Source: Based on data in *Bankers Almanac and Yearbook*, 1968–69.

2 Federal and State Regulation

Regulation of foreign banking embraces all of the complexities of overlapping jurisdiction. These problems focus on the operational relationships between firms domiciled in one country, the governments and regulatory agencies of the country of domicile, and the governments and regulatory agencies of the country in which that bank conducts its overseas operations. The U.S. situation is further confounded by a federal system in which state and national governments share regulatory authority and in which a multiplicity of regulatory agencies operate at the national level. Discussion of the regulation of foreign banks operating in the United States is deferred until Chapter 7.

A. GENERAL OUTLINE OF REGULATION

The greater part of federal regulatory authority over U:S. international banking is concentrated in the hands of the Board of Governors of the Federal Reserve System. In general the Board is responsible for authorising the establishment of foreign branches of member banks of the Federal Reserve System, as well as approving requests to establish international banking (Edge Act) affiliates.

The federal system in the United States provides for state

jurisdiction over these matters. The states enjoy parallel jurisdiction in cases where state member banks participate in international banking business. This parallel jurisdiction has not
presented a serious threat or deep-seated problems thus far.
Also, in cases where non-member banks seek to conduct an international banking business the state banking department
with jurisdiction represents the only regulatory authority. Only
a few non-member banks conduct a significant amount of international banking operations by means of overseas branches.

In general state laws tend to be silent on matters falling into
the international banking category. The few exceptions include
important international banking states such as New York and
California, where the international operations of banks domiciled in these states have become of major significance. Both New
York and California have provided a fairly comprehensive legal
and administrative framework for the regulation and supervision of the international activities of their respective banks.

B.   FEDERAL REGULATION

U.S. banks have resorted to a variety of organisational
approaches in establishing and expanding their international
operations, ranging from correspondent relationships to direct
branches and foreign affiliates. In this section we discuss federal regulation as it applies to *de novo* establishment of overseas
branches and banking corporations, acquisition of foreign
banking facilities, and examination and supervision of existing
facilities.

1. ESTABLISHMENT OF FOREIGN OPERATIONS

Foreign Branches
Basic authority for the establishment of foreign branches by
U.S. banks is embodied in the Federal Reserve Act. As originally passed in 1913, the Federal Reserve Act, Section 25,
authorised the establishment of foreign branches by national
banks. This authority was subject to the approval of the Federal Reserve Board. The Board also was empowered to establish regulations under which these foreign branches might
operate. Under Section 9, paragraph 3 of the Federal Reserve
Act, the Board is given further authority to approve the terms

and conditions for establishment of foreign as well as domestic branches of state member banks. This Section of the Act stipulates that the same conditions, limitations, and restrictions shall be applicable to state and national banks in obtaining permission to establish such branches. Finally, Regulation H, Section 208.9, which deals with the establishment of branches, describes the type of information to be submitted by state member banks when applying for approval to establish foreign branches.

The Board's jurisdiction does not extend to non-member banks seeking to establish foreign branches. This is unfortunate, since it would be desirable to have a single authority operating in this area. Presumably, state authorities have jurisdiction and authority to approve the establishment of foreign branches by state non-member banks. Apparently, this question did not arise as a practical matter prior to 1969, at least in so far as this writer has been able to ascertain.[1] Since that year several non-member banks have established foreign branches subject to state approval. These cases are referred to in a following section dealing with state regulation.

While neither the Comptroller of the Currency nor the Federal Deposit Insurance Corporation have any direct jurisdiction in the establishment of foreign branches of either national or state banks, the Comptroller of the Currency does require that national banks provide the Comptroller's office with prior notification of their intention to establish a foreign branch: 'Prior notification also is required of a national bank to acquire directly a controlling interest in an Edge Act corporation, Agreement corporation or foreign bank, to establish offices of such controlled corporations or foreign banks, or to acquire a controlling interest in banks or other enterprises through such corporations or foreign banks.'[2] At the present time there exists some doubt as to whether the FDIC has authority to approve an insured non-member bank's application to establish a foreign branch. However, such a branch would be subject to the supervisory jurisdiction of the FDIC, including the power to examine the same and to require information and reports, as provided in the Federal Deposit Insurance Act. Also, FDIC would expect the foreign branch to be operated in conformance with the restrictions applicable to foreign branches of national banks, and other members of the Federal Reserve System.[3]

The principal Regulation issued by the Board of Governors covering the establishment and operation of foreign branches by American banks is Regulation M. The most recent major revision of this Regulation that is significant to this discussion was made in 1963. The 1963 revision came about as a result of the passage of Public Law 87-588 (12 U.S.C. 604a) 'to improve the usefulness of national bank branches in foreign countries'. The statute authorises the Board of Governors of the Federal Reserve System to permit foreign branches of national banks to exercise such additional powers as may be usual in the transaction of the business of banking in places where such foreign branches operate.[4] Illustration 2-A includes a list of the items of information which must be submitted through the District Federal Reserve Bank to the Board of Governors in applications for establishing foreign branches.

ILLUSTRATION 2-A

Information to be Submitted with Applications for Establishment of Foreign Branches

1. Map of area with indication thereon of proposed branch site and other banking facilities.
2. Indication of distance between branch site and each of the other banks.
3. Statement as to competitive situation.
4. Cost to build and equip banking quarters, or cost of rental. Source of funds (whether from home office or overseas sources).
5. Prospects of successful operations.
6. Comments on economic and political situation of the foreign country.
7. Reasons for establishing the branch.
8. Action taken by foreign country's banking authorities.
9. Comments re Voluntary Foreign Credit Restraint Program.

In addition to the above, if there should be any unusual factors of any nature having a bearing on the operation of the

branch, of course we would wish to be informed.
Source: Bank Examinations Department, Federal Reserve Bank of New York.

Prior to passage of Public Law 87-588 foreign branches of American banks were subject to statutory law and the regulatory policies designed for domestic banking institutions, and conditions prevailing in the United States. Foreign branches of American banks attempted to carry these institutional patterns to the country where the branch operated, generally resulting in the branch facing a dual set of regulations. At the Senate and House Hearings on this bill, it was brought out that foreign branches of national banks were unable to engage in many commercial banking practices common to the countries where they were located. Among these practices were acceptance financing, real estate loans, bank guarantees, purchase of public securities, and transactions in securities under repurchase agreements.

While Public Law 87-588 may have been regarded as a non-controversial bill, in that there was little or no opposition to it, the Board of Governors did entertain certain reservations regarding the extent to which additional powers should be granted to foreign branches of American banks. The Board held that underwriting and non-banking (manufacturing and trading) activities should continue to be held in restraint. In the words of Chairman Martin:[5]

> . . . I would not interpret this bill as a *carte blanche* for the full equalization of foreign branch powers with those of foreign banks. Apart from the fundamental limitations in the bill itself, it would not allow foreign branches to exercise any additional powers except as expressly permitted by Board regulations that would be formulated after consideration of actual conditions and with due regard for the integrity and soundness of the American banking system.

Passage of the bill authorising foreign branches to engage in a wider range of activities in August 1962, was followed by the Board's revision of Regulation M, which took effect in August 1963.[6] Several major changes in the status of foreign branches were introduced in the revised version of Regulation M. These included the addition of the following powers for foreign branches:

1. Guarantee customers debts or otherwise agree to make payments for their benefit, subject to stated limitations.
2. Accept drafts or bills of exchange, subject to the usual amount limitations of the Board's Regulation C.
3. Invest in the securities of the central bank, clearing houses, government entities, and development banks of the country in which the branch is located, generally subject to an amount limitation of 1 per cent of a branch's total deposits.
4. Underwrite, distribute, buy and sell obligations of the national government of the country in which the branch is located, subject to stated amount limitations.
5. Take liens on foreign real estate in connection with its extension of credit, whether or not of first priority and whether or not such real estate is improved or has been appraised.
6. Extend credit to an executive officer of the branch in an amount not to exceed $20,000 or its equivalent, to finance the acquisition or construction of living quarters to be used as his residence abroad.

The revision also simplifies the procedure which applies when national banks establish foreign branches. After a national bank has established a branch in a foreign country with Board approval, it may establish additional branches in that country after thirty days notice to the Board in the case of each such branch. A similar amendment to Regulation H, effective in August 1963, provided for state member banks to establish additional foreign branches in the same country by giving the Board thirty days notice prior to the establishment of such branches.

Foreign Banking Corporations

State-chartered international banking corporations existed well before enactment of the Federal Reserve Act. The first American international banking institution to establish a system of foreign branches was the International Banking Corporation of New York City.[7] Originally chartered in Connecticut, the Corporation began operations in 1902 and by the eve of World War I had established seventeen branches in China, England, India, Japan, the Philippines, Panama, Malaya, and Mexico. In 1915 IBC was acquired by the National City Bank of New York. Other international banking corporations established in this early period were the Continental Banking and Trust Company of Panama, the Asia Banking Corporation, and the Park-Union Foreign Banking Corporation.

The existence of a growing number of state-chartered international banking corporations gave rise to an amendment to Section 25 of the Federal Reserve Act in 1916. This amendment authorised national banks with capital stock and surplus of $1 million or more to invest up to 10 per cent of their capital stock and surplus in 'one or more banks or corporations chartered or incorporated under the laws of the United States or of any State . . . principally engaged in international or foreign banking . . .'. The way was now open for national banks to invest in existing state-chartered corporations. A prior condition was that national banks enter into an agreement with the Federal Reserve Board which would contain restrictions on the operations of the corporation. For this reason such state-chartered foreign banking corporations have been titled 'agreement corporations'. Whereas the 1916 amendment permitted national banks to invest in federally chartered international banking corporations, the law made no explicit provision for federal chartering.

The legislative structure controlling the international operations of American banks was nearly completed in 1919 with the passage of the Edge Act, named after its sponsor, Senator Walter Edge of New Jersey. This legislation, which added Section 25(a) to the Federal Reserve Act, provided for federally chartered corporations to engage in 'foreign banking or other international or foreign financial operations . . .'.

The principal features of the Edge Act may be summarised as follows:

1. Foreign banking corporations organised with the approval of the Board must have a minimum capital of

$2 million. This is in sharp contrast with the 1916 amendment to the Federal Reserve Act whereby national banks with $1 million *minimum capital* could purchase stock in state-chartered foreign banking corporations up to a *maximum* of 10 per cent of their capital. Apparently, Congressional thinking had undergone a considerable change in three years regarding the adequacy of capital for foreign banking corporations.

2. The powers of such corporations include the conduct of regular banking operations for international customers, the receipt of deposits in the course of foreign business, the establishment of foreign branches, and investment in the stock of other corporations.

3. The above mentioned powers were not extended to the conduct of domestic business within the United States. Hence, such corporations can receive deposits within the United States only as may be incidental to or for the purpose of carrying out transactions in foreign countries.

4. The Federal Reserve Board was given the authority to prescribe rules and regulations governing the operation of corporations chartered under Section 25(a) and to examine these corporations.

In order to properly implement Section 25(a) the Board has issued regulations from time to time. In the first decade of operation under the 1919 amendment, the Board was concerned with organisation and prior Board consent in the establishment of foreign branches of such corporations. Also, the Board gave attention to acquisition of stock in other companies, and the issuance of debentures. In the 1930s interest in international banking and formation of Edge Act corporations declined. However, during the period following World War II a revived interest in the use of Edge corporations as a means of expanding the international activities of U.S. banks led to a major revision of Regulation K, which is the regulation that most directly applies to the establishment and activities of Edge Act affiliates of American banks. This 1957 change provided for the existence of two types of corporations – banking and financing. The former were allowed to exercise the banking functions permitted in Section 25(a) paragraphs 6 and 7 of the Act, including accepting deposits and holding stock in banking companies. Financing corporations were not permitted to accept deposits or hold stock in corporations engaged in banking, but could hold stock in companies engaged in other pursuits. Moreover, financing corporations could engage in a variety of financial operations including issuance of long-term obligations up to a specified multiple of their capital. This separation of powers tended to preserve the distinction that has prevailed domestically between deposit and investment banking.

The distinction between banking and financing corporations incorporated in the 1957 version of Regulation K led to the establishment of two separate and distinct Edge Act corporations by a number of U.S. banks, including several New York banks. The latter had less need for a banking corporation to conduct their international banking operations than non-New York banks since they already enjoyed a New York location from which to develop their international banking activities.

The 1957 revision of Regulation K aimed at more than simply providing a distinction between commercial and investment banking paralleling that formerly achieved on the domestic scene. A further objective was to 'clarify and delineate' the banking functions a banking type Edge corporation might appropriately conduct within the United States.[8] Section 25(a) clearly states that Edge and Agreement corporations may not carry on any business in the United States except that deemed incidental to the corporations' foreign business. For many years prior to 1957 New York and interior banks had operated subsidiary corporations located in New York. Up to this time a number of questions had remained unanswered regarding the activities that might be carried on in New York by subsidiaries of New York and interior banks. Moreover, the prohibition of interstate branching of domestic banks raised numerous questions regarding where appropriate lines might be drawn between what constituted domestic and international business. The 1957 revision of Regulation K attempted to solve these problems by specifying activities which would be regarded as permissible for Edge Act corporations, and by broadening the scope of activities held to be appropriate. For example, the 1957 revision clearly permitted Edge Act corporations to establish foreign branches, but gave no authority for the establishment of domestic branches. The revised Regulation K held that Regulation Q would apply against deposits received within the United States by banking corporations, and prohibited the receipt of deposits by Edge corporations in the United States except where such could be interpreted as incidental to carrying out transactions abroad. The revision defined the types of credit extensions in the United States that could be considered permissible for banking corporations, detailed the types of securities issues which financing corporations might participate in, and specified the categories of obligations financing corporations could acquire.

In 1963 Regulation K was substantially revised for the second time within six years. In this case the objectives of the Board were to enable Edge corporations to operate more effectively, and to 'shorten and simplify the Regulation'.[9] It should be noted that the highly detailed specifications of what were and were not permissible activities in the 1957 revision reflected a somewhat restrictive approach. Six years later, after some of the revisions had been well exposed to the changing character of international banking, the need for several of the provisions became suspect. The 1963 revision in effect removed the distinction between banking and financing corporations. Moreover, there were several liberalisations of banking operations in the United States.

Under the 1963 revision a partial integration of financing and banking activities was made possible. On the sources of funds side, there is no longer any reference to the strict distinction between banking and financing corporations with specified power to incur deposit and debenture type liabilities respectively. In the 1963 revision, Section 211.9(c), it is stated with respect to aggregate liabilities:[10]

> Except with prior Board permission, a Corporation's aggregate outstanding liabilities on account of acceptances, monthly average deposits, borrowings, guarantees, endorsements, debentures, bonds, notes and other such obligations shall not exceed ten times its capital and

surplus; provided that aggregate outstanding unsecured liabilities under guarantees or similar agreements . . . may in no event exceed 50 per cent of its capital and surplus.

On the uses of funds side the earlier (1957) revision of Regulation K considered that banking corporations would ordinarily extend short-term and medium-term credit by means of purchasing or discounting drafts, making advances, and providing acceptance credits. Financing corporations would ordinarily purchase securities of foreign corporations, acquire obligations covering export of goods and services, make advances and issue letters of credit, and extend credit to corporations in which the financing corporation owned voting stock. The 1963 revision amended this by providing that any Edge corporation could invest in the stock of corporations organised under foreign law if such acquisition (1) is incidental to the extension of credit by the corporation to the foreign firm whose shares are acquired; (2) consists of shares in a foreign bank; or (3) is otherwise likely to further the development of U.S. foreign commerce.

To summarise, the 1963 revision of Regulation K provided more flexible operating rules for Edge Act corporations. First, the six-year-old sharp distinction between banking and financing corporations was removed. Second, additional banking powers were made available to Edge Act corporations. Third, banking and financing corporations were provided additional latitude in obtaining funds via acceptance of deposits or issuance of debenture obligations. Fourth, both types of corporations were afforded the opportunity to pursue a more flexible allocation of funds as between short-term 'banking' credits and equity investments.

2. ACQUISITION OF FOREIGN BANKING AND RELATED ACTIVITIES

National banks and state member banks are generally subject to strict limitations in their investment policies with respect to the purchase of stock in affiliates by Section 23A of the Federal Reserve Act. However, the Congress has, from time to time, given express recognition to the fact that the foreign commerce of the United States should be enhanced by permitting national banks and state member banks to engage in certain investment activities in the international field which are prohibited to them domestically. Specific exemptions, for instance, are granted in the Clayton Act and the Bank Holding Company Act of 1956. Permissive legislation has been codified into Sections 25 and 25(a) of the Federal Reserve Act, both of which specifically delegate regulatory authority to the Board of Governors of the Federal Reserve System. Regulation K, issued by the Board, interprets and expands on these sections of the Act.

Acquisition of Interest in Foreign Banks

U.S. banks may acquire an interest in foreign banks or non-bank firms. Three methods are available for national banks to acquire an interest in a foreign banking concern. The first method is to use an Edge Act subsidiary to invest in a foreign banking firm. A second method is to make use of a holding company for this purpose. The third method is to make a direct investment in a foreign bank. This last option is available to national banks as a result of a 1966 amendment to Section 25 of the Federal Reserve Act, and is subject to the conditions and regulations prescribed by the Board of Governors. Direct stock holdings of national banks in foreign banks are in addition to those permitted to national banks through their subsidiary Edge corporations. As a result of the 1966 legislative amendment, Regulation M was revised effective 15 March 1967 and provides that prior Board consent be required for any investment in a foreign bank under Section 25 of the Act. Regulation M limits the amounts that may be invested in foreign banks (together with investments of the national bank in the shares of Edge Act and Agreement corporations) to 25 per cent of the national bank's capital and surplus.[11]

Prior to the 1966 amendment to Section 25 permitting direct investment in a foreign bank by a national bank, the Board was authorised to allow limited investments in foreign banking companies. In connection with this, on 15 August 1962 Public Law 87-588 was enacted. Titled, 'An Act to improve the usefulness of national banks' branches in foreign countries', it amends Section 25 of the Federal Reserve Act. The amendment permits the Board of Governors to authorise a foreign branch of national bank to exercise such additional powers as may be usual in connection with the transaction of banking in places where foreign branches of U.S. banks operate. The Board of Governors revised Regulation M effective 1 August 1963, so as to implement the changes provided for in the amended legislation. Section 213.4(c) of Regulation M authorises foreign branches to acquire and hold securities including equities in the central bank, clearing house, government entities, and development banks of the country in which the American bank's foreign branch is located, where such holdings are usual for banks of that country. Such investments may not exceed 1 per cent of the deposits of the foreign branch as of the preceding year-end call report date. This authority was added to permit foreign branches to make such investments where required by local law, or where such investments would appear to be advantageous in terms of evidencing co-operation with local government economic development efforts.

In applying for the consent of the Board to acquire and hold stock in a foreign bank, the national bank must furnish the following type of information, as required in Regulation M:

1. cost, number, and class of shares to be acquired
2. recent balance sheet and income statements of the foreign bank
3. brief description of the foreign bank's business
4. list of directors and principal officers and of all shareholders known holding 10 per cent or more of any class of the foreign bank's stock
5. information concerning the rights and privileges of the various classes of shares outstanding.

The 1967 revision of Regulation M, which applies specifically to the acquisition of shares by a national bank in a foreign bank, further indicates that national banks may make loans or extend credit to (or for the account of) such a foreign bank. Further, national banks may make such loans to foreign bank affiliates 'without regard to the provisions of Section 23A of the Act . . .'. The latter section provides various limits and restrictions on loans to and investments in affiliates of national banks, including minimum collateral requirements.

Returning to the question of Edge Act corporation acquisition of stock in foreign banks, any Edge Act corporation has the 'general consent' of the Board to acquire and hold shares in a foreign bank, up to 25 per cent of the voting shares if the amount invested does not exceed $200,000 or its equivalent.[12] An Edge Act corporation may acquire stock in a foreign bank beyond these stated limits, but first must obtain 'specific consent' from the Board. In such cases, the overall limitation of 25 per cent of the national bank's capital and surplus invested (directly or indirectly) in the stock of foreign banks becomes applicable.[13]

Until 1970 the law was silent on the use of the bank holding company as a vehicle for acquiring shares in a foreign bank. Until 1970 a bank holding company would become subject to the Bank Holding Company Act of 1956 whenever it directly or indirectly owned or controlled, with power to vote, 25 per cent or more of the voting shares of each of two or more banks. The language of the 1956 legislation seemingly excluded foreign banks from consideration under the type of bank holding company that was defined in the Act. However, in Section 4(c)(8) of the 1956 legislation it was stated that the prohibitions against acquisitions of 'shares held or acquired by a bank holding company in any company which is organized under the laws of a foreign country and which is engaged principally in the banking business outside of the United States' do not apply. In 1970 the holding company legislation was extended to apply to one-bank holding companies. As of that date four foreign banks were made subject to the Bank Holding Company Act as 'registered bank holding companies'. At the time some concern was expressed by the Board of Governors concerning possible inclusion of foreign banks and foreign bank holding companies under certain versions of the one-bank holding company act as proposed in 1970.[14]

Section 4(c)(13) of the Bank Holding Company Act of 1970 permits bank holding companies to acquire shares of companies which do no business in the United States except as an incident to such companies' international or foreign business. In September, 1971 the Board of Governors, the supervisory agency in matters pertaining to administration of the Bank

Holding Company Act, issued revisions in Regulation Y, the Board's interpretive guideline for enforcement and supervision of the provisions of the Bank Holding Company Act. This amendment permits bank holding companies to acquire ownership or control of the shares of companies in which Edge Act corporations may invest, with the Board's consent and under procedures similar to those presently governing investments by Edge Act corporations. Edge Act corporations may invest in companies engaged in international or foreign banking or other international or foreign financial activities. Also, they may make minority non-controlling investments in other types of companies.

According to Regulation Y as amended in 1971, limitations applicable to Edge Act corporations governing the extent to which and the manner in which they may conduct their activities are generally inapplicable to activities conducted on the basis of section 4(c)(13).[15] Such limitations include minimum capitalisation requirements, capital and surplus limitations on investments, approval with respect to issuance abroad of debentures, bonds and notes, and restrictions concerning acceptance liabilities, liabilities of one borrower, and aggregate liabilities.

Under Regulation Y the Board retains authority to impose conditions regarding the operation of foreign subsidiaries of domestic bank holding companies similar to those conditions that apply to Edge Act corporations and their foreign subsidiaries. Bank holding company *subsidiaries* would be required to obtain the Board's approval for the establishment of branches or agencies in the United States, or for the establishment of banking offices in any foreign country new to their operations. Moreover, Board approval would be required for the issue in the United States of any debentures, bonds, promissory notes, or similar obligations, other than instruments due within one year. As a matter of policy, the Board has indicated that where bank holding companies seek to engage in foreign banking activities that involve the receipt of deposits in the United States, they should do so through Edge Act or Agreement corporations.

Merger or Consolidation With Foreign Banks

When discussing expansion of U.S. international banking through merger or consolidation with foreign banks, we again become tangled in a web of multiple federal agencies. The prevailing statute in this area is Section 18(c) of the Federal Deposit Insurance Act, which gives specific authority to two federal agencies, the Board of Governors of the Federal Reserve System, and the FDIC. Section 18(c) requires prior written consent of the Board before a bank may merge, consolidate, or acquire the assets and assume the liabilities of another bank if the acquiring, assuming, or resulting bank is to be a state member bank.

Under the Bank Merger Act of 1960 the FDIC's prior approval is required in any merger, purchase of assets, or assumption of liabilities transaction in which the *resulting bank is an insured bank*, not a member of the Federal Reserve System, and not located in the District of Columbia. Such approval is also required in any absorption of a *non-insured bank* or institution *by an insured bank*. Both the Board and the FDIC must consider several specific factors before approving a merger including (1) the effect on competition, (2) financial and managerial resources, (3) prospects of the existing and proposed institution, and (4) the convenience and needs of the community to be served.[16]

Acquisition of Non-Bank Firms

At the present time U.S. banks may invest in non-banking foreign firms through their Edge Act affiliates. Such investments or acquisitions of interest are regulated by Section 25(a) of the Federal Reserve Act, Regulation K which pertains to corporations doing foreign banking or financing, and more generally by Regulation M which applies to the foreign activities of national banks. Regulation M applies in that it specifies an overall limitation of 25 per cent of a U.S. bank's capital and surplus which may be invested in foreign banks and companies organised under Sections 25 and 25(a) of the Act. In this way a ceiling is imposed on the total investment of U.S. banks in foreign banks and non-banking firms.

Paragraph 8 of Section 25(a) of the Federal Reserve Act

authorises an Edge corporation, with the consent of the Board,

> to purchase and hold stock or other certificates of owner-
> ship in any other corporation organized under the provi-
> sions of this section, or under the laws of any foreign
> country or a colony or dependency thereof, or under the
> laws of any State, dependency, or insular possession of the
> United States but not engaged in the general business of
> buying or selling goods, wares, merchandise or commodi-
> ties in the United States, and not transacting any business
> in the United States except such as in the judgment of the
> Board of Governors of the Federal Reserve System may be
> incidental to its international or foreign business.

The significant items in this passage refer to (1) the foreign
nature of the business of the firm, and (2) that U.S. operations
be incidental to the foreign business. In addition, the Board
must consider the effect on U.S. foreign trade, and whether a
specific acquisition or investment by an Edge Act affiliate will
be favourable or not to fostering this country's international
trade.

Before considering requests for permission to acquire the
stock of foreign companies the Board requires the submission of
pertinent data by the Edge Act or Agreement corporation.
Generally, this includes the dollar and foreign currency value of
the investment, affiliates of the company to be acquired, a
description of the company in which the investment is to be
made, and financial information relating to the acquisition.

In the past Edge Act affiliates of U.S. banks have invested in a
variety of foreign companies, including national or local development banks, financing companies, leasing firms, and firms
which render services required in the conduct of foreign trade.
In many situations presented to it, the Board may find the
application to be 'marginal' or close in terms of the mix of
foreign and domestic operations. In one such case in 1967 the
Board rendered an affirmative decision. A description of this
case follows.[17]

The Edge Act affiliate of a U.S. bank petitioned the Board to
acquire a non-controlling interest in the stock of a combination
export manager. The company and its clients were located in

the United States. Through designated agents and distributors abroad the company obtained foreign orders for its clients in the United States. Also, against firm orders from abroad the company purchased merchandise and reinvoiced it for export. In no case did the company maintain inventories of unsold merchandise, or make any sales in the United States.

The Board of Governors recognised the closeness of the question whether the company was engaged in the business of buying or selling goods in the United States. The Board's conclusion was that in acting as agent or broker for foreign clients with no market risk, or in acting as principal with offsetting firm orders for foreign clients, the activities of the company would not cause it to be engaged in the general business of buying or selling goods or merchandise in the United States. The Board noted:

> While the activities of the company are closely related to those of companies engaged in a commercial business in the United States, the sole business of the company is to act as an intermediary between domestic manufacturers and foreign consumers.[18]

The Board further elaborated that the company was exclusively concerned with effecting international transactions. Accordingly, the Board judged that the activities of the company were 'incidental to its international or foreign business'. Since the stock acquisition by an Edge corporation would likely further the foreign commerce of the United States, the Board concluded that such an acquisition and holding would be permissible and appropriate.

The Board noted that its decision 'was based on the particular facts of this case . . .'. Moreover, applications by Edge corporations for permission to undertake similar acquisitions would necessarily be decided on their own merits.

3. EXAMINATION AND SUPERVISION OF FOREIGN BRANCHES AND BANKING CORPORATIONS

Part of the process of supervising or regulating banks includes examination in order to judge the soundness of banks and to assure conformity to law and regulations. The past growth in international business and banking imposes even greater emphasis on the need for periodic examination of banks heavily committed to overseas operations and foreign lending. For banks in major financial centres such as New York, Chicago, and San Francisco where foreign business has long been an important factor, the changing character of that business alone warrants more intensive scrutiny by the regulatory agencies.

Due to the somewhat different nature of international banking as compared with domestic banking, examination of the former requires consideration of a number of factors not generally found in domestic banking. To render an informed judgement on the competence of bank management in the foreign field, the examiner must himself be fully conversant with the techniques and problems of international banking, including the problems associated with conducting banking operations in many countries that are at varying levels of financial development. An important operating objective for the supervisory authorities is the development of a staff of examiners with sufficient experience and knowledge in international banking and finance.

A serious question faces the regulatory authorities in that the foreign branches, like the domestic branches, are integral parts of the parent bank. Foreign subsidiary banks, while enjoying a separate and distinct legal status apart from the parent U.S. bank, may be considered as substitutes for branches. Therefore, an examination of a U.S. bank with a well developed overseas organisation would be incomplete if the operations of overseas subsidiaries were disregarded. Fortunately, or unfortunately, both overseas branches and subsidiaries of U.S. banks operate under the banking laws and regulations that apply in the countries in which these overseas offices are located. In a number of cases, 'both are examined by foreign banking authorities'.[19] In several of these countries, including Switzerland and the Bahamas, regulations enforcing banking secrecy prohibit the release of bank records and related information.[20] In such cases examinations of foreign branches by U.S. supervisory authorities can raise questions concerning the application of extra-territorial jurisdiction.

The regulation and supervision of the international banking operations of U.S. banks is fragmented between several federal agencies, as well as between overlapping national jurisdictions. This fragmented approach toward the supervision of international banking creates the possibility of differences in view, approach, and emphasis as between the several federal regulatory agencies that are involved. At present, the international operations of head offices of national banks are supervised and examined by the Comptroller of the Currency, and of head offices of state member banks by the Board of Governors of the Federal Reserve System. The Federal Reserve Board authorises the establishment of foreign branches of national and state member banks, but subsequent supervisory jurisdiction depends on whether the branch adheres to a national or state member bank.[21] The Comptroller of the Currency conducts periodic examinations of the foreign branches of national banks.[22] Although the Board of Governors has the power to conduct special examinations of the foreign branches of national banks, the Board has not exercised this power. Copies of the Comptroller of the Currency examination reports are made available to the Federal Reserve for confidential use.[23] Supervision of the foreign branches of state member banks and all Edge Act and Agreement corporations falls within the jurisdiction of the Board of Governors.[24]

The supervisory jurisdiction described above can lead to an anomalous situation, as the following passage indicates:[25]

> the Bank of America conducts part of its international operation in this country from its California offices and part from its Edge subsidiary in New York; abroad, its operations are conducted partly through branches and partly through subsidiaries. The bank's operations in California, and in foreign branches, are supervised by the Comptroller of the Currency, while those in New York, and in subsidiaries abroad, are supervised by the Federal Reserve Board.

It is conceivable that differences in approach between various regulatory agencies could work against a satisfactory supervision of U.S. international banking. There is no evidence at present to indicate that such has taken place. However, a more unified approach among the respective agencies could augur well for the orderly expansion of international banking in the future.

C.   STATE REGULATION

While the international banking operations of American banks has displayed vigorous expansion, only a few states can boast that they house a large number of banks with substantial international or overseas activities. These include New York, California, Illinois, Massachusetts, and Pennsylvania. In Table 2-1 we can see that New York banks operate three-fifths of the overseas branches and over one-fourth of the Edge and Agreement corporations of state member and national banks. Moreover, close to one-half of the Edge and Agreement corporations of U.S. banks have a New York headquarters. California holds an important second position in number of overseas branches, number of Edge and Agreement corporations, and number of these corporations located in New York. The three states Illinois, Massachusetts, and Pennsylvania are difficult to rank in terms of international banking involvement. In the remaining forty-five states over sixty banks operate eighty-seven overseas branches and twenty-four Edge and Agreement corporations.

If anything, the data embodied in Table 2-1 tend to understate the concentration, especially the dominant role of international banking institutions in New York. New York banks are the largest, and enjoy the highest percentages of foreign operations of all banks in the United States. The concentration of international banking activities of U.S. banks in these five states compared with the level of international banking activity in the remaining forty-five states suggests that any need for state regulation may be similarly concentrated.

1.   NEW YORK

In New York the Superintendent of Banks, with the concurrence of three-fifths of the State Banking Board, may approve requests of state banks and trust companies to establish a branch office in a foreign country. Authority to approve such requests is provided for in Section 105-3(a) of the State Banking Law, which further stipulates that such

Table 2.1

Concentration of Banks with Overseas Branches and Edge-Agreement
Corporations, by State, Year-end 1972

State in which Parent Bank is Located	Number of Banks with Overseas Branches[a]	Number of Overseas Branches	Number of Edge and Agreement Corporations	Edge and Agreement Corporations in New York	Edge and Agreement Corporations in California
New York	18[b]	371[b]	27	19	4
California	10[b]	118[b]	17	6	7
Illinois	8	34	9	4	1
Massachusetts	5	28	7	2	0
Pennsylvania	8	10	9	4	0
All Other States	66	87	24[c]	6[c]	1
Total	115[b]	648	93	41	13

[a] Four banking institutions operate Edge Act corporations but have no overseas branches. These include the Bank of Virginia Co., Richmond, a holding company; U.S. Trust Co., New York; and First New Haven National Bank and South Shore National Bank of Quincy, Massachusetts, both institutions operating the Shorehaven International Bank, Boston.

[b] Eight non-member banks were operating twenty-one overseas branches at year-end 1972. These include Bank of Hawaii with twelve branches in the Pacific Island Territories; Bank of Tokyo of California (Nassau); Bank of Tokyo Trust, New York (London and Nassau); Brown Brothers & Harriman & Co., New York (Nassau); European American Bank & Trust Co., New York (Nassau); First Empire Bank, New York (France); First Israel Bank & Trust, New York (Nassau); and J. Henry Schroder Banking Corp., New York (Nassau).

[c] Includes Allied Bank International, owned by eighteen medium-size banks.

Source: Board of Governors of the Federal Reserve System; Federal Reserve Bank of New York; New York Superintendent of Banks; and Superintendent of Banks, State of California.

banks must have a minimum capital stock and surplus of one million dollars. Approval is in the form of a Formal Authorisation Certificate signed by the Superintendent.[26]

In presenting the application for operation of a foreign branch to the Superintendent, the bank must explain how the proposed facility will promote public convenience and service. In connection with this the application must list the name and location of each banking institution in the service area and adjacent areas. Moreover, the application must describe the proposed site for the foreign branch, including details on the building, options and leases, estimated costs of furniture and fixtures, and the time required to place the proposed branch in operation. Accompanying this information must be projections of deposits, income and expenses, and photographs and maps of the site and immediate neighbourhood. In addition, the application must provide the following information:

1. the dollar amount of international transactions financed by the applicant as of the most recent date for which such statistics were compiled;
2. the names, ages, titles and banking experience of at least the two highest ranking officers of the applicant's international department;
3. the reasons why the establishment of the proposed branch would improve and expand the services available to applicant's customers;
4. evidence of approval of local banking authorities in the foreign country, or evidence no such approval is required.

The New York State Banking Department applies supervisory powers over the foreign branches of state banks that are similar to those used with respect to domestic offices of the same banks. No special liquidity requirements are applied to overseas branches, and liquidity is reviewed on an overall basis. No reserve requirements are imposed, although these foreign branches are subject to Federal Reserve requirements with respect to Eurodollars. Similar loan and investment criteria are applied to overseas and domestic branches. Moreover, no specific balance sheet relationships are required. There are no restrictions on the capital positions of overseas branches.

The credit analysis conducted by examiners with respect to foreign departments of state banks is the same as that applied to domestic loan departments of these banks. In evaluating foreign loans the political and economic stability of the borrowing country is considered, and in the case of loans to foreign banks, the affiliation of the bank with the central bank is given consideration.

In the past the Banking Department conducted examinations of overseas branches every three years. However, such examinations have been discontinued. The Department now conducts desk examinations at head offices in New York every three years, and it is expected that this will be done on an annual basis. These examinations are similar to those that apply to domestic branches in so far as loan evaluation is concerned.

The formation and acquisition of interests by state banks in foreign banking corporations is subject to state jurisdiction. The Banking Department has dual jurisdiction with the Federal Reserve over Edge Act subsidiaries of New York State chartered banks. However, this authority does not extend over Edge corporations of out-of-state banks located in New York. Foreign banking affiliates or subsidiaries of state-chartered banks are examined annually.

2. CALIFORNIA

In California state-chartered banks may establish foreign branches upon obtaining the approval of the Superintendent of Banks and after meeting conditions and under such regulations as he may prescribe. Such banks must have a minimum paid-up capital and surplus of one million dollars, and shall not invest more than 10 per cent of capital and surplus in all foreign branches.[27]

According to Section 531 of the California Banking Code, applications to establish a foreign branch shall specify (1) the place where the foreign branch is to be established, (2) the banking operations proposed to be carried on, and (3) any other information which the Superintendent may require.

The Superintendent has not issued rules or regulations establishing criteria and conditions to be applied in such cases.

However, the following matters are looked into in such evaluations:[28]

1. compliance with legal provisions of Article 2, Section 530 of the California Banking Law, referred to above;
2. the general condition of the bank and its experience and capacity in the field of international banking;
3. the volume of foreign and international business now existing in the foreign country which the applicant banks will be able to serve more efficiently by means of the proposed foreign branch.
4. opportunities for profitable employment of bank funds;
5. the extent of transactional exposure in view of control activities due to the distance of the foreign branch from the head office, including an analysis of the review and approval actions taken at the foreign branch level by the Board of Directors or by senior management at head office;
6. the competitive effect on other banks now engaged in international and foreign banking in the foreign country;
7. compliance with the voluntary foreign credit restraint guidelines;
8. the merit of any protests filed in writing with the Superintendent.

Once a foreign branch has been established, the bank operating this branch must furnish the Superintendent all information required concerning the status of the branch. Moreover, the Superintendent may at any time undertake a special examination of any foreign branch office at the expense of the bank maintaining the branch.[29]

Section 534 of the Banking Law requires that the accounts of each foreign branch be maintained independently of the accounts of each other foreign branch and independently of the accounts of domestic offices. At the conclusion of each fiscal period the bank must transfer to its head office general ledger the 'profit and loss from each foreign branch as a separate item'.

Section 534.1 describes the types of business that a foreign branch may and may not undertake. A foreign branch 'may transact such business as may be usual in connection with the transaction of the business of banking in the places where such foreign branch is located'.[30] However, a foreign branch shall not engage in the general business of producing, distributing, buying or selling goods or merchandise. Moreover, except with respect to securities issued by a foreign state, a foreign branch shall not engage in the underwriting, selling, or distributing of securities.

The Banking Law in California is comprehensive in its coverage of matters concerning investments in foreign banks and banking corporations by banks chartered by the State of California. The law provides for the chartering of international and foreign banking and financing corporations; bank investments in international banking and financing corporations organised under the laws of the United States; bank investments in foreign banking corporations organised under the laws of the various states; and acquisitions of stock in foreign banks. These provisions place California Banking Law on a par with comparable laws of all other states, and provide a flexible situation in which state banks may expand their international operations.

An extremely important part of the California Banking Law, resulting from legislation in 1967, permits state banks to acquire and hold, directly or indirectly, the stock of one or more foreign banks. Several restrictions apply, including that the foreign bank have no activities in the United States except those which are incidental to its international operations and that certain amount limitations apply to the transaction.[31]

In 1969 the United California Bank acquired a 58 per cent interest in the Salik Bank in Basel A.G., Basel, Switzerland. Shortly after the acquisition of the Salik Bank, the name was changed to United California Bank in Basel A.G. Salik Bank had been organised in 1965 with a modest capital of $600,000, and by year-end 1966 had assets of $3 million. The bank offered a variety of services to customers including advice on and executing transactions in foreign currencies, equity investments, commodity speculation, and transactions in gold and silver. For its own account the bank purchased and sold commodities, foreign currencies, and managed a diversified investment account. Unfortunately, in 1969–70 the Basel affiliate experienced difficulties in several areas of its operations, including silver trading, cocoa futures, and investments in an American-based firm called Leasing Consultants, Inc.[32] It was reported that the Swiss affiliate's operations in cocoa futures were so extensive that it was dealing in about half the world's production of cocoa. In August 1970 the Basel affiliate reported a loss of $15–20 million in futures trading to its Los Angeles parent. Soon after this it was recognised that the losses were much greater, probably in the area of $40 million. This compares with balance sheet deposits of close to $75 million. By September 1970 the parent bank had submitted a plan to liquidate its subsidiary to a Basel court. At that time a secretary of the Swiss Banking Commission alleged that fraud and forgery were involved in keeping the commodity position of UCB, Basel secret from the parent bank.[33]

The release of information describing the losses incurred by the UCB affiliate in Basel set off a chain of reactions. These included the threat of and actual suits by shareholders of United California Bank, Los Angeles and Western Bancorporation, the holding company parent of United California Bank; an investigation by the Board of Governors of the Federal Reserve System;[34] an inquiry on the part of Representative Wright Patman, Chairman of the House Banking and Currency Committee;[35] and a probe by the Swiss Banking authorities.[36]

In late December 1970 United California Bank in Basel stated it would turn over its leased premises to Migros Bank, Zurich, and complete the process of court-protected liquidation.

Several important points emerge from this interesting and unfortunate episode in international banking experience. First, special difficulties may be encountered in exercising management control and regulatory and supervisory jurisdiction over the international operations of American banks. Second, based on the experience in this particular case, a branch operation might have proven superior to that of a majority-owned affiliate. The parent bank would have had a more direct control and availability of financial information in the case of an overseas branch. Third, we might raise the question of enforceability of criteria established by either federal or state officials in maintaining a watchful eye on the activities of foreign bank iliates of American banks. Doubtless, as a result of the United California Bank in Basel incident both state and federal authorities will be more watchful than in the past. But in cases of bank-owned foreign affiliates, there remains the question of adequate control by parent banking institutions.

D.   CRITIQUE OF REGULATORY FRAMEWORK

The existing regulatory framework as applied in the United States to international banking activities leaves numerous questions regarding adequacy, efficiency and comprehensiveness. While no serious problems have arisen, or appear imminent, the growing importance of international banking operations places more emphasis on the need for a serious review of this regulatory area. The questions that seem most pertinent at this time may be categorised under the following headings:

> Problem of appropriate jurisdiction
> Problem of gaps in regulatory coverage
> Scope for reciprocal treatment
> Need for special regulatory treatment of international banking

The problem of appropriate jurisdiction focuses on the relationships between various federal agencies, and between federal and state agencies in regulating the international banking activities of American banks. As pointed out above supervisory and examining powers are fragmented among several federal agencies, including the Federal Reserve Board, the Comptroller, and the FDIC. The FDIC probably possesses the smallest degree of supervisory authority over overseas activities of American banks. A strong argument exists for centralising all supervisory authority in one single federal agency. At present the Board of Governors appears to be the most likely candidate for assuming the centralised authority.

The jurisdictional question extends to the relationship between federal and state jurisdiction. State banks that are not members of the Federal Reserve System may establish foreign branches and engage in a variety of other international banking activities provided the state banking department is able to authorise such activities. We have seen that two states, New York and California, provide for a comprehensive system of regulation and supervision of the international activities of the banks in their respective states. However, it is doubtful if all of the fifty states in the United States would be able to provide this supervisory coverage if called upon to do so.

Gaps in regulatory coverage may present greater problems than questions of overlapping jurisdiction. An important gap lies in the non-availability of federal deposit insurance coverage on deposits in foreign branches of American banks and on deposits in foreign banks located in the United States. Availability of deposit insurance presupposes parity of underlying assets, and this poses a real question when one examines the nature of foreign branch deposit and loan activities. The dominant role of Eurocurrency operations in many foreign branches of American banks probably precludes FDIC coverage in such cases. This leaves application of federal deposit insurance on deposits in foreign banks in the United States as a realistic possibility. Another gap relates to the lack of federal jurisdiction over foreign banks operating in the United States. While this matter is discussed briefly in Chapter 7, it must be mentioned in this context also. The only federal regulation over foreign banks operating in the United States is via the 1970 amendment to the bank holding company legislation and in cases where foreign banks qualify to be considered as bank holding companies under that legislation. This gap in federal regulation is important in cases where American banks seek reciprocity in treatment from foreign governments.

Reciprocity refers to the ability of one party to seek and obtain equal treatment from a second party, by according that party the same equal treatment. Where international banking is concerned, American and other banks interested in overseas activities have long been concerned with reciprocity. As pointed out in Chapter 1, a number of countries effectively exclude American and other foreign banks from establishing direct representation by branch, agency, or affiliate operations. In the United States the problem of obtaining reciprocity in treatment for American banks is magnified due to the lack of federal regulatory authority over foreign banks, and to the federal system in which state-chartered banks may seek the immediate assistance of the state banking department and not a federal agency with centralised authority to deal with foreign governments on such matters. While U.S. banks may have an urgent need for reciprocity in only a few countries, there is a general presumption that reciprocity could be better or more effectively sought after by an agency of the federal government with broad authority over domestic and foreign banks alike.

The question of special regulatory treatment of international banking comes to the front when such activities become an important part of overall banking operations, as they have for many American banks. In the United States banking is a highly regulated industry. In the international context supervision of the operations of U.S. commercial banks appears to have two broad objectives in mind. These are to facilitate the foreign operations of banks, and to preserve the essential character and soundness of the U.S. banking system. In substance, departures from the general regulatory framework have been minor, and limited to a few specific statutory restraints. Congress has left the law intact, to be applied in a similar manner to domestic and foreign operations of U.S. banks alike. Perhaps the growth of U.S. international banking would not have been as impressive had laws and regulations created impediments of a magnitude or type more restrictive than those generally applicable to domestic banking operations. The question that now appears to lie before the lawmakers in Washington is whether the growth of international operations has reached a point where balancing considerations should be given more weight. That is, at what point does the foreign content of a U.S. bank's loans and deposits become large enough to warrant 'special treatment' of that banking institution under the laws and administrative processes? Is the nature of international banking such that special rules and regulations may be deemed necessary? Does international banking involve greater risks than domestic banking, and is a more secure or risk-free banking structure required when foreign assets and liabilities become in excess of some specified percentage?

II
ORGANISING
FOR INTERNATIONAL
BANKING

3 Managerial Objectives and Strategies

This chapter focuses on the managerial and organisational aspects of international banking. What prompts American banks to consider and eventually embark on a commitment in international banking? To what extent should banks commit themselves to international activities, and under what organisational forms? What organisational strategies are most suitable for individual banks venturing into the international field, and how is this influenced by size, location and other characteristics of banks?

The four chapters which follow elaborate on various parts of the discussion in this chapter. The overall objective is to present a concise yet comprehensive treatment of the problems and questions relating to decisions to 'go international', and selection of the most appropriate organisational path of development. Numerous alternatives may be available to an individual bank management at any particular time.

Various considerations make it rather difficult to give more than fleeting attention to the time factor in questions relating to organisational choices. Nevertheless, considerations as to developing or breaking into international banking now rather than later, may give greater urgency to acquisitions of interests in existing banks, or to the establishment of 'strategic branches' rather than some alternate expansion path. A time perspective may be of paramount importance in terms of the quality of organisational staff, lines of communication within the total bank organisation, and customer relationships.

A. MANAGEMENT OBJECTIVES AND INTERNATIONAL ORIENTATION

1. MANAGEMENT OBJECTIVES

The success of bank management is measured by its ability to promote the maximum rate of earnings return and growth consistent with maintaining a prudent risk exposure. The familiar trilogy of portfolio management considerations ever-present in the eyes of the bank's directors and principal officers, namely liquidity-profit-safety, has become translated into an operating handbook for successful bankers.

The same basic guidelines function in policy formulation concerning the international activities of a commercial bank. These may be specified in somewhat greater detail as follows:[1]

1. to increase or retain profitable deposit or other relationships with customers,
2. to provide the appropriate services in a competitive context at a reasonable cost to the bank,
3. to obtain the maximum gross returns on services rendered, again in a competitive context,
4. to hold the risk exposure of the bank within tolerable limits.

While international banking may possess its own unique characteristics, these general guidelines prevail. Decisions made by individual banks regarding international operations will be influenced by these guidelines. Questions relating to the establishment of international operations, the extent of foreign commitment undertaken by the bank, and the organisational forms and strategies that will be employed will be moulded by considerations which refer back to this profitability-risk relationship.

2. THE 250 U.S. BANKS IN INTERNATIONAL BANKING

Several years ago it was known that at least a hundred banks possessed a separate foreign department.[2] Generally these were banks with assets of $100 million or more. At present the number of U.S. banks with a foreign or international department is more than double the earlier figure.[3] These same banks hold virtually all of the foreign deposits in American banks, and include the large money market and regional banks.

Over 250 U.S. banks are active in international banking. The extent of their international operations varies, ranging from a small foreign section with one or two men carrying out essentially all of the functions, to a 'bank within a bank' wherein the international division carries out virtually all the functions of the domestic division, except for customers conducting an international business. Approximately one hundred of these 250 banks conduct a full range of international banking services. These include maintaining correspondent relations with a number of foreign banks which execute various transactions for U.S. banks and their domestic customers, extending credit abroad, soliciting foreign deposits, and buying and selling foreign exchange. These are the one hundred largest banks in the United States, each with assets of $500 million or more.

It is possible to distinguish three groups of banks from within the one hundred which stand apart in certain respects relative to their foreign operations. The first group consists of three banks including Bank of America, First National City Bank of New York, and Chase Manhattan Bank. Each bank has over $1 billion in foreign loans and credits outstanding at *domestic offices*, and each has over $1 billion in foreign deposits. Together the three account for one-third of foreign credits extended by U.S. banks. In addition, they accounted for 429 of the 648 foreign branches of U.S. banks operating at year-end 1972.[4] In addition their foreign branches accounted for close to one-half of total foreign branch assets of U.S. banks. Each of these three banks operates a global or world-wide network of foreign branches and affiliates. Moreover, each of the three banks in this group has established four or more Edge Act and Agreement corporations, which round out their world-wide international banking systems.

The second group consists of twenty-eight large banks, including nine from New York, five from Chicago, four from California, and one from Boston. All of these banks have established two or more foreign branches, and the twenty-eight banks at year-end 1972 had a total of 135 foreign branches around the globe. Nearly all of these banks operated one London or Nassau branch, and all had at least one Edge Act corporation or Agreement corporation. These banks account for approximately 30 per cent of foreign loans and deposits at domestic offices of banks in the United States.

A third group is more heterogeneous and consists of eighty-four banks located in a number of major cities around the United States. All of these banks have one foreign branch

Table 3.1

Postwar Expansion of Foreign Branches and Banking Corporations of Federal Reserve Member Banks (1950–1972)

	Number of Banks with Foreign Branches	Number of Foreign Branches	Number of Edge (Section 25[a]) Corporations	Number of Agreement (Section 25) Corporations
1950	7	95	2	4
1952	7	104	2	4
1954	7	106	2	4
1956	7	115	3	4
1958	7	119	5	3
1960	8	124	10	5
1962	10	145	22	4
1964	11	180	33	5
1966	13	244	41	4
1968	26	373	56	5
1970	79	532	70	5
1972	107	627	87	6

Source: Board of Governors of the Federal Reserve System.

and a large number of these banks are affiliated with an Edge Act corporation.

These 115 banks conduct the bulk of the international banking business of U.S. banks, and their overseas branches and affiliates comprise almost the entire foreign banking organisation of the United States. In addition, these banks tend to have the following characteristics in common:

1. International operations are of major importance.
2. Senior bank management includes the heads of their international departments.
3. International department operations have become increasingly integrated into the overall workings of the bank.
4. In the largest of these banks, international lending at domestic and foreign offices ranges from one-third to one-half of total deposits.
5. International deposits range from one-eighth to one-half of total deposits.
6. The contribution of international operations to bank earnings is apparently commensurate with the relative importance of foreign lending and deposit activity.
7. With some exceptions, these banks are major money market banks or major regional banks.
8. These banks rank high among the innovators in the banking industry.
9. Over one-third of assets of commercial banks in the United States are held by these 115 banks.[5]

3. PREREQUISITES FOR AN INTERNATIONAL ORIENTATION

Why do banks develop an interest in international banking? The reasons are not difficult to piece together. Developments external to the bank may impress upon the bank's management the opportunities available in the international banking field. Secondly, the inner workings of the bank may develop in such a manner that international operations become attractive, and possibly even a necessity.

Among the external developments, the first and perhaps most obvious is the growth and intensity of competitive pressures, which have become characteristic of American and overseas banking. A second external factor which has brought about an increased interest in international operations has been a shift in the business mix of corporate customers. More U.S. firms of varying sizes enjoy a large proportion of foreign business, and are in need of international banking services. It is only natural that they should seek out these services from their domestic bank. Many U.S. banks have become more internationally oriented mainly as a result of following the internationalisation of their corporate clients.[6]

When is a bank ready for international operations? A number of considerations are important, and should be looked into prior to a bank's embarking on a substantial foreign commitment.[7] Readiness relates to the inner workings, resources and strengths of the bank. There are four critical areas internal to the bank which should be considered in attempting to ascertain whether or not a bank is ready to go international. These areas include (1) the inclination and ability of management, (2) the size and financial strength of the bank, (3) the ability to provide adequate marketing information to customers in need of international services, and (4) location of the bank.

Very often a U.S. corporation that takes the leadership in its industry in developing and promoting international business does so because its chief executive officers and directors have a keen interest in international operations and regard international contacts as a necessary source of profit and future growth. This has been a fact of life for U.S. corporations such as Pfizer, IBM, and Caterpillar Tractor. An American bank should not embark on an international programme unless the senior management of the bank is fully persuaded that international operations will become a necessary part of the overall banking service rendered on behalf of customers of that bank in the future. There should be a complete understanding of the significance that this course will have on manpower requirements, opportunities and problems, the risks attendant upon international credit-making, and the alterations that gradually take place in the composition of the bank's own customer mix.

Not all banks may reasonably expect to move into the foreign banking business at will. A bank must be large enough and possess resources which make it capable of sustaining heavy start-up costs (and possibly losses). Moreover, it must be prepared to assume credit and equity risks that are not exactly paralleled in its domestic business. For this reason substantial financial resources should be available to the bank which embarks on an international banking career. There are several reasons for this, including the fact that a substantial investment ordinarily will be necessary to establish either an international department, foreign branch, or international banking corporation (Edge Act or other). In the latter case, Section 25(a) of the Federal Reserve Act calls for a minimum capital of $2 million for an Edge Act corporation. In the case of a relatively small bank in which the $2 million represents 10 per cent of its own capital and surplus, we have a parent bank capital totalling $20 million, which might support $200 million to $250 million in deposits. In short, we are talking about figures that characterise only the largest banks in the United States.

Not too long ago a corporate treasurer pointed out that his company was 'more interested in the willingness of a bank to respond to the needs of the company than in the size of the bank'.[8] It is entirely possible that the international orientation of a bank may be the outcome of forces within the bank not directly related to size of the bank.

A marketing orientation is essential for a bank desiring to enter the field of international banking. Corporate customers must be persuaded that the bank 'belongs' in the field of international banking, that there is no question of the bank's ability to service a wide range of possible international financing needs, and that the full package of domestic and international marketing intelligence facilities can be made available on terms equal or superior to those offered by competing American and foreign institutions.

B. BALANCING RETURNS AND RISKS

The decision to undertake a foreign commitment in the form of a branch, affiliate, or Edge corporation involves a dual problem; making the actual decision to proceed with the foreign operation as well as selecting the organisational form to be employed. These two aspects of the problem are in most cases inseparable.

The decision to undertake a foreign investment or international banking commitment involves appropriating a certain sum of the bank's own capital funds in developing an international department, assuming a foreign exchange 'position', organising and operating a foreign branch, establishing an Edge corporation, or investing in banking and financing affiliates. Assuming that the bank is sufficiently interested in a foreign commitment, the decision hinges on balancing the direct and indirect returns on foreign operations against the costs and risks of the undertaking.

1. DIRECT AND INDIRECT RETURNS ON FOREIGN OPERATIONS

The decision to invest in foreign operations may be viewed in a manner similar to the investment decision undertaken by any business organisation motivated essentially by profitability considerations. In such cases the analysis generally involves considering positive and negative inducements, with a view toward striking a balance.

Among the positive factors that might be influential in a bank management's decision to undertake an investment in foreign operations and facilities are the following:

1. Direct return on capital
2. Indirect return on capital
3. Ability to avoid risks characteristic of such operations
4. Willingness to assume risks

The direct return refers to the net earnings realised by a foreign department, branch, or affiliate on the funds invested and utilised in international operations. The indirect return refers to the enhancement of head office earnings contributed by the foreign department, branch, or affiliate in the form of expanded market area, deposit growth, increased international department income, and foreign lending activity. It is highly possible that the indirect returns will become a crucial factor in the analysis and decision to make an investment in a foreign department, branch, or affiliate.

The indirect returns are proportionately so considerable that a foreign branch which has not remitted earnings to the Head Office for an extended period may, after analysis, still qualify as a profitable office due to the significant contribution it makes during the same period to Head Office profit potential.[9]

Positive and negative inducements may be included among the factors prompting a bank to consider a larger foreign commitment in a more favourable manner. Included among the negative inducements are the following:

1. slow growth in domestic deposits,
2. competition with domestic financial institutions,
3. shift toward costly time deposits by U.S. asset holders,
4. the need to offer a broader range of banking services in order to retain domestic corporate customers,
5. limits on branching in many states, such as Illinois, Massachusetts, and Florida.

Direct Returns

The return on capital invested by the parent bank will be influenced by a number of variables, including such matters as the degree of flexibility achieved by the foreign operation, dividend policy of the foreign unit, taxation, and ability to obtain supplementary funds in the overseas area of operation. In the following paragraphs we compare the prospects for maximising the return on capital by direct foreign branches and foreign affiliates, based on considerations enumerated above.

Direct foreign branches of U.S. banks are carefully circumscribed by the various regulations that apply. In general, foreign branches cannot undertake operations that extend beyond those ordinarily permitted domestic banks. Some liberalisation was provided for the operations of foreign branches in the 1963 revision of Regulations K and M. Nevertheless, the U.S. foreign branch must bear the burden of responsibility in justifying the need for conducting operations regarded as beyond the pale of banking in this country. Foreign affiliates and Edge Act corporations do not suffer from this type of inflexibility. Through their Edge corporations and foreign affiliates, such banks as Morgan Guaranty Trust Co. have carried on extensive investment banking and underwriting activities overseas. By means of its foreign affiliates, the First National Bank of Boston has developed a fairly important factoring and commercial financing business overseas. Through their Edge corporations and foreign affiliates U.S. banks have been able to undertake equity positions in foreign development banks, and other types of foreign corporations.

In the area of dividend policy, we should note that the entire net income, after local taxes, of a foreign branch is available to the parent bank as earnings. This assumes no foreign exchange restrictions. Head office management in the United States generally would have complete discretion in the use of profits. In the case of foreign affiliates, only the share of declared dividends of the local venture, in proportion to the stock ownership of the Edge corporation or the parent bank, is available to the parent bank. In the case of a joint venture or minority interest on the part of the U.S. bank investor, there may be insufficient influence over dividend policy to fully satisfy the American bank.

Foreign branches of U.S. banks are subject to the same federal tax on profits as U.S. corporations. In effect, branch profits are taken into parent bank net income as reported for federal income tax purposes, *whether or not* they are actually remitted. Therefore, branch earnings are available for reinvestment by the foreign branch net of taxes (U.S. and foreign).

The Revenue Act of 1962 permits retained profits earned by affiliates in less developed countries to be accumulated without current incidence of U.S. corporate profits taxes. In cases of 'controlled foreign corporations' in developed countries, i.e., more than 50 per cent of voting shares are owned by U.S. interests, earnings from interest and services are taxable to U.S. shareholders of 10 per cent or more of voting stock in proportion to their holdings in the foreign corporation. If the foreign corporation is not 'controlled', the retained earnings not declared as dividends are not subject to U.S. taxes, resulting in delaying taxes payable. Less than 10 per cent ownership is unlikely on the part of U.S. investors, because a tax credit is available only when the U.S. parent holds a 10 per cent or larger interest in the foreign affiliate. The tax credit applies for foreign income taxes paid by the foreign affiliate against U.S. taxes due.

In cases of Edge Act corporations, dividends to the parent

corporation are treated according to Section 342 of the Internal Revenue Code dealing with inter-corporate dividends. Subsidiaries which are 80 per cent or more controlled by a U.S. parent (commercial bank in this case) corporation provide a tax advantage in so far as such dividends are concerned. Fifteen per cent of inter-corporate dividends paid by such subsidiaries to U.S. parent firms are subject to income taxes at normal tax rates.

Indirect Returns

We have indicated that an important consideration in the case of a U.S. bank contemplating establishment of a foreign branch or acquisition of an interest in a foreign bank is the extent of indirect return on capital that results from the investment. These indirect returns fall into the following categories: (1) branch foreign balances; (2) dollar deposits from overseas; (3) dollar balances from the United States; (4) marketing area extension; (5) foreign loans; and (6) exchange of business.

1. *Branch foreign balances*　Foreign branches can make an important contribution to overall deposit growth of the parent U.S. bank. Since they are direct branches, without an individual capital and corporate structure, the local and Eurocurrency deposits which they generate are converted to U.S. dollars and included in the accounting figures on reporting dates. The conversion generally takes place at currently prevailing rates of exchange between the local currency involved and the U.S. dollar. Inclusion of these deposit figures increases the deposit and asset figures on the parent bank's books, which raises the ranking of the bank in the tabulations of banks by size. A bank with an equity participation in a separately incorporated foreign banking affiliate cannot enjoy this deposit advantage.

The accounting conversion of branch figures for reporting purposes should not be confused with the fluidity of funds which a bank with domestic branches may enjoy. With limited exceptions, deposits generated in one country may not be put to work in the United States or third countries with great freedom because of the desire on the part of bank management to balance local currency liabilities with assets denominated in that same currency, due to foreign exchange controls, or because of the comparatively tighter monetary conditions which may prevail in the country than in other regions of the world.

2. *Dollar deposits from overseas*   Tangible gains occur for the parent bank in the form of dollar deposits which the foreign branch must maintain in the United States for the conduct of its business there. These 'captive' balances can provide funds for use in the United States. Moreover, branch loans to head office can provide a substantial means of asset and liquidity 'back-up' for the parent bank in its reserve and liquidity management. Dollar balances in an affiliate in which a U.S. bank has an equity interest are not likely to be captive but may be placed in American banks because of advantages that U.S. banks offer. Branches yield captive deposit balances, but the balances of foreign affiliates may or may not be 'placed' with the head office of the U.S. parent bank. Correspondent balances from a foreign bank are not captive. There is a *quid pro quo* in the form of reciprocal balances and services provided.

3. *Dollar balances from the United States*   Another important source of dollar deposits for the parent bank is 'compensating' balances which are placed by U.S. business concerns in return for the services or overseas financing in which the foreign branch or affiliate participates. Here the overseas establishment of the American bank can provide the extra margin of effective service needed to hold or establish favourable customer relations for the parent bank. Banks customarily make no charges for such services, but obviously expect a return of some sort. This is usually derived from the overall domestic relationship, new or increased deposit balances.

Foreign branches owe allegiance to head office. In addition to directing business to the parent, the overseas branch may offer alternative uses of loanable funds, often an important consideration.

In the case of Edge Act corporation equity participation, there is a lesser, but similar, potential for compensating balances. However, allegiance will be split. A sole U.S. minority ownership would provide an advantage in securing balances held in the United States. For example, Bank of America (New York) is the sole U.S. investor in the Greek Development Bank, as compared with numerous U.S. bank participants in the Private Development Corp. of the Philippines. The local aspect of the profit equation becomes more important for the joint venture.

4. *Marketing area*   Direct branches and equity participations provide the type of facilities which few banks can offer, hence those American banks which extend their services in these directions can expand their marketing areas in a fairly effective manner. Their appeal extends to companies throughout the country which have operations in the same overseas area.

5. *Foreign loans*   Foreign branches and equity participations in overseas banks provide opportunities to become acquainted with local credit market operations, and an advantageous position from which to scout out attractive financing proposals for the head office. Development banks providing local currency financing can frequently refer the dollar portion of a customer's expansion programme to their American (bank) shareholders.

6. *Exchange of business*   The overseas affiliate or correspondent makes a contribution to head office profit through business which it is able to direct to the United States. This takes the form of letter of credit, foreign exchange, collections, and deposit balances. Such business is captive with the direct branch, but in the area of correspondent relationships such business is highly competitive. Experience warrants placing the joint venture between the branch and correspondent in this regard.

The establishment of a foreign branch, or purchase into a foreign affiliate involves a probable loss of volume of referral and exchange business from banks in the foreign country. The branch or affiliate will be regarded as a direct competitor of indigenous banks. 'It is interesting that one bank with major equity interests in foreign commercial banks has found no evidence that the exchange of business with existing correspondents in the same country has been diminished since the investments were made.'[10]

Many joint ventures and bank consortium groups are either non-competitive, or competitive in a peripheral way, with local banking facilities in other countries. Joint ventures may, in fact, have an even greater attraction than a local branch as a business feeder by improving the flow of business between the parent bank in the United States and other investing banks in the same or third countries.

A foreign branch or equity participation may serve in the capacity of providing entry for further foreign business. Eligibility of the parent bank to participate in financing under American foreign assistance or agricultural surplus disposal programmes may be contingent upon evidencing an 'interest' in the economic welfare of the country. Such financing is conducted through private commercial channels on a letter of credit basis under dollar commitments from Washington. Designation of the participating American banks is by policy left to one or another agency of the government of the recipient country.

2. RISK ASSUMPTION AND AVOIDANCE

American banks that engage in international operations assume various types of risks. The variety and degree of risks assumed are greater than what a bank ordinarily would face in pursuing only a domestic business. In this section we isolate for discussion several of the risks which are greater in international than domestic banking, or which are present only in the foreign sphere of banking operations. We close our discussion by referring to measures available for minimising these risks.

Hayes distinguishes three separate types of risks in international banking including the credit risk, country risk, and currency risk.[11] The first refers to the financial status of the borrower, the second to the possibilities of political or economic disturbances in the country of the borrower, and the third to fluctuating currency values when loans are denominated in foreign currencies. A more detailed discussion along these lines is included in Chapter 8 titled 'Foreign Lending'.

Another approach in classifying risks is more general and is related to the foreign investment position taken by a bank holding foreign assets, whether they be in the form of foreign loans, overseas branches, equity interests in foreign bank and finance company affiliates, or in some other form. The risks identified here include business risks, economic risks, and political risks. In the discussion which follows we examine these three types of risks in light of the opportunities for an individual bank to control them.

The ability of an American bank to undertake an investment

in a foreign branch or overseas affiliate depends in part upon the ability of the bank to assume certain business risks. These are controlled by the capital position of the bank, the management responsibility retained, the ability to market the new foreign services to clientele, and the local banking structure.

Capital adequacy relates to the capital position of the parent bank, and the ability of the bank to 'risk' capital in a foreign commitment. The ratio of foreign equity investment to the bank's capital might be indicative of the type of measure involved if it was possible to weight the foreign equity investment with a loss probability factor. Diversification of foreign equity investments in a number of countries around the globe might warrant lowering the probability of loss weight applied. Joint ventures tend to reduce the dollar risk or dollar exposure by reducing the investment per foreign office. Participations with other lenders and government agencies tend to reduce the extent of and likelihood of incurring losses on loans and operations overseas.

Management is high on the list of considerations relating to controlling business risks to a minimum. Experienced personnel in international banking are at a premium, and the selection and training of personnel continues to be a costly factor. The joint venture uses less U.S. personnel and more local manpower. Purchase of a going concern overseas may bring with it a cadre of experienced men. Generally, the smaller the management responsibility (per cent investment and control) the more nearly the joint venture resembles a (lower yielding) portfolio investment. Also, the smaller the percentage investment in a joint venture, the less likely business will be directed to the parent bank. Finally, the lower the U.S. bank's proportionate investment and control, the less servicing its own customers will likely receive from the local bank.

An investment in a foreign banking facility carries with it the assumption that the parent will be able to make its existing and prospective customers in the United States aware of the services that can be afforded through this new operation. It is conceivable that U.S. customers will better perceive the direct advantages in services available when the overseas facility is a direct branch. There is less likelihood they will perceive this service facility in light of their own requirements if it should be a minority interest in a foreign bank. A minority interest in a foreign bank may leave an 'indigenous' impression on the part of U.S. businessmen. This may help in developing new business that is local to the country in which the foreign affiliate is domiciled. However, it may not permit adequate control over risk assumption as would ordinarily be the case with a direct branch.

The local banking structure may be one that presents a variety of problems for direct branches on the one hand, and equity interests in local banks on the other. Banking may be tradition or custom-bound, rather than competitively oriented as in the United States. Loan officers may find it difficult to acclimate themselves to such operational conditions. Second, foreign banks may dominate banking, and this may influence the 'ground rules' should a U.S. bank venture into the banking market through a branch or affiliate operation. Finally, profitability and credit analysis considerations and standards may be far different, necessitating that the U.S. bank adjust its methods of operation and performance goals accordingly.

The economic risks attendant upon a foreign investment commitment include those related to the stage of economic development of the host country, the business cycle, dependence on one or several crops for export and foreign exchange earnings, and problems related to an 'open economy' status. Domestic inflation, declines in export earnings, and cyclical influences often bring about an over-exposure of the foreign banking sector, especially in small or less developed countries.

Foreign branches and affiliates of U.S. banks often depend on a high volume of foreign trade in the foreign country to maintain their profitability of operations. A decline in foreign trade as a result of exchange controls, business cycle developments or commodity price fluctuations will reduce the volume of operations and direct and indirect earnings flowing from the foreign branch or affiliate bank in that country. Such losses in volume of operations and earnings may be offset in part by internal inflation wherein the appreciation of prices of local assets brings forth a higher local currency volume of banking operations. However, currency depreciation may result in a dilution of equity in terms of dollars, caused by a devaluation or depreciation in value of the local currency unit.

Once an international commitment has been made, political risks generally are beyond the control of management. These political risks take the form of reform legislation and its ultimate effects on the environment for doing business, especially banking, in the host country; taxation and its effect on the after-tax performance of the U.S. bank's foreign earnings; and foreign exchange controls which may delay the remission of profits from the foreign branch or affiliate.

American banks have access to a wide variety of measures for avoiding or minimising the risks that are associated with international banking. In doing so, they may enlist the co-operation of foreign banks and governments, as well as agencies of the United States government. Moreover, through their own management policies and practices they may avoid or minimise such risks. One of the most important means available for American banks to limit their exposure on foreign credits is by obtaining guarantees from foreign banks. In cases of loans made to foreign nationals, guarantees are often obtained from indigenous commercial banks, or government agencies including central banks. In the past credits extended by U.S. banks in less developed areas have been protected by guarantees of U.S. agencies including the Agency for International Development (AID),[12] and the Export-Import Bank. In the latter case the Export-Import Bank co-operates with the Foreign Credit Insurance Association (FCIA), a group of marine, casualty and property insurance companies, in writing insurance policies covering a variety of risks associated with the granting of short-term and medium-term export credits. In the past Eximbank has assumed the full political risk under these policies, and in excess of certain limits shares the credit risk with FCIA. Other measures followed by banks include achievement of a long-run diversification of risks by the development of a world-wide network of branches and affiliates, and a short-run policy of establishing country limits on credit extensions.

Foreign currency exposure is limited by denominating loans in U.S. dollars. Other means utilised to reduce currency exposure include complicated third currency loan arrangements,[13] and denominating loans in one of several currencies in which forward cover is available.

C. RELATIVE ADVANTAGES IN ALTERNATIVE ORGANISATIONAL FORMS

U.S. banks conduct their international banking activities by means of foreign correspondent banks, overseas branches, foreign affiliates, and international banking consortium groups. Moreover, they employ a variety of strategies in developing and expanding their international operations. As David Rockefeller, Chairman of the Board of the Chase Manhattan Bank has expressed it, 'no single route is the best for all countries and all conditions'.[14] Chase has utilised a variety of methods and approaches including the purchase of existing banks with trained manpower in South-east Asia, joint ventures which have been supported by the governments of Latin American countries, new branches in the Caribbean area, and a world-wide network of correspondents.

1. RELATIVE ADVANTAGES IN BRANCH, AFFILIATE AND OTHER FORMS

American banks conduct their international banking business through correspondents, international departments, overseas branches, and subsidiary institutions. The bank's choice among these various options depends upon the relative advantages in terms of its own organisational set-up, the type of business it operates, conditions in countries overseas, and other factors. Foreign banking corporations, the so-called Edge and Agreement corporations, are special types of subsidiary institutions chartered in the United States, from which a U.S. bank may conduct international operations separate from its domestic business. These corporations also serve as intermediaries through which U.S. banks may participate with other interests in 'certain phases of foreign and international business'.[15]

The following appear to be the more important advantages or considerations in selecting the appropriate organisational form:

    1. Amount of investment required
    2. Return on investment
    3. Type and volume of foreign business
    4. Control over operations

5. Referral business
6. Taxation
7. New business
8. Flexibility of operation
9. Controls by host country
10. Manpower requirements

Most U.S. banks conducting an international business rely at least in part on correspondent banks to handle their foreign transactions. Under this procedure, a U.S. bank may have an agreement with a foreign bank under which the two banks act as agents for each other. The banks may maintain deposit balances with one another and refer business on a reciprocal basis.

Heavy resort to the correspondent approach reflects the nature of unit banking in the United States. Moreover, it may indicate that the banks employing this method do not have sufficient international business to warrant establishing full-fledged banking offices abroad. The correspondent approach has the advantage of not requiring any substantial investment in international banking facilities and manpower. However, it is a relatively inflexible approach and offers only limited potential for developing new business.

Banks that are large enough and at the same time possess a sufficient volume of international business may establish an international division. While expensive to organise and a heavy drain on skilled manpower of the bank, the international division is not without significant advantages. First, organisation of an international department or division is a necessary initial step in the long-run build-up of a profitable international banking business. Second, the ability to offer a considerable range of services through an international department places the domestic side of the bank in a more favourable position to attract and hold customers. Third, the international department can be an excellent training ground for young bank officers in need of a varied experience. Finally, the international department provides the bank with a management control centre for purposes of evaluating profitability of operations, control and co-ordination of international operations, and evaluation of the relative performance of various departments and operations of the bank.

Banks developing a substantial foreign business may go beyond the establishment of an international department, and organise one or more representative offices in principal overseas cities. Through a representative office a U.S. bank may be able to develop better knowledge of foreign markets and thereby make contact with potential customers doing business in these markets.

A representative office requires at least a modest investment on the part of the U.S. bank. In principal overseas cities where there exist premium rentals on first quality office locations, the investment required of the U.S. bank may be substantial. Banks with representative offices are not permitted to conduct a full range of banking activities from these offices, the major prohibition being against the receipt of deposits. A full branch may receive deposits, as well as conduct such other banking operations as are permitted a representative office. Generally, where deposit taking may be an important part of the international banking operation, a branch must be preferred over a representative office. A representative office may be the only means of direct representation in a country that either limits or outright prohibits branches of foreign banks, or foreign ownership of banking firms. On the other hand a representative office may be helpful in referring new business prospects, and certainly can contribute to the parent bank's ability to respond to inquiries regarding local regulations and business conditions.

Establishment of an overseas branch requires a substantial investment on the part of the U.S. bank, both in terms of dollar amount of investment and manpower. Overseas branches of American banks add a high degree of flexibility to international and domestic operations, and can make an important contribution to the development of new business prospects. Income earned by the branch may be subject to foreign taxes, although double-taxation avoidance agreements between the United States and other countries as well as the provision for a foreign tax credit in the U.S. internal revenue code may result in mitigating any additional tax burden resulting from exposure to foreign tax jurisdiction.

Formation of an Edge Act corporation provides a number of strong advantages for a U.S. bank, but at a substantial cost, since the minimum capitalisation of an Edge Act subsidiary is

$2 million. Moreover, an Edge Act subsidiary providing a fairly complete international banking service requires a considerable staff of highly skilled and specialised men. The benefits derived from an Edge corporation include the opportunity to establish an international banking headquarters in New York or some other major city in the United States, the possibility of establishing foreign branches controlled by the Edge subsidiary, flexibility in terms of a diversified approach toward international banking activities, and the prospects for developing new business through the contacts provided by an ongoing international banking and investing subsidiary. The Edge corporation may be subject to the direct control of the parent bank officer cadre. Moreover, any dividends paid by the Edge corporation to its parent bank are taxable as inter-corporate dividends, i.e., only to the extent of 15 per cent of their amount.

Formation or purchase of an interest in a foreign banking affiliate may provide the U.S. bank with entry into foreign banking markets with only a modest equity investment and with only minor demands on the parent bank's relatively scarce international banking manpower resources. Substantial control is possible when the American bank possesses a majority of the stock in the foreign affiliate. However, a minority interest offers little opportunity for control and limited potential for developing new business through referrals. A minority interest does provide the American bank with a 'foot in the door', and the prospects for developing closer business and banking connections in the foreign country far more rapidly than might be possible by going it alone or establishing a *de novo* banking institution.

2. ORGANISATION STRATEGIES OF BANKS

Now that we have considered the various factors which weigh heavily in determining whether a branch, representative office, Edge corporation, or ownership in a foreign affiliate will be the most appropriate organisational method to be used in a specific international banking investment, we might look into the strategy approaches or strategy mixes that have been used by various banks in organising for international operations. In short, we are interested in describing the mixture of organisational approaches in establishing and

Table 3.2

Analysis of Relative Advantages from
Alternative Organisational Forms

Advantage	Correspondent	International Department	Representative Office	Overseas Branch	Edge Act Corporation	Foreign Affiliate majority owned	Foreign Affiliate minority owned
1. Amount of investment required	None	Moderate	Moderate	Substantial	Substantial	Moderate	Moderate
2. Return on investment.	DEPENDS ON OPERATIONS						
3. Type and volume of foreign business	Correspondent executes for U.S. bank	General intl. banking and servicing multi-national clients	Source of information	General intl. banking and Euro-dollars	Out-of-state intl. dept.	Variety of financial services and joint ventures	Variety of financial services and joint ventures

4. Control over operation	None	Direct control and leverage over Correspondent	Possibility of influence over Correspondent	Direct control exists	Direct control exists	Substantial control	Minor control
5. Referral business	On reciprocal basis	Minor	Positive by location	Most favourable	Most favourable	Potential depends on relation with parent	Minor
6. Taxation	Not applicable	Income is part of head office earnings	Income is part of head office earnings	Must pay foreign tax	Tax is payable on 15 per cent of dividend paid by subsidiary	Tax is payable on 15 per cent of dividend paid by subsidiary	Tax is payable on 15 per cent of dividend paid by subsidiary*
7. New business	From correspondent on reciprocal basis	Favourable	Favourable	Most favourable	Most favourable	Some potential exists	Limited potential

Table 3.2

Analysis of Relative Advantages from
Alternative Organisational Forms

Advantage	Correspondent	International Department	Representative Office	Overseas Branch	Edge Act Corporation	Foreign Affiliate majority owned	Foreign Affiliate minority owned
8. Flexibility of operation	Relatively inflexible	Small amount of flexibility	Relatively inflexible	High degree of flexibility	Most flexible	Some flexibility	Inflexible
9. Controls by host country	Not applicable	Not applicable	May be only means of direct representation in foreign country	May prohibit branch	May limit some activities	May limit foreign ownership	May limit foreign ownership
10. Manpower	No requirement	Requirement depends on size	Some manpower required	May involve heavy commitment	Substantial commitment	Minor	Minor

* A minimum 10 per cent ownership is required for applicability of the foreign tax credit.

developing international banking services that have been employed by individual banks. Naturally, history and accident play their role in this regard. Notwithstanding, there do appear to be some sound management strategies involved in the development of an international banking organisation.

In analysing the combinations of international banking organisations actually employed by large U.S. banks it is possible to single out six patterns or strategies which appear to be fairly characteristic. Nearly all of the banking organisations of the 250 or more U.S. banks actively engaged in international banking fit into one of the six strategies or patterns. The six patterns may be described as follows:

1. *Strategy of a World-wide Network*   These banks enjoy a world-wide network of foreign branches, offices, and affiliates.
2. *Strategy of Numerous Foreign Branches*   This group includes banks with a heavy commitment to international banking. These banks each have two or more foreign branches and at least one Edge Act or similar corporate affiliate.
3. *Strategy of Single Foreign Branch*   These are banks that are internationally oriented, have one foreign branch, possibly one or more overseas representative offices, and almost all have an Edge Act affiliate.
4. *Strategy of Edge Act or Foreign Affiliation*   Banks with a part ownership in an Edge Act corporation, or substantial ownership in a foreign bank affiliate.
5. *Strategy of Representative Offices*   This category includes banks with representative offices and a network of correspondent foreign banks.
6. *Strategy of Correspondent Bank Networks*   This group includes banks which rely mainly on correspondent relationships to conduct much of their international banking operations.

Over 250 American banks fit into one of these six organisational patterns. At year-end 1972 three American banks possessed a world-wide network of branches and affiliates.

Twenty-eight banks owned two or more foreign branches. Eighty-four banks operated one branch, falling into category three. There may be no more than three dozen banks that have gone the affiliate route, placing them in category four. Approximately forty U.S. banks have established representative offices, but enjoy no other international banking facilities except their own international department and correspondent ties with foreign banks. These banks fall into category five. This leaves less than 100 banks which have no direct overseas representation and must rely on foreign correspondents to execute transactions and perform services for them.

In the remainder of this section we examine the organisational patterns developed by several of the large banks active in the international field.

World-wide Network

The First National City Bank of New York enjoys the largest and most developed international banking organisation among U.S. banks. At year-end 1972 the First National City Bank operated close to 240 overseas branches, approximately 37 per cent of the overseas branches of U.S. banks at that time. In addition, FNCB operated over 400 additional overseas offices (offices of affiliate banks, finance and leasing companies, and representative offices) operating in ninety-four countries and territories around the world. At year-end 1972 FNCB operated six Edge and one Agreement corporations.

There appear to be several objectives in the strategy employed by FNCB. The first is to develop a world-wide network of banking and financial services superior to that possessed by any other bank in the field. The second is to retain its considerable lead over U.S. rivals such as Bank of America and Chase Manhattan Bank, also leaders in the international banking field. The third is to derive the many advantages that accrue from a world-wide network of diversified banking and financial service facilities throughout the globe.

Numerous Branches

The First National Bank of Boston was one of the first U.S. banks to espouse a real interest in international banking. It established the First National Corporation, incorporated in

Massachusetts in 1918 as a state-chartered foreign banking corporation under Section 25 of the Federal Reserve Act. Subsequently, the corporate name was changed to the Bank of Boston, International, New York, and a federal charter was obtained under Section 25(a) of the Federal Reserve Act. Bank of Boston International is one of nearly two dozen New York based Edge corporations which provide their non-New York parent bank with an international banking department located in New York. The First National Bank of Boston has a second Edge corporation, Boston Overseas Financial Corp., Boston, which was established in 1960 to make equity investments overseas. Through BOFC affiliates the parent bank provides the following financial services; factoring, leasing, consumer financing, industrial development financing and financial consulting. Through its overseas offices, ownership in International Factors, and ownership in other leasing and financing affiliates, First National of Boston operates in thirty-four countries around the globe. Ownership in the factoring units is shared with one or more major financial institutions in each country.

At year-end 1972 the First National Bank of Boston had twenty-five foreign branches. In addition, the bank operates three Edge Act affiliates. While its overseas branches are concentrated in two areas, Latin America and London, through its foreign affiliates the bank provides a diversified banking and non-bank financial service in Western Europe, South Africa, the Far East, and Australia. Apparently, there are two major differences between the international banking strategy of this bank and that of First National City Bank of New York. First, the New York bank possesses a world-wide network of banking offices, whereby the Boston Bank is restricted mainly to Latin America and London. Second, the Boston Bank emphasises ownership interests in foreign financing and non-bank companies, whereas FNCB undertakes substantial equity interests in foreign banks and non-bank companies.

Single Branch

In 1972 over eighty American banks operated a single overseas branch. In almost all cases these overseas branches were located in London or Nassau. These single branches provide the

U.S. bank with access to foreign sources of deposit funds for lending to international customers, as well as an increased capacity to service internationally oriented customers.

Edge Act and Foreign Affiliation

In 1961 the Mellon National Bank and Trust Co. of Pittsburgh made its first significant loan overseas.[16] At that time it was becoming obvious that lack of international banking facilities threatened Mellon's share of the domestic corporate banking business. A major policy shift in 1962 resulted in upgrading the Foreign Bureau to the status of an International Department. By 1963 Mellon was one of the largest American bank creditors to Japan. In 1963 Mellon formed a Pittsburgh-based Edge corporation, which relocated to New York in 1966. This was still not enough. At this point the Swiss Credit Bank of Zurich approached Mellon and asked it to put together a group of U.S. banks to join with a number of European financial institutions to form Eurofinance, a venture organised to analyse portfolio and other investment opportunities in Europe. The reason for Swiss Credit Bank approaching Mellon was the latter's reputation for a strong trust department. Unfortunately, the Interest Equalisation Tax of 1964 destroyed the usefulness of Eurofinance in so far as U.S. portfolio investment was concerned. By this time the Mellon management recognised the need to move into international banking at a more accelerated pace. The question was how?

The opportunity broke to the surface in 1965, when a formal agreement was made for Mellon to purchase a substantial equity interest in the Bank of London & South America (BOLSA). BOLSA presented the situation of a sterling bank operating in the dollar area (Latin America). BOLSA was in need of additional dollar capital. In 1957 when Sir George Bolton took over the reins of management, BOLSA was a moribund institution. From then until 1965, when the negotiations were concluded, the bank had prospered.

Mellon's investment in BOLSA represented the bank's first major step into the field of international banking, and the core of Mellon's foreign banking activities. This is in contrast with First National City Bank of New York's purchase of a 40 per cent stake in National & Grindlays Bank Ltd and Chase

Manhattan's purchase of a 15 per cent interest in the Standard Bank Ltd. In these two situations the New York banks filled gaps in their world-wide geographic coverage.

Mellon's purchase of a substantial equity in BOLSA was prompted by a number of considerations. First, Mellon would obtain a favoured position in the British money and foreign exchange markets. Second, BOLSA had the only foreign-owned bank branches in Spain and Portugal. Third, BOLSA had a strong regional position in Latin America, with over seventy branches in that area. Fourth, the partnership with BOLSA provided Mellon with access to an expertise in international banking operations that Mellon was lacking. For example, BOLSA helped Mellon establish its only branch in London in 1967, and supplied a foreign exchange trader. BOLSA also helped Mellon establish a Tokyo representative office in 1969. In return Mellon helped BOLSA in a number of important respects. In addition to the infusion of dollar capital, Mellon provided BOLSA with access to U.S. customers, has encouraged the introduction of modern operations, and assisted BOLSA in introducing a credit card operation in Argentina.

During the decade of the 1960s Mellon has caught and surpassed a number of major U.S. banks in the development of international banking activities. At present Mellon ranks among the top thirty American banks in the size, flexibility, and sophistication of its international banking network. The purchase of a substantial interest in BOLSA was a key factor in Mellon attaining this position.

4 The International Department

Prior to World War I, almost the entire export trade of the United States was handled by a dozen New York foreign trade firms, with branches and representatives in major trading centres of the world. American manufacturers sold directly to these exporting firms and received payment from them. The reason for these arrangements were the hesitancy of U.S. manufacturers to extend credit terms to foreign buyers, and the unwillingness of foreign buyers to send cash with their orders. Export merchants were responsible for buying and selling, undertaking credit investigations, invoicing, drawing and negotiating bills of exchange, and holding foreign currency balances.[1] In short, they enjoyed a strongly entrenched position in the foreign trade field.

One might be tempted to ask the question, what were American banks doing in these matters? The answer is quite simple. Very little! American banks, on the other hand possessed little foreign credit information, and were not inclined to carry sizeable deposit balances with foreign banks. They possessed practically no foreign branches, and maintained no foreign or international departments as we know them today. Aside from the New York agencies of several British banks, there were almost no international banking facilities in the United States.

Hence all important foreign banking business gravitated to these agencies, and much of this was transacted in sterling rather than dollars.

This situation was profoundly altered during and after World War I. During the war unusual scarcities of goods developed, and U.S. manufacturers and exporters found foreign buyers literally 'knocking at their doors'. This situation watered down the dominant position in exporting formerly enjoyed by the old-line exporting firms. Moreover, it was quickly reflected in the activities of American banks, who found U.S. manufacturers expecting them to take care of the banking side of their foreign business. American banks met this challenge. The growth of the foreign departments of large New York banks in the period 1917–20 was phenomenal. Moreover, American banks established their own foreign branches overseas, and extended and strengthened their correspondent relationships with foreign banks.

Since these early beginnings, the old-line 'foreign department' approach to international banking has given way to what is the subject of discussion in this chapter, the International Department. The change in name is symbolic of the change in functions—from financing foreign trade as the major function to financing a wide variety of operations throughout the world (including the financing of foreign trade as one continuing aspect).

A.   ROLE OF THE INTERNATIONAL DEPARTMENT

1.   RELATION OF THE INTERNATIONAL DEPARTMENT TO THE BANK

In the relatively short span of fifty years the foreign department found its modest beginnings as a relatively specialised section of the bank, grew to become a major department, and assimilated itself into the highly complex global bank of the modern world. As an integral part of the bank's head office, the international department is controlled by the general management of the bank. In contrast with the early days when the 'foreign department was quite separate from the rest of the bank', today its organisation and operation reflect a close meshing of activities with all other divisions of the bank and much more clear-cut lines of control.[2]

The international department of the early 1970s differs from its progenitors of several decades ago in at least three respects. First, it encompasses a wider range of activities, including securing overseas market intelligence, and engaging in investment management activities. Second, it is not nearly as isolated from other divisions of the bank as it was some years ago, probably reflecting a somewhat less specialised array of responsibilities. Third, the international department is regarded as a more important and prestigious unit of the bank. This can be seen in several ways, including the high rank accorded senior officers in charge of international departments, and the relative position of the department in tables of organisation published by individual banks.[3]

Major U.S. banks have come to regard their respective international departments as more important parts of their total organisation for a number of reasons. These include limited expansion prospects in domestic markets, the expanding demand for international financial services, the lack of efficient and diverse money and capital market facilities in many overseas locations, and the lack of familiarity of many American businessmen with prevailing economic and business conditions abroad.[4]

Fifteen years ago it was considered that a foreign department might be justified on the basis of its 'contribution to the net earnings of the bank as a whole', rather than the profitability of the department itself.[5] It was recognised that foreign department operations could be highly profitable.[6] However, when such operations influence the competitiveness of other departments of the bank, and when direct and indirect returns are associated with international department activities, measurement of contributions to profitability become deceptive and elusive.[7] Nevertheless, in most large banks senior management has become persuaded that provision of a wide range of international banking services is necessary if large corporate customers are to be retained by the bank. In a period within which the foreign orientation of many U.S. corporations and the associated need for international banking and financing services have increased, American banks responded to this by means of establishing international departments, expanding existing ones, and realigning organisational structures so as to permit their international departments to cope better with the demands and problems of their own customers. Parallel with this expansion, the international banking departments of many U.S. banks have enjoyed rapid growth in earnings.

2. TYPES OF INTERNATIONAL DEPARTMENTS

During the 1960s a number of developments converged to cause many U.S. banks to re-examine their international commitments. As a result, a number of American banks established or expanded their international or foreign departments. These banks range from the two dozen leading money market banks with head offices in New York, Chicago, Boston, Philadelphia, and San Francisco; to the forty or fifty regional banks located in such cities as Detroit, Atlanta, Pittsburgh, Miami, Seattle, and Dallas; to the 150 or more medium and smaller-sized banks scattered in smaller cities and population centres throughout the United States. The 250 or more American banks possessing international departments range in size from those with $100–200 million in deposits to the largest, with resources exceeding $20 billion. Clearly, the type of international department operated by these banks covers a broad spectrum.

It is possible to distinguish at least four categories of international departments in American banks. They may be described as follows:

1. Full-fledged department with extensive responsibilities for managing and co-ordinating a world-wide network of branches and Edge Act subsidiary and overseas affiliates.[8]
2. Full-fledged department with limited responsibilities for overseas branches and affiliates usually including at least one branch or an Edge Act subsidiary.
3. Complete department providing a wide range of international services, including maintenance of balances in foreign currencies with foreign correspondent banks.
4. Limited department providing specified services for customers, and relying on domestic and foreign correspondent banks for provision of any other international banking services required by its own customers.

Only three American banks fall in the first category, and these banks possess a large number of overseas branches as well as extensive equity investments in majority and minority owned foreign banks and finance companies.[9] In addition to rendering a wide range of banking services for customers, the international department is responsible for managing and co-ordinating the operations of overseas branches and foreign affiliates. Moreover, activities of Edge and Agreement corporations and foreign exchange operations must be co-ordinated and controlled through the international department.

Over one hundred banks fall in the second category. Most of these are money market banks or regional banks. All possess one or more overseas branches and/or Edge Act corporations. In addition, they may hold interests in several foreign banks and finance companies. The major differences between the international departments of these banks and those of banks in the first group are as follows. (1) The extent and relative importance of the management and co-ordination function applicable to overseas branches and affiliates will be far less for the international departments of banks in the second group as compared with those in the first. (2) The extent of the international commitment of banks in the second group may be somewhat less than of those in the first group. Each of the three banks in the first group have at least one-third of their resources committed to international banking operations of one type or another, and a similarly high percentage of earnings is derived from such activities. In the case of some banks falling in the second group, the extent of their international commitment may be less than 10 per cent.[10] (3) Finally, the size differences are substantial. Some banks in the second group have total resources of perhaps one billion dollars, whereas each of the three in the first group has assets in excess of $20 billion.

The third category includes banks with no overseas branches or Edge Act affiliates, but which operate a foreign exchange trading section. The operations of these departments provide a full range of banking services for internationally oriented customers, including the ability to purchase and sell major foreign currencies. The only overseas activities managed by such departments include correspondent bank relationships and any overseas representative offices maintained by the bank.

The fourth category includes banks with limited international departments, which render only specific services for customers. Generally, these departments do *not* have direct access to their own foreign exchange facilities, but obtain exchange needed by customers from domestic correspondent banks. Moreover, the range of international banking services rendered for customers may be restricted to handling routine letter of credit transactions in connection with export-import trade and processing certain items for collection.

The banks in the four groups described above render a wide range of international services for customers. In addition many large 'country' banks not included in the above groups now issue letters of credit on their own forms, directing them to any of several correspondents in metropolitan centres designated as the settling bank. Similarly, they dispatch documentary drafts to overseas banks, designating the money centre bank as settling agent.

B. ORGANISATIONAL ASPECTS

1. FACTORS INFLUENCING ORGANISATIONAL STRUCTURE

An examination of the organisational structures of international departments leaves only limited opportunity for generalisations. Apparently, many organisational choices are available, and imaginative bankers have been quick to employ a large number of these.

It is possible to single out four sets of factors that seem to explain the wide assortment of organisational structures employed by banks for their international departments. These include:

1. Size, location and extent of international commitment
2. Type of management in the bank
3. Domestic business of the bank
4. Offshore operations—amount, variety and location

Large, internationally oriented banks have sizable international departments, and size of department alone has a bearing on the organisational structure. Interior banks utilising a New York-based Edge corporation often have a relatively small international department. Concentration of foreign exchange trading in the Edge unit further reduces the size, and in other ways influences the department's organisation.

A progressive bank management will probably more readily adopt a marketing oriented concept of organisation for its international department. This will entail consciously identifying customers and related customer services, and aligning the various sections of the international department so as to best perform these services for the bank's customers. The ability and willingness of the bank's management to undertake risks influences the decision to establish foreign exchange trading, and the amount of funds allocated to that purpose.

Here location and type of domestic business of the bank also enter into the picture. A bank located in an area unduly subject to business recessions may be unwilling to assume any substantial foreign exchange position and risks. This influences the overall international commitment, the type of operations carried on, and the structure of the international department.

The domestic business of the bank may exert an influence on the mix of international banking activities and the organisational structure of the international department. A strong money market and bond market orientation domestically is likely to pull the bank in the same direction in its international activities. Consequently, its organisational structure, where such activities are concerned, further reflects this orientation.[11] Such banks play an important role in Eurobond, Eurocurrency, and local money market operations overseas.

Finally, the extent and type of offshore operations will influence the organisation of the international department. A heavy mix of overseas branches and affiliates will necessitate an international department structure that can best cope with the management and control of these offshore units. A preponderance of minority-owned affiliate banks is likely to impose less management control pressures and responsibilities than emphasis on direct overseas branches. However, it increases the co-ordination and control problems for the head office. Operation of representative offices overseas, rather than branches or minority affiliates, commensurately reduces the need for operational service facilities in the head office, and most especially in the international department.

2. ORGANISATIONAL PATTERNS

In this section we examine the organisational structures of large international departments. For various reasons, little or no emphasis is given to the small department or section. One reason for this is that in small departments a number of functions and related organisational segments are 'implicit'. For example, small international departments generally do not identify or possess a separate and distinct Loan-Credit Section with which to oversee credits made in the department; a money management administration responsible for obtaining funds and reviewing their deployment among alternative uses; nor an international liaison group with which to develop international business from American companies.

A number of organisational options are available to a given bank in structuring its international department. However, several features appear to be common to most departments of relatively large banks. These are described below.

1. Many large banks regard the international department or division as a key part of the overall organisation. Therefore they assign the international department a high status in the organisational structure of the bank, and often place an Executive Vice President or similarly high-ranking officer in charge of this department. In most large banks the international department, group, or division will stand out as one of six or seven major divisions of the bank.

2. Today large international departments are organised on the basis of a 'market oriented concept'. This means that the bank appraises the market for its international services and organises its international department in a manner that most enhances the delivery of financial services to customer groups identified in that market. Organisation follows the path of least resistance toward best servicing bank customers, actual and prospective.

3. Generally, customers of the bank, both at home and overseas, are categorised according to a territorial or regional system. An individual bank may designate as few as three or as many as seven or eight overseas territories, each of which is supervised by a Senior Vice President or Vice President.[12] It is the responsibility of these men to develop new customer

accounts, supervise them, and insure that the status of the account is profitable to the bank.

4. Large international departments of necessity must place heavy emphasis on Operations and Business Development. As a result, these areas of responsibility are accorded a definite status within the organisational framework of the international department. This can be seen quite clearly in the organisational table of the International Banking Division (IBD) of the Seattle First National Bank (Illustration 4-A). In this case, IBD is split into two major sections: an Operations Section which includes letters of credit, exchange, and trading; and a Business Development Section which overlaps the territorial administrative units.

Chase Manhattan Bank possesses an international department organisation that resembles this in several respects. Illustration 4-B reflects Chase's international department after the 1970 reorganisation, which was effected on a 'task-oriented management' basis, rather than on a primarily geographic basis as existed in the past. Nine functional areas of responsibility were established to replace the previous system of five geographic areas.[13]

5. Finally, where Edge Act or Agreement companies are a part of the bank's international operation, these corporations have boards of directors consisting generally of senior management from the banks and the international departments. This assures co-ordination of bank and international department policies with those of the corporation as well as satisfactory communications and control regarding the activities of these corporations.

Despite the general similarities in organisational approach that can be found among the international departments of the larger banks in the United States, many differences exist. The following focuses on two major examples of such differences.

First, the development, expansion and diversification function may be given greater or lesser weight, and distributed over several units or concentrated within one section or group of the international department. In the reorganisation that took place in 1970 Chase Manhattan established an 'Expansion and Diversification' group. Chase is one of the few banks in the international fold that has assigned so much importance and

Illustration 4-A

International Banking Division
Seattle First National Bank

Receptionist

International Banking Division
Vice President and Department
Manager

Credit Manager

Operations Section

Operations Manager

Exchange

Letters of Credit

Trading

Business Development Section

Business Development Co-ordinator

Secretary

Latin American Business Development

U.S. and Canada Business Development

Japan Business Development

ILLUSTRATION 4–B

INTERNATIONAL DEPARTMENT
NEW ORGANISATION

CHASE MANHATTAN BANK

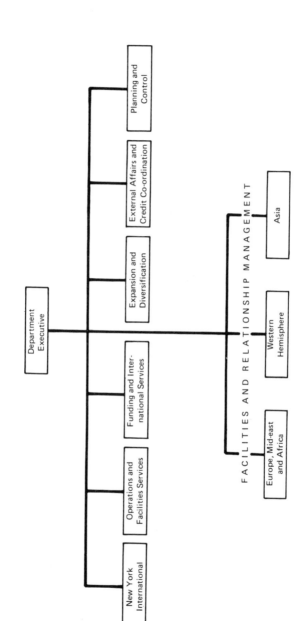

prestige to a unit carrying out these functions. This group is responsible for integrating the planning and development efforts which support long-term growth objectives and strategies; for bringing together the international department's entrepreneurial and innovative talents; and for providing a focal point for senior-level discussion of ideas and projects related to expansion, diversification and innovation.

Second, there exist major differences in the degree to which individual banks and international departments have centralised the supervision of funding or money and credit management. One bank that appears to have achieved considerable progress in centralising and providing more effective control over its credit and money management supervision is Chemical Bank New York. The international division of Chemical Bank contains six territorial sections, as well as two additional administrative groups. One of these, Credit and Money Management Supervision, is headed by the chief credit officer of the international division and centralises the following important activities: overall asset and liability management, review of credits, maintaining a close watch of the money market, insuring that department remains competitive in bidding for deposits, and review of the foreign exchange position of the bank.

C.   FUNCTIONS OF THE INTERNATIONAL DEPARTMENT

The range of activities and services performed by international departments of large banks extends across virtually all facets of banking, and in some cases embraces operations which ordinarily are not vigorously pursued on the domestic scene.[14]

In the sections which follow we discuss the functions of the international department under four headings. These are (1) Service functions for Customers and Correspondents, (2) Overall Asset-Liability Management, (3) Business Development and Diversification, and (4) Management Co-ordination and Control. Small international departments of banks which have recently entered the international banking field are likely to be engaged only in the first – service functions for customers and correspondents. It is possible that such banks will have no foreign correspondent bank relationships, and may depend upon larger domestic correspondents in the money centres of

New York and Chicago to carry out a number of service functions for their customers. As these international departments expand they may be expected gradually to add functions that fall under the other three headings. The largest banks in the United States, those with the most extensively developed international operations, have departments which carry out a wide range of functions under the last three headings.

1. SERVICE FUNCTIONS FOR CUSTOMERS AND CORRESPONDENTS

International department services for customers and correspondents can be broken down into four basic areas: foreign trade oriented functions, loans and credits, foreign exchange activities, and other. The 'other' category includes provision of travel services, collecting and disseminating market and economic intelligence on overseas areas, and providing information to customers and correspondents regarding export credit insurance, prospective buyers, and marine insurance.

Traditionally, the focal point of international department activities has been the servicing of foreign trade transactions. Where the export or import trade of customers (or clients of correspondent banks) is facilitated by letter of credit, 'the bank places the security of its name behind the buyer'.[15] Irrevocable letters of credit authorise the seller to draw drafts on an issuing bank, with the latter's understanding that such drafts will be paid (if a sight letter of credit) or accepted for payment at a later date (if a time letter of credit), provided all documents presented conform to the requirements in the letter of credit. Time letters of credit incorporate the financing of the transaction. In such cases the U.S. bank may 'accept' the time draft drawn on it, thereby creating a banker's acceptance which the bank may hold in its own portfolio until maturity, or sell in the market for banker's acceptances. American banks open import letters of credit in favour of overseas suppliers upon the request of U.S. buyers. Export letters of credit may be issued by U.S. banks on behalf of foreign correspondents for the account of their customers, and advice generally is sent directly to the beneficiary in the United States. Since export letters of credit originate outside the United States, choice of the American bank may depend upon the correspondent ties of the foreign opening bank. However, when American customers specify a preference with regard to the U.S. bank which should advise or confirm, such letters of credit are likely to be channelled through the specified U.S. bank. In such cases the American bank may simply 'advise', or it may 'confirm' the credit. Should the U.S. bank confirm the letter of credit, it assumes the obligation to pay the beneficiary, regardless of action taken by the foreign bank and the availability of dollar exchange in the country of the foreign bank.[16]

In addition to issuing, endorsing, confirming, and paying against letters of credit, international departments provide loans and credits to support foreign trade and the production of goods which enter into foreign trade. Such loans include commodity and warehouse loans, provision of advances against collection, discounting drafts, ship loans, and foreign currency loans.

International departments possessing a foreign exchange trading section carry out a variety of functions for customers and correspondent banks. These include maintaining necessary foreign currency balances with correspondent banks overseas, often on a reciprocal basis; buying and selling foreign exchange by issuing foreign drafts, bank payment orders, and sending cable advices of transfers of foreign deposit balances; and arranging swap transactions. The last refers to simultaneous purchase-sale transactions in the spot and forward markets for a given currency, enabling the customer (1) to engage in interest arbitrage, (2) to adjust his overall position in foreign currencies over time, or (3) to renew or arrange a non-delivery rollover when a customer wishes to continue his investment in a given currency for an extended period of time (this would involve a spot purchase and simultaneous execution of a forward sales contract by that customer in the currency in which the investment is denominated).[17]

2. OVERALL ASSET-LIABILITY MANAGEMENT

Like other divisions of the bank, the international department contributes to the sources of funds available for profitable loan and investment. Moreover, as an integral part of the bank the international department must compete along with other units of the bank for funds to be used in connection with loans, investments, and operating funds. A complaint often made by the divisional officers of banks is that their unit is not allocated resources commensurate with the funds generated by that unit. However, many considerations enter into the question of achieving a favourable allocation of lendable funds within a bank.

Several specific operations must be performed in the large international departments of U.S. banks, where overall asset-liability management is concerned. These include undertaking analyses and reports on the volume and allocation of credit outstanding in the international department, review of credits made by territorial officers and overseas branches, analysis of foreign exchange position of the bank, and engaging in money and bond market operations in overseas locations (including the Euro-currency markets).

An important aspect of international operations involves the management of foreign currency balances, the so-called *nostro* accounts held by the bank in foreign banks. Foreign exchange activities are especially important for several reasons. They include a maximum potential risk-exposure; the profitability from such operations can contribute a high percentage of income to the international department; and they affect deposit balances which are an important means of maintaining favourable correspondent bank relationships overseas. The largest American banks may maintain several hundred separate foreign currency deposit accounts with correspondents, which are denominated in half a dozen major currencies and a number of less important currencies.

As of June 1970 foreign currency deposits of U.S. banks in foreign banks totalled $314 million.[18] An American Banker survey conducted at mid-year 1970 indicated that banks outside the United States held foreign correspondent balances in other banks outside the United States with a dollar value of $11·8 billion.[19] This indicates that American banks play a relatively small role as sources of foreign correspondent deposit balances when compared with all other foreign correspondent banks.

It should be noted that control over foreign currency deposits represents a complicated balancing of considerations from all sides. The Executive Vice President or Senior Vice President must work with senior officers of the bank, including the

Finance Committee of the bank to arrive at a 'total exposure' limit or commitment of the bank's resources denominated in foreign currencies. Second, proper control and co-ordination at head office, through the appropriate unit of the international department must be provided for. Third, implementation must be made by means of the day-to-day operations of the foreign exchange trader, branch operations in foreign currencies, Edge Act subsidiary positions, and the net commitments of other subsidiaries and affiliates. Fourth, regional or territorial officers have the responsibility for maintaining effective correspondent bank relations, and these officers must translate this into recommendations to the international department at head office for placing loans and deposits (in foreign currency) with these foreign correspondents. Fifth, representative officers and Agents must gather and transmit to head office information pertinent to maintaining a constant evaluation of the bank's position in individual currencies.

3. BUSINESS DEVELOPMENT AND DIVERSIFICATION

During the 1960s international banking proved to be one of the most rapidly growing aspects of commercial bank activities, not only because of the existence of favourable economic factors, but also due to the broadly based promotional and innovative activities of U.S. banks. Leading American banks in the field of international banking tend to be the most innovative, as well as extremely competitive.

American bankers have moved ahead rapidly on a number of fronts in achieving growth and diversification of their international operations. They have provided special training for loan and business development officers, who have functioned on a liaison as well as operational basis with the metropolitan and national divisions. In this capacity they have been able to publicise the international services of their respective banks while at the same time engaging in their regular duties.

Secondly, they have purchased equity interests in foreign banks and financial institutions. In this way they have expanded their operating bases, and increased the extent and type of services that can be rendered for customers. This area is explored in detail in Chapter 6.

4. MANAGEMENT CO-ORDINATION AND CONTROL

As the large international department expands, the co-ordination and control of globally dispersed operations becomes more complicated. More basic functions become duplicated in the various territorial sections, and an increasing number of services performed adds to the co-ordination burden. It becomes necessary for senior officers to plan for better control over these many activities, and even more urgent for them to devise standards of performance.

Extending beyond the environs of the head office international department are four types of service-performing units. These are foreign correspondent banks, overseas branches, Edge Act subsidiaries, and foreign affiliate banks and finance companies. It is necessary that the activities generated through these service-performing units be properly controlled and co-ordinated.

American banks depend on their foreign correspondent banks to render services for them in the way of securing credit information, processing foreign collections, and paying against letter of credit. Therefore, the choice of correspondent banks in various countries must be selective. When considering a correspondent relationship, 'financial stability, continuity of management and experience, range of services available and efficiency will all play their part'.[20]

Correspondents co-operate in executing and referring letter of credit business, providing deposit funds for head office and overseas branches, constituting part of the foreign loan business of American banks, and performing a number of important services for U.S. banks such as acting as depositories for foreign currency balances. The largest U.S. international banks, such as Chase Manhattan, Bank of America, and Morgan Guaranty Trust each maintains over one thousand accounts for foreign correspondents. At least half a dozen other major U.S. banks hold 400 or more such deposit accounts for foreign banks.[21]

The activities of overseas branches must be co-ordinated and controlled. The degree of control and supervision is likely to depend on such factors as the relative importance of overseas branches to the bank, the experience and expertise of the bank in international banking, and the length of time over which such overseas branches have been operating. Generally, the international department is likely to exercise close managerial control over the activities of foreign branches when the bank has not had substantial experience in international banking and when the overseas branch is of relatively recent vintage. Banks falling below the 'largest thirty' are likely to follow this pattern. On the other hand very large banks with an extended background in international banking, and which have operated overseas branches for a number of years, are likely to be somewhat more flexible in their managerial control over foreign branches. However, these larger banks will have established an 'Overseas Administrative Group' or similarly titled unit operating within the international department that will maintain a systematic on-going analysis of overseas branch operations. This analysis is likely to encompass the following: internal financial reporting, account analysis, audit control, budget analysis, development of cash flow plans, and review and updating lists of correspondent banks.

Wholly-owned Edge corporations appear to present no more than routine control and co-ordination problems for the head office international department. The overlay of senior bank management and Edge corporation directors tends to assure this. A technical co-ordination problem exists on a daily basis where the Edge corporation headquarters is located in a time zone which differs from that of the parent bank.

Foreign affiliate banks and finance companies present a number of special problems in terms of achieving co-ordination and control over their operations. The difficulties relate to extent of ownership, foreign government regulations, and the role played by the foreign bank or finance company in its own market area. In view of this, it is doubtful that any more than a moderate degree of co-ordination and control can be exercised over these affiliates.

5 Foreign Branches of American Banks

A. ORGANISATIONAL ASPECTS OF OVERSEAS BRANCHING

Like the fabled Hermes American banks have undertaken the great trek, and have moved and extended their field of operations to service a global commerce and travel. This multi-nationalisation could not have proceeded as speedily nor as efficiently as it has in the past decade without resort to the overseas branch. The expansion in number of foreign branches, in number of U.S. banks with foreign branches, and in the assets and deposits held by these branches has been impressive. However, more impressive is the impact this overseas branching has had on the pattern of international bank expansion, the degree of competition, and the channels branching has provided for international short-term capital flows. Foreign branches of American banks provide major links between international financial centres, and permit a more efficient accommodation between the supply and demand for funds in regional sub-markets around the world.

1. FACTORS IN THE DEVELOPMENT OF OVERSEAS BRANCHES*

Despite the surge in foreign branch activity on the part of U.S. banks, overseas branches have not been a common feature of American banking. As recently as year-end 1967 only fourteen U.S. banks had overseas branches. By year-end 1972 this number had jumped to 115 banks. Since in the United States banks are prohibited from opening branches across state borders, and since a number of states do not permit branch banking even within their own state borders, U.S. banks have lacked experience in the field of branch banking. Therefore, foreign branching has been a venturesome undertaking for a number of U.S. banks.

From the organisational standpoint the choice of method of overseas expansion depends on a number of considerations. These include the attitudes of bank management, regulations in the host country, taxation, existing relationships with correspondent foreign banks, and the magnitude of the financial commitment the U.S. bank may feel able and disposed to undertake.[1] In some instances foreign branching is a reaction against state regulations prohibiting the establishment of branch offices.[2] More likely, branching is undertaken due to advantages inherent in the branch form of organisation as compared with other methods of conducting international operations. In a foreign branch the allocation of responsibility is fairly clear. There is a direct line of responsibility from the U.S. head office to the overseas branch manager. As a later section of this chapter will amplify, often there are fairly explicit directions given to the foreign branch regarding authorised lending limits and other matters. Second, the bank's own name is advertised through the foreign branch. Third, U.S. corporate affiliates operating in overseas areas are able to identify easily with the overseas branch, since it carries the name and distinguishing labels of the parent organisation. Overseas branches provide a flexible approach toward the growth and development of international banking activities. While there are fairly substantial start-up costs, the initial investment is not

* This section relies heavily on information generously provided by Frederick R. Dahl, Division of Supervision and Regulation, Board of Governors of the Federal Reserve System.

likely to be anywhere close to that required in establishing a *de novo* institution overseas, or in organising an Edge corporation.[3]

Three American banks may be described as enjoying world-wide branch networks. These are in order of number of foreign branches: First National City Bank of New York; Bank of America, California; and Chase Manhattan Bank, New York. The existence of these world-wide networks gives U.S. international banking a special dimension. By contrast, the British overseas banks have developed many foreign offices, but generally have confined themselves to specific regions rather than establishing a world-wide system. The major continental banks in Europe have engaged in branching abroad to a limited extent only.

Varied circumstances have induced American banks to establish branches overseas. Perhaps the most important development in this regard is the overseas expansion of U.S. foreign business investment. A second important consideration operating as a stimulant to foreign branching has been the opportunity to participate in the local banking market. In many overseas areas local banking facilities are inadequate, and lack the ability to provide a complete range of banking services. Large American banks backed up by massive financial resources and manpower are often in a position to render a variety of sophisticated bank services to local business firms and individuals that could not be provided by smaller indigenous banking institutions.

An important consideration in making a decision to establish a foreign branch relates to the ability to obtain a foothold in the Eurodollar market. Many large United States banks only belatedly came to appreciate the value of an overseas branch, especially in connection with providing funds during periods of extremely tight money. Branches of U.S. banks in safe haven and tax haven centres such as Nassau, Switzerland, and Beirut have been able to attract substantial deposit amounts. Moreover, they have traded on the name and credit standing of the parent bank to attract deposits at relatively low interest rates.

Both the foreign credit restraint programme directed at overseas lending by U.S. banks and the mandatory controls invoked against U.S. direct investment outflows have exerted powerful effects on the growth of U.S. foreign branch banking, as well as on other forms of overseas bank representation. The foreign credit restraint programme inaugurated in 1965 which limited U.S. bank lending to foreigners resulted in many American banks deciding to establish overseas branches to be able to continue servicing their multinational corporate customers in foreign lands. Since foreign branch lending did not fall under the programme, these branches could continue to provide loans to foreign borrowers.

In 1968 the Johnson administration initiated mandatory controls on direct foreign investments of U.S. corporations, and established the Office of Foreign Direct Investments (OFDI) in the Department of Commerce to administer this programme. Briefly stated, the mandatory controls programme established three Scheduled Areas of the world outside the United States, and stipulated percentage ceilings on investment outflows to these areas relative to a base year period. Financial transactions of direct investment affiliates became subject to rather stringent controls, and exceptions had to be approved by OFDI.

The OFDI administered programme affected U.S. international banking in several respects. First, it shifted U.S. corporate borrowing to finance direct investments to offshore areas, resulting in added incentives for U.S. banks to establish foreign branches. Second, the mandatory controls created a demand for special borrowing by U.S. overseas direct investment affiliates including the need for 'dividend funds'. Many U.S. companies end the year with excess direct investments in some Scheduled Areas because they feel they cannot ask their foreign affiliates to reduce retained earnings by declaring dividends to the parent company. It is often poor public relations policy to pull dividends out of a country in the early years of the life of an enterprise, especially if much of the funds used to start the business has been borrowed locally. In such cases the OFDI has insisted that a company declare an extra dividend in the same or another area of the world to compensate for the excess direct investment. The overseas affiliate may borrow the money either on its own credit, or through its parent company guaranty and repatriate the funds to the United States in place of a dividend. If the company demonstrates that it cannot do either

then it can petition OFDI for authorisation for excess investment.[4]

Other effects from the direct investment controls include an
increase in the volume of acquisitions business for U.S. banks to
service as overseas consultants, an increase in the volume of
overseas underwriting activity to finance U.S. corporate expansion, and new opportunities for providing secondary trading
facilities for outstanding corporate debt obligations of U.S.
direct investment affiliates. These last two areas of business
generally accrue to foreign subsidiaries of American banks,
rather than their overseas branches. Finally, we should note
that the mandatory controls have shunted a small amount of
loan business away from U.S. banks. A common practice has
been the use of parallel loans between U.S. and other foreign
investing companies. For example, Raytheon needed sterling
for its U.K. operations but didn't want to borrow abroad or utilise U.S. funds, thereby using up part of its allotted outflows.
Raytheon got together with British Petroleum, which needed
dollars in its U.S. operations but was experiencing difficulties
in getting funds out of the U.K. Raytheon loaned a U.S. subsidiary of British Petroleum $4.8 million while British Petroleum
lent the equivalent in sterling to Raytheon's British subsidiary.
No money crossed the foreign exchanges, and repayment was
scheduled out of earnings of the respective subsidiaries.

Foreign branches have extended the global network of the
United States parent. The momentum of an expanding international branch network carries important advantages in the
way of easier transfers of funds, collection of bills, and reduced
commissions and collection time. Foreign branches operating
in the less developed countries where there is a scarcity of adequate banking facilities, have brought immeasurable benefits
to these countries. In addition, they have proven to be important innovators of efficiency.

In a number of cases foreign branches of U.S. banks have
been established at the urging of American military authorities.
While the original rationale of these branches might have been
to attend to the needs of military personnel, the function of
several of these branches has changed as these countries
emerged from occupied or reconstruction status.

Another factor responsible for the expansion of foreign

branches has been the needs of the U.S. Treasury for depository institutions for funds held abroad. Most of these funds have arisen from operations connected with Public Law 480 whereby agricultural surpluses of the United States have been disposed of among needy nations in return for local currencies. Other sources of funds include U.S. government assistance programmes requiring counterpart funds and surplus property disposals. As a result, U.S. banks expanding abroad frequently receive their first major deposits from U.S. government sources.[5]

Given the many reasons for the increase in foreign branching, we might analyse the factors that underlie the strong growth in foreign branch assets. First, the Eurodollar market has been an essential factor in the expansion in branch assets. The London and Paris branches of American banks are a major channel through which changes in money market conditions in the United States are transmitted internationally. These changes in market conditions provide the incentives for international flows of funds, and for the entry and exit of funds into and out of the Eurodollar market. Second, the growth in foreign branch loans has been fostered by the voluntary credit restraint programme as applied *vis-à-vis* foreign lending by U.S. banks. Head offices of U.S. banks have sold loans to foreign branches in order to comply with the foreign credit restraint programme as well as booked many new loans through their foreign branches. Third, foreign branches have served as redistribution centres for Eurodollars and other currency balances obtained by these branches. Finally, a special set of factors has assisted in the growth of assets in Japanese branches of U.S. banks. Much of the rise in their assets is due to their serving as intermediaries in what are essentially head office rather than branch operations. These branches are the depositories of official Japanese balances, which they redeposit with their U.S. head offices and which then serve as the base of dollar balances employed by head offices for financing Japanese foreign trade and industry, including joint ventures between U.S. and Japanese business interests. The branches carry these funds on their books as liabilities to their head offices and as claims against Japanese banks and business firms.

A number of impediments have been working against the

expansion of overseas branching by U.S. banks. Many American bankers have expressed the fear that overseas branches could not be justified in terms of the relation between risk and expected profits.[6] Moreover, an awareness of the extent to which any area is overbanked could be sufficient cause for an American bank ruling out a particular foreign branch proposal. A second factor would be the size potential of the market for banking services.

Another negative factor is uncertainty on the part of some bankers regarding the status and treatment of foreign source income under the U.S. internal revenue code. There are numerous questions in this area relating to determination of the geographic source of income, applicability of foreign tax credit, and protection afforded by double taxation agreements. It is also possible that such negative factors resulted in favour of establishing foreign branches in particular locations where reasonably attractive options were available. While it was not possible to develop this point clearly in discussions with individual bankers, there is a possibility that the apparent preference of some American banks for Nassau branches as compared with branches in other locations is based upon the absence of corporate income taxes applicable to foreign branch income in that area.

Many American banks rely heavily on correspondent banks to service their customers' international banking needs. Reluctance on the part of the American bank to antagonise its correspondent banks abroad may provide sufficient grounds for turning down a branch proposal. U.S. banks are not uniform in their attitudes on this question. Several American bank managements have expressed the view that an overseas branch can introduce U.S. manufacturing affiliates to foreign correspondent banks to the mutual benefit of all parties concerned.

A major consideration causing many American banks to become luke-warm on the subject of foreign branching has been the lack of suitable personnel to staff foreign branches. One writer has noted that even after utilising a number of attempted solutions, including training of American personnel, recruitment of expensive host country nationals, and provision of costly hardship factor allowances, many U.S. banks have faced residual overseas manpower problems.[7]

Legal deterrents have worked against the development of overseas branches. Banking laws in Australia, Canada and South Africa do not permit the establishment of foreign banks. Restrictions in some countries make branching impractical. Discriminatory treatment has placed foreign branching by U:S. banks at an operational disadvantage. Peru does not permit foreign bank branches to receive savings deposits; in several countries foreign branches do not have access to the discount window of the central bank; and in some countries branches of American banks are at a disadvantage, since as foreign banks they must conform scrupulously to existing statutes, even more so than local banks. U.S. commercial banks may not underwrite corporate stock or bonds, and legal provisions that prevent U.S. banks from participating in the underwriting of corporate securities may have impaired their competitive position in a number of foreign financial centres. Taxation of U.S. banks or their prospective corporate customers also may impede the development of branch business abroad.[8]

Finally, negative considerations may also play an important role in the decision made by a U.S. bank to enter a particular country. This is likely to have been the case with respect to decisions made by American banks regarding entry into Israel. Considering the growth in prosperity in that country over the past two decades, negative considerations must have been considerable. These are derived largely from the lingering tensions between the Arab countries and Israel, and the substantial amount of oil royalty revenues placed on deposit in international banks. When the Exchange National Bank of Chicago received permission from the Bank of Israel to establish a branch in Tel Aviv in 1970, it was pointed out that this was the first request received from a U.S. bank since 1948 when the State of Israel was established. Since 1970 the same bank has established a second branch in Jerusalem.[9]

2. GROWTH AND DISTRIBUTION OF FOREIGN BRANCHES AND ASSETS

The postwar expansion of international banking has been characterised by a steady increase in the direct representation of American banks through overseas branches. In 1949 member banks of the Federal Reserve System operated ninety-two foreign branches. By 1972 the number had increased to 627.[10] The growth of deposits in overseas branches also has been impressive. From 1955 to 1971 the number of branches increased from 117 to 577, and deposits in these overseas branches increased from $2 billion to $51 billion. Branches of U.S. banks were located in twenty-six different countries in 1955, but in 1971 they were located in as many as seventy-one countries.

In 1971 the largest part of the assets and deposits in foreign branches of U.S. banks was concentrated in branches in the United Kingdom (Table 5-1 indicates that 52 per cent of assets were in branches in England and Ireland). The bulk of these assets were in the London branches of American banks. London overshadows all other areas in importance of foreign branch assets and is a focal point for Eurodollar and Euro-currency operations of U.S. and other banks actively engaged in international banking. In the City, the square mile financial district of London, over forty leading American banks have found it to their advantage to establish a branch. In addition, several U.S. banks have established a second branch in London's West End, to service U.S. tourist and embassy personnel. Deposit banking in London is geared to serving the substantial corporate treasurers' market, where temporary surplus funds of the larger U.S. and foreign multinational corporations are placed, and where tax and dividend accruals also may be employed on a one to three month maturity basis. Moreover, a substantial sterling and dollar certificate of deposit market has developed in London since 1966. The London deposit structure is heavily oriented in the direction of inter-bank deposit balances, where wholesale and retail oriented banks clear internationally mobile funds.

The second most important region for the foreign branches of U.S. banks is Continental Europe. At year-end 1971, 19 per cent of the assets of U.S. foreign branches were located in this region. Branches of American banks in Paris are able to benefit from the substantial Eurosterling and EuroSwiss franc business in that centre. In Germany foreign branches service the substantial operations of U.S. manufacturing affiliates located in that country, as well as receive balances from German banks that do not wish to add to their holdings abroad. In keeping

their liquid balances in Germany these banks have preferred
the branches of foreign banks, which do not compete effectively
with them in local deposit and loan markets.

The Bahamas and Far East rank third and fourth in the concentration of foreign branch assets of American banks.
Branches in the Bahamas hold close to 12 per cent of branch
assets, and offices in the Far East hold 9 per cent of the total.

The size of foreign branches of American banks differs considerably from one region to another. Size comparisons by
region are summarised in Table 5-1. The largest overseas
branches are located in the United Kingdom and the figures are
heavily biased by the weighted importance of the London
branches. At year-end 1971 branches in the United Kingdom
held assets averaging $732 million per branch. This places
these foreign branches on a par with many U.S. institutions
that might be included in the hundred largest banks in this
country. Second in rank by size are the Continental branches of
American banks, with average assets of close to $160 million
per branch. Again, the absolute size figures are impressive. The
smallest average size, measured by assets per branch, can be
found in Latin America. Here the average works out to slightly
less than $11 million per branch, reflecting the retail banking
orientation characteristic of branches of American banks in
that region.

3. REGIONAL CHARACTERISTICS

Banks tend to reflect the local or regional peculiarities of the
area in which they are located. This is especially true on the international scene, where one bank may operate a number of
branches in many different countries. This section describes
several of the characteristics that are significant to the conduct
of foreign branch activities by American banks in various
regions of the world.

London

Any discussion of U.S. overseas banking must begin with
London, since it is the most important centre for U.S. foreign
branch activity and because London banking is unique unto
itself. London's special status in international banking stems

from its ability to function as a financial entrepôt, and its excellent money and capital market facilities (discussed in Chapter

Table 5.1

Geographic Distribution of Foreign Branch Assets and Assets per Branch by Region, December 31, 1971

REGION	Number of Branches	Branch Assets ($ millions)	As percentage of Total	Assets per Branch ($ millions)
United Kingdom and Ireland	48	35,143	52.4	732
Continental Europe	80	12,913	19.3	160
Bahamas	73	7,849	11.7	108
Latin America	229	2,519	3.7	11
Far East	83	6,221	9.3	75
Near East and Africa	17	384	0.6	23
U.S. Overseas Areas and Trust Territories	47	2,025	3.0	43
TOTAL	577	67,054	100.0	116

Source: Board of Governors of the Federal Reserve System.

10). Beyond these London has long enjoyed international leadership in shipping, foreign exchange, and international commodities trading. The presence of many large U.S. industrial corporations in the United Kingdom has served as a magnet attracting branches of U.S. banks.

London has become the centre of Eurodollar trading, and as a result many banks have found it to their advantage to establish connections and representation in London. This provides them with more ready contact with the inter-bank market for dollars and other Eurocurrencies. Finally, the pivotal role played by London merchant banks and issuing houses in international bond issues has made this city an important underwriting centre for both Western Europe and North America.

Continental Europe

The European Continent is the second most important region for foreign branches of American banks. Like London, international banking is extremely competitive on the Continent. The presence of numerous local banks and the recent entry of many U.S. banks via their branches have intensified this competitive situation. In countries such as Germany and Switzerland absence of exchange controls has permitted inter-bank competition to prosper.

One aspect of banking on the Continent is the multi-currency activities of many banks. This results in large part from their participation in the Eurocurrency markets. Large multinational corporations are important customers of banks in this region, and banking institutions vying for their favour must be prepared to render a wide variety of services on their behalf.

High per capita income levels, strong saving habits, and substantial institutional channels for aggregating and allocating loanable funds offer banks operating on the Continent multi-fold opportunities for arbitraging in the inter-bank markets, domestic money markets, Eurocurrency markets, and longer-term financial markets. Hundreds of banks participate in the Eurocurrency markets alone, offering foreign branches of U.S. banks many opportunities to acquire wholesale funds without undertaking the credit risks attendant upon serving as ultimate lender. In-depth foreign exchange facilities in most European countries provide additional opportunities for branches of major American banks to further develop their international banking activities.

The Far East

Branches of American banks in the Far East rank fourth in importance by amount of assets held, second by number of branches, and fourth by average size of branch in that region. There are several business and financial centres in the Far East which have tended to attract a concentration of branches and branch assets; these are Japan, Hong Kong, India and Singapore.

Hong Kong is an important depository for funds owned by

overseas Chinese and other residents of South-east Asia threatened by political turmoil and social clashes.[11] In this sense Hong Kong is an important safe haven centre, or collecting point for internationally mobile funds. Much liquid wealth has been brought to Hong Kong by Chinese families that have taken up residence there. There are several factors which explain the attraction of Hong Kong. First, balances in Hong Kong dollars, which are tied to sterling, can be deposited with some of the leading banks of the world that have established banking offices in that centre. The three largest U.S. banks, with world-wide branch networks, are represented in Hong Kong. Second, funds held in Hong Kong can be converted into U.S. dollars, Swiss francs, or any other currency on demand by virtue of the free exchange market that prevails there.

Japan is an important source of overseas business for American banks. The rapid expansion in Japan's foreign trade has created a substantial demand for financing facilities. Moreover, the rapidly growing Japanese economy has tended to be continually in need of additional credit facilities, which American banks under the watchful gaze of the Japanese authorities have been ready to provide. The Japanese authorities have been extremely careful in giving permission for foreign banks to establish branches, as they have been in permitting Japanese banks to open branches in other countries.

The Tokyo branches of U.S. banks are major channels for head-office operations in Japan. The assets held by these branches reflect the following types of transactions: short-term claims on Japanese banks resulting from refinancing of Japanese foreign trade; medium-term dollar loans to Japanese industry; Yen loans to Japanese affiliates of U.S. companies and joint ventures; call loans to Japanese banks; and working capital loans to large business enterprises.

Trade financing generally involves dollar bills of exchange drawn by a Japanese bank or commercial firm on the American branch's head office and accepted by the latter. American banks with branches in Tokyo carry these acceptance credits on their books as a claim on the overseas branch. The branch services the instruments and in turn carries a claim on its own books against the Japanese company or bank, which must put the branch into funds on maturity. Similarly term loans and other types of advances are carried on the books of branches, even though they are typically made out of funds advanced by the head offices or some other branches.

To a considerable extent the funds advanced by the head offices to the Japanese branches are the counterpart of balances deposited in the branches by the Ministry of Finance and the Bank of Japan, in the form of time deposits and redeposited by the branches in their head office. Thus, the large balance sheet totals of the Japanese branches reflect in substantial measure what are essentially head office transactions.

Singapore is an important centre of international trade in the Far East region. However, an influx of manufacturing investment from the United States, Japan, Australia, Hong Kong, and other countries is rapidly converting Singapore into an important manufacturing hub as well. The two most important trading partners are Malaysia and Indonesia. Much of this trade is handled through firms controlled by the overseas Chinese in Singapore and Indonesia. Singapore is a free port, situated at the crossroads of important international shipping lanes, and in terms of tonnage ranks as the fourth largest port in the free world. There is only minimal control over capital movements in and out of Singapore. Capital, dividend, and profit remittances abroad generally are permitted without hindrance. The number of banks is considered adequate. The foreign banks account for close to 60 per cent of total bank loans and advances in Singapore. Over 200 companies are listed on the Stock Exchange, representing commercial, industrial, plantation, and mining companies.

Latin America

Foreign branches of U.S. banks in Latin America play a somewhat different role from those in Western Europe and the Far East. Latin America outranks all other regions in number of branches, holding close to half the overseas branches of American banks. However, as measured by assets per branch these are the smallest branches. American branches fulfil a retail banking role in Latin America, serving local banking needs and the relatively small foreign investment affiliates of U.S. companies operating in that region. Important operations of

U.S. branches in that region include financing foreign trade and processing collections for business firms and retail establishments associated with retail instalment credit.

Per capita incomes in Latin American countries are low, ranging from $200 to $800 annually. Consequently, per capita savings tend to be low, and individuals do not utilise the banking system for effecting transactions nearly as much as in industrialised countries. The demand for credit is quite strong in Latin America, which contrasts with the relative scarcity of funds available to the banking system. Business firms have large needs for working capital because substantial inventories are carried due to transportation deficiencies and the desire to hedge against inflation.[12] Because of the poor development of capital and money markets, business firms depend more heavily on the banking system to satisfy their credit needs than their counterparts in more developed countries. In addition to the problems of short supply and heavy demands for funds, banks operating in Latin America must cope with the following problems:[13] (1) the relatively small financial markets in most countries restrains the expansion and diversification of banks and financial institutions; (2) the issue and transfer of financial assets are inhibited by periodic inflation; (3) the central banks play a dominant role, and in twelve countries in Latin America the resources held by these institutions account for at least one-third of the total assets of the banking system; and (4) the prevalence of foreign exchange controls.

Inflation in Argentina and other Latin American countries has made U.S. banks operating in this region reluctant lenders, while at the same time the inflationary conditions have brought forth an unlimited demand for loans. Consequently U.S. branches have had to confine their lending to short-term loans to borrowers in a position to provide reciprocal business profitable enough to offset the shrinkage in the value of the loans in dollars. At times they have had to charge loan commissions or interest premiums to offset at least partially the erosion of purchasing power of the currency. Inflation and the depreciation of the Argentine peso have tended to retard the growth of branch assets in dollar terms and have been the cause of sizeable losses to U.S. branches during recurrent periods when profit remittances were blocked.

Panama is another important centre for foreign branches of American banks in Latin America. Panama City has prospered as a commercial and agricultural centre, and the cattle industry has been rendered important assistance through financing provided by branches of American banks operating there. In the early 1960s branches of American banks in Panama suffered substantial deposit losses as a result of the exodus of many U.S. corporations after enactment of the U.S. Revenue Act of 1962. That legislation deprived tax haven areas of much of their attractiveness for U.S. companies that had hoped to defer taxes through base companies incorporated in such areas.

Nassau

Nassau is commonly referred to as a safe haven or tax haven centre. Branches of American banks have been established in a number of safe haven centres around the globe, including such cities as Nassau (Bahamas), Beirut, Panama City, Hong Kong, Geneva and Zurich. Most important, these centres are attractive deposit receiving points, and play a key role within the overseas branch networks of U.S. banks. There are several reasons which explain the selective attractiveness of these safe haven centres. First, they provide valuable business and financial advantages not available elsewhere. Second, they are free from exchange controls. Third, they enjoy a generally favourable tax climate. Fourth, these areas have retained a high measure of political stability. Finally, banks in these areas more carefully adhere to the generally recognised principle of privacy of information regarding customers' loan and deposit business with the bank.

Beginning early in 1969 Nassau branches became a substantial factor in U.S. overseas branching.[14] Nassau branches bid for balances of corporations that have set up base or offshore companies in the Bahamas to accumulate earnings there. At least three significant advantages may be derived by firms incorporating in Nassau. They avoid incurring tax liabilities on earnings reinvested. They minimise the risks of expropriation or nationalisation. Finally, they are in a position to remove taxable income from high tax countries by diverting to Nassau such activities as advertising, insurance, and the performance of technical services.

Branches in Nassau also benefit from the activities and size-able deposits of trust companies set up by their parent banks. These branches also are in a position to obtain an impressive amount of offshore dollars from wealthy families in South and Central America. The Nassau offices have been referred to as 'shell' branches for the reason that they may undertake very little activity except to provide a banking office which houses offshore deposits and loans.

Africa and the Near East

In 1971 there were 17 branches of American banks located in the Near East and Africa. Africa has not presented favourable opportunities for U.S. banks interested in establishing foreign branches.[15] There are several reasons for this including the entrenched position of British and French banks in this area, the lack of economic development and related narrow base on which to build banking operations, and the exclusive attitude of the governments in the more advanced African nations where opportunities have been more favourable. In some parts of North Africa and the Near East banking and payment of inter-est runs counter to religious and cultural beliefs of the indigen-ous population.

A large part of the American banking presence in the Near East is focused in Lebanon. Beirut is the leading financial centre in the Near East, and has become one of the more important centres of operations for U.S. overseas banking. Branches in Beirut attract safe haven funds from neighbouring countries where political and economic conditions leave much to be desired. Whereas much of the fast growing liquid wealth of the oil-producing countries bordering the Persian Gulf is deposited in London, New York, and Zurich, Beirut branches have obtained a substantial share. The balances in Lebanese branches of U.S. banks by far exceed the amounts that can be employed in the local loan market. Therefore, substantial amounts of these funds have been redeposited in head office accounts, and in the London and other branches of U.S. banks operating there.

B.   FOREIGN BRANCH OPERATIONS

1.   OVERVIEW OF BRANCH OPERATIONS

We now examine the aggregate balance sheet of foreign branches to obtain an overall view of their activities. Caution must be used in relying on balance sheet figures of foreign branches for several reasons. First, details are often lost sight of due to aggregating smaller and often dissimilar categories. Second, end of quarter and end of year 'window dressing' efforts of non-bank and bank customers of overseas branches tend to distort the relative importance of specific balance sheet items. Third, the float created by in-transit items tends to be large in volume in international banking. These 'clearings' effected by overseas branches swell their 'due from' and 'due to' accounts, magnifying them out of proportion. Finally, many items do not appear directly in the balance sheets, and therefore cannot be reflected. These include forward contracts outstanding for delivery and receipt of foreign exchange, and items in process of collection.

Total assets of foreign branches expanded from $7\frac{1}{2}$ billion in mid-1965 to nearly $70 billion at mid-year 1972. This expansion reflects the establishment of additional foreign branches as well as internal growth of existing branches. On 30 June 1972, 106 Federal Reserve member banks had 558 foreign branches, compared with 13 member banks with 188 branches at year-end 1965.[16] The aggregate balance sheet for the 558 overseas branches of member banks at June 1972 is reproduced in Table 5-2. Over two-thirds of the nearly $70 billion in assets and liabilities is payable in U.S. dollars, the remainder payable in local currencies and other currencies.

Transactions with U.S. head offices are reflected in the items 'Claims against parent bank' and 'Due to parent bank'. In the period 1968–70 foreign branch claims against parent banks reached a peak of $14 billion, and then declined gradually. These borrowings of U.S. head offices from foreign branches reflected extremely tight money in the United States, and the impact of Regulation Q ceilings on bank liquidity. In 1969 the Board of Governors applied marginal reserve requirements on net borrowings of head offices from their foreign branches, and in 1971 these reserve requirements were increased from 10 to 20 per cent. As conditions in U.S. domestic money markets eased, head offices reduced their borrowings from foreign branches. Since 1971 the foreign branches have not been an important source of funds for their head offices, and by June 1972 these borrowings had declined to $2.3 billion.

The foreign branches engage in a small volume of transactions with residents of the United States other than their parent banks. Since September 1969 loans to residents of the United States by foreign branches have been subject to reserve requirements parallel to those that apply to borrowings by head offices. An exception is made in loans to U.S. corporations to enable them to comply with the foreign direct investment programme. American banks have been requested not to accept deposits from U.S. residents at their foreign branches unless such deposits are connected with international business, since deposits at foreign branches are exempt from reserve requirements and from regulation on maximum rates of interest payable on deposits.

The balance sheets of foreign branches reflect a heavy mix of transactions with commercial banks in foreign countries. In some cases these transactions result in a net liability position since these foreign banks represent a primary source of funds. Moreover, much of the Eurocurrency activity is carried on with banks in other countries. In the period 1970–72 claims on foreign banks grew more rapidly than liabilities to these banks. This reflects the reduction in head office borrowings from foreign branches, and the branch placement of these funds with foreign banks. In the period September 1969 to June 1972 foreign branches reduced the net amount of funds raised from foreign banks from $11.4 billion to $5.6 billion (Table 5-2).

In June 1972 foreign branches were net suppliers of funds to non-bank customers in the amount of $9.3 billion. The growth in claims on non-bank borrowers is a continuation of a trend that began in 1965 when the voluntary foreign credit restraint programme was initiated. Some of the increase in claims on non-banks is attributable to the heavy credit demands of large multinational corporations in support of their world-wide operations. While term claims (more than one year maturity) on non-bank foreign borrowers had expanded by 150 per cent in the period 1969–72, they represented less than one-tenth of the total assets of foreign branches ($5.5 billion) at the later date.

On a net basis transactions with foreign official institutions provide a substantial amount of funds to the foreign branches of American banks. In the period September 1969 to June 1972 liabilities to foreign official institutions at foreign branches increased from $2.1 billion to $7.2 billion, of which $5.6 billion was denominated in dollars. These funds have enabled these foreign branches to expand dollar loans to foreign borrowers, and this expansion in credits has probably

Table 5.2

Assets and Liabilities of Foreign Branches of U.S. Banks —
June 30, 1972

ASSETS		$ billions	LIABILITIES		$ billions
Claims on U.S.			Due to U.S.		
Against parent			Due to parent		
bank	2.3		bank	0.6	
Other	2.6		Due to other		
Total		4.9	U.S. residents	2.4	
Claims on foreigners			Total		3.1
Against other branches			Due to foreigners		
of parent bank	11.5		Due to other branches		
Against other			of parent bank	11.1	
banks	30.6		Due to other		
Due from official			banks	36.1	
institutions	1.3		Due to official		
Due from non-bank			institutions	7.2	
foreigners	19.5		Due to non-bank		
Sub-Total		62.9	foreigners	10.2	
Other Assets		1.9	Sub-Total		64.6
			Other Liabilities		1.9
Total Assets		69.6			
Payable in U.S. dollars		44.9	Total Liabilities		69.6
% Payable in U.S. dollars		67	Payable in U.S. dollars		47.8
			% Payable in U.S. dollars		71

Source: *Federal Reserve Bulletin.*

resulted in further additions to foreign official reserves.

2. FUNDING THE OVERSEAS BRANCH

Differences between deposit banking in the United States and overseas hinge on the wholesale aspect of international deposit taking, the increased volatility of internationally mobile funds, and the multicurrency aspect of overseas branch deposits. This multicurrency aspect presents a number of operational distinctions that are not faced by branches located in the United States. Foreign branches generally attempt to balance assets and liabilities by currency of denomination as well as by maturity.

American overseas branches hold deposited funds which are by their nature internationally mobile. This is not generally true of the deposits of domestic banking offices. Only the largest U.S. banks hold substantial amounts of deposited funds in domestic offices which could be considered to be internationally mobile.

American commercial banking is characterised by a conscious effort on the part of the larger banks to solicit deposits from smaller banks and from non-financial corporations. The foreign branches of U.S. banks have attempted to solicit deposits from internationally oriented U.S. corporations which have operations and are located in the same foreign countries as they are. However, the high degree of competition in the international markets for deposits has reduced the effectiveness of direct solicitation. The type of funds involved tends to work against direct solicitation. Eurocurrency deposits, a mainstay of the London, Continental and Nassau branches lend themselves to over-the-counter foreign exchange type placements.[17]

It should be noted that the sources of deposits for many overseas branches of U.S. banks are not as widely diversified as in the case of domestic branches. Deposit business is often at the wholesale level, which naturally works against a wide diversification. Moreover, individual branches often rely heavily on one specific type of deposit source.

In the modern vocabulary of the multinational banker 'funding' has become a commonplace expression. Today bankers recognise that it is necessary to operate with a plan for procuring funds that is properly attuned to their projected end-use.

Liability management has grown to be as important as portfolio management.

The foreign branch finds itself in a far different position from its U.S. head office or domestic branch counterpart in competing for funds. Overseas branches operate from a local currency or Eurocurrency base, whereas domestic offices operate from a dollar fund base. This difference is important for several reasons including the fact that dollar resources at home may be expected to be more plentiful and elastic in supply. Foreign branches find themselves more limited in their ability to attract deposits because they are competing against entrenched indigenous institutions. U.S. banks generally have followed a policy of requiring that overseas branches provide all or very nearly all of the funds required to support their own lending activities. In the long-run these branches must work within the limits of their own capacity to generate deposits.

In many countries outside the United States and United Kingdom, the local money market consists largely of inter-bank operations where banks may place their excess funds with other banks on a short-term basis. This type of market is highly developed in countries such as Germany where there is an abundance of banking institutions of various sizes and types. The inter-bank market provides an important source of liquidity adjustment for banks. In addition, it renders an important service to the foreign branches of American banks by providing them with lendable funds which they otherwise would not have access to. However, in bidding for these funds foreign branches may have to pay a somewhat higher price or premium, especially when there is an energetic effort on their part to build up a substantial base of lendable funds in this manner.

In 1968–9 many American banks with only a modest or medium-sized international operation were beginning to search for á means of expanding their overseas representation, and simultaneously increase their ability to attract internationally mobile funds which could be used both for international lending and domestic liquidity adjustment. In part this was in response to events in 1966 when the few U.S. banks with London branches were able to relieve their reserve positions by obtaining advances from these overseas offices.

London branches possess two shortcomings which are important considerations to medium-sized U.S. banks, especially those which are relative newcomers to the field of overseas branch operations. These shortcomings include the high cost involved in establishing a London branch, and the time zone difference between business hours in New York and London.

It is possible for American banks to avoid these difficulties by establishing a branch in Nassau and to further prosper from the low tax and other benefits which permit Nassau branches to attract a substantial volume of deposits. With the exception of branches established by a few U.S. banks that have long operated in Nassau, branch offices in this location have been of the 'shell' variety. Generally they are staffed with only a few employees, the bulk of the operations being conducted from a New York head office where telephone and cable connections permit instant communication with customers and the Nassau office.

In the period 1968–70 the new Nassau branches provided a means of attracting Eurocurrency deposits, but this barely satisfied the lending requirements of these offices as tight credit market conditions persisted. Subsequent to the rapid easing of monetary pressures in 1970–72 the situation was reversed, with U.S. banks striving to maintain the substantial loan portfolios in Nassau branches which had grown under conditions of credit scarcity.

Another source of funds for overseas branches is in the form of dollar advances from head office, which can be swapped for local currency, used in foreign exchange transactions, or employed in the form of dollar loans. In recent years American banks have made only limited use of this means of providing funds to their foreign branches. Two basic reasons include the desire to limit the exchange risks associated with employment of dollar funds swapped into local currencies, and because this form of capital outflow is applied against the foreign credit guidelines which have been used to curb head office lending to overseas borrowers since 1965.

Eurocurrency deposits provide close to half of total funds at the disposal of foreign branches of American banks, but account for three-quarters of the funds available to branches in the United Kingdom and Nassau. Branches in the United Kingdom supplement Eurocurrency sources through sale of sterling and dollar certificates of deposit, but this does not provide more than a small percentage of the funds available to them.

London banks also carry a substantial amount of deposits related to the shipping and ship-building business. Here, ship-building loans handled by banks in London and elsewhere provide for amortisation related to charter-hire receipts. Such receipts are placed on deposit in these London banks.

On a global basis deposits of multinational corporations, local business firms, and individuals provide approximately one-fifth of total sources of funds of American branches. Restrictions imposed by the U.S. government on direct investment capital outflows of American corporations and the extent of their overseas liquidity holdings have prevented these corporations from contributing substantially to the deposit growth of overseas branches. However, their offshore direct investment activities continue to expand vigorously and this has furnished a larger base from which foreign branches have derived additional opportunities for loan and deposit activity.

Other sources of funds for foreign branches include deposits from central banks and official institutions, and liabilities to other foreign branches of the parent bank. In 1972 deposits of foreign central banks and official institutions accounted for close to 10 per cent of total resources. These deposits represent part of a network of reciprocal relationships between the U.S. head office, the foreign central bank, and the foreign branch of the American bank, whereby the head office may render services for the central bank in return for the latter placing deposits with a foreign branch of the U.S. bank. The services rendered may include providing dollar swap facilities for the central bank, or straight dollar lines of credit.

3. PROBLEMS IN OVERSEAS DEPOSIT STRUCTURE

The structure of deposits in overseas branches of American banks contains a number of built-in weaknesses, which reflect the special character of foreign branch sources of funds. Foreign branches rely on short-term, high cost, volatile deposits. These are bid for in highly competitive international money markets. Overseas branches of American banks cannot easily obtain stable deposits. In a number of cases major customers are overseas affiliates of U.S. corporations, highly leveraged and cash poor, in some instances without adequate working capital.[18] Since the advent of the U.S. balance of payments programme in 1965 American parent corporations have made their overseas affiliates develop their own sources of financing and liquidity.

The volatility of foreign branch deposits has been intensified as interest rate consciousness has increased around the world. Corporate treasurers tend to hold unused funds to a minimum, and money has become more professionally managed as local markets for funds have become increasingly interdependent and sophisticated. Hence, foreign branches of U.S. banks cannot disregard even slight changes in money rates in major and outlying financial centres.

Overseas branches operate on a deposit base that is more short-term than their loan portfolio. This is especially true of branches in London. To some extent the problem of deposit volatility is mitigated by the fact that many foreign branches hold sizeable dollar balances with their U.S. head offices, and in an emergency can fall back on their head offices to ease them over temporary periods of stress and strain. London branches can make use of their head office dollar balances whenever they suffer sizeable losses of sterling deposits. However, swapping dollar balances into sterling may be costly. The deposits at head office may also cushion the effects of seasonal and other pressures in the Eurodollar market.

Other problems in the deposit structure of overseas branches include the increasing sophistication of many sources of funds, especially in the Middle East countries; the need for new branches to pay generous rates to attract a viable base of Euro-currency funds; the need to offer costly special services such as paycheck accounting to attract deposits; and the special problems associated with deposit banking in an inflationary environment. The struggle for deposits is difficult in countries suffering from inflation for two reasons. First, deposits are in a state of flux, and asset holders try to avoid maintaining large deposit balances on a regular basis. Second, U.S. banks with single branches in inflation-ridden countries suffer, since they do not have the branch network necessary to retain deposits. In part they must depend on transactions float as a source of funds and therefore may be required to follow a policy of making loans only to borrowers who maintain substantial deposit balances.

4. USES OF FUNDS

Foreign branches of American banks have utilised the funds at their disposal in a variety of ways. These include providing liquidity support for the operations of U.S. head offices, direct loans to overseas business borrowers including affiliates of U.S. corporations, operating as an intermediary in the inter-bank and Eurocurrency markets, providing interim and short-term credits to other foreign branches of the parent bank, and extending loans and credits to others including foreign central banks and U.S. banks. Transactions in the Eurocurrency markets overshadow the lending as well as deposit-taking activities of foreign branches of American banks.

During the late 1960s providing liquidity support to head offices became the most important factor in the allocation of foreign branch funds. The largest means of providing such liquidity support to U.S. head offices was by direct advances. At year-end 1969 'due from head offices and U.S. branches' accounted for 35 per cent of aggregate foreign branch assets, and 40 per cent, 44 per cent and 28 per cent respectively, of United Kingdom, Bahamas, and Continental Europe branch assets. A second method by which U.S. overseas branches have provided a considerable supplement to the liquidity of their head offices has been through outright purchases of loans from these head offices. Such purchases also have contributed a great deal to the ability of domestic offices to comply with the foreign credit restraints administered by the Federal Reserve. Some of these loans have been sold to foreign branches under repurchase agreements. In addition, at times head offices have instructed their foreign branches to make dollar loans that would have been made out of head offices in the absence of the restraint programme or heavy domestic loan demands. These sales of loans have proven to be an extremely flexible method for adjusting liquidity and complying with foreign lending restraints. For example, in the short period December, 1969 to July, 1970 the amount of loans outstanding that had been sold outright by U.S. commercial banks to foreign branches, holding companies and other affiliates increased from $4.7 billion to $8.0 billion. From July to December 1970 this amount declined to $2.7 billion.[19]

Loans to foreigners other than banks has represented the second most important overall use of funds by foreign branches. Approximately half of these loans are to U.S. multinational corporations operating overseas and their foreign subsidiaries. Where loans are made to foreign subsidiaries of domestic corporations, the U.S. parent may provide its own guarantee. Much of this lending is carried out in Eurocurrencies, the favoured currency generally being the dollar. Non-U.S. corporations including European, Canadian and Japanese firms generate a large demand for funds which foreign branches of American banks attempt to service through Eurocurrency loans. In addition, overseas branches extend credits to U.S. and other business borrowers in local currencies, the proceeds of which may be utilised to finance operations in the respective countries.

The bulk of the loans to non-bank borrowers provided by foreign branches located in London and Western Europe are large denomination credits to U.S. and indigenous corporations. A similar pattern prevails in Japan where branches of U.S. banks extend a mixture of short-term and medium-term loans to industrial corporations. In the less developed countries foreign branches seek to establish deposit and loan relationships with large American and indigenous corporations. However, the opportunities are more restricted than in Western Europe and Japan. In addition, foreign trade financing requirements are substantial in the developing countries partly due to the relative scarcity of appropriate bank and foreign exchange facilities. As a result, American banks operating in these countries allocate a larger proportion of their resources to foreign trade financing.[20]

Foreign branches also provide Eurodollar revolving credits, which may involve a half per cent commitment fee. Under this approach the U.S. bank agrees to make a series of six month loans renewable for a period of up to seven years. At each renewal the bank resets the rate charged which ranges from a half per cent up to $1\frac{1}{4}$ per cent more than the London inter-bank rate on Eurodollars.

Deposits in other foreign banks also represent a sizeable use of funds for overseas branches. Only a small portion of this represents deposits deliberately placed with foreign banks to provide them with credit facilities. Nearly all of these funds can be accounted for by the Eurocurrency transactions in which many foreign branches are heavily involved. The Eurocurrency markets are inter-bank oriented, and American foreign branches find themselves taking an intermediary position both as takers and suppliers of funds.

Contrary to popular belief, foreign branches of American banks do not extend sizeable credits to foreign banks, nor do they place any significant amount of deposits in foreign banks. Foreign branches generally lack the resources to support such financing activities on a large scale. However, this type of lending or placing of deposits may be undertaken by the U.S. head office for special purposes, but usually only to banks in less developed countries where alternative sources of funds are lacking and in cases where the U.S. bank can establish a favourable reciprocal working relationship with the foreign bank.

Although not large as a percentage of assets, claims on other foreign branches of the parent bank permit overseas branches to fulfil an important international banking role. One of the most important functions of foreign branches is to facilitate the movement of funds from relatively low interest rate or surplus areas to markets that can employ these funds more profitably. By carrying out this function American overseas branches contribute materially to the integration of the international money and loan markets.

Foreign branches of American banks often pass funds on to branches or banks in other areas, often under instructions from the U.S. head office. Occasionally they may swap dollars for third currencies for deposit in other markets, or pass sterling deposits to newly-established branches in the overseas sterling area that have inadequate deposit resources but attractive lending opportunities. Inter-branch transactions provide important intermediation facilities. Several large American banks prefer to centralise the redistribution of international balances in the head office, rather than have one overseas branch supply another directly.

5. SERVICE FUNCTIONS PERFORMED FOR HEAD OFFICE

As the number and size of foreign branches of American banks expand, they become an increasingly important mechanism for performing services for the parent bank. Services performed by overseas branches are rendered in large measure on behalf of foreign affiliates of U.S. industrial corporations.

Head offices of American banks may call on their overseas branches to service clients who wish to establish subsidiary operations in the area serviced by the branch. The services called for may range from locating factory and office building sites, obtaining information regarding the regulations affecting joint ventures with foreign partners, and finding merger and acquisition prospects. Existing customers of the head office or foreign branch may wish to have the branch pave the way for local borrowing, especially if the customer grows beyond the branch's lending capacity. Moreover, the foreign branch may render considerable assistance to U.S. corporate affiliates in obtaining licences from the local government, in solving exchange control problems, responding to trade inquiries, and following up on credit file investigations.

Foreign branches can assist in the loan analysis activities of U.S. head offices considering loan requests made by foreign companies with manufacturing or distributing facilities in the United States. When a German company with a U.S. manufacturing operation submits a loan request to a U.S. bank that has a branch in West Germany, it is possible for the American bank to request information from its German branch regarding the prospective borrower. The foreign branch renders the following key services for the U.S. head office: (1) it provides credit information about the German borrower, (2) it establishes initial contact with the German firm, and (3) it strengthens the relation with the German corporation by means of its role in facilitating U.S. domestic credits. As foreign direct investment in the United States expands, the role of overseas branches of American banks in providing these offshore contacts with foreign business firms will become even more important.

Foreign branches speed up the collection of receivables and cheques, and accelerate inter-bank and intra-bank transfers of cash for corporate treasurers and other banks. A foreign branch network can provide immediate credit for funds in various parts of the globe, and can effect economies in the cash requirements of clients.

Another important service rendered by the foreign branch is to collect cheques for customers that receive payment in drafts drawn on U.S. banks. The foreign branch sends them by air freight for collection at its head office. These cheques are credited to the customers accounts one day after they are received at the overseas branch. This service makes possible substantial postal savings and economises on customers' cash balances.

Foreign branches are listening posts for political and economic developments in overseas areas. They service head office loan accounts, accelerate payments, and establish valuable deposit and custody relationships between the central bank of the host country and the parent bank in the United States. Most important, by providing these and other important services, they assist the head office in retaining valuable U.S. corporate deposit balances.

C. MANAGEMENT AND CONTROL

1. HEAD OFFICE CONTROL

Control of overseas branches at the head office is usually the responsibility of an Executive or Senior Vice President in charge of international operations, who may delegate responsibility to another senior officer. Day-to-day supervision is usually assigned to officers in charge of the territories or regions where the branches and representative offices are located. These territorial officers conduct periodic tours of the regions they are responsible for.

The degree of supervision over foreign branches exercised from head office varies from bank to bank. Generally, the larger banks with many years of experience and numerous overseas branches follow a policy of decentralised authority and relaxed supervision. On the other hand, in the case of smaller banks operating one or only a few overseas branches head office control and supervision of foreign branches is very close and quite detailed. In larger banks with numerous branches such offices are managed by a Vice President in charge of a particular region, who may be given fairly wide latitude in decisions involving credit administration and branch operations. Generally these officers are given a great deal of discretion and operate their branches with very little interference from head office. However, among the smaller banks supervision of the foreign branch by the parent bank is often so close that many branch managers resent it and feel it stymies their activities.

Loan, foreign exchange, and other areas of authority of branch management are generally circumscribed in policy guides and operating procedures manuals. The loan authority of the branch manager is typically the same as that of a parent bank officer of the same rank, and in aggregate terms is likely to be somewhat limited. Some banks provide for emergency loan authority to permit branch managers to make quick decisions without reference to head office. In the main, loan and other operations of the branch are subject to review and approval by the parent bank, usually by the Senior Loan Committee of the bank, unless that branch is under exceptionally strong management.

Among the larger banks, especially those with more than one foreign branch, supervision of foreign exchange positions and trading activity tends to be decentralised. In such cases each branch may be relatively free to participate in the local foreign exchange market as it deems necessary, subject to the currency limits and specific spot and forward limits established by the head office. There are two practical reasons which dictate against centralisation of foreign exchange operations. First, it is difficult to funnel pertinent information to head office on an hourly or even daily basis. Second, given a large network of overseas branches, time zone differences make it necessary to allow individual branches to buy and sell and contract for forward exchange in a relatively flexible manner.

There are many unsolved problems in the area of sharing responsibility between the head office and branch managements. As foreign operations expand the basic question of the degree of centralised versus decentralised decision-making in areas of salary administration, promotions, housekeeping operations, and in other specialised functions becomes a more pressing issue.

2. CREDIT ANALYSIS AND CONTROL

The global credit analysis and review procedures instituted by major banks generally includes three major components. In addition, several large banks have more specialised review and analysis procedures, including periodic audit of overseas branches and affiliates, and the development of a special regional loan analysis and review administration.

The three major components of the credit analysis and review procedures of major U.S. banks engaged in international banking include:

1. provision of lending limits for each branch loan officer;
2. adherence to the three Cs of foreign branch credit-making, i.e., customer limits, country limits, and currency limits;
3. procedures for centralised record-keeping and loan review by an appropriate committee or section of the administrative structure of the bank.

Each loan officer assigned to a foreign branch is given a lending limit based upon his prior experience in evaluating credits, his rank, the type of clientele of the branch to which he is assigned, and other factors. The limit may be $500,000 which limits this officer to authorising individual loans up to that amount on his own responsibility. He may work with another loan officer with the same limit, which would permit the two officers jointly to sponsor a single loan of up to $1,000,000 in amount. Obviously, on very large loans extended by a foreign branch the lending authority of all officers may have to be assembled to push through the loan.

Territorial loan officers, usually stationed at head office, may utilise their lending authority in cases where there is insufficient lending authority on the part of branch loan officers. Finally, the lending authority of senior officers of the International Banking Division may have to be drawn upon in cases of requests for very large loans.

The Board of Directors of the bank generally must approve all loans which exceed certain amount limits. For very large banks this may involve all loans in excess of $5–6 million. For smaller banks engaged in foreign branch lending the Board may have to approve all loans of $1 million or more. These safeguards provide a built-in check on foreign as well as domestic branch lending activity.

A second component of the credit analysis and control procedures which apply is the three Cs of foreign branch credit extension. These include limits on credits to individual customers, limits on aggregate credits located in any one country, and limits in the amount of actual and contingent assets and liabilities denominated in specific foreign currencies. Branches are usually subject to specific limitations regarding the amount of loans, acceptance lines, and overdrafts permitted to any one account, and special procedures generally insure that an individual customer's liabilities to branches and head office do not exceed pre-determined credit lines.

Thus there are limits on the amount a branch may place on deposit with any given bank; on its currency and country exposures; and on its overnight foreign exchange positions, not only in the aggregate but also in spot and future transactions and with regard to each currency and each customer. For example, a branch in Brazil will have specific limits on the D-mark or Swiss franc positions it may take. Virtually all the U.S. parent banks and branches themselves tightened their controls over foreign exchange operations since the devaluation of the pound in 1967, at which time several banks suffered sizeable losses.

Many banks have indicated that they apply country limits to the aggregate credits extended to borrowers located in specific countries. There are several sound reasons for this practice, including the desire to provide geographic diversification of risks, and the need to allocate some portion of funds to an increasing number of new borrowing countries where opportunities for business development appear favourable. It is possible that some bankers do not make a fine distinction between country and currency risks, and for that reason identified for the author 'country limits' which may represent limits on particular types of currency exposures.

A final aspect of the credit analysis and review procedures is the review of loans and credits by an appropriately designated committee or section of the bank's administrative structure. There exists somewhat greater variation in actual practices in this area than in other aspects of credit analysis and review, especially where loans and credits initiated by foreign branches are concerned. Some banks utilise a single loan and discount review committee, while others employ more than one. Where a single committee is used, it generally consists of the senior credit officers of the bank, representing national, local (metropolitan), and international credit-making divisions. This committee usually is headed by an executive level officer, with the rank of Executive Vice President. This committee ordinarily reviews new loans that exceed certain amount limits, generally those of $1 million or more. Subject to the approval of this committee, many of these loans will also have to be approved by the Board of Directors of the bank.

Several banks utilise more than one loan and discount review committee. In such instances one committee will review domestic credits and a second committee will review foreign or international credits. In a few cases, loans extended by foreign branches may be subject to the review of a branch, regional or territorial review committee. Thus loans extended through a Frankfurt or Paris branch of an American bank may be reviewed by a European regional loan committee, if the amounts exceed certain pre-determined limits.

3. CO-ORDINATION OF INTERNATIONAL CREDIT AND CUSTOMER RELATIONS

In addition to establishing effective operating guidelines for the analysis and review of new foreign loans and credits, American banks expose their foreign branches and the loans they have extended to an ongoing review. In part this is designed to achieve a reasonable degree of co-ordination between domestic and international banking operations. In addition it aims at insuring that the quality of international loans is maintained at a high level, and that overseas branches conform to the same standards of efficiency and safety that prevail in domestic branches. In this section we discuss briefly four aspects of this review and co-ordination role. These include reporting, centralised record-keeping, audit, and co-ordination of multinational credits.

First, foreign branches must submit periodic reports to their head offices describing their activities, statements of condition, foreign exchange position, status of loans outstanding, and other matters. These reports may be required on a daily, weekly or monthly basis. Minimally, foreign branches must submit their statement of condition on a monthly basis, and loan status reports may be required more frequently. There is considerable variation from bank to bank relative to the frequency at which these reports are required, the general pattern being that larger banks with more numerous overseas branch locations require less frequent reporting than smaller banks. As one officer of a relatively large New York bank expressed it, 'Daily reporting on an across-the-board basis would result in a paper jungle at head office.'

In most banks with foreign branches centralised record-keeping and auditing arrangements are comprehensive and elaborate. Duplicate files are generally maintained at U.S. head offices and a representative of the bank's comptroller may be permanently assigned to foreign branches, or may visit and audit them periodically. Several large banks indicated that their overseas auditing teams are kept quite busy examining and auditing overseas branches and subsidiaries. In several instances there was a definite impression that this area of review and analysis was far more demanding with respect to foreign as compared with domestic operations of the same bank.

The expansion of overseas branch operations on the part of American banks increases the complexity of maintaining a constant review and control over their global credits to multinational corporations. Both from the account relationship and legal points of view it is considered necessary for U.S. banks to maintain a close scrutiny over their aggregate credits to individual corporations. Moreover, with the expanding nature of multinational corporate activities, including the maintenance of banking relationships with many banks in each of a number of different countries, it becomes necessary for U.S. banks to be in a position to summarise the global importance of a particular corporation (U.S., European, Canadian, or Japanese) so that a remote Far Eastern branch may assess the overall impact on the customer relationship of its own decision on a particular loan request of the same customer.

For example, should a well-known multinational firm such

as Pfizer request a loan from the Singapore branch of Bank of America, that bank's head office should be in a position to advise the Singapore branch of the total (global) account relationship between Pfizer and all operating offices of Bank of America. Moreover, the officer of Bank of America in California responsible for the Pfizer account should be in a position to advise Singapore regarding the credit limit fixed for that particular customer, and the extent of its utilisation at any particular time. Finally, that bank may have a country lending limit in Malaysia, which may operate as a constraint in this particular situation.

At the present time there are at least 800 multinational corporations, U.S. and foreign, which potentially could turn up at any of the foreign branches of American banks around the globe with a loan request. The largest of the U.S. banks engaged in international banking have established limits or ceilings on the total credits they are willing to extend to a long list of companies which includes most of these multinational firms. American banks have found it increasingly necessary to establish the following procedures to record and evaluate the status of their account relationships with such customers:

1. to establish a global lending commitment and limit for each multinational customer;
2. to provide a centralised facility where records may be maintained showing the extent to which such customers have utilised outstanding credit lines;
3. to establish a system to estimate the overall value of the account relationship to the bank and employ this system on a regular basis to determine profitability and worth-whileness of individual accounts;
4. to periodically reassess and evaluate the system of estimating the value of account relationships.

Several decades ago many of the largest American banks began to conceive of a 'national division' or 'corporate division' which would have primary responsibility for developing, maintaining, and in part evaluating business connections with large national corporations. At the present time a similar development is taking place whereby the largest American banks are according similar status and treatment to multinational corporations.

6 Edge Act and Agreement Corporations

In the first two decades of this century American banks depended on their international banking affiliates as the major vehicle for expanding their foreign banking activities. Until 1925 these corporations operated more overseas branches than did the banks themselves.[1] Thereafter, as U.S. international banking activities declined, less emphasis was given to the use of this means of conducting foreign operations. More recently, attention has focused on the international banking corporation for at least two reasons. First, these corporations permit their parent banks to undertake international banking activities across state lines. Second, these corporations have the power to purchase and hold the stock of foreign companies.

In the sections which follow we examine the legislative and supervisory conditions under which these corporate affiliates operate. Moreover, we examine the various functions performed by these corporations and analyse how these functions fit into the overall international banking role played by U.S. banks.

A. GROWTH AND DEVELOPMENT OF INTER-NATIONAL BANKING CORPORATIONS

1. AGREEMENT AND EDGE CORPORATIONS

There are two types of international banking corporations in which national and state member banks of the Federal Reserve System may purchase stock. These are known as Agreement corporations and Edge corporations. The 1916 amendment to Section 25 of the Federal Reserve Act permits banks to invest in the stock of corporations principally engaged in international or foreign banking, subject to certain conditions. These are that the bank have a capital and surplus of $1 million or more, that it invest no more than 10 per cent of its capital and surplus in such stock, that the bank secure permission of the Board of Governors of the Federal Reserve System, and that the corporation enters into an agreement with the Board of Governors regarding limitations on its operations. Because of the last-mentioned condition these corporations have been given the name 'Agreement corporations'.

The 1916 amendment to Section 25 did not provide for federal chartering of international banking corporations. This omission was rectified three years later by the addition of Section 25(a) of the Federal Reserve Act. Senator Walter Edge of New Jersey sponsored this legislation, which explains why corporations chartered under Section 25(a) have come to be known as 'Edge corporations'.

There are a number of important differences between Edge corporations and Agreement corporations. First, Edge corporations are federally chartered and not subject to the corporation or banking laws of the various states,[2] while Agreement corporations are normally chartered under and directly subject to state laws.[3] Second, Edge corporations must have a minimum capital of $2 million, while there is no minimum for Agreement corporations. Since the maximum investment permitted a parent bank in each type of corporation is 10 per cent of the bank's capital and surplus, to have an Edge subsidiary requires that a bank have a minimum of $20 million in capital and surplus, while only the statutory minimum of $1 million in capital and surplus is necessary for a bank to have an Agreement subsidiary.

Third, the majority of shares of an Edge corporation must be owned by citizens of the United States, and all directors must be citizens. There are no equivalent restrictions imposed on Agreement corporations. Fourth, all national and state member banks are given statutory authorisation to invest in the stock of an Edge corporation, whereas they must receive specific approval from the Board of Governors to invest in the stock of an Agreement corporation. Finally, there are several differences in the scope of activities of both type of corporations. Edge corporations may engage in international banking or other foreign financial operations, whereas Agreement corporations must engage principally in international or foreign banking. Therefore the operations of Edge corporations may specifically include other financial activities while those of Agreement corporations are generally confined to banking.

Restrictions on the operations of Edge corporations seem to be directed primarily to operations conducted in the United States. Edge corporations are permitted to carry on only those activities in the United States which are incidental to their international or foreign business. This applies specifically to receipt of deposits within the United States. Moreover, they cannot purchase the stock of any company which deals in merchandise or commodities in the United States, nor of any company which transacts any business in the United States, except where such may be incidental to its international or foreign business. Other restrictions include a limitation on the issuance of bonds and debentures, a minimum reserve on deposits in the United States, and a maximum limit on the amount a corporation may invest in any one stock.

In the period since World War II the Edge corporation has been utilised far more extensively than the Agreement corporation. At present there are only two basic reasons for choosing the latter form. In situations where state banking laws provide for state banks to acquire the stock of state-chartered international banking companies, but not that of an Edge corporation, there is no choice available. This was true of California several years ago. The other reason for utilising an Agreement corporation is where the purpose of the corporation does not require a capital of $2 million, which is the minimum required for an Edge corporation. This use is illustrated by Bankers Company of New York, The Gallatin Company, Inc., and First Foreign Investment Corporation, which have been utilised to acquire and hold a single stock issue.

2. REGULATION AND SUPERVISION

The most important regulation which the Board has utilised in implementing its responsibilities of regulating and supervising these international banking corporations is Regulation K. Prior to 1957 Regulation K dealt only with Edge corporations, and the Board exercised its supervisory power over Agreement corporations solely through individual agreements and amendments to these agreements. These agreements generally paralleled the requirements of Regulation K, at least to the extent that such requirements pertained to the Agreement corporation in question.[4]

In 1957 Regulation K was revised, and part of this revision provided for including Agreement corporations within the scope of authority of the Regulation. Other significant changes incorporated in the 1957 revision were the creation of two types of corporations, 'banking' and 'financing'; establishment of specific restrictions on operations of corporations in the United States; and provision for financing corporations to obtain limited general consents for the purchase of stock in foreign companies.

The sharp distinction between commercial and investment banking in the 1957 revision followed the separation provided for in the banking legislation of the 1930s. Banking corporations were permitted to accept deposits and create banker's acceptances, and were prohibited from issuing bonds and debentures. Their stock acquisitions for the most part were limited to foreign banks and bank related companies. Financing corporations were prohibited from receiving deposits, creating acceptances and acquiring stock in companies engaged in banking. This strict division of functions led to the creation of twin corporations by a number of U.S. banks. This development is discussed in a later section of this chapter.

Prior to 1957, regulatory provisions for the acquisition of

shares of stock in foreign companies fluctuated between the extremes of requiring specific consent of the Board of Governors for all acquisitions and granting a blanket consent. The 1957 revision of Regulation K continued the latter approach, which had been in effect since 1943. Moreover, it provided that financing corporations could obtain from the Board a 'limited general consent' to acquire stock that fell within a specified programme.

The 1963 revision of Regulation K incorporated two fundamental changes. These were modification of the formal distinction between banking and financing corporations, and creation of the regulatory 'general consent'.

Since 1963 Regulation K provides for one type of corporation, which may engage in both banking and financing operations. However, the revised Regulation K retains certain restrictions on the operations of those corporations 'engaged in banking'. Corporations are defined as 'engaged in banking' when their aggregate demand deposits and acceptance liabilities exceed their own capital and surplus. Such corporations are severely restricted in securities underwriting activities.

Corporations 'engaged in banking' may not undertake lending commitments to any one borrower exceeding 10 per cent of capital and surplus, whereas the limitation is 50 per cent if the corporation is not engaged in banking.

> In terms of a rough distinction between the former banking and the former financing corporations, those active in banking either do a variety of business typical of that of the international department of a commercial bank or function as holding companies for equity investments in foreign banks. In some cases, they fulfil both functions. The former financing corporations have tended to operate in a different area, with investments in the stock of nonbank financial concerns, development corporations, or commercial and industrial firms.[5]

Banking corporations hold demand and time deposits of foreign parties, issue or confirm letters of credit, finance foreign trade, extend loans and create banker's acceptances, receive items for collection, remit funds abroad, purchase and sell securities, hold securities for safe keeping, issue certain guarantees, act as paying agent for securities issued by foreign governments and certain foreign corporations, and engage in spot and forward foreign exchange transactions.[6]

Provision in the 1963 revision of Regulation K of a general consent for the acquisition of certain stocks brought considerably more flexibility into this aspect of the activities of corporations. With the 1963 revision corporations were permitted to acquire stock of a foreign company if (1) it was in connection with an extension of credit, (2) it represented less than a 25 per cent interest in a foreign bank, or (3) was a small (not over $200,000) investment likely to further U.S. foreign commerce.[7] A somewhat more detailed discussion of general and specific consent provisions in the various revisions of Regulation K follows in Section D below.

In addition to being responsible for the issuance of Regulation K, the Board also enjoys supervisory responsibilities relating to the status of this Regulation. A number of operations carried out by the corporations require specific Board approval. Moreover, the Board enjoys overall responsibility for supervising activities of the corporations that fall within the purview of other Regulations.

The Board has at its disposal a number of means by which to execute its supervisory responsibilities over corporations. First, the Board may rely upon examinations and require reports to keep abreast of the activities of the corporations. Each corporation is examined annually and the resulting report is reviewed by the Board's staff.[8] While foreign subsidiaries are not examined, it is expected that the parent corporation will have on file information necessary for effective management control. In addition, the Board receives half-annual Reports of Condition from each corporation. At least one of the two reports received each year contains financial accounts, currency breakdowns, and affiliated relationships. Quarterly reports are filed with the Board showing all acquisitions and dispositions of stock by the corporation and its subsidiaries.

Applications for Board approval cover a wide variety of areas, including requests for increases in capital, for branches, for permission to exceed regulatory limitations, and for reversal of examiners' findings. One area stands out in importance, namely requests for consent to purchase stock in foreign companies. Applications for approval to purchase shares of stock are the most numerous, and raise the most difficult policy questions. While some requests for permission to acquire and hold shares of stock in a given company can be fairly routine, others can raise difficult questions as to the propriety of such a holding (due to the type of business involved), the degree of control involved, or the political situation in the country. At times the Board has seen fit to grant consent to the acquisition subject to certain conditions. Since the 1963 revision the Board's consent to the acquisition of minority stock interests has usually not been subject to any conditions.[9]

Prior to the 1957 revision of Regulation K the Board exercised its supervisory powers over Agreement corporations primarily through the agreements concluded with those corporations, and examinations and reports. The earlier agreements had a considerable degree of variation. Since the 1957 revision brought Agreement corporations within the purview of Regulation K, the new agreements generally have been confined to the corporations' acceptance of Regulation K.

3. EARLY YEARS

Prior to 1930, eighteen corporations came under the Board's jurisdiction, of which three were Edge corporations and fifteen were Agreement Corporations. Only three Agreement corporations survived beyond the thirties, and one of these dropped its agreement in 1947. Another converted to an Edge corporation in 1957.[10]

Of the eighteen corporations only five originated as wholly-owned subsidiaries. Three of these were owned by the same bank. All of the others had multiple ownership, a feature which reappeared in the late 1960s. In three cases foreign banks held an interest, and several corporations had industrial or other financial companies as stockholders. In two instances one corporation held some of the stock of another corporation.

The early corporations emphasised overseas operations, through direct branches or through subsidiaries. Eight of the corporations maintained foreign offices, with one corporation holding twenty-one overseas branches. All but three of the corporations maintained their head office in New York, but eight (mainly those with overseas branches) also maintained one or more other offices in the United States.

During the 1930s and World War II there was a decline in the international activities of American banks. By 1947 there were only four Agreement and one Edge corporation in operation.

4. POSTWAR EXPANSION

Revival in the use of international banking corporations after World War II was slow in coming. As late as 1954 there were only six corporations in existence. However, by the end of 1972 there were ninety-three corporations operating. These were owned by sixty-one banks and bank holding companies. In addition, three Edge corporations were owned by groups of two or more banks (multi-bank ownership). In short, the 1960s was highlighted by a surge of renewed interest in this mode of achieving expansion in the international banking field.

The dramatic growth in utilisation of Edge and Agreement corporations during the 1960s is indicated in Table 6–1. Between 1954 and 1967 there was a nine-fold expansion in the number of corporations and their total capital accounts. Moreover, in the same period total assets of these corporations expanded seven-fold.

The postwar expansion of international banking by means of forming Edge Act and Agreement corporations has been highlighted by a number of distinguishing characteristics. These are as follows:

1. establishment of New York-based corporations by interior and west coast parent banks,
2. establishment of twin and multiple corporations,
3. establishment of non-New York-based corporations,
4. establishment of corporations with multi-bank ownership,
5. establishment and ownership of corporations by bank holding companies.

The first New York-based corporation established by a west coast bank, and the first corporation established in the postwar period, was Bank of America, New York, appropriately named after its parent California bank. Formed in 1949, Bank of America provided a New York presence for its Pacific Coast

Table 6.1

Postwar Growth of Edge and Agreement
Corporations

Year-end	Number of Parents	Number of Corporations	Total Assets	$ thousands Equity Holdings (at cost)	Capital Accounts
1954	6	6	231,916	2,004	41,019
1955	9	7	252,654	3,956	52,424
1956	9	7	400,984	3,980	57,688
1957	7	7	429,027	16,002	78,115
1958	7	7	471,572	16,466	79,969
1959	7	9	427,856	20,479	84,826
1960	10	15	550,177	26,353	91,484
1961	10	16	592,950	28,487	98,221
1962	13	27	665,356	48,816	150,059
1963	22	36	635,388	68,992	179,906
1964	25	38	888,672	90,891	200,342
1965	29	42	1,016,142	146,314	254,389
1966	33	49	1,387,604	199,588	311,531
6-30-67	36	51	1,626,176	218,904	359,886
1967	37	53			

Source: Allen F. Goodfellow, *International Corporations of American Banks*, 1968, p. 35.

parent. Rapid growth and an expanded scope of operations demonstrated the potential of New York-based Edge corporations. However, it was ten years before another bank established a new subsidiary corporation, and twelve years before another was formed with a New York headquarters.

While during the early 1950s all Edge and Agreement corporations were located in New York, in 1972 these corporations were scattered among twenty-two cities and the Virgin Islands. Despite this geographic spread, New York remains the dominant centre of international banking activities of corporations, as well as of international banking operations in general. In 1972 forty-one of the ninety-three corporations were located in New York, and this number included the largest-sized Edge Act corporations in operation at that time.

At year-end 1972, nineteen of the forty-one Edge and Agreement corporations based in New York were affiliates of New York banks. The remaining twenty-two New York-based corporations were established by non-New York banks.

During the 1960s many non-New York banks began to appreciate the benefits to be derived from operating a New York corporation. These benefits include the ability to operate the equivalent of an international department in New York City, and to compete effectively for the international deposit, loan and other service business of large corporate clients. In 1962, three New York-based corporations were established by non-New York banks, and in 1963 Northwest Bancorporation, a Minneapolis based bank holding company, organised Northwest International Bank, an Edge corporation with its headquarters in New York. In the three year period 1965–7, four new corporations owned by non-New York banks were established in New York. Moreover, three existing corporations moved their head offices to New York.[11]

A second outstanding feature of the postwar period in the development of international banking corporations has been the establishment of twin and multiple corporations. At year-end 1972, nineteen U.S. banks either possessed twin corporations or were operating more than one international banking corporation. Seven of these were New York parent banks. Twin corporations developed from the distinction made between 'banking' and 'financing' corporations in the 1957 revision of Regulation K. During the period that the 1957 revision was in effect eleven banks established twin corporations. Under the 1957 revision of Regulation K only banking corporations could conduct an international banking business or hold stock of foreign banks, and only financing corporations were permitted to hold stock in non-banking companies, issue debentures, or engage in underwriting operations abroad. In four instances where twin corporations had been established the parent bank acquired one additional corporation, so as to have twins. In seven other cases the parent bank chartered two completely new corporations.[12] The 1963 revision of Regulation K removed the major distinctions between these two types of corporations, and as a result the regulatory reason for continuing to operate separate banking and financing corporations vanished. However, nearly all of the banks retained their twin corporations intact. A variety of practical or administrative considerations seems to have influenced this. These include the desirability of maintaining a New York location for the parent bank, the need to have a corporate unit to hold the stock of subsidiary or foreign banks, and the advantages derived from specialising in project financing or underwriting by means of an Edge Act affiliate.

Multiple corporations have existed in at least half a dozen cases. The reasons for establishing a second (or third) corporation have varied considerably. In two instances an Agreement corporation was acquired to hold the stock of an English fiduciary. In another case an Agreement corporation was acquired to conduct a local banking business in the Virgin Islands. In this case, the Agreement corporation is the Virgin Islands National Bank, which in 1972 operated eight branches in the U.S. Virgin Islands, and is owned by the First Pennsylvania Banking and Trust Co., Philadelphia. A fourth case involves the formation of additional Edge corporations by First National City Bank of New York, including San Francisco, Los Angeles, Miami, Houston, and Chicago-based corporations. Another example is the establishment by Bank of America of additional Edge Act corporations based in Chicago, Miami, and Houston.

A third feature of the past several decades has been the establishment of corporations with headquarters outside New York. In 1972, fifty-two of the ninety-three corporations in existence were located in cities other than New York. This indicates that a number of regional 'markets' for international banking and financing services have developed; and that non-New York banks have grown to challenge New York banks for the international corporate clientele. The cities which rank behind New York in number of corporations are as follows: Los Angeles (7 corporations), Miami (7), San Francisco (6), Chicago (6),

Boston (6), Houston (3), Philadelphia (3), and Detroit (3).

A fourth development in the postwar years has been the establishment of corporations with multi-bank ownership. In the postwar period four multi-bank owned corporations have been established.[13] The first, American Overseas Finance Corporation, was formed in 1955 to extend foreign credits in co-operation with the Export-Import Bank of Washington.[14] Satisfactory arrangements could not be concluded and the business of the corporation was sold and the corporation liquidated.[15]

The second and third multi-bank owned corporations have been far more successful. American International Bank and Allied Bank International were both established in 1968 with New York head offices. American International Bank was organised as an affiliate of the Fidelity Bank, Philadelphia and the Wachovia Bank and Trust Co., Winston-Salem. A third partner, Zilkha & Sons, contributed a substantial part of the management expertise. In 1971 Fidelity Bank acquired 100 per cent ownership in AIB and the name of this Edge corporation was changed to Fidelity Bank International, New York.

Allied Bank International was originally affiliated with seventeen parent banks, all of which are major regional banks.[16] In 1970 the seventeen shareholding banks had combined assets of more than $16 billion, and over 675 banking offices across the nation. Heavily capitalised, Allied quickly assumed second position among the corporations subject to the Board's authority.[17] As stated in its *Annual Report*, Allied's principal objectives are as follows:[18]

1. To complement the facilities of parent bank international divisions, by providing broad geographic coverage and capability of services.
2. To assemble outstanding professional talent for financing international trade and investment.
3. To furnish banks and clients abroad with access to U.S. markets through its nation-wide network of shareholding banks.
4. To create a strong international banking operation in New York, stressing fast and efficient service for multinational corporations and foreign traders.

It is interesting to note that in 1919 when the Edge Act was passed the advantages of establishing multi-bank owned corporations was considered a prime motivating factor. It was expected that banks which were unable to maintain a full-fledged international operation themselves, would utilise this device to pool their resources and more effectively compete with the larger banks. It was not until nearly half a century later that this rationale became a genuine motivating factor.

One final note should conclude our discussion of multi-bank owned corporations. As part of the export promotion drive in the United States during the late 1960s a Private Export Funding Corporation, PEFCO, was organised to co-operate with the Export-Import Bank in financing big ticket U.S. exports. Approximately forty banks have participated in PEFCO, by purchasing over $9.8 million of stock in the company. In 1970 the Board of Governors approved purchase of shares in PEFCO by Girard International Corp., an Edge Act subsidiary of Girard Trust Bank. In a letter to Nelson Schaenen, Chairman of PEFCO, the Board indicated it would be prepared to authorise the establishment of a new Edge corporation to be formed for the purpose of enabling smaller banks, unable independently to establish an Edge affiliate, to participate in PEFCO.[19]

A fifth characteristic in the postwar growth and evolution of international banking corporations has been the appearance of corporations which are wholly-owned subsidiaries of bank holding companies. Such corporations are in a position to serve a number of banks in their international operations by providing overseas contacts and relationships, and more particularly in serving the interior banks through the corporation's head office in New York. In 1972 there were five corporations owned by bank holding companies. These included subsidiaries of Bank of Virginia, Co., Richmond; First Wisconsin Bankshares, Corp., Milwaukee; Northwest Bancorporation, Minneapolis; United Virginia Bankshares, Inc., Richmond; and Southeast Bancorporation, Miami. Other Edge corporations were owned by bank holding companies and subsequently transferred to affiliate banks. These included Marine Midland Banks, New York and Western Bancorporation.

The formation and ownership of Edge Act and Agreement

corporations by means of multi-bank and bank holding company structures raises the question of how far the growth and expansion of these corporations may proceed. Based on an analysis of the capital accounts of the 178 Reserve City member banks as of December 31, 1969, which amounted to $19.3 billion, the potential investment in Edge Act and Agreement corporations may be estimated at $1.9 billion (10 per cent of capital funds). In 1970 aggregate capital accounts of Edge and Agreement corporations then operating exceeded $547 million and total resources of these corporations stood at $3 billion. If we assume that nearly all New York and Chicago Reserve City member banks are adequately serviced in this respect, it is only in the remaining category of other Reserve City banks that we can expect additional infusions of capital investment into Edge and Agreement corporations. This suggests the possibility of an additional $1.3 billion capital investment by these banks, compared with the $547 million in capital accounts in such corporations in 1970.

B.   BANKING FUNCTIONS

Growth in the number of corporations and of their parent banks has been accompanied by a marked expansion in the variety of operations undertaken by these corporations. While some completely new types of operations have appeared, many have resulted from the development and subdivision of operations carried on several decades ago.

Despite the wide-ranging variety of current operations of the corporations, these fall into four basic groups, namely:[20]

1. Foreign banking operations in the United States
2. Direct overseas operations
3. Specialised financing, including underwriting
4. Equity investments

Some of these functions, while easily distinguishable, have certain common features. Thus, the first two categories ordinarily require that the corporation be 'engaged in banking', whereas the others do not. Some functions can be combined into a single corporation more easily than others. For example, corporations utilising any of the other three functions may also have stockholdings, but it is unlikely that those 'engaged in banking' could also engage in specialised financing to any great extent.

In this section we examine the first three types of functions. Section C is reserved for consideration of equity investments.

1. BANKING OPERATIONS IN THE UNITED STATES

Among the banking type operations of Edge and Agreement corporations, the full-fledged international banking business has been the centre of interest and the principal focus of growth. Direct overseas operations and specialised financing each have played a distinct but somewhat lesser role.

New York is the focal point for international banking operations in the United States, and for this reason a number of west coast and interior banks have established Edge Act affiliates based in New York. While only a little less than half of the Edge Act and Agreement corporations are based in New York, they are by far the largest of these institutions, and probably account for close to 90 per cent of the assets and capital funds of all such corporations.

This concentration in New York can be explained by the fact that this city is financial centre of the nation, leading deposit centre of the world, corporate headquarters for a major share of the leading industrial firms in the United States, and information centre for international business developments, and a major shipping and foreign trade port.

It is not surprising that interior and west coast banks that have been aggressively developing their international business have seen distinct advantages in establishing a New York location. In attempting to maintain or enlarge their share of the national and international business of major U.S. industrial corporations, the larger banks throughout the country have found they must be in a position to extend a broad range of services. On the foreign side many of these services must be made available in U.S. cities other than where the bank's head office is located, and the first choice beyond the head office city invariably is New York.

Prior to 1949 the only non-New York bank with a New York banking operation was the First National Bank of Boston. In 1918 that bank established an Agreement corporation with a

New York office. This corporation was converted into an Edge corporation in 1957, with the title Bank of Boston, International. In 1949 Bank of America established a New York-based corporation, which today is the largest of all corporations with banking operations. Not until 1962 was another corporation organised by an interior bank to conduct banking operations with a New York headquarters.[21]

The degree of independence accorded individual banking corporations is limited by the need to co-ordinate the overall international operations of the parent bank. Two factors appear to determine the degree of independence extended to corporations in their operations. These are the geographic-time zone differences between the corporation and its parent, and the role that the parent establishes for the corporation. The greater the geographic distance separating parent from corporation, the greater the tendency towards more independence. This pattern can also be observed in branch banking operations, especially in cases where foreign branches are involved. The reasons for this are fairly obvious. Increased communication costs make for increased independence. Moreover, where different time zones are involved, various integrated types of operations become more impracticable.

Individual parent banks may visualise a variety of distinct roles for a corporation located in another state. They may regard it as an extension of the international department's loan operation; as a domestic branch with limited independence; as a foreign branch possessing a high degree of autonomy; as an independent unit requiring co-ordination only at the policy level; or as a centre for managing and operating certain of the banks international operations.[22] Moreover, the degree of independence may vary according to the functions involved. In the foreign exchange area it may transact and manage all such operations for the bank. By contrast, its lending activities may be very closely tied to the parent's policies and operations.

According to Goodfellow, two general patterns emerge in viewing the relationship between banking corporations and their respective parents.[23] First, they act as out-of-state extensions of the parents' international banking department. In such cases these corporations may develop independent operations such as maintaining deposit accounts, making loans, and performing other services, but the bulk of transactions handled are for the account of the parent bank. The second group operates more as independent entities. These corporations develop substantial customer relationships which have no direct connection with the parent bank. In addition these corporations may assume prime responsibility for one or more of the parent banks' international functions.

In all cases the directors and many principal officers of the corporation include the top executive officers of the parent bank. Therefore, at the policy making level there exists nearly complete co-ordination.

Writing in 1968 Goodfellow analysed the types of operations carried on by corporations with international banking activities in New York. His analysis provides a most useful summary of this facet of Edge Act and Agreement corporation activities.[24]

At mid-1967 all eleven corporations with international banking operations in New York were maintaining a deposit and loan business, and ten of the eleven also had customer acceptance finance outstanding. Seven of these eleven corporations had sufficient demand deposits and acceptances outstanding so as to appear to be technically 'engaged in banking' under Regulation K.[25] Only six of the eleven corporations appeared to be funding their loan operations through deposits received, and in these six cases loan to deposit ratios varied widely.

To obtain a somewhat better perspective, we may comment on the aggregate balance sheet relationships for all Edge Act and Agreement corporations as reflected in Table 6–2. The following points appear to warrant attention:

1. In 1967 close to two-thirds of funds were derived from deposits.
2. Capital accounts represented close to 22 per cent of total funds available to these corporations.
3. On the assets or uses side of the balance sheet, Cash & Due from Banks represented the largest single item, 50 per cent of total uses of funds. This reflects the sizeable foreign exchange operations of these corporations, both spot and forward, which have an important influence on balance sheet relationships. According to the custom of the New York market, foreign exchange

Table 6.2

Assets and Liabilities — Edge and Agreement Corporations
1954 and 1967

$ thousands

ASSETS	1954	1967	LIABILITIES	1954	1967
Cash and Due from Banks	69,901	808,553	Total deposits	170,973	1,078,115
U.S. Government	61,849	32,750	Time deposits	28,561	141,091
Other bonds	15,075	34,895	Borrowings	3,092	94,016
Equities	2,004	218,904	Liabilities on acceptances	12,710	84,609
Security reserve	(192)	(16,991)	Other liabilities	4,122	9,550
Loans	71,462	459,309	Capital	20,498	244,693
Loan reserve	(807)	(7,729)	Surplus	14,683	91,961
Customers liabilities for			Undivided profits	5,662	11,661
acceptances	11,155	81,735	Contingency reserves	176	11,571
Fixed assets	176	4,535	Total capital accounts	41,019	359,886
Other assets	1,293	10,215			
Total Assets	231,916	1,626,176	Total Liabilities	231,916	1,626,176

Note: 1954 data are year-end figures; 1967 data reflect June 30 condition.

Source: Allen F. Goodfellow, *International Corporations of American Banks*, 1968, pp. 141–2.

transactions and other international payments are payable in Clearing House Funds (unless Federal Funds are specified). Clearing House Funds are not payable until the following day, whereas Federal Funds are payable on the same business day. Therefore, in liquidating foreign exchange transactions or other payments of funds, the amounts appear overnight in both the 'Due From Other Banks' and 'Deposits-Officers Checks Outstanding' accounts. The effect of this 'float' on New York Edge Act Corporation balance sheets is substantial.

4. Loans represent the second largest asset item, and applying the unadjusted total deposit figure yields a loan-deposit ratio in 1967 of 42.6 per cent. Unfortunately, this figure is meaningless unless some adjustment can be made for the substantial float referred to above. If we could assume that all of the Cash & Due from Banks amount represented float, our adjustment would involve reducing that account as well as the deposit account by $808,553 thousand. This would leave an 'adjusted' deposit figure of $269,562 thousand, less than the amount outstanding in the loan account.

5. Customers Liability for Acceptances represents the fourth largest asset category, and approximately 5 per cent of total assets. When compared with total dollar acceptances outstanding in the United States at mid-1967 of $4,131 million, we find that these corporations accounted for less than 2 per cent of dollar acceptances outstanding. Considering that virtually all major acceptance-creating banks in the United States possessed an international banking corporation at this time, we might conclude that the parents' own international departments continue to generate the bulk of acceptances outstanding.

2. DIRECT OVERSEAS OPERATIONS

American banks have achieved representation overseas by a variety of methods and organisational forms. These include establishment of overseas branches and representative offices by parent banks, purchase of interests in foreign affiliates, and the organisation of foreign branches by Edge Act and Agreement corporations.

Prior to 1930 the major avenue used by American banks to achieve overseas representation was through the branch offices of international banking corporations. Until 1925 Edge and Agreement corporations operated more overseas branches than the parent banks themselves. Following this, there was a period of consolidation, and the direct overseas operations of the corporations declined in number.

Since 1960 direct overseas operations have been undertaken by several Edge Act and Agreement corporations. In 1960 the Virgin Islands National Bank signed an agreement with the Board, and its controlling stock was acquired by the First Pennsylvania Bank and Trust Co., Philadelphia. While the Virgin Islands National Bank operates under an agreement with the Board, it was chartered by and continues to be subject to the jurisdiction of the Comptroller of the Currency. As of 1972 this bank operated eight branches in the Virgin Islands. This Agreement corporation enjoys several distinctions. It is the only corporation located outside the United States, the only one under the direct jurisdiction of the Comptroller, and one of the few with overseas branches. It conducts a general banking business, and is not mainly concerned with financing international trade.

In 1964 the International Bank of Commerce, organised a year earlier by its Seattle based parent, opened a branch in Hong Kong. Since that time four additional branches have been established in the Crown Colony. These branches concentrate on loans to local businesses and individuals. In addition to this important Far Eastern presence, the parent bank operates a London branch.

In 1967 Philadelphia International Investment Corporation opened a London branch. In part this office may be considered a substitute for the establishment of a direct branch by the parent bank, with a major objective of tapping the Eurodollar market. In addition this London office provides the parent organisation with a close contact with the European area and financial developments in the region.

In 1969 Allied Bank International, organised a year earlier, established a London branch. At the same time plans for a second branch in Nassau were being formulated. Allied quickly developed a strong foreign exchange and Eurodollar trading capacity, in large part by means of establishing the London branch. In 1969 Allied moved to second rank among the corporations subject to the Board's authority. Only Bank of America, New York, possesses larger capital accounts and assets.

In addition to the four institutions described above, six additional corporations enjoy direct overseas representation via foreign branches. These include Bank of America, New York (Nassau); Detroit Bank & Trust International (Nassau); Bank of Boston International (Luxembourg); First National City Overseas Investment Corp. (Nassau); International Bank of Detroit (Nassau); and State Street Bank of Boston International (Nassau).

3. SPECIALISED FINANCING

Several corporations not 'engaged in banking' have undertaken a variety of specialised financing activities, ranging from relatively simple term loans to more complicated syndicated loan-equity financing packages. Perhaps the simplest form of specialised financing is where the corporation's parent does not wish to include certain loan types in its own portfolio. These might include term loans which the parent bank's loan committee regards as more suitable for inclusion in the corporation's loan portfolio.

Several corporations have undertaken the financing required when corporate customers establish or expand overseas operations. This has involved organising syndicates to underwrite the financing requirements of the new enterprise. Some of these arrangements have required locating local or foreign partners, placing of bonds or debentures, arranging loan facilities in foreign or local currencies, and public sale of equity interests.

C. EQUITY INVESTMENTS

Utilisation of Edge and Agreement corporations to make equity investments in foreign companies has grown dramatically since the late 1950s. In 1954 the corporations had a total of eight stock holdings representing an acquisition cost of $2 million. By mid-1967 they held 327 separate equity investments representing an acquisition cost of $219 million.

Only one of the eight equity investments in 1954 represented an investment in a foreign bank (a minority interest). The remaining seven included a minority interest in a foreign finance company, one holding in a New York discount house, and several equity investments in companies servicing the parent's foreign branches.[26]

In 1967 over 60 per cent of the dollar value of investments was in foreign banking institutions (Table 6-3). In large part these investments are alternatives for direct foreign branching, or serve to strengthen correspondent bank relationships overseas. Investments in finance, development finance, and investment companies make up the bulk of the remaining equity holdings. There has been only a modest investment in non-financial companies, and usually these have been acquired in connection with an extension of credit or in participation with the International Finance Corporation.

1. NATURE OF INVESTMENTS

In 1967 the more than 300 investments of Edge and Agreement corporations were located in sixty countries. Over one-third of the investment cost was represented by holdings in Europe; close to one-fourth in Latin America; and approximately one-sixth in Africa. Since 1960 the importance of investments in Europe has not kept pace, due to rapid growth of equity investments in other areas of the globe. Moreover, the types of investments in Europe have undergone a substantial change. In the mid-1950s only one investment was in a bank, whereas in 1967 over two-thirds of investments were in banks and bank holding companies. In 1954 only three European countries were represented by equity investments of corporations, as compared with representation in all but very few European countries in 1967.

The first equity investment in Africa was made in 1955. By 1967 at least seventeen African countries were the focal point of forty-three corporation investments totalling $37 million. Almost $35 million of this was in banks and bank holding companies.

In 1960 corporation investment activity in Latin America began to increase noticeably. In that year the cumulative investment in Latin America by corporations was only $1.7 million. However, by mid-1967 there were eighty-seven invest-

Table 6.3

Equity Holdings of the Corporations

Year-end[a]	Banking Institutions[b]		Finance Companies[c]		Non-financial Companies		Totals	
	Dollars	No.	Dollars	No.	Dollars	No.	Dollars	No.
1954	*	6	*	2	—	—	2,004	8
1955	*	7	*	5	—	—	3,956	12
1956	*	7	*	4	—	—	3,980	11
1957	*	9	*	5	—	—	16,002	14
1958	*	10	*	5	*	2	16,466	17
1959	*	13	5,580	7	*	3	20,479	23
1960	16,356	20	9,997	12	—	—	26,353	32
1961	18,533	27	9,848	18	106	2	28,487	47
1962	31,460	37	16,552	36	804	14	48,816	87
1963	44,932	46	22,969	79	1,091	18	68,992	143
1964	50,099	54	39,006	129	1,786	24	90,891	207
1965	91,924	70	50,776	159	3,614	31	146,314	260
1966	128,833	82	66,175	182	4,580	43	199,588	307
6/67	143,632	94	70,173	188	5,099	45	218,904	327

* Data deleted to preserve confidentiality.

[a] As of December 31, except 1967, as of June 30.

[b] Includes bank, bank holding companies, trust companies, nominee companies, and realty holding companies — bank premises.

[c] Includes development finance companies and finance and investment companies.

Source: Allen F. Goodfellow, *International Corporations of American Banks*, 1968, p. 72.

ments with an aggregate value of over $50 million. In contrast with Europe and Africa, investments in Latin America were closely balanced between banks and finance companies. One-half of the number of equity holdings was in non-financial businesses, but they represented only 5 per cent of the value of Latin American investments.

Investments in the developed areas of the Bahamas, Bermuda and Canada are few in number but large in dollar value. Many of these investments have been in 'alter-ego' type affiliates. The alter-ego subsidiary usually offers the same range of services and operations as the parent corporation. A distinguishing feature of these subsidiaries 'is that neither their operations nor those of their parent corporations can really be considered in isolation . . .'.[27] These firms are an integral part of the parent corporations' activities, and their operations should be viewed on a consolidated basis. The first of these alter-ego subsidiaries was Arcturus Investment and Development Ltd., Montreal, Canada, established in 1955 by Chase International Investment Corp. More recently Bankers International Corporation organised a Luxembourg company of this type, and in 1967 First Pennsylvania Overseas Finance Corp. established a similar subsidiary in the Bahamas. These companies have been utilised to lessen the impact of the Interest Equalisation Tax and the voluntary foreign credit restraint programme.

Investments in Asia and the Near East have been predominately small in amount, and generally confined to minority holdings. Over 80 per cent of the total dollar amount has been invested in non-bank financial companies.

In 1967 over 44 per cent of the dollar value, and nearly two-thirds of the number of equity investments of corporations were located in less developed countries. This contrasts sharply with the situation in 1954 and the later 1950s when only one out of eight investments was located in a less developed country. In 1957–9 only slightly over 6 per cent of the dollar value (cumulative) of investments was located in less developed countries. In 1962 a rapid turnabout came, as a result of thirty investments in less developed countries with an investment cost of over $13 million. Between 1961 and 1962 the percentage of equity holdings in less developed countries jumped from 17.6 to 38.5.

In the period 1954–67 a number of changes took place in the degree of ownership of the equity holdings of Edge and Agreement corporations. During the 1950s major emphasis was given to investments in wholly-owned subsidiaries. In 1961 a transition began, with the number of minority investments exceeding the number of investments in wholly-owned subsidiaries. In 1962 controlled subsidiaries (Table 6-4) appeared on the investment scene for the first time. Beginning in this year and continuing through 1967 holdings in wholly-owned subsidiaries became a declining percentage of total investments. By mid-1965 minority interests (45 per cent or less) represented over half of the equity portfolio of corporations, and continued to increase in importance to 55.7 per cent of total holdings at mid-1967.

Table 6.4

Distribution of Equity Holdings by percentage of
Stock Ownership
June 30, 1967

	Amount ($ thousands)	Number of Holdings	As percentage of Total
Almost wholly-owned (over 90 per cent)	53,927	37	24.6
Controlled subsidiary (45–90 per cent)	42,999	18	19.7
Substantial minority interest (10–45 per cent)	72,436	74	33.1
Small minority interest (under 10 per cent)	49,542	198	22.6
Totals	218,904	327	100.0

Source: Allen F. Goodfellow, *International Corporations of American Banks*, 1968, p. 151.

Some patterns can be observed with respect to the geographic concentration and degree of equity investments. Together, Europe and the Bahamas, Bermuda and Canada account for over nine-tenths of the dollar investment in virtually wholly-owned subsidiaries. Nearly nine-tenths of dollar investments in controlled subsidiaries (45-90 per cent ownership) is in Latin America and Europe. Over two-fifths of dollar investments in substantial minority interest subsidiaries is in Africa, one-fourth in Latin America, and one-fifth in Europe. Europe and Latin America account for the bulk (three-fourths) of the dollar investments in small minority interests.

2. INVESTMENTS IN BANKING INSTITUTIONS

In 1967 equity investments of the corporations in banks represented two-thirds of the value of all types of investments. These investments include English fiduciaries, trust companies, bank holding companies, and nominee companies. These investments function in lieu of branches, as an alternative to establishing a branch network, and to strengthen foreign correspondent relationships. The exact function performed by a specific investment is usually related to the degree of control, although this relationship is not perfectly or immutably determined. However, the realisation of specific functions often seems to tend toward investments with certain degrees of control vested in the owning corporation.

In 1967, sixteen corporations held twenty-seven direct investments in foreign banks representing Substantial Minority Holdings. Since 1967 major U.S. banks have undertaken a number of additional investments of this type. The Chase Manhattan Bank, and First National Bank of Chicago, through their respective corporations, hold respectively 25 per cent of the Nederlandsche Credietbank, N.V., Netherlands; and 11 per cent of N.V. Slavenburgs Bank, Rotterdam (sixty branches throughout the Netherlands). Such investments provide opportunities for U.S. banks to obtain representation on the Boards of Directors of foreign affiliates, as well as other advantages.[28] Other major U.S. banks with substantial minority interests in foreign banks which appear to function in lieu of direct branches include Continental Illinois National Bank and Trust Co., Chicago; Bankers Trust Company, New York; and Morgan Guaranty Trust Company of New York.

Investments in foreign banks yielding small minority interests appear to be influenced by the need to strengthen correspondent relations, as well as utilise such affiliates in lieu of direct branches. Such investments are influenced by the Interest Equalisation Tax, which applies to foreign equity interests of less than 10 per cent. Where such stock holdings are of sufficient size to bring a directorship, it is not difficult to see the advantages for the foreign correspondent bank, as well as for the parent.

3. INVESTMENTS IN FINANCE AND INVESTMENT COMPANIES

Investments in finance and investment companies fulfil a broad range of purposes for the parent corporations and U.S. banks. Only during the 1960s was there an acceleration of interest and activity in this type of investment by American banks and their respective corporations. As late as 1960 there were only six such investments on the books of the corporations, and only two were wholly-owned subsidiaries. However, by mid-1967 there were 188 investments in financial companies, with an investment value of over $70 million. Over 40 per cent of this amount was in small minority holdings, half of these in Latin America. Over 25 per cent of the dollar investment at that time was in wholly-owned subsidiaries, many located in the Bahamas, Bermuda, and Canada. The range of operations of these finance companies is almost limitless. Three categories may be noted as important. These are: wholesale or development financing, specialty financing, and companies engaged in counselling on financial and investment matters.

In the wholesale type of operation the most common investment has been in the development finance companies. These companies allocate their resources on the basis of the national development needs of the domestic economy, and many are sponsored by the governments and governmental agencies of the developing countries. The International Finance Corporation has provided financial assistance to a number of these development finance companies, as have other international lending institutions in the World Bank Group.

The private development finance companies are of two types, the national and international. The national private development finance companies are often given special tax concessions. Many Edge and Agreement corporations have made investments in these national companies, including the Private Development Corporation of the Philippines. Perhaps the best known international private development finance company is ADELA Investment Company, South America. A Luxembourg corporation, all of its loans and investments are in Latin America. In 1969 seventeen U.S. banks held an equity interest in ADELA, and the complete list of stockholders is most prestigious, including large European and Japanese banks and industrial corporations.[29]

The specialty financing type companies generally restrict their operations to one country and one specialty area of financing, e.g. leasing, factoring, or instalment finance. The First National Bank of Boston's Corporation Financiera de Boston, S.A.F. yC. in Argentina is an example of this type, which services the automotive industry through the purchase of its instalment paper. Other examples include Wells Fargo's interest in one of Mexico's largest financial leasing firms (Interamericana de Arrendamientos, S.A.), First National Bank of Boston's acquisition of a leasing company in Australia, and Manufacturers Hanover Trust's investment in an Australian investment management concern (Development Finance Corp., Ltd, Sydney). Edge and Agreement corporations of American banks have invested in a number of companies specialised in investment counselling, and in one case at least the company acts as the investment adviser and distribution manager for a European mutual fund.

The reasons for investments in financial companies generally focus on use of the companies as sources of funds. This is true in connection with the Eurodollar market, where American banks (even those with overseas branches) obtain better geographic coverage and improved contacts with local sources of funds. Finance companies make an attractive investment because of their ability to generate local funds, either by selling short-term commercial paper or obtaining loans from banks and other sources. In the case of government sponsored development finance companies, such investments are regarded as politically advantageous.

4. INVESTMENTS IN NON-FINANCIAL COMPANIES

Equity investments in non-financial businesses have accounted for a small part of total investments made by international banking corporations.[30] Only in 1961 did these corporations begin to undertake such investments, and as of 1967 their portfolio of share investments in non-financial businesses consisted of forty-five separate holdings, representing a cost of approximately $5 million. This was less than 2.4 per cent of the aggregate value of all equity holdings of these corporations. Two-thirds of these holdings had been acquired as a result of credit extensions made by the corporations, and half of these were participations resulting from co-operative arrangements with the International Finance Corporation.

A basic reason for the relatively small amount of equity investment by corporations in non-financial companies lies in the question of their appropriateness for bank affiliates. The Board of Governors 'has taken a rather narrow approach to equity acquisitions or participations in joint ventures'. In approving such acquisitions by Edge corporations, the Board has insisted that the acquired company

> confine its activities to those permissible to an Edge Corporation . . . such functions must be confined to the area of banking and financing and that it is inappropriate for an Edge Corporation to acquire control of a company engaged in a nonfinancial business.[31]

In 1969 the Board withheld authorisations for the Edge Corporation of a New York bank to acquire a Taiwan life insurance company. In 1970 the Board denied another Edge corporation permission to acquire, indirectly, effective control of a Caribbean company engaged in real estate development.[32] In the same year the Board required a partial disinvestment by an Edge corporation of interest in a cattle feeding operation in Argentina.

Understandably, it is difficult to draw the line between financial and non-financial, and often it is a matter of degree. According to Governor Mitchell the Board has been compelled to approach the problem on a case by case basis. Since 1963, when Regulation K was revised, the 'trend has been slowly toward somewhat increased permissiveness'.[33]

Only three of the forty-five non-financial companies included in the equity holdings of corporations were located in major industrial nations, the majority of investments being in companies located in the less developed countries, including Latin America. All but one of these holdings represented minority interests, and half involved under 2 per cent of the outstanding shares of the companies involved.

The ability of corporations to acquire equity interests in non-financial businesses has been a useful adjunct to the parent banks' lending operations, and has made some credit operations feasible that might otherwise not have been undertaken. Share 'sweeteners' have permitted extensions of credit at rates acceptable to overseas borrowers. In cases where the corporation has organised project financing, shares or stock options have been received as a commission for these services.

5. JOINT VENTURES

Joint or co-operative ventures between a United States bank and one or more other U.S. and/or foreign banks have been of recent vintage. According to Goodfellow, 'They are found in their purest form when two institutions hold in equal parts the controlling stock of another enterprise.'[34] The situation becomes complicated where two institutions have share holdings in several organisations, some unequal. According to Light,

> the term 'joint venture' . . . refers to an equity participation by an American bank, through its 'Edge Act', or 'Agreement' subsidiary in an overseas banking facility, or other kind of financing venture, in which ownership, return and risk are shared with others.[35]

One distinction that can be made is between joint ventures involving direct bank ownership and those involving ownership by corporations. Three examples of the former include (1) the seventeen-bank group which jointly established Allied Bank International, (2) the three partners that organised American International Bank, and (3) direct acquisitions of equity interests in foreign banks by American banks, now possible as a result of the 1966 amendment to the Federal Reserve Act and subsequent revision of Regulation M.

In the area of ownership by corporations, an example of a joint venture involving fifty-fifty equity interests on the part of

both partners is that of Bank of America and Banco de San-
tander in Banco Commercial para Americana and Banco Intercontinental Espanol. It appears that this partnership does not
extend to activities outside Spain. A somewhat more complex
situation is that involving Continental International Finance
Corporation (CIFC) and Netherlands Overseas Bank
(NOB).[36]

In the late 1960s and early 1970s a number of U.S. banks,
through their corporations, made investments in joint ventures
located in countries which restrict or limit foreign banking
operations. These investments were made in merchant banking
institutions, acceptance-discount houses, companies specialising in international finance, and medium-term lending in
stitutions. For example, in 1970 Chase Manhattan Bank joined
A.C. Goode Associates and the National Bank of Australasia in
forming a $6 million merchant banking and commercial bill
financing enterprise in Australia.

D. GENERAL AND SPECIFIC CONSENT OF THE BOARD

As indicated earlier in this chapter, the 1963 revision of Regulation K provided for 'general consent' equity acquisitions by
Edge and Agreement corporations. This represented a somewhat more liberal treatment than had been available under
the 1957 revision, which failed to mention general consent in
the section describing stock investments by Banking
Corporations.[37] Since 1963 the Board found it necessary, due to
balance of payments considerations, to temporarily suspend
the general consent provision with regard to share acquisitions.
This change became effective in February 1968, and called for
specific Board approval of all stock acquisitions by corporations. Effective January 1969, the Board restored the general
consent provisions in Regulation K.[38]

The wording of the 1969 revision, restoring general consent,
appears to be somewhat more liberal than that found in the
1963 revision of Regulation K. The pertinent paragraph is
reproduced below:[39]

> . . . the Board hereby grants its general consent for any
> corporation to invest, directly or indirectly, in the shares
> of foreign corporations not doing business in the United

States; but no investment hereunder shall cause the corporation to have invested more than $500,000 in the shares, or to hold more than 25 per cent of the voting shares, of any such corporation.

We should note that the amount limitation under this general consent provision is $500,000 as compared with only $200,000 in the 1963 revision. Under the 1963 revision the most widely used of the three general consent provisions, that permitting stock acquisitions of up to $200,000 which are likely to further the development of U.S. foreign commerce, represents the broadest of the general consent provisions. The majority of investments made under this subsection has been in companies engaged in various phases of financing. Hence, the expansion of the dollar limitation in this area to $500,000 may prove to be conducive to a substantial increase in utilisation of the general consent provision of Regulation K.

7 Foreign Banking in the United States

Since 1960 foreign banks have achieved a substantial expansion in their activities and operations in the United States. This has taken place within a world-wide environment of rapid growth in international banking. The purpose of this chapter is to review the growth of foreign banking in this country, to describe the types of operations performed and their effects, and to discuss the regulatory environment as it applies to foreign banks.

A. BACKGROUND AND STRUCTURE OF FOREIGN BANKING

1. EARLY DEVELOPMENT

Foreign banks doing business in the United States are supervised and licensed by the various states, in accordance with the relevant provisions of the state banking laws. At present there is no provision for chartering or effective overall supervision of foreign banks at the national level.[1]

A number of foreign banks were represented in New York prior to World War I. In 1911 New York passed a licensing statute because the increase in number of foreign banking offices was becoming a matter of concern. By 1915, twenty-three foreign licensees were operating banking agencies in New York State.[2] During the 1920s foreign banks opened representative offices, agencies and state-chartered trust companies in New York State. In the early 1920s several foreign banks expressed a desire to establish branches in New York. In 1920 and again in 1923 a bill was introduced in the New York Legislature which would have permitted branching by foreign banks. The bill was rejected, in part on the basis that there might be an invasion of the New York market by larger and more experienced foreign banks.

While the bulk of foreign banking operations during the 1920s was focused in New York City, several foreign banks established agencies and branches in California, Oregon, Washington and Illinois. In three states – California, Washington, and Illinois, foreign branches preceded prohibiting legislation. The foreign branch in Washington State continued operative under a grandfather clause while the other branches converted to subsidiary banks or closed down. Economic conditions from 1929 onwards severely circumscribed the level of foreign banking activities in this country, and not until after 1946 was there a revival.

2. GROWTH AFTER WORLD WAR II

At the termination of hostilities in 1946 the role of the United States and the dollar were dominant factors in international finance. As trade between this country and other countries increased, foreign banks felt a pressing need for American financial assistance. Foreign banks similarly realised that failure to establish their own operation in the United States could result in their eventually becoming excluded from an important share of the international banking business.

Between 1946 and 1960 the most important methods used by foreign banks to expand their operations in this country were by opening agencies and establishing representative offices in New York and other cities.[3] The bulk of these offices were located in New York and San Francisco. During the 1960s a number of foreign banks established branches in this country, largely due to enabling legislation passed in New York State. In the same period a number of state-chartered banking affiliates was established. As of 1972 there were 141 representative offices, forty-nine agencies and sixty-six branches of foreign banks in the United States. Parallel with this, foreign banks had established twenty-nine state-chartered commercial bank subsidiaries, in large part to complement operations of their agencies which by law are prohibited from engaging in trust activities (Table 7-1). Fourteen of these subsidiaries are located in New York. While they are authorised to accept deposits, an informal understanding with foreign bank subsidiaries located in New York and the New York State Banking Department confines their activities mainly to corporate trust and international services. In California especially, the subsidiary form has been utilised to circumvent that state's prohibition against foreign branching.

3. NEW YORK STATE LEGISLATION

During the 1950s several American banks that were in the process of expanding their overseas branch networks began to encounter resistance on the part of some countries. The explanation offered was that the prohibition against branches of foreign banks in several states, especially New York, made the governments of these countries resentful. Lack of reciprocity in the exchange of banking privileges threatened the future expansion of U.S. international banking.[4] As a result, in 1959 the First National City Bank proposed that the New York State Banking Law be changed to permit foreign branch banking. Together with other major New York banks and the State Banking Department, First National co-operated in drafting acceptable legislation. After some debate and compromise a foreign branching amendment was presented to the 1960 legislature. Four arguments were used to support this legislation, including (1) the desirability of removing discrimination against foreign banks, (2) the need to reduce the possibility of retaliatory legislation by foreign countries, (3) the need to increase the status of New York as an international financial centre, and (4) the benefits to be derived from establishment of foreign branches, including the expansion of

foreign trade financing. The New York State Legislature
passed the bill, which became effective on 1 January 1961.

Since the 1961 amendment permitting foreign banks to

Table 7.1

Offices of Foreign Banks in the United States
by type of Office and by State
1972

	Representative Offices	Agencies	Branches	State-chartered Subsidiaries
California	19[a]	21	—	11
District of Columbia	5	—	—	—
Florida	—	—	—	1
Hawaii	—	1	—	1
Illinois	12	—	1	2
Massachusetts	—	—	1[b]	—
New York	98	26	42[c]	14
Oregon	—	—	2	—
Pennsylvania	1	—	—	—
Texas	6	—	—	—
Washington	—	1	1	—
Puerto Rico	—	—	10[d]	—
Virgin Islands	—	—	9[e]	—
Totals	141	49	66	29

[a] Includes two offices of Canadian Imperial Bank of Commerce.

[b] Branch of Barclays Bank International, to open in 1973.

[c] Includes branches of 24 foreign banks.

[d] Includes branches of 2 foreign banks.

[e] Includes branches of 3 foreign banks.

Sources: *American Banker*, July 31, 1972; New York State
Superintendent of Banks; California Superintendent of Banks;
Moodys, *Banks and Finance 1972*.

establish branches, accept deposits, and engage in a broader range of banking functions, forty-two branches have been established in New York. In addition, a few foreign banks converted their agencies to branches.[5] Outside New York, there are only a few branches of foreign banks operating in the territories of Puerto Rico and the Virgin Islands. From the preceding it can be seen that foreign banking activity is still not a major factor in the United States, despite the substantial growth in recent years.

4. CHOICE OF ORGANISATIONAL FORM

Any discussion of choice of organisational form by foreign banks allows very limited application. There is one important banking market for foreign banks, and that is New York which allows foreign banks to operate through any organisational form of their choosing. Only two other states permit as wide a latitude among organisational forms, namely Massachusetts and Oregon. Three other states are important in this context. These are California, Hawaii, and Washington, which authorise foreign banking, but limit the choice of organisational forms.

Most foreign banks have preferred to establish branches rather than subsidiaries. If a foreign bank wishes to conduct a deposit receiving business it must establish either a branch or a state-chartered subsidiary. In either case a fairly large volume of deposits is necessary to make the operation profitable. Considerations other than profit which motivate in favour of establishing branches in the United States include prestige, representation in the market, and service to nationals doing business in the United States. The branch offers a much less complicated organisational problem for the foreign bank. A subsidiary may require American stockholders and board of directors, while the branch does not. American stockholders are not a statutory requirement in New York State (except U.S. directors who are needed for qualifying shares). The New York law does not require U.S. directors but permits the Superintendent to allow up to one-half of the board to be foreign nationals. It can be argued that the home office can more effectively control branch operations than those of a subsidiary. Also, less capital is generally required for a branch. This consideration extends itself into loan operations since the capital position of the subsidiary or the branch's parent bank ordinarily dictates lending limits. Naturally, the loan limit of a branch is likely to exceed that of a subsidiary. In many instances the foreign banks operating branches are relatively large, therefore their branches enjoy fairly substantial lending limits. The infusion of sufficient capital in a subsidiary to have comparable lending limits would probably be most difficult. Finally, a subsidiary may have a name and identity quite distinct from that of the parent bank, whereas a branch can take full advantage of the prestige and reputation associated with the parent's name.

State-chartered subsidiaries hold certain advantages over branches. Branches of foreign banks operating in New York must comply with requirements relating to submission of reports and asset-liability ratios. Subsidiaries are exempt from these requirements. In the practical sense the submission of monthly reports is not onerous. In fact, more than one foreign banker has stated that the reporting requirement is a worthwhile discipline since it requires a periodic review of operations. Subsidiaries are eligible for FDIC insurance, which may be helpful in soliciting consumer type deposits. However, they are subject to administrative capital requirements which relate capital funds to the extent of risk inherent in their asset structures. This is the same approach that is applicable to state-chartered banks.

Despite certain advantages inherent in subsidiaries, the majority of foreign banks have preferred to establish branches. The small number of foreign banks which have opted for the subsidiary form (where branching is possible) have most often done so with the intent of utilising the subsidiary plus agency combination. To understand this approach, we turn to the advantages enjoyed by agencies.

In many instances the choice between agency and branch hinges on prospects for attracting deposits. Where a large enough volume of deposits can be attracted, the higher initial and operating costs of a branch may be justified. However, many foreign banks have preferred to operate a combination of subsidiaries and agencies, rather than branches. In New York, establishment of a branch precludes operating an agency. Therefore resort to the subsidiary plus agency method may hinge on the advantages of the agency over the branch.

Branches of foreign banks suffer from the following disadvantages: they are required to maintain the same fractional reserves against deposits as domestic banks, and to conform to the same loan restrictions. According to a 1969 amendment to the Banking Law, New York State branches and agencies must maintain assets in the state equivalent to 108 per cent of liabilities. Moreover, agencies and branches are subject to the same usury limitations.

In the past a number of foreign banks have concluded that the relative freedom which agencies enjoy, along with the ability to receive deposits in affiliated subsidiaries, is preferable. The agency plus subsidiary arrangement has been preferred by Canadian banks. This is explained by the lack of an alternative, since the Canadian banks cannot meet the reciprocity requirement for branching called for by the amended New York law. In a similar fashion the subsidiary plus agency route has been employed by foreign banks operating in California. This is because California law as amended in 1964 required that a foreign bank must first be approved for FDIC insurance. Since FDIC insurance has not been made available to branches of foreign banks, California remained closed to foreign branches. However, as a result of legislation enacted by the 1969 State Legislature, California agencies are now permitted to accept deposits that originate in foreign countries, without the requirement of FDIC insurance but subject to the approval of the Superintendent of Banks. As of December 1970 three banks had applied for permission to accept deposits. This change makes it possible for agencies to operate as 'branches', excluding the authority to accept *domestic* deposits.[6]

B.   OPERATIONS OF FOREIGN BANKS

1.   REPRESENTATIVE OFFICES

In 1972 foreign banks operated 141 representative offices in this country. The exact number of foreign banks and the number of representative offices cannot be ascertained with certainty due to the nature of and function served by the representative office. Representatives of foreign banks are individuals who represent one or more foreign banks at the same time. Representative offices disseminate information regarding the parent bank and attempt to develop and improve customer-bank relationships. They also function as information gathering centres for foreign banks. Representative offices are not permitted to accept deposits or perform other banking functions. Hence, they are generally exempt from supervision by banking authorities on the basis of their not directly carrying out banking functions.

Important legal questions arise in the area of distinguishing between a representative office on the one hand and an agency or branch on the other. These pertain to the type and extent of bank-related operations which a representative may engage in without operating as an agency or branch, and the scope of permissible tax-free activities available to a representative. For example, if a representative accepts a cheque for deposit with the parent, is he providing a convenience for the parent by forwarding the draft to the parent's head office, or is he conducting a banking transaction? Because of the difficulties involved in drawing a sharp line of demarcation between representative offices and agencies or branches, many representatives are reluctant to discuss their activities in any detail.

2. SUBSIDIARIES

Generally foreign banks establish state-chartered subsidiaries with one of two objectives in mind; namely to engage in general banking activities when the branching alternative is prohibited or less attractive, or to perform trust functions which 'complete' the overall international activities of the parent bank. As of 1972 there were twenty-nine state-chartered subsidiaries of foreign banks operating in the United States. Their location by state and parent bank affiliation are indicated in Table 7-2.

The New York subsidiaries fall into two general categories. The first includes subsidiaries which exist principally to conduct corporate trust activities. These subsidiaries exercise mainly paying agent functions. The deposits which they obtain are incidental to their trust work. The Canadian subsidiaries fall into this group. The remaining subsidiaries in New York carry on a substantial commercial banking type business, and their balance sheet configurations approximate those of domestic banks. New York State subsidiaries engaged in this type of banking are administratively required to have FDIC insurance.

The California subsidiaries have been established primarily to engage in commercial loan-deposit type activities. The bulk of their deposits are domestic as is the major portion of their loans. These state-chartered subsidiaries compete with domestic banks, and are insured by FDIC. Several of these subsidiaries also operate licensed agencies in California. In the past the non-availability of FDIC insurance to branches of foreign banks has prevented establishment of such branches in California. Consequently, foreign banks have relied on the subsidiary and/or agency form of doing business in that state. The 1969 change in California law removing the FDIC insurance requirement for foreign source deposits should result in a shift toward use of the branch form in that state.

3. BRANCHES OF FOREIGN BANKS

As of 1972 there were sixty-six branches of foreign banks in the United States, the largest number of which (forty-two) have been established in New York. Between 1962 and 1968 assets in branches of foreign banks in New York State grew from $0.3 billion to $1.6 billion. In the period 1968–71 assets in these branches expanded further to $3.6 billion. This growth was facilitated in large part by advances from parent bank head offices to the New York branches (Table 7-3). The major activities of these branches are foreign trade financing, short-term investment of dollar funds, foreign deposit solicitation, and commercial lending. In addition, they provide letter of credit, acceptance, transfer of funds, remittances, and collection services. Trade financing accounts for a major portion of the business of these branches of foreign banks. Often the trade financing involves a foreign country other than that of the parent bank. American branches of these foreign banks serve as points of contact for world-wide banking networks, and enhance the competitive strength of their respective parent organisations. In addition to the European and Japanese banks, several banks from the developing nations have established New York branches in the late 1960s.

A number of foreign bank branches serve as depositories for U.S. dollar funds of foreign institutions and individuals. British, Swiss, Lebanese, and Israeli branches attract deposits from individuals in South America, the Middle East, and

Table 7.2

State-chartered Subsidiaries of Foreign
Banking Corporations, 1972

Subsidiary	Parent Bank	Number of Offices
In New York State		
American Bank & Trust Company	Swiss-Israel Trade Bank	1
Atlantic Bank of New York	National Bank of Greece	1
Bank of Montreal Trust Company	Bank of Montreal	1
Bank of Nova Scotia Trust Company	Bank of Nova Scotia	1
Bank of Tokyo Trust Company	Bank of Tokyo, Ltd and Industrial Bank of Japan	4
Barclays Bank of New York	Barclays Bank International	1
Canadian Bank of Commerce Trust Company	Canadian Imperial Bank of Commerce	1
European American Bank & Trust Company	Amsterdam-Rotterdam Bank; Creditanstalt Bankverein; Deutsche Bank; Midland Bank Ltd; Societe Generale (France); Societe Generale de Banque, Brussels	4
First Israel Bank & Trust Company	Bank Leumi Le-Israel	1
Israel Discount Trust Company	Israel Discount Bank Ltd	1
Republic National Bank of New York	Trade Development Bank, Geneva, Switzerland	1
Royal Bank of Canada Trust Company	Royal Bank of Canada	1
Schroder Trust Company	J. Henry Schroder Wagg & Co.	1
Toronto Dominion Bank & Trust Company	Toronto Dominion Bank	1

	Parent bank	
In California		
Barclays Bank of California	Barclays Bank Ltd, and Barclays Bank International	26
Bank of Montreal, California	Bank of Montreal	4
Bank of Tokyo, California	Bank of Tokyo, Ltd	13
California Canadian Bank	Canadian Imperial Bank of Commerce	19
Chartered Bank of London, San Francisco	The Chartered Bank	3
Hong Kong Bank of California	Hong Kong & Shanghai Banking Corporation	10
French Bank of California	Banque Nationale de Paris	1
Mitsubishi Bank of California	Mitsubishi Bank Ltd	1
Sanwa Bank of California	Sanwa Bank Ltd	1
Sumitomo Bank of California	Sumitomo Bank Ltd	14
Toronto-Dominion Bank of California	Toronto Dominion Bank	1
In Florida		
Inter National Bank, Miami	Royal Trust Company	1
In Hawaii		
Central Pacific Bank, Honolulu	Sumitomo Bank Ltd	
In Illinois		
Chicago-Tokyo Bank	Bank of Tokyo Ltd	1
First Pacific Bank of Chicago	Dai-Ichi Kangyo Bank Ltd	1

Sources: Same as in Table 7.1.

Table 7.3

Condensed Composite Balance Sheet for all Branches
of Foreign Banks Licensed in New York State

	Dec. 31, 1962	Dec. 31, 1968	Dec. 31, 1971
Number of Branches	8	27	40
ASSETS		$ millions	
Cash and balances with other banks	38	387	1,240
Bonds and corporate stocks	67	177	226
Loans and overdrafts	166	849	1,384
Customers' liability on acceptances	4	35	80
Due from own head offices and branches	22	103	129
Other assets	10	26	531
Total Assets	309	1,576	3,594
LIABILITIES			
Deposits of foreign governments, central banks, and other foreign banks	147	209	441
Other deposits	24	768	1,202
Liabilities for borrowed money	11	42	123
Acceptances outstanding	9	40	90
Other liabilities	2	66	122
Total liabilities, exclusive of amounts due to own head offices and branches	194	1,126	1,980
Due to own head offices and branches	114	450	1,614
Total Liabilities	309	1,576	3,594

Source: Superintendent of Banks, New York State, *Annual Reports*.

Europe. A number of branches enjoy a strong potential for facilitating the purchase and sale of American securities for the account of foreign customers, especially via the third market. During periods of monetary ease, Swiss and British bankers make street loans to brokers and dealers, and place federal funds. Many branches make loans and solicit deposits from the local office of home airline or steamship companies. Several branches obtain business through ethnic bonds. The Israeli branches obtain substantial banking business from Jewish businessmen. The Puerto Rican branches offer services to Spanish speaking businessmen and individuals in New York.

In addition, these branches offer personal banking services: checking accounts; loans to individuals; and safe deposit facilities. However, these branches do not enjoy personal trust powers. They do not actively solicit personal accounts, exceptions being those deposits which can be traced to their international business and deposits obtained as a result of ethnic appeal (the Puerto Rican and Israeli bank branches).

4. AGENCIES

The U.S. agencies of foreign banks play an important role in two connections, namely in the money market and in financing international transactions. Foreign agencies have enjoyed a strong growth in assets, in part attributable to the increased volume of money market loans made largely by the Canadian agencies to securities brokers and dealers. At year-end 1971 the New York agencies of foreign banks reported assets of $8.1 billion, which compares with assets of $5.3 billion in 1968, and with $3.2 billion at year-end 1962 (see Table 7-4).

Agencies carry on a wide range of activities. Their trade financing activities consist largely of issuing letters of credit, and buying, selling, paying and collecting bills of exchange ensuing from U.S. home nation trade. They manage the dollar balances of their respective head offices and their world-wide networks. Some agencies are involved in the purchase and sale of securities for their home office and customers, and a number are fairly active in the foreign exchange market.

Of the forty-nine agencies operating in the United States in 1972, twenty are affiliates of Japanese banks. The Bank of Tokyo New York Agency stands apart from the other agencies

Table 7.4

Condensed Composite Balance Sheet for all Agencies
of Foreign Banks Licensed in New York State

	Dec. 31, 1962	Dec. 31, 1968	Dec. 31, 1971
Number of agencies	27	27	28
ASSETS	\$ millions		
Cash and balances with other banks	422	825	1,209
Bonds and corporate stocks	581	699	418
Loans and overdrafts	1,489	2,204	3,458
Customers' liability on acceptances	147	705	870
Due from own head office and branches	525	659	1,733
Other assets	47	233	418
Total Assets	3,213	5,327	8,110
LIABILITIES			
Due to foreign banks	341	342	384
Due to other customers	88	166	319
Liabilities for borrowed money	7	68	493
Acceptances outstanding	100	325	605
Other liabilities	55	302	920
Total liabilities, exclusive of amounts due to own head offices and branches	594	1,206	2,723
Due to own head offices and branches	2,618	4,120	5,386
Total Liabilities	3,213	5,327	8,110

Source: Superintendent of Banks, New York State, *Annual Reports.*

since it acts as the fiscal agent of the Japanese Government, and consequently handles sizeable amounts of official dollar balances as a foreign exchange bank. The remaining agencies of Japanese banks are largely engaged in financing trade between the United States and Japan. A large portion of Japanese borrowings in the United States effected through agencies are short-term and directly related to export-import transactions. These agencies rarely engage in the complicated money market operations that the Canadian agencies undertake. The agency form has appealed to the Japanese banks in part because the legal lending limits do not apply to them. These agencies lend substantial amounts to large Japanese trading companies and application of the lending limitations could seriously hamper their lending activities.

In the course of their operations the Japanese agencies generate a large volume of trade acceptances in which American banks invest. This has provided profitable outlets for domestic banks, and has introduced a number of medium-sized U.S. banks to international banking under relatively favourable circumstances.

The Canadian agencies in New York probably account for half of the total agency assets in the State. According to Zwick's analysis, the following factors account for the relative importance of these agencies.[7]

1. Canadian province and municipal bond flotations have yielded sizeable U.S. dollar balances for management by N.Y. agencies.[8]

2. Residents of Canada prefer to hold precautionary balances of U.S. dollars when the Canadian exchange rate is expected to fluctuate.

3. Agencies can attract short-term balances for parent banks by paying higher rates of interest than domestic banks are permitted under Regulation Q. This factor may be expected to exert less influence, given the more liberal Federal Reserve posture on Regulation Q ceilings since 1970.

4. A substantial volume of U.S.-Canadian trade has created large dollar balances held by New York agencies.

5. Fractional reserve requirements do not apply to agency operations, permitting the agencies to borrow New York funds in the parent bank name and lending out the proceeds.

Since Canada severely restricts American bank solicitation of business at home, the agencies derive a substantial advantage in handling the Canadian side of the transaction. The existence of American-based agencies permits the Canadian banks to compete successfully for handling the U.S. side of the transaction as well.

In the past the Canadian agencies have been heavily committed to interest rate arbitrage and operations in the foreign exchange forward markets.[9] This activity has involved the agencies in Eurodollar lending in Europe, and selling short-term CDs and lending funds obtained at medium terms. Such practices contribute to an unstable deposit-loan structure. In connection with this, the Canadian agencies have been extremely active in providing 'street' loans to brokers and dealers, which are convenient investment media for short-term volatile balances.[10] The agencies enjoy cost advantages (absence of FDIC insurance assessments and fractional reserve requirements) in obtaining lendable funds, and are therefore in a position to offer attractive rates on street loans. During periods of tight money the volume of street loans extended by Canadian agencies approximates that of New York City banks. At times of monetary ease, when domestic banks are in a position to lay out an increased volume of funds in the form of street loans, the Canadian agency competition is still present.

The existence of the Canadian agencies in the New York money market has done much to enhance the degree of competition, the alternatives, and the depth of the market. In the late 1960s several developments tended to dampen the growth of Canadian agency activities. These include the voluntary restraint programme which resulted in a withdrawal of U.S.-owned dollar balances in Canada, higher interest rates in the United States, accelerated growth of the commercial paper and CD markets, and the higher ceilings under Regulation Q. Nevertheless, agency resources have continued to grow. Given a relaxation of the U.S. capital restraint programme relative to dollar outflows, the Canadian agencies may experience a more favourable competitive status in the New York money market.

5. NEW YORK STATE INVESTMENT COMPANIES

A small number of foreign banks are represented in New York by means of their affiliated investment companies, which are chartered under the New York State Investment Company Act. These include the European-American Banking Corporation,[11] the French-American Banking Corporation, J. Henry Schroeder Banking Corporation, and the American-Swiss Credit Company.

These companies finance high risk trade and participate in venture capital schemes. A large part of their business is related to trade and investments in Latin America. They enjoy close working relations with exporters and importers, in particular industry lines who conduct their business in specific areas of the globe. They often finance small, unknown firms which might have difficulties obtaining commercial bank financing.

C. REGULATORY ENVIRONMENT

1. EXTENT OF STATE REGULATION

In the main, governmental bodies at both the federal and state levels in the United States have remained silent on the matter of providing for the licensing and administration of foreign banks in this country. The federal government has enacted no legislation in this area, and as recently as 1966 only seven states had seen fit to codify the regulations pertaining to foreign banking operations.[12] An exception to the complete absence of federal supervision and control appeared recently as a by-product of the 1970 amendments to the Bank Holding Company Act. Under authority available in the amended act, the Board of Governors of the Federal Reserve System holds jurisdiction over foreign banks which operate banking subsidiaries in this country. The Board must authorise foreign banks to become holding companies and operate newly chartered affiliates in this country. In 1971 the Board approved three Japanese holding company affiliate investments under this amendment to the Bank Holding Company Act. In the absence of federal legislation foreign banks have turned to the various states to obtain banking privileges. Domestic banks in this country have in general supported the requests of these foreign banks. In the few states which have specific provision for the charter or licensing of foreign banking operations, fairly distinct treatment has been accorded each of the organisational forms, namely representative offices, subsidiaries, agencies and branches.

In establishing state-chartered subsidiaries, foreign banks have generally been supervised in a manner similar to that which applies to domestic banks. Foreign banking institutions are required to establish a board of directors composed at least partially of state residents. The two states which license agencies of foreign banks, New York and California, operate on the understanding that these institutions will not accept deposits within the state. While agencies may not accept deposit accounts, they may and do maintain 'credit balances' or 'current accounts'. These are balances derived from or incidental to trade financing or other services performed by these agencies. In New York, the State Banking Department determines what constitutes a credit balance based on the source of funds and usage of the account. Examples of sources of funds constituting credit balances held in New York agencies of foreign banks include proceeds from purchase of a bill of exchange, funds received from collection of bills of exchange, proceeds from sale of customers' securities, funds placed with the agency to pay a customer's maturing obligation, and margin or cash collateral accounts for letters of credit issued for a customer's account.[13]

The typical agency examination conforms closely to that used for foreign branches or domestic banks. The examination incorporates an analysis of the conduct and affairs of the agency, a statement of assets and liabilities, analysis of the extent of diversification of the investment portfolio, a review of the foreign exchange position, analysis of contingent liabilities, and the examiners' comments and suggestions on operating procedures, internal controls and auditing. In cases where agencies operate in conjunction with subsidiaries chartered in the same state, transactions between the agency and state-chartered subsidiary are also looked into.

Regulatory officials have long regarded branches of foreign banks as the most difficult to supervise. The reasons for this are not hard to understand. Branches are in effect appendages of the foreign bank, and it might be difficult to adequately protect depositors when the parent institution lies largely outside the jurisdiction of state supervisors and examiners. Moreover, it has been contended that assets of branches could be withdrawn by the foreign parent with relative ease. Once removed, it would be difficult for American courts to recover these assets.

Careful attention and consideration was given to the preceding questions when the legislature of New York State drafted the foreign branching act, passed in 1960. The New York State law provides that a branch must maintain within the state dollar assets equivalent to at least 108 per cent of all its liabilities. In addition, the branch must maintain a 'deposit' equal to 5 per cent of its liabilities. These funds must be maintained under a restricted deposit agreement in another domestic bank or in government securities. These amounts are subject to withdrawal only with the consent of the Superintendent of Banks.

In the event of financial difficulties, creditors of the branch are preferred with respect to *branch* assets, without prejudice to their right to share in other assets of the *bank*. In effect, New York State law provides that branches be operated as if their liabilities extended only to branch depositors. This amounts to a 'separate entity concept' of deposits in branches, which has been fully recognised by the courts in the United States.[14] However, the Superintendent may take possession of *any assets* of the foreign banking corporation in the state even if not on the books of the branch.

A provision to permit foreign branching in California was passed in 1964. While virtually identical to the New York branching amendment, the California law differs in one important respect. In order to obtain a branching licence in California the branch must first be approved for FDIC insurance. The 1969 amendment to California's banking law permits branch operations including acceptance of foreign source deposits without the FDIC insurance requirement.

2. THE INTRA BANK EPISODE

On 15 October 1966 the Intra Bank, S.A. of Beirut, Lebanon closed its doors, ending a fifteen-year life studded with numerous successes and amazing growth. At the time the bank held assets with a book value of over $200 million, and controlled close to 20 per cent of Lebanon's banking business.[15] As the largest bank in Lebanon, Intra enjoyed a pivotal role in Lebanese banking, serving as a bankers' bank for many of the domestic banks in the country. In addition, Intra had developed an extensive world-wide network of branches and affiliates.

'The entrepôt nature of Beirut's banking business has led many to refer to it as the Switzerland of the Middle East. More specifically, one could refer to the high educational and social development, the influx of oil revenues from the Persian Gulf, the safe haven status of Beirut relative to surrounding unstable areas, Moslem prohibitions against payment of interest (though Lebanon has a large proportion of Christians in its population), the migrant nature of Lebanese businessmen, the high gold coverage of the Lebanese pound, and a banking secrecy law as factors that were important in contributing to the growth of Beirut as a regional financial entrepôt.[16]

Various reasons have been offered to explain the Intra Bank failure. Some accounts refer to a series of plots against Intra Bank, with the identities of the conspirators ranging from King Faisal of Saudi Arabia, the Russian Moscow Narodny Bank, the British and French Governments, to the Central Bank.[17] Other explanations hinge on the substantial withdrawals that took place in August-September 1966, the associated weakening of confidence in Intra Bank, and the inevitable demise of a sound institution unable to weather the storm of a run on the bank.[18] A third approach is to refer to the extremely illiquid assets held by the bank, in part the outcome of the peculiarities of Lebanese banking which permitted an injudicious blending of investment company, savings bank, and commercial bank operations.

With the closing of the head office of Intra Bank in Lebanon, the New York Superintendent of Banks took possession of the New York branch so as to protect its depositors and creditors. A short time later New York Superintendent Frank Wille announced that the New York branch of Intra Bank had direct liabilities of $2.150 million and assets of $2.435 million.

In 1967 the New York Superintendent received claims by depositors on the New York branch of Intra Bank totalling $32 million, of which only $1 million was initially accepted as valid. In 1970 it was announced that the New York State

Superintendent had paid more than $1 million to 759 former depositors and creditors of the New York branch of Intra Bank.[19] All depositors were paid in full on balances outstanding at the New York branch of Intra Bank.

The implications and lessons to be learned from the Intra Bank demise, and the general Lebanese financial crisis of October 1966 are numerous. A deep insight is provided concerning the prospects for successful and sound banking operations when a strong central bank and proper banking laws are lacking. The central bank in Lebanon was established as recently as 1964, and at the time of the Lebanese banking crisis did not have a strong, qualified staff. The laws governing operations of the central bank were inadequate, and did not specify what forms of discounting or direct lending the Bank might engage in to assist the Lebanese commercial banks.[20] One of the main factors contributing to the downfall of Intra was its role as bankers' bank, functioning as a repository for volatile bankers' deposits.

3. REGULATORY PROPOSALS

During 1967 there was much discussion and debate in Washington concerning the desirability of establishing direct federal control over domestic offices of foreign banking corporations. The initial impetus came from the release in July 1966 of the Zwick report by the Joint Economic Committee of Congress, prepared at the direction of Representative Wright Patman, Chairman of the House Banking and Currency Committee. Reasons offered for the legislative proposals that appeared at this time were the following:

1. the Intra Bank failure;
2. discrimination against U.S. banks abroad and the desire to provide reciprocal treatment by a single federal agency;
3. recognition of inequities both favouring and discriminating against foreign banks operating here;
4. need for control over the operations of foreign banking in the United States, especially at a time when there was much concern over the balance of payments and monetary policy.

Proposals for extending federal regulatory jurisdiction over foreign banking operations in the United States followed several approaches. One approach called for extending the availability of FDIC insurance coverage to foreign bank branches in the United States. A second approach provided for federal chartering and regulation of foreign banking corporations in the United States.

Several proposals were made in 1967 for federal chartering of foreign banks operating in the United States. Early in that year Representative Patman, Chairman of the House Banking Committee, introduced a bill which would bring foreign branch banks under exclusive federal control. The bill required all foreign banks with branches in the United States and those seeking to establish branches to acquire a federal charter, giving the Comptroller of the Currency authority to issue charters. Under the Patman proposal foreign banks would be prohibited from establishing branches in more than one state. Shortly after this, Senator Javits proposed a Foreign Banking Control Act (S 1741) aimed at encouraging activities of foreign banks in the United States, and encouraging foreign countries to grant reciprocal privileges to U.S. banks in their overseas activities.[21] The bill aimed at providing a more uniform admissions policy in accordance with national interests. This bill provided for federal or state chartering of agencies, branches and controlled subsidiaries. Other important aspects of this bill included provision for periodic examination of foreign banks in the United States by national bank examiners, application of the same limitations and regulations to foreign banks as apply to national banks, and the requirement that within ninety days of enactment of the bill the FDIC must submit a legislative proposal to include insurance coverage for branches and controlled subsidiaries of foreign banking corporations.

Other legislation proposed included the Fino Bill. The Fino Bill was similar to the Javits Bill, except that it provided for federal chartering of existing operations within one year of its passage. The Fino Bill also would have permitted foreign banks to establish operations within any state or territory of the United States.

State objections to these regulatory proposals focused on the possible adverse effects on the dual banking system, the subordination of state interests to wider international interests, and the heretofore successful operation of foreign banks under state jurisdiction. In the years since 1967 the question of federal regulation and supervision over foreign banks operating in this country has been dwarfed in importance by the rapid growth of U.S. overseas banking.

III
ROLE AND FUNCTION
OF OVERSEAS BANKING

8 Foreign Lending

In this chapter we examine the role and importance of foreign lending by American banks. American banks are not the only source of short-term or long-term credits for non-resident borrowers. However, the role of U.S. banks is strategic, since they provide a major part of the credits to foreign borrowers that finance U.S. exports and imports, investment transactions, and foreign business development. Foreign loans provided by U.S. banks may serve to bolster the U.S. balance of payments position and facilitate a broad spectrum of international transactions carried on by U.S. residents.

A. SCOPE AND IMPORTANCE OF FOREIGN LENDING BY U.S. BANKS

1. IMPORTANCE AND GROWTH IN FOREIGN LENDING

Foreign lending by American banks plays an important role in a number of contexts. Foreign loans made by banks in the United States are necessary to support a large part of U.S. foreign trade, as well as trade between second and third countries. They support the overseas investment activities of U.S. companies and foreign affiliates, and may be necessary to permit a foreign country to undertake an exchange stabilisation programme by refunding its scheduled debts denominated in hard currencies. Such loans help to maintain friendly relations with the governments of host countries where foreign branches and affiliates of American banks operate. Moreover, they support the economic development programmes of host countries and can be instrumental in developing local food production, thereby contributing to the long-range solution of expanding food and nutritional requirements in certain developing countries.[1] Finally, foreign loans make important contributions to bank profitability.

Lending by U.S. banks through their overseas branches often provides banking and credit facilities in less developed countries of the world that would not be available but for the American presence.

Foreign loans of U.S. banks have provided much needed foreign exchange for countries attempting to stabilise their economies. Moreover, they have contributed to strengthening the position of many foreign banks that at times were in need of credits from some 'lender of last resort'.

Foreign loans made by U.S. banks have exerted a variety of pressures on the U.S. financial markets, both from the direct effects of siphoning off or adding to funds available in the United States for bank lending, and from the indirect effects generated by causing monetary authorities to react to international flows of funds, thereby setting off a series of policy measures designed to hold funds in New York or some other financial centre. By the late 1960s balance of payments considerations relating to these capital flows led to the imposition of several types of controls over the foreign lending activities of U.S. banks.

The discussion of foreign lending which follows is confined largely to head office lending to foreign borrowers located in other countries of the world. Only peripheral attention is given to foreign branch lending activities, which have been discussed in Chapter 5.

It is difficult to assemble complete data on the international lending activities of American banks for several reasons. First, much of the data that is gathered is the by-product of programmes not necessarily oriented toward simple fact gathering. Therefore, information generated from the Voluntary Foreign Credit Restraint Programme administered by the Board of Governors, or the Balance of Payments estimates of the U.S. Department of Commerce are not necessarily geared to measuring foreign lending by U.S. banks, but is collected for other purposes. For example, in the reporting systems of the previously cited programmes, foreign branches of American banks are treated as foreigners. Hence, credits made by U.S. head offices to their foreign branches may be included in the data published by U.S. government agencies or the Board of Governors as *foreign assets*, even though such credits simply finance foreign branch lending activity. Second, the relatively small number of U.S. banks directly engaged in international banking presents disclosure problems, and as a result information gathered for supervisory purposes cannot be published in detail.[2] Third, a substantial part of the foreign lending undertaken by U.S. head offices is funnelled through foreign banks in the form of deposits or currency swaps. In turn the foreign bank makes the loan to an overseas business firm. Such credits may be a specific objective of the original deposit made by the U.S. bank, but will not appear in the statistics describing foreign lending by head offices of American banks. Fourth, many loans extended by U.S. banks to resident borrowers in the United States may finance foreign trade, the purchase of materials from an overseas affiliate of a U.S. industrial corporation, or be used to acquire foreign assets where the probable source of repayment is to be cash flows from domestic operations.[3] Therefore, these loans may be playing an important role in supporting international transactions but they will not be included in published data on foreign loans.

Despite these reservations fairly useful and comprehensive data has been supplied regarding foreign lending and credits outstanding by U.S. banks. This data is a by-product of the balance of payments reporting network which attempts to reflect short-term and long-term capital movements in the form of changes in outstanding claims on foreigners of U.S. banks. Table 8-1 summarises the changes in these outstanding claims over the period 1955–70. The data represents head office claims only. Foreign branches are treated as non-residents in this series. Two observations are worthy of mention at this point in our discussion. First, in each of the five year periods 1955–60 and 1960–65 both short-term and long-term claims reported by U.S. banks more than doubled in amount. Second, the growth in long-term claims outstanding outpaced that of short-term claims until 1965, increasing as a percentage of total bank claims until that year. After this long-term claims declined in importance, the reason for this being application of the Interest Equalisation Tax (IET) against U.S. bank lending abroad, which became effective in 1965.[4]

Table 8.1

Claims on Foreigners Reported by Banks in the United States
1955–1970

	Short-Term	Long-Term	Total	Percentage Long-Term
1955	1,549	671	2,220	30
1960	3,614	1,698	5,312	32
1965	7,728	4,517	12,245	37
1970	10,751	3,049	13,800	22

Amounts are in millions of dollars.
Source: Board of Governors of the Federal Reserve System.

2. TYPES OF FOREIGN LENDING

The focal point of this chapter is foreign lending by the head offices of U.S. banks. Included in this are the various credit-debt relationships that develop between U.S. head offices and their international banking departments on the one hand, and foreign individuals, corporations and banks which are on the other side of the balance sheet. These credit-debt relationships include direct loans, acceptances created by American banks for the account of foreign banks, claims of U.S. banks on foreign banks and non-banks that are in process of being collected (collections), and other types of outstanding claims on foreigners resulting from transactions, loans or clearing activities.

Bank lending from the United States is conducted almost exclusively in U.S. dollars. Only a small amount of foreign currency loans is made, based upon the special needs of customers. A fairly high proportion of term loans is extended by U.S. banks from their head offices, and as early as 1963–64 more than half of the foreign loans extended were term in nature. The maturities tend to cluster in the three to five year range. In the period 1960–65 the costs of borrowing for medium-term from U.S. banks appears to have declined, probably due to growing experience of U.S. banks in this area and the ability to evaluate credit risks more appropriately, and due to increasing competitive pressures.

We should remember that U.S. commercial banks are not the only institutions engaged in making foreign loans, especially loans to finance export-import trade. However, they provide a major portion of the credit in this area. In addition to commercial bank lending to foreign borrowers, U.S. government institutions such as the Export-Import Bank, commercial factoring firms, finance companies, and leasing firms provide a large volume of foreign credits, and undertake a variety of types of loans to non-residents. These non-bank lenders compete with commercial bank foreign lending, but also collaborate and participate with banks in extending foreign loans.

U.S. government financing facilities are made available because of the desire to provide economic assistance to foreign countries with lower per-capita income than the United States, while at the same time pursuing the objectives of American foreign policy. The institutions involved in this connection include the Agency for International Development (AID); the Department of Agriculture, and the Export-Import Bank. AID has provided financing for foreign enterprises through the Development Loan Programme and the Cooley Loan Programme. Under the former, long-term loans are provided in dollars, with repayment in the same currency. Direct development loans are made available to international corporations in a two-step programme, whereby the host country acts as the first borrower on a soft-term basis, with the international corporations functioning as second borrower. Development loans have been made available indirectly through local development banks. Under this programme AID supplies dollar loans to the local development bank which in turn extends local currency loans to the business firm. The so-called Cooley Loans are local currency funds received in payment for export sales of U.S. agricultural products. These local currency funds are loaned to American firms and their subsidiaries engaged in business in the host country, and to private firms in the host country whose activities facilitate the expansion of overseas markets of American agricultural products.

The Department of Agriculture makes long-term credits in local currency with funds obtained through the sale of U.S. agricultural products. An international concern that seeks this local currency financing must first sell U.S. agricultural products, usually financed by a line of credit provided through the U.S. Commodity Credit Corporation. After the sale the international firm may invest the proceeds in projects previously approved by the Department of Commerce Foreign Agricultural Service.

The Export-Import Bank was created to supplement private capital in financing and facilitating exports between the United States and other countries. This includes long-term financing directly connected with U.S. exports, emergency credits to foreign governments, credits to foreign institutions, and the issuance of guarantees and provision of war risk and expropriation insurance for commodities owned by U.S. citizens and located in overseas areas.

3.   CHANGING CHARACTER OF INTERNATIONAL LENDING

The growth, relative importance, and format of international lending has changed over the past ten to twelve years, reflecting developments in domestic and overseas financial markets, government regulation of international transactions, a widening scope for global sources and uses of funds by corporate spenders and investors, and a more competitive environment in the international markets for loanable funds.

The relative cost of borrowed funds in the United States and overseas experienced a significant shift during the 1960s. In the first half of that decade U.S. sources of funds were generally less expensive than comparable sources of funds obtainable overseas.[5] This situation reversed itself beginning in 1966 and the United States continued as a relatively high cost source of funds until 1970. As a result, foreign sources of loan funds became relatively more attractive to overseas borrowers, and this tended to divert foreign borrowing away from U.S. financial markets. In the period 1970–72, U.S. source funds have become relatively lower-priced, and bank credits have become more competitive in the financial markets overseas.

A 1965 amendment to the Interest Equalisation Tax Act made foreign loans by U.S. banks subject to the IET. This tax, which was originally enacted in 1964, imposed an excise duty on medium and long-term lending by U.S. residents to foreigners located in developed countries. The tax was designed to curb a rapidly growing portfolio investment capital outflow which was placing severe pressure on the U.S. balance of payments position. Application of the IET to term lending by American banks cut off a substantial part of foreign loan demand.

Except for the direct financing of U.S. exports, the Interest Equalisation Tax cut off further growth in term lending to corporations in developed countries. That lending has since shifted to foreign sources including foreign branches of U.S. banks. Subsequent broadening of Eurodollar, Eurobond, and foreign medium-term credit sources of funds suggests that U.S. banks might encounter some difficulty in re-establishing this lending should the IET be removed. Interest rate considerations doubtless would play a more exclusively determining role in the share of this international credit demand enjoyed by U.S. banks. In the less developed countries longer-term credits are granted mainly to governments and quasi-government institutions in connection with large-scale development projects or for exchange stabilisation purposes. Other principal borrowers are financial institutions, private or government sponsored. In part these credits have taken the form of participations in shorter maturities of loans made by the World Bank, the International Finance Corporation (IFC), and other international financial institutions. Loans to private business borrowers are selectively made, generally with guarantees from foreign banks.

The growth in term lending in the less developed countries has been slower than elsewhere because of problems of financial and political stability. Concern for the availability of foreign exchange for repayment of credits at maturity is reflected in the uneven geographic distribution of term loans in those countries – and in the extensive use of bank and foreign government guarantees.

The organisational format of international lending has undergone drastic changes since 1966. At that time U.S. head offices provided 70 per cent of the $14.4 billion of loans to overseas borrowers then outstanding. In 1969 head offices accounted for only 58 per cent of the $22.0 billion of overseas loans. By 1972 the importance of head offices had declined further to 49 per cent of overseas loans.[6]

As a result of the expansion in international lending by U.S. banks, and the more important role foreign branch lending has taken, American banks now enjoy a far more diversified loan portfolio. Short-term foreign credits provided at the head offices of major U.S. banks are extended to a wide variety of non-bank borrowers. Financing of seasonal foreign exchange needs of certain governments, international transactions of major oil and shipping companies, interim foreign exchange requirements pending funding of external debt, pre-export financing of crops and commodity processing, are all examples of the areas of financing undertaken by U.S. banks.

Lending done abroad at *foreign branches* of U.S. banks and subsidiaries is even more diversified. Such lending varies according to the banking markets in which overseas banking offices are located. Lending is done in local currencies, U.S. dollars, and in foreign currencies. Individual U.S. overseas branches may lend mainly to other banks, to finance foreign trade transactions, or engage in general local and retail type lending in competition with indigenous banks. In Europe the principal loan operations of branches are now in Eurodollars. The main borrowers are large international corporations – U.S. and European – seeking finance for international transactions and for general corporate purposes. A developing practice is to offer lines of credit that provide for drawings in dollars or in European currencies at offices throughout Europe. This practice can involve complex swaps into and out of a number of currencies. Other loans at European branches arise from purchases of foreign credits originally booked from head offices in the United States to reduce outstanding claims under the Foreign Credit Restraint Programme.

Another important change that has taken place is an expansion in the number of alternatives available to U.S. banks in meeting the global credit needs of their customers. Conversely, there is a wide variety of means through which U.S. and foreign corporations can meet their credit requirements on a worldwide basis. Networks through which funds can be channelled – to bring together surplus and deficit money and loan markets – are made available through the international branch systems of U.S. banks. The multicurrency lending arrangements that have developed in Europe offer an example of the evolving integration of credit market facilities without regard to national boundaries. Credits can be transferred from branch to head office or in reverse, or participated among branches and head office in response to the needs and conveniences of borrower and various banking offices within the branch system.

Members of the branch network, affiliated banks, or representative offices serve as collecting points or agents in certain areas through which liquid funds are passed on to areas where they may be more profitably employed. Beirut, Hong Kong and Nassau figure prominently among the centres which attract such funds for safe keeping, tax haven, or other reasons. These foreign funds may gravitate to offices in the United States as deposits, or may be funnelled by head offices to other branches or into London offices. London is the central redistribution point for balances in some branch networks, and in any event is the principal link to the Eurodollar market.

A rechannelling of international financing to London and the Eurodollar market has followed balance of payments restrictions in the United States. Use of London branches of U.S. banks to obtain funds to support head office operations in the United States became important in the late 1960s. In 1966 as monetary conditions tightened and certificate of deposit (CD) runoffs took place head office borrowings from foreign branches increased rapidly. This brought about an increased understanding of the new role of the Eurodollar market. In these ways U.S. banks have become an important force in the integration of international money and loan markets, and they provide major channels in transmitting changing conditions from one market to another.

B.   FOREIGN LENDING BY HEAD OFFICE OR INTERNATIONAL DEPARTMENT

1.   REVIEW OF FACTORS INFLUENCING FOREIGN LOAN PORTFOLIO

Since the mid-1960s a number of factors have influenced the composition of the foreign loan portfolio of the international departments of U.S. banks. First, the Interest Equalisation Tax has reduced the scope of term lending to foreigners, leaving borrowers in the less developed areas as a more important potential source of customers. Second, the Foreign Credit Restraint Programme has imposed a ceiling on foreign credits by U.S. banks. Third, tight money in the United States in the period 1966–70 increased the relative cost of funds from this country, thereby influencing the ability of American banks to compete for foreign business. Fourth, slack domestic loan demand in the United States along with easy credit market conditions in 1970–72 enhanced the ability of U.S. head offices to compete for foreign business. As a result of these factors in combination, in the period 1965–70 total claims of U.S. banks on foreigners exhibited only modest growth, outstanding term loans in Europe have fallen, and only a very small amount of new term loans have been made in Europe. In addition, foreign loans of U.S. head offices have been transferred or sold to foreign branches and foreign correspondents. In the period 1970–72 short-term claims of U.S. banks on foreigners increased significantly, with claims on Canada and Western Europe rising most rapidly. Much of this expansion resulted from the 1971 exemption of export credits from the Foreign Credit Restraint ceilings. Most of this expansion took the form of dollar loans to banks and other foreign borrowers. Moreover, long-term and medium-term claims of U.S. banks on foreigners increased in the two year period from $3.1 billion to $4.9 billion.

Foreign lending is not conducted in the same manner as domestic lending in the United States. Generally, there is little or no balance sheet information available on customers overseas, and unsecured credit is often made available on the strength of the name and reputation of the borrower. Often, U.S. head office lending is channelled through foreign banks, through direct loans, deposits, or acceptance credits on their behalf. In turn the foreign bank provides credit to a foreign borrower based on that bank's previously established working relationship with that customer. In Western Europe and Japan the term lending portfolio of foreign branches of U.S. banks involves tailoring maturities to the borrowers' projected cash flow. In Hong Kong there exist special difficulties in the way of obtaining credit information, due to the large in-migration of new businessmen. Foreign lending by American banks is characterised by a diversity of credit types and channels through which loaned funds may be directed.

Variations in lending rates depend on whether credits are long-term or short-term, to Europe or LDC areas, and whether borrowers are banks, governments, or other categories of borrowers. Short-term loans to developed areas call for interest charges which are slightly above the U.S. prime rate. Rates in developed areas are lower than rates charged on credits to less developed countries. Rates on long-term credits exceed the U.S. prime rate to a larger extent than short-term credits. In the area of acceptances, differential rates do not apply. In the U.S. market for acceptances, buyers go by the name of the U.S. bank.

Differentials between market-determined rates on acceptances and administratively-determined rates on loans and advances can lead to shifts in the composition of short-term foreign credits in U.S. banks. In the early 1960s acceptance financing was decidedly cheaper, but in the later 1960s direct loan borrowing became preferable (the higher interest rate structure was reflected in sensitive market rates). Compensating balances rule in domestic credits made by U.S. banks, but this is not so in international lending. Since the rise in interest rates in 1966 and later years, U.S. banks have been more active in requesting compensating balances of between 10 and 20 per cent.

While the discussion which follows largely focuses on the foreign lending of U.S. head offices, it is necessary to consider foreign branch lending for several reasons. First, the activities of foreign branches of American banks may enhance the opportunities of head offices to develop favourable loan and deposit relationships with foreign customers. Second, head office lending may be important to support the relationship developing between the foreign branch and the overseas customer. Third, to an increasing extent head office lending has been influenced by the growing importance of foreign branch loan activity. The nature of this influence extends into the types of loans extended by U.S. head offices and loan participation relationships between head office and foreign branches.

Head office lending has been undergoing a number of changes in the past several years in connection with the increased overall importance of foreign lending. Head offices now participate with foreign branches in loans to foreign borrowers. The head office share of the participation may be in the form of a Eurocurrency loan, with the interest rate set at an appropriate margin above the London inter-bank rate on Eurodollars. The head offices of major U.S. banks engaged in international lending often arrange loans booked at head office in this way. As a result of such arrangements the domestic prime rate tends to lose significance, and increased flexibility is injected into the arrangements for compensating balances.

The utilisation of Eurocurrency revolving credits in recent years has represented a small but growing part of head office lending to several multinational corporate borrowers with which U.S. banks have close connections. These credits may have a three month, six month, or longer maturity, and are subject to renewal. Rates charged are based on the inter-bank rate in London for Eurodollars, and are adjusted periodically. Such credits may be booked at the foreign branch, or at head office, or participated in by both.

A fairly recent development in foreign lending by U.S. banks is the floating rate note issue. This type loan comes close to bridging the gap between bank term lending and straight bond issues. Two of the first issues of this type were offered by an Italian state agency and Pepsico International. Loans arranged in this manner may carry a five to seven year maturity, and in some cases the maturities extend on to ten years. These loans may be arranged by single U.S. banks or by groups of banks. An international syndicate may be assembled consisting of U.S. banks and foreign banks. Such floating rate note issues may be held in the loan portfolios of foreign branches of the

U.S. bank, or participated in by the U.S. head office. In addition, part of the note issue may be sold to other medium-size banks, including European banks, private banks and portfolio managers in Switzerland, Germany and Luxembourg, and to other investors. The rate on such loans is adjusted periodically based on the inter-bank rate prevailing in the Eurodollar market.

Borrowers who have sold floating notes of this type include governments and government agencies in the less developed countries. As a result of their entry into this market for lendable funds, the less developed country borrowers have increased their ability to tap foreign sources of portfolio investment capital.

In the early 1960s there was a strong foreign demand for U.S. bank credits. However, a number of constraints operated in limiting the expansion of foreign lending. These included the assessment of political and other risks in lending in particular countries and to specific foreign borrowers. A lack of experienced and adequately trained personnel further engendered a cautious attitude on the part of American banks. Finally, in many cases there was a situation of institutional indigestion. Individual American banks could not cope with more than a three or four-fold increase in overseas lending activity.

2. MAIN FEATURES OF LOAN PORTFOLIO

The statistics on American bank short-term claims on foreigners embraces a wide mixture of loan and credit relationships. In part U.S. bank claims include direct loans made to foreign banks and business firms. Acceptance credits constitute a large part of the claims of U.S. banks on foreign banks. Under various types of agreements with overseas correspondent banks major U.S. banking institutions accept time drafts drawn on them, to finance transactions for customers of foreign banks. The U.S. bank has a claim on the foreign bank for which it provided the dollar exchange in creating the acceptance. U.S. banks also provide collection services for customers. In connection with this, items such as drafts, time bills of exchange, and securities due at maturity may be forwarded to foreign correspondent banks for collection. When the funds are available in the normal process of presenting the documents or securities to the overseas payer, they are made available to the U.S. bank. Until such time, the U.S. bank holds a 'claim' on the foreign bank or business firm liable for payment.

Foreign claims of U.S. banks arise in connection with their extending stabilisation and standby credits, development credits, budgetary credits, and the more traditional commercial credits covering merchandise shipments or the capital needs of subsidiaries of U.S. companies abroad. An interesting development has been the participation of U.S. banks in comprehensive stabilisation programmes with the International Monetary Fund and U.S. government lending agencies. Such credits were provided in the 1950s and 1960s to Chile, Argentina, and France.[7]

In 1970 Manufacturers Hanover Trust Co. of New York led a group of thirty-three U.S. banks which agreed to reschedule $247 million of short and medium-term loans made to the central bank of the Philippines. This debt payment rescheduling followed the granting of an IMF standby credit of $27.5 million and additional credit arrangements concluded between the Philippines and a group of fifteen Japanese banks.[8]

In the development loan field U.S. banks have been quite active in participating in the loans of the World Bank, Export-Import Bank, and the International Finance Corporation. In addition, they have underwritten or subscribed for bonds and notes issued by the regional development banks, including the Asian Development Bank and the Inter-American Development Bank. U.S. banks have found such loans attractive for several reasons including the fact that many have proven to be high quality credits, such participations provide ready access to further business and financing contacts in the borrowing country, and central banks and official institutions in these countries are able to place deposit balances and provide collateral business opportunities for U.S. banks which extend such credits. U.S. banks generally take the earlier maturities of World Bank loans, and have found a number of workable formulas for participating in Export-Import Bank credits. These include providing supplementary credit to borrowers independent of the Export-Import Bank loan, participating directly with the Eximbank in loan packages, extending advances under a letter of credit guaranteed by the Export-Import Bank, and in a few instances U.S. banks have purchased seasoned loans from the Bank. In recent years American banks have provided a substantial part of Eximbank loan packages in financing U.S. capital goods exports, including jet aircraft and machinery.[9]

Short-term lending from the United States is dominated by the borrowings of *foreign banks*. Over two-thirds of short-term loans and acceptance credits outstanding are for the account of foreign correspondent banks.[10] Nearly all of the acceptance credits extended by U.S. banks are for the credit of foreign banks. Lines of credit established for these banks provide for acceptance and advance facilities to finance foreign trade transactions generally, or to refinance overall bank operations. Principal borrowers have been banks in Japan and the less developed countries where credit is in short supply and foreign exchange is relatively limited. Banks in Europe and other developed countries make relatively little use of the substantial lines of credit granted them by U.S. banks.

Japanese banks have been the largest single borrowers of short-term funds from U.S. banks. Their borrowings have the added significance of having played a catalytic role in the development and spread of international activities among U.S. banks. Credits to Japan have undergone a thirty-fold expansion since the mid-1950s, much of this concentrated in the period 1960–65. In 1960 Japanese banks began to solicit credit facilities from leading U.S. banks, offering a prime outlet for lendable funds. Implicit backing by the Japanese government added to this attractiveness. Borrowings of Japanese banks have generally taken the form of acceptance credits—directly or indirectly associated with the financing of Japan's foreign trade. Acceptance credits to Japanese banks account for more than half of all such credits extended to foreigners. The larger part finances Japanese trade outside the United States. Growth of such third country trade financing, of which Japan has been a prime user, is one of the principal changes in the foreign lending done by U.S. banks.

Direct loans to foreign governments and other official institutions on both a short-term and long-term basis have accounted for close to 6 per cent of all foreign claims of U.S. banks. In 1970 this category was somewhat less important than it had been in previous years. American banks play an important role in providing financial resources to foreign governments and their agencies and institutions.

3. REGIONAL ASPECTS

Since 1955 short-term loans and credits have become more diversified geographically. At that date close to 50 per cent of outstanding claims were in Latin America, and another 25 per cent were in Europe. In the five years from 1955 to 1960 foreign loans and credits had more than doubled, and their distribution had become somewhat more diversified. In 1960 credits to Latin America and Europe accounted for 38 and 20 per cent of total credits respectively. In the same period short-term credits to Canada and Asia increased in relative importance. This trend persisted into 1965 when approximately 30 per cent of short-term loans and claims were in Latin America, and only 15 per cent in Europe. At that time also a larger proportion of claims of U.S. banks was against borrowers in Asia, Africa and Canada. In part there was a somewhat better distribution of loans and claims in the sense that the more important borrowing countries appeared to offer less uncertainty about economic and political risks than in 1955. For example, Japanese credits increased absolutely and relatively in the ten year period 1955–65, and Japan has enjoyed a strong balance of payments position and stable economy.

In 1970 credits to Japan exceeded 36 per cent of all short-term claims outstanding, but by 1972 had declined in importance to 27 per cent of short-term claims. In 1970–72 short-term credits in Latin America represented nearly 30 per cent of the total. In 1970 Europe ranked as the third most important user of U.S. bank credits, with nearly 14 per cent of the total outstanding. By 1972 short-term claims of U.S. banks in Western Europe had increased to 20 per cent of the total outstanding (Table 8-2).

In 1970 there was considerable variation in the regional use of different types of short-term credits. For example, nearly two-thirds of straight dollar loans were to 'Other Countries', which includes mainly less developed countries (Table 8-3). Aggregate credits to these borrowers represented 41 per cent of total short-term claims outstanding. Over half of the dollar acceptance credits outstanding represented claims of U.S. banks *vis-à-vis* Japan. Another 34 per cent of dollar acceptance credits was included among the short-term claims of U.S. banks against borrowers in 'Other Countries'. Nearly all of the dollar collections outstanding represented claims against Japan and countries in the 'Other' category. Finally, over half of the foreign currency deposits and other claims of U.S. banks represented claims against borrowers in Canada.

The nature of commercial bank foreign lending varies considerably from one area of the globe to another. The following paragraphs attempt to focus on some of these differences, as well as elaborate on the special types of credit needs found in different regions.

Credits to Japan

At year-end 1972 aggregate short-term and long-term claims of U.S. banks on Japan totalled $4.5 billion. Since 1955 there has been a thirty-fold increase in loans and credits to Japan. This came about as a result of the aggressive solicitation of dollar credits by Japanese banks commencing in the early 1960s.

By United States standards Japanese banks are continuously overloaned and illiquid. They depend heavily on borrowing from the Bank of Japan to supplement deposit sources of funds. Utilisation of alternative sources of funds depends essentially on their relative costs – thus Bank of Japan authorities can exercise direct control over the foreign borrowings of Japanese banks by placing limitations on the amounts each bank may borrow overseas, setting maximum rates banks may pay on their foreign borrowings, specifying maximum maturities of credits (120 days in the case of acceptances), and prescribing required ratios of foreign assets to foreign liabilities.

In 1970 over half of all acceptance credits extended by U.S. banks were to Japanese banks (Table 8-3). Japanese acceptance credits differ materially from traditional banker's acceptances, since they are not drawn by the exporter but by a Japanese bank or its agency in the United States.[11] These acceptances are drawn in round amounts to cover a number of international trade shipments, and are 'backed' by trade bills held by the Japanese banks covering imports into Japan from the United States and elsewhere. They indirectly refinance that

Table 8.2

Short-term Claims on Foreigners reported by Banks in the United States, by Region and Type
1972

$ millions		
By Type		
Payable in Dollars		
Loans to		
Official Institutions	166	
Banks	2,976	
Others	2,589	
Total	5,730	
Collections	3,273	
Acceptances	3,215	
Other	2,478	
Total Dollar Claims		14,695
Payable in Foreign Currencies		
Deposits with Foreigners	441	
Foreign Government Securities, Commercial		
Papers and Finance Paper	223	
Other	181	
Total Non-Dollar Claims		845
Total		15,540
By Region		
Europe		2,921
United Kingdom		856
Canada		1,927
Latin America		4,445
Mexico		1,204
Asia		5,606
Japan		4,172
Africa		308
Other		334
		15,540

Source: *Federal Reserve Bulletin*.

trade. In essence these are unsecured credits to Japanese banks, and the volume of these credits depends more directly on the proportion of import bills Japanese banks choose to use as backing for their external borrowings than on the amount of those bills in their portfolios.

In the short-run, variations in the amount of Japanese acceptances outstanding are largely at the initiative of the borrowing banks, since credit lines exceed normal utilisation by a fairly wide margin. Thus the Japanese banks are able to use their acceptance and advance lines in accordance with their liquidity positions and with the relative costs of borrowing as between U.S. banks and the Bank of Japan.[12]

In 1963–65 term loans extended by U.S. banks in Japan increased, financing the capital expansion of major Japanese industrial firms. Japanese banks arranged the placement of these loans with U.S. banks, and also guaranteed their repayment. U.S. banks with branches in Japan tended to extend term credits from the branches rather than head office. American banks have found that lending in Japan has proven virtually riskless.

Europe

In Europe credits are mainly to non-bank, non-government borrowers. Medium-term lending tends to be important. Two interesting categories of credits involved in U.S. bank lending in this region are:

1. ship loans – mainly to Scandinavian borrowers,
2. loans for general corporate purposes.

1. *Ship Loans* In the past International Departments of American banks have made ship loans a specialty. Because of limited capital facilities in Norway, Norwegian shipping companies have been required to obtain foreign financing for expansion and modernisation of their fleets. Such financing has tended to remain relatively expensive in other European countries, and U.S. banks have bid successfully for this lending business.

Mortgage loans covering 70–75 per cent of the value of the vessel have been provided, and the cash flow afforded by prime

Regional Distribution of Short-term Claims on Foreigners reported by U.S. Banks
1970

$ millions

	U.S. Dollar Loans	U.S. Dollar Acceptance Credits	U.S. Dollar Collections Outstanding	Other Claims in U.S. Dollars	Foreign Currency Deposits & Other Claims	Total
Canada	271	96	23	336	335	1,061
United Kingdom	92	89	54	103	41	379
EEC	151	72	148	36	103	510
Other W. Europe	184	197	96	16	30	523
Japan	428	2,140	1,214	67	41	3,890
Other Countries*	1,914	1,372	880	121	101	4,388
Total	3,040	3,966	2,415	679	651	10,751

As Percentage of Column Totals

	U.S. Dollar Loans	U.S. Dollar Acceptance Credits	U.S. Dollar Collections Outstanding	Other Claims in U.S. Dollars	Foreign Currency Deposits & Other Claims	Total
Canada	9	3	1	49	51	10
United Kingdom	3	2	2	15	6	4
EEC	5	2	6	5	16	5
Other W. Europe	6	5	4	2	5	5
Japan	14	54	50	10	6	36
Other Countries*	64	34	37	18	16	41
Total	100	100	100	100	100	100

*Mainly less developed countries.

Source: *Survey of Current Business*, March 1971, p. 50. This is the last year in which these regional breakdowns were

charters of the vessel upon entry into service has been used as a basis for liquidating the loan. Borrowers agree to assign charter earnings to the lending bank, or in the case of cargo liners, to channel voyage receipts through the bank. Prime Norwegian banks guarantee repayment of most loans extended to Norwegian shipping companies. Maturities generally range from five to seven years, with 10 per cent amortisation per year, and a 30 per cent balloon payment in the final year.

No compensating balances are required since Norwegian foreign exchange regulations do not permit holding balances abroad. Shipping companies hold working balances in U.S. banks in New York or in sterling in London branches and provide collateral business in handling international payments and receipts.

2. *General Corporate Lending in Europe*　Loans extended by U.S. banks to corporations have been used for capital expenditures, working capital, and refinancing short-term debt. The 200 largest corporations in Europe are prime credit risks by any standards. These corporations have business operations on a global scale, and consequently require substantial international banking services. Credits to subsidiaries of U.S. corporations formed a *minor* part of the overall lending in Europe in the early 1960s. These subsidiaries had access to long-term funds through their parent companies, and any short-term credits provided by U.S. banks were mainly through European branches.

Since the middle 1960s lending to European corporations and European-based affiliates of U.S. corporations has shifted to the foreign branches of American banks. Moreover, term loans made by U.S. head offices to these European borrowers were allowed to run down in amount. In part these changes reflect bank willingness to comply with the voluntary credit restraint programme. In the late 1960s U.S. head offices began to participate in Eurocurrency loans to corporate borrowers initiated by their London and Continental branches. These loans generally have taken the form of revolving Eurodollar credits and floating rate note issues.

Less Developed Countries

There are four major categories of credits to the less developed countries:

1. Commercial credits to banks and major exporters
2. Foreign exchange credits to governments and central banks extended under stabilisation programmes.
3. Development loans to governments and their instrumentalities
4. Term credits to corporations for capital expenditure purposes

In Mexico the banks and instrumentalities of the government are the principal borrowers from U.S. banks. The *Nacional Financiera*, the largest credit institution in Mexico, provides loans and guarantees on certain categories of credits. In Panama U.S. bank credits finance purchases of ships by companies that use Panama as a 'flag of convenience'.

South America has been plagued with slow growth and economic and political vicissitudes. The economies of several countries have been characterised by inflation, balance of payments crises, currency devaluation, and exchange controls. In Argentina and Brazil credit lines have been cut back during periods of economic difficulty. U.S. banks have confined eligibility of non-bank borrowers to those foreign or major indigenous companies with substantial foreign exchange earnings that would enable repayment of credits – on condition that these earnings be channelled through the lending bank. Also U.S. banks have required that the Central Bank provide loans to banks and to the coffee federation covering production, storage and export shipments.

Central Banks have obtained significant amounts of short-term credit in the form of *dollar exchange acceptances* to meet seasonal and other reserve drains. Also, medium-term credits have been provided for exchange stabilisation purposes. In 1965 a syndicate of banks furnished Peru with $40 million in such credits at the time of a sharp deterioration in that country's balance of payments. In addition, there has been co-operation with the IMF in the granting of credits of this type.

In 1967 the Argentine peso was devalued and a new stabilisation programme adopted by the Argentine government. The IMF provided standby credit facilities of $125 million, and foreign exchange loans of close to $100 million were obtained from U.S. banks.

Interest rates are not used as a means of rationing credit in South America, nor do they fully reflect relative risks. A certain amount of lending has to be undertaken even under the most adverse circumstances if banking relationships are to be maintained.

In the Philippines, as in Latin America, lending consists of (1) exchange stabilisation credits, (2) development loans, (3) foreign trade financing, (4) loans for capital expenditures, and (5) loans to the central bank.

Governments of the less developed countries often exhibit a preference for borrowing from U.S. head offices rather than foreign branches of American banks. One reason is that credits from the head offices of large U.S. banks, especially the New York banks, carry a certain mark of distinction in so far as that borrower's credit-worthiness is concerned, especially in the eyes of the non-banking public.

4.   HEAD OFFICE CO-ORDINATION OF GLOBAL CREDITS

The internationalisation of American bank lending that has taken place since 1955 has compounded the problem of co-ordinating and effectively controlling the extension of foreign credits. Major American banks generally establish currency and country credit limits. Currency limits are designed to control the exposure of the bank resulting from foreign currency revaluations within amounts considered reasonable in light of the size of the bank, its capital accounts, and the importance of foreign business connections. Currency limits are established for those currencies in which the bank may hold assets, and apply to spot and forward positions in that particular currency. Foreign branch operations generally fall within the purview of these limits.

Country limits assure a regional diversification in the global credits made by the bank. Credits made by head office, by Edge Act corporations, and by foreign branches are generally included in the bank's analysis of credits extended to borrowers located in individual countries. The actual limits established for each country are a matter of bank management policy, and reflect the type of representation of the bank in that country, the prospects for increased business connections in the country, and general economic and financial conditions.

Major U.S. banks generally establish global credit limits for domestic and foreign corporate, and foreign bank customers. To make these limits operative, it is necessary that credit records on global borrowers be centralised at head office. Centralisation at the U.S. head office permits the bank's loan review committee, which consists of the senior lending officers of the bank, to more effectively keep abreast of the loans outstanding *vis-à-vis* specific borrowers, as well as have a clearer picture of the overall customer relationship. Moreover, it is possible to more easily analyse the role played by a specific loan to be undertaken by a foreign branch, in light of the global credit allocation of the bank, while at the same time considering the effect this loan may have on the currency and country limits which may be applicable to it.

C.   PROBLEM AREAS IN FOREIGN LENDING

Foreign lending by U.S. banks may be exposed to more diverse risks than domestic lending. Moreover, foreign lending is subject to more governmental pressures and influence than domestic lending. The role of government can be especially important in providing basic and supplementary credits to stimulate exports, and in guaranteeing or insuring foreign loans and investments made by banks and business investors.

Since foreign lending involves the assumption of risks not generally present when domestic loans are made, the decision framework faced by the U.S. banks is more complex and involves problems and policy resolutions not ordinarily encountered on domestic credits. These include (1) problems and policy decisions on risk exposure; (2) problems of adapting credits to the international economic policies of U.S. and foreign governments while at the same time maximising customer services; (3) policies on an appropriate decision structure for foreign credits; and (4) policies to guide the choice of alternative implementation options on foreign credits.[13]

Through their foreign lending American banks have played an important positive role in at least four distinct connections. First, they have assisted in financing a general economic expansion in world business. Foreign loans by U.S. banks have supported business investment spending in many parts of the globe where financial market facilities and banking services are scarce, and where alternative sources of capital funds would have been lacking or available only at far higher cost. Second, through their acceptance credits and other loans and advances U.S. banks have contributed to a healthy increase in world exports, originating from the United States as well as from other countries. Third, American banks have become important channels of credit for U.S. and foreign multinational corporations. Bank credits, money transfer services, and other facilities provided by major U.S. banks have facilitated the growing activities of multinational corporations. Finally, stabilisation credits and other loans made to a number of less developed countries have contributed to the stability of the international monetary system, inspired confidence in the viability of existing exchange rate relationships, and helped avoid the imposition of trade and capital controls that would have reversed gains previously achieved in the volume of international transactions.

In the sections which follow we discuss the voluntary foreign credit restraint programme of the U.S. government, the adequacy of foreign lending and the role it plays today, the special problems of financing capital equipment exports, and the measures available to banks to reduce or minimise foreign credit risks.

1. VOLUNTARY FOREIGN CREDIT RESTRAINT

Beginning in 1963 the United States adopted a number of measures aimed at strengthening the balance of payments through restraints on foreign lending and investment. The first step in this direction was the Interest Equalisation Tax (IET). The IET was designed to reduce the attractiveness of the New York capital market to foreign borrowers by imposing a tax on U.S. purchases of foreign securities. In 1964 outstanding foreign credits of banks in the United States rose by more than $2 billion. Extensions of short-term credits to foreigners and acceptance credits accelerated throughout 1964, and late in that year bank commitments on new long-term loans were being made at nearly double the rate of a year earlier.[14]

A flood of lending abroad by U.S. banks was a major element

in the record $6 billion outflow of U.S. private capital in 1964.[15] This upsurge in capital outflows offset an increased export surplus in that year and prevented any improvement in the U.S. payments position. Facing this situation President Johnson sent to the Congress on 10 February 1965 a message proposing a comprehensive programme aimed at achieving a substantial improvement in the balance of payments position. A major part of this programme provided for a voluntary foreign credit restraint (VFCR) on the part of U.S. banks engaged in foreign lending. Administration of this part of the President's programme was placed in the hands of the Federal Reserve System, and shortly after the Presidential message, the Board of Governors through the Federal Reserve Banks issued guidelines to be followed by banks and non-bank financial institutions in their foreign lending activities.

A basic objective of the VFCR as originally proposed in 1965 was to insure that bank credit to non-residents rose by no more than 5 per cent of the amount outstanding at the end of 1964. The base was subject to downward adjustment by an amount equivalent to participations in individual loans arranged by the Export-Import Bank or made with Export-Import Bank guarantees. Such loans also were excluded from the 5 per cent target. Further, an escape clause was provided for individual banks to allow their foreign loans to run in excess of the 5 per cent target as a result of binding commitments entered into prior to announcement of the VFCR, the extension of bona fide export credits, or the extension of credits at the request of an agency of the U.S. government.[16]

The *Guidelines* published by the Board of Governors spelled out a number of loan priorities to be followed by banks including export credits and loans to less developed countries. Banks were urged to avoid restrictive lending policies that would unduly burden countries such as Canada and Japan which were heavily dependent on U.S. financing, and the United Kingdom which at the time was suffering from balance of payments difficulties. In 1968 Canada was exempted from the bank lending guidelines when the Canadian government took steps to insure that Canadian financial institutions would not serve as a 'pass through' for U.S. funds.

Various types of bank credits to advanced countries were

indicated that could be cut back with the least adverse side-effects. These included (1) credits to finance third-country trade, (2) credits to finance local currency expenditures outside the United States, (3) credits to finance fixed or working capital requirements, and (4) all other non-export credits to those developed countries that are not suffering from balance of payments difficulties.

The guidelines issued in 1965 made no provision for banks with no previous foreign lending experience and therefore no foreign lending base, except for bona fide export loans to foreigners in 'reasonable amounts'. In the case of banks whose previous foreign business had consisted almost entirely of export financing, 'reasonable amounts in excess of the target from time to time would not be considered in conflict with the programme'. However, these banks were expected to exert every effort to keep their foreign lending within their respective ceilings.

Foreign branches and Edge Act corporations were discussed briefly in the 1965 guidelines. U.S. banks were admonished against using foreign branches to avoid the credit restraint programme. However, it was pointed out that these foreign branches 'have independent sources of funds in the countries in which they are located' as well as from third countries, and that the programme is not designed to hamper their lending activities 'in so far as the funds utilized are derived from foreign sources . . .'.[17] Edge Act and Agreement corporations were included in the programme from its inception. Foreign loans and investments of these corporations could be combined with those of the parent bank for purposes of complying with the programme, or separate targets may be set for the parent bank and its subsidiary. In cases of Edge Act corporations that have not undertaken a significant volume of loans and investments, they have been permitted to take as a lending base their paid-in capital and surplus, up to $2.5 million.

Banks have been advised that under the guidelines they should avoid granting credit to domestic customers if the result would be to aid the latter in making foreign loans or investments inconsistent with the programme. Finally, banks that have placed their own funds abroad for short-term investment, including U.S. dollar deposits outside the United States, should refrain from increasing such deposits or investments, and even undertake to reduce them. While the guidelines have not called for reductions in working balances maintained with foreign correspondents, such balances are and have been considered claims on non-residents for purposes of the programme.

The voluntary programme has influenced the structure and growth of U.S. international banking through at least three avenues, including incentives for establishing foreign branches, relative advantages of organising and expanding Edge Act corporations, and the activities of small banks which are newcomers to the field of international banking and foreign lending. After 1965 American banks with modest or substantial international operations have become increasingly more aware of the advantages inherent in possessing one or more foreign branches. These advantages have been expanding in scope and possible influence as the VFCR programme has been extended. These advantages include the ability of parent banks to continue to expand foreign services for their customers, including a key advantage in possessing the ability to provide offshore financing not subject to the credit restraint guidelines. We should note that the existence of foreign branches permits U.S. head offices to sell foreign loan assets to these branches, thereby providing yet another element in the options available to U.S. banks in complying with the VFCR. In general the establishment of new Edge corporations does not result in an expansion of lending ceilings under the guidelines. Edge Act or Agreement corporations established after 3 March 1965 share the guideline ceilings of their parent banks.[18] In cases of one-bank owned corporations the Edge affiliate and its parent bank may employ individual ceilings or combined ceilings. In cases of multi-bank owned corporations foreign lending ceilings are separate from those of parent banks, and are related to the adjusted ceiling as of 30 November 1969.[19] It would appear that greater incentives to establish or expand Edge Act corporations would operate under the guidelines in cases where banking functions predominated as compared with financing functions, where export credits comprise a major portion of the foreign loans extended by the Edge corporation, and where the Edge affiliate is more involved in extending loans and investments in less developed countries than in developed countries.

It has been asserted that the activities of small banks in the foreign lending field have been inhibited as a result of the VFCR programme. The reasons for this assertion lie in the manner of calculating the foreign lending base in the original version of the VFCR. In the early years of the programme small newcomer banks to the field had no foreign loan base and had to petition the Federal Reserve authorities for special leeway. In short, the pattern of allocating foreign loan ceilings became frozen in the programme.

Four changes incorporated in the 1970 phase of the VFCR programme brought about a substantial advance toward improving the status of small and newcomer banks. These changes increased aggregate ceilings under the guidelines from $10.1 billion to $11.4 billion, introduced separate Export Term-Loan Ceilings, related loan ceilings of individual banks to their total assets rather than previously outstanding loans, and made special provision for foreign lending ceilings for banks which had no ceilings under previous guidelines. The Export Term-Loan Ceilings aggregated $1.3 billion and were made separate from the General Ceilings (which totalled $10.1 billion).

Interest in the possible effects from the VFCR programme points toward its influence on U.S. exports. In 1970 an inquiry was directed at determining whether the restraint programme had led to denial of export credit requested of a bank on behalf of foreign customers and whether the denial had in turn led to loss of an export sale. In October 1970 the Board of Governors sent sample questionnaires to each of the twelve Federal Reserve Banks with a request that they obtain information on this question from VFCR reporting banks and exporters in their respective Districts. Of the close to 170 banks that report under the VFCR programme, 113 were included in the survey and 109 banks responded. The four banks that did not respond had outstanding credit subject to the VFCR of $2.4 million. The information sought in this study referred to refusals of credit by banks, and particulars of loan requests in cases of refusal.

Nearly all of the responding banks indicated that they had not refused loans in 1970 because of the VFCR ceilings. Only seven banks reported having refused a total of eleven requests for export financing during the first ten months of that year amounting to about $2.75 million.[20] The outstanding foreign claims of these seven banks represent less than 3 per cent of total VFCR outstandings and only one of the seven banks had VFCR outstandings over $100 million.

Five of the seven banks indicated that their refusals were attributable to lack of room under their General Ceilings, two stated that their substantial outstanding short-term claims on residents of developed countries prevented their making the export loan. One of the banks stated it was purposely maintaining some unused credits to accommodate new customers. Five of the seven banks had foreign branches to which other outstanding foreign claims could have been transferred to provide room under the General Ceiling. Most of the loans refused were for capital equipment going to less developed countries. Three of the requests were for short-term lines of credit. Follow-up questionnaires to five exporters actually denied bank credit indicated that the export transaction had been completed.

In addition to the five exporters specifically identified as having been denied bank credit, questionnaires were sent to exporters who had made sales involving Eximbank financing or FCIA insurance. Of the 120 exporters who responded to this survey, eight indicated they had been denied credit because of the VFCR. Two of the exporters did not identify specific transactions but simply asserted that the VFCR had been a problem. The remaining exporters reported that the sales eventually were made in all but three cases.

According to the Federal Reserve study, the close to 170 VFCR banks had substantial leeway late in 1970 with which to expand export credits and non-export credits. This leeway amounted to $1.25 billion under both the General Ceilings and Export Term-Loan Ceilings. In cases where individual banks possess no leeway, they may make a loan to a domestic exporter who can extend credit to the foreign buyer, they may arrange for an Eximbank guarantee or FCIA insurance which exempts the credit from the VFCR limits, or they may make the loan from a foreign branch or transfer it to a foreign branch after originally booking it at head office.

While the Federal Reserve study conducted in 1970 suggests that very few foreign loans were turned down in that year due to the VFCR, and that the impact on U.S. exports might have been very modest, several questions remain unanswered. First, what number of export credit requests have never reached U.S. banks due to 'general knowledge' regarding the foreign lending ceilings and the need for banks to comply with the guidelines? Second, the nature of the relationship of the bank and the customer is such that formal requests often are not made for specific credit approvals unless the prospective applicant is reasonably certain that approval will be made by the bank. Unfortunately, existence of the ceilings and the resulting need to ration foreign loan funds on the part of some banks inject another dimension of uncertainty into these arrangements. The study and its findings do not reflect the extent to which some U.S. banks may have failed to expand their foreign lending activities over an extended number of years due to the existence of the VFCR ceilings and the uncertainties surrounding their continuation and possible revision.

2. FINANCING U.S. EXPORTS

Adequate financing of U.S. exports poses a number of problems for U.S. international banking, which reflect on the ability of private commercial banks motivated by considerations of profit to perform in the public interest. Problems which have persisted within the area of export financing include the need for and role of public institutions in supplementing private export credit, government controls and credit restraints on foreign lending, special problems in financing capital equipment exports, and the tendency for international competition in export finance to accelerate.

The Export-Import Bank is the largest single institution whose purpose it is to assist in the financing of U.S. exports. Since its inception in 1934 up to fiscal year 1970 Eximbank authorised loans totalling $24.3 billion, covering a wide variety of types of credits including short-term and medium-term direct loans and participation financing, relending credits for non-U.S. financial institutions, discount loans to commercial banks, aviation export financing, and nuclear power financing.

Eximbank resources can be utilised by U.S. banks and exporters in several ways, including joint or participation financing and the commercial bank export loan discount programme. Under participation financing the Export-Import Bank will accept a part of the buyer's obligation in co-operation with one or more private financial institutions. The private institution charges its regular rates, and if necessary the Eximbank will guarantee the lender against political and commercial risk. Also, Eximbank accepts the later maturities, giving the buyer the benefit of the lower interest rate resulting from the mix of the Bank's 6 per cent rate and the prevailing market rates charged by banks and other lending institutions.

The second important operation involving direct use of Eximbank resources is the commercial bank discount programme. Under this programme the Export-Import Bank makes loans to commercial banks on the basis of outstanding loan obligations. The purpose of this programme is to provide a safety valve, or emergency outlet, for commercial banks who from time to time need relief from a shortage of liquidity.[21]

During fiscal year 1970 the Bank undertook a review of the commercial bank discount loan facility. As a result of this review, in October 1970 Eximbank announced the following changes in this programme. First, the discount facility would be made more flexible on maximum maturities and repayment terms. Eximbank will extend terms on discount loans beyond the previous five year limit, and repayment will be tailored to the specific needs of U.S. banks. Second, Eximbank will purchase notes issued by foreign buyers which have been sold by the U.S. exporter to a commercial bank. By purchasing the note from the U.S. commercial bank rather than merely making a direct advance to the bank, Eximbank accomplishes the following. The bank's debt level is lowered, thereby providing the bank with additional flexibility in terms of outstanding liabilities relative to reserves. A third revision in the discount facility permits Eximbank to make its commitments available to commercial banks for periods extending beyond a year. Often it takes longer for a U.S. company to produce capital goods ordered by a foreign buyer.

In 1970 the Board of Governors of the Federal Reserve System undertook an inquiry to determine the portion of foreign lending by U.S. banks consisting of export credits.

Under the VFCR programme banks and other financial institutions had been asked to give priority to loans to finance U.S. exports. Considerable attention has focused on the scope open to individual banks under the guidelines to engage in export financing, and the net effect of such financing on merchandise exports. It has been recognised by the Board that unrestrained U.S. export credit might expand without being accompanied by a matching increase in exports.[22] In such cases foreign credits could increase more rapidly than merchandise exports and the U.S. balance of payments would suffer.

On the whole, the findings may be regarded as indicative of the share of export credit to total bank credit to foreigners, of average maturities of export credit, and of the amount of exports covered by bank credits to foreigners. Moreover, the results indicate some differences among large, medium, and small banks in the emphasis given to export financing.[23]

The survey, conducted by the Federal Reserve Banks, directed a number of questions to major U.S. foreign lending banks and a sample of smaller banks. Seventy-two banks responded, including the twenty largest. These banks cover 93 per cent of the outstanding foreign credits subject to the VFCR General Ceilings. Coverage was limited to U.S. bank credit extended to foreigners and either subject to VFCR ceilings or exempted from the VFCR due to exemptions applicable to Eximbank and Department of Defence related credit. Among the exclusions from scope of the survey were (1) U.S. bank lending to U.S. residents, (2) U.S. bank credits extended to a foreigner under a general line of credit which could be drawn in part to finance U.S. exports, (3) credits to residents of Canada, and (4) credit extended by foreign branches of U.S. banks.

For the seventy-two banks which reported, 17 per cent of their loans subject to the VFCR General Ceiling or Export-Term-Loan Ceiling consisted of export credits. The relative importance of export credits varied among these reporting banks, with seventeen banks which had $100 million or more in foreign loans under VFCR ceilings reporting that 16 per cent of these loans were export credits, and the other fifty-five banks indicating that 22 per cent of their loans under these ceilings were for financing exports. Until 1971 export credits which were Export-Import Bank guaranteed, FCIA insured, or Department of Defence guaranteed were exempt from VFCR ceilings. (In 1971 all export credits were made exempt from the VFCR ceilings.) When these exempted export credits are added to the total credits subject to VFCR ceilings, the ratio of export credits to aggregate foreign credits of reporting banks rises from 17 per cent to 23 per cent.[24] On this expanded basis the ratio of export credits to aggregate foreign credits for the seventeen largest U.S. foreign lending banks is 22 per cent, compared with 28 per cent for the remaining fifty-five smaller banks.

The shares of export credit in total foreign lending varied considerably from bank to bank, ranging from zero to almost 80 per cent. For the seventeen largest banks with $100 million or more in outstanding foreign loans subject to VFCR ceilings, the variation was moderate, between 7 per cent and 28 per cent. The findings further indicated that during 1970 the seventy-two reporting banks extended approximately $3.8 billion in export credits subject to VFCR ceilings, and that extrapolating the experience of the seventy-two reporting banks to all U.S. banks (the 167 VFCR banks accounted for roughly nine-tenths of all U.S. bank claims on foreigners except Canadians) would result in a total export credit figure of $5.2 billion. This represents about 16 per cent of U.S. merchandise exports in 1970.

The findings of this survey are significant in at least two respects. First, they point to the opportunity available to U.S. banks to allocate a somewhat larger share of foreign credits to export financing. Second, the findings suggest that a relatively small share (16 per cent) of U.S. export is financed by U.S. commercial banks, leaving the remainder financed by other sources or paid for in straight cash transactions (e.g., open book account, or direct investment inter-corporate transactions).

Unfortunately the Federal Reserve study did not go into the specific question of financing capital equipment exports, which is a special problem area within the general field of export credits. The difficulties inherent in providing adequate financing for capital equipment exports have been disguised, partly as a result of increased international competition to support exports by means of providing more liberal export credits. During the 1960s there were substantial increases in export credit by most industrialised countries for three interrelated reasons. These are as follows:[25]

1. The proportion of world trade represented by capital goods has been increasing.
2. A large proportion of the demand for capital goods has come from the developing countries which have limited access to alternative sources of finance.
3. Balance of payments problems of the industrial countries have led them to seek to stimulate exports by offering more generous credit terms, especially in the area of capital goods.

In a study published in 1966 Nehrt pointed to three factors which affect the competitiveness of U.S. exporters of capital goods, especially in developing countries. These are the attitudes of company export managers, the ability of capital equipment exporters to self-finance export credit, and the availability of such credit from outside sources.[26] Prior to 1955 export managers enjoyed sellers' markets. According to Nehrt too many of these men still follow the old policies of selling their exports on a lettter of credit or ninety-day note basis. At the same time European suppliers look for every possible source of credit.

In the past U.S. companies have tended to be far more liquid than their counterparts in Europe and Japan, and have also enjoyed access to much more efficient domestic money and capital markets. For these reasons many U.S. capital equipment exporters are in a position to self-finance their export credit. However, smaller companies cannot do this, since they lack the established reputation that would enable them to obtain extensive financing from their banks or from the domestic financial markets. Therefore, the smaller company must rely more heavily for export financing on U.S. commercial banks, or other sources of export finance.

The third item influencing capital equipment exports, medium-term export credit, is generally available from three major sources, which include the Export-Import Bank, U.S. commercial banks, and non-bank sources including factoring houses and special export finance firms.[27] During the 1960s emphasis shifted away from Eximbank direct lending in the medium-term credit area to its guaranty programme, which makes available full faith and credit guarantees of the U.S. government to U.S. commercial banks and exporters who provide credits to foreign buyers. Nevertheless, the Export-Import Bank still provides a substantial amount of credit each fiscal year, most of which falls into the medium-term category. For example, in fiscal year 1970 the Bank provided $1.6 billion in credits and made $2.2 billion in new loan authorisations. One-fourth of the dollar amount of new loan authorisations in that year financed the sale of jet aircraft and parts. The shift in emphasis from medium-term direct loans to provision of guarantees to banks and exporters extending such credits has resulted in the development of an efficient guaranty system, which is discussed in the next section of this chapter.

As recently as 1960 only a few U.S. commercial banks had entered the field of medium-term lending to finance capital equipment exports.[28] At that time U.S. banks expressed a preference to make direct loans to the American exporter, rather than provide export credit to foreign purchasers. Moreover, some major banks were attempting to interest well-known customers in the use of Eximbank export credit facilities. Between 1960 and 1963 there was an appreciable increase in bank activity in providing medium-term export financing. Credit market conditions were easing in the United States in this period, which probably accounts for the increased interest of many banks in this category of lending. During the early 1960s several Edge Act financing corporations undertook term lending, in part associated with providing export credits to finance capital equipment sales.[29]

Effective in 1970 the Board of Governors of the Federal Reserve System announced the creation of new Export Term-Loan Ceilings under the VFCR of $1.3 billion. Further liberalisation came in 1971 when Export Term-Loan Ceilings for commercial banks were set at one-half of 1 per cent of their asset holdings at year-end 1968. Of critical importance in shaping the overall financial competitiveness of U.S. capital equipment exports is the extent to which other exporting countries have provided credit terms which are better than those available in the United States. For example, in 1966 it was reported that five leading industrial nations provide distinct advantages for their domestic exporting industries where export credit insurance, rediscount facilities, and cost of credit comparisons are made with those available in this country. The export credit insurance programme is owned or financially backed by the government in all five of these countries (United Kingdom, Japan, France, Germany, and Italy), and all but Italy provide coverage against both political and commercial risks. In Italy the insurance covers only political risks. There is considerable variation in the five countries in the degree to which commercial banks become involved in the financing of medium-term export credit. In Italy the banks act as agents for the exporter. However, the Japanese Export-Import Bank participates in the financing of nearly all of Japan's medium-term exports. In the remaining three countries there exists a relatively high degree of bank participation, either because of the availability of rediscounting privileges on export paper, or due to the opportunity to obtain insurance on the credit.

Four of these countries have a government supported rediscount facility, which makes it possible for the commerical banks to rediscount medium-term export paper.[30] Italy possesses a publicly-owned financing organisation, Mediocredito, whose sole purpose is to rediscount medium-term paper. Mediocredito only rediscounts insured credits. The Bank of England began to discount this type of paper in 1961. The Deutsche Bundesbank rediscounts medium-term paper for German commercial banks, and in addition a consortium of major commercial banks functions as a private rediscount facility for member banks (Ausfuhrkredit, A.G., better known as AKA). In France the Banque de France or the Credit National rediscount insured medium-term export credits.[31]

3. RISK SHARING AND REDUCTION

American banks employ a wide range of techniques and measures to reduce or minimise the assumption of risk in foreign lending. These measures include loan selection and structuring, participation in loan agreements with other lenders, use of guarantees and insurance, and minimising exchange rate exposure by denominating a major part of their foreign lending in U.S. dollars.

Loan selection and structuring represents the first line of

defence employed by American banks in their foreign lending. Credit risks are carefully analysed and specific loan limits are applied. In loan operations in the less developed countries the demand for credit often is so large that only the highest quality borrowers are able to obtain loans from U.S. banks. In some cases American banks provide link credits, which are loans or deposits in foreign banks which in turn extend loans to intended borrowers in the same country. Advantages to the U.S. banks in such arrangements include maintaining better relationships with the 'link' bank, extending better quality credits to banks rather than credits to commercial or manufacturing borrowers, and strengthening the possibility of building foreign correspondent bank connection.

The above is not meant to imply that foreign lending is devoid of problems or risks special to the international nature of the credits extended. Eurocurrency loan and deposit activities of American banks have, at times, been criticised due to the volatility of this market and the emphasis given to 'interest rate banking'. Eurocurrency operations and related short-term flows of internationally mobile funds make it possible for relatively small banks with limited resources to take advantage of float and delayed clearing situations, and earn a handsome profit on a highly leveraged financial structure. In one instance a European bank reportedly capitalised at $13 million asked a large New York bank to make $300 million in payments for it in one day. The New York bank immediately ceased handling this account, which carried a $100 thousand deposit with the New York institution.[32] In many cases adequate check of a corporate borrower's credit standing is difficult if not impossible. In some cases U.S. bankers may not feel disposed to expend the energy and resources necessary to complete an exhaustive credit investigation of a foreign borrower.[33] If the loan does not carry adequate collateral, in terms of marketability and margin, creditors may have to accept whatever collateral can be assembled in case of default. In the case of a bank failure in Ecuador the forty foreign creditors were given shares of the reorganised bank and five year notes as collateral for rolling over their loans.[34]

Banks attempt to limit their risks by establishing country and currency limits to their foreign lending. In addition, U.S.

banks maintain a careful review of the balance of payments situation in each of the countries where they hold substantial loan accounts. An adverse change in the balance of payments and foreign exchange position of a given country can result in loan defaults even though debtors in that country have every desire to meet their commitments. With respect to currency risks, prevailing U.S. banking policy is to eliminate all currency risks beyond those actually required to conduct an active foreign exchange operation in which minimal positions in foreign currencies may be taken. This policy has been implemented by denominating virtually all head office loans in dollars and two-thirds of foreign branch assets in dollars (where the borrower assumes the currency risk); denominating loans in currencies on which forward cover is available; or through 'parallel transactions' where the U.S. bank functions as a money broker on a fee basis.

In their foreign lending U.S. banks have made extensive use of formal and informal loan participation arrangements. These include the organisation of international loan syndicates in which the bank participants provide credits to government agencies for stabilisation purposes and to industrial corporations for planned expansion, acquisition of portions of floating rate Eurocurrency note issues, the note issues of regional development banks, and the short maturities of World Bank bonds.

In 1970 several major U.S. banks participated with the International Finance Corporation (IFC) in assembling financing packages to support the expansion of industrial production in developing countries. In one case a $29 million financing was arranged to help establish an integrated petrochemical products plant in Brazil, Poliolefines, S.A. In addition to subscribing for $2.3 million of a total $11.4 million share capital offering, IFC and several other investors provided $17.6 million in loan capital. Bank of America, New York provided $2.5 million of the loan capital, and the two U.S. institutions participated in IFC's commitment. These were Bamerical International Financial Corp., a subsidiary of Bank of America, California; and Manufacturers Hanover Trust Co. of New York.[35] In a larger financing package, IFC, the World Bank, and several other investors including Fiat S.p.A. assembled a $105.8 million package which is expected to double the production of Yugoslavia's integrated automobile manufacturer. Girard International Investment Corp., a subsidiary of Girard Trust Bank of Philadelphia, and Franklin International Corporation, a subsidiary of Franklin National Bank of New York, participated in IFC's commitment.

'U.S. banks have minimised the risks on foreign lending by obtaining guarantees or insurance coverage on their overseas credits. Guarantees have been obtained from parent corporations of foreign affiliates, foreign banks, the Export-Import Bank, foreign governments, and the U.S. Agency for International Development (AID) Private Investment Centre. Insurance coverage has been provided through the FCIA-Export-Import Bank programme.

U.S. export credits have not been guaranteed or insured by government sponsored export credit programmes to the same extent as in other countries. Writing in 1965, Francis X. Scafuro, Vice President of Bank of America, New York, reported that less than 5 per cent of U.S. merchandise exports were covered by Eximbank and FCIA guarantees and insurance. This compared with coverages of 25 per cent of British exports (by the Export Credits Guarantee Department –ECGD), 11 per cent of French exports, 10 per cent of German exports, and 50 per cent of Canada's exports.[36]

A substantial part of foreign lending by U.S. banks consists of loans to overseas affiliates of U.S. corporations. In such cases the American bank will attempt to obtain a guarantee from the parent company for repayment of the loan. In cases of loans made to foreign nationals, particularly in Latin America and Japan, guarantees are often obtained from indigenous commercial banks or government agencies including central banks. The reasons for U.S. bank reliance on government or bank guarantees are fairly clear. In many areas of the world there exists close government supervision of credits and exchange availability on private sector loans. Second, there can exist innumerable difficulties and costs in assessing the credit status of many foreign companies. Finally, correspondent relations have dominated the international credit operations of most U.S. banks engaged actively in international banking.

Credits extended by U.S. banks in the less developed

countries are likely to be protected by the guarantees of U.S. agencies. However, existing guarantee and insurance programmes covering export credits extended by U.S. banks and exporters also cover credits extended to borrowers in developed countries as well. At present there are three broad government operated or sponsored guarantee and investment programmes affording protection to bank and non-bank foreign lenders. These include programmes of the Export-Import Bank, the Foreign Credit Insurance Association (FCIA), and the AID Private Investment Centre.

The Export-Import Bank guarantee programme began in the late 1950s. Any U.S. commercial bank or Edge Act corporation is eligible for guarantees under the Commercial Bank Exporter Guarantee programme. These guarantees provide protection against credit and political risks of non-payment, and are available to the commercial bank upon its purchase of the foreign buyer's promissory notes without recourse to the U.S. exporter. Under this programme the commercial bank bears the commercial credit risk on the early maturities of notes and the Eximbank guarantee covers the commercial credit risks on the remaining instalments. The Eximbank covers the political risks on all maturities of notes associated with the financing. Eximbank charges on guarantees vary, based on the length of the credit period and the classification accorded the country of import because of economic and political conditions. During the period 1966–70 new export guarantees provided for commercial banks by the Export-Import Bank ranged between $700 million and $900 million annually.

In 1962 the Eximbank spun off part of the export credit protection it had been providing into the private sector. The Foreign Credit Insurance Association was formed, initially representing a small number of insurance companies able to underwrite export credit risks relating to commercial and political developments overseas. The FCIA does not insure this credit by itself, but operates in partnership with the Eximbank. The FCIA insures commercial risks up to specified dollar amount limits, beyond which point the Export-Import Bank and FCIA share the risk on a fifty-fifty basis. The entire political risk is insured by Eximbank, although FCIA functions as an agent in writing the individual policies.

The Private Investment Centre of the Agency for International Development (AID) administers programmes designed to promote, insure and finance U.S. private investments in the less developed countries. These programmes are designed to stimulate productive investments rather than finance U.S. exports *per se*. However, AID's extended risk guarantees of private U.S. investments can provide less developed country borrowers with the support required to obtain U.S. private loans for the purchase of U.S. goods and services. The AID investment guarantee programme covers commercial as well as political risks.

4. PROPOSALS FOR REFORM

Increasingly throughout the 1960s and into the early 1970s, U.S. public policy has given greater weight to proposals for improving export potential, with a view toward strengthening the balance of payments. In this section we examine several of these proposals which have a close connection with the structure and operating framework of U.S. international banking.

It has been well stated that there is need for a Federal Reserve type of central rediscounting facility for export paper.[37] A facility of this type would round out the U.S. system of providing international trade credit, as well as make it possible for U.S. exporters to provide credit on terms equivalent to other countries which already possess a centralised rediscount facility.

Closely related to the first proposal is that which suggests lengthening the maturities of banker's acceptances which may be created by member banks. This would require amendment of the Federal Reserve Act, as well as revision of the pertinent Board of Governors regulation. Longer-term drafts with maturities of up to five years could be drawn on and accepted by U.S. banks, broadening the role of banker's acceptances and facilitating the flow of medium-term money into export financing.

Various proposals have been offered to enlarge the activities of the Export-Import Bank in the direction of export financing. In general the Bank has been criticised for its strict credit policies, and tendency to earn substantial profits each fiscal year. Such criticisms are difficult to resolve in the context of an abbreviated discussion. Several considerations are involved, including the effect of 'profits' on continuing Congressional appropriations, from what type operations the profits result, and whether in fact the administration of credit and guarantee programmes can be so finely tuned as to generate a close to break-even position for Eximbank.

A fourth proposal, that U.S. international banks be encouraged by the government to co-operate in a joint venture to create a super export finance rediscount corporation, has been approximately realised. An original proposal described by Scafuro in 1965 called for a super Edge Act corporation jointly owned by a number of U.S. banks, which could sell its own bonds or debentures to tap the money market for funds with which to purchase insured export receivables from banks.[38] In 1971 the final steps were taken to organise the Private Export Funding Corp. (PEFCO). Formed as a result of a Dillon, Read study commissioned by the Bankers Association for Foreign Trade (BAFT), PEFCO is expected to become a major factor in the financing of American exports. The basic purpose of the company is to mobilise heretofore untapped sources of private capital to help finance U.S. exports.[39] PEFCO purchases medium and long-term financial obligations generated by U.S. exports that have been guaranteed by the Export-Import Bank.[40] Early in 1971 forty-six major commercial banks subscribed for $12.7 million of PEFCO's shares. Prior arrangements included obtaining Federal Reserve agreement that U.S. banks could make equity investments in PEFCO through their Edge Act subsidiaries and that participating banks without Edge units of their own would join a communally-owned Edge corporation established for that purpose.[41] Additional funds for PEFCO operations will be obtained by the company selling its own obligations in the private financial markets.

9 Relations with Domestic and International Financial Markets

In recent years the financial markets of the world have become more closely linked together. Three major forces have operated to bind these markets together including the global corporation, the universality of the dollar, and the ability and ingenuity of the international banks and investment banking concerns.[1] The intertwining of world financial markets is reflected clearly by the manner in which markets abroad felt the effects from the severe credit restraint in the United States in 1968–9, and from the international currency crises of 1971 and 1973. The purpose of this chapter is to provide an analysis of the interplay between the domestic and international financial markets and the global operations of internationally oriented banks. Moreover, this chapter examines the role played by New York as an international financial centre; its relation to international banking activities; and the offshore investment banking operations of U.S. banks.

A. NEW YORK AS AN INTERNATIONAL FINANCIAL CENTRE

1. REQUIREMENTS OF AN INTERNATIONAL FINANCIAL CENTRE

New York functions as a clearing house for a large volume and variety of international transactions. It operates as a bank for the entire world, as an underwriter for new issues from developing countries, and as a stock exchange for trading in shares of well-known foreign corporations. Moreover, New York provides financing for many types of commercial transactions, and foreign exchange facilities for clearing international payments.

New York has served as an international financial centre because it possesses a number of favourable features. These include:

1. The universality of the dollar.
2. A variety of financial institutions and banks, possessing considerable capacity for servicing international payments.
3. The substantial demand for dollar funds.
4. The United States provides relative freedom of international transactions for residents as well as non-residents. This is especially important where the centre is equipped to service the underwriting, secondary trading, and investment management needs of an international clientele. In this regard the United States suffers several modest shortcomings, including the Interest Equalisation Tax and the restraints upon direct investment outflows and commercial bank foreign lending.

2. FUNCTIONS PERFORMED

Not until after World War II did New York develop rapidly in servicing the financial needs of the rest of the world. New York does not possess the long-standing international orientation of London, although this is fast changing. Moreover, New York's role as an international centre has been conditioned by its larger role as financier to the nation. New York grew as a financial centre by financing internal development by means of foreign capital inflows, London by financing external development via the export of capital.[2] New York's pre-eminence rests solidly on the usefulness of the dollar as a world currency. By contrast, London's importance and comeback in the 1960s has been related to the special financial institutions and facilities developed for foreign use. New York's usefulness as an international money market is due in no small part to its massive size, and only to a much smaller degree to the development of special facilities for international use. Not until after 1960 did New York become an effective provider of short-term and long-term credits to the rest of the world, and aside from loans to Canada and the World Bank, there was only a modest net flow of capital into foreign issues in the decade 1946–55.

During the first decade and a half after World War II New York's unchallenged leadership as an international financial centre rested heavily on the strength of the dollar, the large volume of savings generated domestically, the breadth and depth of the money and capital market facilities in the United States, and the well-developed foreign exchange market and trading facilities. After 1960 a number of changes took place including a rapid increase in short-term bank credits to foreign borrowers, and acceleration in foreign bond new issue activity, increased scope for short-term investments by non-residents in the New York market, and development of a substantial two-way traffic in portfolio investment in bonds and stocks through New York.

The functions performed by New York as an international financial centre may be summarised as follows:

1. It provides opportunity for short-term deposit and investment of liquid funds denominated in U.S. dollars. This may take the form of foreign owned bank deposits of various maturities, and marketable instruments including government securities, commercial paper and banker's acceptances.
2. It provides investment outlets for long-term funds, within the context of broad, relatively stable stock and bond markets.
3. It affords an adequate variety of financing alternatives

for business and other types of borrowers, both short-term and medium-term. This may include loans provided by banks, commercial finance houses, and other institutional lenders.

4. It possesses adequate new issues and secondary trading market facilities. This includes a wide range of underwriting, stock brokerage, bond dealer, specialist institutions, and stock exchange firms.

5. It affords adequate opportunities for financial intermediation and security substitution. Thus, investors may purchase bank deposits, investment company shares, life insurance policy claims, and other liabilities of financial intermediaries.

6. It provides clearing and money transfer facilities for domestic and foreign business firms and investors. As an entrepôt New York is able to take funds provided by foreign lenders, 'turn them around' and make them available to foreign borrowers on reasonable and attractive terms.

7. Finally, New York makes available a relatively low cost hedging mechanism, through forward markets in major currencies, through commodities futures contracts, and through various types of option contracts available on securities transactions.

B. NEW YORK AS AN INTERNATIONAL MONEY MARKET

1. GROWTH AND INTERNATIONAL ORIENTATION

New York stands at the centre of the money market in the United States. Apart from the Federal Reserve, the two groups of institutions that represent the most important elements in the New York money market are the large commercial banks and dealers in government securities. The principal market sectors include those for U.S. Treasury obligations, and federal funds. Important subsidiary markets include those for commercial paper, banker's acceptances, and negotiable certificates of deposit.

The Treasury bill market occupies a special place of

prominence in the money market. This is due to the large volume outstanding, representing nearly half of money market instruments in dollar value. The largest holders of Treasury bills are the Federal Reserve Banks, commercial banks, state and local governments, and non-financial corporations. During the 1960s the share of bills held by commercial banks declined due partly to the emergence of other investment outlets, the lengthened maturities of bank deposit liabilities, and the high level of loan demand that persisted in the late 1960s.[3] The market for government securities is served by approximately twenty non-bank and bank dealers. The most active market is in Treasury bills, representing over 75 per cent of the total dollar volume of trading in all government securities. New offerings of bills are made weekly on the basis of competitive bids.

Commercial banks can adjust their cash reserves by participating in the inter-bank market for federal funds. Briefly stated, federal funds are sight claims on the Federal Reserve Banks.

Claims and cheques drawn by member banks on the Federal Reserve Banks become immediately available funds for replenishing the reserves of member banks. By contrast, funds in the form of cheques drawn on commercial banks become available at the Federal Reserve Banks on the following business day, when clearing house balances are settled on the books of the Federal Reserve Banks. Federal funds are immediately available to the purchaser, whereas Clearing House funds become available only the next day. Growth in the volume of transactions has brought a number of major banks into the market as dealers in federal funds, 'accommodating' correspondents and smaller banks by operating on both sides of the market. Experience in the market during the fifties and sixties has provided large U.S. banks with a better understanding of coping with the time zone differences subsequently encountered by them as they increased their international activities.

The market for banker's acceptances first obtained Federal Reserve support in the 1920s. Maturities of acceptances generally range from thirty to 180 days. As eligible paper they may be discounted by member banks at the Federal Reserve Bank. Most acceptances arise from financing foreign trade, and the largest volume of this paper is generated in New York. Major purchasers are the commercial banks, Federal Reserve Banks,

Table 9.1

U.S. Money Market Instruments — Volume Outstanding
(Year-end Figures)

	\$ billions							
	1928	1938	1950	1960	1968	1969	1970	1972
Federal Funds[a]	—	—	0.1	1.2	6.7	9.9	16.2	30.9
Time certificates of Deposit[b]	—	—	—	—	23.5	10.9	26.2	44.8
Broker's loans at Banks	6.4	0.8	1.8	3.3	6.6	5.7	6.3	10.2
U.S. Treasury bills[c]	1.3	1.2	31.9	39.4	75.0	80.6	87.9	103.9
Banker's acceptances[d]	1.3	0.3	0.4	2.0	4.4	5.5	7.1	6.9
Commercial Paper	0.4	0.2	0.3	4.3	20.5	31.6	31.8	34.1
Totals	9.4	2.4	34.6	50.3	136.8	144.3	175.5	230.8
Money supply[e]	25.9	29.7	110.2	144.4	197.4	203.6	214.6	246.8
Money market instruments as percentage of Money Supply	36.14	8.01	31.40	34.82	69.20	70.80	81.80	93.40
GNP[f]	98.2	85.2	284.8	503.7	865.0	931.4	974.1	1152.0
Money market instruments as percentage of GNP	9.5	2.8	12.1	10.0	15.8	15.5	18.0	20.0
U.S. short-term Liabilities to Foreigners[g]	2.9	3.6	11.7	21.3	31.7	40.1	41.7	60.7

Short-term liabilities to foreigners as percentage of money market instruments	30.98	155.40	33.90	42.93	23.20	27.80	23.80	26.30

Notes:

[a] Prior to 1965 Federal Reserve figures included Federal Funds sold with Total Loans and Loans to Banks.

[b] While there have been small amounts of time certificates of deposit issued by banks as far back as 1900, no comparable figures are readily available.

[c] For years prior to 1960 data includes certificates of indebtedness outstanding.

[d] Banker's acceptances represent dollar acceptance liabilities of U.S. banks.

[e] Money supply refers to demand deposits adjusted and currency outside banks.

[f] GNP is expressed in billions of current dollars.

[g] This figure has been estimated by interpolation between years, for the years 1928 and 1938. Liabilities are those reported by U.S. banks.

Source: *Federal Reserve Bulletin*, and *Historical Statistics of the United States*.

foreign bank agencies and other financial institutions. Commercial banks buy acceptances for the account of foreign and domestic correspondents. The demand for banker's acceptances from foreign sources has been strong for many years since they provide a safe outlet for temporarily idle funds. Moreover, the income earned on acceptances acquired by non-resident corporations has been held by the Treasury to be exempt from federal income taxes, whereas the income on Treasury bills is subject to a 30 per cent withholding tax.

The commercial paper market is much larger than that for banker's acceptances. Moreover, it is the oldest of the several sectors of the money market. Commercial paper consists of short-term unsecured notes of well-known corporations. This paper is sold in large denominations for specified maturities, either through dealers or placed directly. As of 1970 there were ten dealers in commercial paper, including Goldman Sachs, A.G. Becker, Lehman Brothers, Salomon Brothers and Hutzler, Merrill Lynch, First Boston Corp., and Eastman Dillon. The dealers buy paper as principals and then sell to their clients. Interest rates on commercial paper fluctuate widely along with changing conditions in the money market.

Broker's loans at banks are collateralled by corporate stocks, bonds, and other forms of property. This sector of the market includes broker's loans (also termed street loans) made on a demand or time basis, to finance (1) customers' purchases of securities on margin, (2) dealers' own positions in securities held in investment or trading securities, (3) carrying new securities issues pending distribution, and (4) delivery and receipt of traded securities.

In February 1961 the First National City Bank of New York introduced the Negotiable Time Certificate of Deposit. Other major money market banks soon followed, and an active market quickly developed. Rates that were paid on CDs were subject to the Regulation Q ceilings of the Federal Reserve, which resulted in alternating waves of growth and contraction of CDs outstanding as interest rates on competing money market instruments fluctuated above and below the Regulation Q limits.

In the past fifty years the U.S. money market has improved in size, quality of performance, and in its ability to service international trade. In 1928 money market instruments outstanding represented 9.5 per cent of gross national product, but by 1972 represented 20.0 per cent of GNP (Table 9-1). Relative to money supply, the growth of the money market displays even more striking comparisons. In the same time period (1928–72) the ratio of money market instruments to money supply increased from 36 to 93 per cent.

Quality of performance of the money market may be judged by the stability of the market, in turn reflected by the volume of money market securities outstanding and the conditions and tone of the market. In both respects the money market in the United States has improved considerably over the past several decades. First, the importance of broker's loans at banks has declined from two-thirds of money market instruments outstanding in 1928 to barely 4 per cent in 1972. This highly unstable component represented a most important source of bank liquidity adjustment prior to the U.S. banking reforms of the 1930s. Since that time a considerable centralisation of monetary powers in the hands of the Board of Governors, a growth in U.S. government securities outstanding, and a more important role for commercial paper and other money market instruments has injected added dimensions of stability to the market.

The role of the money market in servicing international needs has improved in several ways over the past fifty years. Major money market banks hold deposit funds of foreign and domestic depositors, in part via the sale of negotiable CDs, and through adjustments in the holdings of money market assets. U.S. banks may finance merchandise trade transactions through the banker's acceptance market, which minimises the commitment of their own liquid funds in such activities. As the following section describes, the New York money market also functions as an important international deposit centre.

The New York money market is much more efficient in servicing financial and non-financial corporations, as well as resident and non-resident participants. The market has indicated it can handle a much greater volume of commercial paper than heretofore expected.[4] Moreover, growth in the negotiable CD market has provided a ready outlet for surplus corporate treasury funds. Understandably, a number of multinational corporations have grown beyond the domestic money market, and have been increasingly resorting to deposit facilities outside the United States in the way of overseas branches of U.S. banks, Eurodollar market facilities, and the money markets of financial centres in other countries.

The New York market services foreign central and commercial banks, individuals, and business firms in numerous ways. These services are broadly reflected in the growth of short-term liabilities to foreigners reported by U.S. banks. These liabilities grew from $11.7 billion in 1950 to $41.7 billion in 1970, and to $60.7 billion in 1972. If we were to relate these liabilities to the size of the money market, we could see the relative importance and potential pressures that can arise from the short-term investment activities of non-residents. For example, the ratio of short-term liabilities to foreigners to money market instruments was 26.3 per cent in 1972. This ratio has fluctuated considerably over the past several decades. Between 1928 and 1938 the ratio advanced rapidly as the depression-induced decline in money market credit took place and as foreigners brought funds into the United States for safe keeping. By 1950 money market instruments outstanding had gained ground, largely associated with increases in Treasury bills issued to finance World War II. Between 1950 and 1960 the ratio increased, reflecting a more balanced government budget position, and steady growth in foreign dollar balances. Since 1960 the ratio has declined and then increased again. The decline reflects a substantial inflation in credit, especially during the late 1960s. The ratio increased sharply in 1969 due to a surge in liabilities to foreigners associated with American bank head office borrowings from overseas branches. A more moderate increase in 1972 can be related to currency uncertainties since 1971 and speculative outflows of dollar funds from the United States, and related foreign central bank intervention in the foreign exchange markets.

Money market instruments outstanding have displayed a persistent and at times amazing propensity to expand. During the last half of the 1960s this expansion has been connected with federal budgetary deficits and the associated rise in Treasury bill issues, tight money and the resort of corporate treasurers to commercial paper financing, and the appearance in 1961 of the market for negotiable certificates of deposit.

Ordinarily, we might expect the growing internationalisation of our major banks, businesses, and money market institutions to result in a gradual rise in the ratio of short-term liabilities to foreigners to money market instruments. The decade of the 1960s witnessed several interruptions in this expected trend. A persistent growth in the role of New York as an international deposit and investment centre could result in a resumption of the upward trend in this ratio in the future.

2. NEW YORK AS AN INTERNATIONAL DEPOSIT CENTRE

Short-term foreign dollar balances serve manifold purposes. Most of these funds are held with United States banks or in the form of money market instruments. They have displayed a persistent growth over the past several decades for the following reasons:[5]

1. Despite several devaluations and currency crises the U.S. dollar has continued to serve as a reserve and investment currency.
2. American financial institutions have become bankers for a more internationally oriented clientele.
3. The United States is the world's leading foreign trader.
4. New York and Chicago are central market places for international commodity transactions.
5. New York is a leading global investment centre.

As an international deposit centre and resting place for internationally mobile funds, the New York money market inevitably competes with other centres. By far New York holds the largest amount of international funds, which at September 1972 amounted to $58.7 billion in short-term money market assets and bank deposits of non-residents. If we include other liquid liabilities to foreigners (holdings of longer-term U.S. government securities), non-resident funds in New York total $79.7 billion. This compares with non-resident funds in the United Kingdom of $68.2 billion.[6] New York also competes with other financial centres such as Switzerland, Germany, Paris, Singapore, and Japan for internationally mobile funds. However, some distinctions must be made between noncompeting sectors, since not all international funds can be expected to be free to move to any financial centre. Some funds are directed to New York for one purpose and to London or another centre to achieve entirely different objectives. The operations of foreign banks through branches and agencies in the United States has contributed substantially to holdings placed in New York.[7] Data published on short-term liabilities distinguishes three categories of foreign holders of dollar assets. These include (1) official institutions (mainly central banks, foreign central governments and their agencies, and the Bank for International Settlements), (2) foreign banks, and (3) other foreigners. In the relatively short period 1969–72 short-term liabilities to these three groups increased by over $20 billion. In this period foreign banks reduced their dollar holdings from $23.4 billion to $14.4 billion, largely as a result of uncertainties regarding dollar convertibility and possible reform of the international monetary system. Official institutions increased their holdings from $11.1 billion to $40.0 billion, in connection with their support of the dollar in the foreign exchange markets. In this period other foreigners maintained approximately the same dollar holdings.

In analysing the ownership distribution and types of short-term claims held by residents of foreign countries we should remember that reported data may be difficult to interpret. Official forward exchange operations by United States and foreign monetary authorities bring about temporary shifts in liquid dollars held in the United States from official to private hands. Increased deposits by official institutions in the Eurodollar market may be accompanied by a rise in private foreign liquid holdings in the United States. Finally, dollar deposits placed by residents in one country with banks in another foreign country and lent to another party appear in the U.S. reported data as liabilities to the ultimate holder. In 1972 two-thirds of the short-term dollar assets of foreigners was held by official institutions, nearly one-fourth by foreign banks, and the remainder by other foreigners, including foreign financial institutions, business corporations and individuals. The motives and reasons for holding dollar balances differ considerably from one type of holder to another.

A large part of the foreign dollar balances held in the United

States represents the international monetary reserves of official institutions. Such institutions hold sizeable dollar deposits in the United States for settlement and clearing purposes. Foreign central banks require operating balances to intervene in the New York foreign exchange market, to sell dollar balances to the commercial banks of their own countries, and for other current needs. Balances are held by central banks and exchange control authorities to provide dollar exchange for repayment of maturing loans, to pay interest on outstanding loans, and to provide funds for purchasing missions.[8] Some monetary authorities hold deposit balances which represent 'commensurate balances' for loans extended to them or to compensate U.S. commercial banks for loans and other services rendered on behalf of private banks in these countries.

Foreign commercial banks hold substantial amounts of dollar deposits in the United States for settlement and clearing purposes. However, the primary reason for their holding balances here is for day-to-day operating purposes. This includes trading in foreign exchange, execution of orders for clients outside the United States in settlement of trade and investment transactions, as compensating balances, and as cover for letters of credit. Commercial banks abroad often lack adequate local money market facilities of their own in which to employ liquid funds. Therefore, they commit sizeable balances in the U.S. money market, particularly at times when interest rate relationships here and abroad are favourable. The dismantling of foreign exchange controls and spread of non-resident convertibility has tended to augment the dollar resources available to foreign banks for short-term investment in dollar assets. Foreign banks include the overseas branches of U.S. banks. At year-end 1970 gross liabilities of large American banks to their foreign branches were $7.7 billion, over half of the demand deposit liabilities due to foreign banks. By year-end 1972 gross liabilities to foreign branches had declined to $1.4 billion.

Other foreigners holding short-term dollar assets include insurance companies, securities dealers and brokers, business corporations, and individuals. Foreign insurance companies hold substantial dollar assets which comprise the premium reserves they must hold according to the state laws under which they operate. Another component of these dollar funds reflects balances whose actual or beneficial owners are affiliates of United States corporations that do not wish to repatriate profits from abroad. Part of the short-term holdings of other foreigners represents safe haven funds held by individuals who wish to keep their dollar assets beyond the reach of foreign government tax revenue commissioners and exchange control authorities. Balances held in the United States for these reasons experience substantial fluctuation, in response to political and financial disturbances in other countries.

Types of Foreign Asset Holdings

At year-end 1972 U.S. Treasury bill holdings represented over 80 per cent of the short-term liabilities to foreign official institutions reported by U.S. banks. By contrast foreign banks and other foreigners held only negligible amounts of Treasury bills. Treasury securities have proven to be an attractive investment for foreign central banks and other foreign official institutions. In part this is attributable to two measures taken by the Kennedy administration in 1961 to make Treasury securities more attractive to foreign holders. In that year Congress enacted legislation which made the interest income of foreign central banks from obligations of the U.S. government exempt from the 30 per cent withholding tax. The new law had the effect of providing the same tax treatment to income of central banks from U.S. government securities as applied to their income from time deposits and banker's acceptances. The second measure provided for the Secretary of the Treasury to issue securities at special rates of interest for subscription by foreign governments and monetary authorities. Under this provision the U.S. Treasury has issued special non-marketable obligations.

Foreign monetary authorities have temporarily acquired liquid dollars in the form of special U.S. Treasury certificates of indebtedness. This is a result of central bank reciprocal currency operations. For example, the United States may initiate a swap drawing on a foreign central bank, exchanging Treasury bills or special Treasury certificates for foreign currency. These foreign currency balances are used to purchase dollars held by the foreign central bank, pending reversal of the swap contract. The U.S. Treasury also has issued foreign currency denominated securities, which were first introduced in 1963.

While obligations of the U.S. government have constituted an important part of the short-term assets of foreign monetary authorities, deposits in U.S. banks have been the largest component of the short-term balances of foreign banks and other foreigners. At year-end 1972 deposits in U.S. banks represented 33 per cent of the short-term assets of foreign banks, and close to 87 per cent of the short-term assets of other foreigners. In 1972 interest bearing time deposits represented over $5.4 billion of the $12.4 billion of deposits in U.S. banks held by residents of foreign countries. This does not consider non-resident holdings of negotiable time certificates of deposit. In addition, substantial amounts of foreign deposits represent funds that are ultimately employed in the domestic money and credit markets in the United States, or in foreign credit markets. This is especially true in the case of balances held by foreign banks in their New York and California agencies which place a large part of their funds in the form of loans with securities brokers and dealers. Agencies of the Canadian chartered banks and Japanese commercial banks place U.S. dollar and convertible free yen deposits with their parent head offices for the account of non-residents of Canada and Japan. In turn their parent institutions place 'sight deposits' with the agencies, for investment in dollar assets. Since these agencies are regarded as domestic institutions for statistical reporting purposes, balances placed with them by their head offices are included in the deposit liabilities of U.S. banks to foreigners. In actuality, most of these balances are placed in the New York market as loans to brokers and dealers, investments in Treasury bills and federal agency issues, and other short-term credits. Hence, these foreign deposits may be viewed as ultimately taking the form of money and credit market investments held for foreign account by banks in the United States.

The Japanese agencies, like the Canadian agencies, are regarded as domestic institutions in the U.S. balance of payments, therefore the funds deposited with them by their head offices in Japan are regarded as foreign liquid assets. The agencies employ the dollars to finance Japan's international trade. Part of the agencies' liabilities to their head offices represents trade bills drawn on U.S. importers and forwarded by the head offices in Japan to the U.S. agencies. The agencies in turn accept the instruments, credit their head offices with the amount of the instrument, and hold the latter to maturity. In recent years increasing amounts of foreign owned balances represent funds obtained in the Eurodollar market by foreign branches of United States banks. These branches are regarded as 'foreign' and their claims on U.S. head offices appear in the statistics as foreign dollar deposits. At year-end 1968, 1969, and 1970 these claims on U.S. head offices were quite high, $6.0 billion, $12.8 billion, and $7.7 billion respectively.[9]

Time deposits held by foreigners have failed to demonstrate any growth in the period 1966–72. Nevertheless they represent a substantial portion, close to 10 per cent, of short-term assets of non-residents in the United States. Foreign time deposits are subject to some fluctuation based on changing yield relationships with Treasury securities and other investment outlets.[10] The yield relationships between time deposits, Treasury securities, and banker's acceptances depend on the tax status of holders. Income earned by *all* foreign residents from time deposits and banker's acceptances is exempt from federal income tax, whereas with the exception of official institutions (central banks) the discount on Treasury bills and interest on other Treasury securities is subject to a 30 per cent withholding tax.

While relative yield considerations may play an important role in the demand of foreign institutions, banks and others for time deposits, there is evidence that a segment of time deposits held by foreigners is inelastic to changes in rate differentials. According to Klopstock, several foreign central banks are 'habitual investors in time deposits', while other central and foreign banks consider time deposits unsuitable for their dollar holdings.[11] Reasons for this insensitivity to interest rate changes include appreciation for loan facilities extended, maintenance of minimum balances in return for open credit lines, desire to continue favourable letter of credit facilities, and expectation that U.S. banks will channel collection and other banking business to foreign banks maintaining dollar balances in U.S. banks.

While the foregoing helps to account for some measure of stability in the volume of foreign owned time deposits maintained in U.S. banks, it should not be interpreted that American banks have not experienced the problem of temporary runoffs in foreign time deposits. Regulation Q ceilings on interest rates have presented difficulties for American banks in periods of rising interest rates in terms of time deposit runoffs. To counter such problems U.S. banks have arranged for foreign banks to participate in some of their loans, in which case the foreign bank may retain some of its funds as time deposits. This practice permits the foreign banks to earn a higher average return on dollar balances. Secondly, banks have arranged 'link financing' deals, whereby foreign holders of dollar balances supply funds to banks as compensating balances. Interest on these funds is paid by the borrower, and the return to the depositor exceeds that obtainable on a straight deposit. Link financing may require the services of a money broker, who may be located either in the borrower's country or abroad.[12]

In order to provide greater flexibility in the working relationships between U.S. banks as deposit takers and foreign official institutions as holders of short-term dollar assets, in 1962 the U.S. Congress amended Section 19 of the Federal Reserve Act, exempting deposits of foreign governments and certain foreign institutions from regulation by the Board of Governors as to the rates of interest which member banks may pay on time deposits. Accordingly, the Board amended Regulation Q, incorporating this exemption.[13]

Banker's acceptances rank behind time deposits in the short-term dollar assets held by residents of foreign countries. Of the $6.9 billion outstanding at year-end 1972, $2.5 billion was held in the portfolios of accepting banks. Another $0.3 billion was held by the Federal Reserve Banks, of which $199.1 million was held for foreign correspondents. The remaining $4.1 billion was held by foreign central banks who have traditionally been important buyers, foreign commercial banks, and domestic investors. Foreign banks have been attracted to banker's acceptances due to their safety, and to the fact that the discount earned has not been subject to federal income taxation.

C. NEW YORK AS A NEW ISSUES MARKET AND SOURCE OF LONG-TERM CAPITAL

Despite the variety of controls and restrictions imposed on U.S. foreign investment and lending since 1963, the United States remains the most important capital supplier in the world. In part this role continues because of the superiority and strength of the capital and money markets, and because of the ability and resourcefulness of American bankers and underwriting firms. As an international capital market, New York provides certain functions which can be duplicated in only a few other national capital markets. These include providing a substantial volume of long-term capital funds to foreign borrowers, providing opportunities for international security substitution, and providing facilities for secondary trading in existing foreign and domestic securities for the account of foreign investors. In connection with the first point, New York is especially qualified as a centre for new issues, and affords an efficiency and low cost equalled in only a few other financial centres.

1. NEW FOREIGN ISSUES

The importance of the United States in the international capital markets can be traced to World War I and the decade of the 1920s. It was at this time that major foreign loans were made to European governments and that American investment banking houses began underwriting issues of foreign securities. During the depression of the 1930s the market for foreign issues dried up almost entirely. Banking reform legislation in the United States in the 1930s altered the structure and operations of banking, and these changes have persisted until today. The Banking Act of 1933 required the separation of commercial banking from investment banking. Commercial banks spun off their underwriting departments, and since that time have confined their domestic new issues activities to subscribing for U.S. government securities, municipal bonds and securities issued by the World Bank and similar international institutions.

After World War II American investors cautiously began to renew their foreign investment activity. This slow return to foreign portfolio investment accelerated during the 1950s and 1960s. Throughout the postwar period the less developed countries have not made extensive use of the U.S. capital market to obtain funds. Several reasons are offered to explain this, including the record of past debt defaults, political instability, existing debt burden, the cost of borrowing, and legal and administrative obstacles to their floating bond issues in the international markets.[14] Even after passage of the Interest

Equalisation Tax Act in 1964, which exempted securities issues from less developed countries from the tax, new foreign bond issues from the less developed countries have accounted for only 15–20 per cent of total foreign issues placed in the United States.

In the years leading up to 1963 New York was increasingly becoming a more important centre for new foreign issues, and for the trading and listing of international equity securities.[15] A distinguishing feature of publicly issued bonds in this period was that the foreign selling groups, consisting mostly of non-United States banks, placed large amounts of such issues abroad. During the period 1945–63 Morgan Stanley managed eighteen bond issues with an aggregate value of $463 million in the U.S. market for the Commonwealth of Australia. Over one-half of this amount was placed with investors outside the United States. In the period 1959–62 issues such as those placed for the Kingdom of Belgium, Cassa per il Mezzagiorno, and Credit Foncier de France were placed to the extent of 79 to 90 per cent abroad. The international entrepôt role of New York which is evident in these figures was becoming more important year by year. This role proved to be shortlived.

U.S. Capital Restraint

Enactment of the Interest Equalization Tax in 1964 had an immediate impact on U.S. purchases of foreign long-term securities. New issues of taxable foreign securities in the United States declined by over $300 million between the first half of 1963 and the first half of 1964, and net purchases of outstanding European and Japanese securities in the first half of 1963 became net sales in the first half of 1964. In addition to reducing the scope for new foreign issues in the United States, the IET deflected a substantial amount of demand for funds away from the New York market and toward the European financial markets. New foreign issues on the European capital markets nearly trebled between 1963 and 1964.[16]

While taxable outflows declined in amount after the IET, non-taxable outflows rose to fill the gap. The most substantial increase was in the area of term bank loans to European business firms. While part of this increase may have been independent of the tax, the rapid development of this type of lending

could have been accelerated by the tax.[17] Other types of outflows which increased substantially in 1964 were short-term
bank lending to non-residents and direct investment by U.S.
corporations. While it is difficult to associate these three forms
of capital outflows with the direct effects of the IET, several
connections may be possible. The deflection of Japanese borrowing from the United States to Europe could have made it
more difficult for German and Italian firms to raise funds at
home, so that they were induced to borrow from American
banks instead. Some U.S. direct investment may have been
stimulated as a result of the depressed state of the European
and Japanese stock markets at this time and the resulting
opportunities for U.S. corporations to acquire shares in existing
companies in these areas.

The overall balance of payments effects of the IET are difficult to estimate due to the possibility of its having induced large
outflows of capital from the United States. Doubtless, some
arbitrage took place as a result of the tax. The substantial
increase in U.S. long-term bank lending and direct investment
abroad led to the promulgation of a new series of restrictions on
U.S. capital outflows. These included the voluntary restrictions
on U.S. bank lending abroad and the mandatory controls on
U.S. business investments overseas financed by direct investment outflows. These developments in the mid-1960s led to the
shifting of a substantial part of the new issues business to the
European Continent. In turn this influenced the attitudes of
major U.S. banks regarding the development of offshore
underwriting and new issues activities.

Underwriting Goes International

In America underwriting has tended to remain the most stable
element in the ferment of an embattled Wall Street financial
community. However, the underwriting field has also been
exposed to serious inroads on its formerly entrenched position.
Many of these intrusions are of an international character,
stemming from the growth of the multinational firm and the
expanding capital pool outside the United States. Several European banking firms have been 'elbowing their way into U.S.
underwriting syndicates in recent years'.[18] The motivation for
this appears to be a desire to gain representation in all the

major capital markets, including New York, and a desire to share in the attractive underwriting profits which accrue to syndicate members. The leverage used by these foreign firms to gain admittance to U.S. syndicates includes reciprocal arrangements providing the U.S. sponsor entry into foreign underwriting activities and demonstration of selling ability both in the United States and overseas. U.S. syndicate managers cite at least two reasons for granting foreign firms a privileged position in U.S. underwritings. These are the recent shrinkage of the dealer organisations and distributing houses, and the overtaxed capital resources of U.S. investment bankers.

Certain activities of U.S. banks complicate the task of assessing the impact of foreign banks on the underwriting situation in the United States. Although barred from underwriting and selling securities by the Glass-Steagall Act, American banks have been cultivating corporate business not specifically barred by the provisions of this legislation. Moreover, they have been increasingly energetic in offering their corporate financial consulting services, often on a fee basis, to corporations which had previously relied exclusively on investment bankers for such advice. Finally, commercial banks have been making a major assault from abroad. Through their joint ventures and affiliations with foreign banking houses the large U.S. commercial banks are moving into the underwriting business on an international basis.

By expanding the facilities available, and thereby the efficiency, in the Eurobond market, American banks may have pulled a substantial volume of underwriting activity from New York. As a matter of fact, the distinctions between a New York and Eurobond underwriting are fast melting away, and are confined in large part to certain technical questions relating to the residency status of underwriters and investors, and SEC registration requirements. According to one well-informed observer, if the 30 per cent withholding tax was abolished on the interest income received by foreign holders of U.S. bonds, these bonds would yield more to foreigners and would be purchased by overseas investors. As a result, the Eurobond market eventually would merge itself into the U.S. bond market, and New York would become the main international issuing centre, even though the apparatus of underwriting and selling groups would continue outside the United States. A foreign bond market would continue to operate for the benefit of those companies unable to register in the United States under the 1933 Securities Act.[19] Given such changes, the composition of underwriting groups handling new issues of U.S. corporations could be expected to become more international.

2. SECONDARY TRADING

In 1971 foreign investors purchased $2.3 billion of corporate and state and local government securities in the United States. At the same time American investors acquired $0.9 billion of foreign securities. In part the build-up of portfolio investment between U.S. and foreign investors represents a two-way exchange of securities based largely on financial considerations. The classical economic rationale for international capital movements is that they shift productive resources from regions of lower to regions of higher return, raising global output. International portfolio investment may take place for many reasons other than national differences in the rate of return on capital. Financial considerations include the effects of monetary policy on securities yields, relative liquidity preference at home and overseas, taxation, and the size of the capital stock which is relatively inelastic in the short-run.[20] In addition, time preferences may differ from country to country, and expectations that there will be an alteration in the foreign exchange rate may influence the prices at which securities are traded. Both of these factors can exert an influence on security values and yields, and consequently bring about an international flow of portfolio investment. According to Cooper, even when yields on securities and real assets are well aligned, differences in transaction costs, the breadth of markets, and in the variability of returns may 'redirect international capital movements'. The attraction of New York as an international centre for securities trading hinges in part on the low cost of transactions, the liquidity afforded by active trading and a large number of participants, and the relative degree of predictability of security prices.

There are four avenues available for U.S. investors and investors in other countries to acquire the securities of a foreign company. These include purchase of depositary receipts, purchase of shares in a domestic company with extensive foreign operations or owning foreign subsidiaries, acquisition of shares in a mutual fund which invests in foreign securities, and direct purchase of foreign shares.[21] The facilities for securities trading in New York and other financial centres in the United States lend themselves well to U.S. and foreign investors utilising all four of these approaches.

New York commercial banks facilitate U.S. ownership and trading of foreign stocks by issuing American Depository Receipts (ADRs) registered in the owner's name upon deposit of foreign bearer shares with selected branches or correspondents. The leading banks in this field have been Chemical Bank, Irving Trust Company, and Morgan Guaranty Trust Co. Similarly, beginning in 1955 Bearer Depository Receipts (BDRs) have been issued by U.S. banks to foreign investors, representing shares in U.S. companies.

While the market for foreign securities has much in common with the market for domestic securities, the former has its own special features. These include (1) specialised brokers and dealers, (2) a two-way market aspect, which includes selling U.S. securities to foreign investors and foreign securities to domestic investors, (3) a tendency for securities prices to be determined by trading taking place in the 'home' country, (4) a time zone factor which provides opportunities for arbitrage, (5) and a more difficult and demanding research effort.

D. INTERNATIONAL FINANCIAL MARKET OPERATIONS

American banks have played an important role in facilitating the rebirth of the international financial markets. A direct contribution lies in the linkages which American banks provide through their global branch and affiliate networks in connecting separate national financial markets. U.S. banks act as collectors, intermediaries and end-use allocators in the international transfer of lendable funds. A second important contribution relates to the numerous specialised investment banking and investment management services which American banks and their overseas banking and financing affiliates provide. These include the more traditional underwriting functions, but also encompass the provision of secondary market trading facilities of various kinds.

1. INVESTMENT BANKING ACTIVITIES

An important component of the international financial market operations of U.S. banks has been their investment banking activity. This includes underwriting, arranging mergers and acquisitions, providing information regarding expansions and mergers, and supporting secondary market trading of existing securities. American banks which have been especially active in underwriting new issues in the international bond market through overseas affiliates include Morgan Guaranty Trust, Bankers Trust, First National City Bank, Bank of America, and Manufacturers Hanover Trust Co.[22]

In 1969 Manufacturers Hanover Ltd, a merchant bank affiliate of the similarly named New York bank, opened its doors for business. During 1970 this merchant bank managed borrowings totalling over one billion dollars, was a member of the management group of six major international issues, and participated as major underwriter in a third of the international issues floated during the year.[23] Among its Euro-underwritings in that year were included Beatrice Foods, City of Copenhagen, Courtaulds International Finance, European Coal and Steel Community, Fuji Photo Company Ltd, IBRD, Massey Ferguson, Mitsubishi Electric, and Olivetti.

The international departments of American banks possess their own staff members who analyse merger and acquisition prospects for customers, provide advice on long-term and medium-term financing options, and supply information to customers regarding interest rate, exchange rate, and financial market trends and developments around the world. To supplement their resources in this direction several American banks have become charter members as well as participating shareholders in Union International d'Analyse Economique et Financière (Eurofinance). Eurofinance is especially well qualified to penetrate the veil of secrecy which tends to surround financial data regarding European corporations and business firms, as well as to obtain investment information and make critical analyses of specific investment opportunities. Imposition of the Interest Equalisation Tax closed off the foreign securities channels formerly open to American investors, who now have less use for this data. The three original U.S. bank participants in Eurofinance include the Mellon National Bank & Trust Co., Northern Trust Co., and Wells Fargo Bank.

As of 1967 Eurofinance was producing 200 to 300 confidential reports a year, on leading European companies and industries. These reports are sent to participating banks for their internal confidential use. Backing up this reporting system are Eurofinance's 20,000 files on British and Continental firms, a multilingual staff, and the general support and backing of the participating banks which include some of the largest in the world.[24] An important aspect of its services includes studies of mergers, acquisitions and new investments in plant and equipment. In one instance an American manufacturer, without European advice, decided to invest $2 million in a plant and supporting organisation in Europe to make and sell a single product. When the manufacturer had completed nearly all arrangements except site location, he consulted his American bank, a member of Eurofinance. Through his bank, Eurofinance was able to tell him that a German firm in a related industry had an identical project much further along toward completion, and would possess a considerable competitive advantage. The American company cancelled its European plans. The American bank's service to its corporate customer, available through its affiliation with Eurofinance, unquestionably saved the American firm from an unprofitable capital outlay.

2. OFFSHORE TRADING FACILITIES

The investment banking functions performed by U.S. banks and their overseas affiliates include supporting secondary market trading activities of securities in the international securities markets. The approaches taken in this connection include purchase of interests in foreign banks actively conducting a securities business, and providing specialised instruments and clearing facilities for trading securities in overseas areas. The first approach has been followed by Bankers Trust Company, which in 1970 purchased a majority interest in Deutsche Unionbank, Frankfurt from the Swedish Match Company Group. The Frankfurt institution specialises in wholesale industrial accounts and the securities business. Unlike the

American situation, in Germany commercial banks are permitted to engage in a wide variety of securities business activities.

In 1970 another United States bank, Southern California First National Bank, through its one bank holding company affiliate Southern California First National Corporation, agreed to purchase a 40 per cent interest in Heusser & Company, a private Swiss bank, subject to U.S. regulatory approval. Nearly one-third of this Swiss bank's revenue is derived from brokerage fees and commissions accruing from membership on the Basel Stock Exchange.

The second approach, providing specialised instruments and clearing facilities, has been vigorously followed by Morgan Guaranty Trust Company, through issuing American Depository and International Depository Receipts, and by providing a clearance service for internationally traded securities (Euroclear). Depository receipts are instruments that simplify the international buying, selling and holding of securities. The issuance of depository receipts involves an agreement between the depository and the holder of the receipt, in which a substitute instrument evidences the international ownership of shares in a company. The substitute instrument, the depository receipt, is utilised where use of the original stock certificate issued by the company would entail inconvenience, delay, added expense, and unnecessary risk.

While American Depository Receipts were developed to facilitate U.S. portfolio investment in foreign companies, Bearer Depository Receipts (BDRs) were introduced in 1955 to provide a medium for investment in U.S. companies by overseas investors. In turn, these were the forerunner of the International Depository Receipts (IDRs) made available by Morgan Guaranty in 1970 for the offshore trading of shares of many U.S. and Japanese companies.

The rapid growth in dollar securities issued outside the United States since 1965, in the form of Eurodollar issues or Eurobonds, has led to the development of an active secondary market in such securities. Hundreds of transactions occur daily in this market, in which the major participants are banks, brokerage firms, and investment houses. The Eurobond market extends to all the main financial centres of Europe, and also to

New York. During the 1960s growth in foreign ownership of U.S. corporate equities and an active market in several Euro-bond and U.S. corporate equity issues increased the need for improved trading facilities in these securities in Europe. Moreover, the fact that the market is dispersed among numer-ous cities and countries created numerous problems in the settling of transactions. Morgan Guaranty established the Euroclear service to cope with the problems associated with physical shipment of securities, the risk of paying for or surren-dering certificates prior to the completion of the transaction, and the mounting costs of handling stock and bond certificate transfers. Participants in Euroclear hold two accounts in the system, a securities clearance account and a U.S. dollar account. These are centralised at Morgan Guaranty's Brussels office. Securities purchased by a participant are credited to his clearance account and payment is made by a charge to his dollar account. When both parties to a securities sale are Euro-clear participants, simple entries on Morgan Guaranty's books complete the transaction. In transactions where only one party is a Euroclear participant, the securities are delivered into or out of the system to accomplish settlement. Syndicate members in new underwritings who are participants in Euroclear can have their bonds credited directly to their Euroclear securities accounts with no requirements for intermediate delivery.

3. INVESTMENT ADVISORY SERVICES

American banks perform investment advisory and manage-ment services for foreign as well as domestic customers through their trust and investment management divisions. Among the banks that have been prominent in this respect are Morgan Guaranty Trust, Bankers Trust, and U.S. Trust Company. In addition, a number of U.S. banks have established offshore mutual funds. These offshore funds managed by U.S. banks and securities firms 'have revolutionised the savings and invest-ment habits of the burgeoning middle classes in many parts of the world where stock ownership by small investors was vir-tually unknown'.[25]

U.S. managed offshore funds prospered in the late 1960s for good reasons. First, such offshore companies based in Panama, the Bahamas, Luxembourg or Bermuda are not subject to the

U.S. Internal Revenue Code. This provides exemption from the Interest Equalisation Tax when foreign securities are acquired and certain restrictions relative to gains from sale of securities held for relatively short periods of time. Second, foreign investors can obtain professional management of an international equities portfolio that might contain a high dollar content. Third, offshore companies are typically headquartered in low tax jurisdictions. Fourth, individuals holding shares in offshore funds generally are not subject to the United States estate tax. Foreign buyers of U.S. mutual funds could incur such a liability.

While these funds have been profitable for both U.S. banks and non-bank investment advisers, more general advantages have accrued to the United States. Some of the funds sponsored by U.S. banks are committed under their statutes to be invested primarily in common stock issued by United States corporations. Also, such advisers have a predilection to invest in the New York market, since their knowledge of U.S. securities is based on long experience in this field. The resulting flow of foreign funds into U.S. equities has exerted an important favourable influence on the international accounts of the United States. In the relatively brief period of two and three-quarter years (Spring 1967 to year-end 1969) close to $4.5 billion of foreign money was placed in United States equities. This inflow was attributable in large part to the growth and development of offshore mutual funds.

10 Banking in Major Countries

A. GREAT BRITAIN
B. FRANCE
C. WEST GERMANY
D. SWITZERLAND
E. CANADA
F. JAPAN
G. HONG KONG
H. SOVIET UNION

The domestic banking scene in each country shapes the opportunities and prospects for favourable development of international banking operations. The following brief description of the banking systems of selected countries mirrors the fairly wide contrasts that can be observed in major countries. The British banking system reflects a long-standing international orientation. Nearly half of the deposits in U.K. banks are domiciled in specialised institutions that have evolved from London's pivotal international financing role. In France, we have a system that stands apart in terms of the new competitive environment, public ownership of major banks, and recently strengthened monetary powers of the Bank of France. By contrast, banking in Germany is characterised by numerous banks, both in number and types. The three big banks in Germany conform closely to the mixed banking pattern, explaining their orientation toward underwriting and international finance. Switzerland offers another interesting special situation. Swiss banks receive substantial foreign funds for deposit and investment management. This has given these banks considerable leverage in the international lending arena, especially as sources of Eurocurrency and participants in foreign bond issue underwriting. The Canadian banking system is noteworthy for its large, well-managed banks, and in the prestige these banks have earned in the international markets for deposits and banking services. The Japanese banking system has made impressive accomplishments in financing a high rate of domestic economic growth. The Hong Kong banks represent a small but highly strategic mechanism for money exchange and services performed for international business in the Far East. Finally, Soviet banking offers additional sharp contrasts in terms of reflecting the crucial role of banks in facilitating economic growth and economic planning.

A.   GREAT BRITAIN

British banking is unique in several respects. London, the focal point of British banking, enjoys a broad diversity of banking types ranging from the large clearing banks to the smaller but no less important merchant banking institutions. No other financial and banking centre is nearly so immersed in international banking as is London, and no other centre provides as wide a variety of banking and financial services as London. British banking has reflected an amazing propensity to adapt to changing conditions. During the past decade the number of London clearing banks has been cut in half as a result of mergers. The growth in foreign currency deposits in U.K. banks has outpaced all other aspects of bank operations,[1] and the appearance of new market sectors including the parallel markets has been a factor in inducing British banks to reorganise themselves for greater participation in the new credit market sectors. Finally, central bank control has been revamped, in part as a response to the many changes taking place in banking and money market structure, and in part in response to the anticipated need of providing a more competitive and flexible posture upon entry into the Common Market.

The London clearing banks have long stood at the centre of the British banking system. As of June 1972 sterling deposits held in the London clearing banks represented close to one-half of all sterling deposits in banks in the United Kingdom. The bulk (95 per cent) of these deposits are due to U.K. residents, only 5 per cent representing deposits due to overseas residents.[2] The clearing banks issue negotiable sterling certificates of deposit, and in 1972 these banks accounted for close to one-fourth of CDs outstanding. In 1972 the clearing banks began issuing certificates of deposit denominated in U.S. dollars. Nearly two-thirds of the assets of the clearing banks are allocated to advances, principally to U.K. companies and financial institutions, and loans to local authorities. Close to one-eighth of their resources are held in the form of short and medium-term government securities. The remainder of their assets, slightly over one-fifth, is held in liquid money market assets and balances with the Bank of England. Liquid assets consist of money at call to the discount market, sterling bills discounted including British government Treasury bills, and balances with other U.K. banks.

Approximately one-half of the deposits in U.K. banks is in other (non-sterling) currencies. Nearly all of these foreign currency deposits are placed with deposit banks other than the clearing banks. These institutions include the Accepting Houses, British Overseas and Commonwealth banks, American banks, and other banks. These institutions cover a wide range of operations, interests and specialisations. They are characterised by a high proportion of non-sterling to total deposits; a high ratio of transactions with overseas residents; and specialised operations in the newly developing money market (parallel market) sectors such as sterling and U.S. dollar certificates of deposit, loans to local authorities, Euro-currency loans and deposits, and inter-bank transactions.

In any discussion of British banking and finance specific mention must be made of the merchant banks headquartered in London. Nearly two dozen old line merchant banks and a number of more recently organised institutions constitute the merchant banking group.[3] Their main activities fall into three areas, including banking, company services, and portfolio management. Banking activities include sterling and foreign currency deposits, short and medium-term loans, foreign exchange and acceptances, and money market operations. Company services are wide-ranging and include new issues in the domestic and international capital markets, acquisitions and mergers, capital reorganisations, and corporate planning. Several of the older line merchant banks have been active in managing Eurobond issues. A third area of activity includes portfolio management for pension funds, trust funds, unit trusts, offshore funds and private individuals. Many of the

London merchant banks have extensive overseas representation through branch offices, wholly-owned affiliates, and consortium banks.

The British banking system enjoys the distinction of possessing the oldest central bank in the world. Organised in 1694 under royal charter as a private commercial bank, the Bank of England gradually evolved into a bankers' bank with responsibility for preserving the integrity of the circulating medium. Central banking institutions and monetary policy in Britain are still evolving and changing, as is evidenced by the launching of a new monetary policy in 1971.

Briefly stated, the new monetary and credit policy aimed at (1) permitting a more competitive financial environment, (2) more flexible reliance on interest rate changes in the allocation of lendable funds, and (3) increased emphasis on changes in money supply as a monetary policy target. Specific changes in the framework of Bank of England control over credit include the application of new reserve requirements to all banks, and extending reserve requirements to cover deposits in foreign banks and London merchant banks. Formerly only the clearing banks had been subject to reserve and liquidity requirements. In addition, the 'near banks', the discount houses and finance houses were made subject to their own reserve requirements.

Further changes affect interest rate determination in the United Kingdom. The London and Scottish clearing banks abandoned their agreements on interest rates, permitting bank lending rates, deposit rates, and Bank Rate of the Bank of England to move more flexibly relative to one another. Moreover, the previous collective bid of the discount houses for weekly offerings of Treasury bills has been discontinued.

In the past the Bank of England has used a variety of credit control measures to achieve employment, growth, and balance of payments objectives. These include changes in Bank Rate, moral suasion, suggested bank credit ceilings, special deposit requirements, and open market operations.[4] While it is too early to note definite patterns or departures from previous policy approaches, it seems likely that in future the Bank of England may continue to employ a wide variety of credit control instruments. The difference probably will be in the increased flexibility and competitive movement of money market rates of interest that has now become possible.

B. FRANCE

Prior to 1966 French finance and banking was tradition-bound, rigidly state controlled, and dominated by the nationalised banks and insurance companies. This pattern had been established as a result of the banking legislation of 1945 which nationalised the Bank of France and the largest deposit banks, and demarcated areas of operation between deposit banks, investment banks (banques d'affaires), and long and medium-term credit banks.[5] In 1966–7 major banking reforms were introduced. These suspended the long standing separation between deposit banking and investment banking. The objectives of the 1966–7 reforms were to facilitate the transfer of lendable funds to important areas of investment, to make the credit and banking system more flexible, and to promote efficiency via increased competition.

Until the reforms of the 1960s deposit banks could not receive deposits for terms in excess of two years. Moreover, the long and medium-term credit banks could not accept deposits for terms under two years, and the investment banks were severely restricted in their deposit taking. The reforms abolished limits on opening new branches, extended the terms of deposits taken by deposit banks beyond two years, and prohibited payment of interest on current and checking accounts. In the years since 1966 banks have sought to widen their deposit bases, and as a result the banking system has experienced a rapid growth in bank branches and an increase in the ratio of term and savings deposits to total deposits.[6] By 1971 the structure of deposits in deposit banks included approximately equal amounts of company and private customer deposits. Nearly 30 per cent of company deposits are term deposits. Savings accounts of private customers, certificates of deposit and bonds constitute approximately one-sixth of total deposits. Inter-bank items, which include much of the foreign currency operations of deposit banks represent an important part of assets and liabilities.

Since the changes in 1966, the deposit banks have increased their lending at medium-term and long-term. However, short-term credit of less than two years still accounts for the larger part of aggregate lending. Close to three-fourths of short-term credit is secured by means of discounted bills and promissory notes. Some short-term lending is in the form of overdrafts to customers of high credit standing. Credit facilities with maturities of three to seven years are provided for equipment and export financing. Most of this is in the form of bills eligible for discount at the central bank. The 1966–7 reforms eased the restrictions on acquisition of ordinary shares in companies by deposit banks. Up to one-fifth of the equity capital of an industrial or business firm may be acquired with an overall limit equal to the bank's own capital funds.[7]

In the past investment banks catered to a relatively narrow clientele. Their major sphere of activity was participation in and management of business enterprises. They assist in the issue of securities, arrange mergers and acquisitions, and make investments for their own account. More recently the investment banks, through mergers, have extended their activities into deposit banking.

The French banking system also includes a number of private banks, several hundred savings banks, mortgage credit institutions, small loan companies, and other specialised institutions.

Monetary policy has not escaped the recent reform and changes taking place in the French banking sector. The Wormser Report published in 1969 noted various deficiencies in French monetary controls and made proposals for strengthening the central bank's power over credit expansion. The Report noted the need for a more flexible, market-oriented interest rate pattern, and the illogic in a rate structure where the discount rate remained fixed below open market rates. A central thesis of the Report was the proposal to establish a mechanism whereby the discount rate at which the Bank of France intervened in the money market would be above flexible open market rates. Beginning in 1971 the Wormser Report proposals were implemented as follows:

1. Open-market policy became a key aspect of the Bank of France's monetary powers. Open market rates were permitted to fall below the discount rate. Open market operations are conducted in eligible paper which includes Treasury bills and other public debt, and first

class paper including short and medium-term credits (banker's acceptances and export bills). Eligible paper also includes certain types of commercial paper and hire purchase paper on which higher intervention rates prevail. The Bank intervenes by outright purchases or by temporary rediscounts.

2. In 1967 a system of fractional reserves was introduced whereby French banks must maintain deposits with the Bank of France up to a maximum of 15 per cent of each deposit category. As of late 1972 these requirements were set at 10 per cent of sight deposits and 5 per cent of time deposits of residents, and 12 per cent and 6 per cent respectively for deposits of non-residents. In 1971 a system of compulsory reserves based on bank credits was brought into effect. This operates parallel to the reserves required on deposits. At mid-1972 this rate was fixed at 4 per cent of specified credits.[8]

3. The discount rate has declined in overall importance. Movements in the rate have been relatively small, and represent an adjustment according to market tendencies. Nonetheless, a change in the discount rate still has a psychological effect and may reflect a change in direction of monetary policy. Moreover, the discount rate functions as a base which banks use in establishing interest rates they charge their own customers.[9]

On several occasions in the past the Bank of France has utilised a general credit restraint. This takes the form of a percentage ceiling on the monthly increase in bank credit in restricted loan categories. This was last used in 1968–70. Generally, this type of control is reserved for use in periods of monetary crisis, and suffers the disadvantage of freezing competition between banks and being excessively burdensome on small and dynamic banks.

C. WEST GERMANY

Frankfurt is the leading banking and financial centre in West Germany, housing the head offices of the central bank (Bundesbank), the big three commercial banks, the largest internationally oriented domestic and foreign companies, and the Frankfurt stock exchange which is the largest in Germany. In the pre-1914 period Berlin held the centre of financial gravity in Germany. However, German banking has always tended to be decentralised and at present Hamburg enjoys a lead in the financing of foreign trade, and Düsseldorf retains a measure of leadership in industrial financing.

German banking is competitive, due to the large number and types of banking institutions and near banks. There are over 300 commercial or deposit type banks, among them the big three (Deutsche, Dresdner, and Commerz), 130 other commercial banks, and approximately 170 private banks. In the past German commercial banks thought of themselves primarily as bankers to industry. The savings banks tended to specialise in small savers' money, mortgages, public authority loans, and long-term securities. In between were sandwiched a third group of institutions, the co-operative banks, lending mainly to local retail trade. In large part these functional distinctions have been washed away, and each of these types of institutions offers full service banking facilities.

Over 850 savings banks operate 14,000 branches throughout Germany. These savings banks have their own clearing organisation in each of the eleven regions and Berlin—the Girozentralen. Several of these have invested part of their resources in general banking and international finance. For example, the Westdeutsche Landesbank-Girozentrale embarked on an ambitious programme to build its international business and in 1969 participated in the management of 40 per cent of all international D-mark issues. The savings banks are steadily assuming broader functions along the lines of universal banking. Their massive resources and tax advantages place them in a favourable competitive position. The co-operative banks, of which there are about 750 industrial and 8,000 agricultural, have their own central institutions. The banking structure in Germany also includes the trade union banks, building and loan associations, mortgage banks, and hire purchase finance houses.

In addition to the large number and wide variety of bank types, banking in Germany has become especially competitive for the following reasons:[10] (1) relative ease of opening new branches, (2) free movement of interest rates, (3) freely convertible D-mark, and (4) free access of foreign banks to the German markets.

At one time the big banks in Germany had a virtual monopoly in financing the larger industrial firms. Their equity holdings and seats on boards of directors gave them a 'tacit claim' on the company's financing business.[11] Some of the large industrial groups retain their own 'house banks' which render important services in such areas as clearing cash balances and regulating the timing of new issues. However, the individual operating companies in the group are free to use outside banks.

The structure of commercial bank balance sheets has not shifted markedly over the past decade, but several features are worthy of discussion. The proportion of savings deposits has increased, reflecting competition for sources of funds. Savings deposits exceed sight deposits but are considerably less than other time deposits. At year-end 1971 approximately half of time deposits were for terms of under three months. Deposits and borrowings from other banks represent 30 per cent of funds. The asset structure of commercial banks is heavily weighted by loans to non-bank customers (48 per cent of assets), and with the expansion in longer-term deposits the banks have been providing medium and long-term finance to industry. Nearly half of the lending to non-banks falls in the over one year maturity. Second in importance among bank assets is lending to other banks (21 per cent of assets). This reflects the nature of money market operations of banks in Germany. The German money market is heavily oriented in the direction of call money transactions wherein banks lend and borrow sight deposits placed with the Bundesbank without security. In this respect the German call money market bears similarity with the London inter-bank market.[12] Ancillary components of the German money market include the commercial bill, Treasury bill, and banker's acceptance markets.

The commercial banks are not substantial holders of Treasury securities, and at year-end 1971 this represented less than 1 per cent of total assets. However, the German banks do hold a substantial amount of corporate securities and bank bonds, these representing close to 9 per cent of asset holdings. The banks are actively involved in the securities market and stock exchanges, functioning as underwriters, brokers and dealers, and managing investments on behalf of customers. Since they are free to purchase corporate securities including equities, they can offer their customers a wide range of services including long-term debt and equity financing. Share and loan issues are as a rule placed through banking syndicates. In 1957 the major issuing banks established a Central Capital Market Committee to make recommendations on the timing of new security issues so as to preserve stability in the capital markets. The scale on which banks operate as buyers of securities depends on their liquidity situation and the current demand for direct credits. For this reason, the dominant role of the banks in the capital markets results in a rapid transmission of monetary policy pressures to that sector of the financial markets.

The central bank uses a variety of measures to control bank credit and liquidity. One of the most important is changes in reserve requirements relative to deposit liabilities. At year-end 1971 cash and balances with the central bank represented 7 per cent of total assets and 13 per cent of non-bank deposits. Reserve requirements may be met on the basis of a monthly average of deposits, which permits bank flexibility in effectively employing working balances.[13] Reserve requirements vary according to term of deposits, size of bank, whether deposits are due to residents or non-residents, and location of the bank. As of year-end 1972 minimum reserve ratios ranged between 7 and 17 per cent for resident deposits. For non-residents minimum reserve ratios were 40 per cent of sight deposits, 35 per cent of time deposits under four years maturity, and 30 per cent of savings deposits. Minimum reserve ratios are changed frequently as a weapon of policy. During 1972 these ratios were increased on three occasions for deposits of residents and once for non-residents.[14]

In addition to its power to change reserve ratios, the Bundesbank has at its disposal a wide array of monetary policy instruments. These include open market operations, establishing conditions for access to rediscount credit from the central bank, fixing the rate for advances on securities, and the right to intervene in the foreign exchange markets, for example by offering favourable terms to cover forward exchange risks (swap policy). Section 19 of the Bundesbank Act authorises the Bundesbank, in dealings with banks, to buy and sell bills at its fixed discount rate including Treasury bills issued by the Federal Government and Länder. The total volume of rediscount credit at the disposal of each bank is limited by the rediscount quotas. These quotas depend on the capital funds of the bank and the applicable multiplier, which may vary for different groups of banks. The rediscount quotas are calculated individually and communicated to the banks. In addition, the Bundesbank may grant 'lombard credits', which are interest bearing loans against the pledge of specified securities. The Bundesbank uses its discretion in providing such advances on securities, depending on the general credit situation and other factors. In general, bank lending rates in Germany quickly reflect changes in central bank discount rate and rates on lombard credits.

Banking in West Germany is especially exposed to international financial pressures. Exports represent close to 23 per cent of GNP. Relative freedom of international capital movements permits substantial flows of funds across the German foreign exchanges. Such developments pose problems for the Bundesbank as well as for the German banks. In 1970 when the banking system was relatively illiquid, German business firms obtained substantial amounts of funds from overseas sources. The German banks were in the position of watching their local business clientele obtain credits from overseas at a time when the Bundesbank was increasing minimum reserve ratios to counter expansion in the domestic money supply resulting from the inflow of foreign funds. Since 1970 the Bundesbank has altered its policy by recycling dollar funds into the U.S. money market, rather than into the Euromarkets. Moreover, German banking law has been amended, providing for reserve requirements applicable to business firms that obtain credits from abroad (Bardepot).

D. SWITZERLAND

With a population of only six million, Switzerland ranks third as a market for foreign and international bond issues and as an international banking centre. Moreover, the constant influx of funds, mainly of short-term maturity, supplements domestic savings in providing a substantial capacity for the export of capital. While the Swiss franc may never become a key currency, due to the small size of the Swiss economy, the Swiss franc is considered the world's safest and most stable currency.

Switzerland has developed into an important financial entrepôt for several reasons. Substantial inflows of funds can be explained by the stability of value and gold cover of the Swiss franc,[15] the high reputation of the Swiss banks which has been earned from careful investment management and respect for confidentiality,[16] political stability, relatively low tax rates, and the availability of facilities for securities trading and transactions in precious metals.[17] The Swiss banks and other investment managers have been as efficient in placing capital in overseas loans and investments as they have been in attracting foreign funds.

The Swiss banks include the 'big three' (Credit Suisse, Swiss Banking Corporation, and Union Bank of Switzerland); twenty-eight Cantonal Banks which offer complete banking services as well as trust services; and thirty-nine Local and Savings Banks. In addition, Switzerland has over a hundred private banks, many of which enjoy an international reputation. The private banks combine regular deposit banking with securities and underwriting operations. Foreign owned banks in Switzerland include branches of several American banking firms: namely Bank of America, First National City Bank of New York, and Morgan Guaranty Trust Company; and affiliates of U.S. and European banks.[18]

Switzerland also possesses a considerable number of finance companies. These companies play a prominent role in financing instalment notes and other paper. The insurance companies, investment management houses, and the investment trusts play an important role in the capital and securities markets in Switzerland. Finally, the financial holding companies, foreign owned or controlled, maintain large share holdings in major industrial firms around the world.

While inflows of funds to Switzerland are attracted by the political and financial stability of the country, the stability of the Swiss franc, and the many investment and deposit options afforded in Swiss banks and financial institutions, the Swiss have also proven themselves extremely competent foreign lenders and investors. In 1971 the Swiss banking system derived 46 per cent of assets and 48 per cent of liabilities from foreign business.[19] Switzerland itself is far too small to absorb large amounts of short or medium-term capital inflows without inflating the currency and the entire domestic economy. In short, foreign funds may not be welcome in Switzerland unless investment opportunities abroad are found for them. However, such opportunities depend on world conditions, which extend beyond the pale of Swiss central bank and governmental policy influence. For this reason, the Swiss National Bank has at times imposed restrictions on payment of interest on foreign deposits, and has also 'frozen' funds from abroad by requiring that the banks deposit such funds in blocked accounts with the Swiss National Bank.

The Swiss banks play a key role in purchasing and managing foreign loan issues, and Switzerland is an important centre for foreign borrowers who wish to obtain funds in the international money and capital markets. Interest rates are generally considerably lower than those prevailing in other major centres. And while underwriting costs and taxes applicable to an issue on the Swiss capital market are higher than on Eurobond issues, total borrowing costs have been lower in Switzerland.[20] In the past the Swiss authorities and the central bank have screened applications for foreign issues carefully, largely with a view toward not exceeding the capacity of the Swiss capital market. Foreign borrowers able to place new bond issues in the Swiss market generally have been those with a high grade credit standing. More recently with the international exchange crises of 1971–3 Switzerland applied the most liberal policy on capital export that it has ever had. Swiss franc loans amounting to 60–80 million Swiss francs have been approved.[21]

A large part of the funds transferred to Switzerland from other countries is invested in Swiss franc loans to foreign borrowers. These afford exchange security as well as an attractive yield. Issuance of foreign loans is in the hands of a banking syndicate which consists of the large banks and several private banking groups. The banking syndicate dominates the Swiss capital market like a cartel and apportions excess participations of the banking consortium to a number of non-member banks.

The central bank enjoys a unique relationship with the banks in Switzerland. In large part this is due to the private character of the Swiss National Bank as well as the marked degree of federalism that prevails in that country. The central bank does not have at its disposal the instrument of compulsory reserves, and must rely heavily on voluntary (gentlemen's) agreements with the banks. These agreements cover such matters as the interest rates paid on bank bonds, foreign-held Swiss franc balances, stock exchange dealing in foreign securities, and restriction of bank credit.[22]

The Swiss credit institutions enjoy considerable freedom of action. Nevertheless, the Swiss National Bank has been highly successful in executing the main task allotted to it by law, namely maintaining a stable gold value of the Swiss franc, i.e., safeguarding the internal value of the currency. This task is made difficult in light of the relative openness of the financial markets and banking system, and the influence that massive capital inflows can exert on domestic liquidity and money supply. In 1971 capital inflows were equivalent to nearly 15 per cent of Swiss gross national product.[23] Aside from voluntary agreements with the banks, the major instruments of monetary policy are discount rate changes, open market policy, and capital export policy. Due to substantial inflows of funds the Swiss banks have remained in a relatively liquid condition. Therefore, they have not made extensive use of rediscount facilities which by statute the Swiss National Bank must provide. However the local banks and savings banks have relied on advances against bonds to obtain funds from the central bank.

Switzerland does not have an active secondary market in Treasury bills, and this has limited the scope of open market policy. The commercial banks usually comply with the central bank's requests to buy from it or sell to it bills or securities, even though their liquidity and ready access to the discount facility give the Swiss banks a high degree of independence. To ease tight money conditions on the eve of window dressing dates, the Swiss National Bank buys Eurodollars from Swiss banks or concludes swap arrangements with them.[24] Due to the facilities provided by the Eurocurrency market, the Swiss banks have no urgent need to develop an active domestic money market. In fact it is possible to regard the closely connected Euro-Swiss franc market in foreign countries as a developing offshore extension of the Swiss money market.

E. CANADA

Canada's banking system is one of the strongest and most highly regarded in the world. For a relatively small country with a population of only twenty-two million, this prestige in itself is quite an accomplishment. Canadian banking is unique and important in a number of respects. The geography of Canada, a large sprawling land mass, has compelled the Canadian banks to develop an efficient and competitive branch banking system with continental scope. Development of efficient securities markets in Canada has provided large corporations with an effective bond financing alternative to bank credits, thereby sharpening the corporate-banker relationship. Adoption of a floating currency has permitted the central bank to focus more clearly on the management of internal economic performance, including regulation of bank credit expansion as a central aspect of overall credit creation. Finally, we should note that there is virtually no direct representation of foreign banks in Canada, in part an outgrowth of Canadian policy toward foreign ownership of domestic business and banking institutions.

The five large chartered banks dominate the banking scene in Canada. All five rank among the fifty largest banks in the world. These banks operate over 6,000 branch offices in all parts of Canada, and control over 90 per cent of banking resources. Four smaller banking institutions complete the list of Canada's federally chartered banks. Canadian banking requirements are also served by a number of smaller institutions including over fifty trust companies (an area in which the chartered banks are not permitted to operate), provincial savings offices, credit unions, and other lending institutions.

One interesting aspect of Canadian banking is that federal

charters are given for a period of only ten years, and must be renewed with the revision of the Bank Act. The 1967 bank legislation was designed to increase competitive attitudes among banks and financial intermediaries. Included among the new provisions in the 1967 legislation are the following:

1. The 6 per cent interest rate ceiling on loans was removed, and interest rate agreements between banks were prohibited.
2. Banks were permitted to extend their mortgage lending to non-guaranteed mortgages.
3. Increased capital needs of banks could be met by issue of debentures as well as ordinary shares.
4. Complementary legislation provided for establishment of the Canada Deposit Insurance Corp. (CDIC) to insure deposits in Canadian banks up to a maximum of $20,000.

The Bank of Canada was established in 1934. Its operations closely resemble those of its counterpart central bank in the United States. It engages in open market operations, discounts for the chartered banks, holds the legal reserves of the chartered banks and periodically revises the required reserve ratio. The Porter Commission and the subsequent legislation in 1967 incorporated several changes in the reserve and liquidity requirements that apply to the banks. First, different reserve ratios are now applied to time (4 per cent) and demand (12 per cent) deposits. Second, these reserve requirements must be met on the basis of a two week average. Third, informal secondary reserves held in the form of Treasury bills and day-to-day loans (loans to investment dealers with government security collateral) were given legal sanction. The 1967 Bank Act empowered the monetary authority to vary these secondary reserves between zero and 12 per cent of Canadian dollar deposits.[25]

The Bank of Canada is the focal point of the money market. Its open market operations in government securities are comparable in scope with those of the Federal Reserve in the United States money market.[26] The Bank of Canada provides lender of last resort facilities to authorised dealers in government securities by means of making purchase and resale agreements

(PRAs) in short-term government securities and banker's acceptances. The amount of such facilities is limited, and the Bank of Canada periodically reviews the ceilings on these lines of credit available to securities dealers.[27]

The international activities of Canadian banks are well developed. International operations extend principally into three areas, namely foreign trade financing, direct overseas representation, and foreign currency activities. Since Canada exports 24 per cent of domestic product, it is no surprise that the Canadian banks are active in financing this trade. In addition to providing short-term letter of credit and documentary draft servicing, the banks have been extending longer-term equipment credits to finance exports, and medium-term financing, in part in U.S. dollars. Direct overseas representation is accomplished by means of several agencies (all located in the United States), over 250 foreign branches, and numerous foreign affiliate institutions. Several large Canadian banks have formed merchant banks based in London and other important cities.

A large proportion of international business is conducted on a foreign currency basis. Between 1960 and 1972 the foreign currency assets of the Canadian chartered banks grew from $2.7 billion to $15.7 billion, representing 28 per cent of total assets. The foreign currency business of Canadian banks extends into swapped deposits (largely for corporate customers), North American U.S. dollar business, merchant banking, and local (offshore) commercial banking.[28]

F. JAPAN

While the financial system in Japan is lacking in depth and variety of institutions, the banking sector is highly developed and efficient. A dozen large city banks include several which rank among the largest twenty banks of the world. The city banks cater to large corporate customers and conduct an extensive international banking operation as well. Another sixty local banks operate numerous branches throughout Japan and serve a clientele consisting mainly of smaller enterprises and households.

Rapid growth of the Japanese economy over the past two decades has strained the rather limited resources of Japan's domestic capital market, and consequently large enterprises have made heavy demands for funds on the city banks. As a result the city banks have been perpetually short of funds and in debt to the Bank of Japan. This has tended to place the city banks in an over-borrowed condition, and particularly sensitive to central bank controls and changes in bank rate.[29]

A permanent feature of Japanese banking over the past decade and a half has been the regular dependence of the city banks on loans from the Bank of Japan. The undeveloped state of the capital market and lack of alternative sources of funds for industrial corporations has at times placed severe pressures on the large commercial banks in Japan. Fortunately, the advanced state of development of Japan's banking system, a co-operative central banking policy, and the willingness and ability of the big banks in Japan to extend their activities into the capital market sector have provided a mechanism for financing rapid economic growth. The Japanese banks provide substantial loan facilities to industrial corporations which are heavily leveraged and dependent upon bank credits. Moreover, the Japanese banks invest in capital market assets including government securities, bank debentures, and industrial bonds and shares. In 1971 the banks acquired the equivalent of one-fourth of new share issues, and one-fifth of new industrial bond issues. Moreover, they acquired nearly 30 per cent of local authority and public enterprise bond issues, and one-fifth of debentures issued by financial institutions.[30]

The ability of the Japanese banking system to generate a substantial portion of both short and long-term credit can be traced to the fact that the banks effectively mobilise the major part of household saving and financial asset accumulation. In 1971 three-fourths of the household sector's increase in financial assets was in the form of cash and bank deposits. Financial intermediaries in Japan other than the banks account for a relatively small share of household savings. This, coupled with the continued injection of central bank credit into the banking system has made it possible for the Japanese banks to satisfy a considerable part of the economy's demand for credit.

In addition to the commercial banks, the Japanese banking system has three long-term credit banks. The oldest, the Industrial Bank of Japan, was established in 1892 to channel foreign capital into appropriate domestic industries. The long-term credit banks issue debentures, the proceeds of which finance their loans and investments in Japanese industry.

Japan has seven trust banks, which conduct a commercial banking business in addition to their regular trust activities. The trust banks carry on a variety of trust activities including money trusts and loan trusts where broadly specified investments are made, pension trusts, securities investment trusts, and real estate trusts.

Monetary policy carried out by the Bank of Japan enjoys special status for several reasons. First, fiscal policy has remained in disuse for much of the postwar period. Second, the banking sector plays a far more important role in credit making than in most other industrial countries.

The Bank of Japan is banker for the government, as well as a bankers' bank. It holds deposit funds for the government, handles the issue of government securities, and functions as agent for the Minister of Finance in buying and selling foreign exchange. The central bank enjoys a variety of monetary policy instruments including Bank Rate, supervision of the discount facility, open market operations, and reserve deposit requirements. Bank Rate changes and administrative supervision of the discount window have been the most effective measures of control in the past. Relatively small changes in Bank Rate generate a considerable change in the banking and financial sector in Japan. Monetary policy in Japan operates as a strong conditioning force on the flow of funds and business activity.

G.   HONG KONG

During the past two decades Hong Kong has enjoyed a vigorous economic growth. Hong Kong possesses an efficient government that has provided needed infrastructure with minimum interference with business. Taxes are low and government budgetary surpluses are frequent. Despite pressures from a growing population, Hong Kong has achieved impressive results. The 1970 per capita income is estimated at $650, which is high by Asian standards. Exports exceed those of any other nation in Asia except Japan. The Crown Colony functions as an investment centre; its banks safeguard the wealth of residents of many countries surrounding Hong Kong; gold can be purchased and sold; and the banks offer a wide variety of clearing, collection and foreign exchange trading services. The presence of official Chinese Communist banks lends weight to the argument that the city serves as a necessary financial agent for that government.

While Hong Kong is a member of the Sterling Area the bulk of the large international capital inflow goes through the free dollar market. Hong Kong operates its own Exchange Funds. The 14.3 per cent devaluation of the pound in 1967 had several effects on the Sterling Area ties of Hong Kong. In 1967 the Hong Kong dollar was devalued, and subsequently revalued upward, yielding a residual devaluation of 5.7 per cent. Second, negotiations were concluded in 1968 for protection against future possible exchange rate adjustments, whereby the United Kingdom agreed to maintain the U.S. dollar value of 90 per cent of official sterling reserves held by Hong Kong. Finally, there was a shift from financing Hong Kong foreign trade with sterling bills to U.S. dollars. The shift to dollar invoicing was in keeping with the fact that nearly half of Hong Kong exports go to the United States, and that American banks have been actively promoting dollar financing and letter of credit services in Hong Kong-United States trade.

Hong Kong's banking structure is something of a paradox. While it has no central bank, it has weathered the storms of financial crises and bank runs as if it had. Approximately one-fourth of Hong Kong's banking resources are devoted to foreign trade financing. The major organs of this international finance are the seventy-three banks, which operate over 360 offices. In addition to these, there are some two dozen representative offices of foreign banks. The banks and branch offices in Hong Kong fall into three groups: (1) the thirty-two foreign banks, which include the Hongkong & Shanghai Banking Corporation and the Chartered Bank; (2) the Hong Kong Chinese banks, some of which are large, and highly efficient; and (3) the thirteen mainland Chinese banks, of which the Bank of China is the most influential.[31] As of year-end 1969 bank deposits totalled in excess of $US 2 billion, probably equal to the national income. Between 20–25 per cent of bank deposits are believed to be owned abroad and because of this the Hong Kong banks maintain fairly comfortable liquidity ratios.[32] Enjoying a wide diversity of financial expertise, Hong Kong rivals better known banking centres.

In terms of functions, the banks may be distinguished in several ways, although these differences are tending to break down with the growth of the local economy. The banks originating in China form a distinct group, and tend to be more occupied with financing sales of mainland exports and accumulating foreign exchange reserves for the Peking Government. Hong Kong is also a collecting point for remittances from the overseas Chinese in South-east Asia and other parts of the world, who wish to send money back to China to support relatives. The Colony represents the largest source of foreign exchange earnings for the Chinese Government.

The foreign banks specialise in financing foreign trade, and especially trade with their own home countries. The British banks, which issue bank-notes in their own names, and several of the larger local Chinese banks handle the bulk of the business of financing industry, by providing working capital loans and term financing. The local Chinese banks established themselves by attracting deposits at relatively high interest rates, and cannot compete in the same areas of credit as the expatriate banks. Consequently, they concentrate on property finance, and personal loans.

The American banks are well represented in Hong Kong due to the large volume of trade with the United States and the fact that over 500 U.S. companies have operations in Hong Kong. U.S. banks have experienced difficulties in attracting lendable funds, in part due to the large base of deposits held by several of the long established foreign banks. The latter do not participate in the inter-bank market for lendable funds. Another problem has been the lack of familiarity of U.S. banks with Chinese businesses, which are 'intricately woven family affairs'.[33] U.S. branches have little opportunity to attract funds by offering higher interest rates to the public. While there are no restrictions on lending rates, the bankers association sets ceilings on rates banks may pay for deposit funds.

Hong Kong possesses no central bank, although the Hong-kong & Shanghai Banking Corporation performs functions associated with such an institution, such as undertaking note issue, serving as principal banker to the government, and performing certain clearing functions.[34] The bank is the largest underwriter of new issues in the Colony.

Hong Kong has enjoyed substantial inflows from abroad for several reasons. First, the political stability and freedom from controls—including the free exchange market—have made Hong Kong one of the world's money havens. Free enterprise, a minimum of government interference, and a free and stable exchange market generally provide conditions which attract capital. Second, Hong Kong functions as a 'money changer' for many countries. Money directed to Indonesia, Taiwan, the Philippines and other countries in South-east Asia is directed through Hong Kong, where on the free market currencies can often be purchased more cheaply than at the official exchange rate prevailing in the receiving country. Third, overseas Chinese in countries such as Indonesia and the Philippines move their wealth and direct excess funds to Hong Kong for safe keeping or investment in factories and real estate. Fourth, business firms in the developed countries such as the United States have brought funds into Hong Kong for investment in joint enterprises and manufacturing establishments. Fifth, nationals of the various countries in South-east Asia have brought funds to Hong Kong, motivated by fears of currency depreciation or inflation at home, or for other reasons. Much of the funds that flow into Hong Kong go out again in the form of money market loans or portfolio investment in other countries. However, a small proportion remains behind, adding to bank liquidity, reserves and deposit growth.

H.   SOVIET UNION

Money and the banking system perform essentially the same tasks in the Soviet Union as they do in other countries. However, the overall environment of banking, credit, and finance is far different. In the Soviet Union production and the distribution of income is by economic plan rather than by market mechanism and free competition. Therefore, individuals are not free to use their money to invest in a business, nor are they free to determine the amount of money balances they maintain. Business investment is restricted to state enterprises, and money and credit are allocated in accordance with the planning blueprint and the needs of productive enterprises.

The banking system plays an important role in the execution of the Soviet financial plan. The State Bank (Gosbank), with its head office in Moscow and over 8,000 branch offices, is the most important banking institution in the Soviet Union. The State Bank's prime function is to provide working capital credits for government enterprises. The Bank holds the deposit accounts of all Soviet firms, has strict control of wage funds, and supervises payments between enterprises. It is in this capacity that the Bank acts as an essential part of the economic control mechanism, insuring that cash resources are used only in accordance with the economic plan. The State Bank also functions as banker for the Treasury, including holding funds on deposit, maintaining close financial supervision of enterprises, and handling budgetary receipts and disbursements of the government.[35]

The Gosbank serves as a central bank by issuing bank-notes, keeping the gold reserve, effecting foreign payments, and providing important fiscal services for the Treasury.[36] The Soviet currency, the rouble, is nominally on the gold standard. The practical significance of this is in establishing an official rate of exchange with other currencies.

During the financial reforms of 1930–32 provision for long-term investment capital was assigned to four special investment banks. Several reorganisations have left one Investment Bank to service the capital needs of the Soviet Union. The Investment Bank is largely a disbursing agent which supervises the expenditure of investment funds made available to state enterprises from the government budget, retained profits, or depreciation reserves. Most of the long-term investment in the Soviet Union has come from interest-free grants paid into the State Bank account of the enterprise undertaking the investment. Since the 1965 reforms, more emphasis has been placed on levying interest charges on bank credits so as to make state enterprises more aware of the economic value of such credit facilities.

The Savings Banks are an important segment of Soviet banking. They are primarily concerned with safeguarding the deposits of tens of millions of individuals. They pay interest at 2–3 per cent per annum and invest all funds in State Bonds. The

Savings Banks perform numerous financial services including issue of travellers' cheques, sale of government bonds to individuals, collection of Communist Party dues, collection of fees for public utility services, and management of the state lottery.

As in capitalist oriented economies, the bulk of money transactions in the Soviet Union takes place by means of transfers of deposit balances maintained by state enterprises in the Gosbank. Only a small per cent of the value of transactions is effected in currency. Workers receive their wages in currency and purchase consumer goods with it. The State Bank operates a quarterly Cash Plan which relates the issue of currency to state transactions with households and to interregional transfers of state enterprises. Credit instruments to assist financing of consumer purchases hardly exist in the Soviet Union.[37] The consumer money circuit in currency is almost completely insulated from the state enterprise money circuit, which consists of giro transfers against deposits in State Banks.

Before concluding our discussion of Soviet banking, brief mention should be made of the International Bank for Economic Co-operation (IBEC). IBEC began to operate in 1964 with the purpose of promoting increased foreign trade and facilitating multilateral settlements between the Comecon countries of Eastern Europe. Located in Moscow, IBEC operates as an agency to facilitate clearing and settlement of current transactions between member countries, much like the now defunct European Payments Union did in the period 1950–58. Clearing is carried out in transferable roubles, which have the same nominal gold content as the domestic rouble. Member countries report all transactions at the end of each day, and the accounting surplus or deficit of each member is determined. That member's net position in the clearing is settled by an increase in deposits with the Bank if that member is in surplus, or by use of revolving short-term credit if that member is in deficit. Use of credit by deficit members beyond a stipulated limit calls for payment of interest. A member country may be authorised to swap transferable roubles in its account at IBEC for convertible currencies. Outside countries that acquire transferable roubles in this way are free to use them for purchase of goods in any of the Comecon countries. IBEC has established correspondent relations with commercial banks in the West, providing for exchange of small amounts of reciprocal balances in convertible currencies including dollars and sterling.[38]

11 The Eurocurrency Market

Probably the most discussed money market of the 1960s and 1970s is the Eurocurrency market. This market is regarded by some as a safe haven for expatriate funds, by others as a much-needed cement for solidifying the international money markets, by others as an international money market in itself, and by still others as a leak in the circuits through which central bankers attempt to enforce their monetary policies.[1]

A generally accepted definition of the market refers to dollar balances deposited in banks outside the United States including the foreign branches of U.S. banks. However, the market is broader since it also consists of other currency balances deposited in banks outside the currency area. Hence the Eurosterling, EuroSwiss franc and EuroD-mark markets extend throughout and beyond Continental Europe. The Eurodollar component of this market is by far the largest, representing nearly three-fourths of the total. The market is largely interbank oriented, consisting of Euro-banks in Western Europe with affiliations extending into Canada, Lebanon, Nassau and Singapore. As one of the largest markets for short-term funds in the world, the Eurocurrency market enjoys a high degree of flexibility and freedom. The market facilitates the rapid transfer of capital throughout the globe, and in this way tends to iron out discrepancies in interest rate relationships between various money centres.

A.   ORIGIN AND NATURE OF THE MARKET

1.   EARLY BEGINNINGS

How and why did the Eurodollar market begin? Einzig traces the origins of the market to 1957 when U.K. authorities, during a serious balance of payments crisis, imposed restrictions on the use of sterling credits for financing non-sterling areas. At the same time the British authorities promoted the use of London facilities in financing third-country trade, and the international deposit-taking banks in London eagerly substituted the dollar for the pound as a financing currency. The liberalisation of exchange controls at the end of 1958 resulted in the development of markets for all major European currencies in addition to the dollar, although Eurodollars have continued to dominate the scene.[2]

The Eurodollar market can be compared to an international banking system based on foreign currency deposits. Major requirements for the growth and development of this type of money market system are: (1) interest rate differentials between national credit markets, and between international money centres; (2) freedom from exchange controls so that investors may take advantage of rate differences; and (3) confidence in the vehicle currency. In the context of postwar history the key currency role of the dollar and continuing U.S. balance of payments deficits have provided some of the requirements for development of the market.

Beginning in 1958 when major European currencies became convertible, interest rates in the United States set the lower limits for Eurodollar deposit rates and the approximate upper limits for Eurodollar loan rates.[3] In 1958–59 when the removal of exchange controls had set the stage for development of the market, rate discrepancies and artificial limits to interest rate flexibility in the United States and elsewhere became crucially important. Eurodollar deposit rates of close to 4 per cent were well above the $2\frac{1}{2}$ per cent Regulation Q ceiling in effect in the

United States on 90–180 day deposits. In the U.S. market for bankers' deposits no interest could be earned on a deposit of less than thirty days. U.S. banks were charging the equivalent of $5\frac{3}{4}$ per cent on business loans, including the compensating balance, while Euro-banks were offering dollar loans at rates of 5 per cent and under. No doubt, artificial limits on interest rate adjustments including Regulation Q were of significance in the early development of this market. Restrictions of more recent vintage, such as the Interest Equalisation Tax and the voluntary foreign restraint lending programmes to assist the U.S. balance of payments also supported the growth of the market since these measures forced European borrowers to resort to Eurodollar channels for funds.

2. NATURE AND SIZE OF THE MARKET

In the Eurocurrency market foreign commercial banks trade demand deposit claims held against U.S. banks. These deposits are converted into earning assets by interest arbitrage operations with other foreign banks or through direct conversion into loans or investments. Trading units are usually in multiples of $1 million. Maturities of deposits and loans vary from call to seven days, one month, three months, and longer. In addition to direct deposits, Euro-banks issue negotiable time certificates of deposit in Eurodollars and Eurosterling.

The Eurodollar market is an inter-bank, over-the-telephone market. In these and other respects it resembles a foreign exchange market.[4] However, the market operates more like an international money market in which liquidity positions may be adjusted, and in which funds may be provided on a relatively short-term basis.

Individual banking participants play a variety of roles in this market, dictated by the extent of their own resources, their willingness to assume long or short positions, types of clientele they serve, location and relative strength or weakness of their own currency *vis-à-vis* principal Eurocurrencies. Some Euro-banks play the role of intermediaries, bridging the gap between supply and demand sides of the market. Some banks are mainly suppliers, while others are mainly users of deposits. The manager of the money position of a Euro-bank determines that bank's position in the market.

Limiting the amount loaned to any one customer or any one country is one of the few safeguards Euro-banks employ. Many Euro-banks act as intermediaries only, dealing primarily with banks, and having minimum contact with commercial and international borrowers. By doing this they keep their risk to a minimum, yet perform a useful service by bringing together major international banks with loanable funds but with no knowledge of local loan markets. Thus, the market is largely a wholesale one, characterised by a high proportion of inter-bank activity, and relatively narrow profit margins. Since Eurodollar transactions usually involve prime customers, inter-bank loans can be arranged in a few minutes or hours, with actual transfers of funds by telephone or teletype with a letter of confirmation for documentation.

Eurodollar transactions are considered practically costless for several reasons. They are large-scale, and are generally considered to carry a low risk. Moreover, few additional facilities or personnel are required. Banks in this market are willing to work with narrower margins than in the case of domestic currency transactions. At mid-1969 for example, the margin for prime name banks was $\frac{1}{32}$ per cent and $\frac{1}{4}$ per cent, while that for prime industrial or commercial firms was about $\frac{1}{2}$ per cent. In some cases margins may be as large as $2\frac{1}{2}$ per cent, depending on the type of borrower and other factors.[5]

The Bank for International Settlements reports its own estimates on the size of the Eurocurrency market. In 1960 the size of the market was probably in the area of \$1–2 billion.[6] By 1966 the Bank for International Settlements estimated the market had grown to approximately \$18 billion, and by 1972 to \$131 billion. In part this growth is due to the strong competitive position of the European banks which do not have to maintain cash reserve requirements, or conform to restrictions on payment of interest on varying categories of deposits.

Growth of the market has depended upon a parallel expansion in demand and supply for funds. On the demand side important factors have been tightening credit conditions in the United States, the balance of payments restraint programme imposed by U.S. authorities, and unrest in the currency markets.[7] On the supply side major influences have been the relative ease of monetary conditions in some Continental European countries, substantial currency fears with respect to sterling, the French franc, and more recently the U.S. dollar, and the U.S. mandatory controls programme which stimulated U.S. corporate Eurobond flotations and the temporary deposit of these funds in the Eurodollar market.[8]

Over the decade of the 1960s and early 1970s significant changes took place in the geographic origins of these Eurocurrency funds. In 1964 Western Europe, North America, and Japan were net users of Eurodollars. The Middle East, Latin America, and 'other' Western Europe countries were net suppliers. By the late 1960s Western Europe became the most important supplier of funds, while North America's role as a supplier of funds became more accentuated. London and Canada are to a great extent intermediaries in the system. London generally receives funds from all areas except the United States. Canada generally receives funds from Western Europe and the rest of the world, and supplies funds to the United Kingdom and United States.

3. SOURCES AND USES OF FUNDS

Originally, primary suppliers of funds to the Eurodollar market were central banks. During the 1960s the relative importance of central banks as suppliers of funds diminished. In part this may be explained by the 1962 Federal Reserve Board amendment to Regulation Q which exempted foreign official dollar holdings from the interest rate ceilings. Until 1971 central banks and official agencies remained an important source of funds for the market. Central banks have been motivated by a variety of factors in deciding to add or subtract funds from the market, including the desire to influence domestic liquidity and to neutralise the effect from short-term international flows of funds on liquidity, to maintain orderly conditions in the international financial markets, and to establish desired swap situations for commercial banks operating in the foreign exchange markets.[9] In the spring of 1971 the Group of Ten central banks agreed not to increase their reserve holdings in the Euro-market, and during the 1971 currency crisis shifted more of their placements out of the market and into the U.S. money market.[10] However, in the same year central banks outside the Group of Ten placed a substantial amount of dollars in the Eurodollar market, and

converted some dollar holdings into other currencies for placement in the Eurocurrency market. Central banks may place
funds in the market through their own domestic commercial
banks, through the Bank for International Settlements, or
through foreign commercial banks.

In addition to the central banks, other primary suppliers include commercial banks, non-financial institutions, and individual investors. Commercial banks constitute a second major
group of depositors in the Eurodollar market by receiving
dollar deposits in countries without organised money markets
and utilising the Eurodollar market as an outlet for short-term
funds, or by accepting domestic currency liabilities and converting the corresponding excess reserves into dollars. Not
unlike the central banks, foreign commercial banks find the
abundance of short-term investment opportunities and favourable yields very attractive. In countries such as Germany,
France and Italy where broad and diversified money market
facilities have been slow to develop, the commercial banks welcome the opportunity to diversify their investments and to
equalise the average maturity of their liabilities and assets.

Large financial corporations including insurance companies, and non-financial corporations, constitute a third
group of suppliers of funds to the Eurodollar market. These
sources of funds are motivated by considerations of interest
rates, safety and convenience. Large international corporations
may deposit the proceeds of Eurobond issues until such time as
these funds are needed for corporate purposes. Cash flow and
liquidity considerations might prompt financial corporations
to maintain Eurocurrency deposits in various Euro-banks.
Until 1965 United States direct investment affiliates were depo-
siting substantial sums in banks in Western Europe, Canada
and other areas. Upon initiation of the voluntary balance of
payments programme in that year the major portion of these
funds was repatriated to parent corporations in the United
States.

Borrowers of funds in the Eurodollar market include commercial banks, investment brokers and dealers, firms engaging
in foreign trade, international corporations, and government
units. Canadian banks use funds obtained through U.S. dollar
deposits in making overnight loans to securities firms in New

York. U.S. commercial banks have borrowed dollar deposits from their foreign branches to rebuild their own reserve positions. Many commercial banks rely on Eurodollars to extend loans to exporters and importers, as well as other types of customers. Euro-banks often swap Eurodollars into local currency in order to make loans to domestic borrowers. This practice is followed by London banks to provide funds for U.K. hire-purchase companies and local government authorities. International corporations are major borrowers of Eurodollars and other Eurocurrencies, including Norwegian shipping firms, Japanese commercial trading firms, American petroleum and chemical companies, and Italian State corporations.[11] American companies doing business abroad rely heavily on the market as a means of complying with the mandatory balance of payments controls programmes of the United States government.

B. STATUS OF LONDON IN THE MARKET

1. LONDON AS AN INTERNATIONAL DEPOSIT CENTRE

While London may no longer function as a major source of long-term capital for the rest of the world, due to the U.K. balance of payments situation and underlying economic relationships, the City of London has enjoyed a comeback during the 1960s as an entrepôt for short-term and long-term international capital flows. In recent years London banks have been competing vigorously and successfully with New York institutions for a larger share of the international deposit business. In part, the competition has been intensified by the presence in London of many overseas branches of American and other foreign banks. Branches of American commercial banks became a prominent part of the London financial scene in the late 1960s.

Why is London the centre of the Eurodollar market? There is probably no other financial centre capable of competing for this role, except New York, and it is quite simple to rule New York out of consideration. New York is a 'high cost' banking centre, if only because formal reserve requirements, FDIC assessments, and other cost elements raise the price that must be charged for loan funds by New York banks. Second, Regulation Q interest ceilings and the prohibition on payment of interest for demand deposits prevent American banks from competing freely for funds. Third, since 1965 foreign lending by U.S. banks has been subject to the voluntary credit restraint programmes whereby American banks could not expand the amount of their loans to foreigners. Finally, American authorities probably would be unwilling to see U.S. banks accept foreign currency deposits and at the same time be further exposed to the abrupt inflows and outflows of funds that accompany an international deposit business.

2. LONDON'S SHARE OF THE MARKET

London's central role in the Eurodollar market strengthened during the later part of the 1960s.[12] According to Scott, in 1965 U.K. banks accounted for 47 per cent of U.S. dollar liabilities reported by banks in the eight country reporting area. By 1968 the U.K. share had increased to 57 per cent. Apparently this dominant role persisted beyond 1968. Bank for International Settlements figures indicate that dollar liabilities in U.K. banks relative to total dollar liabilities in the Eurodollar market were 56 and 54 per cent at year-end 1969 and 1970 respectively.[13] The U.K. banks have enjoyed a sizeable share of the Eurocurrency business due to London's strong position in the dollar sector of that market. In 1971 as the non-dollar component of the Eurocurrency market increased in importance, the share of U.K. banks in the overall market decreased from 47 to 45 per cent. The share of U.S. bank branches in London's Eurocurrency business declined relatively in 1971 as loans to their U.S. head offices were reduced and as London branches of U.S. banks placed much of these funds with other banks in London, which loaned them abroad.

During 1971 there was a large expansion in U.K. bank lending of foreign currency to residents. Most of this lending was to finance U.K. companies' overseas investment. U.K. residents deposit funds in the Eurocurrency market, provided they have exchange control permission to hold foreign currencies. Direct investment by U.K. companies in non-sterling countries is often financed by borrowing foreign currencies and pending investment, redepositing the funds in U.K. banks. Trading and commercial companies with world-wide operations, including shipping and oil companies, are permitted to hold foreign currency balances to finance their operations. Funds obtained from disinvestment of U.K. residents' foreign securities are frequently held in the London Eurocurrency market pending reinvestment. These balances tend to fluctuate according to developments on overseas securities markets, especially New York.

We should recognise that a number of 'parallel' or complementary markets have developed within London, which are supported by and lend support to the Eurocurrency market in London. These include the market for local authority loans (actually deposits held by these borrowers), finance company deposits, and inter-bank sterling balances.[14]

3. OTHER EUROCURRENCY CENTRES

In addition to London, other financial centres around the globe have carried out specialised Eurocurrency functions, and therefore have attracted branch offices of U.S. and other foreign banks. These include the major cities of Western Europe – particularly Paris, Zurich, Brussels and Rome – as well as Beirut, Nassau, Hong Kong and Singapore.

Paris and several other Continental cities are clearing centres for Eurocurrency transactions. Paris is a focal point for Euro-sterling and EuroSwiss franc dealings. During 1971 the French banks recorded the largest increase in external foreign currency liabilities of any group of banks on the European Continent. In major financial centres in Switzerland, Euro-banks engage in Eurosterling and other Eurocurrency transactions. The Swiss banks are the largest net suppliers of Eurocurrency funds. Generally, the funds placed by the Swiss banks at their customers' own risk, trustee funds, are excluded from Eurocurrency totals. Luxembourg has also become an important centre for Eurocurrency deals, especially in connection with balances resulting from Eurobond flotations. The Belgium-Luxembourg banks transact the largest volume of business in Eurocurrencies other than dollars and are the largest direct lenders to foreign non-bank residents.[15] The Continental cities are the converging and redistributing centres for Eurocurrency balances sent from outlying centres such as Beirut, Nassau, and Hong Kong.

The so-called safe haven centres have developed into important collecting points for Eurodollars and other Eurocurrencies.

These centres include Nassau, Panama City, Hong Kong and Beirut. They share similar advantages in the form of favourable tax climate, political stability, and absence of exchange controls. Branches of American and other foreign banks have been attracted to all of these centres in large part because of the ability to attract Eurodollar and other types of deposits.

The idea of developing an Asian dollar market in Singapore came in 1968 when the Singapore branch manager of Bank of America suggested that foreign currency deposits should be attracted to that city. At the time there was a 40 per cent tax on foreign currency deposits, which effectively eliminated this aspect of the deposit business for banks located in Singapore.[16] Discussions with the Singapore Finance Minister resulted in elimination of the tax, and the commercial trading hub of Malaysia also became the focal point of a newly emerging regional money market. Singapore has become the centre of the market because of its political stability, strategic location, sound financial policy, and moderate approach to taxation.

Other centres in Asia might have challenged Singapore for this role. For example, Hong Kong is a major trade and financial centre. However, Hong Kong also taxes interest on deposits. Japanese exchange controls were probably too rigid to permit Tokyo to serve as a centre for foreign currency deposits and lending operations. Moreover, the Japanese authorities apparently would not wish to have their money market exposed to the swings of supply and demand pressures characteristic of the Eurodollar market in Western Europe.

Since the Singapore authorities relaxed their posture on foreign currency deposits, a number of banks have obtained a licence to accept deposits there, including Bank of America, First National City Bank, Chase Manhattan, the Chartered Bank, Hongkong & Shanghai Bank, the Bank of Tokyo, and General Bank of the Netherlands. The size of the market in 1969 was approximately $100 million. In 1969 a Singapore official estimated that deposits in the market could reach $400 million by year-end 1970. By 1971 the market had reached a level of $1 billion and in 1972 was reported between $2-3 billion. Loan operations are small-scale relative to lending taking place in the Eurocurrency market in London and on the European continent. Transactions are also carried out in Asian D-marks and Asian sterling.

The Asian dollar market is closely linked to the Eurodollar market, and interest rates are closely aligned to those prevailing in London and Paris. The hope of bankers is that the Asian dollar market will attract much of the loose money that is owned by the overseas Chinese, and that Asian governments will begin switching some of their liquid reserves to Singapore. This could result in a substantial expansion of the market.

C.   ROLE OF SPECIALISED INSTITUTIONS

Development of Eurocurrency banking operations in London has attracted numerous foreign banks and specialised institutions, capable of providing the type of services required in this large and steadily expanding market. In the two sections which follow we examine the role played by London branches of American banks and the type of Eurocurrency operations now familiar to the medium-term consortium banks operating in London.

1. U.S. BANKS IN LONDON

One of the most significant developments in international banking in the late 1960s was the invasion of London by American banks. In the period 1966 to 1972, U.K. branches (almost all in London) of U.S. banks increased in number from twenty-one to forty-five. At year-end 1972 these branches held $42 billion in assets, representing 56 per cent of the total assets of foreign branches of American banks. This means that at year-end 1972 the average assets per U.K. branch was close to $975 million.

From the data contained in Table 11-1 we can observe that in the period 1963–9 London branches of American banks grew in relative importance in the Eurocurrency aspect of international banking. However, since 1969 their share of the non-sterling business levelled off and even declined somewhat. These changes have taken place within an environment of substantial growth in non-sterling liabilities in all U.K. banks.

American branches in London enjoy several advantages over their competitors in attracting deposits. They have been exposed to prior banking relationships with firms that have had contacts with the head offices of banks in the United States.

Moreover, they are better known to U.S. firms operating in Western Europe. Not restricted by the Regulation Q ceiling

Table 11.1

Non-sterling Liabilities in U.K. Banks
(Year-end Figures)

£ million

Year	Total Non-sterling Liabilities in U.K. Banks	Held by American Banks	Percentage held by American Banks
1963	1,798	440	24
1965	2,930	1,091	37
1967	6,329	2,847	45
1969	16,902	9,110	54
1970	21,072	10,605	50
1971	24,028	11,540	47
1972*	30,878	13,890	45

* Data reflect October 18, 1972 figures.

Source: Bank of England, *Quarterly Bulletin*, 'The Euro-currency Business of Banks in London', March 1970, p.48; also same *Bulletin*, March 1972 and December 1972 issues, Table 8.

applicable to domestic operations, London branches of American banks can pay rates competitive with non-regulated money market rates in New York.

Eurodollar lending policies of American overseas branches have varied. Some branches carry on a full range of lending operations. Others concentrate on lending to other banks, or on loans which finance foreign trade. A number of banks apply various restrictions to their lending activities. Branch lending activities are generally subject to specific instructions from the head office, including limits on lines of credit and amounts to be loaned in specific loan categories.

In a study of the lending and deposit activities of American branches in London, Saunders found that Eurodollar deposits were put to four primary uses.[17] These included swaps into foreign currency loans, loans to corporate customers, loans in the inter-bank Eurodollar market, and repatriation to the bank's head office. Due to operational necessities, it is not always feasible for banks to match forward and spot positions in various currencies although they make an effort to do so. American banks have covered their foreign currency purchases as far as possible.

Sterling is the currency usually swapped, with the proceeds finding short-term outlets in deposits with U.K. local authorities and loans in the discount market. Local authorities represent one of the main outlets for funds raised in the 'complementary markets' in London.[18] Their borrowing is secured by local rate revenue. In the short end of the market the maturity terms range from overnight to almost one year. The minimum sum taken on deposit is usually £50,000, although lesser amounts can be negotiated.[19] Eurodollars have also been swapped to make commercial loans in sterling.

Dollar loans in London are largely to foreign affiliates of U.S. corporations. While head offices have attempted to insure that London branches lend at rates no lower than the head offices, it has been extremely difficult to enforce this policy. In order to compete successfully for dollar business, American branches have been forced to lend at rates below those prevailing in New York. An important exception to this might exist in a period of unusually tight money.

In the period 1969–70 the largest single use of Eurodollars by American branches was in relending to U.S. head offices. This pattern was reversed in late 1970 and 1971. It appears that American banks have been net borrowers in the market, with this net borrowing reflected as U.S. deposit liabilities to the British banking system. The borrowing bank acquires a deposit at another U.S. bank, which may be carried as a correspondent balance, or more likely, clears through the Federal Reserve machinery. Member banks have found this 'use' of Eurodollars an important means of reconstituting their own reserve positions. However, Eurodollar claims on the United States by London contain substantial balances which serve a function that is quite removed from head office adjustment of reserve positions at the Federal Reserve. These claims contain substantial loans to the American money market by banks in London, mostly Canadian banks, through their New York and San Francisco agencies. In order to earn yields competitive with London rates the Canadian banks have made commercial loans and broker's loans.[20] In his study Altman found that Canadian bank street lending varied positively with total stock broker loans in New York.[21]

The Eurodollar market has come to play an essential role for major money market and multinational U.S. banks. In general, the market opens up a greater variety of options for American banks, in the direction of further extending profitable branch office locations, in the sources and uses of international funds, and in the character and variety of loan and foreign exchange operations from which U.S. banks may choose. In the paragraphs which follow we shall confine our discussion to four areas in which access to the Eurodollar market provides American banks with significant operating advantages.

The market's attraction for the money desk manager of the large U.S. commercial bank should be clear. Depending upon a wide variety of conditions and circumstances in and around the money markets the money manager will call upon one or more of the following sources of liquidity to adjust the bank's reserve position on a day-to-day basis: the federal funds market, the Federal Reserve discount window, sale of securities, more aggressive sale of CDs, and the purchase of Eurodollars. The last two of these items have come to be regarded as direct offsets, in the sense that conditions of tight money in 1966 and 1968–9 were accompanied by CD runoffs and partially offsetting increases in the liabilities of U.S. banks to their foreign branches.[22] Not only does the U.S. bank provide a key link between the markets for funds entering the Eurocurrency market, but these markets in turn provide opportunities by which the money position of the bank may be more flexibly managed. In recent years the Federal Reserve has employed the interest ceiling on time deposits as an instrument of anti-inflationary policy. Through open market operations money market rates are driven through the ceilings on interest rates which U.S. head offices may pay on CDs under Regulation Q. As a result, holders of CDs permit them to mature, investing the proceeds in other more attractive money market instruments. The banking system thus experiences a shift from time to demand deposits which call for a higher reserve requirement, placing banks in a generally contractionary position. These CD runoffs affect individual banks through adverse clearings, and the banking system via a shift toward the demand deposit category, which calls for somewhat higher overall reserve requirements. During the first half of 1969, the increase in head office liabilities to foreign branches nearly equalled the decline in large CDs of weekly reporting banks.[23] Until 1969 the attractiveness of the Eurodollar market as a source of funds for U.S. banks was quite favourable due to the fact that borrowings of head offices from foreign branches were not subject to reserve requirements. An individual bank could increase its reserves by borrowing from an overseas branch, except that the reserves one bank gained were lost by another. Such borrowing could be varied as a defensive operation by individual banks attempting to maintain the level of deposits.[24] During the first three quarters of 1969 Eurodollar borrowings of large U.S. money market banks increased by $8.7 billion, but their growth tapered in the final quarter of that year. The levelling off in growth of head office liabilities to overseas branches was partly the result of amendments to Regulations D and M, which deal with reserve requirements and foreign activities of member banks.[25]

An amendment to Regulation D requires that member banks count outstanding cheques or drafts arising out of Eurodollar transactions as demand deposits subject to reserve requirements. This action increased the required reserves of the large money market banks by close to $600 million.[26] In August of the same year the Board of Governors amended both Regulation D and M. These amendments placed a 10 per cent marginal reserve requirement on net borrowings of banks from their foreign branches to the extent that these borrowings exceed a base period amount. Reserve requirements were also placed on direct bank borrowings from foreign sources other than their own foreign branches.

A second area of importance for U.S. banks is that the Eurodollar market permits these banks to bid for business that might be unobtainable in the United States. The foreign credit restraint restricts the volume of foreign lending that head offices may undertake. The Eurodollar market permits the overseas branches of U.S. banks access to massive flows of funds, which are needed in large amounts to satisfy the enormous demands of U.S. corporate affiliates operating overseas.

Another important consideration is that the facilities of the Eurodollar market tend to round out the foreign operations of major American banks. This rounding out process refers to the world-wide 'network' of channels through which lendable funds flow, to the variety of currencies which American banks may lend and borrow, and to the mixture of wholesale and retail deposit and lending operations provided by individual American banks.

Finally, the Eurodollar market provides considerable growth opportunities for U.S. banks. Sophisticated American banks have taken advantage of such opportunities by opting for branches in London, Nassau, and other Eurocurrency deposit centres. London branches especially have afforded excellent opportunities for American banks, due to the rapid growth and large volume of Eurocurrency operations there.

While on the surface it is possible to detect a number of advantages for U.S. banks from their presence in the Eurodollar market via overseas branches, there are a number of important implications regarding the structure and soundness of banking operations. Moreover, the large relative role of American bank operations in the Eurodollar market and international banking in general, raises serious questions regarding the profitability of Eurodollar operations for U.S. banks.

Prior to 1965, the structural relationships between interest rates in the Eurodollar market and the United States could be compared to a sandwich within a sandwich.[27] The outside sandwich consisted of Regulation Q interest rate ceilings and the effective U.S. prime rate. These constituted the buying and selling rates for corporate treasurer funds in the United States. The Eurodollar buying and selling rates constituted the inside sandwich, and permitted Euro-banks to compete successfully against U.S. banks for dollar deposits, and to offer Eurodollars at loan rates well below those prevailing in the U.S. Early in 1965 the Eurodollar prime loan rate cut across the effective U.S. prime rate, and from 1965–9 continued to hover close to the U.S. rate. In effect the cost of U.S. loans to foreigners provided a partial ceiling. The changes that have taken place since 1965 when the foreign credit restraint programme was instituted were to shift foreign loan demand to Western European sources of funds, including the Eurocurrency market. Since 1965 Eurodollar loan rates have been relatively free to rise as high as the cost of domestic (U.S.) funds.[28]

Whether this new relationship between U.S. and Eurodollar prime rates has influenced the profitability of U.S. bank operations in the Eurocurrency market depends upon several considerations, including the effect of Eurodollar growth on deposit and loan volume, and the margins between deposit and lending rates of interest.

Participation in the Eurodollar market by U.S. banks can expand the volume of their loan-deposit operations in several ways. First, the multinational banks, of which some twenty have been identified,[29] are better able to expand their lending volume both at home and overseas during periods of tight money than other U.S. banks.

Second, volume increases may follow from a multiplier effect operating within the Eurocurrency market. The Eurodollar credit multiplier, which has been compared with the money (deposit) expansion process within a commercial banking system, has been described as 'potentially large'. Its size has been estimated as less than one,[30] and in the range of 1.5 to 2.0.[31] This is because many European banks are not required to hold dollar reserves relative to Eurodollar deposits, and Eurobanks often achieve a close balance in the respective maturities of their Eurodollar deposits and loans. Any sizeable leakages from the market would tend to reduce the size of the multiplier. An important drain in 1968–9 was the large borrowings from the market by U.S. banks.

A third source of increases in volume could come from non-dollar Eurocurrency operations of foreign branches of American banks. While the volume in this area thus far has been dwarfed by Eurodollar volume, the amount probably runs into several billions of dollars.

Doubtless, profit margins for American banks have been narrower in the Eurodollar market than for comparable transactions effected at home. This imputes a 'marginal' tone to business volume in the market. This is probably not a correct view of the situation. Competitive pressures at home and abroad have made it clear to major U.S. banks that retention of large corporate customers and other equally mobile bank customers calls for a flexible strategy, and one designed to defensively safeguard existing and new business connections. American banks have 'given' to the changing competition of what has increasingly become an international bank loan and deposit environment. Therefore, the dynamics of the situation in the late 1960s strongly suggests that American banks were compelled to offer lower margin Eurodollar services to corporate and other customers who would have found alternative banking connections willing to offer these services in the absence of this flexible posture on the part of major U.S. banks. Fortunately, for American banks, the relatively low margin Eurodollar loan and deposit volume may be displacing only a small proportion of domestic business, perhaps no more than 10 per cent of loan and deposit volume in U.S. banks. However, the percentage would be much higher if we compared this Eurodollar volume to total loans and deposits of the two dozen or more U.S. banks which derive a sizeable portion of their aggregate volume through overseas branch operations in the Eurodollar market.

2. MEDIUM-TERM CONSORTIUM BANKS

Medium-term consortium banks appear to have become a permanent feature in the Eurocurrency market in London. At year-end 1972 close to twenty such banks could be identified, most with a London headquarters, several located in Paris and Brussels. These institutions have been organised and are owned by shareholding banks from the United Kingdom, Continental Europe, the United States, Canada and Japan. In 1972 asset holdings of these institutions ranged between £25 million and £500 million.[32]

The consortium banks have strong connections through their parent institutions, which has resulted in a rapid expansion in their Eurocurrency operations. The list of shareholder parent banks includes most of the fifty largest banks in the world. Several shareholder banks have interests in more than one consortium institution. For example, Midland Bank has an interest in Midland and International Bank, London (MAIBL), and

Banque Européenne de Credit à Moyen Terme, Brussels (BEC). Hambros Bank has interests in Western American Bank, London, and Interunion Bank, Paris.

The consortium banks have tended to concentrate on longer term lending while depending on relatively short-term non-sterling deposit sources of funds. Bank of England published statistics indicate that in 1971 the consortium banks in London as a group held £1,314 million in non-sterling claims compared with total outstanding claims of £24,743 million. This represents approximately 5 per cent of non-sterling claims outstanding at that time. On the other hand the London consortium banks held £581 million in Eurocurrency loans with maturities of one year or more, or 17 per cent of same maturity loans outstanding held by all London institutions.[33] Most of these were claims on overseas residents other than banks.

During 1972 demand for Eurocurrency credits, including medium-term maturities, remained low. Therefore the consortium banks had to rely on lending to established customers in countries such as Mexico and Canada. Moreover, conditions throughout 1972 made lending in developing countries more attractive, and it is likely that consortium banks increased their loans to governments and banks in these countries. It was for this reason that some criticism was levelled at Euro-banks which decline to participate in term loans to 'reasonably leveraged' corporations, but turn around and make a term deposit with a bank whose capital position is 'less than the three-year average after tax cash flow' of the corporate credit that was turned down.[34]

While they have made substantial penetration in the area of medium-term Eurocurrency lending, the consortium banks have had relatively little impact in other types of international banking activities in London. For example, they have not extended themselves significantly into investment banking, underwriting, portfolio management, Eurobonds, or dollar certificates of deposit. Nevertheless, diversification may be the pattern these institutions will follow in future.

D. POLICY IMPLICATIONS

The growth and success of the Eurodollar market, and the increasing presence of American banks and other specialised institutions in that market present a number of questions for the effective formulation and implementation of monetary policy in the United States and in other countries whose financial markets possess important links with the Eurocurrency market. The two broad areas of central bank responsibility are concerned with credit control and balance of payments stabilisation.

Since 1966 the Eurodollar market has become an important means of reserve adjustment for American banks. U.S. banks with foreign branches that have access to the market are in a position to attract dollar deposits and their related federal funds (balances at Federal Reserve Banks). While the Eurodollar market cannot in itself create additional bank reserves for the U.S. banking system, it provides a means for more intensive utilisation of existing reserves via their redistribution through the American banking system. The general effect is to shift reserve balances toward major money market banks, an outcome similar to that which followed the development of the federal funds market in the early 1960s.

Access to the Eurodollar market is especially meaningful to U.S. banks during periods of tight money, which are usually accompanied by runoffs of certificates of deposit at large U.S. money market banks. The money market banks are in the position of greatest exposure to CD runoffs during tight money, and likewise have greater access to Eurodollar sources of reserve replenishment should they enjoy the luxury of one or more overseas branches.[35]

According to an analysis made by Governor Andrew Brimmer, banks with ready access to Eurodollar inflows were more successful (in 1969) in cushioning the impact of monetary restraint than were other banks.[36] The implication from this is clear. Monetary policy designed to restrain credit creation may have an important built-in side effect – namely to redistribute bank reserves and deposits toward 'multinational' banks, those with foreign branches. Any uneven incidence of monetary pressures with respect to different categories of banks injects a banking structure aspect into the formulation and implementation of credit policy.

Eurodollar borrowings by overseas branches of American banks, and the placement of these funds with head offices, tends to inject a measure of confusion into the balance of payments measures that are commonly referred to in assessing the strength of the dollar and the international competitiveness of the American economy. This confusion was magnified in 1969, and neither of the two conventional measures of the overall balance of payments position, the liquidity and the official settlements balances, seemed to convey the changes in the underlying relationships. The rationale of the official settlements balance is that only official holdings of dollars represent a meaningful potential claim on U.S. reserve assets. Substantial inflows of interest sensitive private capital, representing an increase in U.S. liabilities to commercial banks abroad, assisted in reducing dollar reserves of foreign monetary authorities, thereby providing a substantially favourable official settlements balance. This balance should not necessarily be interpreted as a sign of fundamental improvement.[37] On the other hand, the liquidity deficit in 1969 greatly exaggerated the extent of worsening in the U.S. balance of payments, by not counting as an offset to borrowings by U.S. banks from foreigners, the increase in U.S. short-term assets abroad.

Finally, we should note that the substantial Eurodollar borrowings of American banks placed severe upward pressures on Eurodollar interest rates, induced foreign investors to demand dollars for Eurodollar investments, thus depleting liquid dollar holdings of several foreign central banks.[38] The impact on the reserve positions of some European countries was a cause for concern in 1969, and resulted in the adoption of various types of regulations designed to limit lending in the Eurocurrency markets. Early in 1969 banks in France were instructed to eliminate net foreign currency asset positions *vis-à-vis* non-residents. The Italian monetary authorities similarly took action to restrain Eurodollar placements by Italian commercial banks.[39] Similar measures were followed in Belgium.

While the prospects for future growth of the Eurodollar market seem favourable, they may be strongly influenced by the monetary policies pursued both in the United States and in certain Western European countries. Early in 1970 the new Chairman of the Board of Governors of the Federal Reserve System, Arthur Burns, proposed that U.S. banks should be allowed to compete more freely for deposits in the domestic money market.[40]

12 International Banking and the Developing Countries

'Currently there is a world shortage of capital for which the developing nations must compete.'[1] In these few pointed words a leading writer on the subject of economic development has summarised the major problem which will face the developing nations for the remainder of the twentieth century. There are two dimensions of this world-wide capital shortage, in so far as the less developed nations are concerned. These hinge on the need to develop domestic financial market institutions and patterns of behaviour necessary to generate and mobilise capital funds, and the need to provide suitable international channels through which capital may be directed toward the developing countries. The former problem reflects the necessity for achieving a proper allocation of internal resources as between capital and consumer goods, whereas the latter is concerned with the requirement that an international transfer of purchasing power and real resources take place.

The connection between financial development and economic growth can be viewed from a number of perspectives. Patrick singles out three distinct contributions that the financial system can make in the direction of enhancing the growth process. These include encouraging a more efficient allocation of wealth, stimulating a more efficient mix of new investment, and providing increased incentives to save, invest and work.[2]

International banking can play a salient role in these areas, as well as make other contributions to the well-being of the developing nations. As we shall see in the pages that follow, American banks operating in the developing nations have addressed themselves to fulfilling important development finance functions, in addition to pursuing the international quest for profit. As the president of a major internationally oriented bank has noted, the prime function of international banks is the creation of 'integrated packages of capital and know how' to stimulate economic development on a world-wide scale.[3]

A. GENERAL RELATIONSHIPS WITH THE DEVELOPING COUNTRIES

1. PAST RELATIONSHIPS

During the decade of the 1960s a growing number of U.S. banking officers have evidenced an increased awareness of the financing needs and business potential in the developing countries.[4] Doubtless, internationally oriented commercial banks are likely to play an important role in the future growth of the emerging nations of Asia, Africa, and Latin America. They have much to offer in satisfying the banking and financial market needs of these developing countries. However, in the course of servicing the development needs of these nations, special problems are likely to appear, if only because of the differing business, social, and economic philosophies and way of life espoused in the less developed nations. Therefore, a review of past relationships is in order, if only to set the picture for recognising the existence of different attitudes and viewpoints from the perspective of the residents in developing and developed countries.

From the point of view of residents of the developing nations the extension of European and subsequently American banking operations into their lands has had a number of negative effects. Under the colonial system that existed prior to 1950 the extension of branches by banks in the metropolitan centres of London and Paris resulted in the integration of the colonial territory 'into the branch banking system of the metropolitan country'.[5] Hence, monetary conditions in the metropolitan country fundamentally influenced those prevailing in the colonial territories, whether such conditions were appropriate in light of current business trends, or not. Thus, if interest rates were raised in the United Kingdom as a result of a rise in Bank Rate, interest rates would be raised by the branches of British banks operating in many parts of the world without special reference to the needs of the individual overseas territories being served by these branches.[6]

A second feature of the international banking activities of expatriate institutions has been the retention of standards and conventions to which the banks had become accustomed in their native (metropolitan) countries, and which they exported in overseas territories. Not infrequently this has presented real operating difficulties in the way of obtaining mortgage security on real property loans, common in more developed countries with highly formalised systems of land tenure. Moreover, it presents real policy difficulties for banks accustomed to providing mainly short-term credit at home, but where indigenous business firms request longer-term credits. Obviously, the capital needs of firms in the less developed countries cannot be satisfied given the absence of long-term capital market facilities, and this places pressure on foreign banks operating in these countries to provide more long-term international credits than they ordinarily would make from their head offices at home.

A third feature of the commercial banking activities of overseas branches and representative offices is that in the past they often concentrated their lending on expatriate industries oriented toward exporting to these developing nations, or that were engaged in relatively narrow occupational pursuits such as the extractive fields and plantations and mining. It has been stated that such industry disseminates only minor benefits to the local economy in the way of stimulating related enterprises and productivity gains. It would not be accurate to make the preceding point without noting that since the middle 1950s there have been distinct policy changes in these areas. Several of the large internationally oriented banks have established development corporations for the purpose of making longer-term loans to indigenous firms. Moreover, many European and

American banks have supported the establishment and operations of national development banks.

As a result of these policies, the expatriate banking system in the developing nations had the effect of channelling funds away from local industrial development and towards the country in which the banks' head offices were located. Based on data assembled by Nevin regarding the British Colonial territories, it is possible to support the criticism that many colonies were credit-exporting areas probably well into the early 1960s.[7]

Despite these criticisms, which may have applied in a fairly widespread fashion for a decade and a half after World War II, the international banks have rendered a number of distinct services to the areas in which they are located. They developed and inculcated high standards of stability, integrity, and safety to the practice of banking. Moreover, they earned for themselves and the banking industry a reputation for maintaining high standards of sound and efficient banking practices.

During the period 1955–72 political independence brought with it many other changes which altered the conditions described in the preceding paragraphs. The former banking ties with London weakened, indigenous banks were formed and grew rapidly in scope, the competition between expatriate banks of various nationalities intensified, and the attitude and operations of existing entrenched metropolitan banks became adjusted to the new order.[8] As a result the great European and American international banks began to recognise that operating in newly established nation states called for different rules of the game as compared with doing business in colonial territories. Distinct credit needs could be identified with each of the newly formed nations. This was reinforced by the creation of monetary areas and units, and membership of new nations in the International Monetary Fund. Further reinforcement was provided by the many instances in which these young nations established their own central banks to regulate money creation and monetary flows. Finally, it has become recognised by bankers operating in all these developing nations that the financial system is intimately bound up with the general programme for economic development. Parallel with this has been an increased focus on providing bank credit to promote the development of local industry.

2. SATISFYING THE BANKING NEEDS OF DEVELOPING COUNTRIES

In the discussion which follows we point to six areas in which international banking has contributed to the development efforts of the less developed countries. The six areas are as follows:

1. It supports foreign trade sector.
2. It assists development of local financial institutions and markets.
3. It facilitates inflows of capital.
4. It promotes thrift and savings habits.
5. It adds to the managerial performance of the banking system.
6. It provides foreign exchange assistance where and when needed.

Foreign trade plays a key role in the well-being and economic growth of the developing nations. Most developing nations simply cannot survive without imports of manufactured goods, and the industrialisation process requires substantial imports of machinery and components. Many less developed nations fit into the category of 'open economies', that is where the ratio of exports or imports to gross national product exceeds 10–15 per cent. Many less developed nations suffer from a lack of product diversification, and rely on the export of surplus production to finance purchase of needed imported goods. Internationally oriented banks support a substantial volume of foreign trade of the developing nations by a variety of measures. Head offices of U.S. banks provide dollar loans directly to foreign correspondent banks which in turn use these funds to finance export-import transactions in their own country. American banks provide acceptance credits on behalf of their foreign correspondent bank and non-bank customers. At year-end 1972 the short-term claims on foreigners reported by banks in the U.S. totalled $15.5 billion. Of this amount, $6.2 billion represented claims on developing nations. At year-end 1971 there were 361 overseas branches of American banks in less developed countries, with approximately $3.4 billion in loans outstanding. No doubt, a substantial portion of these loans outstanding and short-term claims represented the financing of foreign trade. In addition to letter of credit facilities, American banks also make special financing arrangements to support continued and/or expanded sales of U.S. suppliers. This might involve arranging participation loans with overseas banks to provide longer-term financing for purchasers including those located in less developed countries, or providing FCIA comprehensive risk guarantees on longer-term credit lines made available through U.S. suppliers.

American banks have played an important role in the development of local banks, financial institutions, and financial markets in the developing nations. At year-end 1971, the 361 branches operated by U.S. banks in developing countries held total assets of $6.5 billion. This represents an average of $18 million in assets per branch located in the less developed countries, and compares favourably with the U.S. average of $18 million per domestic banking office at year-end 1971. Considering the differentials in per capita income between the United States and less developed countries, we can see that these banking facilities and resources provided by U.S. overseas branches are considerable. In addition to overseas branches, American banks have invested in subsidiary banks, local development banks and a variety of types of finance companies in the less developed countries.

The impact of these banking offices and investments in local banks and financial institutions is immeasurable. Beyond these accomplishments, U.S. banks have provided invaluable assistance as financial advisors to foreign central banks, governments, and financial institutions. For example, in 1965 Bankers Trust Co., New York, through its Philippine affiliate Bancom Development Corp., undertook a five year contract to devise a financial development programme for the Philippines.[9] The Philippine government accepted the idea of starting with plans for a Treasury bill market closely resembling that in the United States. The plan was highly successful, and that country now enjoys all of the advantages which accrue to a nation with a well developed Treasury bill market.

U.S. banks often can facilitate long-term capital inflows, which are essential for furthering the development process. Through their overseas branches and representative offices they can assist U.S. firms to seek out attractive business investment opportunities. Moreover, once a profitable opportunity has been uncovered the American bank may assist the U.S. firm in executing the investment with a minimum of exchange risk. In one such case a mid-west bank had a U.S. client who wished to establish an industrial operation in a country undergoing a severe political crisis. There was danger of exchange blockage and local government interference. The subsidiary could import the machinery but the parent could not insure that the funds could be repatriated. The American bank arranged registration of the capital investment with the host country's Central Bank, and obtained a U.S. government guarantee covering war risk, exchange blockage and expropriation. The bank then arranged a medium-term loan for the purchase of the machinery. Since that time the company has been operating profitably, the loan has been properly serviced, and the parent company has been insured against the risks of doing business in that country.[10]

American banks have made modest contribution to the promotion of thrift and savings habits by providing a retail banking service in areas where such facilities had been lacking. However, they have faced a serious competitive threat in the form of saving and loan associations and credit unions whose formation and growth have been subsidised by the U.S. government and international agencies.[11] While the expansion of these institutions in Latin America has probably enhanced the stability of the financial system in Latin America, it has biased this growth in the direction of non-commercial areas and away from those types of economic and business activity whose expansion might lead to self-generating economic growth.

Banking systems in many of the less developed countries are at the early stages of growth. Consequently, accounting practices, credit investigations, and the standard financial tools of analysis are poorly developed or even rarely used.[12] Contacts with foreign branches and affiliates of U.S. banks can often be helpful in transmitting better management techniques to the indigenous banking institutions in these developing nations.

Finally, American banks have made important foreign exchange loans to the governments and central banks of various less developed countries, often at times when they were experiencing balance of payments difficulties. These credits have supplemented the credit facilities available through the International Monetary Fund and other official channels.

B. ORIENTATION OF U.S. INTERNATIONAL BANKING TOWARD DEVELOPING AREAS

1. BRANCHES AND ASSETS IN DEVELOPING COUNTRIES

American banks are well represented in the developing countries by their direct branches and foreign affiliates. In addition U.S. head offices conduct a substantial volume of business with foreign banks and other customers located in these developing areas. On an overall basis it might be possible to generalise, and in a very broad way suggest that less than one-fourth of U.S. international banking activity is with the developing nations.

The number of foreign branches of American banks located in the developing areas is sizeable, representing 63 per cent of all foreign branches of U.S. banks (Table 12-1). However, these branches tend to be considerably smaller than those located in Europe. Moreover, the operations carried on by the branches in less developed countries differ from those conducted in the larger branches in the U.K. and Western Europe. Branches in Latin America which include nearly two-thirds of the branches of U.S. banks in developing countries, emphasise foreign trade finance, collections, and retail activities, as compared with the wholesale, Eurodollar, money market, and multinational corporate financing activities which tend to predominate in the branches of U.S. banks located in the developed countries.

In Table 12-1 we can see that 35 per cent of the short-term claims on foreigners reported by U.S. banks represent claims on debtors located in developing countries. Approximately three-fourths of the dollar amount indicated stems from claims against Latin American official institutions, banks, corporations, and individuals. The two largest categories included in the short-term claims of U.S. banks are acceptances made for the account of foreigners, and collections outstanding.

Short-term liabilities reported by U.S. banks *vis-à-vis* foreigners located in the developing countries represent close to 12 per cent of total short-term liabilities. Over 30 per cent of these liabilities ($2.1 billion) were due to residents of Asian countries (excluding Japan which is a developed country), and approxi-

Table 12.1

Foreign Branches, Short-term Assets and Liabilities
in Less Developed Countries, Year-end 1971

			Millions of dollars	
	Number of Foreign Branches	Assets in Foreign Branches	Short-term Claims on Foreigners Reported by U.S. Banks	Short-term Liabilities to Foreigners Reported by U.S. Banks
Latin America	229	2,519	3,232	4,052
Far East	68	4,600[a]	1,280	2,134
Near East and Africa	17	384	134	519
U.S. Overseas Areas and Trust Territories	47	2,025	28	42
Total, Less Developed	361	9,528	4,674	6,747
Global Total	577	67,054	13,277	55,430
Less Developed as percentage of Global Total	63	14	35	12

[a] Estimated by author by subtracting estimate of assets in Japanese branches of U.S. banks.

Source: Board of Governors of the Federal Reserve System.

mately 60 per cent ($4.1 billion) were due to residents of Latin American countries.

2. BANKING IN AN INFLATION ECONOMY

Trends in the general price level can exert a fundamental influence on the performance of banks. This is because commercial banks deal in financial assets and liabilities, the demand for which is exposed to rapid change during periods of rising or falling prices. On the domestic scene inflation may influence the savings habits and thereby the flow of deposits to banks and other financial institutions. In international banking where banks may undertake balanced positions in various foreign currencies, or unbalanced asset-liability positions in one or more specific currencies, the impact of inflation becomes even more critical.

U.S. banks operating branch offices or subsidiaries in the developing countries may find themselves exposed to the pressures that result from a rising price level. This statement is not intended to reflect adversely on the integrity of the currencies of developing countries in general, since many less developed countries can lay claim to a far better record in the area of controlling inflation than many industrial countries. However, it would be accurate to note that the excesses of inflation, with annual price level advances of 10 per cent or more, have been encountered somewhat more frequently in the developing countries. During the late 1960s such countries as Vietnam, Chile, Brazil, Korea, and Indonesia have been at the top of the list in so far as the rate of depreciation of money is concerned.

Inflation poses real risks and problems for banks as lenders and deposit-takers. First, inflation may impair the real (U.S. dollar) value of the capital stock and surplus of a bank. Second, it may inhibit the inflow of long-term capital, thereby aggravating credit market stringencies and foreign exchange difficulties. Third, inflation may provide the conditions leading to devaluation or a floating depreciation of the currency. Fourth, devaluation and exchange crises may encourage speculation in commodities and excessive debt financing. These activities tend to reinforce the inflationary and balance of payments pressures. Operating in such an environment, banks must often accept greater credit risks, a possible erosion of capital values, and the need to operate within far greater vehicle currency constraints than would ordinarily be the case. Should a bank operating in a less developed country incur an excessive volume of foreign currency liabilities, it might be thrown into bankruptcy by a devaluation. Similarly, extending local currency loans would impair the dollar value of capital accounts given a devaluation.

Under such circumstances a U.S. bank operating in a less developed country must exert more than average efforts to maintain the value of its assets, whether they are denominated in local or foreign currency. The major question is how? The following alternatives appear to be open to many banks:[13]

1. Undertake equity (inflation hedge) investments.
2. Assume risk and adjust lending operations accordingly.
3. Pass maintenance of value risk on to borrower.
4. Pass risk on to local government.
5. Pass risk on to U.S. government.

Unfortunately, American banks operating overseas ordinarily do not find it possible to make use of the first option since they are prohibited from making equity investments, except in very few special cases. Therefore, this option may be available to foreign banking affiliates of U.S. banks, but not their overseas branches. The second alternative, for the American bank to assume the risk itself, may seriously jeopardise the 'capital' of the overseas branch. Devaluation can decapitalise a bank very quickly when there is a high proportion of dollar liabilities and local currency loans. Use of an interest surcharge to accumulate a reserve for maintenance of value is considered to be inadequate and not recommended for a private institution.[14] Therefore, banks are often forced to fall back upon the device of attempting to balance asset-liability positions in whatever currencies they operate in.

There are several means by which it may be possible for a bank to pass the risk of maintaining the value of assets on to the borrower. These include tying the loan to a stable hard currency (such as the dollar), tying the loan to a commodity, or tying the loan to a domestic price index. Tying loans to the dollar carries dangers, including exposure to the claim that there exists an excessive degree of financial control of the local economy by U.S. financial interests. There are distinct advantages involved in tying loans to commodities or domestic price indexes. Thus, an AID mission to Chile recommended that a wage index be used in adjusting the principal balances on mortgages. Other experiments have been made in Latin America in which corporate bonds were indexed according to changes in the prices of commodities sold by the borrowing corporation. There are a number of practical and conceptual difficulties involved in indexing. Generally, the method of indexing resorted to is likely to be the outcome of a bargaining process by which borrower and lender finally agree on an approach which minimises their potential maximum loss, but which leaves substantial possible minimum losses.

Attempts to shift the risk of maintenance of value on to the government will be successful as long as the government does not assume an inflexible position. The U.S. Extended Risk Guarantee Programme can be used to protect the lender. In the past American banks such as Morgan Guaranty, Bank of America, and Continental Illinois of Chicago have used AID guarantees to cover their investments in intermediate credit institutions in countries such as Columbia, Peru, the Ivory Coast, Morocco, Tunisia, and Turkey. This coverage has been made available for less than 2 per cent of the amount guaranteed. It may also be possible for a U.S. bank to negotiate an agreement or come to an understanding with the government of, or an official agency in, a less developed country regarding repayment of a loan extended, or at least the availability of foreign exchange to cover the servicing of the loan if it should be denominated in a hard currency.

In short, there are a variety of banking risks inherent in an inflationary economy. American banks operating in the less developed countries must be aware of these types of risks and the means which are available to cope with them, understanding that no one of these measures will be capable of mitigating against all types of exposure.

C. RELATIONSHIP WITH PRIVATE AND PUBLIC INTERNATIONAL INSTITUTIONS

1. RELATIONS WITH NATIONAL DEVELOPMENT BANKS

U.S. banks operating in the less developed nations have encountered financial market institutions which differ markedly from those found in the United States. One of the most important types of financial institutions or 'banks' found in the less developed nations is the development bank. In many emerging nations investment, development and commercial banking functions are combined in this type of institution. Development banks focus on the assembly and financing of new enterprises, and undertake to provide medium and long-term funds for productive investment in these enterprises. In 1964 the International Finance Corp. estimated that there were over 125 institutions in the developing world which could be called development banks. A more recent study estimated that there were over 300 such institutions in operation, and that 200 of these development banks held aggregate assets of over $14 billion.[15]

American banks co-operate as well as compete with local development banks. The forms of co-operation range from outright equity investments in these institutions to 'participations' in loan packages to local business firms. The reasons which prompt U.S. banks to invest in development banks are numerous: to open the door for ready access to business situations in that country; to obtain a strong local partner who will become well-entrenched in the domestic capital market; to provide a symbol of the U.S. bank's support for the national development effort; to obtain business leads and contacts for the development of the parent bank's lending and deposit business; to obtain maximum returns from a minimal investment; to establish a satellite or captive affiliate that may not be subject to all of the host country regulations regarding commercial bank activities.[16]

Houk lists seven U.S. banks that enjoy major international status, with a total of twenty-nine equity and thirty-six debt investments in national and other types of development banks.[17] As of 1967 at least thirty-nine U.S. commercial banks had made debt or equity investments in one or more development banks, and since that date many additional U.S. banks have undertaken similar investments.

An interesting example of an early postwar investment by an American bank in a national development institution is the Chase Manhattan interest in the Industrial and Mining Development Bank of Iran (IMDBI). Early in 1958, a Lazard Freres and Chase International Investment Corporation financial team embarked for Iran, and during the negotiations which extended for approximately one year an agreement was firmed up involving the aforementioned U.S. institutions, the World Bank, and officials of the Iranian government. During the next several months organisational matters were completed and a public sale of stock was undertaken. IMDBI opened officially in October 1959. Of the initial capital of $42.2 million, equity totalled $5.3 million, divided sixty-forty between local and foreign investors. Chase and Lazard each subscribed $242,000 in IMDBI, the largest single foreign shares, equivalent to 10 per cent of the institution's capital stock and almost one-quarter of non-Iranian holdings.[18]

2. CO-OPERATION WITH INTERNATIONAL LENDING ORGANISATIONS

American and other banks have shared in a partnership for economic progress with the major international lending organisations, such as the World Bank, the International Development Association, and the International Finance Corporation. The contributions rendered by American banks have assumed a variety of forms, but the net results have been similar in all cases, namely an increased flow of capital, technology, and organisational know-how to the less developed nations of the world.

U.S. banks have played an important development assistance role by subscribing for World Bank bonds, beginning with the first issue marketed in the United States in 1947. These early purchases of World Bank bonds were instrumental in restoring confidence in international lending and represented a turning point in the ebb and flow of portfolio investment. In addition, U.S. banks have participated, on both an equity and debt basis, with the IDA and IFC in a large number of investments in industrial and financial enterprises in the less developed nations. We shall look at a few of these investments with a view to understanding the nature and extent of these co-operative investing efforts. In general two patterns emerge. U.S. commercial banks have made independent investments in IFC assisted projects, as well as purchased portions of existing IFC investments. As of 1970 the IFC had sold over $142 million of its own investments to U.S. and foreign commercial banks and financial institutions.[19] Moreover, American banks have participated with the IFC in investments in a variety of business firms in the less developed countries.

During fiscal 1970 two United States institutions participated in a $5 million IFC commitment to a Brazilian petrochemical producer. These were Bamerical International Financial Corporation, a subsidiary of Bank of America, and Manufacturers Hanover Trust Company. In addition Bank of America, New York, and the Export-Import Bank of the United States provided loan capital. Share capital was made available by a U.S. firm, the IFC, and two Brazilian lending institutions to bring the total financing package to $29 million.[20] In the same year two American banks, along with eleven other European and Japanese banks sponsored an investment package of $11 million in a Congolese financial institution (Société Congolaise de Financement du Développement).[21] The share capital subscribed by these foreign financial institutions was in excess of $1 million. The International Development Association provided $5 million in loan capital, with the balance accounted for by smaller investments by the Congolese government, banks, and the IFC.

These international investment syndicates sponsored by the World Bank and its affiliate institutions afford American banks maximum flexibility in participating in investments in a variety of types of establishments (financial and industrial) in the less developed countries. These investments represent an area of growing importance in so far as the international activities of U.S. banks are concerned.

3. RELATIONS WITH OTHER INSTITUTIONS

During the 1960s American banks have developed close working relationships with several newly formed private investment companies. Association with these companies has been profitable, both in the direct financial sense as well as from the resulting business connections that these relationships have led to. One of the most important of these private institutions is the Atlantic Community Development Fund for Latin American (ADELA) which was organised in 1965. Since that time additional institutions have been organised, including the Private Investment Company for Asia (PICA) in 1969, and the Société Internationale Financière pour les Investissements et le Développement en Afrique (SIFIDA) in 1970.

SIFIDA is a recent addition to the list of multinational private investment companies established to operate in the less developed regions of the world. All of these institutions have in common a sizeable equity capital made up from the relatively modest subscriptions of numerous banks and industrial firms in the industrialised countries. Each institution is regional in character, and is committed to a private sector approach toward supporting economic development. The organisation of SIFIDA was sponsored by the African Development Bank and the Standard Bank. Share ownership limitations insure that the institution operates as a truly multinational unit, and a wide group of sponsors have pledged support, including thirteen U.S. companies, and firms representing twelve other developed countries. The purpose of SIFIDA is to identify, evaluate, promote and finance profitable projects in the industrial and agricultural business sectors of the developing African states.[22]

PICA was formed by prominent financial and industrial concerns in the developed countries, with the purpose of promoting new and expanding enterprises in Asia and the Far East. Headquarters are in Tokyo. PICA has committed itself to purchase participations in IFC loans to several industrial enterprises in Asia. Shortly after it began operations PICA received several dozen investment applications for approximately $50 million in funds. Included among PICA's Board of Directors are Eugene Black, a Director of Chase Manhattan Bank, and Rudolph A. Peterson, President of the Bank of America.

ADELA, a Luxembourg corporation, began operating in 1965 with a paid-in capital of $32 million. ADELA was organised to make investments in industrial and finance companies in Latin America. ADELA has co-operated with the IFC and similar organisations in its investments. Over a hundred banks, financial institutions and industrial concerns originally subscribed to share capital in ADELA. Fourteen U.S. banking institutions were among these investors, and contributed $6.25 million in capital funds.

During the first four and a half years of its operations ADELA sponsored and participated in investment projects whose value aggregated over $1.1 billion. ADELA's own assets totalled $136 million in 1969, nearly all of which consisted of loans, investments, and underwritings in Latin America.

Looking ahead, this institution anticipates greater utilisation of loan syndicates and sale of its own investments to other institutions, increased resort to industrial and financial joint ventures between corporations in various parts of Latin America, and the development of more active internal capital markets in the various countries of Latin America.

13 The Federal Reserve and International Banking

A. OBJECTIVES AND ORIENTATION TOWARD INTERNATIONAL BANKING

The purpose of this chapter is to relate the growth in U.S. international banking activity to the evolving role of the Federal Reserve as a stabilising force in U.S. domestic and foreign economic relationships. An increased international commitment on the part of U.S. banks, and the changes that have taken place in the structure of the international financial markets present challenges and opportunities for the Federal Reserve. While conditions and problems are changing, Federal Reserve objectives remain essentially intact, including the pursuit of domestic economic stability and the preservation of reasonably well-balanced international payments relationships.

1. MONETARY POLICY AND THE CHANGING INTERNATIONAL ECONOMY

The monetary authorities in the United States face a number of constraints in their efforts to pursue domestic monetary objectives and at the same time provide for an orderly evolution of our international banking institutions. For over a decade the United States has been burdened with a large and rapidly growing external floating debt.

Financial market facilities outside the United States have been and are likely to continue to expand more rapidly than those within this country. This in turn reflects more rapid economic growth in Western Europe and Japan, as well as structural and competitive forces that are accelerating financial market growth overseas.

Vital questions of national sovereignty are at stake where international or transnational banking activities are concerned. While developments in the rest of the world may influence the U.S. balance of payments position, U.S. monetary policy and credit market developments play a substantial role in affecting the level of interest rates and financial flows in most other parts of the globe.[1] Expansion of the Eurodollar market, in which American banks play a dominant role, raises serious questions of importing inflation, international credit creation, and the need for central bank co-operation in stabilising a massive international money market.

In a world in which balance of payments statistics repeatedly steal the scene from GNP and other economic series, there is heightened interest in the role of central banks in providing export credits, the relative need for asset reserves and other selective credit control instruments, and the extent to which international banks may have become immunised to domestic credit policies. The past decade has not been an easy one for central bankers, and there is good promise that the next decade will be even more challenging.

In the United States the expansion of international banking has resulted in a synthesis of the dual problems of credit control and supervision of banking structure. These two areas offer strong probabilities of shifting closer together as bankers search for new organisational frameworks with which to improve their global credit-making, and as competitive forces in the international financial markets yield new organisational solutions.

2. OBJECTIVES OF MONETARY POLICY

During the past decade problems related to balance of payments and international banking came to play a major role in monetary policy deliberations in the United States and in other countries. This is evidenced in a number of connections:

1. Foreign exchange operations became an important aspect of Federal Reserve activities, in part related to the system of reciprocal currency arrangements (swap facilities) established between the Federal Reserve and fourteen other major central banks.
2. The Eurodollar market became as important as the federal funds market as a source of reserve adjustment for some sixty U.S. banks with foreign branches and ready access to Eurodollar funds.
3. Major changes in the system of reserve requirements put into effect during the past five years are the outcome of international banking activities of U.S. banks.
4. Proposals for changing the regulatory framework by which the Federal Reserve controls bank credit include removal of Regulation Q and a system of reserve requirements on foreign assets.

If we were to distinguish between the domestic and international objectives of monetary policy, we might find the list of monetary objectives on the domestic side falling behind in overall importance. While domestically oriented objectives reflect concern for full employment, price stability and economic growth, the list of international objectives has become lengthy. This list now includes balance of payments adjustment, stemming the growth of destabilising short-term capital flows, lending assistance to currencies subject to speculative pressures, supporting monetary co-operation and reform of the international monetary system, avoiding credit market restraints which dampen possibilities for export finance, restraining major banks from using offshore funds in a manner that neutralises monetary objectives, and pursuing measures which contribute to exchange rate stability. Offsetting the balance of payments and domestic credit market effects from international flows of funds has become an increasingly important aspect of central banking operations in recent years.

In the section which follows we analyse the methods by which the Federal Reserve has attempted to dampen the amount and undesirable influence of short-term capital flows.

B. MEASURES DESIGNED TO INFLUENCE INTERNATIONAL FLOWS OF FUNDS

1. CLOSING THE HOLES

Massive flows of short-term capital have become a dominant factor which monetary authorities must cope with in order to safeguard their balance of payments and international liquidity positions. In attempting to close the openings through which U.S. resident capital outflows might be directed a series of measures were taken by the Johnson Administration, beginning with the Interest Equalisation Tax enacted in 1964, and which include the Voluntary Foreign Credit Restraint programme (VFCR).

In 1969 special problems began to emerge which served to provide further incentives for international movements of funds. These included widening differences in interest rates in national money and capital markets, increased expectations of changes in exchange rate parities, and the need for American banks to seek additional outlets for adjusting their reserve and liquidity positions beyond those available domestically. During 1969 United States liquid liabilities to foreigners increased by $8.2 billion, of which approximately $6 billion represented additional liabilities of U.S. banks to their overseas branches. It is possible that this increase in liabilities to overseas branches was facilitated by the transfer of corporate funds from the United States to other countries to take advantage of higher yields available abroad.[2]

During 1969 speculative anticipations of a revaluation of the German mark led to substantial flows of funds to Germany, which were reversed after the upward revaluation of the D-mark in October of that year. Between 30 September and 31 December 1969 capital outflows from Germany exceeded

$5.3 billion.[3] It was under these pressures that monetary policy in the United States found itself overly burdened, and in need of additional muscle with which to pursue the twin objectives of dampening short-term international capital flows and stabilising our balance of payments position.

2. NEW RESERVE REQUIREMENTS

The year 1969 was characterised by extremely tight credit markets resulting from Federal Reserve measures designed to check an inflationary spiral. Rising interest rates led to CD runoffs as yields on competing money market assets rose above Regulation Q ceilings. International flows of short-term capital were substantial, and placed pressure on the French franc, contributing to an 11.1 per cent devaluation of the franc in August. Net capital outflows from Italy reached $2.8 billion in 1969, of which two-thirds moved abroad through the export of Italian bank notes.[4]

While CD runoffs and generally tight monetary conditions prevailed in the United States throughout 1969, major American banks with foreign branches were able to utilise an important means of reserve adjustment. During the first seven months of 1969 Eurodollar borrowings of these U.S. banks through their foreign branches advanced by $7 billion to reach a peak of $14.6 billion on the week ending 30 July.

At its 12 August meeting, the Federal Open Market Committee noted in its economic policy directive that the surplus on the official settlements version of the balance of payments had shifted toward deficit, 'as U.S. banks' borrowings of Eurodollars levelled off'. Moreover, notice was made of the possible need to resort to open market operations if bank credit should deviate from projections due to foreign exchange developments or bank regulatory changes.[5] It was at this time that the Board of Governors announced the establishment of new reserve requirements on certain foreign borrowings by member banks.

The purposes of these new reserve requirements were (1) to moderate the flow of foreign funds between U.S. banks and their foreign branches, and (2) to remove special advantages that accrue to member banks that have access to Eurodollars not subject to reserve requirements to counter domestic credit restraint.[6] The new reserve requirements were embodied in amendments to Regulation D which governs member bank reserves, and Regulation M which governs the foreign activities of member banks. The amendment to Regulation D established a 10 per cent reserve requirement on borrowings by member banks from foreign banks. These amendments became effective on 4 September 1969.[7]

The amendments to Regulation M were in two parts.

1. The first established a 10 per cent reserve requirement on net borrowings of member banks from their foreign branches to the extent that these borrowings exceed the daily average amounts outstanding in the base period (the four weeks ending 28 May 1969). This marginal requirement was also applied to assets acquired by foreign branches from U.S. head offices except for assets representing credits extended by head offices to non-residents after 26 June.

2. The second established a 10 per cent reserve requirement on branch loans to U.S. residents to the extent such loans exceed either the amount outstanding on 25 June or 26 June 1969, or the daily average outstanding in the four weeks ending 28 May 1969 (choice of the base would be at the option of the member bank). This amendment includes three exemptions. It does not apply to any foreign branch with $5 million or less in credit outstanding to U.S. residents, to credit extended to enable a borrower to comply with requirements of the Office of Foreign Direct Investments (OFDI), and to credit extended under lending commitments entered into prior to 27 June 1969.

Effective 7 January 1971 the Board of Governors adopted two amendments to Regulations D and M pertaining to reserves against Eurodollar borrowings. The first change was to raise from 10 to 20 per cent the reserve ratio applicable to a member bank's Eurodollar borrowings to the extent they exceed a specified reserve free base. The reserve free base refers to the amount of head office borrowings from foreign branches outstanding in the base period (May,

1969), which are not subject to these reserve requirements.

The second change applied an automatic downward adjustment to the minimum reserve free bases applicable to Eurodollar borrowings.[8] These changes were intended to dampen international flows of funds resulting from changes in the level of commercial bank Eurodollar borrowings, and to induce commercial banks to preserve their reserve free Eurodollar borrowing bases should they need to make use of them, given future tightening of bank reserves and credit markets in the United States.

During 1970 the U.S. balance of payments on an official settlements basis had moved into deficit as a result of the repayment of head office borrowings from foreign branches, and by year-end 1970 liabilities of U.S. banks to their foreign branches had declined to $7.6 billion. In addition to swelling the payments deficit on the official reserve basis, repayments of Eurodollar borrowings to foreign branches tend to feed the build-up of dollars at foreign central banks, thereby straining confidence in the viability of the dollar parity, and forcing U.S. officials to resort to reciprocal swap facilities with European central banks and other means to absorb excess dollars on the foreign exchange markets.

The willingness of American banks to repay Eurodollar borrowings during 1970–71 was based on the difference between domestic and Eurodollar interest rates. Relaxed money and credit market conditions in the United States provided banks with access to relatively low cost funds. The Federal Reserve authorities action in late 1970 of raising marginal reserve requirements to 20 per cent on Eurodollar borrowings above the reserve free base was intended to serve as an incentive for banks to preserve a larger part of this base. The key question is whether the extra cost of preserving the Eurodollar reserve free base is worth the extra cost over the long-run (in late 1970 it represented more than a 1 per cent differential per year, or $60 million a year for the $6 billion of reserve free base held by New York banks).[9] According to William F. Butler, chief economist at the Chase Manhattan Bank, 'it all depends on a bank's forecast of rates over the next few years'. If a bank expects tight money to continue, it will be reluctant to allow its reserve free base to drop.[10]

A final reason explaining the Federal Reserve move to increase the reserve requirement to 20 per cent was the desire to avoid placing undue pressure on the Eurodollar market, and less directly on the European financial markets. The Eurodollar market acts as an efficient transmission belt linking the U.S. and European money markets. Interest rates in the Eurodollar market are responsive to U.S. interest rate changes as well as pressures from increased or reduced U.S. head office borrowings. Small interest rate differentials resulting from these pressures can induce substantial short-term capital flows between the Eurodollar market, European financial markets, and North America. The decline in U.S. interest rates in 1970–71 and the backflow of Eurodollars released by U.S. banks pushed Eurodollar rates down, creating a strong incentive for European firms to borrow Eurodollars. The resulting inflow of funds hampered European, and especially German, monetary authorities in their struggle against inflation.[11]

3. OTHER MEASURES DESIGNED TO INFLUENCE INTERNATIONAL FLOWS

The Federal Reserve has attempted to exert an influence on capital flows in a number of ways that extend beyond the voluntary credit restraint programme and changes in reserve requirements. These range from co-operating with other agencies in offshore 'open-market' operations, the use of moral suasion on foreign banks with U.S. offices, and forward exchange operations. The following is a brief description of these activities.

Beginning early in 1971 the Board of Governors of the Federal Reserve System amended its regulations to permit U.S. banks to count toward maintenance of their reserve free Eurodollar bases any funds invested by their overseas branches in Export-Import Bank securities offered under the programme announced by the Export-Import Bank.[12] Under this programme the Export-Import Bank offered to sell three-month notes to the foreign branches of U.S. banks at a 6 per cent interest rate. The Board provided that this Exim paper held by foreign branches could be counted as part of the reserve free base. Sweeteners provided by the Export-Import Bank and U.S. Treasury included allowing the U.S. banks to pay for such notes by credit to the Treasury's tax and loan accounts, and paying a higher rate (6 per cent) than was available on Federal Agency issues at that time (4.43 per cent).[13] Several months later the U.S. Treasury offered $1.5 billion in special certificates to foreign branches of U.S. banks.[14] The Board made a similar amendment to Regulation M permitting U.S. banks to count funds invested by overseas branches in such securities toward maintenance of their reserve free Eurodollar bases.[15]

A major objective of Federal Reserve support of these open-market sales was to absorb dollars that otherwise might have been added to the official reserve holdings of foreign central banks. Moreover, these offerings paved the way for greater official influence over the Eurodollar market, and helped the U.S. balance of payments by having the Export-Import Bank, which lends dollars to foreign buyers of U.S. wares, obtain the funds overseas.[16] In addition, it was hoped that this type of Eximbank financing would make American banks more willing to maintain their overseas borrowings from foreign branches, since the Export-Import Bank was paying rates on notes sold which exceeded those available in the U.S. market for Federal Agency issues. Domestically, these sales permit the Treasury to raise funds without bumping against the federal debt ceiling, and the Treasury can add to its bank balances without borrowing in domestic markets.[17] Finally, the sale of these notes allowed the Export-Import Bank to repay more expensive funds it had borrowed from the Treasury, meaning a larger profit for Eximbank.

The foreign repercussions from sale of Eximbank and U.S. Treasury issues were considerable. It was held that these sales widened the spread between U.S. and offshore dollar borrowing costs, which could have a favourable impact on the U.S. balance of payments deficit. The contrasting rate movements, including higher Eurodollar rates, were regarded as influential on the borrowing and lending decisions of foreign borrowers, especially German business firms. During the period of credit restraint and high interest rates in Western Germany, business firms in that country had found it convenient to borrow Eurodollars, convert them into local currency, and thereby finance their operations on a relatively inexpensive basis. However, with the upward pressure on the Eurodollar rate, and moderate easing of rates in Europe, foreign borrowers were beginning to find Eurodollar financing more expensive.[18] The balance of payments implications of such a reversal in financing patterns are significant. In April 1971 German businessmen were reported to have $7 billion of short-term Eurodollar liabilities outstanding. A decision to permit these borrowings to run off would result in the loss of a substantial amount of dollars from the German central bank.

In so far as it is concerned with the regulation of domestic credit, the Federal Reserve faces a peculiar situation with respect to the agencies, branches, and subsidiaries of foreign banks either domiciled or operating in the United States. In general, the Federal Reserve can not exert the same leverage on the credit creating activities of foreign banks as it does with respect to domestic banking institutions. There are two reasons for this difference. Many domestically chartered subsidiaries of foreign banks are not members of the Federal Reserve System, and branches and agencies of foreign banks are ineligible for membership. This tends to insulate these institutions from the direct credit control measures employed by the Federal Reserve. Second, the head offices of these foreign banks are able to supply funds to their agencies and branches located in the United States. This means that at times when the Federal Reserve is attempting to check the growth of credit, funds provided to these U.S. branches and agencies by their head offices may finance an expansion of credit.

Another aspect of this problem is that the U.S. agencies of foreign banks are in a position to shift the financing of foreign trade between the United States and the home country of their parent bank, placing pressure on the U.S. balance of payments as a result of the reversed direction taken by short-term capital flows used to finance this trade. For example, in 1969 when money was tight in the United States and interest rates high relative to those prevailing in other countries, a good deal of Japanese import finance shifted from dollars to yen. This helped the U.S. balance of payments because it reduced short-term capital outflows which had taken the form of dollar credits extended to Japanese importers. However, in 1970 this situation was reversed. With interest rates in the United States dropping below levels prevailing in Japan, importers in that country were inclined to borrow in New York. In May of 1970 the Bank of Japan eliminated its strict controls over Japanese bank participation in the U.S. banker's acceptance market, and it was estimated that within one month the level of acceptances held by the Japanese agencies in this country increased by close to $100 million.[19] Late in 1970 it was reported that the Federal Reserve Board had asked the New York agencies of Japanese banks not to permit their holdings of banker's acceptances to exceed the level reached at the end of November 1970. In the eyes of the Federal Reserve, the Board was simply asking the foreign bank agencies in New York 'to follow the spirit of the balance of payments guidelines'. During the six year period ending in late 1970 banker's acceptances held by the Japanese agencies in New York had doubled, reaching a level of about $1 billion.

Another Federal Reserve measure designed to cope with massive international flows of funds has been to engage in forward exchange transactions. By exerting leverage on the forward exchange rate of a given currency the Federal Reserve is in a position to widen or narrow the spread between the spot and forward rates of exchange on a particular currency. This in turn would have the effect of increasing or reducing the cost of forward cover for speculators and those interested in interest arbitrage between New York and financial centres located in other countries. For example, during the month of February 1971 the Federal Reserve Bank of New York attempted to slow the flow of funds into Germany by selling marks in the forward exchange market, thereby making it more expensive for purchasers of spot marks to cover their position in marks. Karl Klasen, President of the German Bundesbank, welcomed the action, since the inflow of funds into Germany had been making it difficult for the central bank to enforce its tight monetary policy.[20]

Backing up these Federal Reserve transactions in the forward and spot markets for foreign exchange are (1) an extensive network of reciprocal currency arrangements in which fourteen central banks, the Bank for International Settlements (BIS), and the Federal Reserve stand ready to provide swap lines of credit to one another in the form of their own currencies, and (2) special arrangements between the U.S. Treasury and several foreign central banks which provide for the sale of U.S.

Treasury securities denominated in foreign currencies.

C.   EFFECTS OF POLICY MEASURES

As we have seen, Federal Reserve policy measures such as the introduction of new reserve requirements, the VFCR programme, currency swaps and foreign exchange operations have exerted important effects on foreign lending, capital flows, and the balance of payments. In addition, Federal Reserve measures have influenced the evolving structure of U.S. banking, have altered competitive relationships in American banking, and exerted numerous side effects.

1. CHANGES IN BANKING STRUCTURE

In a speech delivered before the Board of Directors of the Federal Reserve Bank of Dallas early in 1970, Andrew F. Brimmer, a member of the Board of Governors of the Federal Reserve System commented upon the effects of the foreign credit restraint programme which had been in effect for over five years.[21]

> The program has affected the pattern of U.S. international banking. Competitive inequities among banks have developed, and a network of foreign branches has been stimulated whose long-run impact cannot be seen clearly.

During the first five years of the VFCR programme there was a six-fold increase in the number of banks with branches abroad. The rapid growth in number and importance of foreign branches of American banks could have serious implications for the U.S. balance of payments over the long-run. In the past, U.S. export finance has been focused in the head offices of American banks more than in their overseas branches. The shift in emphasis of foreign operations toward overseas branches could lessen the relative role of export finance in the international activities of American banks, and lessen the possibilities for export expansion. This would follow if (1) the growth in foreign branch funds is at the expense of growth in funds available at U.S. head offices for export finance, (2) the foreign credit restraint programme limiting U.S. bank lending to foreigners is extended in a manner that dampens U.S. head office export credits,[22] and (3) foreign sources of financing U.S. exports do not develop at a rapid enough pace.

2. COMPETITIVE FACTORS

Changes in American banking structure related to the substantial increase in number of foreign branches during the late 1960s have generated shifts in the competitive status of different categories of banks. In turn these competitive differences hinge on the pattern of portfolio adjustment and ability to service the loan demand of large corporate customers.

In 1969–70 it became evident that various categories of commercial banks in this country were responding differently to monetary restraint. In his analysis, Governor Brimmer singled out three categories of banks, including a small number of multinational banks active in both the domestic and international money markets, a larger number of regional banks, and other banks which concentrate mainly on local credit markets. Based on data reflecting operations in 1969, a year of extremely tight credit market conditions, the first group of banks was the most successful in expanding its total loans, and the second group was next in line.

In Brimmer's analysis the multinational bank group, heavily comprised of large Eurodollar banks, was subject to the largest absolute and percentage decline in deposits in 1969. The deposit decline at major regional banks was second largest, and the deposit reduction in the local bank group was the smallest. Despite this disparity in deposit flows the percentage advances in total earning assets at these three groups of banks were similar, suggesting that the imbalances in deposit flows were offset by an opposite imbalance in the growth of non-deposit sources of funds.[23] Total loans and business loans expanded more sharply at the multinational banks than at the other two groups of banks, suggesting that the multinational banks were more successful in avoiding the restraints of a tight monetary policy. Since loan sales, which were heaviest at the multinational banks, were not included in the figures in Brimmers' analysis the foregoing conclusion is strengthened. When adjustment is made for these loan sales, the growth rate of business loans is raised by more than one-half at the multinational banks, by one-quarter at the regional banks, and by only 5 per cent at the local banks. The conclusion is inescapable. The ability of some of the largest commercial banks to sell part of their existing loan portfolios to obtain funds to meet new demands for loans provides another means for them to lighten the impact of monetary restraint. The largest banks with both national and international customers, and which mobilise funds in both the domestic and international financial markets, are able to avoid a substantial proportion of the impact of monetary restraint. In doing so, they are able to maintain or even expand their earning assets. The large regional banks also can succeed in this direction, but not as well as the multinational banks. Finally, the larger local banks can avoid the burden of monetary restraint to a much lesser extent.

3. EFFECTIVENESS OF DOMESTIC CREDIT RESTRAINT MEASURES

Recent experience during the 1960s demonstrates that the internationalisation of American banking and credit markets has blunted the fine cutting edge of monetary policy. The VFCR programme has generated side effects in the form of greater incentives for establishing foreign branches and other forms of overseas representation. In turn, the restructuring of U.S. international banking in favour of foreign branch operations has provided opportunities for U.S. banks to cushion the impact of Federal Reserve policy, and may have introduced a structural bias working against the provision of export finance. Foreign branches are less active in financing U.S. exports than their head offices located in this country.

In 1969 it was evident that the multinational banks were able to offset deposit losses by obtaining non-deposit sources of funds, and by sale of loan assets to foreign branches. The introduction of reserve requirements against Eurodollar borrowings by U.S. head offices has not lessened the impact of short-term capital flows on the U.S. balance of payments, and efforts on the part of Federal Reserve authorities to provide special inducements to commercial banks to preserve their reserve free Eurodollar borrowing bases have been of doubtful success.

If existing monetary policy measures are not successful in restraining credit creation by the multinational and regional banks, it would appear reasonable to search about for additional instruments with which to strengthen the Federal

Reserve in its quest for monetary stabilisation. In the following section we examine two areas of possible reform, which might permit monetary policy to enjoy a greater measure of success in restraining credit expansion. These include the proposals for establishing reserve requirements on foreign assets, and the prospects for regulation or control over the Eurodollar market.

D. RECENT DEVELOPMENTS AND PROPOSALS TO REFORM CREDIT FLOWS

In recent years Federal Reserve authorities have found it increasingly necessary to consider international repercussions when formulating and implementing monetary policy. The complexities involved in a world financial framework where flows of funds and competitive pressures quickly transmit monetary influences from one country to another necessitate that central bankers in large countries such as the United States give heed to the impact of their actions in other countries which jealously safeguard their right to monetary and financial sovereignty.

It is a truism that when monetary authorities possess a larger number of policy measures they gain increased flexibility of action. In the sections which follow we examine several areas in which Federal Reserve and non-U.S. monetary authorities may acquire increased control over foreign and domestic credit creation and allocation. Prominent among these are the establishment of asset reserves on foreign loans made by U.S. banks, and co-ordinated central bank control over the Eurodollar market.

1. RESERVE REQUIREMENTS ON FOREIGN ASSETS

The Federal Reserve Board has shown considerable flexibility in the use of reserve requirements in the last several years. In part this has involved tailoring changes in such requirements to differentiate the impact by size of bank. This took place in 1966 and 1967 with respect to requirements against time deposits, and continued in 1968–9 with respect to reserve requirements which apply against demand deposits.[24] In 1969 reserve requirements were imposed by the Board of Governors against Eurodollar borrowings by American banks.

In a speech delivered in February 1970, Governor Andrew F. Brimmer proposed that reserve requirements against foreign assets be considered as an alternative to the Voluntary Foreign Credit Restraint Programme.[25] This reserve against foreign assets would be in addition to the customary reserves that banks maintain against deposits, and would raise the cost of foreign lending and dampen the outflow of U.S. capital. Such 'supplemental reserves' would not be related to general domestic credit conditions, nor would they be used to raise the average level of reserves required for individual banks. Since the object of utilising such reserves would be to restrain the growth of foreign lending, they might be applied 'only to the amount of lending above some determined volume'.[26] Therefore, they would constitute marginal rather than average required reserves. A variant of this approach might be to apply such foreign asset reserves to all new foreign loans rather than use them as marginal reserve requirements.

Percentage reserve requirements could be varied against different categories of foreign assets held by banks so as to take account of priorities assigned to each area of foreign lending. In this way, different percentage requirements might be applied to export credits, loans to developing countries, and foreign loans which exceed a stipulated percentage of total assets.[27]

Somewhat later in 1970 Governor Brimmer elaborated further on his asset reserve proposal. He noted that thought might be given to adopting asset reserve requirements for domestic purposes as well as for foreign assets. Such reserve requirements would provide the Board of Governors with a better means of influencing the availability of credit in different sectors of the economy. Domestic loans subject to the supplemental reserve requirement could be defined in a manner that would take account of whatever set of priorities might be established, including the financial needs of state and local governments, or the availability of credit to the mortgage sector.

Several advantages exist in the foreign asset reserve proposal. First, the Board of Governors would be provided with an additional flexible instrument of monetary policy. Second, availability of this type of instrument would permit easing domestic credit conditions while at the same time imposing additional credit restraints on capital outflows taking the form of bank lending. Third, the discriminatory effects of domestic monetary policy on different size banks, referred to in section C above, would be minimised. Finally, the Board would have a means of reducing its reliance on Regulation Q as a means of exerting pressure on those banks which conduct the largest part of foreign lending. As pointed out earlier in this chapter Brimmer's analysis suggests that the large multinational banks in the United States have been able to offset much of the disintermediation effects from rising market rates of interest and inelastic Regulation Q ceilings via their foreign branch Eurodollar circuits. In short, Regulation Q has become less effective as a means of imposing reserve pressures on large American banks at times when the Federal Reserve authorities have followed a tight money policy. Unfortunately, the disruptive effects on the U.S. financial markets remain, in the form of disintermediation and unusually severe pressures on certain credit market sectors. Use of foreign asset reserves, it is claimed, would serve to dampen foreign lending, and at the same time provide flexibility in the levels at which the Board of Governors maintains Regulation Q interest ceilings.

In the past, discussion of asset reserve requirements has tended to focus on selective credit control or counter-cyclical objectives. Effectiveness of this measure to achieve balance of payments goals would depend upon the degree of elasticity of foreign demand for bank credit, the existence of rigidities which prevent or slow down adjustments in interest rates, and the absolute level of reserves required per dollar of foreign assets.[28] If the results of the Interest Equalisation Tax are meaningful, the elasticity of foreign demand for U.S. credit *in general* appears to be relatively high, and one would expect a somewhat higher elasticity for U.S. bank credit.

Numerous problems crop up in evaluating the merits of a proposal of this type. These include the equity associated with singling out U.S. banking institutions only, the technical problem of adding another dimension to the multifaceted array of capital flow restraints presently operative *vis-à-vis* banks and other foreign lenders and investors, and the desirability of introducing selective reserve requirements on commercial bank asset holdings.

2. TOWARD REGULATION OF THE EUROCURRENCY MARKETS

We have already discussed the special role of the Eurocurrency markets in the areas of money-credit creation, international transmission of interest rate pressures, and the opportunities for speculative activity against particular currencies. Moreover, attention was focused on the risks and problems associated with the Eurodollar market for individual banks, countries, and the international financial system as a whole. In the discussion which follows we examine the prospects for extending Federal Reserve and other central bank regulatory authority over the Eurocurrency markets. There are several reasons for increased interest in the development of such regulatory authority. First, monetary authorities are concerned regarding the viability of the international monetary system, and rapid expansion of the Eurocurrency markets has added a new dimension of activity in this area. Second, many leading trading nations are recurrently exposed to balance of payments pressures, which can be aggravated by the widened scope for arbitrage and speculative currency transactions now possible through these markets. Third, international bankers and monetary experts are concerned with the strength of the Eurocurrency markets and their ability to support a heavier burden of clearing, credit and money-transfer transactions, all of which constitute the basis of international banking. Finally, many nations are finding that the everyday operations of the Eurocurrency markets have resulted in a serious intrusion upon their sovereignty with respect to control over domestic interest rates, credit markets, and liquidity.

It has been noted that these problems seem to be the outcome of two characteristics of this market: (1) that there is no single institution to which participants can turn as lender of last resort, and (2) that the market has created a set of semi-independent interest rates over which no single country or monetary authority has effective control.[29]

What measures might be utilised to assure a more orderly operation of the Eurocurrency markets, and at the same time solve the problems of conflicting national sovereignty?

Various proposals have been put forth for regulation of the Eurocurrency markets, reflecting wide differences of viewpoint regarding how best to achieve a more efficient functioning of the international monetary system, the extent to which differing national problems may be resolved, and the extent to which central banks operating in unison or alone may be able to influence the market. With respect to the last point several econometric type studies of the Eurodollar market have been attempted, with limited success. In 1967 Hendershott completed a study of the structure of international interest rates which sought to investigate the sensitivity of Eurodollar deposit rates to changes in the U.S. Treasury bill rate.[30] In summary, Hendershott found 'that the Eurodollar rate adjusts completely to changes in the U.S. bill rate', that the adjustment takes about a year, and that the first month impact of a percentage point change in the U.S. bill rate on the Eurodollar deposit rate ranges from 0.14 to 0.23 percentage points.[31] The implications are significant for Federal Reserve policy, since policy actions aimed at raising the U.S. Treasury bill rate to dampen short-term capital outflows may provide only very short-run relief. In order for policy actions to exert a more lasting effect, (1) capital flows must be influenced by foreign interest rates which do not adjust as readily to changes in U.S. rates as Eurodollar rates, (2) capital flows must be more sensitive to changes in U.S. interest rates than to foreign rates, or (3) substantial lags must exist in the adjustment of capital flows to changes in international interest rate differentials.

The Hendershott study was based on data covering the period 1957–64. Subsequently, a study was made by Black of weekly data reflecting U.S. bank Eurodollar borrowings for the period 1966–8. The purpose of this second study was to quantify supply and demand functions for Eurodollar borrowings by New York banks from their own foreign branches.[32] A number of variables were entered into supply and demand functions for Eurodollars, including the interest rate on Eurodollar deposits in London, the rate on U.S. Treasury bills, the rate on U.S. Federal Funds, and the volume of certificates of deposit outstanding in New York banks. In deriving an equation to explain the interest rate level on Eurodollar borrowings, Black found that the U.K. Bank Rate and the level of CDs outstanding 'have only transitory effects on the Eurodollar deposit rate'. Changes in U.S. Treasury bill rates exert their influence on Eurodollar rates with the shortest time lags. Unfortunately, both of these studies covered time periods which preceded the August 1969 introduction of reserve requirements on Eurodollar borrowings of U.S. head offices. Nevertheless, there are several general observations which have important implications for any plans to regulate the Eurodollar market. First, these studies emphasise the high degree of interest sensitivity that attaches to funds located in various money centres, including the Eurodollar market. Second, both studies suggest that an important transmission mechanism now operates linking interest rate levels in the major money centres, namely New York, London, the European Continent, and peripheral centres such as Tokyo, Singapore, and Hong Kong. Finally, both studies clearly reflect the difficulties experienced in empirical investigations of international flows of funds.

3. REFORM PROPOSALS

In the following discussion we review five alternatives for improving the performance of the Eurodollar market. These range from recommendations for modest increases in central bank co-operation to the imposition of tight controls on transactions within the market. Each of these alternatives possesses certain implications for the framework and functioning of international banking, especially the international banking operations of American banks.

On the more moderate side, it has been proposed that central bankers should pursue policies which influence domestic credit market relationships and flows of funds through the foreign exchanges. According to this point of view, it is highly unlikely that any uniform control of the Eurodollar market could succeed. Central banks themselves hold widely differing views about the need for control, as well as the kinds of control measures that might prove to be most workable. Therefore, on an individual basis central bankers should use caution in feeding dollars into the Eurodollar market, should gradually diminish the amount of their reserve assets held in the market, and should more actively utilise internal credit measures and control of commercial bank foreign exchange positions as measures of indirect restraint over the market.[33] This point of view regards minimum reserve requirements, and greater international efforts at aligning interest rate levels among major industrial countries as important instruments to be used in avoiding the inflationary impact of flows of funds through the Eurodollar market. A central part of this line of thinking is that central banks should refrain from placing dollars in the Eurodollar market.[34]

Kindleberger's approach toward the Eurodollar market differs substantially from the foregoing. In his view new sources of instability have become built into what was formerly a pure dollar international monetary system. These include the development of additional money centres around the globe (Japan in the Yen bloc, and London and Frankfurt in the European area) which add to the possibilities for international currency speculation. He proposes two modifications to make the dollar system 'politically acceptable' in today's world.[35] These include inviting the Europeans and Japanese onto the Federal Open Market Committee, and engaging in open market operations in the Eurodollar market on an internationally organised basis. According to Kindleberger, past operation of the dollar system has given the United States control over the world interest rates and the rest of the world control over the U.S. balance of payments. He sees co-ordinated open market operations in the Eurodollar market as a half-way house to full and complete international monetary co-operation.

Kindleberger's proposal differs from the first alternative in several respects. He calls for co-ordinated central bank open market operations in the Eurodollar market as a means to stabilise credit markets on a global basis. The more moderate proposal would have central banks withdraw their international reserves from the market on a more or less permanent basis. Second, Kindleberger's proposal recognises the difficulties faced by individual central banks in attempting to regulate their own domestic credit markets, given the possibilities for Eurodollar transactions by bank and non-bank participants. The first proposal tends to ignore this problem, and even implies that domestic policies followed by individual central banks may exercise sufficient influence.

A third alternative is that offered by Machlup. He views the Eurodollar market as an engine for creating money and credit, and uses the analogy of non-member banks in the United

States.[36] Both the Eurodollar system and the American non-member bank system are additional layers in the pyramid of dollar deposit creation. Cash reserves of both groups of banks (non-member banks in the U.S. and Euro-banks in the Euro-dollar market) are high-powered money and can support multiple deposit expansion. Machlup notes that the practice of European central banks placing dollar deposits with Euro-banks can result in adding to the stock of official reserves.[37] This happens when a central bank places New York dollars with the BIS in exchange for BIS dollars, whereupon the BIS places the New York dollars with a London bank. The BIS gets London dollars and the London bank lends the New York dollars to a multinational firm. The company converts the dollars into a European currency and the New York dollars revert back to a European commercial bank which resells them to a central bank. Thus the New York dollars are back with a central bank, but the central bank continues to hold BIS dollars and therefore now has two dollars in reserves for each dollar that it placed in the Eurodollar market.

As the New York dollars which the central bank placed in the Eurodollar market reappear in its reserves (of necessity due to IMF par value obligations of the country), the supply of domestic money and bank reserves increase, and inflation becomes imported. A restrictive credit policy on the part of the central bank can only serve to aggravate the situation, since rising interest rates serve as an incentive for funds to flow through the Eurodollar market, and the European central bank must acquire additional dollars to defend existing parities. As a result, domestic credit policy tends to be defeated. According to Machlup the central banks 'sabotage their own policies in several ways'. Their major error is in placing dollars in the Euro-dollar market, and Machlup recommends that this practice be discontinued. Formal agreement in this direction may help, but a less informal restraint could prove workable.[38]

Machlup warns against over-regulation of the Eurodollar market, and notes that unless care is exercised, efforts to achieve control over the market could prove to be counter-productive. The Eurodollar system has provided important benefits in the way of integrated and efficient international money and capital markets. The world would lose if improper

regulation was adopted which compartmentalised or seg-
mented these financial markets.

Machlup's position appears to differ from Kindleberger's in
a number of respects. First, Machlup emphasises the money-
credit creation aspects of Eurodollar operations whereas Kindleberger appears to be more concerned with international flows
of funds. Second, Kindleberger's solution is more positive,
namely central bank open market operations in the Eurodollar
market so as to regulate credit availability on a global basis.
Machlup urges that central banks refrain from transactions in
the Eurodollar market.

A fourth proposal, suggested by Guido Carli, Governor of the
Bank of Italy, would impose obligatory reserve requirements on
Eurodollar deposits. Such requirements would have to be
adopted by the eight countries whose banks hold the major part
of Eurodollar deposits, and the reserve requirements themselves would have to be uniform for all countries. Otherwise the
proposal would not be feasible from a technical viewpoint.
According to Carli, Euro-banks are able to mobilise a large
mass of credit which can exert a substantial influence on national capital markets. Moreover, the multiplier effect of the
Eurodollar market on the creation of international liquidity can
be substantial. Carli has estimated that the multiplier effect has
been a factor of 2.5, but that it could rise to 7.0 due to the
absence of any obligatory reserves on Eurodollar deposits.
Imposition of reserve requirements would have the effect of stabilising the multiplier, and utilisation of variable reserve requirements would permit central banks in unison to exert some
pressure on the Eurodollar market by changing the multiplier
factor. Carli's proposal is worthy of consideration. However,
there exists some doubt as to the likelihood of central banks and
their respective governments agreeing to a proposal of this type.
Like Kindleberger's proposal, Carli's approximates to the creation of an international central banking authority.

The fifth proposal is that individual countries in the Eurodollar market area impose exchange controls over domestic
borrowers taking Eurodollars. The possibility that central
banks of major industrial countries will get together and
impose controls on the free flow of funds in order to prevent a
recurrence of the rush of money on the German mark is cause

for concern.[39] This would break the postwar trend toward progressively freer movements of capital funds by major countries that has contributed to the growth of world trade and investment. A move of this type would have to include Western Germany, a major industrial country that has had the freest capital market in the world for over a decade. A major fear is the impact upon credit quality from Eurodollar exchange controls. According to Mr Harry Ekblom, president of European-American Bank & Trust Co., New York, if certain European countries barred their nationals from borrowing Eurodollars, this would create an excess supply of funds in the market. The next step would be a lowering of quality standards in order to put Eurodollar funds to work.[40] Even if there was no problem of credit quality, some of the current borrowers of Eurodollars would have difficulty in obtaining the funds to pay off their maturing loans.

At the American Bankers Association International Banking Conference held in Munich in May 1971, Rinaldo Ossola, Director General of the Bank of Italy, stated that the recent monetary crisis which led to the adoption of a floating rate for the German mark resulted from speculative flows of funds rather than a fundamental disequilibrium between the U.S. dollar and Europe. He called for strong controls over international flows of funds, which would be applied to bank operations in international markets, foreign borrowings by corporations, and non-resident investments.[41] This view apparently runs counter to that espoused by German bankers.

IV
ROLE OF THE
UNITED STATES
AS WORLD BANKER

14 Benefits and Costs for the United States

The United States became a world banker in the twentieth century, and has retained this distinction because of the many international financial and banking functions it performs for itself as well as for the rest of the world. We have already examined these functions in various connections. However, it would be well to review them with the objective of establishing a basis for appraising the balance between the benefits derived and costs incurred by the United States in discharging its role as world banker.

The primary objective of this chapter is to establish a framework for evaluating the assumption that being a world banker results in net gains or benefits for the United States. Closely related to this is the objective of estimating whether the international banking role of the United States results in net benefits or costs.

A. THE U.S. AS WORLD BANKER AND INTERNATIONAL BANKING SPECIALIST

In the Introduction we hinted briefly at the distinction between the United States as a world banker and the United States in international banking. At that point we noted that U.S. international banking, namely service functions performed by U.S. banks for their internationally oriented customers, constitutes only part of the responsibilities and functions of the United States as a world banker. Before embarking on an analysis of the benefits and costs to the United States related to its international banking role, it would be well for us to separate out those functions and areas of responsibility which relate strictly to the international banking function from those which exist as a result of the role of world banker. After doing this we shall be able to analyse the benefits and costs which accrue to the United States in each of these capacities.

As world banker, the United States has rendered the following services:

1. It provides a relatively stable, efficient and convenient means of international payments.
2. It provides an efficient international flow of funds mechanism.
3. It provides international liquidity in the form of short-term dollar assets held by non-residents.

In the period 1934–71 the dollar enjoyed a fixed parity with gold, a boast that can be made for very few currencies. The Swiss franc is the only other important international currency that has maintained a similar record in this respect. On 15 August 1971 President Nixon suspended gold convertibility for official holders of U.S. dollars, and in December 1971 the dollar was devalued relative to other major currencies by approximately 8 per cent. In 1973 the dollar was further devalued by approximately 10 per cent. While it is not clear at the time of writing whether or not the world banker role of the United States will continue in these three connections, there is no evidence that it will not. Therefore, our discussion in this chapter is based on the assumption that the world banker role of the United States will continue.

Provision of an efficient international flow of funds mechanism refers to the long-term capital flows that move to and from the United States. Presumably, the United States is facilitating a more efficient international allocation of investible funds by providing a mechanism through which long-term and short-term capital flows along this two-way street. In addition, an international adjustment of long and short-term asset holdings is accomplished whereby U.S. residents purchase long-term claims on the rest of the world and foreign investors purchase short-term claims in the form of U.S. money market instruments and bank deposits, all denominated in dollars. This gets us to the third world banker function, provision of international liquidity in the form of short-term dollar claims of non-residents. As banker for the rest of the world, the United States lends long and borrows short. This provides foreign non-official holders of short-term dollar assets the opportunity to 'manage their assets' with still one more degree of freedom of choice in making their portfolio selections. Moreover, this provides foreign official holders of short-term dollar claims the opportunity to increase their international reserves in the form of liquid U.S. dollar assets, and possibly to use these dollar assets in the execution of their own monetary policy where this may be called for.

The international banking functions of the United States may be distinguished from the world banker functions, although this distinction is not perfect since there is some overlap. Perhaps the most significant area of overlap is in the provision of international liquidity. The New York money market and deposits in U.S. banks provide a wide assortment of short-term assets denominated in dollars which non-residents may elect to hold. The overlap lies in the area of foreign dollar deposits placed with U.S. banks, which at year-end 1972 totalled close to $14 billion. No doubt, U.S. institutions engaged in international banking facilitate the world banker role of this country in providing international liquidity.

International banking functions which exhibit little or no overlap with the world banker function of the United States include the following: (1) finance of U.S. foreign trade; (2) service to U.S. multinational corporations in their global operations;

(3) conduct of Eurodollar operations; (4) provision of venture capital overseas; (5) provision of banking facilities in less developed countries. In the next section we examine the benefits and costs that accrue to the United States from each of these functions.

B. BENEFITS AND COSTS THAT ACCRUE FROM WORLD BANKER AND INTERNATIONAL BANKING FUNCTIONS

1. TYPES OF BENEFITS AND COSTS

The international status of the United States suggests a variety of benefits and costs, including profits earned from providing international banking services,[1] effect on the balance of payments, effect on central bank ability to regulate credit creation, effect on international allocation of credit, effect on soundness of the banking system, and impact on U.S. foreign trade. Not all of these benefits or costs lend themselves to simple quantification. However, where possible we undertake to develop quantitative estimates of the benefits and costs that might be involved. In developing our estimates we shall treat the United States as an economic unit and measure the income or profit derived from each function, or the cost or loss involved.

2. STABLE MEANS OF PAYMENT

A world banker must manage its affairs so as to achieve a balanced economy, and thereby insure that its currency retains a high measure of stability in terms of its relationship with other currencies and its own internal purchasing power. When a balance of payments disequilibrium exists, the point has been well made that import surcharges are less costly in restoring equilibrium than internal deflation.[2] Extending the argument, it might be contended that the constraints imposed upon a world banker may result in a conflict between the pursuit and achievement of domestic and international policy objectives, resulting in the need either to sacrifice domestic stability (full employment or price stability) or resort to extreme measures in solving an international disequilibrium (devaluation or extensive control over foreign trade).

Aliber has argued that in part the reserve currency role of the dollar has imposed constraints by eliminating easy access to the option to resort to devaluation of the dollar. Moreover, he maintains that:

> The possible conflicts between domestic and international policy objectives appear to arise primarily because the New York financial market enables foreign and U.S. private parties to shift funds easily from dollar assets to foreign currency assets, rather than because of the U.S. reserve-currency role. International shifts of private short-term funds would occur even if the United States were not a reserve-currency country.[3]

Grubel assigns significant weight to the status of the United States as world banker in imposing serious constraints on the use of full employment policies. He distinguishes two aspects of the deflationary bias resulting from world banker status, namely the need to employ policies conducive to price stability, and the large size of the required adjustment, prolonging the existence of external disequilibrium and the period over which deflationary employment levels might persist. An answer to the contention that the status of world banker inevitably carries with it the cost of under-employment equilibrium can be found in Harry N. Goldstein's article in which he raises the crucial question, is it the inevitable outcome of world banker status or the application of 'inefficient monetary and fiscal policies' that contributed to the deflated employment levels of the early 1960s?[4] This question continues to be debated.

If we accept the possibility of an 'output gap' resulting from the need to pursue somewhat deflationary policies in light of world banker status, how large might this gap be? The Council of Economic Advisors has provided estimates of an output gap ranging well beyond the $40 billion figure. However, we shall be far more conservative. We shall assume a potential gap of one per cent of GNP. Applying 1971–2 levels of GNP in the United States we arrive at an output gap of over $12 billion.

A second cost element exists relative to the attainment of a stable means of payment. In order to support existing parity relationships between the dollar and other major currencies it is necessary that the U.S. Treasury maintain a gold and foreign exchange reserve available for settling residual international balances, intervention in the foreign exchange markets, and for psychological reasons. If we assume that U.S. international reserves represent potential international purchasing power which might be invested at a 10 per cent return, we could infer that the cost related to the world banker role of the United States can be estimated at 10 per cent of existing gold and foreign exchange reserves. This implies a cost of approximately $1 billion per year.

3. INTERNATIONAL FLOW OF FUNDS MECHANISM

The coincidence of two factors has made it possible for the United States to function as a world banker in so far as its role in the international flow of funds mechanism is concerned. These are net payments surpluses on current account, and the development of New York as a world financial centre. Between 1950 and 1971 the stock of U.S. investment abroad rose from $33 billion to over $150 billion. In the same period foreign investments in the U.S. increased from $20 billion to nearly $100 billion. A major objective of this analysis is to arrive at some estimate of the net gains or costs to the United States as a result of these long-term capital flows. There exists a vast body of literature which discusses the theoretical and empirical aspects of the profitability of capital outflows from the lending and borrowing country points of view. Our major objective is to arrive at a rough estimate of gains or losses to the United States resulting from foreign investment.

While there may be some question regarding the extent of net gain from foreign investment for the lending country, the large volume of U.S. private foreign investment does argue in favour of this possibility. Department of Commerce figures indicate a somewhat higher return on U.S. overseas manufacturing investment than domestic investment in the period 1950–66, but nearly an equalisation of returns in recent years. If we admit the possibility of higher returns on foreign investment than domestic investment, and therefore, a gain for the United States from overseas investment, we must keep in mind a number of negative factors that lower the net gain. These include losses from seizure of property, devaluation which results in a lower dollar value of foreign-currency investment assets, a reduction in the return on overseas investment resulting from competition by increasing amounts of U.S. invested capital, and the payment of taxes on foreign investment income to foreign governments. U.S. tax laws permit a tax credit for foreign taxes paid. Hence, the payment of foreign income taxes by U.S. investors results in a net loss for the United States, since a part of the foreign-source profits flow into a foreign government's treasury and become unavailable for taxation and expenditure in the United States.

If we compute the benefits from U.S. capital exports, and apply an assumed 1 per cent margin of return on foreign as compared with domestic investment to the total long-term asset position, the benefits appear to be in the order of $1.20 billion. If we assume a 33 per cent foreign income tax, the net benefits are reduced to $0.80 billion.

4. PROVISION OF INTERNATIONAL LIQUIDITY

The United States fulfills a vital role in the world economy by providing non-residents the opportunity to hold short-term liquid dollar assets, in the form of bank deposits or money market instruments such as Treasury bills or similar assets. There is a dual aspect to this function. U.S. banks play an important role in this area, by providing dollar deposit facilities for non-residents. However, the international liquidity function extends well beyond the role of U.S. international banking. The position of the United States as world banker in the functional area of providing international liquidity necessarily includes the attractiveness of the dollar, which is tied to its relative stability of international value, the services of U.S. banks whereby foreign dollar deposits are held in U.S. banking offices, and the facilities and instruments of the New York money market.

In attempting to calculate the value of the benefits derived from providing international liquidity as a world banker, we must use the funds held in the United States by foreign governments, businesses, individuals, and international agencies as a base. This figure was over $60 billion at year-end 1972. If we assume a 10 per cent investment return on these funds for the United States, and a 7 per cent average cost of funds paid to foreigners on the interest earning portion ($8 billion of demand deposits and the remaining $52 billion in interest earning

investment) we arrive at the following net benefits, equal to
$2.36 billion per annum:

Implicit Income on Foreign Short-term Dollar Holdings (10 per cent rate on $60 billion)	$6.00 billion
Interest Paid Non-Resident Holders of Short-term Dollar Assets (7 per cent rate on $52 billion)	3.64 billion
Net Return to United States	$2.36 billion

Functioning as an international banking centre, the U.S.
earns considerably less in the way of net benefits than it does as
a world banker. At year-end 1972 U.S. international banks had
attracted some $9 billion in foreign non-official deposits. At the
estimated 10 per cent rate of return, we have a $0.9 billion bene-
fit. If we assume a 7 per cent average cost of funds on the time
deposit portion of these foreign deposits (nearly $2.6 billion) we
have a $0.2 billion annual cost of funds. This yields a net return
on U.S. international banking head office deposit operations of
$0.7 billion per annum.

To recapitulate, as a world banker the United States enjoys
net benefits equivalent to approximately $2.36 billion per year.
However, as an international banking centre, U.S. banking institutions enjoy net benefits of approximately $0.7 billion per
year.[5]

5. FINANCE OF U.S. FOREIGN TRADE

Provision of international banking services permits the export
of goods and services at prices that may be somewhat higher
than otherwise, thus raising the real income of the United
States. In cases where trade financing is available in the United
States but not so on equal terms in a competing export country,
the advantages of dealing with a U.S. financed credit are likely
to result in permitting U.S. exports to sell on a somewhat more
favourable price basis. The question is how much higher can
U.S. export prices be?

It is within reason to assume that a foreign importer would be willing to pay a higher price equivalent to 1, or 2 per cent of the U.S. supplier's price to obtain credit and documentary services without having to shop around for these services. The extent of imperfection in the market for foreign financing services is not too well known, and the differences from country to country probably are considerable.

In order to provide a figure that will serve as an indication of the possible magnitude of gains available to the United States from this source, we shall assume that the $43 billion of U.S. merchandise exports in 1971 would have brought 1 per cent less revenue in the absence of the credit and documentary services provided by U.S. banks. On this basis, the benefits to the U.S. from its international banking organisation are calculated at $430 million, annual rate.

6. SERVICE TO MULTINATIONAL CORPORATIONS

The international departments of banks service a wide assortment of multinational corporations, financial institutions, and smaller foreign firms conducting international business. In large New York City banks the manpower required for these operations may be proportionately greater than that used by banks in other parts of the United States with a smaller emphasis on international services. How do we measure the benefits derived for the United States from providing these services?

We shall first measure the 'income' derived from provision of these international banking services, and then estimate the portion of this income that represents a gain in the form of a higher return than could have been earned from an alternative (domestic) use of these resources. We first start out by assuming that U.S. income from sale of financial services was equal to one per cent of non-official foreign deposits held in the United States. At year-end 1972 these foreign deposits totalled $14 billion, yielding an estimated income of $140 million. Second, we further assume that the sale of specialised banking services to multinational corporations and foreigners yielded a return that was 5 per cent above what it could have been in domestic use. This yields a gain of $7 million.

7. CONDUCT OF EURODOLLAR OPERATIONS

U.S. overseas banking operations are heavily oriented around the Eurodollar market. At year-end 1971 London branches of American banks held close to half of Eurocurrency deposits in London.[6] Writing somewhat earlier, Scott had reported that between 1965 and 1968 U.S. banks in the United Kingdom had increased their share of Eurocurrency deposits in that market from 44 to 59 per cent.[7]

No doubt, overseas branches of American banks constitute an important part of the Eurocurrency market, and may account for 40–45 per cent of the deposit volume. At year-end 1968 time deposits in these overseas branches totalled $14.9 billion, at which time the Eurodollar market was estimated at $25 billion.[8] The market is estimated to have grown to $100 billion by year-end 1971.[9] If we assign 40 per cent of the market, or $40 billion, to U.S. overseas branches, and assume a $\frac{1}{4}$ of 1 per cent margin of profitability, we arrive at a $100 million gain from Eurocurrency operations of American banks.

8. PROVISION OF VENTURE CAPITAL OVERSEAS

We have seen that U.S. international banking is heavily oriented toward venture capital, or equity type investments. The major part of these investments is funnelled through Edge Act subsidiaries. Therefore, a basic limiting factor in the amount of investments undertaken by Edge Act corporations is their sources of funds. National and state member banks may not invest any more than specified percentages of their capital and surplus in Edge corporations.

The actual amount invested by U.S. banks in their Edge corporations is not a widely published figure. As of year-end 1969 American banks had invested close to $500 million in the capital stock and surplus of their Edge affiliates. In the period 1969–71 this investment probably grew by 10 per cent per annum, reaching approximately $600 million in 1971. If we assume an additional $600 million in borrowed funds available for venture capital type operations (which may be generous), we have a total investment fund of close to $1.2 billion. Further estimating a 2 per cent return on investment differential in favour of foreign investments by Edge corporations over domestic investment outlets, we arrive at a $24 million annual benefit from Edge Act affiliate venture capital investments.

9. SERVICE TO LESS DEVELOPED COUNTRIES

Services performed by U.S. international banking on behalf of the less developed countries in which American banks conduct their operations are of inestimable value to the host countries as well as to the United States. We shall assume that the advantages to the United States will have been included in the various measures estimated in preceding sections.

C. BALANCE BETWEEN BENEFITS AND COSTS

Referring to Table 14-1 we observe that as world banker the United States incurs an annual cost that may well exceed $9 billion. This stems from the need to maintain domestic and external stability, to preserve the stability of the dollar as a means of international settlements, to provide a flow of funds mechanism whereby the international flow of capital is accomplished, and to provide international liquidity.

One might be tempted to assign an excessive reliance on the accuracy of this $9 billion figure. This would represent a gross misinterpretation. Our efforts have been to search for general areas of magnitude, and by so doing have found a significant cost element involved in the United States playing the role of world banker.

No attempt is made here to answer the question whether it is worthwhile for the United States to incur the costs associated with the role of world banker. That might prove to be difficult, if only because while the U.S. underwrites these costs, the world economy benefits, and possibly to an extent that far exceeds the expenses borne by the United States.

By contrast the United States earns a modest net income in return for the international banking services performed by its commercial banks. At an annual rate these gains may exceed $1.2 billion. In a balance of payments context, the earnings from international banking activities may have prevented an unfavourable payments situation from deteriorating into a more serious imbalance. Another way of looking at these relationships is to suggest that the benefits derived from the role of the U.S. in international banking probably offset a substantial part of the costs directly associated with the world banker status of this country.

Table 14.1

Estimates of Annual Net Benefit and Cost from World Banker and International Banking Roles of the United States, based on 1971—72 Figures

Function	$ billions		
	Benefit	Cost	Net Benefit
1. Stable Means of Payment			
a. U.S. Output Gap		12.000	
b. Cost of holding gold and foreign exchange reserve		1.000	
2. International Flow of Funds Mechanism Differential earned after tax on long-term investment	0.800		
3. Provision of International liquidity Earned on non-resident funds			
a. as world banker	2.360		
b. as international banker	0.700		
4. Finance of U.S. Foreign Trade Marginal price on exports	0.430		
5. Service to Multinational Corporations	0.007		
6. Conduct of Eurodollar Operations	0.100		
7. Provision of Venture Capital overseas	0.024		
8. Service to Less Developed Countries	*		
Net Benefit			
as World Banker[a]			−9.840
as International Banker[b]			+1.261

[a] Obtained by subtracting lines 1a and 1b from lines 2 and 3a.
[b] Obtained by adding lines 3b, 4, 5, 6, and 7.
* Included in other functions.

15 The Future of International Banking

Earlier discussion has reflected the changing character of U.S. international banking over the postwar years. This dynamic feature is the result of interaction between changing environmental factors, and bank reaction to an environment in flux. International bankers have had to adjust to new competitive forces both in domestic and international banking, and have had to alter their mode of operations to cope with the realities of growing international opportunities, as well as co-ordinate their activities with new economic policies introduced by host countries. Moreover, the international economic and monetary structure has been subject to constant stress with the alternations in balance of payments deficits and surpluses, the introduction of new exchange rate relationships, the widening of currency areas, and the upsurge of new financial centres around the world. Banks have introduced new organisational forms to more effectively deal with these changing conditions, including multi-bank owned Edge units, venture banking affiliates, joint venture merchant banks, and parent bank organisational structures which are more adaptable to shifting international pressures. Finally, regulatory agencies have reacted to these changes—witness the establishment of an office by the Comptroller of the Currency in the U.S. Embassy in London, and the recent request of the New York State Banking Department to establish a London office to examine overseas branches of New York State chartered banks.[1] The Board of Governors of the Federal Reserve Board announced early in 1973 that it was reviewing the U.S. operations of foreign banks, and the regulations that it has issued concerning the international banking activities of American banks.[2] This review focuses on structural aspects rather than flows of funds through banking institutions.

A. OUTLINE OF FUTURE TRENDS

The future growth and development of international banking will depend upon the health and vitality of the international economy, as well as the political environment. The following summarises the major trends and developments that might be expected in international banking over the near and medium-term future.

1. The growth of international business will continue, including foreign trade, direct investment, and portfolio investment transactions. This expansion will be accompanied by an increased demand for international financial services, especially those provided by commercial banks oriented toward multi-country operations. Financial service requirements will become more heterogeneous as the base of international business operations expands and as individual banks, both American and foreign, attempt to provide distinctive financial service packages in competing for a multi-national clientele.

2. More banks representing a wider base of home countries will become important in international banking, as a result of expanding domestic opportunities in other countries, and as a consequence of the expansion of indigenous businesses into the international sphere. In addition, a number of mergers and amalgamations of existing foreign banking institutions will be likely, so that these banks may better compete at home and overseas.

3. Competitive pressures will continue to increase. Over the past quarter of a century banking institutions in the United States obtained a lead and competitive advantage over banks in other countries in developing their international banking activities. As a result, the U.S. share of international banking activities has remained relatively high, probably close to half of world-wide international banking operations. Over the long-run we

might expect the U.S. share to be reduced as a result of shifts in underlying relationships and a more competitive spirit on the part of European, Japanese, and less developed country banking institutions. The growing competition in international banking is reflected in various ways, including bank mergers, strengthening commercial ties, extension of overseas representation, and in the development of new financial centres that challenge New York and London.

4. The growth and development of the less developed countries will proceed, and in some cases the growth rate of certain developing countries may accelerate. Development finance has become a specialised branch of international banking and has competed with as well as complemented the international activities of major banking institutions. We may expect this pattern to continue, with the major differences that the less developed countries will carry more weight in the global mixture of international finance, and that their own banking and financing institutions will become better equipped to service local needs.

5. Specific countries and regions will play an increasingly important role in international business and global finance. The Common Market countries are in the process of enlarging their operating area to include the United Kingdom and several additional countries. Japan's impressive economic growth record will be extended into the 1970s and give that country a more important status in so far as international banking opportunities are concerned. Japanese and Common Market banking institutions will enjoy the advantage of operating from domestic banking bases that afford wider scope for growth and specialisation. These advantages will have a spill-over effect in so far as international banking is concerned.

6. In the future we may expect to see a larger role played by foreign investment coming into the United States, bringing with it foreign banking. the beginning of this trend has already become apparent, even though the strong inflow of foreign direct and portfolio investment

entering the United States date back only to the late 1960s.

7. In the years to come international bankers may have to resort to new organisational forms to better service their own clientele, and to cope with competition from foreign banks. The Orion Group represents an example of a U.S. bank assuming a major role in the establishment of a multinational banking group. The Chase Manhattan Bank, together with National Westminster Bank, Ltd., London, the Royal Bank of Canada, and the Westdeutsche Landesbank Girozentrale, Düsseldorf, established the Orion Group in 1970. Orion consists of three institutions: Orion Bank, Ltd, a merchant bank; Orion Termbank, a medium-term credit institution; and Orion Multinational Services Ltd, the group's management and planning unit. The Orion Group expects to benefit from the specialised abilities of its parent institutions – Chase and Royal Bank in oil, Westdeutsche in savings, and National Westminster in export finance.

Another development in the area of new organisational forms is the establishment of specialised banks and finance companies equipped to service East-West trade. While U.S. banks have not been especially active in this area, they are likely to follow the initiative offered by a number of European banks. For example, in 1971 Credit Lyonnais and a group of French banks signed an agreement with the Rumanian National Bank to form a Franco-Rumanian bank capitalised at 20 million francs ($3.6 million). The new bank is expected to aid in the financing of trade between Rumania and Western Europe. In the same year seven European banks agreed to form a trading company to promote East-West trade. The new company was given the title Centropa.

8. Further development of national money and capital markets in countries such as Switzerland, West Germany, France, and Italy, and their growth and expansion in financial centres such as Luxembourg, Singapore, Hong Kong, and Beirut will increase the

scope of international competition in finance and banking. Moreover, global flows of funds will have a larger number of alternative routes. Growth and evolution of markets such as the Asian dollar and Riodollar markets will afford increased opportunities for international finance and investment.

9. Improved technical means will be developed to speed up and lower the cost of international payments and communications. Recently, it was announced that 239 banks, including thirty-six from the United States, were organising the Society for Worldwide Interbank Financial Telecommunications (SWIFT).[3] SWIFT will provide user banks with a private international communications system, enabling the banks to transmit among themselves international payments, statements and other messages. The service will be operating in stages, beginning in 1975–6, and a daily input traffic volume of 260,000 messages is expected by 1980.

10. The increased role and importance of U.S. international banking is likely to bring with it numerous changes in the structure of banking in the United States. One important change that has become visible since 1970 is the emergence of regional banking sub-centres. Cities such as Atlanta, Miami, New Orleans, Dallas, San Francisco, and Seattle already function as international banking sub-centres. These sub-centres will depend on domestic and international banking activities for their future growth and development. Growth in international banking will come from (1) diversification of activities by banks in these sub-centres, (2) the formation of Edge Act subsidiaries by large banks headquartered in other centres, and (3) expansion in the number of international banking departments by banks headquartered in these sub-centres or in immediately adjacent cities. International banking has tended to erode a number of structural barriers in banking in the United States that formerly were considered watertight. These include barriers against intra-state branching, interstate banking, and

securities underwriting. The widespread entry of foreign banks into the United States, including their establishment of affiliates in regional sub-centres such as Miami, Chicago, and San Francisco must add to the pressure on legislatures to permit U.S. banking institutions greater freedom to competitively respond.

11. Balance of payments pressures against the United States will persist, at least for several years. The balance of merchandise trade will dip into a deficit position and may hover in that vicinity for extended periods. Capital outflows will persistently operate against the U.S. dollar on the foreign exchanges, and U.S. government grants and loans will inject a marginal payments influence on the U.S. international accounts.

12. United States monetary authorities will continue to shift away from Regulation Q ceilings as a means of credit restraint. This will result in strengthening the deposit attracting status of major U.S. banks, and may indirectly provide New York with additional leverage as an international deposit and money centre.

B. FUTURE PROSPECTS AND PROBLEMS

Looking beyond the initial years of the 1970s it seems clear that U.S. international banking faces numerous challenges and problems. The types of problems that may prove to be especially troublesome for U.S. bankers in the future range from maintaining credit standards in international loans and investments, maintaining a favourable share of the international banking market, coping with outbreaks of nationalist sentiment and resulting confiscatory policies, to adopting new methods and organisational structures that are suitable to the conduct of international banking in a changing world.

Movement toward monetary union in the EEC will intensify the competitive problems facing American banks on the European Continent, but at the same time will open up the possibilities for alliances with British banks which also will feel the competitive pressures from the Continent.

The international deposit role of New York will be influenced by such developments as monetary union in the EEC area, a more important role of the Japanese yen in international finance, the emergence of new international financial centres and expansion of existing centres, and by balance of payments disturbances that appear. New York and the dollar both will face increased competitive pressures, which may result in reducing the relative importance of New York as an international deposit centre.

In the past quarter of a century international bankers have responded competitively to new opportunities and problems. If the past is a prologue to the future, we may expect that these same bankers will respond positively to the problems and opportunities that they face in the future.

Epilogue

The onrush of events in the field of international banking since final revision of the manuscript warrants inclusion of the following sample of important new developments. These developments cover such areas as management strategy, size and scope of international banking operations, regulation, research and analysis, and technical innovations.

In the area of management strategy several of the largest American banks have moved in the direction of diversifying their international operations into retail banking. The First National City Bank of New York has indicated its intention to adjust its European emphasis from a current 80 per cent wholesale corporate lending level down to 40 per cent within the next decade. Similarly, Chase Manhattan has launched a new British subsidiary aimed at the middle market, as well as a retail-oriented family bank in Germany.

In 1973 the Board of Governors of the Federal Reserve System established a special committee to research and analyse various aspects of international banking including the growing role of foreign banks in the U.S. and the effects of international banking on U.S. domestic banking structure. This Steering Committee on International Banking Regulation has been asked to recommend changes in existing regulation, where deemed appropriate.

On the regulatory front numerous developments have materialised since the early months of 1973. The Board of Governors of the Federal Reserve System extended the Voluntary Foreign Credit Restraint programme to U.S. agencies and branches of foreign banks, requesting that these institutions should not increase their foreign assets covered by the programme above the levels of June 1973. At May 1973 sixty-four U.S. agencies and branches of foreign banks had total foreign assets of about $6.2 billion. Of this amount $3.6 billion was sub-

ject to the VFCR programme. In the year and a half leading up
to this extension of the VFCR to foreign banks their assets outside the United States had approximately doubled. On 1 June
1973 the Board of Governors requested the agencies and
branches and non-member bank subsidiaries of foreign banks
to maintain voluntary reserves against Eurodollar borrowings
in excess of a base level.

Regulation of foreign bank activity by the various states
became more active during 1973, largely in connection with the
increased scope of activity of foreign banks operating in the
United States. Conflicting trends are evident. In some cases
state banking commissioners appear to be preserving the 'little
monopolies' enjoyed by domestic banks, witness the denial by
the New York Superintendent of Banks of Barclays Bank Ltd's
request to acquire the Long Island Trust Company. Fortunately, such cases are in the minority. On the other hand, states
such as Illinois and Washington have enacted legislation permitting foreign banks to establish branches in their respective
states. In the case of Illinois, the expectation is that ten or more
foreign banks will have established branches in Chicago within
one year of passage of the enabling legislation. In California a
restrictive bill was defeated that would have prohibited foreign
banks from establishing branches in that state except under
rather rigorous conditions of reciprocity.

International banking made important advances in terms
of its size and scope of operations. Commercial banks in the
U.S. and abroad set a record for a single Eurobond financing
with a $1 billion ten-year loan to the British Electricity Coun-
cil. There was virtually no participation by non-commercial
banking investment bankers. The loan carries the guarantee
of the U.K. Treasury, and was managed by Lazard Bros. &
Co. Ltd., Western American Bank (Europe) Ltd., and National Westminster Bank Ltd.

On the technical front international banks have been
streamlining their money transfer, message communication,
and account transactions. As of September 1973 the First
National City Bank machine-readable telegraphic input service (MARTI) had signed over two hundred customers.
MARTI provides a computer-connected telegraphic system
wherein transactions created on telex machines in Europe are

transmitted through a regional computer to New York. The system segregates messages into several types of transaction, and further is linked with the New York Clearing House Interbank Payments System. In a similar development several hundred of the largest international banks are establishing a European-based computer message and payments system. This system (SWIFT) will provide facilities for instant payments, account reconciliation, and message transfer between any of the several hundred banks linked into the system. The SWIFT facility is expected to be operational in 1976.

The world of international banking continues to grow and evolve at an accelerated pace. The linkages and transfers of skills and knowledge afforded by this revolution in banking can have much influence on the world economy and world business in the years to come. Hopefully, the regulatory agencies will exercise prudent judgement and caution in the execution of their responsibilities. If they do, international banking will continue to thrive and prosper, and generate its own external economies for the betterment of society and world business.

Notes

CHAPTER 1

1. Fred H. Klopstock, 'A New Look at Foreign and International Banking in the United States', in *Private Financial Institutions*, Prentice Hall, 1963, p. 342.
2. Harold S. Taylor, 'Antitrust, Lack of Trust and Foreign Deposits', *The Bankers Magazine*, Autumn 1968, pp. 36–7.
3. World Bank and IDA, *Annual Reports* of 1972, 1970 and 1968, pp. 68–70 and 92–3; pp. 46–8; pp. 60–61, respectively.
4. Joint Economic Committee of the U.S. Congress, *A Description and Analysis of Certain European Capital Markets*, 1964.
5. 'Banking Regulation in Britain, by Suasion not Statute', *Midland Bank Review*, November 1967, pp. 12–13.
6. Joint Economic Committee of the Congress of the United States, *Foreign Government Restraints on United States Bank Operations Abroad*, U.S. Government Printing Office, 1967, p. 7.
7. *American Banker*, 2 June 1970.
8. 'United States Banks and Foreign Trade Financing', *Federal Reserve Bulletin*, April 1955, pp. 364–5.
9. See Tables 6 and 7 of the study cited above.

CHAPTER 2

1. Based on correspondence with Paul M. Horvitz, Director of Research, Federal Deposit Insurance Corporation, dated 26 September 1969.
2. Comptroller of the Currency, 'International Operations Regulation 20', Section 20.1 (b)(3).
3. Correspondence with Robert E. Mitchell, Assistant General Counsel, FDIC, dated 22 October 1969.
4. This discussion is based on material found in Ronald E. Covault, 'Foreign Branches and Edge Act Corporations', *National Banking Review*, December 1963, pp. 247–51.
5. Covault, p. 248, as cited from Hearings on S. 1771 before the House Committee on Banking and Currency, 87th Congress (1962).
6. The text of the 1962 act may be found in *Federal Reserve Bulletin*, September 1962, p. 1154. The text of the 1963 revision of Regulation M may be found in *Federal Reserve Bulletin*, August 1963, pp. 1068–70.

7. Clyde W. Phelps, *The Foreign Expansion of American Banks*, Ronald Press, 1927, p. 147.
8. Frederick R. Dahl, 'International Operations of U.S. Banks: Growth and Public Policy Implications', *Law and Contemporary Problems*, Duke University School of Law, Winter 1967, p. 119.
9. *Federal Reserve Bulletin*, September 1963, p. 1238.
10. Ibid., p. 1241.
11. The original version of the Edge Act passed in 1919 limited national banks to invest only up to 10 per cent of their capital and surplus in Edge Act and Agreement corporations.
12. Regulation K, Section 211.8(a) as amended effective 1 September 1963.
13. Regulation M, Section 213.4(a) as amended effective 15 March 1967.
14. The four foreign banks subject to the 1956 Act in 1970 were Barclays Bank, Ltd, Bank of Montreal, Canadian Imperial Bank of Commerce, and the Bank of Tokyo, Ltd. As a result, in 1970 it was necessary for Barclays Bank Ltd, the largest free world bank outside the United States to obtain permission from the Federal Reserve Board to acquire a 6 per cent interest in another British-based bank, the Bank of London and South America Ltd, which operates a branch in New York. The Board's approval was necessary because Barclays is a registered bank holding company, due to its ownership of more than 25 per cent of Barclays Bank, DCO, London, which at the time operated three branches in New York, and in Barclays Bank of California, San Francisco, a state-chartered bank. *American Banker*, 3 September 1970.
15. Board of Governors of the Federal Reserve System, *Press Release*, dated 20 September 1971, Regulation Y, Part 222, Bank Holding Companies, Foreign Activities of Domestic Holding Companies.
16. FDIC, *Annual Report 1968*, p. 18; and Board of Governors of the Federal Reserve System, *Annual Report 1968*, p. 348.
17. 'Acquisition by Edge Corporation of Stock of Combination Export Manager', *Federal Reserve Bulletin*, May 1967, pp. 752–3.
18. Ibid., p. 752.
19. Dahl, p. 125.
20. Dahl, pp. 125–6.
21. There exists an important non-parallel wherein the Comptroller's office has jurisdiction for approving requests for establishing domestic branches, but the Board of Governors holds jurisdiction for approving requests for establishing overseas branches. The non-parallel as between domestic and foreign regulatory powers in this area was put to the test without success, in 1963. On 23 December of that year the Comptroller, James J. Saxon, sent a letter to the presidents of all national banks with foreign operations. In the letter he proposed that the Comptroller's office rule on national bank applications for acquisition of stock in foreign banking corporations (Edge Act corporations), and acquisitions of controlling interest in foreign corporations or state-chartered foreign banking corporations. Earlier that year Representative Fernand St. Germain of Rhode Island introduced HR 5800, with the intent of transferring from the Board of Governors to the Comptroller of the Currency the

power to authorise and examine foreign branches of national banks.

22. In these examinations two areas are emphasised: namely credit review and foreign exchange transactions. The credit review considers lines and extensions of credit, loan appraisals and possible weaknesses in loans. The analysis of foreign exchange transactions considers risk exposure.

23. Correspondence with Wallace R. Anker, Director, International Division, The Administrator of National Banks, Comptroller of the Currency, dated 22 July 1969.

24. The Board of Governors does not conduct regular examinations of the foreign branches of state member banks, this practice having been discontinued in 1954. However, a pilot programme was launched in 1969 whereby two London branches of member banks were examined.

25. Dahl, p. 126.

26. This information was obtained through correspondence with Mr Frank A. Carlson, Assistant to Deputy Superintendent, New York State Banking Department, dated 29 December 1970.

27. Sections 530 and 535, California Banking Law.

28. This information was provided through private correspondence with Mr John H. Sherman, Chief Deputy, California State Banking Department, dated 29 December 1970.

29. Article 2, Section 532, California Banking Law.

30. This provision was added to the California Banking Law in 1969, and places foreign branches of California chartered banks on a par with the foreign branches of national banks and New York chartered banks in their ability to compete effectively with banks established in the countries where the branches are located.

31. Article 4, Section 3580.

32. *Wall Street Journal*, 8 October 1970, p. 30, and 9 October 1970, p. 30.

33. *American Banker*, 24 September 1970. In connection with this seven former employees of the Basel affiliate were arrested on suspicion of fraud.

34. *United States Investor*, 9 November 1970. Vice-Chairman J. L. Robertson, of the Board of Governors of the Federal Reserve System stated that the commodity speculation that took place was in direct violation of the conditions under which the Federal Reserve had approved United California Bank's acquisition of the Swiss bank.

35. *American Banker*, 8 October 1970.

36. *American Banker*, 10 September 1970. The Swiss Banking Commission launched an investigation of the losses experienced by the Basel affiliate soon after information was made public concerning these losses. Swiss bankers expressed the view that this experience could create pressure for a tightening of Swiss law on the supervision of all banks in that country. They further expressed satisfaction that the parent bank had gone well beyond the requirements of the law in providing for depositors and creditors.

CHAPTER 3

1. Douglas A. Hayes, 'A Bankers' Primer on International Banking', *The Bankers Magazine*, Spring 1970, pp. 32–3.
2. Commission on Money and Credit, *The Commercial Banking Industry*, Prentice Hall, 1962, p. 251.
3. In 1969 *Business Abroad* published a 'Banking Directory for Foreign Traders', which listed 210 American banks with 'active foreign departments', January 1969, pp. 44–6. A 1972 Correspondent Banking Survey conducted by the *American Banker* lists over 260 U.S. banks with foreign deposits, 18 December 1972, pp. 49–61.
4. Nearly all of these foreign branches were operated by Federal Reserve member banks. At year-end 1972, twenty-one of these overseas branches were operated by eight non-member banks.
5. In a similar analysis, Andrew F. Brimmer, Governor of the Federal Reserve Board in Washington, D.C., reported on the comparative international deposits and assets of twenty multinational and sixty regional U.S. banks. This report, presented as a paper to the American Economic Association meeting in Toronto, December 1972, was summarised in the *American Banker*, 10 January 1973.
6. It has not always worked out in this manner. According to a survey conducted by John R. Kreidle and Paul O. Groke, many local banks are reluctant to encourage international business or give advice on export financing or international finance in general. Often, local banks refer customers to metropolitan correspondents, and then lose the business to the large city bank. 'Local Banks Lose Out in Overseas Business', *American Banker*, June 1969, p. 25.
7. A list of pointers can be found in Herbert Bratter, 'Pointers for Directors of Banks Entering International Fields', *Banking*, March 1966, p. 54.
8. 'Ralston Prefers U.S. Bank Branches Abroad', *American Banker*, 4 March 1970.
9. Prescott B. Crafts, Jr, *A Management Re-Examination of Expansion Overseas by American Banks*, a dissertation completed at the Stonier Graduate School of Banking, 1957, p. 64.
10. John Light, *Joint Ventures: An Approach to International Banking*, a dissertation completed at the Stonier Graduate School of Banking, 1964, p. 53.
11. Hayes, pp. 35–7.
12. The Overseas Private Investment Corp. was created in 1969 with the intention of taking over and building on the investment insurance programmes of the Agency for International Development. It was established as a private corporation to encourage the participation of businessmen in the programme's operations.
13. Hayes, pp. 38–9.
14. David Rockefeller, *Creative Management in Banking*, McGraw-Hill, 1964, p. 75.
15. Frank M. Tamagna and Parker B. Willis, 'United States Banking Organization Abroad', *Federal Reserve Bulletin*, December 1956, p. 1284.
16. 'Bolsa Investment Holds the Key to Mellon's International Goals', *American Banker*, 28 January 1970.

CHAPTER 4

1. William S. Shaterian, *Export-Import Banking*, Ronald Press, 1956, pp. 3–4.
2. Walter B. Wriston, 'The International Department', in *The Bankers' Handbook*, Dow-Jones-Irwin, 1966, p. 886.
3. For example, in its *Annual Report 1969*, Morgan Guaranty Trust Company devoted two and a half pages of its eight page organisational layout to the International Banking Division and the International Council, pp. 26–33. In 1969 the same bank operated *eight overseas branches* compared with *only five domestic offices*. Naturally, this comparison represents an over-simplification, since the head office of Morgan Guaranty is so large.
4. Hugh Chairnoff, 'Philadelphia Bankers are International Bankers', *Business Review*, Federal Reserve Bank of Philadelphia, May 1968, pp. 2–3.
5. Charles N. Henning, *International Finance*, Harper, 1958, p. 256.
6. Shaterian, p. 20.
7. Two obstacles in the way of management evaluation of success of an international department are the time factor and the accounting methods employed in apportioning costs and earnings. A new foreign department may not show a profit for three years or longer. Smaller banks may be ill-advised to consider direct international operations. According to Lee, 'a number of interior banks are earnestly trying to garner some letter of credit business . . . Frequently the commission income fails to cover the direct expense of processing these generally complicated credits, and often there would appear to be little in the way of collateral benefits particularly in the light of the risks assumed.' Robert E. Lee, 'International Banking on Main Street', *The Bankers Magazine*, Winter 1969, p. 48.
8. In the late 1950s international departments acquired the pseudonym 'bank within a bank'. This term has fallen into disuse and at present bank management tends to regard the international department as 'a major operating division of the bank'.
9. These are Bank of America, Chase Manhattan Bank, and First National City Bank of New York.
10. However, a number of these banks obtain 20–30 per cent of their deposits from foreign branches and international department customers. In addition, several of these banks in the second category have international loans in the $1 billion range.
11. Morgan Guaranty Trust and Bankers Trust tend to fit into this pattern.
12. For example, Chase Manhattan Bank identifies three territorial groups, while First National City Bank identifies five.
13. Robert A. Bennett, 'Chase Reshapes International Department on Task Basis', *American Banker*, 14 December 1970.
14. The activities which are not normally a part of the domestic operations of U.S. banks but which do fit into the activities of a number of international departments include assembling and providing information on the investment climate in individual countries, syndicating credits for overseas borrowers, finding and evaluating merger and acquisitions prospects overseas, engaging in liaison with foreign and U.S. government agencies,

and operating leasing-factoring-commercial credit affiliates in certain overseas areas.

15. Chemical Bank New York Trust Company, *Financing Imports and Exports*, 1967, p. 11.

16. It is understandable that some exporters, especially when unfamiliar with the foreign issuing bank, would prefer to have some kind of commitment in the way of a confirmed letter of credit from their own U.S. bank. A fuller discussion of this may be found in *Commercial Letters of Credit*, published by the International Banking Department, Continental Bank, pp. 4–5.

17. *Foreign Exchange and Foreign Remittances*, published by International Banking Department, Continental Bank.

18. *Federal Reserve Bulletin*, August 1970, page A83, Table 14.

19. *American Banker*, 18 December 1970, pp. 62–3. It should be noted that this figure excludes the dollar deposits of foreign banking institutions in U.S. banks. At June 1970 deposit liabilities of U.S. banks to foreign banking institutions were as follows: demand deposit liabilities $15.3 billion, time deposit liabilities $1.8 billion. *Federal Reserve Bulletin*, August 1970, page A78, Table 8.

20. J. G. Bickford, 'Reciprocal Arrangements Buoy International Service', *American Banker*, 18 December 1970, p. 18.

21. These include Marine Midland Bank, New York; National Bank of North America; United California Bank; and the Philadelphia National Bank.

CHAPTER 5

1. Robin Pringle, 'Why American Banks Go Abroad', *The Bankers Magazine*, Autumn 1967, pp. 53–4.

2. 'Pro-Branching Lobby in Illinois Closes Down as Funding Slows after Decade of Defects', *American Banker*, 30 April 1970. This article comments that the First National Bank of Chicago had withdrawn its support of the Illinois Council for Branch Banking, and had become disenchanted with what it considered to be a futile branching cause. Instead First National 'has devoted its energies toward the expansion of its international operations and eventually of its one bank holding company'.

3. 'Foreign Banks in London: A British Bankers View', *The Banker*, October 1969, pp. 1063–64. This article notes that rents in the square mile of the City are already very high, and American banks coming to London have created a seller's paradise for good sites.

4. Sanford Rose, 'Capital is Something That Doesn't Love a Wall', *Fortune*, February 1971, p. 103.

5. Joint Economic Committee, U.S. Congress, *Foreign Government Restraints on United States Bank Operations Abroad*, 1967, pp. 16–17.

6. In a speech delivered at a biennial business conference in New York John A. Waage, Senior Vice President of Manufacturers Hanover Trust Co., warned of the dangers from over-rapid expansion of overseas branches, including increased tendencies toward expropriation and nationalisation. Cited in *American Banker*, 7 December 1970.

7. Maximo Eng, *U.S. Overseas Banking – Its Past, Present, and Future*, Business Research Institute, St John's University, September 1970, p. 22.

8. A deterrent that operated until 1966 when the U.S. tax laws were changed diverted from U.S. overseas branches the sizeable liquid holdings of the so-called Delaware Corporations. In order to obtain an exempt status with respect to the 30 per cent withholding tax on non-resident bond purchases these corporations must obtain more than 80 per cent of their income from overseas sources. Prior to 1967 interest paid on deposits by overseas branches of U.S. banks was not regarded as meeting this requirement.

9. 'First U.S. Bank Opening in Israel', *New York Times*, 29 August 1970; and *American Banker*, 5 January 1973.

10. These figures exclude foreign branches of non-member banks. At the time of writing the author could identify twenty-one foreign branches of eight non-member banks. It should be noted that most of these banks are affiliates of larger foreign banks.

11. The wealth and influence of the overseas Chinese residing in many of the countries of the Far East is often ignored. Close to 98 per cent of the population of Hong Kong is Chinese, and in Singapore, Malaysia, and Thailand the overseas Chinese constitute 75, 47, and 10 per cent of the total population, respectively.

12. Federal Reserve Bank of Atlanta, 'Banking in a Developing Economy: Latin American Patterns', *Monthly Review*, November 1970, p. 155.

13. Ibid., pp. 155–6.

14. On 31 December 1968 there were eight branches of Federal Reserve member banks in the Bahamas; one year later there were thirty-one branches.

15. American banks have tended to use affiliates to develop their banking representation in Africa.

16. 'Recent Activities of Foreign Branches of U.S. Banks', *Federal Reserve Bulletin*, October 1972, pp. 855–65. The discussion in this section is based on this source.

17. Contrary to European practice, American banks and their overseas branches generally do not station their Eurocurrency and foreign exchange traders in the same immediate physical location of the banking premises. On the Continent Eurocurrency trading essentially becomes a foreign exchange type function.

18. This has been the case especially since the voluntary direct investment controls programme began in 1965. As a result of this programme equity investments in foreign affiliates of U.S. companies have been severely restricted, and foreign debt financing has been more aggressively pursued, resulting in a highly leveraged situation.

19. *Federal Reserve Bulletin*, various issues in 1970–71, Table A-32.

20. This is not possible in the developed countries. This is because the commission and interest income on this form of financing is attractive and vigorously competed for by local banks that have long been established in this area.

CHAPTER 6

1. Frank M. Tamagna and Parker B. Willis, 'United States Banking Organization Abroad', *Federal Reserve Bulletin*, December 1956, p. 1289.
2. There is an exception to this, in that the state banking department may share dual jurisdiction with the federal agency over Edge Act subsidiaries of that same state's chartered banks. For example, the New York State Banking Department has dual jurisdiction over Edge Act subsidiaries of New York State chartered banks, but not over those of out-of-state banks located in New York.
3. An exception to this is the Virgin Islands National Bank, an Agreement Corporation holding a national bank charter and thereby subject to federal laws.
4. Allen F. Goodfellow, *International Corporations of American Banks*, unpublished thesis, Stonier Graduate School of Banking, Rutgers, June 1968, p. 9.
5. George H. Bossy, 'Edge Act and Agreement Corporations in International Banking and Finance', *Monthly Review*, Federal Reserve Bank of New York, May 1964, p. 89.
6. Ibid., p. 89.
7. Regulation K, Section 211.8(a), as revised effective 1 September 1963. See Section D of this chapter for a description of more recent revisions concerning general and specific consent provisions.
8. Goodfellow, p. 21.
9. Ibid., p. 20.
10. Frank M. Tamagna and Parker B. Willis, 'United States Banking Organization Abroad', *Federal Reserve Bulletin*, December 1956, p. 1292.
11. Late in 1970 one New York-based Edge corporation, Northwest International Bank, received Board approval to relocate to Minneapolis, where its parent institution (Northwest Bancorporation) is located. Northwest International Bank was formed in 1963 to function as the international department of the group's seventy-five affiliate banks. *American Banker*, 14 December 1970.
12. Goodfellow, p. 43. For example, First National City Bank of New York retained its Agreement corporation, International Banking Corporation, as its banking corporation and established a new Edge corporation to function in the financing area. In 1967 FNCB established a second Edge corporation to conduct a banking business with headquarters in San Francisco.
13. Application to form the fourth multi-bank owned corporation was made by the South Shore National Bank of Quincy, Mass. and the First New Haven National Bank in 1970. Approval of this application has resulted in these banks being the smallest in the United States with an Edge Act unit. The subsidiary is known as Shorehaven Bank, International, Boston.
14. The parent institutions were Chase Manhattan Bank, Chemical Corn Exchange Bank, First National Bank of Boston, Mellon National Bank and Trust Co., and National Bank of Detroit.

15. The purchaser was American Overseas Finance Company, another Edge corporation wholly-owned by American Overseas Investing Co., Inc., controlled by industrial interests. In 1960 the new AOFC entered liquidation.

16. The origins of Allied can be traced back to the period 1961–6 when James J. Saxon served as U.S. Comptroller of the Currency. Shortly after Saxon resigned from the Comptrollers office he joined American Fletcher National Bank and Trust Co., Indianapolis as its co-chairman. During his term as Comptroller, Saxon envisaged the formation of a strong new international banking organisation that could contribute materially to American exports and other profit-making business activities abroad, and thereby add to the nation's badly needed store of foreign exchange. American Fletcher took a leading role in founding Allied Bank International (originally known as American Overseas Banking Corp.). 'The Bank of the Year and its Banker', *Finance*, October 1969, pp. 8–11.

17. The largest such corporation is Bank of America, New York. Not only was Allied heavily capitalised, it also sought and recruited the best international banking talent available. Its President, Jacques R. Stunzi, has a long record of success in business and finance with Hanover Bank, Celanese Corp., American Express Co., and Continental Bank International, New York.

18. Allied Bank International, *Annual Report 1969*, p. 1.

19. *American Banker*, 22 October 1970.

20. Goodfellow, p. 49.

21. There were three corporations organised in that year, two by interior banks (Continental Bank International and First Chicago International Banking Corp.), and one by a west coast bank (United California Bank International).

22. Goodfellow, p. 57.

23. Ibid., pp. 57–8.

24. Ibid., pp. 59–63.

25. Under Regulation K, Section 211.2(d) a corporation is 'engaged in banking' whenever it has aggregate demand deposits and acceptance liabilities exceeding its capital and surplus.

26. Goodfellow, p. 70.

27. Ibid., p. 96.

28. In 1969 First National City Bank had three representatives on the Board of National and Grindlays Bank (40 per cent ownership), and four on the Board of Iranians Bank (35 per cent ownership). However, these stock holdings were purchased directly by FNCB, as permitted in the 1966 and 1967 amendments to the Federal Reserve Act and Regulation M, respectively.

29. The American banks and corporations with equity interests in ADELA as of 1969 were Bamerical International Financial Corp. (Bank of America), Chemical International Finance, Ltd, Continental International Finance Corp., Crocker-Citizens International Corp., The Fidelity International Corp., First Chicago International Finance Corp., First National City Overseas Investment Corp., First Pennsylvania Overseas Finance Corp.,

Irving International Financing Corp., Manufacturers-Detroit International Corp., Manufacturers Hanover International Finance Corp., Mellon Bank International, Northwest International Bank, Republic International Company, Shawmut International Corp., and Wells Fargo Bank International Corp. ADELA Investment Co., *Annual Report*, 1969, pp. 40–41.

30. A possible alternative to Edge and Agreement corporation equity investments is the purchase of an interest by a bank holding company. For example, in January 1971 it was announced that the First National City Bank, via its holding company parent, had acquired Cresap, McCormick & Paget, Inc., an international management consulting firm. *American Banker*, 5 January 1971.

31. Speech delivered by Governor George W. Mitchell at the Annual Legal Seminar of the California Bankers Association, Santa Barbara, California, on 10 April 1970, titled 'The Intent and the Letter of Bank Regulation', pp. 10–11.

32. Chase Manhattan Overseas Banking Corp. holds an interest in Housing Development Corp., San Juan, Puerto Rico. Under the Board's ruling, Chase will not be permitted to continue to hold the HDC shares when the Puerto Rican firm acquires an interest in a new resort complex.

33. Mitchell speech, p. 12.

34. Goodfellow, p. 101.

35. John Light, *Joint Ventures: An Approach to International Banking*, dissertation completed at Stonier Graduate School of Banking, 1964, p. 1. Writing in 1964 Light identified eighty-four such investments by American banks (pp. 10–11). Somewhat earlier, Farley identified only two joint ventures entered into by U.S. banks. The banks involved were Morgan Guaranty Trust Company and the First National Bank of Boston. T. M. Farley, *The Edge Act and United States International Banking and Finance*, dissertation completed at Stonier Graduate School of Banking, 1962, p. 48.

36. Goodfellow, p. 102.

37. The section containing provision for general consent in the 1957 revision of Regulation K is Section 9(c), which states that 'the Board of Governors may grant its general consent for a Financing Corporation to purchase and hold stock, up to such amounts and in such circumstances as the Board may prescribe, in generally designated types of corporations which are not engaged in banking . . .'.

38. This change was published in the *Federal Reserve Bulletin*, January 1969, pp. 51–2.

39. Regulation K, Section 211.8(a), effective 7 January 1969.

CHAPTER 7

1. There are two exceptions to this. In cases where foreign banks establish national banks subject to federal jurisdiction, or where state-chartered subsidiaries of foreign banks obtain FDIC insurance coverage or become members of the Federal Reserve System, federal jurisdiction applies.

Second, the 1970 amendment of the federal bank holding company legislation gave the Federal Reserve Board jurisdiction over one-bank holding companies. This gave the Board jurisdiction over the activities of foreign banks with state-chartered affiliates in the United States.

2. Cadogan A. Gordon notes that as early as 1880 the Hongkong & Shanghai Banking Corporation established a New York office, followed by the British Colonial Bank in 1890, The Chartered Bank in 1902, and the National Bank of South Africa in 1915; 'British Banking in New York', *The Banker*, July 1969, p. 673. According to Robert F. Cassidy, at least two Canadian banks predate 1880 – in 1879 the Bank of Montreal successfully engaged in investment banking through its New York Agency. *The Friendly Invasion – Foreign Banks in New York State*, unpublished dissertation, 1968, pp. 14–15.

3. Jack Zwick, *Foreign Banking in the United States*, Joint Economic Committee, U.S. Congress, 1966, p. 3.

4. This point is documented statistically in an early article by Andrew Brimmer, which points to the small number of foreign bank offices in the United States and the larger number of Canadian banking offices in Latin America as compared with U.S. banking offices in that region. Andrew F. Brimmer, 'Foreign Banking Institutions in the U.S. Money Market', *The Review of Economics & Statistics*, February 1962, pp. 80–81.

5. The amended New York State law stipulates that a bank cannot maintain both an agency and a branch.

6. This information was supplied by Donald E. Pearson, Superintendent of Banks, State of California, and Bertwing C. Mah, Director of Research, State Banking Department, through private correspondence dated 4 December 1970.

7. Zwick, p. 14.

8. Canadian issues are exempt from the Interest Equalisation Tax.

9. This experience was earned during periods in which the Canadian dollar was allowed to 'float' in terms of its rate of exchange with the U.S. dollar and other pegged currencies.

10. Brimmer's study published in 1962 indicates that at that time foreign agency banks were not significant factors in the Federal Funds market, but that they accounted for a substantial volume of loans to brokers and dealers. Brimmer, pp. 78–9.

11. Formerly the Belgium-American Banking Corporation, which in 1968 reorganised under its present name. Until that date this corporation was wholly owned by Société Generale de Banque. In 1968 the Deutsche Bank, Midland Bank and Amsterdam-Rotterdam Bank made substantial investments to form the present institution. At year-end 1968 European-American Banking Corp. had equity capital of $42 million and combined assets of $255 million. An affiliate, European-American Bank and Trust Company, conducts a general banking business to service customers of both institutions, as well as clients of the four parent banks.

12. A survey of state governments conducted by Jack Zwick at that time revealed only seven states with specific legal provision for foreign bank operations within their jurisdiction. See Zwick, pp. 22–3.

13. Cassidy, pp. 45–6.
14. A somewhat fuller discussion of the legal concept can be found in Zwick, pp. 24–5.
15. Phillips Perera, *Development Finance: Institutions, Problems and Prospects*, Praeger, 1968, p. 131.
16. George N. Sfeir, 'Banking the Lebanese Way', *The Bankers Magazine*, 1965, pp. 28–9.
17. Harold S. Taylor, 'The Day They Shorted the Intra Bank', *The Bankers Magazine*, 1967, pp. 13–15.
18. The Lebanese banking system has relied to a considerable extent on funk money, internationally mobile money which is subject to constant geographic relocation based on changing interest rate and safety considerations. Rising interest rates in September 1966 caused large amounts of this money to exit from Lebanon, much of it moving into the Eurocurrency market.
19. *American Banker*, 30 July 1970.
20. Perera, p. 135.
21. This was actually a reintroduction of S 3765, which had been introduced in the 89th Congress in 1966. One important revision it contained was the addition of a concept of dual federal-state supervision. Cassidy, pp. 135–6.

CHAPTER 8

1. In a book published in 1964 David Rockefeller described the many foreign lending activities of Chase Manhattan Bank in such areas as modernisation of ranches, stimulating scientific programmes of seeding and breeding, accepting liens on cattle as loan collateral, and for general agricultural purposes. *Creative Management in Banking*, McGraw-Hill, pp. 65–6.
2. Hugh Chairnoff, 'Philadelphia Bankers Are International Bankers', *Business Review*, Federal Reserve Bank of Philadelphia, May 1968, p. 5.
3. The mandatory direct investment controls programme does not apply to U.S. companies which are *not* direct investors.
4. This is the so-called Gore Amendment to the IET.
5. Naturally there are exceptions to this. For example, over the past decade Switzerland has tended to remain a relatively low cost source of funds.
6. At year-end 1966 foreign loans totalled $14.4 billion, consisting of $4.3 billion in foreign branch loans to foreigners *other than banks* and $10.1 billion in head office claims on foreigners. In 1969 foreign loans totalled $22.0 billion, consisting of $9.2 billion in foreign branches and $12.8 billion at head offices. In 1972 foreign loans totalled $42.1 billion, consisting of $21.6 billion in foreign branches and $20.5 billion at head offices.
7. Klopstock, *Private Financial Institutions*, p. 336.
8. *American Banker*, 17 March 1970 and 19 October 1970; *Wall Street Journal*, 15 June 1970.
9. In 1970 Bankers Trust Co. of New York headed a syndicate of U.S. banks that extended loans of $27 million to the Marinduque Mining and

Industrial Corp. of the Philippines. This was part of a $119 million loan to the company guaranteed by the Philippine government. Other parts of the loan package consisted of a $27 million loan by the Export-Import Bank, $60 million of suppliers' credits by Kobe Steel Ltd. of Japan, and a $5 million credit from Bankers Trust London branch. *American Banker*, 9 December 1970. According to George Budzeika, Economist of the New York Federal Reserve Bank, foreign lending by New York banks, especially term lending, is closely related to purchases by foreign businesses of heavy capital equipment from American companies. Public utilities and metal manufacturers carry heavy weight among these foreign borrowers. *Lending To Business By New York City Banks*, Bulletin No. 76–77 of the Institute of Finance, New York University, September 1971, p. 24.

10. We should also note that two-thirds of short-term claims of U.S. banks denominated in foreign currencies represent deposits with foreign banks, adding a third major component to the credit facilities U.S. banks provide to their foreign correspondents.

11. This is counter to U.S. bank experience in trade with Europe, where drafts generally are drawn by the exporter.

12. Japanese banks also borrow on the Eurodollar market, and costs in that market are a third variable in determining the extent of their borrowing in the United States.

13. Douglas A. Hayes, 'A Bankers Primer on International Banking', *The Bankers Magazine*, Spring 1970, p. 35.

14. 'Bank Credits to Foreigners', *Federal Reserve Bulletin*, March 1965, p. 361.

15. Ibid., p. 362.

16. 'Guidelines For Banks and Non-bank Financial Institutions', *Federal Reserve Bulletin*, March 1965, p. 372.

17. Ibid., p. 374.

18. Federal Reserve Bank of New York, *Revised Guidelines for Banks and Nonbank Financial Institutions Under the President's Balance of Payments Programme*, Circular No. 6669, 11 January 1971, p. 5.

19. Board of Governors of the Federal Reserve System, 'Revised Guidelines for Banks and Nonbank Financial Institutions', *Press Release*, 17 December 1969, p. 7.

20. Board of Governors of the Federal Reserve System, *Inquiry Into Possible Effects of VFCR in 1970 On Export Financing and On Exports*, 7 January 1971, p. 4.

21. Henry Kearns, 'Eximbank Resources and Facilities and How To Use Them', *Proceedings of the Fifty-Sixth National Foreign Trade Convention*, 1970, pp. 261–2.

22. For example, Arthur F. Burns, Chairman of the Board of Governors, has argued that not all Export-Import Bank loans result in additional export sales. Frequently Eximbank extends export credit that only substitutes for other financing in the U.S. or abroad. Whenever such credits substitute for foreign financing the U.S. balance of payments suffers. Burns feels that the Export-Import Bank might do more to help the U.S. trade balance by diverting some of the funds used to finance jet aircraft to credits for goods where U.S. exporters face sharper world competition. 'Burns Opposes

Lifting Eximbank Loan Limit', *The Journal of Commerce*, 24 September 1970.

23. Bernard Norwood and Barbara R. Lowrey, *Survey of Export Credit as a Portion of U.S. Bank Credit to Foreigners*, Report prepared for the Board of Governors of the Federal Reserve System, 3 March 1971, pp. 5–6.

24. Ibid., p. 7.

25. D. E. Fair, 'Export Credit Problems', *The Three Banks Review*, December 1970, p. 24.

26. Lee C. Nehrt, *Financing Capital Equipment Exports*, International Textbook Co., 1966, p. 77.

27. Leading factoring houses include Intercontinental Credit Corp. and James Talcott, Inc. In 1963 the Export Procurement Corporation (EPC) was organised with the purpose of financing medium-term export credits.

28. Nehrt, p. 94.

29. Machinery and Allied Products Institute, *Financing U.S. Exports and Overseas Investment*, MAPI, 1964, pp. 17–20.

30. The Japanese Export-Import Bank is authorised to rediscount such paper, but at the time of the study had not exercised this authority.

31. Nehrt, pp. 108–109.

32. These remarks are attributed to John. H. Andren, Executive Vice President in charge of the International Division, Manufacturers Hanover Trust Co., New York. *American Banker*, 23 June 1970.

33. Remarks attributed to Frederick Heldring, Vice Chairman, Philadelphia National Bank, *American Banker*, 27 November 1970.

34. Ronald Hart, 'Banks Rush To Offer Credit in Latin America Criticised', *American Banker*, 26 February 1971.

35. International Finance Corporation, *Annual Report 1970*, p. 18.

36. Francis X. Scafuro, 'How Adequate Are Present Export Financing Facilities?', *Bankers Monthly Magazine*, 15 February 1965, p. 28.

37. Scafuro, p. 44.

38. Scafuro, pp. 40–41.

39. *Wall Street Journal*, 8 January 1970.

40. Dillon, Read & Co., Inc., *Prospectus*, 'PEFCO' Private Export Funding Corp. Common Stock, 20 April 1971, pp. 9–10.

41. *American Banker*, 12 March 1971.

CHAPTER 9

1. Walter H. Page, 'The One World of Finance', *Proceedings of the Fifty-Sixth National Foreign Trade Convention*, National Foreign Trade Council, Inc., New York, 1970, pp. 118–19.

2. Paul Meek, *New York – International Financial Center*, dissertation completed at the Stonier Graduate School of Banking, Rutgers University, April 1962, pp. 3–4.

3. J. S. G. Wilson, 'Money Markets in the United States of America', *Quarterly Review*, Banca Nazionale del Lavoro, December 1970, pp. 345–6.

4. Several foreign corporate borrowers have begun to tap the commercial

paper market in the United States. Both Mitsubishi and Mitsui have issued commercial paper in the U.S. with domestic bank guarantees. Ben Weberman, 'Mitsubishi to Sell Paper in U.S.; Could Lead Way for European Firms', *American Banker*, 19 January 1971.

5. Fred H. Klopstock, 'A New Look at Foreign and International Banking in the United States', in *Private Financial Institutions*, Prentice Hall, 1963, p. 372.

6. These figures are not strictly comparable, since the U.K. total includes $54.9 billion of liabilities to overseas residents denominated in nonsterling currencies. Bank of England, *Quarterly Bulletin*, December 1972, Tables 23–24.

7. Federal Reserve Bank of New York, 'Foreign Liquid Assets in the United States 1957–67', *Monthly Review*, June 1968, p. 117.

8. Klopstock, p. 371.

9. *Federal Reserve Bulletin*, February 1971, Table 21, p. A86.

10. In times of easy money conditions interest rates paid on time deposits tend to exceed prevailing market yields on Treasury bills and other instruments.

11. Klopstock, p. 376.

12. For a detailed description of link financing techniques see Reimann and Wigglesworth, *The Challenge of International Finance*, McGraw Hill, 1966, pp. 564–9.

13. *Federal Reserve Bulletin*, October 1962, pp. 1279–80; August 1965, p. 1084; and February 1968, p. 167.

14. In a book published in 1969 Hang-Sheng Cheng asserts that these explanations are not as significant as is commonly accepted. *International Bond Issues of the Less Developed Countries*, Iowa State University Press, 1969, pp. 26–51.

15. John M. Young, 'U.S. Role in the International Capital Market', *The Banker*, July 1969, p. 642.

16. Richard N. Cooper, 'The Interest Equalization Tax: An Experiment in the Separation of Capital Markets', *Finanz-Archiv*, Vol. 24, No. 3. Reprinted by the Yale Economic Growth Centre, 1966, pp. 455–6.

17. Richard N. Cooper, *The Economics of Interdependence*, McGraw Hill, 1968, pp. 137–8.

18. Samuel L. Hayes, 'Investment Banking: Power Structure in Flux', *Harvard Business Review*, March-April 1971, p. 150. The better known of these European banking firms include Paribas, Société Générale, and Credit Lyonnais (co-owner with Commerzbank A.G. of Euro-Partners Securities Corp.).

19. These remarks are attributed to Evan Galbraith, Managing Director, Bankers Trust International, Ltd, *American Banker*, 19 March 1971.

20. Richard N. Cooper, *The Economics of Interdependence*, p. 113.

21. Wilford J. Eiteman and David K. Eiteman, *Leading World Stock Exchanges*, University of Michigan, 1964, pp. 84–90.

22. This has been accomplished through overseas affiliates such as Morgan & Cie International, S.A., Bankers Trust International, Ltd, and Manufacturers Hanover Ltd. Morgan Guaranty Trust indirectly holds a minority

interest in Morgan & Cie International, S.A. through Morgan Guaranty International Financial Corp. (an Edge corporation) which owns Morgan & Cie, S.A., which in turn holds the minority interest in Morgan & Cie International, S.A. Morgan Stanley holds the majority interest in Morgan & Cie International, S.A.

23. *American Banker*, 10 February 1971.
24. Arthur Van Vlissinger, 'Eurofinance – Window to Western Europe', *Burroughs Clearing House*, February 1967, pp. 75–6.
25. Fred H. Klopstock, 'Foreign Demand for United States Equities – The Role of Offshore Mutual Funds', *Monthly Review*, Federal Reserve Bank of New York, July 1970, p. 166.

CHAPTER 10

1. In the relatively short period 1966–72 sterling deposits in U.K. banks advanced from £12.7 billion to £26.7 billion, whereas non-sterling deposits increased from £7.2 billion to £27.2 billion. In the period sterling deposits declined in relative importance from 63 to 49 per cent of total deposits in U.K. banks. Bank of England, *Quarterly Bulletin*, various issues.
2. Bank of England, *Quarterly Bulletin*, September 1972, pp. 380–82.
3. 'London's Merchant Banks', *The Banker*, December 1972, pp. 1605–44.
4. Beginning in 1970, the Bank of England has published detailed information concerning Bank of England intervention in the money market. Details include number of days in each month where open market intervention has taken place, amount of intervention, and whether intervention took the form of last resort lending, purchase or sale of Treasury bills, or other. Bank of England, *Quarterly Bulletin*, September 1972, Table 6.
5. Richard Fry, 'A Brisk Awakening', *The Banker*, January 1973, p. 41.
6. Jonathan Radice, 'French Banking', *The Banker*, January 1973, pp. 51–2.
7. Peter Brunsden, 'Controls Over Banking in France – Part I', *The Banker*, September 1972, p. 1162.
8. Peter Brunsden, 'Controls Over Banking in France, Part II', *The Banker*, October 1972, p. 1267.
9. Ibid., p. 1271.
10. Juergen Ponto, 'Expansion and Competition in German Banking', *The Banker*, January 1971, p. 53.
11. Richard Fry, 'German Banks Look Outwards', *The Banker*, January 1971, p. 44.
12. Paul Einzig, *Parallel Money Markets*, Volume Two, Macmillan-St. Martins, 1972, p. 173.
13. Deutsche Bundesbank, *Instruments of Monetary Policy in the Federal Republic of Germany*, 1 July 1971, p. 42.
14. 'European Banking Systems', *Midland Bank Review*, February 1973, p. 12.
15. Switzerland has long been able to boast a currency enjoying the largest percentage gold cover in the world. During the 1960s the ratio of monetary gold reserves to bank notes in circulation far exceeded 100 per cent. As recently as 1966 it was reported at 121.5 per cent. In 1972 the ratio edged

down to 84.1 per cent. Union Bank of Switzerland, *Economic Survey of Switzerland, 1972,* January 1973, p. 15.

16. The Swiss numbered or coded accounts have been given much attention by writers, but unfortunately many misconceptions exist regarding these accounts. The numbered accounts follow an old tradition which flourished at time of war and political persecution. Only under exceptional conditions will the courts require a Swiss bank to reveal the identity of the numbered account to the court. C. J. Devine Institute of Finance, *Switzerland, An International Financial Center,* New York University, 1964, p. 9.

16. Also, T. R. Fehrenbach, *The Swiss Banks,* McGraw-Hill, 1966, pp. 36–43 and pp. 51–5.

17. Switzerland possesses several stock exchanges, the largest in Zurich. A large number of U.S. companies shares are listed on the Zurich, Basel and Geneva exchanges, providing investment and arbitrage opportunities.

18. In 1965 Dow Chemical Company formed the Dow Banking Corporation, Zurich, with the purpose of insuring that its customers would have access to the European capital market. The bank engages in wholesale operations and has a small staff of men working on Eurodollar and European currency loans, export financing, multiple currency overdrafts and other international money market operations. 'Dow Chemical Owns Bank in Zurich', *New York Times,* 20 March 1968.

19. Max Ikle, 'Swiss Invisible Earnings', *The Banker,* February 1973, p. 188.

20. Chase Manhattan Bank, *Euro-Dollar Financing,* 1968, p. 29.

21. Heinz Portmann, 'Swiss Finance – More International Still', *The Banker,* January 1972, p. 39.

22. Bank for International Settlements, *Eight European Central Banks,* Praeger, 1963, pp. 298–300.

23. Bank for International Settlements, *Annual Report,* 1972, p. 103.

24. Einzig, p. 188.

25. D. D. Peters, 'Competition and Canada's Banking Structure', *The Banker,* October 1971, p. 1204.

26. Einzig, p. 122.

27. J. S. G. Wilson, 'The Money Market in Canada', *Banca Nazionale del Lavoro Quarterly Review,* June 1972, pp. 175-6.

28. Forrest L. Rogers, 'Canadian Banks Overseas', *The Banker,* October 1971, pp. 1217–20.

29. K. Bieda, *The Structure and Operation of the Japanese Economy,* Wiley, 1970, pp. 136–7.

30. OECD, *Financial Statistics,* 1972, Volume I, pp. 312–13.

31. P. A. Graham, 'Hong Kong's Banks and Financial Institutions', *The Banker,* July 1970, pp. 747-50.

32. This information was provided to the author by Y. C. Jao, University of Hong Kong, in private correspondence dated 2 February 1971.

33. Robert A. Bennett, 'Hongkong and Shanghai Bank is the Tai-pan', *American Banker,* 10 June 1970.

34. Richard Fry, 'A Financial Entrepôt for East Asia', *The Banker,* July 1970, p. 731.

35. Howard J. Sherman, *The Soviet Economy*, Little Brown & Co., 1969, pp. 241–2.
36. Alec Nove, *The Soviet Economy: An Introduction*, Praeger, 1966, p. 117.
37. Michael Kaser, *Soviet Economics*, McGraw-Hill, 1970, p. 127.
38. Eugene Babitchev, 'The International Bank for Economic Co-operation', in *Money and Plan*, Gregory Grossman (ed.), University of California Press, 1968, p. 144.

CHAPTER 11

1. In connection with the last point, it has been suggested that in 1967 U.S. Treasury Department officials encouraged American businessmen to use the Eurodollar market to cope with the problem of tight money and rising interest rates. In one case a large U.S. conglomerate borrowed $50 million in the Eurodollar market to assist in financing acquisitions of meat packing and sporting goods subsidiaries. '1969 Loans Urged by U.S., Ling Says', *New York Times*, 23 April 1970. The chairman of the company, (Ling-Temco-Vought), indicated that Treasury officials had passed this suggestion on to a number of U.S. business firms.
2. Paul Einzig, *The Eurodollar System*, St. Martins Press, 1967, p. 7.
3. Jane Sneddon Little, 'The Euro-dollar Market: Its Nature & Impact', *New England Economic Review*, Federal Reserve Bank of Boston, May-June 1969, p. 5.
4. The other respects refer to the variety of abritrage-type operations that are available with Eurodollars, including interest, place, time, and type of currency balance. See Paul Einzig, *The Euro-Dollar System*, pp. 42–51.
5. Little, p. 3.
6. There is little agreement on this figure. See Oscar Altman, 'Foreign Markets for Dollars, Sterling and Other Currencies', IMF *Staff Papers*, December 1961, p. 140.
7. Bank for International Settlements, *Annual Report*, 1972, pp. 148–9.
8. Bank for International Settlements, *Annual Report*, 1969, p. 140.
9. In the fall of 1967 German, Swiss, Dutch and Belgium central banks and the Bank for International Settlements channelled $1.4 billion into the market to prevent Eurodollar interest rates from rising abruptly. This was at the time of the sterling crisis.
10. Bank for International Settlements, *Annual Report*, 1972, p. 149.
11. In April 1970 the Italian State Electricity Authority arranged for a $425 million Eurodollar financing including a $125 million public offering of notes that contain an unusual rate escalating clause. This was the largest financing ever negotiated in the Eurodollar market, and included a $300 million loan from a consortium of banks managed by Bankers Trust International, Ltd, and several other banks and investment firms. Both the $125 million of notes (due in 1980) and the $300 million bank loan will carry interest rates tied to the going rate on six-month Eurodollar deposits in the London market (3/4 percentage point above this rate). The seven year bank loan calls for repayments to commence in 1974, and the notes

have provision for a sinking fund. *Wall Street Journal*, 30 April 1970.

12. Bank of England, *Quarterly Bulletin*, March 1970, p. 32. According to Bank of England commentary, the growth in London's Eurocurrency liabilities accelerated. In the period 1963–5 these liabilities grew at a rate of 25 per cent per annum. In the period 1965–8 the rate of increase was 50 per cent per annum. During 1969 the growth rate further accelerated to 75 per cent.

13. Ira O. Scott, 'That Controversial Euro-Dollar Market', National Westminster Bank *Quarterly Review*, August 1969, p. 16. Also, Bank for International Settlements, *Annual Report*, 1971, p. 161.

14. 'Recent Developments in London's Money Markets', *Midland Bank Review*, November 1969, pp. 1–12.

15. Bank for International Settlements, *Annual Report*, 1972, p. 159.

16. *Wall Street Journal*, 29 December 1969.

17. Philip Saunders, Jr, 'American Banks in London's Eurodollar Market', *National Banking Review*, September 1966, pp. 22–3.

18. By the complimentary markets, or parallel markets, we refer to the short-term markets for funds which have developed in the 1960s around the nucleus of the London money market. The four complementary markets include those dealing in short-term deposits with local authorities, with instalment finance houses, Eurodollars, and inter-bank sterling balances. 'Recent Developments in London's Money Markets', *Midland Bank Review*, November 1969, pp. 3–12.

19. Ibid., p. 6.

20. Saunders, p. 24.

21. Oscar L. Altman, 'Canadian Markets for U.S. Dollars', *Factors Affecting the United States Balance of Payments*, Washington, D.C. Subcommittee on International Exchange and Payments of the Joint Economic Committee, 1962, p. 533.

22. Ira O. Scott, 'That Controversial Eurodollar Market', National Westminster Bank *Quarterly Review*, August 1969, pp. 13–14.

23. Federal Reserve Bank of New York, *Annual Report*, 1969, pp. 24–5.

24. Saunders, p. 28.

25. These amendments were announced in July and August 1969, respectively.

26. Federal Reserve Bank of New York, *Annual Report*, 1969, pp. 25–6.

27. Paul Einzig, *The Eurodollar System*, pp. 79–82.

28. Jane Sneddon Little, 'The Euro-dollar Market: Its Nature & Impact', Federal Reserve Bank of Boston, *New England Economic Review*, May-June 1969.

29. Andrew Brimmer, 'The Banking Structure and Monetary Management', speech delivered in San Francisco, California, 1 April 1970, pp. 3–5.

30. Fred H. Klopstock, 'The Euro-dollar Market: Some Unresolved Issues', *Essays In International Finance*, Princeton University, March 1968.

31. Jane Little, pp. 5–6.

32. *The Banker*, June 1972, pp. 799–800.

33. Bank of England, *Quarterly Bulletin*, March 1972, pp. 60–61.

34. *The Banker*, June 1972, p. 794.

35. The ability of overseas branches to attract Eurodollars for the use of head offices was bolstered in 1968 by heavy speculative flows of funds, from sterling and the French franc. Board of Governors of the Federal Reserve System, *Fifty-fifth Annual Report*, 1968, p. 53.
36. Andrew Brimmer, 'The Banking Structure and Monetary Management', speech delivered in San Francisco, California, April 1970, pp. 2–3.
37. 'U.S. Balance of Payments and Investment Position', *Federal Reserve Bulletin*, April 1970, p. 317.
38. Federal Reserve Bank of New York, *Annual Report*, 1969, pp. 35–6.
39. 'Euro-Dollars: A Changing Market', *Federal Reserve Bulletin*, October 1969.
40. 'Burns Proposals May Cut Eurodollar Growth', *American Banker*, 29 April 1970.

CHAPTER 12

1. Benjamin Higgins, *Economic Development, Problems, Principles, and Policies*, Norton, 1968, p. 568.
2. Hugh T. Patrick, 'Financial Development and Economic Growth in Under-developed Countries', *Economic Development and Cultural Change*, January 1966, pp. 177–8.
3. Speech delivered by Rudolph A. Peterson, president of Bank of America at the annual meeting of the American Bankers Association. Cited in *American Banker*, 20 May 1970.
4. For example, in a speech delivered in Hong Kong celebrating the opening of a regional representative office of the Security Pacific National Bank, Los Angeles, Frederick Larkin, chairman of Security likened South-east Asia to Europe of fifteen years ago, as the new frontier for world investment. *American Banker*, 24 September 1970.
5. Edward Nevin, *Capital Funds in Underdeveloped Countries*, Macmillan, 1963, p. 45.
6. Ibid., p. 46.
7. Ibid., pp. 50–51.
8. F. W. Crick, *Commonwealth Banking Systems*, Oxford, 1965, pp. 33–5.
9. 'Treasury Bills for the Philippines', *Fortune*, December 1966, pp. 99–100.
10. The U.S. bank involved in this transaction, Northwest International Bank, is an Edge Act corporation.
11. Joint Economic Committee, *Thrift Institution Development in Latin America*, study prepared for the Subcommittee on Inter-American Economic Relationships, Congress of the United States, 4 June 1970. This study points to the inadequacy of thrift institutions in Latin America, and describes the role played by the Agency for International Development and the Inter-American Development Bank in promoting the expansion of savings and loan associations and credit unions.
12. Richard Elliot Benedick, *Industrial Finance in Iran*, Harvard, 1964, pp. 76–7.

13. These alternatives have been described in J. T. Dock Houk, *Financing and Problems of Development Banking*, Praeger, 1967, pp. 20–36.
14. Houk, p. 22.
15. This study was undertaken by J. D. Nyhart, 'Analysis of Global Data for Development Banks', Mass. Inst. of Technology, as cited in Phillips Perera, *Development Finance*, Praeger, 1968, p. 151.
16. This discussion is based in part on several points made by Houk, pp. 95-8. According to Perera, commercial banks operating in Peru created privately controlled financieras as captive affiliates to provide risk capital at rates of interest exceeding those permitted the bank in its lending operations. The maximum interest commercial banks could charge was 12 per cent plus a 1 per cent commission. On the other hand loans made by financieras generally carried an effective rate of 20–30 per cent and were extended for terms longer than the one year maximum applicable to commercial banks.
17. Houk, pp. 15–152.
18. Benedick, pp. 120–21.
19. The American banks include Bank of America, First National City Bank, Manufacturers Hanover Trust, The Northern Trust Co., Girard International Investment Corp., and First Pennsylvania Overseas Development Corp., IFC, *Annual Report 1970*, p. 13.
20. IFC, *Annual Report 1970*, p. 18.
21. Ibid., p. 21. The two American banks were Morgan Guaranty International Banking Corp., and Philadelphia International Investment Corp.
22. Sir Henry Phillips, 'A Private Investment Company for Africa', *The Banker*, August 1970, pp. 826–9.

CHAPTER 13

1. Union Bank of Switzerland, 'Does the U.S.A. Determine Europe's Interest Rates?', *Business Facts and Figures*, February 1971, p. 9.
2. Joint Economic Committee of the U.S. Congress, *Joint Economic Report 1970*, 25 March 1970, pp. 49–50.
3. Deutsche Bundesbank, *Annual Report 1969*, pp. 15–16. The new rate of 3.66 marks per dollar established on 24 October 1969 represented a 9.3 per cent revaluation.
4. Charles A. Coombs, 'Treasury and Federal Reserve Foreign Exchange Operations', *Federal Reserve Bulletin*, March 1970, p. 237.
5. *Federal Reserve Bulletin*, November 1969, pp. 886–7.
6. Board of Governors of the Federal Reserve System, *Press Release*, 13 August 1969.
7. The first change in reserve requirements relative to Eurodollar transactions came somewhat earlier. Effective 31 July 1969 banks could no longer reduce reserve requirements through Eurodollar float. Regulation D was amended to include 'bills payable' and 'London cheques' in deposits subject to reserve requirements, cancelling the initial savings in

required reserves. *Federal Reserve Bulletin*, August 1969, pp. 655–6.

8. *Federal Reserve Bulletin*, December 1970, pp. 940–41.

9. Ben Weberman, 'Fed, Banks Perplexed on Best Policy In Wake Of Eurodollar Moves', *American Banker*, 8 December 1970.

10. *American Banker*, 2 December 1970. Developments since 1970 have borne out this view. During 1970–71 interest rates in the United States and Europe declined, indicating that bankers were correct in allowing their Eurodollar borrowing bases to be reduced.

11. First National City Bank, 'The Future of the Dollar', *Monthly Economic Letter*, November 1970, p. 125.

12. Board of Governors of the Federal Reserve System, *Press Release*, 15 January 1971. An amendment to Regulation M governing reserves against Eurodollar borrowings of member banks.

13. *American Banker*, 19 January 1971.

14. 'Treasury Slates Offering To Plug Eurodollar Drain', *Wall Street Journal*, 2 April 1971.

15. Board of Governors of the Federal Reserve System, *Press Release*, 1 April 1971.

16. Robert A. Bennett, 'Sale of Exim Notes Abroad to Aid U.S. Balance of Payments, May Increase Official Leverage in Euromarket', *American Banker*, 24 February 1971.

17. At this time the Administration was pursuing an aggressive easy money policy.

18. *American Banker*, 6 April 1971.

19. Robert A. Bennett, 'Fed Is Talking To Japanese Banks in N.Y. Requesting Them To Put Limit On Foreign Loans', *American Banker*, 22 December 1970. At that time the Fed declared that it would not purchase or hold acceptances that were offered to the public at rates above those of similar paper issued or guaranteed by U.S. banks, since it could not be considered prime paper.

20. 'Germany Gains Dollars Despite N.Y. Fed Moves', *American Banker*, 4 March 1971.

21. Andrew F. Brimmer, 'Capital Outflows and the U.S. Balance of Payments', speech delivered at Dallas, Texas, 11 February 1970, pp. 4–5.

22. Fortunately, in November 1971 the Board of Governors of the Federal Reserve exempted head office export credits from the VFCR programme ceiling on foreign lending.

23. Andrew F. Brimmer, 'The Banking Structure and Monetary Management', speech delivered at the San Francisco Bond Club, 1 April 1970, p. 15.

24. Andrew F. Brimmer, 'The Banking Structure and Monetary Management', speech delivered at the San Francisco Bond Club, San Francisco, California, 1 April 1970, pp. 22–3.

25. Andrew F. Brimmer, 'Capital Outflows and the U.S. Balance of Payments', speech delivered at the Fairmont Hotel, Dallas, Texas, 11 February 1970, p. 23.

26. Ibid., p. 24.

27. According to Brimmer, the Board of Governors may already possess

authority to establish this type of reserve programme with respect to member banks. Further, Executive Order 11387, issued in January 1968 authorises the Board to regulate or prohibit any transaction by any bank or other financial institution if necessary to strengthen the balance of payments position of the United States. Possible additional authority is the Credit Control Act which empowers the Board to prescribe maximum ratios of loans of particular types to assets of particular types. This power requires Presidential determination that such regulation is necessary to control inflation. Ibid., pp. 27–8.

28. Warren L. Smith, 'Reserve Requirements in the American Monetary System', published in *Monetary Management*, Commission on Money and Credit, 1963, pp. 283–4.
29. E. Wayne Clendenning, *The Euro-Dollar Market*, Oxford, 1970, pp. 168–9.
30. Patric H. Hendershott, 'The Structure of International Interest Rates: The U.S. Treasury Bill Rate and the Eurodollar Deposit Rate', *The Journal of Finance*, September 1967, pp. 455–65.
31. Ibid., p. 465.
32. Stanley W. Black, 'An Econometric Study of Euro-Dollar Borrowing By New York Banks and the Rate of Interest on Euro-Dollars', *The Journal of Finance*, March 1971, pp. 83–8.
33. These views were expressed by a panel of experts at the annual meeting of the Foreign Exchange Dealers Club held in Copenhagen in May 1971. Panel members included Irving Friedman, Economic Adviser to the World Bank; Roy Bridge, formerly with the Bank of England; Dr F. E. Aschinger, Economic Adviser to the Swiss Bank Corp.; Dr Kurt Richebacher, of the Dresdner Bank; and S. Schmiegelov, Director of Privatbanken, Copenhagen. *American Banker*, 24 May 1971.
34. This aspect of regulation which has been implemented is discussed in greater detail below.
35. Charles P. Kindleberger, 'The Dollar System', *New England Economic Review*, Federal Reserve Bank of Boston, September/October 1970, p. 8.
36. Fritz Machlup, 'Euro-Dollar Creation: A Mystery Story', *Quarterly Review*, Banca Nazionale Del Lavoro, September 1970, pp. 234–6.
37. Fritz Machlup, 'The Magicians and Their Rabbits', *Morgan Guaranty Survey*, May 1971, pp. 11–12.
38. Ibid., p. 13. It should be noted that in May 1971, shortly after the severe international monetary crisis in which the D-mark was allowed to float and the Swiss and Austrian currencies were revalued, it was noted that shifts of funds by European central banks from the Eurodollar market to New York were considered responsible for strength in the U.S. government securities market. According to Governor J. Dewey Daane of the Board of Governors of the Federal Reserve System, foreign central banks had begun channelling their surplus dollars into U.S. government securities via the New York market. 'Foreign Dollars Spur Treasury Price Jumps', *American Banker*, 27 May 1971.
39. Ben Weberman, 'Ekblom Frowns on the Possibility of Concerted Exchange Controls', *American Banker*, 25 May 1971.
40. Ibid.

41. Robert A. Bennett, 'Long Mark Float, Capital Flow Curbs Seen by Emminger', *American Banker*, 26 May 1971.

CHAPTER 14

1. Herbert Grubel uses this approach in 'The Benefits and Costs of Being the World Banker', *National Banking Review*, December 1964, p. 191.
2. Richard N. Cooper, *The Economics of Interdependence*, McGraw Hill, 1968, pp. 257–9.
3. Robert Z. Aliber, *The Future of the Dollar as an International Currency*, Praeger, 1966, p. 48.
4. Harry N. Goldstein, 'Does it Necessarily Cost Anything to be the World Banker?', *National Banking Review*, June 1965, p. 411.
5. At the same date there was some $13.6 billion in official dollar deposits in U.S. banks.
6. Bank of England, *Quarterly Bulletin*, September 1972, pp. 380–87.
7. Ira O. Scott, Jr., 'The Euro-Currency Business of Banks in London', *National Westminster Bank Quarterly Review*, August 1969, pp. 15–16.
8. Bank for International Settlements, *39th Annual Report*, 1969, p. 149.
9. Bank for International Settlements, *42nd Annual Report*, 1972, pp. 148–9.

CHAPTER 15

1. 'NYS Bank Department Seeks to Open London Office', *American Banker*, 18 January 1973.
2. Board of Governors of the Federal Reserve System, *Press Release*, dated 1 February 1973.
3. *American Banker*, 3 May 1973.

Index of Proper Names

Index of Subjects

Voluntary Foreign Credit Restraint Program (VFCR), 20, 99, 100, 102, 115, 119, 158, 195, 201, 202, 217–23, 256, 293, 346, 377

Wall Street community, 256
war risk insurance, 198
widening currency areas, 369
withholding tax, 242, 252, 257
World Bank bonds, 231, 326

world banker, 4, 357, 358, 363
    and international banker, 358–60, 362, 364
World War I, 4, 23, 79, 80, 168, 254
World War II, 4, 24, 137, 238, 254
worldwide banks, 99
Wormser Report, 270–1

Yugoslavia, 232

Zwick Report, 187

crepúsculo

Livro Primeiro do Ciclo
Luz e Escuridão

STEPHENIE MEYER

crepúsculo

STEPHENIE MEYER

GAILIVRO

CREPÚSCULO
Título original: Twilight
Texto copyright © Stephenie Meyer 2005

Traduzido para a Língua Portuguesa por
Vera Falcão Martins
Coordenação Editorial Andrea Alves Silva
e Ema Rodrigues
Design da capa © Roger Hagadone
Composição de Svetlana Tomnikova
Impressão e acabamento de Multitipo

EDIÇÕES GAILIVRO
Rua Cidade de Córdova, n.º 2
2610-038 Alfragide
Portugal
Telef. +351214272200
Fax +351214272201
www.gailivro.pt

Uma editora do grupo Leya

Depósito legal n.º 287 627 / 09
ISBN 978-989-557-270-0

9.ª Edição, Junho de 2009

Para a minha irmã mais velha
— sem o seu entusiasmo esta história
poderia estar ainda por terminar.

Agradecimentos:

Agradeço aos meus pais, Steve e Candy, pelo amor e apoio de uma vida, por me lerem grandes obras quando era pequena e por ainda segurarem na minha mão quando estou nervosa.

Agradeço ao meu marido, Pancho, e aos meus filhos, Gabe, Seth e Eli, por me partilharem tão amiúde com os meus amigos imaginários.

Agradeço aos meus amigos da *Writers House:* a Genevieve Gagne-Hawes, por me ter dado aquela primeira oportunidade, e a Jodi Reamer, por ter transformado os meus sonhos mais fantasiosos em realidade.

Agradeço aos meus irmãos, Paul e Jacob, pela sua ajuda de peritos em todas as minhas questões relacionadas com automóveis.

Agradeço ainda à minha família *online*, os bestialmente talentosos escritores de *fansofrealitytv.com* — em particular a Kimberly «Shazzer» — pelo incentivo, pelos conselhos e pela inspiração.

*É Ele quem conhece o que se esconde nas trevas
e a luz mora junto d'Ele.*

Daniel 2,22

PREFÁCIO

Nunca reflectira longamente sobre a forma como morreria — ainda que, ao longo dos meses anteriores, tivesse tido motivos de sobra para tal —, mas, mesmo que o tivesse feito, jamais teria imaginado que seria assim.

Olhei fixamente para o lado oposto da longa sala, sem respirar, fitando os olhos negros do caçador, e este lançou-me também um olhar amável.

Era decerto uma boa maneira de morrer: morrer no lugar de alguém, de alguém que eu amava. Chegava mesmo a ser nobre. Esse facto deveria ter alguma importância.

Eu sabia que, se nunca tivesse ido para Forks, não estaria, naquele momento, a enfrentar a morte, mas, apavorada como estava, não conseguia sentir-me arrependida de tal decisão. Quando a vida nos oferece um sonho que ultrapassa largamente todas as nossas expectativas, não é razoável sentir pesar quando o mesmo chega ao fim.

O caçador sorria de um modo amistoso à medida que avançava vagarosamente para me matar.

Capítulo Um

Primeira Vista

A minha mãe levou-me ao aeroporto, de automóvel, com os vidros abertos. Estava uma temperatura de trinta e cinco graus em Phoenix e o céu tingido de um azul perfeito e sem nuvens. Usava a minha camisa preferida — sem mangas, de renda branca com ilhós; vestira-a como um gesto de despedida. A peça de vestuário que trazia na mão era um anoraque.

Na Península Olímpica do Noroeste do estado de Washington, existe uma pequena localidade chamada Forks que se encontra imersa num quase permanente manto de nuvens. Nesta insignificante localidade chove mais do que em qualquer outro lugar dos Estados Unidos da América. Foi desta localidade e da sua sombra carregada e omnipresente que a minha mãe fugiu, levando-me consigo, quando eu tinha apenas alguns meses de idade. Nesta cidade fui obrigada a passar um mês todos os Verões até completar catorze anos. Mas nesse ano, finalmente, protestei; em vez disso, nos últimos três Verões, o meu pai, Charlie, passou duas semanas de férias comigo na Califórnia.

Foi em Forks que eu agora me exilei — um acto que assumi com grande horror. Eu detestava Forks.

Adorava Phoenix. Adorava o Sol e o calor escaldante. Adorava a cidade vigorosa e desordenada.

— Bella — disse-me a minha mãe, pela derradeira vez, após o ter repetido outras mil, antes de eu entrar no avião —, não tens de fazer isto.

A minha mãe parece-se comigo, excluindo o facto de ter cabelos curtos e rugas de expressão. Senti um acesso de pânico ao fitar os seus olhos arregalados, quase infantis. Como podia deixar a minha mãe terna, excêntrica e estouvada a cuidar de si mesma? É claro que agora tinha Phil, pelo que as contas seriam provavelmente pagas, haveria comida no frigorífico, gasolina no carro dela e alguém a quem ela poderia telefonar quando se perdesse, mas mesmo assim...

— Eu *quero* ir — menti.

Nunca soube mentir mas, ultimamente, repetia esta mentira com tanta frequência que já quase parecia convincente.

— Dá cumprimentos meus ao Charlie — disse-me, resignada.

— Fá-lo-ei.

— Ver-te-ei em breve — insistiu ela. — Podes regressar a casa quando desejares, eu voltarei assim que precisares de mim.

No entanto, eu conseguia ver o sacrifício que os seus olhos reflectiam por trás da promessa.

— Não te preocupes comigo — exortei. — Será óptimo. Eu gosto muito de ti, mãe.

Abraçou-me firmemente durante um instante e, em seguida, embarquei no avião e ela partiu.

A viagem aérea de Phoenix a Seattle tem a duração de quatro horas, seguidas de mais uma hora num pequeno avião até Port Angeles e outra de automóvel até Forks. Viajar de avião não me incomoda; estava, porém, um pouco preocupada com a viagem de uma hora de carro na companhia de Charlie.

Na verdade, Charlie encarara toda aquela situação com bastante simpatia. Parecia sinceramente satisfeito com o facto de, pela primeira vez, eu ir viver com ele com a intenção de prolongar a minha estada por algum tempo. Já me matriculara no liceu e ia ajudar-me na compra de um carro.

A convivência com Charlie prometia, porém, ser marcada por alguma falta de à vontade. Nenhum de nós era aquilo que qualquer pessoa designaria por *verboso* e, de qualquer forma, eu não sabia o que dizer. Tinha consciência de que ele estava mais do que apenas um pouco confundido com a minha decisão. Tal como a minha mãe antes de mim, eu não fizera questão de esconder a minha antipatia por Forks.

Quando aterrei em Port Angeles, estava a chover. Não considerei este facto como um presságio — apenas como algo inevitável. Já me despedira do Sol.

Charlie aguardava-me no carro de rádio-patrulha, o que também não me supreendeu. Ele é o chefe Swan da polícia das boas gentes de Forks. A minha principal motivação para a compra de um carro, apesar da escassez dos meus fundos, era o facto de me recusar a percorrer a cidade numa viatura com luzes azuis e vermelhas no tejadilho. Nada abranda o fluxo do tráfego como um agente da polícia.

Charlie deu-me um desajeitado abraço com apenas um dos braços depois de eu ter desembarcado do avião com passos vacilantes.

— É bom ver-te, Bells — exclamou ele, sorrindo, ao agarrar-me automaticamente e devolver-me o equilíbrio. — Não mudaste muito. Como está a Renée?

— A mãe está óptima. Também é bom ver-te, pai.

Não me era permitido chamar-lhe «Charlie» abertamente.

Tinha apenas algumas malas. A maioria das roupas que eu usava no Arizona eram demasiado permeáveis para poder vesti-las em Washington. Eu e a minha mãe tínhamos reunido os nossos recursos para reforçar o meu guarda-roupa de Inverno, mas este continuava a ser escasso. Tudo coube perfeitamente no porta-bagagem do carro de rádio-patrulha.

— Encontrei um bom carro para ti, a um preço bastante reduzido — comunicou-me ele depois de entrarmos no carro e de termos colocado os cintos de segurança.

— Que género de carro?

A forma como ele dissera «um bom carro para *ti*», em vez de apenas «um bom carro», suscitou em mim algumas suspeitas.

— Bem, na verdade, é uma *pick-up,* uma Chevrolet.

— Onde a encontraste?

— Recordas-te do Billy Black, que mora lá em baixo, em *La Push*?

La Push é a minúscula Reserva Índia junto à costa.

— Não.

— Ele costumava ir pescar connosco durante o Verão — relembrou Charlie.

Isto explica por que motivo não me recordava dele. Sou bastante bem sucedida nas minhas tentativas de apagar factos dolorosos e desnecessários da minha memória.

— Ele encontra-se agora numa cadeira de rodas — prosseguiu Charlie ao verificar que eu não retorquia —, pelo que não pode conduzir e propôs vender-me a sua *pick-up* a um preço reduzido.

— De que ano é?

Apercebi-me, pela mudança de expressão no seu rosto, que esta era a questão que ele esperava que eu não colocasse.

— Bem, o Billy já procedeu a muitos melhoramentos no motor. Na verdade, tem apenas alguns anos.

Esperava que ele não me tivesse em tão pouca consideração a ponto de acreditar que eu desistiria assim tão facilmente.

— Quando é que ele a comprou?

— Comprou-a em 1984, creio eu.

— E era nova quando a comprou?

— Bem, não. Penso que era nova no início dos anos 60 ou, no máximo, no final dos 50 — reconheceu timidamente.

— Me... Pai, não percebo realmente nada de carros. Não seria capaz de a arranjar se surgisse algum problema e não pudesse pagar a um mecânico...

— A sério, Bella, a coisa funciona às mil maravilhas. Já não se fabricam *pick-ups* como aquela.

"A *coisa*", pensei para comigo... "tinha potencial, como alcunha, no mínimo."

— A que te referes quando falas em preço reduzido?

No fim de contas, era sob este aspecto que não podia comprometer-me.

— Bem, querida, eu, de certa forma, já ta comprei. Como um presente de regresso a casa.

Charlie olhava-me pelo canto do olho com um ar esperançoso.

"Ena. De borla."

— Não precisavas de fazer isso, pai. Eu própria ia comprar um carro.

— Não me importo. Quero que sejas feliz aqui.

Olhava em frente, para a estrada, quando proferiu estas palavras. Charlie não se sentia à vontade ao exprimir verbalmente as suas emoções. Herdei esta característica dele. Logo, olhava em frente quando repliquei:

— É muito simpático da tua parte, pai. Obrigada. Agradeço-te muito.

Não havia necessidade de acrescentar que ser feliz em Forks era para mim uma impossibilidade. Ele não precisava de compartilhar do meu sofrimento. Além disso, nunca tinha observado o motor de uma *pick-up*.

— Ora, não tens de quê — balbuciou, embaraçado com o meu agradecimento.

Trocámos mais alguns comentários a respeito do tempo, que estava húmido, e a conversa resumiu-se praticamente a isso. Lançávamos, em silêncio, o olhar fixo através das janelas.

A paisagem era, evidentemente, bela; eu não podia negá-lo. Tudo era verde: as árvores, os troncos revestidos de musgo, os ramos em forma de abóbada, o solo coberto de fetos. O próprio ar, filtrado pelas folhas, assumia uma tonalidade verde.

Era demasiado verde — um planeta extraterrestre.

Finalmente, chegámos a casa de Charlie. Vivia ainda na pequena casa com dois quartos que comprara em conjunto com a minha mãe nos seus primeiros tempos de casados — os únicos tempos que o casamento de ambos durou. Ali, estacionada na rua, em frente à casa que nunca alterava, encontrava-se a minha nova — bem, nova para mim — *pick-up*. Caracterizava-se por um tom vermelho desbotado, grandes pára-choques arredondados e uma cabina abaulada. Para minha grande surpresa, adorei-a. Não sabia se funcionaria, mas conseguia imaginar-me dentro dela. Além disso, era um daqueles veículos de ferro sólido nos quais nunca se consegue fazer uma mossa — do género daqueles que se vêem no local onde ocorreu um acidente, sem um único risco na pintura, rodeado pelos destroços do carro que destruíra.

— Ena, pai, adoro-a! Obrigada!

A partir deste momento, o meu dia horrível já se tornava muito menos pavoroso. Não seria confrontada com a escolha entre percorrer três quilómetros a pé, à chuva, até à escola ou aceitar uma boleia no carro de rádio-patrulha do chefe.

— Ainda bem que gostas — afirmou Charlie de modo rude, novamente embaraçado.

De uma só vez, conseguimos levar todos os meus pertences para o andar superior. Fiquei no quarto virado para Oeste, que tinha vista para o pátio em frente à casa. O quarto não me era estranho; pertencera-me desde que eu nascera. O piso de madeira, as paredes pintadas de azul-claro, o tecto em ogiva, as cortinas de renda amarelada na janela — todos estes pormenores faziam parte da minha infância. As únicas alterações a que Charlie alguma vez procedera foram a substituição do berço por uma cama e a colocação de uma secretária à medida que fui crescendo. A secretária suportava agora um computador em segunda mão, com o cabo telefónico para ligar ao modem fixo ao longo do piso até à tomada telefónica mais próxima. Esta fora uma condição que a minha mãe impusera, de modo a que pudéssemos permanecer facilmente em contacto uma com a outra. A cadeira de balouço dos meus tempos de bebé ainda se encontrava ao canto.

Havia apenas uma pequena casa de banho ao cimo das escadas, que teria de partilhar com Charlie. Tentava não me deter muito sobre este assunto.

Uma das melhores características de Charlie é o facto de não me controlar. Deixou-me sozinha para desfazer as malas e me instalar, um feito que, para a minha mãe, seria absolutamente impossível. Era agradável estar só, não ter de sorrir e parecer satisfeita; era um alívio olhar, de forma deprimida, a chuva copiosa através da janela e deixar escapar apenas algumas lágrimas. Não estava com disposição para desatar numa autêntica choradeira.

Reservaria o desabafo para a hora de deitar, ao pensar no dia seguinte.

O Liceu de Forks contava com um inquietante total de trezentos e cinquenta e sete — agora trezentos e cinquenta e oito — alunos; na cidade de onde provinha, só na escola do terceiro ciclo do ensino básico havia mais de setecentas pessoas. Em Forks, todos os miúdos tinham crescido juntos — os seus avós aprenderam a andar juntos. Eu seria a nova aluna da cidade grande, uma curiosidade, uma aberração.

Se aparentasse ser uma rapariga de Phoenix, talvez pudesse tirar partido desta situação. Em termos físicos, porém, eu nunca me integraria em parte nenhuma. *Devia* ter a pele bronzeada, ser loura e dada à actividade desportiva — talvez uma jogadora de voleibol ou chefe de claque — tudo coisas inerentes à vida no vale do Sol.

Em vez disso, a minha pele era ebúrnea, não tendo sequer a desculpa dos olhos azuis ou dos cabelos ruivos, apesar de o Sol brilhar de forma constante. Sempre tivera um corpo esbelto, mas, de certo modo, flácido, o que não correspondia, obviamente, ao corpo de uma atleta; não possuía a coordenação entre as mãos e os olhos necessária para praticar desporto sem ser sujeita a uma humilhação, lesionando a mim própria, ou a quem estivesse demasiado perto de mim.

Quando acabei de colocar as roupas na velha cómoda de pinho, peguei na bolsa que continha os produtos de higiene pessoal e dirigi-me à casa de banho comum para me lavar depois de um dia de viagem. Olhei-me ao espelho, enquanto escovava o cabelo húmido e emaranhado. Talvez se devesse à luz, mas eu já parecia mais lívida, pouco saudável. A minha pele podia ser bonita — era muito clara, tinha um aspecto quase translúcido —, mas tudo dependia da cor. Ali, era completamente descorada.

Encarando o meu pálido reflexo no espelho, fui obrigada a admitir que estava a mentir a mim mesma. Não era apenas em termos físicos que eu jamais me integraria. Se eu não conseguia encontrar o meu lugar numa escola com três mil pessoas, quais seriam as minhas hipóteses ali?

Não me relacionava de forma satisfatória com as pessoas da minha idade. Na verdade, talvez não me relacionasse de forma satisfatória com as pessoas — ponto final. Nem com a minha mãe, a pessoa a quem neste mundo eu era mais chegada, conseguia manter uma relação harmoniosa, nunca estando propriamente em sintonia. Por vezes, interrogava-me se, através dos meus olhos, via as mesmas coisas que o resto do mundo via através dos seus. Talvez o meu cérebro tivesse um problema técnico.

A causa, porém, não era relevante. O único aspecto relevante era o efeito. O dia seguinte seria apenas o princípio.

Não dormi bem nessa noite, mesmo depois de ter acabado de chorar. O som constante provocado pela chuva e pelo vento ao fustigarem o telhado recusava-se a enfraquecer e a ser reduzido a ruído de fundo. Puxei a velha e desbotada colcha para tapar a cabeça e, mais tarde, recorri também à almofada, mas só consegui adormecer depois da meia-noite, quando a chuva finalmente amainou e se transformou em chuviscos mais silenciosos.

De manhã, através da minha janela, conseguia ver apenas um denso nevoeiro e sentia a claustrofobia a assaltar-me. Ali, nunca se conseguia ver o céu; era como uma gaiola.

O pequeno-almoço tomado com Charlie foi tranquilo. Desejou-me boa sorte para o primeiro dia de escola. Agradeci-lhe, sabendo que as suas esperanças eram vãs. A boa sorte tendia a evitar-me. Charlie foi o primeiro a sair, dirigindo-se para a esquadra da polícia, que era a sua esposa e a sua família. Depois de ele ter saído, sentei-me à velha mesa quadrada de madeira de carvalho numa das três cadeiras, diferentes umas das outras, e examinei a pequena cozinha, com paredes escuras, armários de um tom amarelo-vivo e piso de linóleo branco. Nada sofrera alterações. A minha mãe pintara os armários, há dezoito anos, numa tentativa de iluminar um pouco a casa como se do brilho do Sol se tratasse. Por cima da pequena lareira da sala de estar, que tinha as dimensões de um lenço, encontrava-se uma sucessão de retratos. Em primeiro lugar, um retrato do casamento de Charlie e da minha mãe em Las Vegas; depois, um no qual figurávamos os três, no hospital, depois de eu ter nascido, que fora tirado por uma prestável enfermeira, seguido pela procissão dos meus retratos escolares, até ao do ano passado. Era embaraçoso olhá-los — teria de ver o que podia fazer para convencer Charlie a colocá-los noutro lugar, pelo menos enquanto eu ali morasse.

Estando naquela casa, era impossível não perceber que Charlie jamais esquecera a minha mãe, o que me causou um certo incómodo.

Não queria chegar demasiado cedo à escola, mas já não conseguia ficar em casa. Vesti o casaco — que, ao toque, parecia tratar-se de um fato de protecção contra riscos biológicos — e saí, expondo-me à chuva.

Continuava apenas a chuviscar, o que não foi suficiente para ficar imediatamente encharcada, enquanto tentava alcançar a chave de casa, que estava sempre escondida debaixo do beiral, junto à porta, que tranquei. O chapinhar das minhas botas novas à prova de água era enervante. Senti a falta do habitual ruído do cascalho enquanto caminhava. Não podia deter-me e admirar novamente a minha *pick-up* conforme pretendia; tinha pressa de me abrigar da humidade brumosa que rodopiava em torno da minha cabeça e aderia ao meu cabelo debaixo do capuz.

O interior da *pick-up* estava seco e agradável. Era evidente que Billy ou Charlie lhe tinham feito uma limpeza, mas, dos bancos com estofos castanho-amarelados, emanava ainda um odor a tabaco, gasolina e hortelã-pimenta. O motor pegou rapidamente, para meu alívio, mas de forma sonora, roncando no princípio e, em seguida, começando a falhar ao atingir o volume máximo. Bem, uma *pick-up* tão velha tinha de ter, obrigatoriamente, algum defeito. O antigo rádio funcionava, um aspecto positivo com que eu não contava.

Não foi difícil encontrar a escola, apesar de nunca ali ter estado antes. Situava-se, tal como a maior parte das outras coisas, logo à saída da estrada nacional. À primeira vista, não parecia tratar-se de uma escola; apenas a tabuleta, que indicava ser o Liceu de Forks, me fez parar. Aparentava ser um aglomerado de casas similares, construídas com tijolos de cor castanho-avermelhada. Havia tantas árvores e arbustos que, a princípio, não consegui aperceber-me da sua dimensão. O que era feito da sensação de instituição? – interroguei-me nostalgicamente. O que era feito das vedações de rede metálica, dos detectores de metais?

Estacionei em frente ao primeiro edifício. Por cima da porta encontrava-se um letreiro onde se podia ler CONSELHO EXECUTIVO. Nenhum outro carro estava ali parado, pelo que tive a certeza de que o estacionamento era proibido, mas resolvi ir pedir indicações no interior em vez de andar às voltas, debaixo de chuva, como uma idiota. Saí de má vontade da aconchegante cabina da *pick-up* e percorri um pequeno caminho empedrado ladeado por sebes escuras. Respirei fundo antes de abrir a porta.

O interior estava intensamente iluminado e mais quente do que eu esperava. O gabinete era pequeno: uma pequena zona de espera com cadeiras articuladas almofadadas; um tapete comercial com manchas cor-de-laranja; avisos e prémios a preencherem desordenadamente as paredes; um grande relógio a marcar o tempo de forma sonora. Cresciam plantas por toda a parte, dentro de grandes vasos de plástico, como se não houvesse verdura suficiente no exterior. A sala estava dividida ao meio por um balcão comprido, atulhado de cestos de arame repletos de papéis e com folhetos intensamente coloridos colados na sua parte frontal. Por trás do balcão, havia três secretárias, uma das quais ocupada por uma corpulenta mulher de cabelos ruivos e que usava óculos. Tinha vestida uma camisola roxa de mangas curtas, o que imediatamente fez com que me sentisse vestida com exagero.

A mulher de cabelos ruivos ergueu o olhar.

– Posso ajudá-la?

– Chamo-me Isabella Swan – informei-a e vi que os olhos se lhe iluminaram de imediato. Eu era esperada e, sem dúvida,

tema de mexericos. Filha da volúvel ex-mulher do chefe, finalmente regressada a casa.

— É claro — retorquiu ela.

Revistou uma pilha de documentos precariamente amontoa-
dos na sua secretária até encontrar aqueles que procurava.

— Tenho o teu horário aqui mesmo, assim como um mapa da
escola.

Trouxe várias folhas até ao balcão para mas mostrar. Enu-
merou-me as aulas a que eu assistiria, salientando, no mapa,
o melhor itinerário para chegar a cada sala, e deu-me um pequeno pedaço de papel, que teria de ser assinado por cada
professor e devolvido no final do dia. Ela sorriu-me e, tal como Charlie, afirmou esperar que eu gostasse de estar em Forks.
Retribuí o sorriso da forma mais convincente que consegui.

Quando regressei à minha *pick-up*, começavam a chegar outros alunos. Contornei a escola, seguindo a fila de trânsito. Fiquei
contente ao verificar que a maioria dos carros era mais velha, tal
como o meu, e nada tinham de demasiado ostentosos. Na terra onde antes vivera, morava num dos poucos bairros para famílias de
rendimentos mais baixos que pertenciam ao distrito de Paradise
Valley. No entanto, era comum ver um Mercedes ou um Porsche
novo no parque de estacionamento para os estudantes. Aqui,
o automóvel mais vistoso era um Volvo reluzente. Mesmo assim,
desliguei o motor logo que estacionei, para que o ruído atroador
não chamasse a atenção sobre mim.

Consultei o mapa dentro da *pick-up*, tentando fixá-lo imediatamente na memória; com alguma sorte, não teria de andar
pela escola com ele diante do nariz durante todo o dia. Guardei
tudo dentro da mala, coloquei a alça ao ombro e inspirei profundamente. Consigo fazer isto, menti a mim mesma sem grande convicção. Ninguém há-de morder-me. Por fim, expirei e saí
da *pick-up*.

Mantive o rosto escondido pelo capuz ao dirigir-me para o
passeio, apinhado de adolescentes. O meu simples casaco preto
não dava nas vistas, observei com alívio.

Assim que contornei a cantina, foi fácil localizar o edifício três. Na esquina oriental, estava pintado um «3» grande e preto num quadrado branco. Senti-me a ficar gradualmente mais ofegante à medida que me aproximava da porta. Tentei suster a respiração ao seguir duas gabardinas unissexo que se dirigiam para o interior.

A sala de aula era pequena. As pessoas que caminhavam à minha frente detiveram-se logo a seguir à porta para pendurarem os seus casacos numa longa fileira de cabides. Imitei-as. Tratava-se de duas raparigas: uma delas era loura e com pele cor de porcelana, e a outra caracterizava-se igualmente por uma tez pálida e tinha cabelos castanho-claros. Pelo menos, a minha pele não sobressairá aqui.

Levei o pequeno pedaço de papel ao professor, um homem alto, no qual a calvície começava a alastrar-se, cujo nome se encontrava numa placa sobre a secretária, identificando-o como sendo o Professor Mason. Fitou-me com um ar espantado ao ver o meu nome — o que não foi uma reacção animadora — e, como é evidente, fiquei vermelha como um tomate. No entanto, pelo menos, ele mandou-me sentar numa carteira vaga ao fundo da sala sem me apresentar à turma. Era mais difícil para os meus colegas de turma olharem-me fixamente estando eu sentada ao fundo da sala, mas, de alguma forma, conseguiam fazê-lo. Mantive o olhar baixo, fixado na lista de leituras que o professor me dera. Esta era relativamente elementar: Brontë, Shakespeare, Chaucer, Faulkner. Este facto era reconfortante... e entediante. Perguntei-me se a minha mãe me enviaria a pasta que continha trabalhos antigos ou se consideraria que o facto de eu recorrer aos mesmos equivalia a copiar. Enquanto o professor falava monotonamente, revivi, em pensamento, diversas discussões que se tinham desenrolado entre nós.

Quando a campainha tocou, emitindo um som que lembrava um zumbido nasalado, um rapaz esgalgado, com problemas cutâneos e cabelo que se assemelhava a um derrame de petróleo, inclinou-se para a coxia para falar comigo.

— És a Isabella Swan, não és?

Parecia ser o género de rapaz demasiado prestável que pertence ao clube de xadrez.

— Bella — corrigi.

Todos os que estavam sentados num raio de três lugares se viraram para mim.

— Onde é a tua próxima aula? — perguntou ele.

Tive de confirmar tal informação na minha mala.

— Hum, Administração Pública, com o Jefferson, no edifício seis.

Não havia para onde dirigir o olhar sem deparar com olhos curiosos.

— Eu vou em direcção ao edifício quatro, posso indicar-te o caminho...

É, sem dúvida, excessivamente prestável.

— Chamo-me Eric — acrescentou.

Sorri com uma certa hesitação.

— Obrigada.

Pegámos nos nossos casacos e dirigimo-nos para o exterior, onde a chuva caía agora mais intensamente. Poderia jurar que, atrás de nós, caminhavam várias pessoas a uma distância suficiente para escutar a conversa. Esperava não estar a ficar paranóica.

— Então, isto é muito diferente de Phoenix, não é? — perguntou ele.

— Muito.

— Lá, não chove muito, pois não?

— Três ou quatro vezes por ano.

— Ena, como é o clima lá? — quis saber.

— Soalheiro — informei-o.

— Não pareces estar muito bronzeada.

— A minha mãe é parcialmente albina.

Ele examinou o meu rosto de forma apreensiva e eu suspirei. Aparentemente, as nuvens e o sentido de humor não eram conciliáveis. Bastam alguns meses neste ambiente para eu me esquecer de como se fazem observações sarcásticas.

Voltámos a contornar a cantina, encaminhando-nos para os edifícios que se situavam a Sul, junto do ginásio. Eric acompanhou-me mesmo até à porta, apesar de o edifício estar notoriamente assinalado.

— Bem, boa sorte — exclamou quando eu toquei no puxador. — Talvez tenhamos outras aulas em conjunto.

Parecia esperançoso. Sorri-lhe vagamente e entrei.

Passei o resto da manhã sensivelmente da mesma forma. O meu professor de Trigonometria, o professor Varner, o qual, de qualquer modo, eu teria odiado devido à disciplina que leccionava, foi o único que me fez ficar especada diante da turma e apresentar-me. Gaguejei, ruborizei e tropecei nas minhas próprias botas ao dirigir-me para o meu lugar.

Passadas duas aulas, comecei a reconhecer vários rostos em cada uma das que se seguiram. Havia sempre alguém mais corajoso do que os restantes, apresentando-se e fazendo-me perguntas a respeito do que achava de Forks. Tentava ser diplomática, mas, na maior parte das vezes, limitava-me a fazer bastantes afirmações que não correspondiam à verdade. Pelo menos, nunca precisei de recorrer ao mapa.

Uma rapariga sentou-se a meu lado nas aulas de Trigonometria e de Espanhol, fazendo-me companhia na caminhada até à cantina para almoçarmos. Era baixinha, com estatura bastante inferior aos meus 1,62m de altura, mas os seus cabelos escuros rebeldemente encaracolados compensavam grande parte da nossa diferença de alturas. Não conseguia recordar-me do seu nome e, por conseguinte, sorria e acenava com a cabeça enquanto ela tagarelava a respeito dos professores e das aulas. Não me esforçava por lhe seguir o raciocínio.

Sentámo-nos na extremidade de uma mesa ocupada por vários amigos seus, que ela me apresentou. Esqueci os nomes de todos eles logo que os proferiu. Pareciam impressionados com a valentia dela ao falar comigo. O rapaz que conheci na aula de Inglês, Eric, acenou-me do lado oposto da sala.

Foi ali, enquanto estava sentada no refeitório, tentando

conversar com sete desconhecidos curiosos, que os vi pela primeira vez.

Estavam sentados a um canto, tão afastados quanto possível do local onde eu me encontrava na longa sala. Eram cinco. Não conversavam e não comiam, apesar de cada um deles ter um tabuleiro com comida intacta diante de si. Não me fitavam imbecilmente, ao contrário da maioria dos restantes alunos, sendo, portanto, seguro olhá-los fixamente, sem receio de deparar com um par de olhos excessivamente interessado. Não foi, todavia, nenhum destes aspectos que despertou e prendeu a minha atenção.

A sua aparência não se assemelhava em nada. Dos três rapazes, um era grande — musculado como um autêntico halterofilista, com cabelo escuro encaracolado. Outro era mais alto, mais esguio, mas, ainda assim, musculoso, com cabelo louro, da cor do mel. O último era esgalgado, menos corpulento, com cabelo cor de bronze desalinhado. Tinha um aspecto mais pueril do que os restantes, que aparentavam ter idade para frequentar a faculdade ou mesmo ser professores em vez de alunos.

As raparigas constituíam perfeitos opostos. A mais alta era escultural. Tinha uma bela silhueta, do género daquelas que figuram na capa da edição dedicada a fatos de banho da revista *Sports Illustrated* e que fazem aumentar a auto-estima de todas as raparigas em seu redor simplesmente por se encontrarem na mesma sala. Tinha os cabelos dourados, ondulando suavemente até ao meio das costas. A rapariga baixa parecia um duende, extremamente magra, com traços delicados, cabelos curtos, tingidos de um negro acentuado e que apontavam em todas as direcções.

Apesar de tão diferentes, todos eram idênticos. Todos eles eram pálidos como giz, os mais pálidos de todos os estudantes que viviam naquela terra sem Sol. Mais pálidos do que eu, a albina. Todos se caracterizavam por olhos extremamente escuros, apesar de haver uma grande variedade de tonalidades de cabelo. Tinham também sombras escuras sob os olhos — sombras arroxeadas, semelhantes a hematomas, como se todos tivessem passado uma noite sem dormir ou estivessem na fase final de recuperação de um nariz partido, ainda que os seus narizes e todos os seus traços fisionómicos fossem rectos, perfeitos, angulares.

Não era, contudo, por nenhum destes motivos que eu não conseguia afastar o olhar.

Olhava-os fixamente devido ao facto de os seus rostos, tão diferentes, mas tão similares, serem todos avassaladora e desumanamente belos. Eram rostos que nunca se esperava ver, a não ser, talvez, nas páginas aerografadas de uma revista de moda ou pintados por um velho mestre como correspondendo à face de um anjo. Era difícil determinar quem era o mais belo — talvez a rapariga loura ou o rapaz de cabelo cor de bronze.

Todos eles desviavam o olhar; desviavam-no uns dos outros, dos restantes alunos, de tudo em particular, tanto quanto me foi possível verificar. Enquanto os observava, a rapariga pequena levantou o seu tabuleiro — refrigerante por abrir, maçã por trincar — e afastou-se com rápidos e graciosos passos largos que seriam bem empregues numa pista de corrida. Observei-a, espantada com o seu delicado andar de bailarina, até que ela despejou o tabuleiro e deslizou pela porta das traseiras, de forma mais ágil do que eu pensara ser possível. Os meus olhos precipitaram-se novamente sobre os outros, que permaneciam inalteradamente sentados.

— Quem são *eles?* — perguntei à rapariga que conhecera na aula de Espanhol, cujo nome já tinha esquecido.

Quando ela erguia o olhar para ver a quem eu me referia — embora, provavelmente, já soubesse, devido ao meu tom de voz — ele olhou subitamente para ela, o mais magro, o mais pueril, talvez o mais novo. Olhou para a rapariga que se encontrava a meu lado, durante apenas uma fracção de segundo e, em seguida, os seus olhos escuros cruzaram-se com os meus.

Ele desviou o olhar rapidamente, mais rapidamente do que eu poderia fazê-lo, ainda que, num assomo de embaraço, eu tenha baixado os olhos de imediato. Naquele breve relance de olhos, o seu rosto não revelou qualquer interesse — era como se ela tivesse entoado o seu nome e ele tivesse olhado numa reacção involuntária, tendo já decidido não responder.

A rapariga junto de mim soltou risinhos de embaraço, olhando, tal como eu, para a mesa.

— São o Edward e o Emmett Cullen, a Rosalie e o Jasper Hale. A que se foi embora era a Alice Cullen; vivem todos com o Dr. Cullen e a sua esposa — proferiu em voz segredada.

Relanceei o olhar de lado na direcção do belo rapaz que, agora, olhava para o tabuleiro, desfazendo um pão em pedaços com os dedos longos e pálidos. A boca mexia-se muito rapidamente, mal abrindo os seus lábios perfeitos. Os restantes três continuavam a desviar o olhar e, mesmo assim, tive a sensação de que ele lhes dirigia palavras discretas.

"Que nomes estranhos, impopulares", pensei eu. Nomes do género daqueles com que os avós eram baptizados. Talvez, porém, tal estivesse em voga naquela localidade — nomes de cidade pequena? Lembrei-me, por fim, de que a rapariga junto de mim se chamava Jessica, um nome perfeitamente comum. Na cidade onde eu vivera, havia duas raparigas chamadas «Jessica» na minha aula de História.

— São... muito bem-parecidos — debati-me com o conspícuo eufemismo.

— Pois são! — concordou Jessica com outro risinho. — Todos estão, porém, comprometidos uns com os outros — o Emmett com a Rosalie e o Jasper com a Alice, quero eu dizer. Além disso, vivem juntos.

A sua voz continha todo o choque e condenação da pequena cidade, pensei eu, de modo crítico. No entanto, se quisesse ser sincera, tinha de reconhecer que, mesmo em Phoenix, tal facto seria motivo de mexericos.

— Quais são os Cullen? — perguntei. — Não parecem ser aparentados...

— Oh, e não são. O Dr. Cullen é extremamente jovem; encontra-se na casa dos vinte ou dos trinta. São todos adoptados. Os

Hale é que são irmãos, mais precisamente gémeos — os louros — e foram colocados numa família de acolhimento.

— Parecem já ter demasiada idade para serem colocados numa família de acolhimento.

— Agora têm. Tanto o Jasper como a Rosalie têm dezoito anos, mas estão ao cuidado da Sra. Cullen desde os oito. Ela é tia deles ou algo semelhante.

— É bastante simpático da parte deles, o facto de cuidarem de todos aqueles miúdos dessa forma, sendo eles também tão jovens.

— Suponho que seja — reconheceu Jessica com relutância, tendo eu ficado com a impressão de que, por algum motivo, ela não gostava do médico nem da esposa. Com os olhares que lançava aos filhos adoptados de ambos, poderia presumir que o motivo seria inveja. — Julgo, porém, que a Sra. Cullen não pode ter filhos — acrescentou, como se tal diminuísse a bondade do casal.

Durante toda esta conversa, os meus olhos vaguearam uma e outra vez na direcção da mesa, à qual a estranha família se encontrava sentada. Continuavam a fitar as paredes e a não comer.

— Viveram em Forks desde sempre? — perguntei.

Decerto teria reparado neles num dos Verões que ali passei.

— Não — exclamou num tom de voz que insinuava que tal facto deveria ser óbvio, mesmo para uma recém-chegada como eu. — Mudaram-se para cá há apenas dois anos, vindos de algures no Alasca.

Fui invadida por um sentimento de piedade e alívio. Senti piedade, pois, sendo tão belos, eram forasteiros, claramente não aceites. Por outro lado, senti alívio por não ser a única recém-chegada naquele local, nem, de forma manifesta, a mais interessante segundo qualquer critério.

Enquanto eu os examinava, o mais novo, um dos Cullen, ergueu o olhar cruzando-o com o meu, desta vez com uma curiosidade evidente patente na expressão do seu rosto. Ao desviar rapidamente o olhar, pareceu-me que o dele transmitia uma certa impressão de expectativas não correspondidas.

— Qual deles é o rapaz com cabelo castanho arruivado? — perguntei.

Espreitei-o pelo canto do olho e ele continuava a olhar-me fixamente, mas não de um modo espantado como os restantes alunos tinham feito nesse dia — tinha uma expressão de ligeira frustração estampada no rosto. Voltei a baixar o olhar.

— É o Edward. É lindo, como é evidente, mas não percas tempo. Ele não sai com raparigas. Pelos vistos, nenhuma das raparigas daqui é suficientemente atraente para ele.

Ela torceu o nariz, um caso explícito de despeito. Perguntei-me quando é que ele a teria rejeitado.

Mordi o lábio para disfarçar o sorriso. Em seguida, voltei a olhá-lo de relance. O seu rosto estava voltado na direcção oposta, mas pareceu-me que estava elevado, como se também ele estivesse a sorrir.

Volvidos mais alguns minutos, Edward não voltou a olhar-me.

Permaneci sentada à mesa com Jessica e os seus amigos durante mais tempo do que teria feito se estivesse sozinha. Estava ansiosa por não chegar atrasada às aulas no meu primeiro dia. Uma das minhas novas conhecidas, que me lembrava recorrentemente de que o seu nome era Angela, tinha Biologia II comigo na hora seguinte. Caminhámos juntas para a aula, em silêncio. Também ela era tímida.

Quando entrámos na sala de aula, Angela foi sentar-se a uma bancada de laboratório com tampo preto idêntica àquelas a que eu estava habituada. Já tinha uma colega de carteira. Na verdade, todas as bancadas estavam completamente ocupadas, excepto uma. Ao lado da coxia central, reconheci Edward Cullen devido ao seu cabelo invulgar, estava sentado junto do único lugar vago.

Ao percorrer a coxia para me apresentar ao professor e lhe pedir que assinasse o pequeno pedaço de papel que me fora dado, observava-o sub-repticiamente. Então, no preciso momento em que eu passava, ele adoptou de súbito uma postura rígida no seu lugar. Voltou a fitar-me, fixando os olhos nos meus com a mais estranha das expressões estampada no rosto — revelava hostilidade, fúria. Apressei-me a desviar o olhar, chocada, enrubescendo novamente. Na passagem, tropecei num livro e tive de procurar o equilíbrio na borda de uma bancada. A rapariga que estava ali sentada soltou alguns risinhos.

Reparara no facto de que os olhos dele eram negros — negros como o carvão.

O professor Banner assinou-me o papel e entregou-me um livro sem proceder a quaisquer apresentações disparatadas. Percebi que nos daríamos bem. Como é evidente, não teve alternativa senão mandar-me sentar no único lugar vago no meio da sala. Mantive os olhos baixos enquanto caminhava para ir sentar-me a seu lado, desconcertada com o olhar hostil que ele me lançara.

Não levantei o olhar ao pousar o livro na carteira e ao sentar-me, mas, pelo canto do olho, vi a sua postura alterar-se. Inclinara-se, distanciando-se de mim, ficando sentado mesmo à beirinha da cadeira e desviando o rosto como se tivesse sentido um odor desagradável. Discretamente, cheirei o meu cabelo. Exalava uma fragrância a morango, o aroma do meu champô preferido. Parecia um odor bastante inócuo. Deixei os meus cabelos caírem sobre o ombro direito, criando uma cortina negra entre nós, e tentei prestar atenção ao professor.

Infelizmente, a lição tinha como tema a anatomia celular, algo que eu já estudara. De qualquer forma, tomei notas cuidadosamente, mantendo sempre o olhar baixo.

Não conseguia evitar espreitar, de vez em quando, através do biombo do meu cabelo, o estranho rapaz que se encontrava a meu lado. Durante toda a aula, nunca relaxou a posição hirta na borda da cadeira, estando sentado tão longe de mim quanto possível. Conseguia ver que a sua mão, pousada na perna direita, estava fechada, formando um punho cerrado, com os tendões a sobressaírem sob a pele pálida. Também este nunca relaxou. Tinha as longas mangas da camisa branca arregaçadas até aos cotovelos e o antebraço era surpreendentemente firme e musculoso sob a pele clara. Não era, de modo nenhum, tão franzino como aparentava quando estava junto do seu corpulento irmão.

A aula parecia arrastar-se durante mais tempo do que as restantes. Dever-se-ia ao facto de o dia estar finalmente prestes a terminar ou de eu esperar que o seu punho tenso se distendesse? Tal nunca chegou a acontecer; permaneceu de tal modo estático que parecia não respirar. O que se passava com ele? Seria este o seu comportamento normal? Questionei a minha interpretação a respeito do azedume de Jessica ao almoço. Talvez não estivesse tão despeitada como eu pensara.

Aquela atitude não podia, de forma alguma, estar relacionada comigo. Não me conhecia de lado nenhum.

Espreitei-o uma vez mais e arrependi-me de o ter feito. Lançava-me novamente um olhar irritado, estando os seus olhos negros repletos de repulsa. Estremeci ao afastar-me dele, encolhendo-me contra a minha cadeira e a expressão *«se o olhar matasse»* atravessou-me o espírito.

Nesse momento, a campainha tocou de forma sonora, sobressaltando-me, e Edward Cullen moveu-se do seu lugar. Ergueu-se com naturalidade — era muito mais alto do que eu pensara — de costas voltadas para mim e transpôs a porta antes que mais alguém tivesse saído do seu lugar.

Permaneci imóvel no meu lugar, lançando o olhar vazio na direcção em que ele seguira. Ele era tão mau. Não era justo. Comecei a recolher os meus pertences lentamente, tentando refrear a raiva que me invadia, com receio de que os meus olhos se enchessem de lágrimas. Por algum motivo, havia uma ligação estabelecida entre o meu temperamento e os meus canais lacrimais. Costumava chorar quando estava zangada, o que era uma tendência humilhante.

— Não és a Isabella Swan? — perguntou uma voz masculina.

Levantei o olhar e deparei com um rapaz giro com cara de bebé, cabelo louro-claro cuidadosamente moldado com gel, alinhadamente espetado, que me sorria de um modo amistoso. Era evidente que ele não pensava que eu exalava um odor desagradável.

— Sou a Bella — corrigi-o, esboçando um sorriso.

— Eu chamo-me Mike.

— Olá, Mike.

— Precisas de ajuda para encontrar a sala onde vai ser a tua próxima aula?

— Na verdade, vou para o ginásio. Julgo que consigo encontrá-lo.

— Essa é também a minha próxima aula.

Pareceu radiante, ainda que tal facto não fosse uma grande coincidência numa escola tão pequena.

Caminhámos juntos para a aula; ele era um tagarela — encarregou-se de grande parte da conversa, o que facilitou a minha tarefa. Vivera na Califórnia até aos dez anos e, por conseguinte, queria saber o que eu pensava do sol. Veio a verificar-se que ele também fazia parte da minha turma de Inglês. Foi a pessoa mais simpática que conheci neste dia.

No entanto, quando estávamos a entrar no ginásio, ele perguntou:

— Então, apunhalaste o Edward Cullen com um lápis ou quê? Nunca o vi agir daquela forma.

Eu retraí-me. Não fora, então, a única a reparar e, pelos vistos, aquele *não era* o comportamento normal de Edward Cullen. Decidi fazer-me despercebida.

— Referes-te ao rapaz ao lado do qual me sentei na aula de Biologia? — perguntei com naturalidade.

— Sim — respondeu ele. — Parecia estar em sofrimento ou algo do género.

— Não sei — repliquei. — Não falei com ele.

— É um tipo estranho.

Mike demorava-se na minha companhia em vez de se dirigir ao vestiário.

— Se eu tivesse tido a sorte de me sentar a teu lado, teria falado contigo.

Sorri-lhe antes de passar pela porta do balneário feminino. Ele era amável e um manifesto admirador meu, mas tal não era suficiente para atenuar a minha irritação.

O professor de Ginástica, o treinador Clapp, arranjou-me um equipamento, mas não me obrigou a vesti-lo para participar na aula deste dia. Na minha terra, eram necessários apenas dois anos de Educação Física. Aqui, a disciplina de E. F. era obrigatória durante os quatro anos. Forks era literalmente o meu inferno na Terra.

Assisti a quatro partidas de voleibol que decorriam simultaneamente. Ao lembrar-me das lesões que sofrera — e infligira — quando jogava voleibol, senti-me um pouco enjoada.

O derradeiro toque da campainha finalmente soou. Encaminhei-me vagarosamente para o Conselho Executivo para devolver os documentos que me foram entregues. A chuva afastara-se, mas o vento estava forte e mais frio. Apertei os braços em torno do meu corpo.

Quando entrei no gabinete aconchegante, quase dei meia volta e saí pelo mesmo caminho.

Edward Cullen estava de pé, junto da secretária, à minha frente. Voltei a reconhecer aquele desgrenhado cabelo cor de bronze. Não pareceu aperceber-se da minha entrada. Fiquei de pé, encostada à parede do fundo, esperando que a recepcionista pudesse atender-me.

Ele discutia com ela num tom de voz grave e sedutor. Depressa compreendi o cerne da questão. Estava a tentar mudar a aula de Biologia ao sexto tempo para outra hora — qualquer outra hora.

Simplesmente não queria acreditar que era eu o móbil de tal atitude. Devia tratar-se de algo mais, de algo que acontecera antes de eu entrar na sala onde decorria a aula de Biologia. A expressão estampada no seu rosto deveria ser motivada por uma exasperação completamente distinta. Não era possível que aquele desconhecido tivesse sentido uma antipatia tão intensa e repentina por mim.

A porta abriu-se de novo e o vento frio irrompeu subitamente pela sala, soprando os documentos que se encontravam sobre a secretária e fazendo com que os meus cabelos redemoinhassem à volta do meu rosto. A rapariga que entrou limitou-se a dirigir-se à secretária, colocar um bilhete no cesto de arame e sair, mas as costas de Edward Cullen ficaram rígidas e ele virou-se lentamente para me fitar – o seu rosto era absurdamente formoso – com um olhar penetrante e repleto de ódio. Por um instante, senti um frémito de autêntico medo, que fez com que os pêlos dos meus braços se eriçassem. O olhar durou apenas um segundo, mas enregelou-me mais do que o vento gélido. Virou-se novamente para a recepcionista.

– Então, esqueça – disse ele apressadamente num tom de voz que parecia aveludado. – Vejo que é impossível. Muito obrigado pela sua ajuda.

Em seguida, deu meia volta sem voltar a pousar os olhos em mim e desapareceu porta fora.

Aproximei-me devagarinho da secretária, com o rosto inusitadamente branco em vez de vermelho, e entreguei o pedaço de papel assinado à recepcionista.

– Como correu o teu primeiro dia, querida? – perguntou maternalmente.

– Muito bem – menti, com a voz débil.

Não pareceu ficar convencida.

Quando entrei na *pick-up*, esta era praticamente a última viatura que se encontrava no parque de estacionamento. Parecia um refúgio, sendo já o que eu tinha de mais semelhante a um lar naquele buraco verde e húmido. Permaneci sentada no seu interior durante alguns momentos, lançando apenas o olhar vazio pelo pára-brisas, mas depressa tive frio suficiente para necessitar do aquecimento, pelo que liguei a ignição e o motor roncou ao entrar em funcionamento. Dirigi-me de regresso a casa de Charlie, tentando conter as lágrimas ao longo de todo o percurso.

Capítulo Dois

Livro Aberto

O dia seguinte foi melhor... e pior.

Foi melhor porque ainda não chovia, embora as nuvens fossem densas e opacas. Foi mais fácil, pois eu sabia o que esperar do meu dia. Mike sentou-se a meu lado na aula de Inglês e acompanhou-me até à sala da aula seguinte, sob o constante olhar feroz de Eric, do Clube de Xadrez, o que era lisonjeador. As pessoas já não me olhavam tanto como tinham feito no dia anterior. Ao almoço, sentei-me a uma mesa com um grande grupo, que incluía Mike, Eric, Jessica e várias outras pessoas de cujos nomes e caras agora me recordava. Comecei a ter a sensação de que caminhava sobre água, em vez de me afogar nela.

Foi pior porque estava cansada; ainda não conseguia dormir com o vento a assobiar em torno da casa. Foi pior porque o professor Varner me chamou na aula de Trigonometria quando a minha mão não estava levantada e eu dei a resposta errada. Foi péssimo porque tive de jogar voleibol e, da única vez que não me afastei da trajectória da bola, atingi a minha colega de equipa na cabeça. Foi, por fim, pior porque Edward Cullen não apareceu na escola.

Durante toda a manhã, receei o almoço, temendo os seus bizarros olhares irados. Parte de mim desejava confrontá-lo e exigir saber qual era o seu problema. Enquanto estava deitada, sem sono, na cama, cheguei a imaginar o que diria, mas conhecia-me demasiado bem para pensar se teria mesmo coragem para o fazer. Fiz com que o leão cobarde parecesse o exterminador.

No entanto, quando entrei na cantina com Jessica — tentando evitar que os meus olhos esquadrinhassem o local em busca dele e fracassando redondamente —, vi que os seus quatro irmãos de aparência diversa estavam sentados à mesma mesa e ele não se encontrava lá.

Mike interceptou-nos e conduziu-nos até à sua mesa. Jessica parecia enlevada por aquela atenção e os seus amigos depressa se juntaram a nós. Porém, enquanto tentava escutar a sua trivial tagarelice, sentia-me terrivelmente pouco à vontade, aguardando com nervosismo o momento da sua chegada. Esperava que ele simplesmente me ignorasse quando aparecesse e demonstrasse que a minha suspeita era falsa.

Não vinha e, à medida que o tempo passava, eu ficava cada vez mais tensa.

Caminhei até à aula de Biologia de forma mais confiante depois de, até ao final do almoço, ele ainda não ter aparecido. Mike, que assumia as qualidades de um *golden retriever*, caminhava fielmente a meu lado até à aula. Sustive a respiração ao chegar à porta, mas Edward Cullen também não estava presente. Respirei fundo e dirigi-me ao meu lugar. Mike seguiu-me, falando sobre uma iminente viagem até à praia. Permaneceu junto da minha bancada até ao toque da campainha. Então, sorriu-me melancolicamente e foi sentar-se junto de uma rapariga com aparelho dentário e uma permanente mal conseguida. Parecia que eu teria de tomar uma atitude quanto a Mike e tal não seria fácil. Numa cidade como esta, onde todos controlavam todos, a diplomacia era essencial. Eu nunca tivera grande tacto; não tinha qualquer tipo de prática em lidar com rapazes excessivamente amáveis.

Fiquei aliviada por ter a bancada só para mim, por Edward estar ausente. Disse isto a mim própria repetidas vezes, mas não conseguia livrar-me da incómoda suspeita de que era eu o motivo da sua ausência. Era ridículo e egotista pensar que eu podia afectar alguém de maneira tão intensa. Era impossível, mas, mesmo assim, não conseguia deixar de me preocupar com a possibilidade de tal corresponder à verdade.

Quando o dia de aulas finalmente terminou e o rubor provocado pelo incidente no jogo de voleibol começava a desvanecer-se das minhas faces, voltei rapidamente a vestir as minhas calças de ganga e a camisola azul-marinho. Apressei-me a sair do balneário feminino, satisfeita por constatar que, por enquanto, me esquivara com êxito do meu amigo *retriever*. Encaminhei-me agilmente para o parque de estacionamento, agora apinhado de alunos que partiam. Entrei na minha *pick-up* e remexi no interior da minha mala para me certificar de que tinha aquilo de que necessitava.

Na noite anterior, descobrira que Charlie não sabia cozinhar muito mais do que ovos estrelados e toucinho fumado. Por isso, pedi que me fossem confiadas as tarefas da cozinha durante a minha estada. Morto por isso estava ele. Cheguei também à conclusão de que ele não tinha comida em casa. Assim, com a lista de compras e o dinheiro do frasco que era guardado no guarda-louça e em cujo rótulo podia ler-se «dinheiro para comida», dirigi-me para o *Thriftway*.

Liguei o ensurdecedor motor da *pick-up*, fazendo-o entrar em funcionamento, ignorando as cabeças que se voltavam na minha direcção e recuei cuidadosamente, ocupando um lugar na fila de carros que esperavam para sair do parque de estacionamento. Enquanto esperava, tentando fingir que o atroador ribombar era originado pelo carro de outra pessoa, vi os dois Cullen e os gémeos Hale entrarem no seu carro. Tratava-se de um Volvo novo reluzente. Claro. Ainda não reparara nas suas roupas — ficara demasiado hipnotizada com os seus rostos. Agora, ao prestar atenção, tornava-se óbvio que todos estavam excepcionalmente bem vestidos; de modo simples, mas com roupas que denotavam subtilmente origens de marca. Com a notável boa aparência e o estilo do seu porte, podiam envergar trapos sem que ninguém notasse. Parecia excessivo o facto de eles terem boa aparência e, ao mesmo tempo, dinheiro, mas, tanto quanto me é possível verificar, a vida funciona desta forma na maior parte das vezes. Não parecia, porém, proporcionar-lhes a aceitação naquele lugar.

Não, eu não acreditava inteiramente nisto. Deviam ser eles

que desejavam viver isolados; não conseguia imaginar nenhuma porta que não fosse aberta por aquele grau de beleza.

Olharam para a minha ruidosa *pick-up* ao passar por eles, tal como as outras pessoas. Continuei a olhar em frente e fiquei aliviada quando finalmente saí do recinto da escola.

O *Thriftway* não ficava longe da escola: situava-se apenas a algumas ruas de distância, para Sul, à saída da estrada nacional. Era agradável estar no interior do supermercado; transmitia uma sensação de normalidade. Em casa, era eu que me encarregava das compras e dediquei-me de boa vontade à tarefa com que já estava familiarizada. O interior da loja era suficientemente grande para que eu não conseguisse ouvir a chuva a bater no telhado e não fosse relembrada do local onde me encontrava.

Quando cheguei a casa, descarreguei toda a mercearia, guardando-a onde quer que conseguisse encontrar um espaço livre. Esperava que Charlie não se importasse. Envolvi batatas em papel de alumínio e coloquei-as no forno para assarem, mergulhei um bife numa marinada e equilibrei-o em cima de uma embalagem de ovos no frigorífico.

Quando concluí esta tarefa, levei a pasta com os livros para cima. Antes de me debruçar sobre os trabalhos de casa, vesti umas calças de fato de treino, apanhei o cabelo húmido num rabo-de-cavalo e consultei o meu correio electrónico pela primeira vez. Tinha três mensagens.

«Bella», escrevia a minha mãe.

«Escreve-me assim que chegares a casa. Diz-me como correu a tua viagem de avião. Está a chover? Já sinto saudades tuas. Estou quase a acabar de fazer as malas para a viagem à Florida, mas não consigo encontrar a minha blusa cor-de-rosa. Sabes onde a coloquei? O Phil manda-te cumprimentos.

Mãe.»

Suspirei e passei à seguinte. Foi enviada oito horas depois da primeira.

«Bella», escrevia ela.

«Porque é que ainda não me contactaste por correio electrónico? De que é que estás à espera?

Mãe.»

A última datava daquela manhã.

«Isabella,
Se não tiver recebido notícias tuas até às 17h30 de hoje, telefono ao Charlie.»

Olhei para o relógio. Ainda dispunha de uma hora, mas a minha mãe era conhecida por se antecipar aos acontecimentos.

«Mãe,
Acalma-te. Estou a escrever-te neste preciso momento. Não tomes nenhuma atitude precipitada.
Bella.»

Enviei esta mensagem e recomecei.

«Mãe,
Está tudo óptimo. É claro que está a chover. Estava à espera de ter algum assunto acerca do qual escrever. As aulas não são más, apenas um pouco repetitivas. Conheci alguns miúdos simpáticos que se sentam a meu lado ao almoço.
A tua blusa está na lavandaria — devias ter ido buscá-la na sexta-feira.
O Charlie comprou-me uma *pick-up*, acreditas? Adoro-a. Sabes, é velha, mas verdadeiramente robusta, o que é bom para mim.

Também sinto saudades tuas. Voltarei a escrever em breve, mas não vou consultar o meu correio electrónico de cinco em cinco minutos. Descontrai-te, respira. Gosto muito de ti.

Bella.»

Decidira ler *O Monte dos Vendavais* — o romance que estávamos a estudar, naquele momento, na disciplina de Inglês — uma vez mais apenas pelo gozo, e era isso que estava a fazer quando Charlie chegou a casa. Tinha perdido a noção do tempo e precipitei-me para o andar de baixo a fim de retirar as batatas e colocar o bife a grelhar.

— Bella? — gritou o meu pai quando me ouviu descer as escadas.

«Quem haveria de ser?» pensei.

— Olá, pai, bem-vindo a casa.

— Obrigado.

Pendurou o seu coldre e descalçou as botas enquanto eu me afadigava na cozinha. Tanto quanto eu sabia, ele nunca disparara a arma em serviço, mas mantinha-a a postos. Quando eu ia àquela casa durante a infância, o meu pai retirava sempre as balas assim que passava a porta. Suponho que agora me considerava com idade suficiente para não me alvejar a mim mesma acidentalmente e que não estava deprimida o bastante para o fazer de propósito.

— O que é o jantar? — perguntou de forma cautelosa.

A minha mãe era uma cozinheira imaginativa e nem sempre as suas experiências eram comestíveis. Fiquei surpreendida, mas também triste, por ele parecer conservar lembranças tão antigas.

— Bife com batatas — respondi.

Pareceu ficar aliviado.

Dava a impressão de estar constrangido ao ficar especado na cozinha sem fazer nada; arrastou-se pesadamente até à sala de estar para ver televisão enquanto eu trabalhava. Ambos nos sentíamos mais à vontade desta forma. Preparei uma salada enquanto os bifes cozinhavam e pus a mesa.

Chamei-o quando o jantar ficou pronto e ele sentiu o cheiro da comida de forma apreciadora ao entrar na cozinha.

— Cheira bem, Bell.

— Obrigada.

Comemos em silêncio durante alguns minutos. Não era constrangedor. Nenhum de nós ficava incomodado com o silêncio. Sob alguns aspectos, éramos talhados para coabitar um com o outro.

— Então, que tal te pareceu a escola? Fizeste algumas amizades? — perguntou enquanto se servia uma segunda vez.

— Bem, tenho algumas aulas com uma rapariga chamada Jessica. Sento-me na companhia dos amigos dela ao almoço. Há também um rapaz, o Mike, que é muito amável. Todos parecem bastantes simpáticos. Com uma excepção de relevo.

— Deve ser o Mike Newton. Bom rapaz, boa família. O pai dele é o proprietário da loja de material desportivo logo à entrada da cidade. Ganha a vida de modo bastante folgado com todos os turistas que passam por aqui.

— Conheces a família Cullen? — perguntei de modo hesitante.

— A família do Dr. Cullen? Com certeza. O Dr. Cullen é um grande homem.

— Eles... os filhos... são um pouco diferentes. Não parecem integrar-se muito bem na escola.

Charlie surpreendeu-me ao parecer zangado.

— Pessoas desta cidade — resmungou. — O Dr. Cullen é um cirurgião brilhante que poderia, provavelmente, trabalhar em qualquer hospital do mundo e ganhar dez vezes o salário que aufere aqui — prosseguiu, elevando o tom de voz. — Temos muita sorte em tê-lo aqui, por a sua esposa ter querido viver numa cidade pequena. Ele é uma mais-valia para a comunidade e todos esses miúdos são educados e bem-comportados. Quando eles se mudaram, tive as minhas dúvidas relativamente a todos aqueles adolescentes adoptados. Pensei que poderíamos vir a ter problemas com eles, mas são todos muito maduros. Nenhum deles me causou o mais pequeno incómodo. O mesmo já não posso dizer dos filhos de algumas pessoas cujas famílias aqui habitam há várias gerações. Além disso, mantêm-se unidos como uma família deve fazer — vão acampar fim-de-semana sim, fim-de-semana não... Só por serem recém-chegados, as pessoas têm de bisbilhotar.

Foi o discurso mais longo que eu jamais ouvira Charlie proferir. Devia sentir-se fervorosamente afectado pelo que quer que fosse que as pessoas comentavam.

Retrocedi.

— A mim, pareceram-me bastante simpáticos. Só reparei no facto de serem reservados. São todos muito atraentes — acrescentei, tentando ser mais elogiosa.

— Devias conhecer o médico — afirmou Charlie, rindo. — Ainda bem que ele tem um casamento feliz. Muitas das enfermeiras do hospital tiveram dificuldade em concentrar-se no trabalho com ele por perto.

Caímos novamente no silêncio ao terminarmos a refeição. Ele levantou a mesa enquanto eu começava a tratar da louça. Voltou para diante da televisão e, depois de eu ter acabado de lavar a louça à mão — não havia máquina de lavar —, dirigi-me de má vontade ao andar superior para me dedicar aos meus trabalhos de casa de Matemática. Conseguia pressentir uma tradição a estabelecer-se.

Finalmente, tive uma noite calma. Adormeci depressa, sentindo-me exausta.

Durante o resto da semana, não se deram grandes acontecimentos. Habituei-me à rotina das aulas. Quando chegou a sexta-feira, eu já era capaz de reconhecer, se não mesmo chamar pelo nome, quase todos os alunos da escola. Na aula de Ginástica, todos os membros da minha equipa aprenderam a não me passar a bola e a colocar-se rapidamente à minha frente se a equipa adversária tentasse tirar proveito da minha fraqueza. Eu, de bom grado, não me atravessava no caminho deles.

Edward Cullen não voltou à escola.

Todos os dias, eu permanecia ansiosamente atenta até os restantes Cullen entrarem na cantina sem ele. Então, podia sossegar e participar na conversa que se desenrolava durante a hora de almoço. Esta centrava-se sobretudo numa viagem ao *Parque Marítimo de La Push* que teria lugar dentro de duas semanas e que Mike estava a organizar. Fui convidada e acedera a ir, mais por delicadeza do que por vontade. As praias deviam ser quentes e secas.

Quando chegou a sexta-feira, eu já me sentia perfeitamente à vontade ao entrar na aula de Biologia, não estando preocupada com a presença de Edward. Tanto quanto sabia, desistira da escola. Tentei não pensar nele, mas não conseguia eliminar de vez a preocupação relativamente ao facto de eu ser responsável pela sua ausência continuada, por mais ridículo que parecesse.

O meu primeiro fim-de-semana em Forks decorreu sem quaisquer incidentes. Charlie, não estando habituado a passar o tempo na casa normalmente vazia, trabalhou durante a maior parte do fim-de-semana. Procedi à limpeza da casa, adiantei os trabalhos da escola e escrevi à minha mãe mais mensagens de correio electrónico falsamente animadas. No sábado, cheguei a dirigir-me à biblioteca, mas ela estava tão mal fornecida que não me dei ao trabalho de obter um cartão; em breve, teria de marcar um dia para uma ida a Olympia ou a Seattle e encontrar uma boa biblioteca. Perguntei-me futilmente qual seria o consumo da *pick-up* em termos de gasolina... e estremeci só de pensar.

A chuva manteve-se fraca durante o fim-de-semana, silenciosa, e, por conseguinte, eu consegui dormir bem.

As pessoas cumprimentaram-me no parque de estacionamento, na segunda-feira de manhã. Não sabia o nome de todas, mas retribuía o aceno e sorria a toda a gente. Nesta manhã, estava mais frio, mas, felizmente, não chovia. Na aula de Inglês, Mike ocupou o seu lugar habitual a meu lado. Foi-nos dado um teste surpresa acerca de *O Monte dos Vendavais*. Era directo, extremamente fácil.

Na verdade, eu sentia-me bastante mais à vontade do que pensara. Mais à vontade do que alguma vez esperara sentir-me aqui.

Quando saímos da aula, o ar estava repleto de farrapos brancos que giravam num torvelinho. Conseguia ouvir as pessoas gritarem de forma empolgada umas para as outras. O vento açoitava-me a face e o nariz.

— Ena! — exclamou Mike. — Está a nevar.

Olhei para os pequenos pompons de algodão que estavam a acumular-se ao longo do passeio e a rodopiar erraticamente diante do meu rosto.

— Que horror! Neve. Lá se vai o meu bom dia.

Ele pareceu surpreendido.

— Não gostas de neve?

— Não. Significa que está demasiado frio para chover. É óbvio. Além disso, pensei que devia cair em flocos, tu sabes, cada um é único e tudo isso. Estes assemelham-se apenas às extremidades dos cotonetes.

— Nunca assististe à queda de neve? — perguntou ele incredulamente.

— Claro que já assisti — detive-me. — Na televisão.

Mike riu-se. Então, uma bola grande e mole de neve gotejante atingiu-o na nuca. Ambos nos voltámos para ver de onde provinha. Eu desconfiei de Eric, que se afastava, de costas voltadas para nós, caminhando na direcção errada para a sua aula seguinte. Mike, pelos vistos, tinha a mesma opinião. Inclinou-se e começou a formar um monte com aquela macia polpa branca.

— Encontramo-nos ao almoço, está bem?

Continuei a andar enquanto falava. "Quando as pessoas começam a arremessar substâncias húmidas, abrigo-me."

Ele limitou-se a acenar com a cabeça, tendo os olhos pousados na figura em retirada de Eric.

Ao longo da manhã, todos tagarelaram empolgadamente a respeito da neve; pelos vistos, tratava-se do primeiro nevão do novo ano. Eu mantive-me calada. É claro que era mais seca do que a chuva — até se derreter nas nossas meias.

Caminhei de modo vigilante até à cantina, na companhia de Jessica, depois da aula de Espanhol. Bolas de polpa macia voavam por toda a parte. Eu mantive uma capa nas minhas mãos, pronta para usá-la como escudo de protecção se tal fosse necessário. Jessica achou-me hilariante, mas algo na expressão do meu rosto a impedia de ser ela própria a lançar-me uma bola de neve.

Mike alcançou-nos quando entrámos, rindo, com gelo a derreter-se no cabelo, anulando o efeito espetado. Ele e Jessica conversavam animadamente acerca da luta na neve quando entrámos na fila para comprar comida. Olhei para a mesa do canto por uma questão de hábito e, em seguida, fiquei paralisada no local onde me encontrava. Estavam cinco pessoas sentadas à mesa.

Jessica puxou-me pelo braço.

— Sim? Bella? O que desejas?

Baixei o olhar; tinha as orelhas a ferver. Não tinha qualquer motivo para me sentir inibida, relembrei a mim mesma. Não fizera nada de errado.

— O que se passa com a Bella? — perguntou Mike a Jessica.

— Nada — respondi eu. — Hoje, vou tomar apenas um refrigerante.

Voltei para o final da fila.

— Não tens fome? — perguntou Jessica.

— Na verdade, sinto-me um pouco enjoada — declarei, com os olhos ainda pregados no chão.

Esperei que eles recebessem a comida e, posteriormente, segui-os até uma mesa, com os olhos pousados nos meus pés.

Sorvi o meu refrigerante lentamente, com o estômago às voltas. Mike perguntou duas vezes, com desnecessária preocupação, como é que me sentia. Disse-lhe que se tratava de algo sem importância, mas interrogava-me se deveria fazer uma encenação, escapar até à enfermaria e ali permanecer durante a hora seguinte.

Que ridículo. Eu não devia ter de fugir.

Decidi permitir-me um olhar de relance para a mesa da família Cullen. Se ele estivesse a olhar-me com um ar feroz, eu faltaria a Biologia, como cobarde que era.

Mantive a cabeça baixa e olhei por baixo das minhas pestanas. Nenhum deles estava a olhar na minha direcção. Levantei um pouco a cabeça.

Estavam a rir-se. Tanto Edward como Jasper e Emmett tinham o cabelo completamente repleto de neve a derreter-se. Alice e Rosalie afastavam-se enquanto Emmett sacudia o seu cabelo gotejante na direcção delas. Desfrutavam do dia nevoso, tal como todos os outros — só que eles pareciam mais formar uma cena retirada de um filme do que o resto de nós.

No entanto, além do riso e do espírito de brincadeira, havia algo diferente e eu não conseguia determinar ao certo em que é que consistia essa diferença. Examinei Edward de forma mais minuciosa. Cheguei à conclusão de que a sua pele estava menos pálida — talvez enrubescida pela luta na neve — e os círculos sob os seus olhos menos perceptíveis. Havia, porém, algo mais. Ponderei, olhando-os fixamente, tentando isolar a mudança.

— Bella, para que é que estás a olhar? — intrometeu-se Jessica, seguindo o meu olhar fixo.

Nesse preciso momento, os olhos dele deslocaram-se para se cruzarem com os meus.

Baixei a cabeça, deixando os cabelos caírem para me ocultarem o rosto. Tinha, todavia, a certeza de que, no instante em que os nossos olhares se cruzaram, ele não parecia descortês ou hostil como acontecera da última vez que o vira. Parecia, de novo, meramente curioso, insatisfeito sob algum aspecto.

— O Edward Cullen está a olhar-te fixamente — comentou Jessica ao meu ouvido, soltando risinhos.

— Não parece zangado, pois não? — não consegui evitar a pergunta.

— Não — respondeu ela, parecendo confusa com a minha pergunta. — Devia estar?

— Acho que ele não gosta de mim — confessei.

Sentia-me ainda indisposta. Pousei a cabeça no braço.

— Os Cullen não gostam de ninguém... bem, não se mostram delicados o suficiente para que as pessoas gostem deles. Mas ele continua a olhar-te fixamente.

— Pára de olhar para ele — murmurei com alguma exasperação.

Soltou um riso abafado, mas desviou o olhar. Levantei a cabeça o suficiente para me certificar de que ela o fazia, encarando a possibilidade de recorrer à violência se ela oferecesse resistência.

Mike interrompeu-nos nesta altura — estava a preparar uma épica batalha da nevasca no parque de estacionamento depois das aulas e queria que nós participássemos. Jessica acedeu com entusiasmo. A forma como ela olhava para Mike deixava pouca margem para dúvidas relativamente ao facto de que estaria disposta a alinhar no que quer que fosse que ele sugerisse. Eu mantive-me calada. Teria de me esconder no ginásio até que o parque de estacionamento ficasse vazio.

Durante o resto da hora de almoço, mantive, com extremo cuidado, os olhos pregados na minha própria mesa. Decidi honrar o compromisso que firmara comigo mesma. Como ele não tinha um ar zangado, eu assistiria à aula de Biologia. O meu estômago dava pequenas voltas de pavor ao pensar que iria sentar-me novamente ao seu lado.

Não queria propriamente caminhar até à aula na companhia de Mike, como era hábito — ele parecia ser um alvo privilegiado para os atiradores furtivos de bolas de neve —, mas, quando chegámos à porta, todos os que se encontravam junto de mim se lamentaram em uníssono. A chuva caía, apagando todos os vestígios de neve em faixas límpidas e glaciais que escorriam pela berma da passagem para peões. Coloquei o capuz na cabeça, estando, no meu íntimo, satisfeita. Estaria livre para ir directamente para casa após a aula de Ginástica.

A caminho do edifício quatro, Mike não parou de se lamuriar.

Assim que entrámos na sala de aula, verifiquei, com alívio, que a minha bancada ainda se encontrava desocupada. O professor Banner circulava pela sala, distribuindo um microscópio e uma caixa de diapositivos por cada bancada. Ainda faltavam alguns minutos para o início da aula e na sala imperava o burburinho das conversas. Mantive o olhar afastado da porta, rabiscando indolentemente a capa do meu caderno de apontamentos.

Ouvi nitidamente a cadeira que se encontrava a meu lado mover-se, mas os meus olhos permaneceram cuidadosamente concentrados nos motivos que eu estava a desenhar.

— Olá — disse uma voz suave, melodiosa.

Ergui o olhar, aturdida por ele estar a dirigir-me a palavra. Estava sentado tão distante em relação a mim quanto a bancada o permitia, mas a sua cadeira estava virada na minha direcção. Tinha o cabelo molhado ao ponto de gotejar, em desalinho — mesmo assim, parecia alguém que acabara de participar na filmagem de um anúncio publicitário a gel capilar. O seu rosto deslumbrante tinha uma expressão amigável, aberta, com os lábios perfeitos a esboçarem um ligeiro sorriso. Os olhos, porém, espelhavam algum cuidado.

— Chamo-me Edward Cullen — prosseguiu. — Não tive a oportunidade de me apresentar na semana passada. Deves ser a Bella Swan.

A minha cabeça girava de tão confusa. Será que tudo aquilo fora fruto da minha imaginação? Ele estava, agora, a ser perfeitamente delicado. Eu tinha de falar, ele estava à espera. Não me ocorria, contudo, nada de convencional para dizer.

— Como é que sabes o meu nome? — balbuciei.

Ele riu-se de uma forma suave e encantadora.

— Oh, acho que todos sabem o teu nome. Toda a cidade tem estado a aguardar a tua chegada.

Esbocei um esgar. Sabia que tal correspondia mais ou menos à verdade.

— Não — insisti estupidamente. — O que eu queria perguntar-te era por que motivo me chamaste Bella.

Ele pareceu confuso.

— Preferes Isabella?

— Não, gosto de Bella — retorqui. — Mas julgo que o Charlie — quero dizer, o meu pai — deve chamar-me Isabella nas minhas costas — parece que é por esse nome que todas as pessoas daqui me conhecem — tentei explicar, sentindo-me como uma completa débil mental.

— Ah.

Deu o assunto por encerrado. Eu desviei o olhar com algum constrangimento.

Felizmente, o professor Banner deu início à aula nesse momento. Tentei concentrar-me enquanto ele explicava o trabalho laboratorial do dia. Os diapositivos que se encontravam na caixa estavam desordenados. Trabalhando como parceiros de laboratório, tínhamos de separar os diapositivos referentes às células da extremidade da raiz da cebola consoante as fases de mitose que representavam e classificá-los em conformidade com estes aspectos. Não podíamos consultar os livros. Vinte minutos depois, ele faz uma ronda pelas bancadas para ver quem acertara.

— Comecem — ordenou.

— Primeiro, as senhoras, parceira? — perguntou Edward.

Eu levantei o olhar e vi-o a esboçar um sorriso constrangido tão belo que eu conseguia apenas fitá-lo como uma idiota.

— Ou, se desejares, posso ser eu a começar.

O sorriso esbateu-se; ele começava evidentemente a perguntar-se se eu seria mentalmente apta.

— Não — disse eu, ruborizando. — Eu começo.

Estava a exibir-me, apenas um pouco. Já realizara este trabalho laboratorial e sabia o que procurar. A tarefa adivinhava-se fácil. Coloquei o primeiro diapositivo sob o microscópio e regulei este rapidamente para a objectiva de 40X. Examinei o diapositivo durante breves instantes.

A minha avaliação era segura.

— Prófase.

— Importas-te que dê uma olhadela? — perguntou ele quando

eu começava a retirar o diapositivo. A mão dele segurou a minha, para me deter, enquanto fazia a pergunta. Os seus dedos estavam gelados, como se, antes da aula, os tivesse colocado numa acumulação de neve. Não foi, porém, por este motivo que retirei a minha mão tão bruscamente. Quando ele me tocou, senti uma dor pungente na mão, como se um fluxo de corrente eléctrica nos tivesse atravessado.

— Desculpa — sussurrou ele por entre dentes, retirando imediatamente a mão.

No entanto, continuou a tentar alcançar o microscópio. Observei-o, ainda desconcertada, enquanto ele examinava o diapositivo, o que fez num instante ainda mais breve do que eu fizera.

— Prófase — concordou ele, registando a designação com uma caligrafia impecável no primeiro espaço da nossa ficha de trabalho. Substituiu agilmente o primeiro diapositivo pelo segundo e, em seguida, olhou-o rapidamente.

— Anáfase — murmurou, anotando a denominação ao pronunciá-la.

Mantive um tom de indiferença na minha voz.

— Posso?

Ele esboçou um sorriso afectado e aproximou o microscópio de mim.

Olhei através da ocular de modo ansioso, apenas para sofrer uma desilusão. Raios! Ele tinha razão.

— Passamos ao terceiro diapositivo?

Estendi a mão sem lhe dirigir o olhar. Entregou-mo; parecia estar a ser cauteloso de modo a não voltar a tocar a minha pele.

Olhei para o diapositivo da forma mais fugaz que consegui.

— Intérfase.

Passei-lhe o microscópio antes de ele ter tido tempo para o pedir. Deu uma rápida espreitadela e, em seguida, apontou a designação. Eu tê-lo-ia feito enquanto ele olhava para o diapositivo, mas a sua caligrafia clara e elegante intimidava-me. Não queria conspurcar a página com as minhas toscas garatujas.

Terminámos antes de o resto da turma estar perto de o fazer. Conseguia ver Mike e o seu parceiro a comparem dois diapositivos uma e outra vez e um outro grupo tinha o livro aberto debaixo da bancada.

Assim, fiquei sem nada para fazer, a não ser tentar não olhar para ele... sem sucesso. Olhei para cima e ele fitava-me, com aquele mesmo ar de frustração inexplicável reflectido nos olhos. Subitamente, identifiquei aquela diferença subtil no seu rosto.

— Puseste lentes de contacto? — disse de forma abrupta e impensada.

Ele pareceu ficar perplexo com a minha pergunta inesperada.

— Não.

— Oh — balbuciei. — Pensei que havia algo diferente nos teus olhos.

Ele encolheu os ombros e desviou o olhar.

Na verdade, eu tinha a certeza de que havia algo diferente. Lembrava-me nitidamente da uniforme cor negra dos seus olhos da última vez que ele me lançara um olhar hostil — a cor destacava-se ao contrastar com o fundo da sua pele pálida e do cabelo castanho-avermelhado. Neste dia, os olhos dele tinham uma cor completamente diferente: um estranho ocre, mais escuro do que caramelo de manteiga, mas com o mesmo tom dourado. Não compreendi como tal poderia ser possível, a não ser que, por algum motivo, ele estivesse a mentir a respeito das lentes de contacto ou talvez Forks estivesse a enlouquecer-me na verdadeira acepção da palavra.

Baixei o olhar. As suas mãos estavam novamente fechadas, com os punhos cerrados.

O professor Banner veio, então, até à nossa bancada para ver por que motivo não estávamos a trabalhar. Olhou por cima dos nossos ombros para ver o trabalho laboratorial concluído e, em seguida, examinou-o com maior atenção para conferir as respostas.

— Então, Edward, não achaste que deveria ser dada à Isabella a oportunidade de utilizar o microscópio? – perguntou o professor Banner.

– À Bella – corrigiu Edward automaticamente. – Na verdade, ela identificou três das cinco fases representadas nos diapositivos.

O professor Banner olhava agora para mim, com uma expressão de cepticismo estampada no rosto.

– Já realizaste este trabalho laboratorial? – perguntou ele.

Eu sorri acanhadamente.

– Com raiz de cebola, não.

– Com blástula de coregono?

– Sim.

O professor Banner acenou com a cabeça.

– Em Phoenix, estavas integrada num programa de colocação avançada?

– Estava.

– Bem – exclamou ele após alguns instantes. – Suponho que o facto de vocês os dois serem parceiros de laboratório seja proveitoso.

Balbuciou algo mais ao afastar-se. Depois de se ter ido embora, comecei novamente a rabiscar no meu caderno de apontamentos.

– Foi pena aquilo da neve, não foi? – perguntou Edward.

Tinha a sensação de que ele estava a obrigar-se a estabelecer um diálogo de ocasião comigo. A paranóia invadia-me novamente. Era como se ele tivesse escutado a minha conversa com Jessica ao almoço e estivesse a tentar provar que eu estava errada.

– Nem por isso – respondi de forma sincera, em vez de fingir ser normal como todas as restantes pessoas. Estava ainda a tentar afastar a estúpida sensação de suspeição e não conseguia concentrar-me.

– O frio não te agrada. – Não era uma pergunta.

– Nem o tempo chuvoso.

– Deve ser difícil para ti viver em Forks – devaneou.

– Nem fazes ideia – murmurei por entre dentes de modo enigmático.

Por algum motivo que eu não conseguia imaginar, ele parecia

fascinado com aquilo que eu dizia. O seu rosto constituía uma tal fonte de distracção que eu tentava não olhá-lo mais do que aquilo que a cortesia permitia.

— Então, porque vieste para cá?

Ninguém me colocara tal questão — não tão directamente como ele fizera, exigindo tal informação.

— É... complicado.

— Acho que consigo acompanhar-te — pressionou.

Após um longo momento de silêncio, cometi o erro de o fitar directamente nos olhos. Os seus olhos dourado-escuros baralharam-me e respondi sem pensar.

— A minha mãe casou pela segunda vez — declarei.

— Não parece ser algo assim tão complexo — discordou ele. No entanto, subitamente, mostrou-se solidário. — Quando é que isso aconteceu?

— No passado mês de Setembro.

A minha voz parecia triste, mesmo aos meus próprios ouvidos.

— E tu não gostas dele — conjecturou Edward, ainda com um tom de voz gentil.

— Não, o Phil é uma boa pessoa. Talvez um pouco jovem de mais, mas é bastante simpático.

— Porque não ficaste com eles?

Não conseguia determinar o motivo do seu interesse, mas ele continuava a fitar-me com um olhar penetrante, como se a entediante história da minha vida tivesse, de algum modo, uma importância vital.

— O Phil viaja muito. Ganha a vida a jogar à bola.

Esbocei um sorriso irónico.

— Já ouvi falar dele? — perguntou, retribuindo o sorriso.

— Provavelmente não. Ele não joga bem. Joga na segunda liga e desloca-se muito.

— E a tua mãe mandou-te para cá de modo a poder viajar com ele — disse como se se tratasse novamente de uma suposição e não de uma pergunta.

O meu queixo elevou-se um pouco.

— Não, ela não me mandou para aqui. Vim por vontade própria.

O seu sobrolho ficou carregado.

— Não compreendo — confessou, parecendo desnecessariamente frustrado com este facto.

Suspirei. Porque é que estava a explicar-lhe esta situação? Ele continuava a olhar-me fixamente com uma curiosidade evidente.

— A princípio, ficava comigo, mas sentia saudades dele. A separação fazia-a infeliz... logo, decidi que estava na altura de passar algum tempo útil com o Charlie.

Quando acabei de falar, a minha voz estava soturna.

— Agora, porém, és tu quem está infeliz — referiu ele.

— E daí? — desafiei-o.

— Não parece ser justo.

Encolheu os ombros, mas o olhar continuava a ser intenso. Ri sem vontade.

— Nunca ninguém te disse «A vida não é justa.»?

— Creio *já ter ouvido* isso algures — assentiu secamente.

— Então, é tudo — insisti, perguntando-me por que motivo é que ele continuava a fitar-me daquela maneira.

O seu olhar fixo tornou-se analítico.

— Disfarças bem — disse ele lentamente. — Mas estaria disposto a apostar que estás a sofrer mais do que demonstras a todos.

Fiz-lhe um esgar, resistindo ao impulso de mostrar a língua como uma criança de cinco anos, e desviei o olhar.

— Estou enganado?

Tentei ignorá-lo.

— Bem me pareceu que não — murmurou presunçosamente.

— Porque é que isso te interessa? — perguntei, irritada.

Mantive os olhos afastados, observando o professor enquanto este fazia as suas rondas.

— Essa é uma excelente pergunta — sussurrou por entre dentes, num tom de voz tão abafado que me interroguei se ele não estaria a falar consigo mesmo. No entanto, após alguns instantes de silêncio, concluí que esta seria a única resposta que eu iria obter.

Suspirei, olhando com o sobrolho carregado para o quadro.

— Estou a aborrecer-te? — perguntou ele com um ar divertido.

Olhei-o de relance sem pensar... e voltei a dizer a verdade.

— Não propriamente. Estou mais aborrecida comigo mesma. Sou tão transparente... a minha mãe chama-me sempre o seu livro aberto — respondi franzindo o sobrolho.

— Pelo contrário; considero-te muito opaca.

Apesar de tudo o que eu dissera e ele supusera, parecia estar a falar a sério.

— Então, deves ser um bom avaliador de carácter — retorqui.

— Normalmente.

Esboçou um sorriso rasgado, exibindo uma dentadura perfeita e extremamente branca.

O professor Banner restabeleceu, então, a ordem na sala e eu virei-me para prestar atenção. Não queria acreditar que acabara de expor a minha vida monótona àquele bizarro e lindo rapaz que devia, ou não, desprezar-me. Parecia absorto na nossa conversa, mas, agora, eu conseguia ver, pelo canto do olho, que ele estava novamente a afastar-se de mim, com as mãos a segurarem na borda da mesa com inequívoca tensão.

Tentei parecer atenta enquanto o professor Banner ilustrava, com acetatos no retroprojector, aquilo que eu observara, sem dificuldade, através do microscópio. Os meus pensamentos, porém, estavam ingovernáveis.

Quando o toque da campainha finalmente soou, Edward apressou-se a sair da sala de forma tão ágil e graciosa como fizera na segunda-feira anterior e, tal como nesse mesmo dia, fixei, com assombro, o olhar na direcção em que ele seguira.

Mike avançou rapidamente para junto de mim e pegou nos meus livros. Imaginei-o com uma cauda a agitar-se.

— Foi horrível — lamentou-se. — Todas pareciam exactamente iguais. Tiveste sorte em ter o Cullen como parceiro.

— Não tive quaisquer dificuldades em identificá-las — afirmei, ofendida com a sua pressuposição, arrependendo-me imediatamente da reprimenda. — Mas também já fiz este trabalho laboratorial – acrescentei antes que ele considerasse que eu acabara de ferir os seus sentimentos.

– Hoje, o Cullen parecia estar bastante simpático – comentou ele enquanto vestíamos as nossas gabardinas.

Não pareceu satisfeito com aquele facto.

Tentei mostrar-me indiferente.

– Pergunto-me o que teria ele na passada segunda-feira.

Não conseguia concentrar-me na conversa de Mike enquanto caminhávamos para o ginásio e a aula de Educação Física também não cativava muito a minha atenção. Hoje Mike fazia parte da minha equipa. De forma cavalheiresca, ocupou a minha posição e também a dele, pelo que a minha abstracção era apenas interrompida quando chegava a minha vez de servir; a minha equipa desviava-se prudentemente sempre que tal acontecia.

Quando me dirigi ao parque de estacionamento, a chuva não passava de neblina, mas senti-me mais confortável quando entrei na cabina seca da *pick-up*. Liguei o aquecimento, não me importando, pela primeira vez, com o embrutecedor ronco do motor. Abri o fecho do casaco, tirei o capuz e soltei o cabelo húmido para que, com o calor, secasse no trajecto para casa.

Olhei ao redor para me assegurar de que o caminho estava desimpedido. Foi então que reparei na figura branca e imóvel. Edward Cullen estava encostado à porta dianteira do Volvo, a três carros de distância de mim, e a olhar atentamente na minha direcção. Desviei rapidamente o olhar e procedi a uma manobra de marcha-atrás com a *pick-up*, quase embatendo num Toyota Corolla ferrugento, com a minha pressa. Para sorte deste, travei a tempo. Tratava-se precisamente do género de carro do qual a minha *pick-up* faria sucata. Respirei profundamente, ainda olhando para o lado oposto do meu carro, e voltei a recuar cautelosamente, com maior êxito. Olhei fixamente em frente ao passar pelo Volvo, mas, através de um vislumbre periférico, podia jurar que o vira rir-se.

Capítulo Três

FENÓMENO

Quando abri os olhos, de manhã, algo estava diferente.

Era a claridade. Caracterizava-se ainda pela tonalidade verde-acinzentada de um dia nublado na floresta, mas, de alguma forma, estava mais luminosa. Apercebi-me de que não havia nevoeiro a velar a minha janela.

Levantei-me de um salto para olhar para o exterior e, então, soltei um gemido de horror.

Uma fina camada de neve cobria o jardim, empoava o tejadilho da minha *pick-up* e embranquecia a estrada. Porém, isto não era o pior. Toda a chuva que caíra no dia anterior gelara e solidificara — revestindo as agulhas das árvores de configurações deslumbrantes e fantásticas e fazendo da estrada uma mortífera superfície gelada. Já tinha bastante dificuldade em manter-me de pé quando o piso estava seco; talvez fosse mais seguro para mim voltar agora para a cama.

Charlie já saíra para o trabalho antes de eu descer. Sob muitos aspectos, o facto de viver com Charlie equivalia a ter a minha própria casa e dei por mim a deliciar-me com a solidão, em vez de me sentir só.

Tomei apressadamente uma taça de cereais e um pouco de sumo de laranja directamente do pacote. Sentia-me animada por ir para a escola e isso assustava-me. Sabia que não era pelo estimulante ambiente de aprendizagem que eu esperava ansiosamente, nem por ver o meu novo grupo de amigos. Se quisesse ser honesta comigo mesma, tinha consciência de que estava impaciente por chegar à escola porque iria encontrar Edward Cullen, o que era uma grande, grande idiotice.

Devia tentar evitá-lo por completo depois da minha insensata e embaraçosa verborreia do dia anterior. Além disso, tinha as minhas desconfianças em relação a ele; porque haveria de mentir a respeito dos seus olhos? Estava ainda assustada com a hostilidade que, por vezes, sentia emanar dele e ficava ainda sem palavras sempre que visualizava o seu rosto perfeito. Estava absolutamente ciente de que o meu mundo e o mundo dele eram pólos que não se tocavam. Logo, eu não deveria, de modo algum, estar ansiosa por vê-lo neste dia.

Foi necessária toda a minha concentração para conseguir percorrer a glacial entrada de tijolo e chegar ao fim com vida. Quase perdi o equilíbrio quando finalmente cheguei junto da *pick-up*, mas consegui segurar-me ao espelho retrovisor lateral e manter-me a salvo. Este dia seria manifestamente um pesadelo.

Ao conduzir até à escola, o meu medo de cair e as minhas indesejadas especulações acerca de Edward Cullen afastaram-se do meu espírito, ao pensar em Mike e Eric e na óbvia diferença da forma como os rapazes adolescentes reagiam à minha pessoa nesta cidade. Tinha a certeza de que a minha aparência era exactamente a mesma que tinha em Phoenix. Era natural que isso estivesse apenas relacionado com o facto de os rapazes da minha terra terem assistido à minha lenta passagem por todas as estranhas fases da adolescência e ainda fizessem esta ideia de mim. Talvez esta realidade se devesse ao facto de eu ser uma novidade nesta cidade, onde as novidades eram poucas e surgiam muito de longe a longe. Possivelmente, a minha incapacitante falta de jeito era encarada como sendo enternecedora em vez de patética, projectando de mim a imagem de uma donzela em apuros. Qualquer que fosse a razão, o comportamento típico de um cachorrinho que Mike assumia e a aparente rivalidade que existia entre ele e Eric eram desconcertantes. Não sabia ao certo se não preferia ser ignorada.

O desempenho da minha *pick-up* não parecia ser, de modo algum, dificultado pelo gelo negro que cobria as estradas. Apesar disso, eu conduzia muito lentamente, não querendo deixar um rasto de destruição na Rua Direita.

Quando saí da minha *pick-up*, na escola, vi por que motivo tivera tão escassas dificuldades. Algo prateado chamou a minha atenção e dirigi-me à parte traseira da *pick-up* — segurando--me cuidadosamente ao flanco para me apoiar — para examinar os pneus. Havia finas correntes entrecruzadas em forma de diamante em torno deles. Charlie levantara-se sabe Deus quão cedo para colocar correntes de neve na minha *pick-up*. Senti subitamente a garganta apertada. Não estava habituada a que cuidassem de mim e a tácita preocupação de Charlie apanhou--me de surpresa.

Encontrava-me junto do canto traseiro da *pick-up*, esforçando-do-me por conter a súbita onda de emoção que as correntes de neve geraram, quando ouvi um ruído estranho.

Tratava-se de um guincho estridente e estava depressa a tornar-se dolorosamente sonoro. Ergui o olhar, sobressaltada.

Vi várias coisas em simultaneo. Nada se movia em câmara lenta, como acontece nos filmes. Em vez disso, o afluxo de adrenalina parecia fazer com que a actividade do meu cérebro acelerasse significativamente e eu fui capaz de assimilar, com grande pormenor, várias coisas ao mesmo tempo.

Edward Cullen encontrava-se a quatro automóveis de distância de mim, olhando-me fixamente com um ar horrorizado. O seu rosto sobressaía num mar de rostos, estando todos paralisados com a mesma máscara de choque. No entanto, o factor de importância mais imediata era a carrinha azul-escura que derrapava, com os pneus bloqueados e a chiarem sob o efeito dos travões, fazendo piões fora de controlo no gelo do parque de estacionamento. Ia embater na traseira da minha *pick-up* e eu estava de permeio. Não tive sequer tempo para fechar os olhos.

Precisamente antes de ouvir o esmagador estrépito da carrinha a embater contra a plataforma da *pick-up*, moldando-se a ela, algo me atingiu, com violência, mas não vindo da direcção que eu esperava. A minha cabeça bateu no alcatrão gelado e senti algo sólido e frio a prender-me ao chão. Estava estendida no passeio por trás do automóvel castanho-amarelado ao lado do qual eu estacionara, mas não tive oportunidade de reparar em mais nada, pois a carrinha continuava a avançar na minha direcção. Enfaixara-se com um ruído irritante na traseira da *pick-up* e, ainda rodopiando e patinando, estava prestes a colidir novamente comigo.

Uma imprecação proferida em voz baixa fez-me perceber que estava alguém comigo e era impossível não reconhecer aquela voz. Duas mãos longas e brancas precipitaram-se de forma protectora à minha frente e a carrinha estremeceu até parar a trinta centímetros da minha cara, com as grandes mãos a encaixarem-se providencialmente numa mossa profunda da parte lateral da carroçaria da carrinha.

Então, as mãos dele moveram-se tão rapidamente que se desfocaram. Uma estava subitamente a agarrar a parte inferior da carroçaria da carrinha e algo me arrastava, sacudindo as minhas pernas como se das de uma boneca de trapos se tratasse, até que estas bateram no pneu do carro castanho-amarelado. Um áspero baque metálico feriu-me os tímpanos e a carrinha ficou imobilizada, com vidro a saltar sobre o asfalto — exactamente onde, há um instante, estavam as minhas pernas.

Durante um longo momento, fez-se um absoluto silêncio, até que os gritos começaram. Na abrupta confusão, conseguia ouvir mais do que uma pessoa a gritar o meu nome, mas, mais distintamente do que todos os clamores, conseguia escutar a voz grave e frenética de Edward Cullen ao meu ouvido.

— Bella? Estás bem?

— Estou óptima.

A minha voz soava-me estranha. Tentei sentar-me e apercebi-me de que ele me apertava contra a parte lateral do seu corpo com uma força férrea.

— Tem cuidado — advertiu-me enquanto eu me debatia. — Acho que bateste com a cabeça com bastante violência.

Apercebi-me de uma dor latejante localizada acima da orelha esquerda.

— Au! — exclamei, surpreendida.

— Bem me parecia.

Espantosamente, a sua voz parecia dar a entender que ele estava a conter o riso.

— Que diabos... — As minhas palavras perderam intensidade, tentando aclarar as minhas ideias, recompor-me. — Como é que chegaste aqui tão depressa?

— Estava mesmo a teu lado, Bella — disse ele, novamente com um tom de voz sério.

Virei-me para me sentar e, desta vez, ele deixou-me fazê-lo, retirando o braço que me envolvia pela cintura e afastando-se de mim tanto quanto podia no espaço exíguo. Olhei para a sua expressão preocupada, inocente, e fiquei mais uma vez desorientada com a intensidade dos seus olhos de cor dourada. O que é que eu estava a perguntar-lhe?

Então, uma concentração de pessoas com lágrimas a escorrerem-lhes pelos rostos acorreu, gritando umas com as outras, gritando connosco.

— Não se mexam! — recomendou alguém.

— Tirem o Tyler da carrinha! — bradou outra pessoa. Houve grande movimentação ao nosso redor. Tentei levantar-me, mas a mão fria de Edward empurrou-me para baixo pelo ombro.

— Fica quieta por agora.

— Mas está frio — queixei-me.

Fiquei admirada quando ele soltou um riso abafado. Havia uma certa veemência no som.

— Tu estavas além — lembrei-me de repente, tendo o seu riso cessado bruscamente. — Estavas junto do teu carro.

A expressão do seu rosto tornou-se dura.

— Não, não estava.

— Eu vi-te.

Em tudo aquilo que nos rodeava, imperava o caos. Conseguia ouvir as vozes mais rudes de adultos que chegavam ao local, mas eu persistia obstinadamente na nossa discussão; tinha razão e ele haveria de o reconhecer.

— Bella, eu estava contigo e puxei-te para te afastar da trajectória da carrinha.

Fitou-me com todo o avassalador poder dos seus olhos, como se tentasse transmitir algo crucial.

— Não.

Cerrei os maxilares. O tom dourado dos seus olhos resplandeceu.

— Por favor, Bella.

— Porquê? — interroguei.

— Confia em mim — suplicou, com a sua irresistível voz suave.

Já conseguia ouvir as sirenes.

— Prometes explicar-me tudo mais tarde?

— Tudo bem — disse de modo incisivo, bruscamente exasperado.

— Tudo bem — repeti agastada.

Foram necessários seis técnicos de emergência médica e dois professores — o professor Banner e o treinador Clapp — para afastar suficientemente a carrinha de nós, de modo a abrir caminho para as macas. Edward recusou com veemência a sua e eu tentei fazer o mesmo, mas o traidor disse-lhes que eu batera com a cabeça e, provavelmente, sofrera uma contusão. Quase morri de humilhação quando me colocaram o colar cervical. Parecia que toda a escola estava presente, assistindo circunspecta enquanto me colocavam na parte de trás da ambulância. Edward sentou-se à frente. Era exasperante.

Para piorar ainda mais a situação, o chefe Swan chegou antes que pudessem ter-me levado em segurança.

— Bella! — gritou em pânico ao aperceber-se de que era eu que me encontrava estendida na maca.

— Está absolutamente tudo bem comigo, Char... pai — disse, suspirando. — Não há nada de errado comigo.

Virou-se para o técnico de emergência médica mais próximo para pedir uma segunda opinião. Deixei de lhe prestar atenção para reflectir sobre a miscelânea de imagens inexplicáveis que se encadeavam caoticamente na minha cabeça. Quando me levantaram, afastando-me do automóvel, vi a mossa profunda do pára-choques do carro castanho-amarelado — uma mossa extremamente distinta cuja forma coincidia com os contornos dos ombros de Edward... como se ele tivesse fincado o corpo no carro com força suficiente para causar danos na estrutura de metal...

Além disso, ali encontrava-se também a sua família, observando à distância, com expressões que variavam entre reprovação e fúria, mas não evidenciavam qualquer laivo de preocupação relativamente à segurança do seu irmão.

Tentei pensar numa explicação lógica que justificasse aquilo que eu acabara de ver — uma explicação que excluísse a hipótese de eu estar demente.

Naturalmente, a ambulância foi escoltada pela polícia até ao hospital distrital. Senti-me ridícula durante todo o tempo que demoraram a retirar-me da mesma. O que piorou a situação foi o facto de Edward ter passado com naturalidade pelas portas do hospital. Cerrei os dentes.

Levaram-me para o serviço de urgência, uma longa sala com uma sucessão de camas separadas por cortinas com motivos em tons pastel. Uma enfermeira colocou-me um medidor de tensão arterial no braço e um termómetro debaixo da língua. Como ninguém se dava ao trabalho de puxar a cortina para me conceder alguma privacidade, decidi que já não era obrigada a usar o colar cervical, que me fazia parecer uma idiota. Quando a enfermeira se afastou, apressei-me a desapertar o velcro e a atirar aquele para debaixo da cama.

Deu-se um novo afluxo de pessoal hospitalar e uma outra maca foi trazida para junto da cama ao meu lado. Reconheci Tyler Crowley, que fazia parte da minha turma da disciplina de Administração Pública, sob as ligaduras manchadas de sangue que lhe envolviam e apertavam a cabeça. Tyler aparentava estar cem vezes pior do que eu, mas fitava-me com um ar ansioso.

— Bella, lamento imenso!

— Eu estou óptima, Tyler. E tu estás com péssimo aspecto. Estás bem?

Enquanto falávamos, as enfermeiras começaram a desenrolar as suas ligaduras manchadas, expondo miríades de cortes superficiais em toda a sua testa e face esquerda.

Ele ignorou-me.

— Pensei que ia matar-te! Estava a conduzir com demasiada velocidade e não adequei a marcha ao piso gelado...

Estremeceu quando uma enfermeira começou a limpar-lhe o rosto.

— Não te preocupes com isso; não me acertaste.

— Como é que te afastaste tão depressa? Estavas ali e, de repente, já tinhas desaparecido...

— Hum... O Edward puxou-me e afastou-me da trajectória da carrinha.

Pareceu confuso.

— Quem?

— O Edward Cullen estava junto a mim.

Nunca soubera mentir; as minhas palavras não pareceram, de todo, convincentes.

— O Cullen? Não o vi... ena, suponho que tudo aconteceu muito rapidamente. Ele está bem?

— Julgo que sim. Está algures por aqui, mas não o obrigaram a deitar-se numa maca.

Eu sabia que não estava louca. O que sucedera? Não havia forma satisfatória de explicar aquilo que eu vira.

Transportaram-me, então, para outro local, a fim de submeter a minha cabeça a um exame radiográfico. Disse-lhes que não havia nada de errado e tinha razão. Nem sequer uma contusão. Perguntei se podia ir-me embora, mas a enfermeira afirmou que eu tinha de consultar primeiro um médico. Estava, então, presa no serviço de urgência, aguardando, incomodada pelos constantes pedidos de desculpa e promessas no sentido de ser compensada por parte de Tyler. Por mais que eu tentasse convencê-lo de que eu estava óptima, ele insistia em martirizar-se. Acabei por fechar os olhos e ignorá-lo. Ele continuou a resmonear, cheio de remorsos.

— Ela está a dormir? — perguntou uma voz melodiosa.

Os meus olhos abriram-se imediatamente.

Edward encontrava-se aos pés da minha cama, sorrindo afectadamente. Olhei-o irritada. Não foi fácil — teria sido mais espontâneo fitá-lo ternamente.

— Ei, Edward, lamento profundamente — principiou Tyler.

Edward ergueu a mão para detê-lo.

— Não havendo sangue, não há problema — declarou ele, exibindo os seus dentes brilhantes. Deslocou-se até à cama de Tyler, à beira da qual se sentou, de frente para mim. Voltou a esboçar um sorriso afectado.

— Então, qual é o veredicto? — perguntou-me.

— Não há absolutamente nada de errado comigo, mas não me deixam ir embora — lamentei-me. — Porque é que não estás amarrado a uma maca como nós?

— Tudo depende dos nossos conhecimentos — respondeu ele. — Mas não te preocupes, vim libertar-te.

Em seguida, um médico contornou a esquina e eu fiquei boquiaberta. Era jovem, louro... e mais bonito do que qualquer estrela de cinema que eu alguma vez vira. Estava, porém, pálido, com um ar cansado e olheiras vincadas. De acordo com a descrição traçada pelo meu pai, só podia tratar-se do pai de Edward.

— Então, menina Swan — disse o Dr. Cullen com uma voz extraordinariamente cativante —, como se sente?

— Estou óptima — afirmei, esperando tê-lo feito pela última vez.

Dirigiu-se ao negatoscópio que se encontrava na parede por cima da minha cabeça e ligou-o.

— As suas radiografias parecem estar bem — disse ele. — Dói-lhe a cabeça? O Edward comentou que bateu com a cabeça com bastante violência.

— A minha cabeça está óptima — repeti com um suspiro, lançando um rápido olhar mal-humorado na direcção de Edward.

Os seus dedos frios perscrutaram levemente o meu crânio. Reparou no meu estremecimento.

— Está dorido? — perguntou.

— Nem por isso. — Já sentira dores mais profundas.

Ouvi um riso abafado e ao olhar, deparei com o sorriso condescendente de Edward. Semicerrei os olhos.

— Bem, o seu pai está na sala de espera; já pode ir com ele para casa, mas volte cá se sentir tonturas ou se tiver qualquer problema de visão.

— Não posso voltar para a escola? — perguntei, imaginando Charlie a tentar ser atencioso.

— Talvez devesse repousar por hoje.

Olhei de relance para Edward.

— E *ele*, pode ir para a escola?

— Alguém tem de espalhar a boa notícia de que nós sobrevivemos — afirmou Edward com comprazimento.

— Na verdade — corrigiu o Dr. Cullen — a maior parte da escola parece estar na sala de espera.

— Oh, não — lastimei-me, tapando o rosto com as mãos.

O Dr. Cullen franziu o sobrolho.

— Quer ficar?

— Não, não! — exclamei com insistência, colocando as pernas fora da cama e levantando-me rapidamente. Demasiado rapidamente — titubeei e o Dr. Cullen amparou-me. Parecia preocupado.

— Estou óptima — assegurei-lhe novamente.

Não havia necessidade de lhe dizer que os meus problemas de equilíbrio nada tinham a ver com a pancada que eu sofrera na cabeça.

— Tome Tylenol para as dores — sugeriu ao devolver-me o equilíbrio.

— Não dói assim tanto — insisti.

— Parece que teve imensa sorte — afirmou o Dr. Cullen, sorrindo, enquanto eu assinava a minha ficha com um floreado caligráfico.

— Tive a sorte de o Edward se encontrar junto de mim — rectifiquei, lançando um olhar firme ao alvo da minha afirmação.

— Oh, bem, sim — concordou o Dr. Cullen, subitamente ocupado com os documentos que tinha diante de si.

Em seguida, desviou o olhar, pousando-o em Tyler, e dirigiu-se à cama ao lado. A minha intuição vacilou; o médico estava ao corrente dos factos.

— Receio que o Tyler tenha de nos fazer companhia apenas durante mais algum tempo — disse-lhe ele, começando a examinar-lhe os golpes.

Assim que o médico virou costas, aproximei-me de Edward.

— Posso falar contigo por um instante? — interroguei baixinho, manifestando desagrado.

Ele recuou um passo, afastando-se de mim, com os maxilares subitamente cerrados.

— O teu pai está à tua espera — disse ele por entre dentes.

Olhei de relance para o Dr. Cullen e para Tyler.

— Gostava de falar contigo a sós, se não te importares — insisti.

Lançou-me um olhar cruel e, em seguida, voltou-me as costas e atravessou a longa sala com grandes passadas. Quase tive de correr para conseguir acompanhá-lo. Assim que contornámos a esquina, entrando num pequeno corredor, ele deu meia volta para ficar de frente para mim.

— O que queres? — perguntou ele, com um olhar frio e parecendo aborrecido.

A sua atitude hostil intimidou-me. As minhas palavras saíram menos severas do que eu pretendia.

— Deves-me uma explicação — relembrei-lhe.

— Salvei-te a vida, não te devo nada.

Recuei de forma titubeante perante o ressaibo patente na sua voz.

— Tu prometeste.

— Bella, bateste com a cabeça, não sabes o que estás a dizer.

O seu tom de voz era incisivo. Agora, o meu génio inflamava-se e eu olhava-o com um ar de desafio.

— Não há nada de errado com a minha cabeça.

Ele retribuiu o olhar.

— O que queres de mim, Bella?

— Quero saber a verdade — declarei. — Quero saber por que motivo estou a mentir por tua causa.

— O que *julgas* que aconteceu? — perguntou com brusquidão. Tais palavras foram proferidas num ímpeto.

— Sei apenas que não estavas próximo de mim; o Tyler também não te viu, portanto, não me venhas dizer que bati com a cabeça com demasiada violência. Aquela carrinha ia esmagar-nos a ambos, tal não se verificou e as tuas mãos deixaram mossas na parte lateral da viatura. Deixaste ainda uma mossa no outro carro e não tens qualquer ferimento. A carrinha ter-me-ia esmagado as pernas, mas tu estavas a erguê-la no ar...

Apercebi-me de quão disparatado parecia tudo isto e não consegui prosseguir. Estava tão enfurecida que sentia as lágrimas virem-me aos olhos; tentei reprimi-las rangendo os dentes.

Ele fitava-me incredulamente, mas o seu rosto estava tenso, defensivo.

— Pensas que levantei uma carrinha de cima de ti?

O seu tom de voz punha em causa a minha sanidade e contribuiu apenas para aumentar ainda mais a minha desconfiança. Parecia uma deixa perfeita proferida por um actor experiente.

Limitei-me a acenar uma vez com a cabeça, com os maxilares cerrados.

— Ninguém vai acreditar nisso, sabes?

A sua voz tinha agora uma ponta de troça.

— Eu não vou contar a ninguém.

Pronunciei cada palavra devagar, controlando cuidadosamente a minha raiva.

A surpresa atravessou-lhe o rosto.

— Então, que importância é que isso tem?

— Para mim, tem — insisti. — Não gosto de mentir; logo, é bom que haja um excelente motivo para estar a fazê-lo.

— Não podes apenas agradecer-me e superar isso?

— Obrigada.

Eu esperava, encolerizada e expectante.

— Não vais esquecê-lo, pois não?

— Não.

— Nesse caso... espero que gostes de sofrer desilusões.

Olhámo-nos mutuamente com um ar colérico, em silêncio. Fui a primeira a falar, tentando manter-me concentrada. Corria o risco de ser distraída pelo seu rosto lívido e sublime. Era como tentar vergar um anjo destruidor com um olhar.

— Porque te deste sequer àquele trabalho? — perguntei friamente.

Ele deteve-se e, por um breve momento, o seu rosto de uma beleza estonteante tornou-se inesperadamente vulnerável.

— Não sei — sussurrou.

Em seguida, virou-me as costas e afastou-se.

Eu estava tão zangada que só após alguns minutos consegui mexer-me. Quando consegui começar a andar, encaminhei-me vagarosamente para a saída, ao fundo do corredor.

O confronto com a sala de espera foi mais desagradável do que eu temera. Parecia que todas as caras que eu conhecia em Forks estavam ali, olhando-me fixamente. Charlie precipitou-se para junto de mim; eu levantei as mãos.

— Não há nada de errado comigo — assegurei-lhe taciturnamente. Estava ainda irritada, sem disposição para conversas.

— O que disse o médico?

— O Dr. Cullen observou-me e disse que eu estava óptima e podia ir para casa — declarei, suspirando.

Tanto Mike como Jessica e Eric estavam presentes, começando a convergir na nossa direcção.

— Vamos embora — exortei.

Charlie envolveu-me as costas com um braço, não me tocando inteiramente, e conduziu-me às portas de vidro da saída. Acenei timidamente aos meus amigos, esperando transmitir a ideia de que já não precisavam de se preocupar comigo. Foi um enorme alívio — a primeira vez que me senti assim — entrar no carro de rádio-patrulha.

Seguimos em silêncio. Estava tão absorta nos meus pensamentos que mal notava a presença de Charlie. Tinha a certeza de que o comportamento defensivo de Edward no corredor era a confirmação das bizarras ocorrências que ainda mal acreditava ter presenciado.

Quando entrámos em casa, Charlie falou finalmente.

— Hum... tens de telefonar à Renée.

Baixou a cabeça, invadido por um sentimento de culpa.

Fiquei aterrada.

— Contaste à mãe!

— Desculpa.

Ao sair bati com a porta do carro do meu pai com um pouco mais de violência do que a necessária.

A minha mãe estava histérica, como é evidente. Tive de lhe dizer que me sentia optimamente no mínimo trinta vezes até que se acalmasse. Implorou-me que regressasse a casa — esquecendo o facto de que esta, naquele momento, se encontrava vazia —, mas foi mais fácil resistir às suas súplicas do que eu teria pensado. Estava consumida pelo mistério que Edward representava e mais do que um pouco obcecada pelo próprio Edward. Parva, parva, parva. Não estava ansiosa por fugir de Forks como deveria estar, como qualquer pessoa normal e sã de espírito estaria.

Decidi que mais valia deitar-me cedo nessa noite. Charlie continuava a vigiar-me cheio de cuidados e este facto começava a enervar-me. Ao dirigir-me para o quarto, fiz uma paragem na casa de banho para ir buscar três comprimidos Tylenol. Surtiram, de facto, efeito e, à medida que a dor se atenuava, eu adormecia.

Essa foi a primeira noite em que sonhei com Edward Cullen.

Capítulo Quatro

Convites

No meu sonho, estava muito escuro e a luz esbatida que existia parecia irradiar da pele de Edward. Eu não conseguia ver-lhe o rosto, mas apenas as costas, à medida que se afastava de mim, deixando-me no negrume. Por mais depressa que corresse, não conseguia alcançá-lo; por mais alto que o chamasse, ele nunca se virava. Agitada, acordei a meio da noite e não consegui voltar a adormecer durante aquilo que me pareceu um longo lapso de tempo. Depois disso, ele esteve presente nos meus sonhos praticamente todas as noites, mas sempre na periferia, nunca ao meu alcance.

O mês que se seguiu ao acidente foi intranquilo, tenso e, a princípio, embaraçoso.

Para minha consternação, dei por mim a ser o centro das atenções durante o resto daquela semana. Tyler Crowley estava impossível, seguindo-me para todo o lado, obcecado com a ideia de me ressarcir de alguma forma. Tentei convencê-lo de que o que eu queria, acima de tudo, era que ele esquecesse tudo aquilo — dado que não me acontecera nada de grave — mas ele manteve-se insistente. Seguia-me nos intervalos das aulas e ao almoço sentava-se à nossa mesa, que estava agora apinhada de gente. Mike e Eric mostravam-se ainda mais hostis relativamente a ele do que um em relação ao outro, e preocupou-me o facto de ter conquistado um novo admirador indesejado.

Ninguém parecia preocupado com Edward, embora eu tenha explicado repetidas vezes que fora ele o herói — como me afastara da trajectória da carrinha e quase fora também esmagado. Tentei ser convincente. Jessica, Mike, Eric e todos os restantes comentavam sempre que nem sequer o tinham visto lá até a carrinha ter sido removida.

Perguntei a mim mesma por que motivo é que ninguém o vira de pé a uma distância tão considerável antes de estar súbita e incrivelmente a salvar-me a vida. Com desgosto, apercebi-me da causa provável – mais ninguém estava tão atento a Edward como eu sempre estava. Ninguém o observava da mesma forma que eu. Que lástima!

Edward nunca esteve rodeado por multidões de curiosos espectadores ávidos do seu relato em primeira mão. Como de costume, as pessoas evitavam-no. Os Cullen e os Hale sentaram-se à mesma mesa, como sempre, não comendo, mas apenas conversando entre si. Nenhum deles, sobretudo Edward, voltou a olhar na minha direcção.

Quando se sentou a meu lado na aula, tão longe de mim quanto a bancada permitia, parecia totalmente alheio à minha presença. Só às vezes, quando os seus punhos se cerravam subitamente – com a pele esticada a ficar ainda mais branca sobre os ossos –, é que eu me interrogava se estaria tão absorto como aparentava.

Ele gostaria de não me ter afastado da trajectória da carrinha de Tyler – não havia outra conclusão a que eu pudesse chegar.

Queria muito conversar com ele e, no dia posterior ao acidente, tentei. Da última vez que estivemos juntos, à entrada do serviço de urgência, estávamos ambos imensamente furiosos. Eu estava ainda zangada com o facto de ele se recusar a confiar-me a verdade, ainda que eu estivesse a cumprir à risca a minha parte do acordo. No entanto, ele salvara a minha vida, independentemente da forma como o fizera, e, de um dia para o outro, o calor da minha raiva extinguira-se para se transformar em temerosa gratidão.

Ele já estava sentado quando cheguei à aula de Biologia, olhando em frente. Sentei-me, esperando que se voltasse na minha direcção. Não evidenciou qualquer sinal de que se apercebera da minha presença.

— Olá, Edward! — exclamei de forma amável, para lhe mostrar que iria portar-me bem.

Ele virou um pouco a cabeça na minha direcção sem cruzar o seu olhar com o meu, acenou uma vez com a cabeça e, em seguida, olhou no sentido oposto.

Este foi o último contacto que tivemos, embora ele estivesse ali, a trinta centímetros de distância, todos os dias. Por vezes, observava-o, não sendo capaz de o evitar — ainda que à distância, na cantina ou no parque de estacionamento. Via os seus olhos dourados tornarem-se perceptivelmente mais escuros a cada dia que passava. Na aula, todavia, eu não aparentava dar-lhe mais importância do que ele a mim. Estava infelicíssima. E os sonhos continuavam.

Apesar das minhas mentiras francas, o teor das minhas mensagens de correio electrónico alertou Renée para a minha depressão e ela telefonou-me algumas vezes, preocupada. Tentei convencê-la de que era apenas o tempo que me fazia sentir desanimada.

Mike, pelo menos, ficou satisfeito com a manifesta frieza que existia entre mim e o meu parceiro de laboratório. Eu via que ele estava preocupado com a possibilidade de o ousado resgate que Edward protagonizara me ter impressionado e ficou aliviado por tal parecer ter surtido o efeito contrário. Tornou-se mais confiante, sentando-se na beira da minha bancada para conversar antes da aula de Biologia ter início, ignorando Edward tanto quanto ele nos ignorava.

A neve desapareceu definitivamente depois daquele único e perigoso dia. Mike estava desiludido por não ter chegado a organizar a sua luta na neve, mas satisfeito pelo facto de a viagem à praia poder realizar-se em breve. A chuva, porém, continuava a cair copiosamente e as semanas foram passando.

Jessica informou-me acerca de um outro acontecimento que começava a surgir no horizonte — telefonou na primeira terça-feira de Março pedindo a minha permissão para convidar Mike para o baile de Primavera, que decorreria dentro de duas semanas, e para o qual eram as raparigas que escolhiam o seu par.

— Tens a certeza de que não te importas... não tencionavas convidá-lo? — insistiu ela quando lhe disse que não me importava minimamente.

— Não, Jess, eu não vou — assegurei-lhe.

A dança não era claramente um dos meus talentos.

— Vai ser extremamente divertido.

A sua tentativa no sentido de me convencer era desprovida de entusiasmo. Suspeitava que Jessica preferia a minha inexplicável fama à minha companhia propriamente dita.

— Diverte-te com o Mike — incentivei-a.

No dia seguinte, fiquei surpreendida com o facto de Jessica não se mostrar efusiva como era seu hábito nas aulas de Trigonometria e Espanhol. Permaneceu calada enquanto caminhava ao meu lado nos intervalos das aulas e eu receava perguntar-lhe o motivo. Se Mike recusara o seu convite, eu era a última pessoa a quem ela quereria contar.

Os meus medos foram reforçados durante o almoço, quando Jessica se sentou tão longe de Mike quanto possível, conversando animadamente com Eric. Mike estava invulgarmente calado.

E continuava calado ao acompanhar-me até à aula, sendo a expressão de pouco à vontade estampada no seu rosto um mau sinal. No entanto, só abordou o assunto quando eu me sentei no meu lugar e ele se empoleirou na minha carteira. Como sempre, eu estava electricamente ciente da presença de Edward, sentado ao alcance do meu toque e tão distante como se fosse um mero fruto da minha imaginação.

— Pois — disse Mike, olhando para o chão —, a Jessica convidou-me para o baile de Primavera.

— Isso é óptimo. — Fiz com que a minha voz parecesse animada e entusiástica. — Vais divertir-te imenso com a Jessica.

— Bem... — hesitou ao examinar o meu sorriso, nitidamente nada satisfeito com a minha reacção — eu disse-lhe que tinha de reflectir sobre o assunto.

— Porque farias isso?

Deixei que a reprovação marcasse o meu tom de voz, embora

tivesse ficado aliviada com o facto de ele não lhe ter dado um não rotundo como resposta.

O seu rosto estava tingido de uma tonalidade vermelho-viva ao baixar novamente o olhar. Um sentimento de pena abalou a minha determinação.

— Estava a perguntar-me se... bem, se estarias a pensar convidar-me.

Detive-me por um momento, odiando a onda de culpa que me assolava, mas vi, pelo canto do olho, a cabeça de Edward inclinar-se na minha direcção.

— Mike, acho que devias aceitar o convite dela — afirmei.

— Já convidaste alguém?

Será que Edward reparou na forma como os olhos de Mike tremularam na sua direcção?

— Não — assegurei-lhe. — Nem sequer vou ao baile.

— Porque não? — perguntou Mike.

Não queria correr os riscos de segurança que a dança representava, pelo que fiz rapidamente novos planos.

— Vou a Seattle nesse sábado — expliquei.

De qualquer modo, precisava de sair da cidade — subitamente, surgiu a altura ideal para o fazer.

— Não podes ir noutro fim-de-semana?

— Lamento, mas não — respondi. — Não deves, portanto, fazer a Jess esperar mais. É uma falta de educação.

— Sim, tens razão — resmungou ele e voltou-se, abatido, para regressar ao seu lugar.

Fechei os olhos e exerci pressão com os dedos sobre as têmporas, tentando expulsar a culpa e a compaixão da minha cabeça. O professor Banner começou a falar. Suspirei e abri os olhos.

Edward estava a fitar-me com um ar curioso, sendo agora aquele já conhecido laivo de frustração ainda mais distinto nos seus olhos negros.

Retribuí-lhe o olhar, surpreendida, esperando que ele se apressasse a desviar o seu, mas, em vez disso, continuou a fixar os seus olhos nos meus com uma intensidade inquisidora. Não se colocava sequer a questão de eu desviar o olhar. As minhas mãos começaram a tremer.

— Sr. Cullen? — chamou o professor, pretendendo a resposta a uma pergunta que eu não ouvira.

— O ciclo de Krebs — respondeu Edward, mostrando relutância ao virar-se para dirigir o olhar para o professor Banner.

Olhei para o meu livro assim que os seus olhos me libertaram, tentando situar-me. Cobarde como sempre, coloquei o meu cabelo sobre o ombro direito para ocultar o rosto. Não conseguia acreditar na torrente de emoção que pulsava no meu íntimo — apenas porque, por acaso, ele me olhara pela primeira vez em meia dúzia de semanas. Não podia permitir que exercesse tamanha influência sobre mim. Era patético. Mais do que patético: era doentio.

Esforcei-me enormemente por me alhear da sua presença durante o tempo que restava da hora de aula e, visto que tal era impossível, pelo menos por não dar a perceber que lhe dava importância. Quando a campainha finalmente tocou, virei-lhe as costas para reunir os meus pertences, esperando que ele saísse logo, como era habitual.

— Bella?

Eu não deveria estar tão familiarizada com a sua voz, como se tivesse conhecido o seu som durante toda a minha vida e não apenas durante umas escassas semanas.

Voltei-me lentamente, de má vontade. Não queria sentir o que sabia que *iria* sentir quando olhasse para a sua face demasiado perfeita. Tinha uma expressão de cautela estampada no rosto quando finalmente me virei para ele; a do seu era indecifrável. Ele nada disse.

— O que foi? Já voltaste a falar comigo? — perguntei finalmente, com um laivo de petulância não intencional na minha voz.

Os seus lábios contorceram-se, tentando conter um sorriso.

— Não, nem por isso — confessou.

Fechei os olhos e inspirei lentamente pelo nariz, consciente de que estava a ranger os dentes. Ele esperou.

— Então, o que queres, Edward? — perguntei, mantendo os olhos fechados; assim, era mais fácil conversar de forma coerente.

— Desculpa. Eu sei que estou a ser muito indelicado, mas é melhor assim, a sério.

Parecia sincero. Abri os olhos. O seu rosto estava extremamente sério.

— Não sei a que te referes — afirmei, com uma voz cautelosa.

— É melhor que não sejamos amigos — explicou. — Confia em mim.

Semicerrei os olhos. Já ouvira aquelas palavras antes.

— É pena que não tenhas percebido isso antes — disse, com raiva, por entre dentes. — Terias evitado todo esse arrependimento.

— Arrependimento?

O termo e o meu tom de voz apanharam-no desprevenido.

— Arrependimento em relação a quê?

— Em relação ao facto de não teres simplesmente deixado que o raio daquela carrinha me tivesse esmagado.

Ele ficou atónito. Olhava-me com um ar de incredulidade.

Quando finalmente falou, quase parecia enfurecido.

— Julgas que eu me arrependo de te ter salvado a vida?

— Eu *sei* que te arrependes de tê-lo feito — disse com brusquidão.

— Tu não sabes nada.

Estava, sem dúvida, enfurecido.

Virei-lhe a cara bruscamente, cerrando os maxilares para travar todas as desenfreadas acusações que queria dirigir-lhe. Reuni os meus livros e, em seguida, levantei-me e encaminhei-me para a porta. Queria realizar uma saída dramática da sala, mas, como é evidente, fiquei com a biqueira da bota presa na ombreira da porta e deixei cair os meus livros. Fiquei ali especada por um instante, pensando deixá-los ali. Depois, suspirei e curvei-me para apanhá-los. Ele estava ali; já os empilhara. Entregou-mos, com uma expressão dura no rosto.

— Obrigada — disse glacialmente.

Ele semicerrou os olhos.

— Não tens de quê — retorquiu ele.

Endireitei-me agilmente, tornei a voltar-lhe as costas e segui altivamente em direcção ao ginásio sem olhar para trás.

A aula de Educação Física foi brutal. Começáramos a praticar basquetebol. A minha equipa nunca me passava a bola, o que era bom, mas eu estava constantemente a cair. Por vezes, arrastava alguém comigo. Nesta aula, o meu desempenho estava pior do que o habitual, pois a minha cabeça estava predominantemente povoada por Edward. Tentei concentrar-me nos meus pés, mas ele insistia em voltar a imiscuir-se nos meus pensamentos, no exacto momento em que eu precisava realmente de manter o equilíbrio.

Ir-me embora foi, como sempre, um alívio. Quase corri até à *pick-up*; havia tantas pessoas que eu queria evitar. A *pick-up* sofrera apenas danos mínimos no acidente. Tivera de substituir os faróis traseiros e, se tivesse mandado pintá-la, teria retocado esses mesmos danos. Os pais de Tyler tiveram de vender a sua carrinha para que as peças fossem aproveitadas.

Quase tive um ataque quando contornei a esquina e vi uma figura humana alta e morena encostada à parte lateral da minha *pick-up*. Então, apercebi-me de que se tratava de Eric. Retomei a marcha.

— Olá, Eric — exclamei.

— Viva, Bella.

— O que se passa? — perguntei enquanto destrancava a porta.

Não estava a prestar atenção ao laivo de pouco à vontade patente na sua voz, pelo que as palavras que ele proferiu de seguida me apanharam de surpresa.

— Aah, estava apenas a pensar... se irias ao baile da Primavera comigo.

A sua voz falhou na última palavra.

— Pensei que eram as raparigas que escolhiam o seu par — disse eu, demasiado assustada para ser diplomática.

— Bem, e são — reconheceu, envergonhado.

Recuperei a compostura e tentei esboçar um sorriso caloroso.

— Obrigada por me convidares, mas eu estarei em Seattle nesse dia.

— Ah — exclamou ele. — Bem, talvez para a próxima.

— Claro — concordei, mordendo, em seguida, o lábio. Não queria que ele levasse as minhas palavras demasiado à letra.

Afastou-se cabisbaixo, dirigindo-se novamente para a escola. Ouvi um riso abafado.

Edward estava a passar pela dianteira da minha *pick-up*, olhando em frente, com os lábios cerrados. Abri a porta com um puxão e saltei para o interior, batendo sonoramente com a mesma depois de ter entrado. Embalei o motor de forma ensurdecedora e fiz marcha-atrás até ao corredor de passagem. Edward já se encontrava no seu carro, a dois lugares de distância, recuando suavemente à minha frente, bloqueando-me a passagem. Parou ali — para esperar pela sua família; conseguia ver os quatro a encaminharem-se naquela direcção, mas ainda junto da cantina. Considerei a hipótese de arrancar a traseira do seu Volvo reluzente, mas havia demasiadas testemunhas. Olhei pelo meu espelho retrovisor. Começava a formar-se uma fila. Logo atrás de mim, no seu Sentra usado, recentemente adquirido, encontrava-se Tyler Crowley, a acenar. Eu estava demasiado exasperada para demonstrar que reparara na sua presença.

Enquanto ali permanecia sentada, olhando em todas as direcções, excepto na do carro que se encontrava à minha frente, ouvi bater na janela do lado do passageiro. Olhei; era Tyler. Voltei a olhar pelo espelho retrovisor, confusa. O motor do seu carro estava ainda ligado, tendo a porta ficado aberta. Inclinei-me para abrir o vidro. Estava perro. Consegui abri-lo até ao meio e, depois, desisti.

— Desculpa, Tyler, estou encurralada atrás do Cullen.

Estava aborrecida. Como era óbvio, não era eu a responsável pelo engarrafamento.

— Oh, eu sei; queria apenas pedir-te algo enquanto estamos aqui presos.

Esboçou um sorriso rasgado.

Isto não podia estar a acontecer-me.

— Convidas-me para o baile da Primavera? — prosseguiu.

— Estarei fora da cidade, Tyler.

A minha voz parecia um pouco incisiva. Tinha de ter presente que ele não tinha culpa de Mike e Eric já terem esgotado a minha quota diária de paciência.

— Pois, o Mike falou nisso — confessou.

— Então, porque é que...

Ele encolheu os ombros.

— Estava com esperança de que estivesses apenas a recusar o convite dele de uma forma simpática.

Muito bem, a culpa era toda dele.

— Desculpa, Tyler — disse eu, esforçando-me por dissimular a minha irritação. — Eu vou mesmo sair da cidade.

— Tudo bem. Ainda temos o baile de finalistas.

Então, antes que eu pudesse replicar, já ele se dirigia novamente para o seu carro. Conseguia sentir a irritação estampada na minha cara. Olhei em frente para ver Alice, Rosalie, Emmett e Jasper a entrarem no Volvo. Através do espelho retrovisor, os olhos de Edward estavam pousados em mim. Estava indiscutivelmente a tremer de riso, como se tivesse ouvido cada palavra que Tyler pronunciara. O meu pé ansiava por pisar no acelerador... uma pequena colisão não iria magoar nenhum deles, mas apenas danificar aquela lustrosa pintura prateada. Embalei o motor.

No entanto, já todos tinham entrado no carro e Edward partia a grande velocidade. Conduzi até casa lenta e cuidadosamente, resmungando com os meus botões durante todo o percurso.

Quando cheguei, decidi preparar *enchiladas* de frango para o jantar. Tratava-se de uma preparação demorada e manter-me-ia ocupada. Enquanto as cebolas e as malaguetas cozinhavam em lume brando, o telefone tocou. Quase receei atendê-lo, mas podia ser Charlie ou a minha mãe.

Era Jessica e estava radiante; Mike interpelara-a depois das aulas para lhe comunicar que aceitava o seu convite. Festejei com ela durante breves instantes enquanto mexia o preparado. Ela tinha de desligar, pois queria telefonar a Angela e a Lauren para lhes contar. Eu sugeri — com descontraída inocência — que talvez Angela, a rapariga tímida que tinha Biologia comigo, pudesse convidar Eric. Por sua vez, Lauren, uma rapariga reservada que sempre me ignorara à mesa do almoço, poderia convidar Tyler; eu ouvira dizer que ele estava disponível. Jess achou que era uma óptima ideia. Agora que a companhia de Mike estava assegurada, parecia efectivamente sincera ao afirmar que gostaria que eu fosse ao baile. Desculpei-me com a minha ida a Seattle.

Depois de ter desligado, tentei concentrar-me no jantar — sobretudo em cortar o frango em cubos; não queria arriscar uma nova ida ao serviço de urgência, mas a minha cabeça dava voltas, tentando analisar cada palavra que Edward proferira neste dia. O que queria ele dizer quando afirmou que era melhor que não fôssemos amigos?

O meu estômago contorceu-se quando me apercebi daquilo que ele devia ter querido dizer. Ele devia ter percebido quão fascinada eu estava por ele; não devia querer dar-me falsas esperanças... logo, não podíamos sequer ser amigos... pois ele não estava minimamente interessado em mim.

É claro que ele não estava interessado em mim, pensei colericamente, com os olhos a arderem-me — uma reacção retardada às cebolas. Eu não era *interessante*. E ele era. Interessante... e brilhante... e misterioso... e perfeito... e lindo... e, possivelmente, capaz de levantar carrinhas em peso com uma mão.

Bem, não havia problema. Eu podia deixá-lo em paz. Eu *iria* deixá-lo em paz. Iria cumprir a minha pena auto-imposta naquele purgatório e, seguidamente, com alguma sorte, alguma escola no Sudoeste ou, possivelmente, no Havai oferecer-me-ia uma bolsa de estudos. Concentrei os meus pensamentos em palmeiras e praias soalheiras enquanto terminava as *enchiladas* e as colocava no forno.

Charlie pareceu desconfiado quando chegou a casa e sentiu o cheiro dos pimentos verdes. Não podia censurá-lo — a região mais próxima onde existia comida mexicana comestível era provavelmente o Sul da Califórnia. No entanto, ele era polícia, ainda que numa cidade pequena, sendo, por conseguinte, suficientemente corajoso para comer a primeira garfada. Pareceu gostar. Era divertido ver como ele começava lentamente a confiar nos meus dotes culinários.

— Pai? — interpelei quando ele estava quase a terminar a refeição.

— Sim, Bella?

— Hum, queria apenas informar-te de que vou passar um dia em Seattle de sábado a uma semana... se não houver problema.

Não queria pedir autorização — tal estabelecia um mau precedente. Mas senti que estava a ser descortês e, assim, acrescentei aquelas palavras no final.

— Porquê?

Pareceu surpreendido, como se não conseguisse imaginar nada que Forks não pudesse proporcionar.

— Bem, queria requisitar alguns livros... os recursos da biblioteca daqui são bastante limitados e, além disso, talvez pudesse comprar algumas roupas.

Tinha mais dinheiro do que aquele a que estava habituada, visto que, graças a Charlie, nada tivera de pagar para adquirir um automóvel, ainda que a *pick-up* me ficasse bastante cara em termos de despesas com combustível.

— Aquela *pick-up* deve consumir bastante combustível — afirmou ele, reproduzindo os meus pensamentos.

— Eu sei. Farei uma paragem em Montessano e outra em Olympia e, se for necessário, também em Tacoma.

— Vais sozinha? — perguntou ele.

Não consegui perceber se desconfiava que eu tivesse um namorado secreto ou se estava apenas preocupado com a possibilidade de surgirem problemas mecânicos.

— Vou.

— Seattle é uma cidade grande, podes perder-te — disse ele, mostrando-se inquieto.

— Pai, Phoenix é cinco vezes maior do que Seattle. E eu sei interpretar um mapa, não te preocupes.

— Queres que vá contigo?

Tentei ser astuta ao esconder o meu pavor.

— Não é necessário, pai. Provavelmente, limitar-me-ei a passar todo o dia em gabinetes de prova — será extremamente entediante.

— Oh, está bem.

A ideia de estar sentado em lojas de roupa feminina durante qualquer período de tempo demoveu-o imediatamente.

— Obrigada! — exclamei, sorrindo-lhe.

— Estarás de volta a tempo de ir ao baile?

Grrr. Só numa cidade tão pequena é que um *pai* saberia quando é que os bailes do liceu se realizam.

— Não, eu não danço, pai.

Justamente ele devia compreender este facto, uma vez que não herdei os meus problemas de equilíbrio da minha mãe.

De facto, ele compreendeu.

— Oh, é verdade — percebeu.

Na manhã seguinte, quando entrei no parque de estacionamento, estacionei deliberadamente o mais longe possível do Volvo prateado. Não queria deparar com uma excessiva tentação e acabar por ficar a dever-lhe um carro novo. Ao sair da cabina, atrapalhei-me ao pegar na chave e esta caiu numa poça aos meus pés. Ao curvar-me para apanhá-la, uma mão branca precipitou-se e agarrou-a antes de eu ter podido fazê-lo. Endireitei-me de súbito. Edward Cullen estava mesmo a meu lado, descontraidamente encostado à minha *pick-up*.

— Como é que *fizeste* isso? — perguntei irritada.

— Como é que fiz o quê?

Erguia a minha chave no ar enquanto falava. Quando tentei alcançá-la, deixou-a cair na palma da minha mão.

— Aparecer vindo do nada.

— Bella, não tenho culpa de que tenhas uma excepcional falta de poder de observação.

A sua voz estava mais serena do que o habitual — aveludada, abafada.

Lancei um olhar mal-humorado ao seu rosto perfeito. Os seus olhos estavam novamente claros, tingidos de uma carregada cor de mel dourado. Então, tive de baixar os meus, para reordenar os pensamentos agora confusos.

— Qual foi o motivo do engarrafamento da noite passada? — interroguei, desviando ainda o olhar. — Pensei que andasses a fingir que eu não existo e não a matar-me de irritação.

— Foi pelo bem do Tyler, não pelo meu. Tinha de lhe proporcionar a sua oportunidade.

Soltou um riso algo reprimido.

— Seu!... — exclamei, ofegante.

Não me ocorria uma palavra suficientemente desagradável. Tive a sensação de que o fervor da minha raiva poderia queimá-lo fisicamente, mas ele apenas aparentava estar mais divertido.

— E não ando a fingir que tu não existes — prosseguiu.

— Então, *andas* mesmo a tentar matar-me de irritação? Já que a carrinha do Tyler não se encarregou de o fazer?

A raiva passou como um raio pelos seus olhos de um tom amarelo-acastanhado. Cerrou os lábios numa linha dura, tendo desaparecido todos os vestígios de humor.

— Bella, és completamente absurda — afirmou ele, com frieza na sua voz grave.

Sentia formigueiros nas palmas das mãos — desejava ardentemente bater em algo. Fiquei surpreendida comigo mesma. Por norma, não era uma pessoa violenta. Voltei as costas e comecei a afastar-me.

— Espera! — exclamou ele.

Continuei a andar, chapinhando colericamente debaixo de chuva, mas ele estava a meu lado, acompanhando facilmente o meu andamento.

— Desculpa, foi indelicado da minha parte — disse ele enquanto caminhávamos.

Eu ignorei-o.

— Não estou a dizer que não é verdade — prosseguiu — mas, de qualquer forma, foi indelicado da minha parte afirmá-lo.

— Porque é que não me deixas em paz? — resmunguei.

— Queria perguntar-te algo, mas tu desviaste-me dos meus fins — declarou, soltando um riso abafado.

Parecia ter recuperado a boa disposição.

— Sofres de um distúrbio de múltipla personalidade? — perguntei com severidade.

— Lá estás tu outra vez.

Suspirei.

— Então, muito bem. O que queres perguntar-me?

— Estava a pensar se, de sábado a uma semana, tu sabes, o dia do baile da Primavera...

— Estás a tentar ser *engraçado*? — interrompi-o, virando-me na sua direcção. O meu rosto ficou encharcado quando ergui a cabeça para olhar para o rosto dele.

Os seus olhos estavam malevolamente divertidos.

— Fazes o favor de me deixar terminar?

Mordi o lábio e uni as mãos, entrelaçando os dedos, de modo a que não pudesse tomar nenhuma atitude precipitada.

— Ouvi-te dizer que ias a Seattle nesse dia e estava a pensar se quererias boleia.

Desta não estava eu à espera.

— O quê? — não sabia ao certo aonde ele pretendia chegar.

— Queres boleia para Seattle?

— De quem? — perguntei, baralhada.

— De mim, obviamente.

Pronunciou cada sílaba como se estivesse a falar com alguém que possuísse uma deficiência mental.

Eu estava ainda aturdida.

— Porquê?

— Bem, eu tencionava ir a Seattle durante as próximas semanas e, para ser sincero, não sei se a tua *pick-up* resistirá à viagem.

— A minha *pick-up* funciona perfeitamente, muito obrigada pela tua preocupação.

Comecei novamente a andar, mas estava demasiado surpreendida para conseguir manter o mesmo grau de raiva.

— Mas será que a tua *pick-up* consegue realizar a viagem consumindo um só depósito de gasolina?

Seguia novamente ao meu ritmo.

— Não vejo em que medida é que isso possa dizer-te respeito.

Estúpido proprietário de um Volvo reluzente.

— O desperdício de recursos limitados diz respeito a todos.

— Francamente, Edward — senti um frémito perpassar-me quando proferi o seu nome e detestei tal sensação —, não consigo acompanhar-te. Pensei que não querias ser meu amigo.

— Eu disse que seria melhor se não fôssemos amigos e não que não queria que o fôssemos.

— Oh, obrigada, agora está *tudo* esclarecido.

Profundo sarcasmo. Apercebi-me de que parara novamente de andar. Estávamos agora abrigados sob o tecto da cantina, podendo eu, assim, olhar mais facilmente para o rosto dele, o que certamente não favorecia a minha clareza de raciocínio.

— Seria mais... *prudente* que não fosses minha amiga — explicou ele. — Mas estou farto de tentar manter-me afastado de ti, Bella.

O seu olhar tornou-se sublimemente intenso ao proferir aquela última frase, com a voz a evidenciar sinais de raiva reprimida. Não conseguia lembrar-me de como se respirava.

— Vais comigo a Seattle? — perguntou, ainda com intensidade.

Ainda não conseguia falar, pelo que me limitei a acenar com a cabeça.

Ele sorriu por breves instantes e, em seguida, o seu rosto ficou sério.

— Devias mesmo manter-te afastada de mim — advertiu. — Vemo-nos na aula.

Virou-se bruscamente e voltou para trás pelo mesmo caminho que tínhamos trilhado.

Capítulo Cinco

Grupo Sanguíneo

Encaminhei-me para a aula de Inglês num estado de estupe-facção. Ao entrar na sala, não me apercebi sequer de que a aula já começara.

— Obrigado por se juntar a nós, menina Swan — disse o professor Mason de forma depreciativa.

Enrubesci e precipitei-me para o meu lugar.

Só quando a aula terminou é que me apercebi de que Mike estava sentado no seu lugar habitual, ao meu lado. Senti uma pontada de culpa. No entanto, tanto ele como Eric se encontraram comigo à porta como era costume e, assim, deduzi que o seu perdão era possível. Mike parecia tornar-se mais ele próprio à medida que caminhávamos, passando a estar entusiasmado ao referir-se às previsões do boletim meteorológico para o fim-de--semana seguinte. Supostamente, iria haver uma pausa mínima no tempo chuvoso e, deste modo, talvez a sua viagem à praia pudesse realizar-se. Tentei parecer ansiosa, de modo a compensá--lo pela desilusão que eu lhe provocara no dia anterior. Era difícil; com ou sem chuva, a temperatura não ultrapassaria os nove graus, se tivéssemos sorte.

O resto da manhã passou sem que nada ficasse retido na minha memória. Era difícil acreditar que eu não imaginara aquilo que Edward dissera nessa manhã e o seu olhar. Talvez se tratasse apenas de um sonho extremamente convincente que eu confundira com a realidade. Esta hipótese era mais provável do que a de que eu o cativava fosse a que nível fosse.

Assim, estava impaciente e assustada quando eu e Jessica entrámos na cantina. Desejava ver o rosto dele para verificar se voltara a ser a pessoa fria e indiferente que eu conhecera ao longo

das semanas anteriores ou se, por algum milagre, eu realmente ouvira aquilo que pensava ter ouvido nessa manhã. Completamente
alheia à minha desatenção, Jessica tagarelava incessantemente a
propósito dos seus planos para o baile — Lauren e Angela tinham
convidado os outros rapazes e iam todos juntos.

A desilusão invadiu-me quando os meus olhos focaram infa-
livelmente a mesa de Edward. Só os quatro ali se encontravam,
ele estava ausente. Será que fora para casa? Arrasada, segui Jessica, que continuava a tagarelar, ao longo da fila. Perdera o apetite — comprei unicamente uma garrafa de limonada. Desejava
apenas ir sentar-me e amuar.

— O Edward Cullen está, de novo, a olhar-te fixamente —
afirmou Jessica, rompendo finalmente a minha abstracção ao
pronunciar o nome dele. — Pergunto-me porque estará ele hoje
sentado a uma mesa sozinho.

Levantei a cabeça bruscamente. Segui o olhar dela e deparei
com Edward, esboçando um sorriso constrangido, olhando-me
fixamente a partir de uma mesa vazia no lado da cantina oposto àquele em que costumava sentar-se. Assim que os nossos
olhares se cruzaram, levantou uma mão e fez um gesto com o
dedo indicador para que eu fosse fazer-lhe companhia. Enquanto o fitava com incredulidade, ele piscou o olho.

— Está a dirigir-se a *ti*? — perguntou Jessica com uma admiração insultuosa patente na voz.

— Talvez precise de ajuda nos trabalhos de casa de Biologia
— murmurei por entre dentes. — Hum, é melhor ir ver o que ele
deseja.

Sentia o olhar dela fixo na direcção em que eu seguia à medida que me afastava.

Quando cheguei junto à mesa, mantive-me de pé, insegura,
atrás da cadeira que se encontrava defronte dele.

— Porque não te sentas à minha mesa hoje? — perguntou,
sorrindo.

Sentei-me automaticamente, observando-o com cautela. Ele
estava ainda a sorrir. Era difícil acreditar que alguém tão belo

pudesse ser real. Temia que ele desaparecesse numa súbita nuvem de fumo e eu acordasse.

Ele parecia estar à espera que eu dissesse algo.

— Esta situação é fora do vulgar — consegui finalmente afirmar.

— Bem.

Deteve-se e, em seguida, as restantes palavras sucederam-se num ímpeto.

— Decidi que, já que ia para o inferno, mais valia fazê-lo de forma consumada.

Esperei que ele dissesse algo que tivesse sentido. Os segundos passaram.

— Tu sabes que eu não faço a menor ideia daquilo a que te referes — acabei por salientar.

— Pois sei.

Voltou a sorrir e, depois, mudou de assunto.

— Acho que os teus amigos estão zangados comigo por te ter roubado.

— Hão-de sobreviver.

Conseguia sentir os seus olhares a trespassar-me as costas.

— Mas eu posso não te devolver — disse ele com um brilho perverso nos olhos.

Eu engasguei-me. Ele riu-se.

— Pareces preocupada.

— Não — retorqui, mas, ridiculamente, a minha voz falhou. — Na verdade, estou surpreendida... A que se deve tudo isto?

— Já te disse, fartei-me de tentar manter-me afastado de ti. Portanto, desisto.

Ainda sorria, mas os seus olhos ocres estavam sérios.

— Desistes? — repeti num estado de confusão.

— Sim, desisto de tentar ser bom. A partir de agora, faço apenas o que me apetece e o resto que se dane.

O seu sorriso esmoreceu à medida que se explicava e um laivo de rispidez insinuou-se na sua voz.

— Baralhaste-me de novo.

O espantoso sorriso constrangido ressurgiu.

— Falo sempre de mais quando converso contigo — esse é um dos problemas.

— Não te preocupes, não compreendo nada do que dizes — declarei ironicamente.

— Estou a contar com isso.

— Então, sem rodeios, já somos amigos?

— Amigos... — meditou, indeciso.

— Ou não? — murmurei por entre dentes.

Ele esboçou um sorriso rasgado.

— Bem, suponho que podemos tentar, mas aviso-te de que não sou um bom amigo para ti.

Por trás do sorriso, o aviso era autêntico.

— Repetes isso muitas vezes — referi, tentando ignorar o súbito estremecimento no meu estômago e procurando manter a voz isenta de variações.

— Pois, porque não estás a dar-me ouvidos. Ainda estou à espera que acredites no que te digo. Se fores esperta, evitas-me.

— Julgo que também já tornaste bastante clara a tua opinião a respeito do meu intelecto.

Semicerrei os olhos. Ele sorriu como quem pedia desculpa.

— Então, enquanto eu... não estiver a ser esperta, tentaremos ser amigos?

Esforcei-me por sintetizar o confuso diálogo.

— Parece-me que é mais ou menos isso.

Olhei para as minhas mãos a envolverem a garrafa de limonada, não sabendo ao certo o que fazer a partir daquele momento.

— Em que é que estás a pensar? — perguntou curiosamente.

Olhei para os seus olhos de um profundo tom dourado, fiquei confusa e, como habitualmente, deixei escapar a verdade.

— Estou a tentar compreender quem tu és.

O seu maxilar contraiu-se, mas ele manteve o sorriso no devido lugar com algum esforço.

— Estás a fazer progressos nessa empreitada? — perguntou ele, num tom de voz espontâneo.

— Não muitos — confessei.

Soltou um riso abafado.

— Quais são as tuas teorias?

Eu enrubesci. Ao longo do mês anterior, hesitara entre Bruce Wayne e Peter Parker.[1] Não iria, de forma nenhuma, confessar este facto.

— Não me dizes? — perguntou ele, inclinando a cabeça para um lado com um sorriso tremendamente tentador.

Abanei a cabeça.

— É demasiado embaraçoso.

— Isso é *mesmo* frustrante, sabes — lamentou-se.

— Não — discordei rapidamente, com um olhar duro —, não consigo *imaginar* por que motivo tal seria minimamente frustrante, apenas porque alguém recusa revelar-te os seus pensamentos, mesmo que, durante todo esse tempo, essa pessoa teça comentariozinhos obscuros que se destinam especificamente a manter-te acordado à noite, perguntando a ti mesmo qual será o respectivo significado... agora, por que motivo é que tal seria frustrante?

Ele fez um esgar.

— Ou melhor — prossegui, com a irritação reprimida agora a fluir livremente — digamos que essa pessoa também cometeu uma grande variedade de actos bizarros, desde salvar a tua vida em circunstâncias incríveis num dia e a tratar-te como um pária no seguinte, nunca te tendo igualmente dado uma explicação para nenhum desses factos, mesmo depois de ter prometido fazê-lo. Isso também não seria nada frustrante.

— Tens um ligeiro mau feitio, não tens?

— Não me agrada a dualidade de critérios.

Olhámo-nos fixamente, sem sorrir.

Ele olhou por cima do meu ombro e, em seguida, de forma inesperada, soltou um riso algo reprimido.

— O que foi?

— O teu namorado parece pensar que estou a ser desagradável contigo. Está a deliberar se há-de ou não vir interromper a nossa

---

1. N. E. — Figuras humanas correspondentes, respectivamente, aos super-heróis Batman e Homem-Aranha.

discussão — esclareceu ele, voltando a rir-se da mesma forma.

— Não sei a quem te referes — disse eu, glacialmente. — Mas, seja como for, tenho a certeza de que estás enganado.

— Não estou. Já te disse, a maioria das pessoas é transparente.

— Excepto eu, é claro.

— Sim, excepto tu.

O seu estado de espírito alterou-se de repente; os olhos tornaram-se pensativos.

— Pergunto-me porque será.

Tive de desviar os olhos da intensidade do seu olhar. Concentrei-me em desenroscar a tampa da minha limonada. Sorvi um trago, olhando fixamente para a mesa sem a ver.

— Não tens fome? — perguntou, com o espírito perturbado.

— Não.

Não me apetecia dizer-lhe que já tinha a barriga cheia... de nervosismo.

— E tu?

Eu olhava para a mesa vazia que se encontrava diante dele.

— Não, não tenho fome.

Não compreendi a expressão estampada no seu rosto — parecia que estava a divertir-se com algum tipo de piada pessoal.

— Podes fazer-me um favor? — perguntei após um instante de hesitação.

Ficou subitamente desconfiado.

— Depende daquilo que pretendes.

— Não é nada de mais — assegurei-lhe.

Ele esperou, cauteloso mas curioso.

— Pensei apenas... se poderias avisar-me antecipadamente da próxima vez que resolveres ignorar-me para o meu próprio bem? Apenas para que eu esteja preparada.

Olhava para a garrafa de limonada enquanto falava, percorrendo o círculo da abertura com o dedo rosado.

— Parece-me justo.

Quando levantei o olhar, ele estava a contrair os lábios para evitar rir-se.

— Obrigada.

— Sendo assim, podes dar-me uma resposta em troca? — interrogou.

— Só uma.

— Revela-me *uma* teoria.

— Ai, ai! Essa não.

— Não ficaste apurada; prometeste-me apenas uma resposta — relembrou-me.

— Tu também já fizeste promessas que não cumpriste — retorqui-lhe.

— Apenas uma teoria, eu não me rio.

— Sim, ris.

Estava certa quanto a esse facto.

Ele baixou o olhar e, em seguida, olhou na minha direcção, através das suas longas pestanas negras, com os olhos ocres a exercerem um efeito cáustico.

— Por favor? — pronunciou suavemente, inclinando-se na minha direcção.

Eu pestanejei, ficando a minha mente completamente despojada de qualquer pensamento. Santo Deus, como é que ele fez aquilo?

— Hã, o quê? — perguntei, aturdida.

— Por favor, revela-me apenas uma teoriazinha.

Os seus olhos ainda me lançavam fogo.

— Hum, bem, foste mordido por uma aranha radioactiva?

Será que ele era também hipnotizador? Ou seria eu apenas uma pessoa irremediavelmente fácil de convencer?

— Essa teoria não é muito criativa — escarneceu.

— Lamento, é a única que tenho — declarei, aborrecida.

— Não estás nem perto da verdade — disse ele, em tom de provocação.

— Não há aranhas?

— Não.

— Nem radioactividade?

— Nenhuma.

— Raios! — exclamei, suspirando.

— A criptonite também não me afecta — afirmou ele, soltando um riso abafado.

— Não podes rir-te, lembras-te?

Ele esforçou-se por ficar com um ar sério.

— Acabarei por descobrir — adverti-o.

— Quem me dera que não tentasses.

Ficou novamente com um ar grave.

— Porque...?

— E se eu não for um super-herói? E se for o vilão?

Sorriu jocosamente, mas os seus olhos estavam impenetráveis.

— Ah! — exclamei, à medida que várias das suas insinuações se encaixavam subitamente. — Estou a ver.

— Estás mesmo?

O seu rosto tornou-se bruscamente austero, como se receasse ter acidentalmente falado de mais.

— És perigoso? — arrisquei a adivinhar, com a minha pulsação a acelerar quando me apercebi da verdade das minhas próprias palavras. Ele era perigoso. Estivera sempre a tentar transmitir-me esta ideia.

Limitava-se a olhar-me, com os olhos repletos de alguma emoção. Eu não conseguia compreender.

— Mas não és mau — sussurrei, abanando a cabeça. — Não, não acredito que sejas mau.

— Estás enganada.

A sua voz estava quase inaudível. Baixou o olhar, surripiando a tampa da minha garrafa e fazendo-a girar de lado entre os dedos. Fitei-o, perguntando-me por que motivo não sentia medo. Ele estava a falar a sério — isso era óbvio. Eu, porém, sentia-me apenas ansiosa, nervosa... e, acima de tudo, fascinada. Sentia-me como sempre me sentia quando estava perto dele.

O silêncio perdurou até que eu reparei que a cantina estava quase vazia.

Levantei-me de um salto.

— Vamos chegar atrasados.

— Não vou à aula hoje — disse ele, fazendo com que a tampa rodopiasse tão rapidamente que chegava a parecer uma mera névoa.

— Porque não?

— É saudável baldarmo-nos às aulas de vez em quando.

Sorriu-me, mas os seus olhos estavam ainda perturbados.

— Bem, eu vou — informei-o.

Eu era demasiado cobarde para correr o risco de ser apanhada. A sua atenção voltou a incidir sobre a tampa, que servia de recurso de ocasião.

— Então, vemo-nos mais tarde.

Hesitei, sentindo-me arrasada, mas, então, o primeiro toque da campainha fez-me precipitar pela porta, com um último olhar para confirmar que ele não se deslocara um único centímetro.

Enquanto me dirigia para a aula, quase em passo de corrida, a minha cabeça girava mais rapidamente do que a tampa da garrafa. Tão poucas perguntas obtiveram resposta em comparação com a quantidade de novas questões que tinham sido levantadas. Pelo menos, a chuva cessara.

Tive sorte; o professor Banner ainda não estava na sala quando cheguei. Instalei-me rapidamente no meu lugar, ciente de que tanto Mike como Angela me olhavam fixamente. Mike parecia melindrado e Angela surpreendida e um pouco espantada.

O professor Banner entrou, então, impondo a ordem na sala. Fazia malabarismos com algumas pequenas caixas de cartão nos braços. Pousou-as na bancada de Mike, dizendo-lhe para começar a fazê-las circular pela turma.

— Muito bem, meninos, quero que todos retirem um instrumento de cada caixa — disse ele, enquanto sacava um par de luvas de borracha do bolso do seu casaco de laboratório e as colocava. O som estridente produzido pelas luvas ao moldarem--se aos seus pulsos afigurou-se-me como sendo de mau agouro.

— O primeiro deve ser um cartão indicador — prosseguiu ele,

pegando num cartão branco com quatro quadrados desenhados e exibindo-o. – O segundo é um aplicador com quatro dentes – mostrou algo que se assemelhava a um pente praticamente desprovido de dentes. – E o terceiro é uma microlanceta esterilizada.

Mostrou um pequeno instrumento de plástico azul e abriu-o. A farpa era invisível àquela distância, mas o meu estômago revolveu-se.

– Eu vou a cada bancada com um conta-gotas com água para preparar os vossos cartões, portanto, por favor, não comecem antes de eu me ter dirigido aos vossos lugares...

Começou novamente pela mesa de Mike, colocando cuidadosamente uma gota de água em cada um dos quatro quadrados.

– De seguida, quero que piquem cuidadosamente o dedo com a lanceta...

Pegou na mão de Mike e espetou o espigão na ponta do dedo médio deste último. Oh, não. Uma humidade pegajosa invadiu-me a testa.

– Coloquem uma gota de sangue em cada um dos dentes.

Procedeu a uma demonstração, apertando o dedo de Mike até que o sangue começou a correr. Eu engolia em seco convulsivamente, com o estômago às voltas.

– Em seguida, apliquem-no no cartão.

Terminou, erguendo o cartão vermelho e gotejante no ar para que pudéssemos vê-lo. Fechei os olhos, esforçando-me por ouvir algo além do zunido nos meus ouvidos.

– A Cruz Vermelha irá promover uma recolha de sangue em Port Angeles no próximo fim-de-semana e, por conseguinte, julguei que todos deveriam tomar conhecimento do respectivo grupo sanguíneo.

Parecia sentir orgulho em si próprio.

– Aqueles dentre vós que ainda não tiverem completado dezoito anos, necessitarão de uma autorização dos pais. Tenho os documentos a serem assinados na minha secretária.

Continuou a percorrer a sala com as suas gotas de água. Encostei a face ao fresco tampo negro da bancada e tentei manter-me consciente. Em meu redor, conseguia ouvir gritos agudos, reclamações e risinhos à medida que os meus colegas de turma espetavam os dedos. Inspirei e expirei lentamente pela boca.

— Bella, estás bem? — perguntou o professor Banner.

A sua voz soava próximo da minha cabeça e parecia inquieta.

— Eu já sei qual é o meu grupo sanguíneo, professor Banner — disse sem energia.

Receava levantar a cabeça.

— Sentes-te desfalecer?

— Sinto, senhor professor — murmurei, pontapeando-me por dentro por não ter faltado à aula quando surgiu a oportunidade de o fazer.

— Será que alguém pode levar a Bella até à enfermaria, por favor? — bradou.

Não precisava de erguer os olhos para saber que seria Mike a oferecer-se.

— Consegues andar? — perguntou o professor Banner.

— Consigo — sussurrei. — "Deixe-me só sair daqui", pensei eu. "Se necessário, até rastejarei".

Mike parecia ansioso ao envolver-me a cintura com o braço e ao colocar o meu sobre o seu ombro. Encostei-me pesadamente a ele enquanto saíamos da sala de aula.

Atravessou o recinto da escola comigo a reboque. Quando contornámos a cantina, saindo do campo visual do edifício quatro, na eventualidade de o professor Banner estar a observar-nos, parei.

— Deixas-me ficar sentada só por um instante, por favor? — implorei.

Ajudou-me a sentar junto do passeio.

— E, faças o que fizeres, mantém a mão no bolso — avisei-o.

Sentia-me ainda tonta. Deixei-me cair bruscamente de lado, pousando a face no gélido e húmido cimento do passeio. Tal parecia exercer um certo efeito benéfico.

— Ena, estás verde, Bella — exclamou Mike nervoso.

— Bella? — invocou uma outra voz ao longe.

Não! Por favor, que seja eu a imaginar aquela voz horrivelmente conhecida.

— O que é que se passa, ela magoou-se?

A sua voz estava agora mais próxima e ele parecia transtornado. Não era imaginação minha. Forcei as pálpebras umas contra as outras, desejando morrer ou, pelo menos, não vomitar.

Mike parecia tenso.

— Acho que ela desmaiou. Não sei o que aconteceu, ela nem sequer picou o dedo.

— Bella! Consegues ouvir-me?

A voz de Edward soava mesmo a meu lado, transmitindo agora alívio.

— Não — gemi. — Vai-te embora.

Ele soltou um riso abafado.

— Eu ia levá-la à enfermaria — explicou Mike num tom defensivo — mas ela recusou-se a avançar mais.

— Eu levo-a — afirmou Edward. — Podes voltar para a aula.

Conseguia ainda ouvir o sorriso na sua voz.

— Não — protestou Mike. — Sou eu que devo fazê-lo.

De repente, o passeio desapareceu debaixo de mim. Os meus olhos abriram-se rapidamente com o sobressalto. Edward pegara em mim com os seus braços, tão facilmente como se eu pesasse cinco quilos em vez de cinquenta.

— Põe-me no chão! — "Por favor, por favor, que eu não vomite para cima dele", pensei.

Ele já caminhava antes de eu ter acabado de falar.

— Ei! — exclamou Mike, que já se encontrava dez passos atrás de nós.

Edward ignorou-o.

— Estás com péssimo aspecto — disse-me ele, esboçando um largo sorriso.

— Coloca-me novamente no passeio — afirmei, gemendo.

O movimento oscilante do seu andar não estava a ajudar. Ele

segurava-me afastando-me do seu corpo, cuidadosamente, suportando todo o meu peso apenas com os braços — tal não parecia incomodá-lo.

— Com que então desmaias ao ver sangue? — perguntou ele.

Este facto parecia diverti-lo. Não respondi. Voltei a fechar os olhos e debati-me contra as náuseas com todas as minhas forças, apertando os lábios.

— E nem sequer se tratava do teu próprio sangue — continuou, regozijando-se.

Não sei como é que ele conseguiu abrir a porta enquanto me carregava, mas, subitamente, a temperatura ambiente aumentou e, consequentemente, apercebi-me de que estávamos entre paredes.

— Credo! — ouvi uma voz feminina pronunciar, sobressaltada.

— Ela desmaiou na aula de Biologia — explicou Edward.

Abri os olhos. Estava no gabinete do Conselho Executivo e Edward caminhava a passos largos em direcção à porta da enfermaria, passando pelo balcão da frente. A menina Cope, a recepcionista ruiva do Conselho Executivo, precipitou-se à frente dele para segurar a porta. A enfermeira com ar de avó desviou o olhar de um romance, atónita, quando Edward entrou comigo na sala e me pousou delicadamente no papel crepitante que revestia o colchão de vinil castanho da única marquesa. Então, ele afastou-se para se encostar à parede, distanciando-se tanto quanto era possível na estreita sala. Os seus olhos estavam brilhantes, emocionados.

— Ela está apenas um pouco fraca — disse ele, tranquilizando a sobressaltada enfermeira. — Estão a tipificar sangue na aula de Biologia.

A enfermeira acenou com a cabeça de modo sagaz.

— Acontece sempre a alguém.

Ele conteve o riso.

— Deita-te só um pouco, amor; isso passa.

— Eu sei — disse eu, suspirando.

As náuseas começavam já a desvanecer-se.

— Isto acontece-te muito frequentemente? — perguntou ela.

— Às vezes — confessei.

Edward tossiu para disfarçar outra gargalhada.

— Já podes voltar para a aula — disse-lhe ela.

— Devo ficar com ela.

Ele proferiu estas palavras com uma autoridade de tal modo segura que a enfermeira, ainda que tenha franzido os lábios, não voltou a argumentar.

— Vou buscar gelo para colocares na testa, querida — disse-me ela, saindo, em seguida, apressadamente da sala.

— Tinhas razão — gemi, deixando que os meus olhos se fechassem.

— Costumo ter, mas, desta vez, a respeito de quê, em particular?

— Fazer gazeta é mesmo saudável.

Eu ainda praticava exercícios de respiração.

— Por um instante, assustaste-me — confessou ele após um momento de silêncio.

O seu tom de voz levava a crer que estava a confessar uma fraqueza humilhante.

— Pensei que o Newton estava a arrastar o teu corpo sem vida para o enterrar no bosque.

— Ah! Ah!

Tinha ainda os olhos fechados, mas sentia-me mais normal a cada minuto que passava.

— Sinceramente, já vi cadáveres com melhor cor. Estava preocupado com a possibilidade de ter de vingar o teu homicídio.

— Pobre Mike. Aposto que está furioso.

— Ele abomina-me de verdade — disse Edward animadamente.

— Não podes ter a certeza disso — argumentei, mas, depois, perguntei-me subitamente se poderia.

— Vi a cara dele, era perceptível.

— Como é que me viste? Pensei que estavas a fazer gazeta.

Já estava quase boa, ainda que o mal-estar tivesse provavelmente passado mais depressa se eu tivesse comido ao almoço.

Por outro lado, talvez tivesse sido uma sorte o facto de o meu estômago estar vazio.

— Estava no meu carro, a ouvir um CD.

Uma resposta tão normal foi coisa que me supreendeu. Ouvi a porta e abri os olhos, vendo a enfermeira com uma compressa fria na mão.

— Aqui tens, querida — disse e estendeu-a na minha testa. — Estás com melhor aspecto — acrescentou.

— Acho que estou bem — disse eu, sentando-me.

Sentia apenas um zunido nos ouvidos, mas a cabeça já parara de andar à roda. As paredes verde-hortelã permaneciam no seu devido lugar. Pude ver que ela estava prestes a fazer-me voltar a deitar, mas, nesse preciso momento, a porta abriu-se e a menina Cope espreitou.

— Chegou outro — avisou.

Desci da marquesa para deixá-la livre para o enfermo que se seguia.

Voltei a entregar a compressa à enfermeira.

— Aqui tem, não preciso disto.

Então, Mike entrou, cambaleante, amparando agora Lee Stephens, outro rapaz que pertencia à nossa turma de Biologia e que estava com um ar pálido. Eu e Edward recuámos, encostando-nos à parede, para lhes dar espaço.

— Oh, não — resmungou Edward. — Vai para o gabinete, Bella.

Olhei para ele, confusa.

— Confia em mim, vai.

Voltei-me e agarrei a porta antes de esta se fechar, precipitando-me para fora da enfermaria. Sentia a presença de Edward mesmo atrás de mim.

— Tu deste-me mesmo ouvidos.

Ele estava estupefacto.

— Senti o cheiro do sangue — disse eu, torcendo o nariz.

Lee não estava indisposto por ter observado outras pessoas, como era o meu caso.

— As pessoas não conseguem sentir o cheiro do sangue — refutou.

— Pois eu consigo. E é isso que me faz ficar indisposta. Cheira a ferrugem... e sal.

Ele fitava-me com um ar insondável.

— O que foi? — interroguei.

— Não foi nada.

Então, Mike saiu, olhando na minha direcção e na de Edward. O olhar que ele lançou a Edward confirmou o que este afirmara a respeito da abominação. Voltou a olhar para mim, com os olhos sorumbáticos.

— Estás com melhor aspecto — acusou.

— Mantém apenas a mão no bolso — voltei a adverti-lo.

— Já não está a sangrar — murmurou por entre dentes. — Vais voltar para a aula?

— Estás a gozar? Teria apenas de dar meia volta e regressar para aqui.

— Suponho que sim... Então, vais participar na viagem deste fim-de-semana? À praia?

Enquanto falava, lançou um outro olhar hostil na direcção de Edward, que estava encostado ao balcão atulhado, imóvel como uma estátua, olhando o vazio.

Tentei parecer o mais amável possível.

— Claro, eu disse que alinhava.

— Vamos encontrar-nos na loja do meu pai, às dez horas.

Os seus olhos voltaram a tremular na direcção de Edward, perguntando-se se estaria a fornecer demasiada informação. A sua linguagem corporal tornava claro que não se tratava de um convite aberto a todos.

— Lá estarei — prometi.

— Então, vemo-nos na aula de Educação Física — disse ele, deslocando-se irresolutamente na direcção da porta.

— Até já — retorqui.

Ele olhou-me uma vez mais, com o rosto arredondado a mostrar-se ligeiramente aborrecido, e, em seguida, à medida que passava lentamente pela porta, os seus ombros baixaram-se subitamente. Fui invadida por uma onda de compaixão. Reflecti sobre o facto de ir novamente deparar com o seu ar de decepção... na aula de Educação Física.

— Educação Física — murmurei.

— Eu posso tratar disso.

Não reparara que Edward se aproximara de mim, mas ele falava-me agora ao ouvido.

— Vai sentar-te e faz um ar pálido — murmurou por entre dentes.

Não se tratava de um grande desafio; eu estava sempre pálida e o desfalecimento que sofrera pouco antes deixara-me um ligeiro brilho de suor no rosto. Sentei-me numa das cadeiras articuladas que rangiam e encostei a cabeça à parede com os olhos fechados. Os desmaios sempre me deixaram exausta.

Ouvi Edward a falar suavemente ao balcão.

— Menina Cope?

— Sim?

Eu não a ouvira regressar à sua secretária.

— A Bella tem Educação Física no próximo tempo e eu acho que ela não se sente suficientemente bem. Na verdade, estava a pensar se não deveria levá-la já para casa. Acha que podia dispensá-la da aula?

A voz dele assemelhava-se a mel a derreter-se. Conseguia imaginar quão avassaladores estariam os seus olhos.

— Também precisa de ser dispensado, Edward?

A menina Cope agitava-se de um lado para o outro. Porque é que eu não consigo agir dessa forma?

— Não, eu tenho a professora Goff, ela não se importa.

— Muito bem, está tudo tratado. Desejo-lhe as melhoras, Bella — disse-me ela.

Eu acenei com a cabeça sem energia, levantando-a apenas um pouco.

— Consegues andar ou queres que eu te carregue novamente?

De costas voltadas para a recepcionista, a expressão estampada no seu rosto tornou-se sarcástica.

— Eu vou a pé.

Levantei-me cuidadosamente e continuava a sentir-me bem. Ele segurou a porta para eu passar, com um sorriso educado, mas olhos trocistas. Saí, expondo-me à fria e miúda cacimba que acabara de começar a cair. À medida que me lavava o rosto, libertando-o da pegajosa transpiração, transmitia-me uma sensação agradável — esta foi a primeira vez que me agradou a constante humidade que caía do céu.

— Obrigada — disse eu, quando ele me seguiu em direcção ao exterior. — Quase vale a pena ficar doente para faltar a Educação Física.

— Sempre às ordens.

Ele olhava em frente, observando a chuva de soslaio.

— Então, vais? À viagem do próximo sábado, quero eu dizer.

Eu esperava que ele fosse, ainda que parecesse improvável. Não o imaginava a participar numa boleia organizada com os restantes miúdos da escola; ele não pertencia ao mesmo mundo. Eu esperava, todavia, que ele me proporcionasse o primeiro rasgo de entusiasmo que eu já sentira relativamente à excursão.

— Exactamente aonde é que todos vão?

Ele continuava a olhar em frente, impassível.

— Até *La Push*, ao porto.

Perscrutei o seu rosto, tentando decifrá-lo. Os seus olhos pareciam semicerrar-se infinitesimalmente.

Olhou-me de relance pelo canto do olho, esboçando um sorriso forçado.

— Penso que não fui mesmo convidado.

Suspirei.

— Eu acabei de te convidar.

— Não vamos, tu e eu, provocar ainda mais o coitado do Mike esta semana. Não queremos que ele se passe.

Os seus olhos dançavam; a ideia agradava-lhe mais do que ele gostaria.

— Mike-chmike — murmurei por entre dentes, preocupada com a forma como ele dissera «tu e eu». Agradava-me mais do que *eu* gostaria.

Encontrávamo-nos agora perto do parque de estacionamento. Virei para a esquerda, dirigindo-me para a minha *pick-up*. O meu casaco ficou preso em algo que me fez recuar bruscamente.

— Aonde pensas que vais? — perguntou ele, escandalizado.

Estava a agarrar uma parte do meu casaco com uma mão. Eu estava confusa.

— Vou para casa.

— Não me ouviste prometer levar-te a casa em segurança? Julgas que vou deixar-te conduzir no estado em que te encontras?

Na sua voz, a indignação ainda era patente.

— Qual estado? E a minha *pick-up*? — reclamei.

— Peço à Alice que a leve até tua casa depois das aulas.

Ele levava-me, agora, a reboque na direcção do seu automóvel, puxando-me pelo casaco. Nada mais podia fazer para evitar cair de costas. De qualquer modo, se tal tivesse acontecido, ele limitar-se-ia, provavelmente, a arrastar-me ao longo do percurso.

— Larga-me! — exclamei com insistência.

Ele ignorou-me. Eu caminhei aos ziguezagues, de lado, ao longo do passeio molhado até chegarmos junto do Volvo. Então, ele libertou-me finalmente e eu esbarrei na porta do passageiro.

— És tão atrevido! — resmunguei.

— Está aberta.

Foi esta a sua única réplica. Ele entrou pelo lado do condutor.

— Estou perfeitamente apta a conduzir até casa!

Mantive-me especada junto do carro, profundamente irritada. Chovia, agora, com maior intensidade e eu não colocara o capuz, pelo que o meu cabelo gotejava pelas costas abaixo.

Ele abriu o vidro eléctrico e inclinou-se, através do banco, na minha direcção.

— Entra, Bella.

Não retorqui. Estava a calcular mentalmente as minhas hipóteses de alcançar a minha *pick-up* antes de ele me conseguir apanhar. Tinha de admitir que não eram muito favoráveis.

— Limitar-me-ei a arrastar-te novamente até aqui — ameaçou, adivinhando o meu plano.

Tentei manter o máximo de dignidade possível ao entrar no seu carro. Não fui muito bem sucedida. Parecia um pinto encharcado e as minhas botas chiavam.

— Isto é completamente desnecessário — disse eu, obstinadamente.

Ele não retorquiu. Mexia nos comandos, aumentando a potência do aquecimento e baixando o volume da música. Quando saiu do parque de estacionamento, eu estava a preparar-me para lhe aplicar o tratamento do silêncio, colocando o rosto em modo de beicinho total. Mas, de repente, reconheci a música que estava a tocar e a minha curiosidade levou a melhor sobre as minhas intenções.

— «Clair de Lune»? — perguntei, surpreendida.

— Conheces Debussy?

Também ele pareceu surpreendido.

— Não muito bem — reconheci. — A minha mãe põe muita música clássica a tocar em casa. Só conheço os meus compositores preferidos.

— Debussy também é um dos meus compositores preferidos.

Ele lançava o olhar fixo através da chuva, perdido nos seus pensamentos. Eu ouvia a música, descontraindo-me no banco de pele cinzento-clara. Era impossível não reagir à conhecida e tranquilizante melodia. A chuva transformava tudo o que se encontrava do lado de fora do vidro em meras manchas cinzentas e verdes. Comecei a aperceber-me de que seguíamos a grande velocidade; no entanto, o carro deslocava-se com tanta firmeza, com tanta regularidade, que não tinha noção da velocidade. Apenas a vista da cidade, que passava rapidamente, a denunciava.

— Como é a tua mãe? — perguntou-me ele de repente.

Eu olhei-o de relance e deparei com ele a perscrutar-me com olhos curiosos.

— Parece-se bastante comigo, mas é mais bonita — disse eu, enquanto ele franzia o sobrolho. — Tenho demasiada influência genética do Charlie. Ela é mais sociável do que eu e também mais corajosa. É irresponsável, ligeiramente excêntrica e uma cozinheira muito imprevisível. É a minha melhor amiga.

Detive-me. Falar sobre a minha mãe estava a deprimir-me.

— Que idade tens, Bella?

Por algum motivo que eu não conseguia imaginar, era patente alguma frustração na voz dele. Ele parara o carro e apercebi-me de que já estávamos junto da casa de Charlie. A chuva era tão intensa que eu mal conseguia vê-la. Era como se o carro estivesse submerso num rio.

— Tenho dezassete anos — respondi, um pouco confusa.

— Não pareces ter dezassete anos.

O seu tom de voz transmitia censura; fez-me rir.

— O que foi? — perguntou, novamente curioso.

— A minha mãe diz sempre que eu nasci com trinta e cinco anos de idade e que a minha mentalidade se torna mais característica de uma pessoa de meia-idade a cada ano que passa.

Ri-me e, em seguida, suspirei.

— Bem, alguém tem de desempenhar o papel de adulto — disse eu, detendo-me por um instante. — Tu também não pareces um jovenzinho do liceu — observei.

Ele manifestou discordância com um trejeito do rosto e mudou de assunto.

— Então, porque é que a tua mãe casou com o Phil?

Fiquei admirada com o facto de ele se recordar do nome; referira-o apenas uma vez, há quase dois meses. Demorei um pouco a responder.

— A minha mãe... tem um espírito muito jovem para a idade. Penso que o Phil a faz sentir ainda mais jovem. De qualquer modo, ela é louca por ele.

Abanei a cabeça. Esta atracção constituía um mistério.

— Tu aprovas? — perguntou ele.

— A minha opinião tem alguma importância? — contrapus. — Eu quero que ela seja feliz... e é ele quem ela quer.

— É muito generoso da tua parte... Pergunto-me... — devaneou ele.

— O quê?

— Julgas que ela demonstraria a mesma cortesia em relação a ti? Independentemente da pessoa sobre a qual a tua escolha recaísse?

Ele estava subitamente atento, com os seus olhos a examinarem os meus.

— Julgo que sim — tartamudeei. — Mas, afinal, é ela a mãe. É um pouco diferente.

— Então, desde que não se tratasse de alguém demasiado assustador... — disse ele num tom provocador.

Eu respondi-lhe com um sorriso rasgado.

— O que queres dizer com «assustador»? Múltiplos *piercings* faciais e tatuagens generalizadas?

— Suponho que é uma definição possível.

— Qual é a tua definição?

No entanto, ele ignorou a minha questão e colocou-me outra.

— Achas que *eu* poderia ser assustador?

Ele franziu uma sobrancelha e o ténue indício de um sorriso iluminou-lhe o rosto.

Reflecti por um momento, perguntando-me se seria preferível dizer a verdade ou recorrer a uma mentira. Decidi optar pela verdade.

— Hum... Acho que *poderias* sê-lo, se assim o desejasses.

— Agora, estás com medo de mim?

O sorriso desapareceu e o seu rosto celestial ficou, de repente, sério.

— Não.

Respondi, porém, depressa de mais. O sorriso voltou.

— Então, vais agora falar-me sobre a tua família? — perguntei, de modo a distraí-lo. — Deve tratar-se de uma história muito mais interessante do que a minha.

Tornou-se imediatamente cauteloso.

— O que queres saber?

— Os Cullen adoptaram-te? — procurei confirmar.

— Adoptaram.

Hesitei por um momento.

— O que aconteceu aos teus pais?

— Morreram há muitos anos — respondeu num tom de voz objectivo.

— Sinto muito — balbuciei.

— De facto, não me lembro deles assim tão nitidamente. O Carlisle e a Esme já são os meus pais há muito tempo.

— E tu ama-los.

Não era uma pergunta. Tal facto era evidente na forma como falava deles.

— Amo — respondeu com sorriso. — Não consigo imaginar duas pessoas melhores.

— Tens muita sorte.

— Eu sei que tenho.

— E os teus irmãos?

Ele olhou para o relógio no *tablier*.

— Os meus irmãos, assim como, a propósito, o Jasper e a Rosalie, vão ficar bastante aborrecidos se tiverem de ficar à chuva à minha espera.

— Oh, desculpa, suponho que tens de te ir embora.

Eu não queria sair do carro.

— E tu deves querer a tua *pick-up* de volta antes que o chefe Swan chegue a casa, de modo a que não tenhas de lhe contar o incidente que se deu na aula de Biologia.

Ele sorriu-me ironicamente.

— Tenho a certeza de que ele já soube. Não existem segredos em Forks — suspirei.

Ele riu-se e havia uma veemência patente no seu riso.

— Diverte-te na praia... está bom tempo para tomar banhos de sol.

Olhou para a chuva que caía copiosamente.

— Não nos vemos amanhã?

— Não. Eu e o Emmett vamos começar o fim-de-semana mais cedo.

— O que vão fazer?

Uma amiga podia fazer este tipo de perguntas, certo? Eu esperava que a decepção não fosse demasiado notória na minha voz.

— Vamos fazer caminhadas em Goat Rocks Wilderness, a Sul de Rainier.

Lembrei-me de que Charlie referira que os Cullen iam acampar frequentemente.

— Oh, bem, diverte-te.

Tentei parecer entusiástica. No entanto, não me parece que o tenha enganado. Um sorriso adivinhava-se à beira dos seus lábios.

— Fazes algo por mim este fim-de-semana?

Ele virou-se para me olhar directamente no rosto, utilizando todo o poder dos seus ardentes olhos dourados.

Eu acenei com a cabeça, indefesa.

— Não fiques ofendida, mas pareces ser uma daquelas pessoas que atraem acidentes como um íman. Por isso... tenta não cair ao mar, ser atropelada ou algo do género, está bem?

Sorriu de través.

O meu estado indefeso desvaneceu-se à medida que ele falava. Lancei-lhe um olhar irritado.

— Verei o que posso fazer — disse com brusquidão ao sair do carro e ficar à chuva.

Depois de ter saído, bati com a porta com excessiva violência.

Ao partir, ele ainda sorria.

Capítulo Seis

HISTÓRIAS ASSUSTADORAS

Enquanto permanecia sentada no meu quarto, tentando concentrar-me no terceiro acto de *Macbeth*, estava, na verdade, a tentar ouvir a minha *pick-up*. Pensava que, apesar do ruído da chuva fustigante, poderia ouvir o roncar do motor, mas, quando, mais uma vez, fui espreitar pela cortina, de repente já lá estava.

Não estava ansiosa por que chegasse sexta-feira e esta superou a minha ausência de expectativas. Como é evidente, ouvi comentários a respeito do meu desmaio. Era sobretudo Jessica quem parecia entusiasmar-se mais com aquela história. Felizmente, Mike mantivera a boca fechada e ninguém parecia ter conhecimento do envolvimento de Edward. Ela tinha, porém, muitas questões a colocar relativamente ao almoço.

— Então, que é que o Edward Cullen queria ontem? — perguntou Jessica na aula de Trigonometria.

— Não sei — respondi, sendo fiel à verdade. — Não chegou ao cerne da questão.

— Parecias algo furiosa — afirmou, tentando obter informações.

— Parecia?

Eu mantinha o rosto inexpressivo.

— Sabes, eu nunca o vi sentar-se à mesa com alguém que não fosse da sua família. Foi esquisito.

— Esquisito — concordei.

Ela parecia aborrecida; mexia impacientemente nos seus caracóis negros com os dedos. Supus que esperava ouvir algo que constituísse uma boa história para divulgar.

O pior da sexta-feira foi o facto de eu, apesar de saber que ele estaria ausente, ainda esperar encontrá-lo. Quando entrei na cantina com Jessica e Mike, não consegui evitar olhar para a mesa dele, onde Rosalie, Alice e Jasper se encontravam sentados, a conversar, com as cabeças bem próximas umas das outras. Não consegui igualmente evitar a melancolia que me invadiu ao aperceber-me de que não sabia quanto tempo teria de esperar para voltar a vê-lo.

Na minha mesa do costume, todos se referiam com entusiasmo aos nossos planos para o dia seguinte. Mike estava novamente animado, depositando uma grande confiança no apresentador do boletim meteorológico local, que garantia que o tempo iria estar soalheiro. Eu teria de ver para crer. No entanto, no dia em que nos encontrávamos, o tempo estava mais quente, atingindo uma temperatura de quase quinze graus. Talvez a excursão não viesse a ser um fracasso completo.

Interceptei alguns olhares pouco amigáveis por parte de Lauren durante o almoço, que não compreendi até sairmos da cantina. Eu seguia mesmo atrás dela, a apenas trinta centímetros dos seus lisos cabelos louros prateados, e ela não se dera conta.

— ... não sei porque é que a *Bella* — proferiu o meu nome com escárnio — não se senta simplesmente à mesa dos Cullen de agora em diante — ouvi-a segredar a Mike. Nunca reparara na sua desagradável voz nasalada e fiquei admirada com a maldade nela patente. Não a conhecia muito bem seguramente, não o suficiente para que ela não gostasse de mim — ou assim pensava eu.

— Ela é minha amiga; senta-se à nossa mesa — sussurrou Mike de forma leal, mas também um pouco territorial.

Detive-me para deixar Jess e Angela passarem por mim. Não queria ouvir mais nada.

Nessa noite, ao jantar, Charlie parecia entusiasmado com a minha viagem a *La Push* na manhã seguinte. Julgo que se sentia culpado por me deixar sozinha em casa durante os fins-de-semana, mas ele passara demasiados anos a criar as suas rotinas para quebrá-las agora. Evidentemente, sabia o nome de todos os miúdos que iam, dos pais e, provavelmente, também dos avós. Parecia aprovar. Perguntei-me se ele aprovaria a minha intenção de ir até Seattle com Edward Cullen. Não que eu fosse revelar-lha.

— Pai, conheces um lugar chamado Goat Rocks ou algo do género? Acho que fica a Sul do Monte Rainier — perguntei de forma desinteressada.

— Conheço, porquê?

Encolhi os ombros.

— Alguns miúdos estavam a falar em ir acampar para lá.

— Não é um lugar muito bom para acampar — afirmou ele, parecendo admirado. — Há demasiados ursos. A maioria das pessoas frequenta essa região na época da caça.

— Ah — murmurei. — Talvez tenha percebido mal o nome.

Eu pretendia dormir até mais tarde, mas uma claridade invulgar despertou-me. Abri os olhos e vi uma límpida luz amarela que atravessava as janelas do meu quarto. Não conseguia acreditar. Precipitei-me para a janela para averiguar e, de facto, lá estava o Sol. Encontrava-se na posição errada no céu, estando demasiado baixo, e não parecia estar tão próximo como deveria, mas tratava-se, sem dúvida, do Sol. As nuvens cingiam o horizonte, mas, no meio, era visível uma mancha azul. Permaneci junto da janela enquanto consegui, receando que, se me fosse embora, o azul voltasse a desaparecer.

Os Armazéns Olímpicos Newton ficavam precisamente na zona Norte da cidade. Eu já vira a loja, mas nunca lá entrara — já que não tinha grande necessidade de quaisquer provisões necessárias à permanência ao ar livre por um período de tempo alargado. No parque de estacionamento, reconheci o Suburban de Mike e o Sentra de Tyler. Ao estacionar ao lado dos veículos de ambos, vi o grupo que se encontrava em frente do Suburban. Eric estava presente, juntamente com dois outros rapazes com quem eu tinha aulas; estava bastante certa de que os seus nomes eram Ben e Conner. Jess também lá estava, ladeada por Angela e Lauren. Três outras raparigas encontravam-se na sua companhia, incluindo aquela sobre a qual me lembrava de ter caído na aula de Educação Física na sexta-feira. Esta lançou-me um olhar de desagrado quando saí da *pick-up* e sussurrou algo ao ouvido de Lauren. Lauren sacudiu o seu cabelo semelhante a barbas de milho e olhou-me com desdém.

Seria, então, um *daqueles* dias.

Pelo menos, Mike estava contente por me ver.

— Vieste! — exclamou, encantado. — E eu bem disse que o tempo hoje estaria soalheiro, não disse?

— Eu disse-te que vinha — relembrei-lhe.

— Estamos só à espera do Lee e da Samantha... a não ser que tenhas convidado alguém — acrescentou Mike.

— Não convidei — menti sem dificuldade, esperando que a minha mentira não fosse denunciada, mas também desejando que se desse um milagre e Edward aparecesse.

Mike parecia satisfeito.

— Vais no meu carro? Ou isso ou no monovolume da mãe do Lee.

— Claro.

Ele sorriu com um ar de felicidade. Mike era tão fácil de contentar.

— Podes sentar-te no lugar do pendura — prometeu ele.

Ocultei o meu enfado. Não era fácil contentar Mike e Jessica ao mesmo tempo. Conseguia ver Jessica fitar-nos agora com um ar zangado.

No entanto, os números jogaram a meu favor. Lee levou mais duas pessoas e, de repente, todos os lugares se tornaram necessários. Consegui colocar Jess à força entre mim e Mike no banco dianteiro do Suburban. Mike poderia ter encarado a situação com maior graciosidade, mas, pelo menos, Jess parecia tranquilizada.

La Push ficava apenas a quinze quilómetros de Forks, com a estrada ladeada por densas e deslumbrantes florestas verdes durante a maior parte do percurso e o largo rio Quillayute a serpentear debaixo daquela em dois locais. Abríramos os vidros novamente —

o Suburban ficava um pouco claustrofóbico com nove pessoas no seu interior — e eu tentei absorver o máximo de luz possível.

Já frequentara muitas vezes as praias nos arredores de *La Push* durante os Verões que passara com Charlie em Forks, pelo que a meia-lua com um quilómetro e meio de comprimento da First Beach não me era estranha. Caracterizava-a uma beleza de cortar a respiração. A água tinha uma tonalidade cinzento-escura, mesmo à luz do Sol, coroada de branco e elevando-se sobre a praia cinzenta e rochosa. Ilhas erguiam-se das águas do porto de aço com íngremes escarpas, culminando em cumes desnivelados, coroadas de abetos austeros e altaneiros. A praia tinha apenas uma estreita faixa de areia na orla da água, após a qual se transformava em milhões de grandes pedras polidas, que, à distância, pareciam uniformemente cinzentas, mas, ao perto, se revestiam de vários tons: terracota, verde-mar, alfazema, cinzento-azulado, dourado-opalescente. A linha da maré estava juncada de enormes árvores flutuantes, que as ondas salgadas descoloraram e às quais conferiram uma tonalidade branco-osso, estando algumas amontoadas junto à orla da floresta e outras jazendo solitárias, fora do alcance das ondas.

Um vento acelerado soprava das ondas, fresco e salgado. Pelicanos flutuavam na ondulação, enquanto gaivotas e uma águia solitária voavam em círculos acima deles. As nuvens cingiam o céu, ameaçando atacar a qualquer momento, mas, por enquanto, o Sol ainda brilhava com intensidade no seu halo de céu azul.

Caminhámos cautelosamente até à praia, com Mike a indicar o caminho em direcção a um recinto formado por toros flutuantes que já fora manifestamente utilizado para a realização de festas como a nossa. Havia um círculo para fogueiras já a postos, repleto de cinzas negras. Eric e o rapaz que eu pensava chamar-se Ben recolheram ramos quebrados de madeira flutuante a partir dos montes mais secos que se encontravam junto da orla da floresta e depressa se ergueu uma construção semelhante às tendas cónicas dos peles-vermelhas sobre as velhas cinzas.

— Já viste uma fogueira de madeira flutuante? — perguntou-
-me Mike.

Eu estava sentada num dos bancos cor de osso; as restantes
raparigas agruparam-se, bisbilhotando animadamente, tanto à
minha direita, como à minha esquerda. Mike ajoelhou-se junto
da fogueira, ateando alguns dos paus mais pequenos com um
isqueiro.

— Não — disse eu enquanto ele encostava cuidadosamente o
ramo em chamas ao cone formado pela madeira.

— Então, vais gostar disto; observa as cores.

Ateou outro pequeno ramo e colocou-o ao lado do primeiro.
As chamas começaram a consumir rapidamente a madeira seca.

— Está azul — exclamei com espanto.

— É um efeito provocado pelo sal. É bonito, não é?

Ateou mais um galho, colocou-o num ponto ao qual o fogo
ainda não alastrara e, em seguida, foi sentar-se a meu lado. Felizmente, Jess encontrava-se do outro lado. Virou-se para ele e
exigiu a sua atenção. Eu observei as estranhas chamas azuis e
verdes a crepitarem em direcção ao céu.

Após uma hora de conversa, alguns dos rapazes quiseram fazer uma caminhada até às poças residuais da maré que ficavam
nas proximidades. Era um dilema. Por um lado, eu adorava as
poças residuais da maré. Fascinavam-me desde pequena; eram
uma das raras coisas por que eu ansiava quando tinha de ir para Forks. Por outro, também caíra nelas imensas vezes, o que não
é nada de mais quando se tem sete anos e se está acompanhada pelo pai. Isto fez-me recordar o pedido de Edward — que eu
não caísse ao mar.

Foi Lauren quem tomou a decisão por mim. Ela não queria
caminhar e os sapatos que calçara eram, sem dúvida, inadequa-
dos para tal. A maioria das raparigas, além de Angela e Jessica,
decidiu ficar também na praia. Eu esperei até que Tyler e Eric se
comprometessem a permanecer com elas para me levantar discretamente e me juntar ao grupo que era a favor da caminhada. Mike lançou-me um enorme sorriso ao ver que eu ia.

A caminhada não foi demasiado longa, ainda que eu, nos bosques, detestasse perder o céu de vista. A claridade verde da floresta tornava-se estranhamente incompatível com o riso adolescente, sendo demasiado tenebrosa e ominosa para estar de harmonia com os alegres gracejos que me rodeavam. Tinha de calcular com muito cuidado cada passo que dava, evitando as raízes no plano inferior e os ramos no superior, e depressa fiquei para trás. Acabei por conseguir ultrapassar os confins esmeraldinos da floresta e voltei a deparar com a praia rochosa. A maré estava baixa e um rio de maré corria, passando por nós e dirigindo-se para o mar. Ao longo das suas margens juncadas de seixos, poças com pouca profundidade, que nunca secavam por completo, pululavam de vida.

Eu tinha uma extrema cautela em não me debruçar demasiado sobre os pequenos lagos oceânicos. Os outros eram destemidos, saltando por cima das rochas, empoleirando-se precariamente à beira das mesmas. Encontrei uma rocha com um aspecto estável na orla de uma das maiores poças e ali me sentei cautelosamente, enfeitiçada pelo aquário natural que se encontrava debaixo de mim. Os ramalhetes de anémonas brilhantes ondulavam sem cessar na corrente invisível; conchas retorcidas agitavam-se ao longo das orlas, ocultando os caranguejos; estrelas-do-mar permaneciam estaticamente presas às rochas e umas às outras, enquanto uma pequena enguia negra com listas de corrida brancas serpenteava por entre as algas de um verde-vivo, esperando que o mar regressasse. Estava completamente absorta, à excepção de um pequeno recanto da minha mente que se perguntava o que estaria Edward a fazer naquele momento e tentava imaginar o que estaria ele a dizer se estivesse ali comigo.

Por fim, os rapazes ficaram com fome e eu levantei-me contrafeita para segui-los no caminho de regresso. Desta vez, esforcei-me por acompanhá-los ao longo dos bosques, pelo que acabei por cair algumas vezes. Fiquei com alguns arranhões superficiais nas palmas das mãos e as minhas calças de ganga ficaram manchadas de verde na zona dos joelhos, mas podia ter sido pior.

Quando regressámos à First Beach, o grupo que deixámos multiplicara-se. Ao aproximarmo-nos, conseguimos ver os brilhantes cabelos negros lisos e a pele acobreada dos recém-chegados, adolescentes da reserva que foram conviver um pouco. A comida já circulava e os rapazes apressaram-se a reivindicar um quinhão, enquanto Eric nos apresentava à medida que cada um de nós entrava no círculo de madeira flutuante. Eu e Angela fomos as últimas a chegar e, quando Eric disse os nossos nomes, reparei que um rapaz mais novo, que se encontrava sentado nas pedras perto da fogueira, me olhou com interesse. Sentei-me ao lado de Angela, e Mike levou-nos sandes, assim como uma grande variedade de refrigerantes para que escolhêssemos, enquanto um dos rapazes, que parecia ser o mais velho dos visitantes, proferia rapidamente os nomes dos restantes sete que se encontravam com ele. Consegui apenas perceber que uma das raparigas também se chamava Jessica e que o rapaz que reparara em mim se chamava Jacob.

Estar sentada junto de Angela era relaxante; era o género de pessoa cuja companhia era repousante – não sentia necessidade de preencher cada momento de silêncio com tagarelice. Deixou-me à vontade para reflectir, sem perturbações, enquanto comíamos e eu reflectia sobre a forma como o tempo parecia fluir incoerentemente em Forks, passando, por vezes, de modo confuso, com imagens isoladas a destacarem-se mais nítidas do que outras. Outras vezes, cada segundo era significativo, ficava gravado na minha mente. Eu sabia exactamente o que originava a diferença e isso incomodava-me.

Durante o almoço, as nuvens começaram a avançar, movimentando-se furtivamente pelo céu azul, precipitando-se por momentos para diante do Sol, projectando extensas sombras sobre a praia e enegrecendo as ondas. Ao acabarem de comer, as pessoas começaram a afastar-se em grupos de duas e três. Algumas caminharam até à beira das ondas, tentando pular de rocha em rocha através da superfície agitada. Outras reuniram voluntários para uma segunda expedição às poças residuais da maré. Mike — com Jessica a segui-lo como uma sombra — encaminhou-se para a única loja da aldeia. Alguns dos miúdos indígenas acompanharam-nos; outros alinharam na caminhada. Quando já todos se tinham dispersado, eu estava sentada, sozinha, no meu toro flutuante, enquanto Lauren e Tyler se entretinham com o leitor de CD que alguém se lembrara de trazer, e três adolescentes da reserva estavam empoleirados em torno do círculo, incluindo o rapaz chamado Jacob e o mais velho que desempenhara o papel de porta-voz.

Alguns momentos depois de Angela ter partido com o grupo que iria realizar a caminhada, Jacob avançou vagarosamente e ocupou o lugar dela a meu lado. Aparentava ter catorze anos, talvez quinze, e tinha cabelos negros longos e brilhantes, presos com um elástico na nuca. A sua pele era linda, sedosa e de cor castanho-avermelhada; os olhos eram escuros, profundamente encovados acima das elevadas superfícies planas das maçãs do rosto. Tinha ainda apenas um resquício de pueril rotundidade em torno do queixo. No conjunto, um rosto muito bonito. No entanto, a minha opinião positiva a respeito da sua aparência foi afectada pelas primeiras palavras que proferiu.

— És a Isabella Swan, não és?

Era como reviver o primeiro dia de aulas.

— Bella — disse, suspirando.

— Eu sou o Jacob Black — declarou, estendendo a mão num gesto amigável. — Compraste a *pick-up* do meu pai.

— Ah! — exclamei, aliviada, apertando-lhe a suave mão. — És o filho do Billy. Provavelmente devia lembrar-me de ti.

— Não, sou o mais novo da família. Lembrar-te-ias das minhas irmãs mais velhas.

— A Rachel e a Rebecca — recordei-me de repente. Charlie e Billy juntaram-nos muitas vezes durante as minhas estadas em Forks, de modo a manterem-nos entretidas enquanto eles pescavam. Éramos todas demasiado tímidas para fazer com que a nossa amizade evoluísse de forma significativa. Como é evidente, quando completei onze anos, já fizera birras suficientes para pôr termo às pescarias.

— Elas estão aqui?

Examinei as raparigas que se encontravam à beira do mar, perguntando-me se agora as reconheceria.

— Não — disse Jacob, abanando a cabeça. — A Rachel obteve uma bolsa de estudos na Universidade do Estado de Washington e a Rebecca casou com um surfista samoano. Agora, vive no Havai.

— Está casada. Ena. - Eu estava aturdida. As gémeas eram pouco mais de um ano mais velhas que eu.

— Então, que tal te parece a *pick-up*? — perguntou ele.

— Adoro-a, funciona às mil maravilhas.

— Pois, mas é mesmo lenta — riu-se. — Fiquei tão aliviado quando o Charlie a comprou. O meu pai não deixava que eu me dedicasse à construção de outro carro, já que tínhamos um veículo em perfeitas condições ali mesmo.

— Não é assim tão lenta — protestei.

— Já tentaste ultrapassar os cem quilómetros por hora?

— Não — reconheci.

— Ainda bem. Nem tentes.

Esboçou um sorriso rasgado. Não consegui evitar retribuir-lhe o sorriso.

— Sai-se muito bem numa colisão — mencionei em defesa da minha *pick-up*.

— Acho que nem um carro de combate conseguiria dar cabo daquele velho monstro — concordou ele com outra gargalhada.

— Com que então constróis carros? — perguntei, impressionada.

— Quando tenho tempo livre e peças. Por acaso não sabes onde posso arranjar um cilindro principal para um Volkswagen Rabbit de 1986? — acrescentou em tom de graça.

Ele tinha uma voz agradável, rouca.

— Sinto muito — ri. — Não vi nenhum ultimamente, mas ficarei atenta.

Como se eu soubesse do que se tratava. Era muito fácil conversar com ele.

Exibiu um sorriso fulgurante, olhando-me com apreço, de uma forma que eu estava a aprender a reconhecer. Não fui a única a notar.

— Conheces a Bella, Jacob? — perguntou Lauren, naquilo que eu imaginava ser um tom insolente, do lado oposto da fogueira.

— De certa forma, conhecemo-nos desde que eu nasci — riu-se, sorrindo-me novamente.

— Que giro!

O seu tom de voz não transmitia a ideia de franqueza e os seus olhos claros, semelhantes aos dos peixes, semicerraram-se.

— Bella — exclamou ela novamente, observando o meu rosto cuidadosamente —, estava mesmo agora a comentar com o Tyler que era uma pena o facto de nenhum dos Cullen poder ter vindo hoje. Ninguém se lembrou de convidá-los?

O seu ar de preocupação era pouco convincente.

— Referes-te à família do Dr. Carlisle Cullen? — interrogou o rapaz alto, mais velho, antes de eu poder responder, o que provocou bastante irritação em Lauren. Na verdade, ele estava mais próximo de ser um homem do que um rapaz e a sua voz era extremamente grave.

— Sim, conhece-los? — perguntou ela de modo condescendente, virando-se parcialmente na direcção dele.

— Os Cullen não vêm aqui — afirmou ele num tom que encerrava o assunto, ignorando a pergunta dela.

Tyler, tentando reconquistar a atenção de Lauren, perguntou-lhe a sua opinião a respeito de um CD que ela segurava na mão. Ela estava distraída.

Eu olhava fixamente para o rapaz de voz grave, tendo sido apanhada de surpresa, mas ele lançava o olhar na direcção da floresta sombria atrás de nós. Dissera que os Cullen não iam ali, mas o seu tom de voz insinuara algo mais – que a sua presença não era permitida; estavam proibidos de frequentar aquele local. O seu comportamento deixou em mim uma estranha impressão e tentei ignorá-la sem sucesso.

– Então, Forks já está a dar contigo em doida? – perguntou Jacob, interrompendo a minha meditação.

– Oh, eu diria que isso é ser comedido nas palavras – afirmei, fazendo um esgar; esboçou um sorriso largo, demonstrando compreensão.

Ainda com o breve comentário acerca dos Cullen a revolver-me o pensamento, tive uma inspiração súbita. Era um plano idiota, mas não tinha outro melhor. Esperava que o jovem Jacob ainda fosse inexperiente no que se referia ao relacionamento com raparigas, de modo que não se apercebesse das intenções das minhas tentativas de namoriscá-lo, as quais estavam votadas a ser dignas de pena.

– Queres caminhar comigo pela praia? – perguntei, tentando imitar aquela forma que Edward tinha de olhar por debaixo das suas pestanas. Sabia que estava longe de conseguir o mesmo efeito, mas Jacob levantou-se de um salto e de bastante bom grado.

Enquanto caminhávamos para Norte ao longo das pedras com diferentes matizes em direcção ao paredão de madeira flutuante, as nuvens cerraram finalmente fileiras no céu, desencadeando o escurecimento do mar e a diminuição da temperatura. Enterrei bem as mãos nos bolsos do meu casaco.

– Então, que idade tens? Dezasseis anos? – perguntei, tentando não parecer uma palerma ao pestanejar como vira fazer na televisão.

– Acabei de completar quinze – confessou ele, sentindo-se lisonjeado.

– A sério?

O meu rosto estava repleto de falsa surpresa.

– Eu diria que eras mais velho.

– Sou alto para a idade que tenho – explicou.

— Vais a Forks com muita frequência? — perguntei maliciosamente, como se ansiasse por uma resposta afirmativa. Parecia uma idiota aos meus próprios ouvidos. Receava que ele me virasse as costas, manifestando repugnância, e me acusasse de dolo, mas continuava a aparentar sentir-se lisonjeado.

— Nem por isso — confessou, franzindo o sobrolho. — Mas, quando terminar o meu carro, posso lá ir sempre que quiser, depois de tirar a carta condução — corrigiu.

— Quem era aquele outro rapaz com quem a Lauren estava a conversar? Parecia um pouco velho de mais para andar connosco.

Eu juntara-me aos mais novos, tentando deixar claro que preferia Jacob.

— É o Sam, tem dezanove anos — informou-me ele.

— O que é que ele estava a dizer acerca da família do médico? — perguntei inocentemente.

— Os Cullen? Ah, eles não podem entrar na reserva.

Desviou o olhar, na direcção de James Island, ao confirmar aquilo que eu pensara ter ouvido nas palavras de Sam.

— Porque não?

Voltou a olhar na minha direcção, mordendo o lábio.

— Ups. Não posso dizer nada a esse respeito.

— Oh, eu não conto a ninguém, estou apenas curiosa.

Tentei esboçar um sorriso cativante, perguntando-me se estaria a exagerar.

No entanto, ele retribuiu o sorriso, parecendo cativado. Depois, levantou uma sobrancelha e a sua voz ficou ainda mais rouca do que antes.

— Gostas de histórias assustadoras? — perguntou ele de forma ominosa.

— *Adoro*-as! — exclamei com entusiasmo, esforçando-me por lhe lançar um olhar ardente.

Jacob deambulou até uma árvore flutuante cujas raízes se projectavam como as patas adelgaçadas de uma enorme aranha

sem cor. Empoleirou-se sem dificuldade numa das raízes retorcidas, enquanto eu me sentei, abaixo dele, no tronco da árvore. Ele
fixava o olhar nas rochas, com um sorriso a aflorar aos seus lábios grossos. Eu conseguia ver que ele iria esforçar-se para que
aquilo valesse a pena. Concentrei-me para evitar que o interesse vital que eu sentia se reflectisse nos meus olhos.

— Conheces alguma das nossas histórias antigas, a respeito
das nossas origens — dos Quileutes, quero eu dizer? — principiou.

— Nem por isso — confessei.

— Bem, existem imensas lendas, das quais algumas remontam
pretensamente ao Dilúvio; supostamente, os antigos Quileutes
amarraram as suas canoas às copas das árvores mais altas da
montanha para sobreviverem como Noé e a arca. — Ele sorriu,
de modo a mostrar-me quão pouca fé tinha nestas histórias. —
Segundo uma outra lenda, nós descendemos de lobos, e estes
são ainda nossos irmãos. A lei tribal proíbe que sejam mortos.

— Depois, existem as histórias acerca dos *frios* — afirmou,
tendo o tom da sua voz baixado um pouco.

— Dos frios? — perguntei, estando agora sinceramente intrigada.

— Sim. Existem histórias acerca dos frios que são tão antigas
como as lendas sobre os lobos, havendo também algumas muito mais recentes. De acordo com a lenda, o meu próprio bisavô
conhecia alguns deles. Foi ele quem firmou o tratado que os
mantinha longe das nossas terras — disse ele, revirando os olhos.

— O teu bisavô? — incitei-o a continuar.

— Ele era um ancião da tribo, tal como o meu pai. Sabes, os
frios são os inimigos naturais do lobo. Bem, não propriamente
do lobo, mas dos lobos que se transformam em homens, como
os nossos antepassados. Poder-se-ia chamar-lhes lobisomens.

— Os lobisomens têm inimigos?

— Apenas um.

Fitava-o com um ar sério, esperando disfarçar a minha impaciência de admiração.

— Portanto, como vês — prosseguiu Jacob —, os frios são, por tradição, nossos inimigos, mas o bando que chegou ao nosso território no tempo do meu bisavô era diferente. Não caçavam como outros da sua espécie o faziam — não deviam constituir uma ameaça à tribo. Assim, o meu bisavô decretou uma trégua com eles. Se prometessem manter-se afastados das nossas terras, ele não os denunciaria aos caras-pálidas.

Ele piscou-me o olho.

— Se não constituíam uma ameaça, porque é que...? — tentei compreender, esforçando-me por não deixar que ele percebesse quão a sério eu estava a levar a sua história de fantasmas.

— Existe sempre perigo para os humanos ao estarem perto dos frios, mesmo que sejam civilizados como este clã era. Nunca se sabe quando é que eles podem ficar demasiado famintos para conseguirem resistir.

Introduziu deliberadamente um carregado laivo de ameaça no seu tom de voz.

— O que queres dizer com «civilizados»?

— Eles alegavam não caçar humanos. Supostamente eram, de alguma forma, capazes de atacar animais como alternativa.

Tentei manter um tom de voz desinteressado.

— Então, como é que isso encaixa nos Cullen? Eles são como os frios que o teu bisavô conheceu?

— Não — deteve-se teatralmente. — São os *mesmos*.

Ele deve ter pensado que a expressão estampada no meu rosto se devia ao temor inspirado pela sua história. Sorriu, satisfeito, e prosseguiu:

— Agora há mais, uma nova fêmea e um novo macho, mas os restantes são os mesmos. No tempo do meu bisavô, já tinham conhecimento da existência do líder, o Carlisle. Ele estivera aqui e partira antes de a vossa gente ter sequer aqui chegado.

Ele tentava reprimir um sorriso.

— E o que são eles? — perguntei por fim. — O que *são* os frios?

Sorriu misteriosamente.

— Bebedores de sangue — retorquiu num tom de voz arrepiante. — A tua gente chama-lhes vampiros.

Fixei o olhar na ondulação encrespada depois de ele ter respondido, não sabendo ao certo o que o meu rosto expressava.

— Estás com pele-de-galinha — riu-se com satisfação.

— És um bom contador de histórias — elogiei-o, olhando ainda fixamente para as ondas.

— Mas é uma coisa de loucos, não é? Não admira que o meu pai não queira que nós falemos disto a ninguém.

Ainda não conseguia controlar suficientemente a minha expressão facial para olhar para ele.

— Não te preocupes, eu não te denuncio.

— Suponho que apenas violei o tratado — riu-se.

— Este segredo irá comigo para o túmulo — prometi e, em seguida, senti um calafrio.

— Agora a sério, não comentes nada com o Charlie. Ele ficou bastante enfurecido quando soube que alguns de nós não iam ao hospital desde que o Dr. Cullen começou a trabalhar lá.

— Não comentarei, claro que não.

— Então, pensas que nós somos uma súcia de indígenas supersticiosos ou quê? — perguntou ele num tom jocoso, mas com um laivo de preocupação.

Eu ainda não desviara o olhar do mar.

Assim, voltei-me e sorri-lhe com a maior normalidade possível.

— Não, mas penso que tens muito jeito para contar histórias assustadoras. Ainda estou com pele-de-galinha, vês?

Mostrei o meu braço.

— Porreiro! — disse ele, sorrindo.

Então, o ruído das rochas da praia a baterem umas nas outras alertou-nos para o facto de que alguém se aproximava. As nossas cabeças viraram-se rapidamente, ao mesmo tempo, e avistámos, então, Mike e Jessica a cerca de cinquenta metros de distância, caminhando na nossa direcção.

— Aí estás tu, Bella — exclamou Mike com alívio, agitando o braço sobre a sua cabeça.

— É o teu namorado? — perguntou Jacob, alertado pelo laivo de ciúme patente na voz de Mike.

Fiquei admirada por tal ser tão óbvio.

— Não, de modo algum — sussurrei.

Estava tremendamente grata a Jacob e ansiosa por agradar-
-lhe o mais possível. Pisquei-lhe o olho, voltando-me cuidadosamente de costas para Mike para o fazer. Ele sorriu, enlevado
pelo meu inepto galanteio.

— Então, quando eu tirar a carta de condução... — principiou.

— Devias ir visitar-me a Forks. Podíamos passar algum tempo juntos um dia destes.

Senti-me culpada ao proferir tais palavras, tendo consciência
de que usara Jacob, mas simpatizei, de facto, com ele. Era uma
pessoa de quem era fácil ficar amigo.

Mike já chegara junto de nós, encontrando-se Jessica alguns
passos atrás. Eu conseguia ver os olhos dele a examinarem Jacob e mostrando satisfação perante a sua óbvia tenra idade.

— Onde tens estado? — perguntou, ainda que a resposta estivesse mesmo diante dele.

— Jacob estava apenas a contar-me algumas histórias nativas
— mencionei. — Foi realmente interessante.

Lancei um sorriso caloroso a Jacob e ele retribuiu-mo com
um sorriso rasgado.

— Bem. — Mike deteve-se, reavaliando cuidadosamente a situação ao observar a camaradagem que existia entre nós. — Estamos a arrumar as coisas, parece que vai chover em breve.

Todos olhámos para o céu carregado. De facto, parecia mesmo que a chuva estava prestes a cair.

— Muito bem — concordei, levantando-me de um salto. — Eu
vou já.

— Foi bom ver-te *novamente* — disse Jacob, tendo eu percebido que ele estava a provocar Mike um pouco.

— Foi, de facto, muito bom. Da próxima vez que o Charlie
vier visitar o Billy, eu também virei — prometi.

O seu sorriso rasgou-se-lhe no rosto.

— Isso seria porreiro.

— E obrigada — acrescentei com um ar sério.

Coloquei o capuz enquanto caminhávamos pesadamente sobre as rochas em direcção ao parque de estacionamento. Começavam a cair algumas gotas, deixando manchas negras nas pedras em que pousavam. Quando chegámos junto do Suburban, os outros já estavam a colocar tudo novamente dentro do carro. Entrei para o banco de trás, ao lado de Angela e Tyler, comunicando que já tivera a minha oportunidade para viajar no lugar do pendura. Angela limitava-se a olhar, pelo vidro, para a tempestade que se avolumava e Lauren contorcia-se no lugar central para chamar a atenção de Tyler, pelo que eu podia simplesmente recostar a cabeça no banco, fechar os olhos e esforçar-me arduamente por não pensar.

Capítulo Sete

PESADELO

Disse a Charlie que tinha muitos trabalhos de casa para fazer e que não queria comer nada. Na televisão, estava a ser transmitido um jogo de basquetebol a propósito do qual ele estava entusiasmado, ainda que, evidentemente, eu não fizesse a menor ideia do que tinha de especial, não se tendo ele, portanto, apercebido de nada de invulgar no meu rosto ou no meu tom de voz.

Assim que cheguei ao meu quarto, tranquei a porta. Remexi na secretária até encontrar os meus velhos auscultadores e liguei-os ao pequeno leitor de CD. Peguei num CD que Phil me oferecera no Natal. Tratava-se de uma das suas bandas preferidas, mas abusava um pouco do baixo e produzia um som demasiado estridente para o meu gosto. Inseri-o no leitor e estendi-me na cama. Coloquei os auscultadores, premi a tecla «Play» e aumentei o volume até me ferir os tímpanos. Fechei os olhos, mas a luz continuava a infiltrar-se, tendo eu, por conseguinte, colocado uma almofada sobre a metade superior do rosto.

Concentrei-me com muito cuidado na música, tentando compreender a letra, destrinçar os complicados padrões da bateria. A ouvir o CD pela terceira vez, já sabia, pelo menos, todos os refrões. Fiquei admirada por descobrir que, afinal, gostava realmente daquela banda, assim que passei à frente do ruído retumbante. Teria de voltar a agradecer a Phil.

Resultou. As batidas estrondosas impossibilitaram-me de pensar — o que constituía o objectivo do exercício. Ouvi o CD uma e outra vez, até conseguir cantar todas as músicas, antes de, por fim, adormecer.

Abri os olhos num local conhecido. Ciente, em algum recanto da minha consciência, de que estava a sonhar, reconheci a claridade verde da floresta. Conseguia ouvir as ondas a rebentarem contra as rochas algures por perto e sabia que, se encontrasse o mar, seria capaz de ver o Sol. Estava a tentar seguir o som, mas, de repente, apareceu Jacob Black, puxando-me pela mão, querendo conduzir-me novamente na direcção da parte mais sombria da floresta.

— Jacob? O que se passa? — perguntei.

O seu rosto expressava pavor enquanto ele se debatia com todas as suas forças contra a minha resistência; eu não queria embrenhar-me na escuridão.

— Foge, Bella, tens de fugir! — sussurrou ele, aterrorizado.

— Por aqui, Bella! — reconheci a voz de Mike a bradar do âmago soturno das árvores, mas não conseguia vê-lo.

— Porquê? — interroguei, resistindo ainda à força de pulso de Jacob, procurando agora o Sol de forma desesperada.

Jacob, contudo, largou a minha mão e regougou, estando, de repente, a tremer, caindo no indistinto chão da floresta. Contorceu-se no solo enquanto eu o observava, horrorizada.

— Jacob! — gritei.

No entanto, ele desaparecera. No seu lugar, encontrava-se um grande lobo castanho-avermelhado de olhos negros. O lobo virou-se numa direcção oposta àquela em que eu me encontrava, apontando para a praia, com o pêlo na parte de cima dos seus quartos dianteiros a eriçar-se, com graves rosnadelas provenientes dentre as suas presas expostas.

— Bella, foge! — clamou Mike novamente de trás de mim, mas eu não me virei. Estava a observar uma luz que vinha na minha direcção, a partir da praia.

Então, Edward irrompeu dentre as árvores, com a pele a emitir um brilho ténue e com os olhos negros e perigosos. Ergueu uma mão e acenou-me para que fosse até junto dele. O lobo rosnava aos meus pés.

Avancei um passo, na direcção de Edward. Então, ele sorriu e os seus dentes eram bem aguçados.

— Confia em mim — ronronou.

Dei outro passo.

O lobo lançou-se pelo espaço que me separava do vampiro, com as suas presas a apontarem para a jugular deste último.

— Não! — gritei, levantando-me violentamente da cama.

Este movimento brusco fez com que os auscultadores puxassem o leitor de CD e o levassem a cair da mesinha-de-cabeceira, produzindo um ruído sonoro ao embater no piso de madeira.

A luz do meu quarto ainda estava acesa e eu estava sentada na cama, completamente vestida e com os sapatos calçados. Olhei, desorientada, para o relógio que se encontrava sobre a minha cómoda. Eram cinco e meia da madrugada.

Gemi, deixei-me cair de costas e virei-me, pousando a cara e descalçando as botas apenas com os pés. No entanto, estava demasiado desconfortável para conseguir dormir. Voltei a virar-me e desabotoei as calças de ganga, despindo-as desajeitadamente ao tentar manter-me na posição horizontal. Conseguia sentir a trança do meu cabelo, uma incómoda saliência que se estendia ao logo da parte de trás do meu crânio. Virei-me de lado e arranquei o elástico, passando rapidamente os dedos pela trança. Voltei a pousar a almofada sobre os meus olhos.

Como é evidente, nada disso adiantou. O meu subconsciente dragara exactamente as imagens que eu tentava tão desesperadamente evitar. Agora, teria de enfrentá-las.

Sentei-me, e a minha cabeça girou por um instante, enquanto o sangue fluía no sentido descendente. Em primeiro lugar, o mais importante, pensei comigo mesma, disposta a adiar ao máximo o assunto. Peguei na bolsa que continha os meus produtos de higiene pessoal.

O duche, porém, não durou de modo algum o tempo que eu esperava que durasse. Mesmo levando algum tempo a secar o cabelo, depressa esgotei as tarefas a realizar na casa de banho. Embrulhada numa toalha, voltei para o meu quarto. Não sabia se Charlie ainda estava a dormir ou se já saíra. Fui espreitar à janela e o carro de rádio-patrulha desaparecera. Fora pescar novamente.

Vesti o meu fato de treino mais confortável e, em seguida, fiz a cama — algo que eu nunca fazia. Não podia adiar mais aquele assunto. Dirigi-me à secretária e liguei o meu velho computador.

Detestava aceder à Internet ali. O meu modem estava tristemente ultrapassado e o meu serviço gratuito tinha uma qualidade abaixo da média; só a ligação demorou tanto tempo que resolvi ir buscar uma taça de cereais enquanto esperava.

Comi lentamente, mastigando cada colherada com cuidado. Quando terminei, lavei a taça e a colher, limpei-as e arrumei-as. Os meus pés arrastavam-se enquanto eu subia as escadas. Encarreguei-me, em primeiro lugar, do meu leitor de CD, apanhando-o do chão e colocando-o mesmo no centro da mesa. Desliguei os auscultadores e guardei-os na gaveta da secretária. Em seguida, pus o mesmo CD a tocar, baixando o volume no ponto em que a música se resumia a ruído de fundo.

Com um suspiro, voltei-me para o meu computador. Evidentemente, o ecrã estava pejado de janelas de publicidade. Sentei-me na minha rígida cadeira articulada e comecei a fechar todas as pequenas janelas. Acabei por conseguir aceder ao meu motor de busca preferido. Fechei mais algumas janelas de publicidade e, em seguida, digitei uma palavra.

Vampiro.

Como é óbvio, a pesquisa demorou um tempo enfurecedoramente longo. Quando os resultados surgiram, havia muito para esquadrinhar — tudo, desde filmes e séries televisivas a jogos de dramatização, música da pesada e empresas que produziam cosméticos góticos.

Então, encontrei um sítio promissor — Vampiros de A a Z. Esperei pacientemente que carregasse, clicando rapidamente para fechar cada janela de publicidade que surgia no ecrã. Por fim, a imagem ficou completa — fundo branco simples com texto preto, de aspecto académico. Fui saudada por duas citações na página inicial:

*Em todo o vasto mundo sombrio dos fantasmas e dos demó-
nios, não existe figura tão terrível, figura tão temida e abomi-
nada, mas, ao mesmo tempo, paramentada de um tal fascínio
temeroso como o vampiro, que não é fantasma, nem demónio,
mas que, todavia, compartilha das índoles tenebrosas e possui
os misteriosos e terríveis atributos de ambos.* – Rev. Montague
Summers.

*Se existe, neste mundo, um relato devidamente fundamenta-
do, é aquele que se refere à existência dos vampiros. Nada lhe
falta: relatórios oficiais, atestados de pessoas de renome, cirur-
giões, sacerdotes, magistrados; a comprovação judicial está
quase concluída. E, com tudo isso, quem é que acredita em
vampiros?* – Rousseau.

O resto do sítio consistia numa listagem ordenada alfabetica-
mente de todos os diferentes mitos a respeito dos vampiros sustentados em todo o mundo. O primeiro em que cliquei, o *Danag*,
era um vampiro filipino supostamente responsável pelo plantio
de taro nas ilhas, há muito tempo. Ainda segundo o mito, o *Danag* trabalhou com humanos durante muitos anos, mas a parce-
ria chegou ao fim no dia em que uma mulher cortou um dedo e
um *Danag* sugou o seu ferimento, gostando tanto do sabor que
fez com que o corpo dela ficasse completamente exangue.

Li cuidadosamente as descrições, procurando algo que não
me parecesse estranho, já para não dizer implausível. Ao que parecia, a maioria dos mitos relacionados com vampiros centrava-
-se em belas mulheres no papel de demónios e em crianças no
de vítimas; parecia também tratar-se de construções do espírito
criadas para fornecer uma explicação satisfatória para as elevadas taxas de mortalidade de crianças de muito tenra idade e
proporcionar aos homens uma desculpa para a infidelidade.
Muitas das histórias implicavam espíritos incorpóreos e avisos
contra enterros impróprios. Não havia nada de significativo que
tivesse semelhanças com os filmes a que eu já assistira e apenas

um muito escasso número de vampiros, como o hebraico *Estrie* e o polaco *Upier*, se preocupava em beber sangue.

Apenas três entradas me chamaram realmente a atenção: o romeno *Varacolaci*, um poderoso ser morto-vivo que conseguia aparecer como um belo humano de pele clara; o eslovaco *Nelapsi*, uma criatura tão forte e veloz que podia chacinar uma aldeia inteira numa única hora, logo após a meia-noite; e um outro, o *Stregoni benefici*.

A respeito deste último, havia apenas uma breve frase.

Stregoni benefici: um vampiro italiano que, segundo consta, está do lado do bem e é um inimigo mortal de todos os vampiros malévolos.

Foi um alívio aquela pequena entrada, o único mito entre centenas que defendia a existência de vampiros bons.

Na generalidade, todavia, existia pouca informação coincidente com as histórias de Jacob ou com as minhas próprias observações. Eu elaborara um pequeno catálogo na minha mente à medida que fora lendo e comparava-o cuidadosamente com cada mito. Velocidade, força, beleza, pele clara, olhos que mudam de cor; e, depois, os critérios de Jacob: bebedores de sangue, inimigos do lobisomem, de pele fria e imortais. Havia muito poucos mitos que correspondiam a um só factor que fosse.

Havia, além disso, um outro problema, um aspecto que me lembrava de ter visto no pequeno número de filmes de terror a que assistira e que era corroborado pela leitura deste dia — os vampiros não podiam sair durante o dia, já que o Sol os reduziria a cinzas. Dormiam em caixões durante todo o dia e saíam apenas à noite.

Exasperada, desliguei a ficha do computador da fonte de alimentação, não esperando para encerrá-lo devidamente. Através da minha irritação, sentia um embaraço avassalador. Tratava-se de uma tolice tão grande. Estava sentada no meu quarto, a realizar uma pesquisa sobre vampiros. O que se passava comigo? Cheguei à conclusão de que a maior parte da culpa cabia à entrada na cidade de Forks — e, no que a isso diz respeito, também a toda a encharcada Península Olímpica.

Tinha de sair de casa, mas não havia nenhum sítio aonde desejasse ir que não implicasse uma viagem de três dias de automóvel. De qualquer modo, calcei as botas, indecisa quanto à direcção em que seguiria, e desci as escadas. Vesti a gabardina sem ver como estava o tempo e saí porta fora.

O céu estava carregado de nuvens, mas ainda não chovia. Ignorei a minha *pick-up* e comecei a dirigir-me para Leste, a pé, atravessando o pátio de Charlie em direcção à sempre invasora floresta. Não demorou muito tempo até que eu estivesse suficientemente embrenhada nela, a ponto de a casa e a estrada se tornarem invisíveis, e de o único som ser o ruído da terra húmida sob os meus pés e os súbitos gorjeios dos gaios.

Havia ali uma ténue faixa de um trilho que conduzia através da floresta ou eu não arriscaria deambular sozinha daquela forma. O meu sentido de orientação era irremediavelmente mau; podia perder-me em meios muito menos propícios. O trilho adentrava-se cada vez mais profundamente na floresta, avançando sobretudo, tanto quanto eu percebia, em direcção a Leste. Serpenteava em torno das epíceas-de-sitka e dos abetos-do-canadá, dos teixos e dos bordos. Sabia apenas vagamente os nomes das árvores que me rodeavam e tudo o que sabia devia-se ao facto de Charlie mas indicar a partir do vidro do carro de rádio-patrulha quando eu era mais pequena. Havia muitas que eu não conhecia e outras que não conseguia identificar ao certo por estarem de tal modo cobertas de parasitas verdes.

Segui pelo trilho enquanto a raiva que sentia em relação a mim mesma me impeliu a avançar. Ao começar a ficar mais calma, abrandei a marcha. Algumas gotas de humidade pingavam da abóbada acima de mim, mas não conseguia determinar se estava a começar a chover ou se se tratava simplesmente de charcos formados no dia anterior, sustentados bem lá no alto pelas folhas acima de mim, gotejando lentamente para regressarem à terra. Uma árvore recentemente derrubada — sabia que era algo recente, pois a árvore não estava completamente atapetada de musgo — repousava, encostando-se ao tronco de uma das suas irmãs, formando um banquinho abrigado a apenas alguns seguros centímetros do trilho. Passei por cima dos fetos e sentei-me cuidadosamente, certificando-me de que o meu casaco se interpunha entre o húmido assento e as minhas roupas onde quer que estivessem em mútuo contacto e encostei a minha cabeça, coberta pelo capuz, à árvore viva.

Não devia ter ido para aquele lugar. Devia ter calculado, mas que outro sítio havia para onde ir? A floresta caracterizava-se por um verde-carregado e assemelhava-se demasiadamente ao cenário presente no sonho que eu tivera na noite anterior para me proporcionar paz de espírito. Agora que já não se ouvia o som dos meus passos na terra ensopada, o silêncio era cortante. Também os pássaros estavam sossegados e as gotas começaram a cair com maior frequência, pelo que devia estar a chover. Agora que eu estava sentada, os fetos erguiam-se acima da minha cabeça e sabia que alguém podia passar pelo caminho e não me ver.

Ali, no meio das árvores, era muito mais fácil acreditar nos absurdos que, dentro de casa, me causavam embaraço. Nada se alterara naquela floresta desde há milhares de anos e todos os mitos e lendas de uma centena de terras diferentes pareciam muito mais prováveis naquela bruma verde do que na nitidez do meu quarto.

Obriguei-me a concentrar-me nas duas perguntas fundamentais que exigiam resposta, mas fi-lo com relutância.

Em primeiro lugar, tinha de saber se era possível que aquilo que Jacob dissera a respeito dos Cullen fosse verdade.

Imediatamente, a minha mente replicou com uma retumbante resposta negativa. Era uma tolice e uma morbidez albergar ideias de tal modo ridículas. Mas, então, qual era a explicação? Interroguei-me. Não havia qualquer justificação racional para o facto de eu estar viva naquele momento. Voltei a enumerar, na minha cabeça, os aspectos que eu mesma observara: a força e velocidade incríveis, a cor dos olhos a mudar de negro para dourado e vice-versa, a beleza desumana, a pele clara e álgida e ainda mais — pequenas coisas que começaram lentamente a ter sentido —, como o facto de parecer que eles nunca comiam, a perturbadora graciosidade dos seus movimentos e a forma como ele, por vezes, falava, com estranhas cadências e expressões que mais se adequavam ao estilo de um romance da viragem do século do que ao de uma sala de aula do século XXI. Ele faltara a uma aula no dia em que procederamos à tipificação sanguínea. Só recusara o convite para a viagem à praia depois de saber aonde íamos. Parecia adivinhar os pensamentos de todos os que o rodeavam... excepto eu. Dissera-me que era o vilão, que era perigoso...

Seria possível que os Cullen fossem vampiros?

Bem, *algo* haviam de ser. Algo que transcendia a possibilidade de uma justificação racional estava a ocorrer diante dos meus incrédulos olhos. Quer estivesse relacionado com os *frios* de Jacob ou com a minha própria teoria do super-herói, Edward Cullen não era... humano. Era algo mais.

Portanto — talvez. Essa teria de ser a minha resposta por enquanto.

Colocava-se, então, a questão mais importante de todas. O que iria eu fazer se fosse verdade?

Se Edward fosse um vampiro — mal conseguia sequer pronunciar mentalmente as palavras —, o que deveria eu fazer? Implicar outra pessoa estava definitivamente fora de questão. Eu própria não conseguia acreditar; qualquer que fosse a pessoa a quem eu contasse, mandaria internar-me.

Apenas duas opções pareciam viáveis. A primeira consistia em seguir o conselho dele: ser esperta, evitá-lo o mais possível; cancelar os nossos planos, voltar a ignorá-lo tanto quanto conseguisse; fingir que existia um muro de vidro impenetravelmente espesso entre nós na única aula em que éramos obrigados a ficar juntos; dizer-lhe para me deixar em paz — e, desta vez, fazê-lo com intenção.

Fui tomada por um súbito paroxismo de desespero ao encarar essa alternativa. O meu espírito rejeitou o sofrimento, passando rapidamente para a opção seguinte.

Não podia fazer nada de diferente. Afinal, embora ele fosse algo... sinistro, ainda não fizera nada para me magoar até ao momento. Na verdade, eu seria uma mossa no pára-choques de Tyler se ele não tivesse agido com tanta prontidão. Com tanta prontidão, arguía comigo mesma, que podia ter-se tratado de meros reflexos. No entanto, retorqui, se salvar vidas era um reflexo, até que ponto é que ele poderia ser mau? A minha cabeça girava em círculos desprovidos de respostas.

De uma coisa eu tinha a certeza, se é que estava certa de algo. O Edward tenebroso que aparecera no meu sonho na noite anterior era apenas um reflexo do meu medo em relação à palavra que Jacob proferira e não do próprio Edward. Mesmo assim, quando eu gritara de pavor aquando da investida do lobisomem, não fora o receio do lobo que levava os meus lábios a exclamarem «não». Era receio de que *ele* pudesse ser ferido; mesmo quando ele me chamava com presas afiadas, eu temia por *ele*.

Soube, então, que ali residia a minha resposta. Não sabia se chegara sequer a haver uma alternativa. Eu já estava demasiado envolvida. Agora que sabia — *se* é que sabia —, nada podia fazer quanto ao meu segredo assustador, pois, quando pensava nele, na sua voz, nos seus olhos hipnóticos, na força magnética da sua personalidade, nada mais desejava senão estar com ele naquele preciso momento. Mesmo que... mas não conseguia conceber tal coisa. Não ali, sozinha na floresta sobre a qual começava a abater-se a escuridão. Não enquanto a chuva tornasse o ambiente esbatido como o crepúsculo sob a abóbada florestal e tamborilasse como passos no piso de terra atapetado. Eu arrepiei--me e levantei-me rapidamente do meu esconderijo, preocupada com o facto de o caminho poder, de algum modo, ter desaparecido com a chuva.

No entanto, ali estava, nítido e a salvo, serpenteando em direcção à saída do gotejante dédalo verde. Segui-o apressadamente, com o capuz bem chegado ao rosto, ficando surpreendida, enquanto passava praticamente a correr pelas árvores, com a tamanha distância que eu percorrera. Comecei a perguntar-me se me encaminhava, de facto, para a saída ou se seguia pelo caminho para me embrenhar ainda mais nos confins da floresta. Contudo, antes de ter ficado demasiado tomada de pânico, comecei a vislumbrar alguns espaços abertos através dos ramos repletos de teias de aranha. Então, consegui ouvir um carro passar na rua e eu estava livre, com o relvado de Charlie a estender-se diante de mim, a casa a acenar-me, prometendo aconchego e meias secas.

Era apenas meio-dia quando voltei a entrar em casa. Dirigi-me ao andar superior e vesti a roupa do dia, calças de ganga e uma camisola de mangas curtas, visto que ia ficar em casa. Não foi necessário muito esforço para me concentrar na tarefa do dia: um trabalho sobre *Macbeth* cujo prazo de entrega era até quarta-feira. Resolvi, de bom grado, esboçar um rascunho aproximado, estando mais serena do que me sentira desde... bem, desde a tarde de quinta-feira, para ser sincera.

Todavia, essa fora sempre a minha maneira de proceder. Tomar decisões era, para mim, a parte dolorosa, a parte que me afligia, mas, assim que a decisão estava tomada, eu simplesmente a levava até ao fim — normalmente, sentindo alívio pelo facto de a escolha ter sido feita. Por vezes, o alívio era viciado pelo desespero, como foi o caso da minha decisão de vir para Forks, mas tal continuava a ser preferível à luta com as alternativas.

Era ridiculamente fácil viver com esta decisão. Perigosamente fácil.

Assim, o dia foi calmo, produtivo — terminei o trabalho antes das oito horas da noite. Charlie chegou a casa com uma grande quantidade de peixe apanhado e eu anotei mentalmente que deveria requisitar um livro de receitas de peixe quando estivesse em Seattle na semana seguinte. Os arrepios que me percorriam a coluna vertebral, sempre que pensava nessa viagem, não eram em nada diferentes daqueles que sentira antes de fazer a caminhada com Jacob Black. Deviam ser diferentes, pensei. Eu devia ter medo — sabia que devia ter, mas não conseguia sentir o género acertado de temor.

Nessa noite dormi sem sonhar, extenuada por ter começado o dia tão cedo e ter dormido tão mal na noite anterior. Acordei, pela segunda vez, desde que chegara a Forks, para deparar com a intensa claridade amarela de um dia soalheiro. Dei um salto até à janela, espantada por verificar que havia poucas nuvens no céu e as que havia eram apenas pequenos pompons brancos com aspecto de algodão que não podiam, de modo nenhum, trazer chuva. Abri a janela — ficando surpreendida quando esta se abriu sem fazer ruído, sem ficar presa, depois de não ter sido aberta durante sabe Deus quantos anos — e aspirei o ar relativamente seco. O tempo estava quase quente e o vento quase não soprava. O meu sangue fervia-me nas veias.

Charlie acabava de tomar o pequeno-almoço quando eu desci e apercebeu-se logo da minha disposição.

— Está um belo dia lá fora — comentou.

— Pois está — concordei com um sorriso rasgado.

Ele retribuiu o sorriso, com os seus olhos castanhos a enrugarem-se nos cantos. Quando Charlie sorria, era mais fácil perceber por que motivo a minha mãe se lançara demasiado precipitadamente num casamento precoce. Grande parte do jovem romântico que ele fora naqueles tempos desvanecera-se antes de eu o conhecer, à medida que o cabelo castanho encaracolado — da mesma cor, se não mesmo com uma textura idêntica à do meu — fora enfraquecendo, revelando cada vez mais a pele reluzente da sua testa. No entanto, quando ele sorria, eu conseguia ver um pouco do homem que fugira com Renée quando ela era apenas dois anos mais velha do que eu sou agora.

Tomei o pequeno-almoço alegremente, observando os fossos de poeira a agitarem-se sob a luz do Sol que invadia a janela das traseiras. Charlie despediu-se com um clamor e eu ouvi o carro de rádio-patrulha afastar-se. Hesitei ao sair pela porta, com a mão na gabardina. Seria estar a tentar a sorte se a deixasse em casa. Com um suspiro, dobrei-a por cima do braço e saí para deparar com a claridade mais luminosa que vira desde há vários meses.

À custa de muito esforço, consegui abrir os dois vidros da *pick-up* quase completamente. Fui uma das primeiras pessoas a chegar à escola; não olhara sequer para o relógio na minha pressa de ir para a rua. Estacionei e dirigi-me para os raramente usados bancos de piquenique no lado Sul da cantina. Os bancos ainda estavam um pouco húmidos e, por conseguinte, sentei-me em cima da gabardina, contente por lhe dar uma utilidade. Os meus trabalhos de casa estavam feitos — o resultado de uma vida social pouco intensa —, mas havia alguns problemas de Trigonometria cuja resolução se apresentava complicada. Peguei no livro aplicadamente, mas, antes de acabar de conferir o primeiro problema, já estava a sonhar acordada, observando a incidência da luz do Sol sobre as árvores de casca vermelha. Fazia esboços nas margens dos meus trabalhos de casa. Alguns minutos depois, apercebi-me subitamente de que desenhara cinco pares de olhos negros que me olhavam fixamente a partir da página. Apaguei-os com a borracha.

— Bella! — ouvi alguém chamar, parecendo a voz de Mike.

Olhei em volta e verifiquei que a escola ficara povoada enquanto eu permanecia ali sentada, com o espírito ausente. Todos envergavam camisolas de mangas curtas e alguns até tinham calções vestidos, ainda que a temperatura não ultrapassasse seguramente os quinze graus. Mike caminhava na minha direcção com uns calções caqui e uma camisola de râguebi às riscas.

— Viva, Mike! — exclamei, retribuindo-lhe o aceno, incapaz de conter o entusiasmo numa manhã como aquela.

Foi sentar-se a meu lado, com o seu cabelo espetado a reflectir tons dourados à luz do sol e o seu sorriso a rasgar-se-lhe no rosto. Estava tão encantado por me ver que tinha de sentir-me satisfeita.

— Nunca tinha reparado antes, mas o teu cabelo tem reflexos ruivos — comentou ele, pegando com os dedos num fio que esvoaçava sob o efeito da leve brisa.

— Só ao Sol.

Fiquei um pouco constrangida quando ele me colocou o anel de cabelo atrás da orelha.

— Está um dia fantástico, não está?

— Um dia como eu gosto — concordei.

— O que fizeste ontem?

O seu tom de voz era um pouco possessivo de mais.

— Trabalhei sobretudo na minha dissertação — não acrescentei que a terminara, não havia necessidade de parecer presumida.

Bateu na testa com a base da mão.

— Ah, pois — o prazo de entrega é até quinta-feira, certo?

— Hum, até quarta-feira, creio eu.

— Quarta-feira? — franziu o sobrolho. — Isso não é nada bom... Qual é o tema da tua?

— O facto de o tratamento que Shakespeare dá às personagens femininas ser ou não misógino.

Ele olhou-me como se tivesse acabado de falar em linguagem criptofónica.

— Suponho que terei de trabalhar nisso esta noite — disse ele, abatido. — Ia perguntar-te se querias sair.

— Ah! — fui apanhada desprevenida. Porque é que eu já não conseguia ter uma conversa agradável com Mike sem ficar constrangida?

— Bem, podíamos ir jantar ou algo do género... e eu podia trabalhar na dissertação mais tarde. — Sorriu-me esperançosamente.

— Mike... Acho que não seria a melhor das ideias.

Eu detestava que me colocassem em situações desagradáveis.

O seu rosto reflectiu desânimo.

— Porquê? — perguntou, com um olhar cauteloso.

Edward surgiu no meu pensamento e perguntei-me se o mesmo acontecera a Mike.

— Julgo... e se alguma vez repetires o que eu estou a dizer neste preciso momento, eu terei todo o prazer em espancar-te até à morte — ameacei —, mas acho que isso feriria os sentimentos da Jessica.

Ele ficou confuso, sendo óbvio que os seus pensamentos não iam, de todo, *nesse* sentido.

— Da Jessica?

— Sinceramente, Mike, tu és *cego?*

— Ah! — suspirou, claramente aturdido.

Aproveitei esse facto para me escapar.

— Está na hora da aula e não posso voltar a atrasar-me.

Recolhi os meus livros e meti-os na pasta. Caminhámos em silêncio até ao edifício três e a expressão estampada no seu rosto era a de alguém que tinha o espírito perturbado. Eu esperava que, quaisquer que fossem os pensamentos em que ele estava imerso, o conduzissem na direcção certa.

Quando vi Jessica na aula de Trigonometria, ela não cabia em si de tanto entusiasmo. Ela, Angela e Lauren iam a Port Angeles naquela noite para comprarem os vestidos para o baile e ela queria que eu também fosse, ainda que não precisasse de vestido nenhum. Fiquei indecisa. Seria agradável sair da cidade com algumas amigas, mas Lauren também iria. E quem sabia o que eu faria naquela noite? No entanto, não era decididamente por este caminho que devia permitir que o meu espírito devaneasse. É claro que eu estava contente com a luz do Sol, mas esse aspecto nem por sombras era inteiramente responsável pelo estado de euforia que me encontrava.

Assim, dei-lhe como resposta um *talvez*, dizendo-lhe que, primeiro, teria de conversar com Charlie.

Ela não falou de mais nada além do baile ao longo do trajecto para a aula de Espanhol, continuando como se nenhuma interrupção se tivesse verificado quando a aula finalmente terminou, cinco minutos depois da hora, e fomos almoçar. Estava demasiado absorta no meu próprio frenesim de expectativa para prestar atenção a grande parte daquilo que ela dizia. Estava dolorosamente ansiosa por ver, não só a ele, mas a todos os Cullen — para compará-los com as novas suspeitas que assolavam o meu espírito. Ao passar a soleira da porta da cantina, senti o primeiro autêntico formigueiro de temor descer-me pela coluna e assentar no estômago. Seriam eles capazes de adivinhar os meus pensamentos? Então, uma sensação diferente perpassou-me — estaria Edward à espera para se sentar novamente comigo à mesa?

Como era meu procedimento habitual, olhei, em primeiro lugar, na direcção da mesa dos Cullen. Um estremecimento de pânico fez-se sentir no meu estômago ao aperceber-me de que estava vazia. Com uma esperança cada vez menor, os meus olhos fizeram o reconhecimento do resto da cantina, esperando encontrá-lo sozinho, à minha espera. O espaço estava praticamente todo ocupado — a aula de Espanhol fizera com que nos atrasássemos —, mas não havia quaisquer vestígios de Edward nem de nenhum membro da sua família. A desolação apossou-se de mim com uma força avassaladora.

Caminhava tropegamente atrás de Jessica, já não me dando ao trabalho de fingir estar a escutá-la.

Chegámos tão tarde que já todos se encontravam sentados à nossa mesa. Evitei a cadeira vazia ao lado de Mike em favor de uma junto de Angela. Notei vagamente que Mike afastou com delicadeza a cadeira para que Jessica se sentasse e que, em resposta, o semblante dela se iluminou.

Angela fez algumas perguntas discretas a respeito do trabalho sobre *Macbeth*, às quais respondi da maneira mais natural possível enquanto o meu estado de espírito se afundava cada vez mais com tanta infelicidade. Também ela me convidou para acompanhá-las naquela noite e, desta vez, aceitei, agarrando-me a qualquer coisa que me proporcionasse distracção.

Apercebi-me de que conservava uma réstia de esperança quando entrei na sala de Biologia, vi o lugar dele vazio e senti uma nova onda de decepção.

O resto do dia passou lento e triste. Na aula de Educação Física, o professor procedeu a uma explanação acerca das regras do badminton, suplício que me tinham reservado, mas, pelo menos, pude sentar-me e escutar em vez de andar aos tropeções no campo. O melhor disto foi que o treinador não terminou a exposição e, portanto, o dia seguinte seria novamente de descanso. Não importava que, dois dias depois, me munissem de uma raqueta antes de me deixarem à mercê do resto da turma.

Fiquei contente por deixar o recinto da escola, ficando, portanto, livre para amuar e ficar com a neura antes de ir sair, nessa noite, com Jessica e companhia limitada. No entanto, assim que cheguei à porta da casa de Charlie, Jessica telefonou para cancelar os nossos planos. Tentei parecer satisfeita com o facto de Mike a ter convidado para jantar — estava mesmo aliviada por ele finalmente parecer ter percebido —, mas o meu entusiasmo soou a falso aos meus ouvidos. Adiou, para a noite do dia seguinte, a nossa viagem para ir às compras.

Este adiamento não me deixou muito com que me distrair. Colocara peixe a marinar para o jantar, com uma salada e pão que sobrara da noite anterior, não havendo, portanto, nada a fazer neste âmbito. Dediquei meia hora de concentração aos trabalhos de casa, que terminei de seguida. Consultei o meu correio electrónico, lendo as mensagens em atraso que tinham sido remetidas pela minha mãe, as quais se tornavam cada vez mais amargas à medida que avançavam no tempo. Suspirei e digitei uma resposta rápida.

«Mãe,
Desculpa. Tenho estado fora. Fui à praia com alguns amigos e, além disso, tive de redigir um trabalho.»

As minhas desculpas eram relativamente dignas de dó, tendo eu, portanto, desistido de as apresentar.

«Hoje, está sol lá fora — eu sei, também estou admirada —, logo, vou para a rua absorver o máximo de vitamina D possível. Gosto muito de ti,
Bella.»

Decidi empregar uma hora em leituras que não estivessem relacionadas com a escola. Possuía uma pequena colecção de livros que trouxera para Forks, sendo o volume mais gasto uma compilação das obras de Jane Austen. Escolhi esse e dirigi-me para o jardim das traseiras, retirando, ao descer, uma velha e esfarrapada colcha do armário da roupa que se encontrava no cimo das escadas.

No exterior, no pequeno pátio quadrado de Charlie, dobrei a colcha ao meio e estendi-a fora do alcance da sombra das árvores, sobre o denso relvado que estava sempre ligeiramente molhado, por mais que o Sol brilhasse. Deitei-me de bruços, cruzando os tornozelos no ar, folheando os diversos romances do livro, tentando decidir qual seria aquele que me ocuparia melhor o espírito. Os meus preferidos eram *Orgulho e Preconceito* e *Sensibilidade e Bom Senso*. Lera o primeiro há menos tempo e, por conseguinte, comecei por *Sensibilidade e Bom Senso* apenas para me lembrar, depois de ter começado a leitura do terceiro capítulo, de que o herói da história se chamava, por acaso, Edward. Irritada, optei por *O Parque de Mansfield*, mas o herói desta composição literária chamava-se *Edmund*, o que era demasiado parecido. Será que não havia outros nomes disponíveis no final do século XVIII? Fechei o livro violentamente, com irritação, e deitei-me de costas. Arregacei as mangas o máximo possível e fechei os olhos. Não pensaria em nada além do calor na minha pele, disse para comigo mesma com severidade. A aragem que corria era ainda leve, mas fazia com que anéis do meu cabelo esvoaçassem, em torno do meu rosto, o que provocava algumas cócegas. Levantei o cabelo, deixando que formasse um leque sobre a colcha, e concentrei-me novamente no calor que incidia nas minhas pestanas, na face, no nariz, nos lábios, nos antebraços, e no pescoço, deixando-me completamente ensopada, o que era visível através da minha camisa leve...

Só voltei a ter consciência com o som do carro de rádio-patrulha de Charlie a virar para a entrada ladrilhada. Sentei-me surpreendida, apercebendo-me de que a claridade desaparecera, por trás das árvores, e eu adormecera. Olhei em redor, desorientada, com a súbita sensação de que não estava sozinha.

— Charlie? — chamei, ao mesmo tempo que consegui ouvir a porta do seu carro bater em frente da casa.

Levantei-me de um salto, tolamente tensa, pegando na colcha, agora húmida, e no meu livro. Corri para dentro para pôr óleo a aquecer no fogão, apercebendo-me de que o jantar iria atrasar-se. Charlie estava a pendurar o coldre e a descalçar as botas quando eu entrei.

— Desculpa, pai, o jantar ainda não está pronto, adormeci lá fora — reprimi um bocejo.

— Não te preocupes com isso — afirmou ele. — De qualquer modo, queria ver qual era o resultado do jogo.

Vi televisão com Charlie após o jantar, para me entreter. Não estava a ser transmitido nenhum programa a que eu quisesse assistir, mas ele sabia que eu não gostava de basquetebol e, por isso, mudou de canal para uma disparatada série cómica com que nenhum de nós se divertia. Ele parecia, contudo, feliz por estarmos juntos e, apesar do meu desânimo, fazê-lo feliz proporcionava-me uma sensação agradável.

— Pai — exclamei durante um anúncio publicitário —, a Jessica e a Angela vão ver vestidos para o baile amanhã à noite em Port Angeles e queriam que as ajudasse a escolher... Importas-te que vá com elas?

— A Jessica Stanley? — perguntou ele.

— E a Angela Weber — suspirei ao fornecer-lhe os pormenores.

— Mas tu não vais ao baile, pois não? — perguntou confuso.

— Não, pai, mas vou ajudá-las a procurar vestidos, tu sabes, fazer-lhes críticas construtivas.

Não teria de proceder a este tipo de explicações se estivesse a falar com uma mulher.

— Pronto, muito bem — condescendeu, parecendo perceber que estava fora do seu elemento no que se referia aos assuntos de raparigas. — Mas tens aulas no dia seguinte.

— Nós partimos logo após as aulas, de modo a podermos

voltar cedo. Tu desenvencilhas-te com o jantar, certo?

— Bells, eu encarreguei-me da minha alimentação durante dezassete anos antes de aqui chegares — relembrou-me.

— Não sei como é que sobreviveste — murmurei por entre dentes e, em seguida, acrescentei de forma mais perceptível — deixarei algumas coisas no frigorífico para preparares sandes de carnes frias, está bem? Logo em cima.

Lançou-me um olhar divertido, mas tolerante.

Na manhã seguinte, o Sol voltava a brilhar. Despertei com uma esperança renovada que tentei reprimir veementemente. Vesti, para o tempo mais quente, uma blusa azul-escura com decote em V — algo que eu usara em pleno Inverno em Phoenix.

Planeara chegar à escola apenas em cima da hora da aula. Com um aperto no coração, andei às voltas em todo o parque de estacionamento à procura de um lugar, enquanto tentava encontrar o Volvo prateado que, manifestamente, não se encontrava ali. Estacionei na última fila e apressei-me para a aula de Inglês, chegando sem fôlego, mas mais calma, antes do toque final da campainha.

Ocorreu o mesmo que no dia anterior — simplesmente não conseguia evitar que pequenos rebentos de esperança florescessem no meu espírito apenas para serem dolorosamente esmagados — quando perscrutei o refeitório em vão e me sentei diante da minha bancada vazia na aula de Biologia.

O programa de Port Angeles estava novamente pronto a ser executado naquela noite e tornou-se ainda mais apelativo pelo facto de Lauren ter outras obrigações. Estava ansiosa por sair da cidade, de modo a poder parar de olhar por cima do ombro na esperança de o ver aparecer vindo do nada como sempre fazia. Jurei a mim própria que, naquela noite, estaria bem-disposta e não estragaria o divertimento de Angela e Jessica na caça ao vestido. Talvez também eu pudesse comprar algumas roupas. Recusava-me a pensar que iria sozinha às compras a Seattle naquele fim-de-semana, já não estando interessada na combinação anterior. Ele não iria decerto cancelar a viagem sem, pelo menos, mo comunicar.

Depois das aulas, Jessica seguiu-me até casa no seu velho Mercury branco, de modo que eu pudesse ali deixar os meus livros e a *pick-up*. Escovei rapidamente os cabelos enquanto estava dentro de casa, sentindo um ligeiro rasgo de entusiasmo ao pensar em sair de Forks. Deixei um bilhete a Charlie em cima da mesa, explicando novamente onde podia encontrar o jantar, retirei o meu velho porta-moedas da pasta escolar e coloquei-o numa bolsa que raramente utilizava, saindo, depois, a correr para me juntar a Jessica. Em seguida, fomos a casa de Angela que estava à nossa espera. O meu entusiasmo aumentou exponencialmente quando, de facto, saímos dos limites da cidade.

Capítulo Oito

PORT ANGELES

Jess conduzia mais depressa do que o chefe e, por isso, chegámos a Port Angeles por volta das quatro da tarde. Já passara algum tempo desde que eu saíra à noite só com raparigas e o afluxo de estrogénio era vivificante. Ouvimos lamuriosas músicas *rock* enquanto Jessica tagarelava acerca dos rapazes com quem nós nos dávamos. O jantar de Jessica com Mike correra muito bem e ela esperava que, até sábado à noite, já tivessem evoluído para a fase do primeiro beijo. Sorri para dentro, satisfeita. Angela estava mais ou menos feliz por ir ao baile, mas não estava realmente interessada em Eric. Jess tentou levá-la a confessar qual era o rapaz que fazia o seu género, mas eu interrompi-as com uma pergunta sobre vestidos, de modo a poupá-la. Angela olhou agradecida na minha direcção.

Port Angeles era uma bela armadilha para turistas, muito mais aprimorada e peculiar do que Forks, mas Jessica e Angela conheciam-na bem, não tencionando, portanto, perder tempo na pitoresca marginal junto à baía. Jess dirigiu-se imediatamente para a única grande loja da cidade, que ficava a algumas ruas de distância da zona da baía digna do olhar dos visitantes.

O baile fora publicitado como sendo semiformal e nenhuma de nós sabia ao certo o que isso significava. Tanto Jessica como Angela pareceram surpreendidas e quase incrédulas quando lhes disse que nunca fora a um baile em Phoenix.

— Nunca foste sequer com um namorado ou algo do género? — perguntou Jess de forma duvidosa ao entrarmos pela porta da frente da loja.

— A sério — tentei convencê-la, não querendo confessar as

minhas dificuldades relacionadas com a dança. — Nunca tive um namorado nem nada parecido. Raramente saía.

— Porque não? — interrogou Jessica.

— Ninguém me convidava — respondi com sinceridade.

Ela parecia céptica.

— Aqui, há quem te convide para sair — relembrou-me ela — e tu recusas.

Encontrávamo-nos agora na secção juvenil, esquadrinhando as prateleiras em busca de trajes de cerimónia.

— Bem, exceptuando o Tyler — corrigiu Angela tranquilamente.

— Desculpa! — exclamei com voz arquejante. — Que disseste?

— O Tyler contou a toda a gente que vai acompanhar-te ao baile — informou-me Jessica com um olhar desconfiado.

— Contou o quê?

A minha voz soava como se eu estivesse a sufocar.

— Disse-te que não era verdade — segredou Angela a Jessica.

Fiquei calada, estando ainda perdida num sentimento de escândalo que começava a transformar-se em irritação. Tínhamos, porém, encontrado as prateleiras dos vestidos e tínhamos agora trabalho a fazer.

— É por isso que a Lauren não gosta de ti — comentou Jessica, soltando risinhos, enquanto nós remexíamos as roupas.

Rangi os dentes.

— Achas que, se eu o atropelasse com a minha *pick-up*, ele deixava de se sentir culpado pelo acidente? Que talvez desistisse de me compensar e desse o assunto por encerrado?

— Talvez — disse Jessica, soltando um riso abafado. — Se for esse o motivo por que ele está a agir desta forma.

A variedade de vestidos não era muito grande, mas cada uma delas encontrou qualquer coisa para experimentar. Sentei-me numa cadeira baixa mesmo no interior do gabinete de prova, junto do espelho de três faces, tentando controlar a cólera.

Jess estava dividida entre dois vestidos — um comprido, sem alças, com o preto como cor de base e outro azul-eléctrico com alças fininhas, cujo comprimento se ficava pelos joelhos.

Incentivei-a a optar pelo azul; porque não jogar com a cor dos olhos? Angela escolheu um vestido cor-de-rosa pálido que caía lindamente na sua estatura elevada e conferia cambiantes cor de mel aos seus cabelos castanho-claros. Elogiei ambas generosamente e ajudei-as a restituir os artigos rejeitados às respectivas prateleiras. Todo o processo foi muito mais breve e fácil do que certas viagens similares que eu efectuara com Renée em Phoenix. Suponho que a escassez de opções tinha algo a ver com este facto.

Dirigimo-nos para a secção de sapatos e acessórios. Enquanto elas experimentavam artigos sucessivamente, eu limitava-me a olhar e a dar a minha opinião, não estando com disposição para fazer compras para mim, embora precisasse, de facto, de sapatos novos. O entusiasmo relativamente à saída com as raparigas estava a desvanecer-se na sequência do meu aborrecimento com Tyler, deixando espaço para que a melancolia voltasse a instalar-se.

— Angela? — principiei, hesitante, enquanto ela experimentava um par de sapatos de salto alto cor-de-rosa com tiras.

Ela estava radiante por ter um acompanhante suficientemente alto para lhe permitir usar sapatos de salto alto. Jessica afastara-se até ao balcão da ourivesaria e nós estávamos sozinhas.

— Sim? — respondeu ela enquanto esticava a perna, torcendo o tornozelo, de modo a poder ter um melhor ângulo de visão do sapato.

Acobardei-me.

— Gosto desses.

— Acho que vou comprá-los — apesar de não condizerem com mais nada além daquele único vestido — reflectiu ela.

— Oh, compra-os, estão em saldo — incentivei-a.

Ela sorriu, voltando a colocar a tampa numa caixa que continha sapatos num tom branco-pérola com aspecto mais prático.

Tentei novamente.

— Hum, Angela...

Ela ergueu o olhar com curiosidade.

— É normal que os... Cullen — mantive os olhos pregados nos sapatos — estejam muitas vezes ausentes da escola?

Falhei miseravelmente na minha tentativa de demonstrar desprendimento.

— É. Quando o tempo está agradável, eles partem muitas vezes em viagem, com a mochila às costas... até o médico. São todos grandes adeptos do ar livre — revelou-me ela tranquilamente, examinando também os seus sapatos.

Não fez uma única pergunta, ao contrário do que aconteceria com Jessica, que teria debitado centenas delas. Começava a gostar realmente de Angela.

— Ah!

Não insisti mais no assunto, pois Jessica voltou para nos mostrar as jóias de imitação de diamante que encontrara para combinarem com os seus sapatos prateados.

Tencionávamos ir jantar a um pequeno restaurante italiano situado na marginal, mas a compra do vestido não demorara tanto tempo como nós estávamos à espera. Jess e Angela iam levar as suas roupas para o carro e, depois, caminhar até à baía. Disse-lhes que me encontraria com elas no restaurante dentro de uma hora — queria procurar uma livraria. Ambas estavam dispostas a fazer-me companhia, mas instiguei-as a irem divertir-se — não sabiam quão abstraída eu podia ficar quando estava rodeada de livros; tratava-se de uma coisa que preferia fazer sozinha. Partiram em direcção ao carro, conversando alegremente, e eu encaminhei-me no sentido que Jess me indicara.

Não tive qualquer dificuldade em encontrar a livraria, mas esta não era o que eu procurava. As montras estavam repletas de cristais, caçadores de sonhos e livros acerca de cura espiritual. Não cheguei sequer a entrar. Através do vidro, consegui ver uma mulher de cinquenta anos com longos cabelos grisalhos que se lhe estendiam ao longo das costas, envergando um vestido característico dos anos sessenta e sorrindo de forma acolhedora de trás do balcão. Cheguei à conclusão de que podia prescindir daquela mulher. Devia haver uma livraria normal na cidade.

Vagueei pelas ruas, que começavam a encher-se com o trânsito do final do dia de trabalho e esperei estar a dirigir-me para o centro da cidade. Não estava a prestar tanta atenção como devia ao rumo que estava a tomar; debatia-me com o desespero. Tentava com tanta veemência não pensar nele, naquilo que Angela dissera... e, acima de tudo, tentava reprimir as minhas esperanças quanto ao dia de sábado, temendo sofrer uma decepção ainda mais dolorosa do que o resto, quando olhei e deparei com o Volvo prateado de alguém estacionado na rua. Tudo desabou sobre mim. «Vampiro estúpido, que não é digno de confiança», pensei para comigo.

Eu caminhava com um passo pesado para Sul, em direcção a algumas lojas com fachada de vidro que pareciam promissoras, mas, quando cheguei junto destas, não passavam de uma oficina de reparações e de um espaço vago. Ainda dispunha de demasiado tempo para ir ter com Jessica e Angela, e tinha absoluta necessidade de controlar a minha disposição antes de voltar a encontrar-me com elas. Passei os dedos pelo cabelo um par de vezes e respirei fundo antes de prosseguir, contornando a esquina.

Comecei a aperceber-me, ao atravessar outra rua, de que estava a ir na direcção errada. Os poucos peões que vira dirigiam-se para Norte e parecia que quase todos os edifícios que ali se encontravam eram sobretudo armazéns. Decidi virar para Leste na esquina seguinte e, em seguida, dar umas voltas depois de ter percorrido alguns quarteirões e tentar a minha sorte numa rua diferente no caminho de volta para a marginal.

Um grupo de quatro homens, vestidos de forma demasiado descontraída para estarem a efectuar o percurso do escritório para casa, mas muito sujos de fuligem para serem turistas, contornou a esquina para a qual eu me dirigia. Ao aproximarem-se de mim, apercebi-me de que não eram muito mais velhos do que eu. Gracejavam sonoramente entre si, rindo e socando os braços uns dos outros. Afastei-me o máximo que podia para o lado interior do passeio de modo a dar-lhes espaço, caminhando velozmente, olhando, ao passar por eles, para a esquina.

— Viva! — exclamou um deles ao passarem, devendo estar a dirigir-se a mim, visto que não havia mais ninguém por perto.

Olhei automaticamente. Dois deles tinham-se detido, enquanto os outros dois estavam a abrandar o passo. O que se encontrava mais próximo de mim, um homem moreno, de constituição pesada, com vinte e poucos anos, parecia ser o que falara. Envergava uma camisa de flanela aberta por cima de uma camisola de mangas curtas suja, calças de ganga cortadas pelos joelhos e sandálias. Deu meio passo na minha direcção.

— Olá — balbuciei, reagindo instintivamente.

Em seguida, desviei rapidamente o olhar e caminhei mais depressa em direcção à esquina. Conseguia ouvi-los a rirem-se a plenos pulmões atrás de mim.

— Eh, espera! — exclamou um deles, dirigindo-se a mim novamente.

Eu, porém, mantive a cabeça baixa e contornei a esquina com um suspiro de alívio. Ainda conseguia ouvi-los rirem-se às gargalhadas atrás de mim.

Dei por mim num passeio que se estendia ao longo das traseiras de vários armazéns de cor sombria, cada um deles com grandes portas salientes da parede para a descarga de camiões, fechadas a cadeado para a pernoita. O lado Sul da rua não tinha passeio, mas apenas uma vedação de rede metálica encimada por arame farpado que protegia algum tipo de recinto de armazenamento de peças de motor. Distanciara-me significativamente da zona de Port Angeles que eu, enquanto convidada, devia visitar. Apercebi-me de que começava a escurecer, com nuvens a acumularem-se no horizonte a Ocidente, originando um pôr do Sol prematuro. A Oriente, o céu continuava limpo, mas começava a ficar cinzento, raiado de laivos de tons cor-de-rosa e cor-de-laranja. Deixara o casaco no carro e um súbito arrepio fez-me cruzar os braços com firmeza contra o peito. Uma única carrinha passou por mim e, depois, a estrada ficou vazia.

De repente, o céu escureceu ainda mais e, ao olhar por cima do ombro para observar a ofensiva nuvem, apercebi-me, com um sobressalto, de que dois homens caminhavam silenciosamente atrás de mim a uma distância de seis metros.

Pertenciam ao mesmo grupo por que eu passara na esquina, embora nenhum deles fosse o moreno que me falara. Virei logo a cabeça para a frente, acelerando o passo. Um calafrio que nada tinha a ver com o tempo fez-me tremer novamente. A minha mala estava segura por uma alça de pendurar ao ombro e eu trazia-a suspensa, a atravessar-me o tronco, da forma que deve ser usada para não ser roubada por estição. Sabia exactamente onde estava o meu gás de pimenta — continuava na minha mochila, debaixo da cama, nunca tendo chegado a sair dali. Não tinha muito dinheiro comigo — apenas uma nota de vinte dólares e algumas de um — e pensei em deixar cair a minha mala «acidentalmente» e continuar a andar, mas uma vozinha assustada no ponto mais recôndito da minha mente advertiu-me para a possibilidade de eles serem algo pior do que ladrões.

Escutei com atenção os seus discretos passos, que eram demasiado silenciosos quando comparados com a ruidosa agitação que tinham protagonizado há pouco, e não parecia estarem a acelerar ou a aproximar-se mais de mim. «Respira», tinha de lembrar a mim mesma. «Não sabes se estão a seguir-te». Continuei a andar o mais depressa que podia, sem correr, concentrando-me na curva para a direita que estava agora a apenas alguns metros de distância. Conseguia ouvi-los, ficando tão para trás como tinham estado antes. Um automóvel azul virou para a rua vindo do lado Sul e passou por mim a grande velocidade. Pensei em saltar-lhe para a frente, mas hesitei, inibida, não estando certa de que estava mesmo a ser perseguida e, então, já era tarde de mais.

Cheguei à esquina, mas um rápido olhar revelou que se tratava apenas de um beco sem saída que dava acesso às traseiras de outro edifício. Já dera meia volta na expectativa; tive de corrigir apressadamente a minha rota e precipitar-me para o lado oposto da estreita estrada, voltando para o passeio. A rua chegou ao fim na esquina seguinte, onde se encontrava um sinal de «Stop». Concentrei-me nos passos quase inaudíveis atrás de mim, decidindo se havia ou não de fugir. Pareciam, porém, estar mais longe e eu sabia que eles, de qualquer modo, conseguiriam correr mais depressa do que eu. Decerto tropeçaria e estatelar-me-ia no chão se tentasse acelerar ainda mais o passo. O som das passadas ficara, decididamente, mais para trás. Aventurei-me a olhar por cima do ombro e verifiquei, com alívio, que eles se encontravam, agora, talvez a doze metros de distância, mas ambos tinham o olhar fixado em mim.

O tempo que levei a chegar à esquina pareceu uma eternidade. Mantive um ritmo de andamento regular, ficando os homens que se encontravam atrás de mim ligeiramente mais afastados a cada passo que eu dava. Talvez se tivessem apercebido de que me assustaram e lamentassem tê-lo feito. Vi dois carros a dirigirem-se para Norte ao passarem pelo cruzamento para o qual me encaminhava e respirei de alívio. Haveria mais pessoas por perto logo que eu saísse daquela rua deserta. Contornei a esquina de um pulo com um suspiro de agradecimento.

Escorreguei até parar.

A rua era ladeada de paredes despidas, sem portas nem janelas. Ao longe, conseguia avistar, a dois cruzamentos de distância, candeeiros de iluminação pública, automóveis e mais peões, mas tudo estava demasiado longe. Isto porque, encostados ao edifício ocidental, na zona intermédia da rua, encontravam-se os outros dois homens do grupo, assistindo com sorrisos de entusiasmo, enquanto eu ficava paralisada de morte no passeio. Apercebi-me subitamente de que não estava a ser seguida.

Estava a ser direccionada.

Detive-me apenas por um instante, mas tive a sensação de que tal se prolongara por muito tempo. Então, virei-me e precipitei-me para o lado oposto da estrada. Tive a desanimadora impressão de que tal tentativa era vã. Os passos vindos de trás de mim eram agora mais sonoros.

— Aí estás tu!

A voz trovejante do homem entroncado de cabelo escuro quebrou o intenso silêncio e fez-me estremecer de súbito. Na crescente escuridão, parecia que o seu olhar se fixava além de mim.

— Pois! — exclamou sonoramente uma voz vinda de trás de mim, fazendo-me estremecer enquanto me apressava a descer a rua. — Fizemos apenas um pequeno desvio.

Eu tinha agora de abrandar o passo. Estava a encurtar a distância que me separava da indolente parelha demasiado depressa. Tinha uma boa e sonora capacidade vocal e aspirei ar, preparando-me para fazer uso dela, mas a garganta estava tão seca que não sabia ao certo qual a intensidade que aquela conseguiria atingir. Com um movimento rápido, coloquei a minha mala acima da cabeça, segurando a alça com uma mão, pronta para entregá-la ou utilizá-la como arma se a necessidade a tal obrigasse.

O homem atarracado afastou-se da parede quando me detive com cautela e avancei lentamente pela rua.

— Afaste-se de mim — avisei com um tom de voz que devia parecer firme e destemido, mas eu estava certa quanto à questão da garganta seca, a intensidade da voz revelou-se nula.

— Não sejas assim, meu docinho! — exclamou ele. Então, o riso rouco desencadeou-se novamente atrás de mim.

Firmei posição, com os pés afastados, tentando lembrar-me, enquanto superava o pânico, das poucas estratégias de autodefesa que conhecia. Lançar a base da mão em sentido ascendente, partindo, com alguma sorte, o nariz da pessoa visada ou enfiando-lho no cérebro; enfiar o dedo na órbita ocular — tentar colocá-lo em posição de gancho e arrancar o olho; e, claro, a normal joelhada na virilha. Então, a mesma voz pessimista que ecoava dentro da minha cabeça voltou a manifestar-se, relembrando-me que, provavelmente, não tinha quaisquer hipóteses ao defrontar um deles e eles eram quatro. «Cala-te!», ordenei à voz antes que o pavor me incapacitasse. Não ia sucumbir sem levar alguém comigo. Tentei engolir de modo a conseguir soltar um grito decente.

De repente, surgiram luzes de faróis na esquina e o carro quase atingiu o sujeito entroncado, obrigando-o a recuar com um salto na direcção do passeio. Atirei-me para a estrada — *este* carro iria parar ou teria de me atingir. No entanto, o carro prateado fez um pião, derrapando até se imobilizar com a porta do passageiro aberta a escassos metros de distância de mim.

— Entra — ordenou uma voz furiosa.

Foi espantosa a forma como o medo sufocante desapareceu instantaneamente, como, de súbito, uma sensação de segurança se apoderou de mim — mesmo antes de ter entrado no carro — assim que ouvi a voz dele. Saltei para o banco, batendo com a porta depois de ter entrado.

No interior do carro, estava escuro — nenhuma luz se acendera quando a porta fora aberta — e eu mal conseguia ver o seu rosto na luminosidade emanada do *tablier*. Os pneus chiaram quando ele rodopiou para ficar virado para Norte, acelerando demasiado, guinando em direcção aos homens estupefactos que se encontravam na rua. Vi-os de relance a atirarem-se para o passeio enquanto nós retomávamos o rumo e acelerávamos em direcção ao porto.

— Coloca o cinto de segurança — ordenou ele.

Então, apercebi-me de que estava a agarrar-me ao assento com ambas as mãos. Apressei-me a obedecer-lhe; o estalido produzido quando o cinto se prendeu foi sonoro na escuridão. Virou à esquerda numa curva apertada, avançando em grande velocidade, passando como um raio por vários sinais de «Stop» sem a menor quebra da velocidade.

No entanto, sentia-me completamente a salvo, sem querer saber para onde íamos. Fitava o seu rosto com um profundo alívio, um alívio que transcendia o meu súbito salvamento. Examinei os seus traços impecáveis na claridade limitada, esperando que a minha respiração voltasse ao normal, até que me apercebi de que ele tinha estampada no rosto uma expressão de raiva assassina.

— Estás zangado comigo? — perguntei, espantada com a forma como a minha voz estava enrouquecida.

— Não — disse ele secamente, mas com um tom de voz que transmitia fúria.

Permaneci sentada em silêncio, observando-lhe o rosto enquanto os seus olhos ardentes se mantinham fixos no que se encontrava à sua frente, até que o carro parou de repente. Olhei em redor, mas estava demasiado escuro para conseguir ver além do indefinido contorno das árvores sombrias que juncavam a berma da estrada. Já não estávamos na cidade.

— Bella? — interrogou ele, com a voz tensa e controlada.

— Sim? — respondi com a voz ainda rouca.

Tentei aclarar a garganta de forma discreta.

— Estás bem?

Continuava sem olhar para mim, mas a fúria era evidente no seu semblante.

— Estou — respondi com uma voz gutural.

— Distrai-me, por favor — ordenou.

— Desculpa, o que disseste?

Expirou bruscamente.

— Fala apenas sobre algo sem importância até que eu acalme — esclareceu, fechando os olhos e beliscando a cana do nariz com o polegar e o dedo indicador.

— Hum — dei voltas à cabeça em busca de um assunto banal. — Amanhã, antes das aulas, vou atropelar o Tyler Crowley.

Ele ainda comprimia as pálpebras, mas o canto da boca contraiu-se-lhe.

— Porquê?

— Anda a dizer a todos que vai acompanhar-me ao baile de finalistas, ou está louco ou anda ainda a tentar compensar-me por quase me ter matado no outro dia... bem, tu recordas-te, e julga que o baile é, de algum modo, a maneira adequada de o fazer. Logo, calculo que, se eu colocar a vida dele em perigo, ficaremos quites e ele não poderá continuar a tentar compensar-me. Não preciso de inimigos e talvez a Lauren sossegasse se ele me deixasse em paz. Talvez tenha, todavia, de destruir o Sentra dele. Se não tiver um meio de transporte, não pode levar ninguém ao baile... — tagarelei.

— Ouvi falar disso — parecia um pouco mais calmo.

— *Ouviste?* — perguntei incredulamente, com a irritação de há pouco a inflamar-se. — Se estiver paralisado do pescoço para baixo, também não pode ir ao baile de finalistas — murmurei, aperfeiçoando o meu plano.

Edward suspirou e, por fim, abriu os olhos.

— Estás bem?

— Nem por isso.

Aguardei, mas ele não voltou a falar. Encostou a cabeça ao banco, olhando para o tejadilho do automóvel. O seu rosto estava austero.

— O que é que se passa? — as minhas palavras saíram sussurradas.

— Por vezes, tenho problemas com o meu temperamento, Bella — também ele sussurrava e, enquanto olhava pelo vidro, os seus olhos semicerraram-se, transformando-se em meras frechas. — Mas não adiantaria de nada se eu desse meia volta e perseguisse aqueles... — não terminou a frase, desviando o olhar, esforçando-se, por um momento, por controlar novamente a sua raiva. — Pelo menos — continuou — é disso que tento convencer-me.

— Ah! — tal interjeição parecia inadequada, mas não me ocorreu uma réplica melhor.

Ficámos novamente sentados em silêncio. Olhei para o relógio que se encontrava no *tablier*. Já passava das seis e meia da tarde.

— A Jessica e a Angela vão ficar preocupadas — murmurei. — Devia ir encontrar-me com elas.

Ligou o motor sem voltar a proferir uma única palavra, procedendo a uma suave inversão de marcha e acelerando de novo em direcção à cidade. Num ápice, já estávamos debaixo das luzes dos candeeiros de iluminação pública, avançando ainda com demasiada velocidade e passando com facilidade por entre os automóveis que circulavam devagar pela marginal. Estacionou paralelamente aos restantes veículos, junto da borda do passeio, num lugar que eu considerava demasiado pequeno para o Volvo, mas ele ocupou-o sem o mínimo esforço à primeira tentativa. Olhei pelo vidro e vi as luzes de *La Bella Italia*, assim como Jess e Angela a irem-se embora, distanciando-se ansiosamente de nós.

— Como é que sabias onde...? — principiei, mas, depois, limitei-me a abanar a cabeça.

Ouvi a porta a abrir-se e virei-me, vendo-o a sair.

— O que estás a fazer? — interroguei.

— Vou levar-te a jantar.

Esboçou um ligeiro sorriso, mas tinha os olhos duros. Saiu do carro e bateu com a porta. Tentei desajeitadamente libertar-me do cinto de segurança e, em seguida, apressei-me também a sair do carro. Ele esperava-me no passeio.

Falou antes de eu ter tido oportunidade de o fazer.

— Vai atrás da Jessica e da Angela antes que eu tenha também de seguir no seu encalço. Acho que não conseguiria refrear-me se desse outra vez de caras com aqueles teus amigos.

Tremi perante o tom de ameaça patente na sua voz.

— Jess! Angela! — gritei, seguindo atrás delas e acenando-lhes quando olharam.

Precipitaram-se na minha direcção, com a nítida expressão de alívio estampada no rosto de ambas a transformar-se simultaneamente em surpresa ao verem quem se encontrava a meu lado. Hesitaram em avançar a escassos metros de distância de nós.

— Onde estiveste? — a voz de Jessica transmitia desconfiança.

— Perdi-me — confessei timidamente. — E, depois, encontrei-me com Edward por acaso.

Fiz um gesto na direcção dele.

— Não se importam que eu vos faça companhia? — perguntou com a sua voz suave e irresistível.

Pelo ar espantado de ambas, percebi que ele nunca antes usara os seus encantos com elas.

— Aah... claro que não — afirmou Jessica suavemente.

— Hum, na verdade, Bella, nós já comemos enquanto estávamos à espera; desculpa — confessou Angela.

— Tudo bem, não tenho fome — disse eu encolhendo os ombros.

— Julgo que devias comer alguma coisa — Edward falava em voz baixa, mas com muita autoridade. Olhou para Jessica e falou com um tom de voz ligeiramente mais elevado. — Importas-te que eu leve a Bella a casa esta noite? Deste modo, não terão de esperar enquanto ela come.

— Hum, suponho que não há problema...

Ela mordeu o lábio, tentando perceber, através da minha expressão facial, se era aquilo que eu queria. Pisquei-lhe o olho. Nada mais queria senão estar a sós com o meu eterno salvador. Havia imensas perguntas com que só podia bombardeá-lo quando estivéssemos sozinhos.

— Está bem! — disse Angela mais rápida do que Jessica. — Até amanhã, Bella... Edward.

Pegou na mão de Jessica e puxou-a na direcção do carro, que eu conseguia avistar a uma curta distância, estacionado do outro lado da First Street. Ao entrarem, Jess voltou-se e acenou, com o rosto a transparecer uma curiosidade ávida. Retribuí-lhe o aceno, esperando que elas se afastassem antes de me virar de frente para ele.

— A sério, não tenho fome — insisti, erguendo o olhar para lhe perscrutar o rosto. A sua expressão facial era indecifrável.

— Faz-me a vontade.

Dirigiu-se para a porta do restaurante e manteve-a aberta com um ar de obstinação. Obviamente, não haveria mais discussões. Passei por ele, entrando no restaurante, com um suspiro de resignação.

O restaurante não estava muito cheio — vivia-se a época baixa em Port Angeles. Quem recebia os clientes era uma mulher e eu percebi o seu olhar enquanto examinava Edward. Recebeu-o de uma forma mais calorosa do que o necessário. Fiquei espantada com o modo como tal me incomodava. Ela era vários centímetros mais alta do que eu e artificialmente loura.

— Tem uma mesa para dois?

A voz dele era sedutora, quer fosse essa a sua intenção ou não. Vi o olhar dela incidir em mim e, depois, desviar-se, tendo ficado satisfeita com a minha óbvia vulgaridade e com a cautelosa distância que Edward mantinha entre nós. Conduziu-nos até uma mesa suficientemente grande para acomodar quatro pessoas, no centro da zona mais apinhada da sala de jantar.

Estava prestes a sentar-me, mas Edward abanou a cabeça.

— Talvez num local um pouco mais íntimo? — insistiu tranquilamente junto da anfitriã.

Não tinha a certeza, mas parecera que ele lhe dera uma gorjeta de forma subtil. Nunca vira ninguém recusar uma mesa, a não ser nos filmes antigos.

— Com certeza — anuiu ela, tão surpreendida como eu. Conduziu-nos, passando por uma divisória, até um pequeno recinto com cabinas, todas elas vazias. — O que lhe parece?

— Perfeito.

Ele exibiu o seu sorriso resplandecente, deslumbrando-a por momentos.

— Hum! — exclamou ela, abanando a cabeça e pestanejando — a empregada que irá servir-vos não demorará.

Afastou-se com um passo pouco firme.

— Não devias mesmo fazer isso às pessoas — critiquei. — Não é muito justo.

— Fazer o quê?

— Deslumbrá-las dessa forma; neste preciso momento, ela deve estar na cozinha a respirar de forma ofegante.

Ele parecia confuso.

— Oh, vá lá — disse com hesitação. — Tu deves ter noção do efeito que exerces nas pessoas.

Inclinou a cabeça para um dos lados e os seus olhos expressaram curiosidade.

— Eu deslumbro as pessoas?

— Ainda não reparaste? Julgas que todos conseguem alcançar o que pretendem com tanta facilidade?

Ignorou as minhas perguntas.

— E a *ti*, deslumbro-*te*?

— Frequentemente — confessei.

Então, a nossa empregada de mesa chegou, com um ar expectante. A anfitriã tinha, decididamente, embelezado os factos nos bastidores e a nova rapariga não parecia decepcionada. Colocou um fio de cabelo negro curto atrás de uma das orelhas e sorriu com desnecessário entusiasmo.

— Olá. Chamo-me Amber e vou ser a sua empregada de mesa esta noite. O que deseja para beber?

Não me escapou o facto de ela se dirigir unicamente a ele. Ele olhou para mim.

— Eu quero uma Coca-Cola.

A entoação da frase levou a que parecesse tratar-se de uma pergunta.

— São duas Coca-Colas — disse ele.

— Trá-las-ei de imediato — asseverou-lhe ela com outro sorriso desnecessário, mas ele não o viu. Estava a observar-me.

— O que foi? — interroguei quando ela se foi embora.

Os olhos dele permaneceram fixos no meu rosto.

— Como te sentes?

— Estou óptima — retorqui, surpreendida com a sua veemência.

— Não te sentes tonta, enjoada, com frio...?

— Devia sentir?

Ele soltou um riso abafado perante o meu tom de perplexidade.

— Bem, na verdade estou à espera de que entres em estado de choque.

O seu rosto contorceu-se, dando origem àquele perfeito sorriso de través.

— Não creio que isso vá acontecer — declarei depois de conseguir voltar a respirar. — Sempre fui bastante boa a reprimir coisas desagradáveis.

— Mesmo assim, ficarei mais descansado quando ingerires algum açúcar e comida.

Nesse preciso instante, a empregada de mesa apareceu, trazendo as nossas bebidas e um cesto de gressinos. Posicionou-se com as costas voltadas para mim enquanto os colocava em cima da mesa.

— Está pronto para pedir? — perguntou a Edward.

— Bella? — interrogou ele.

Ela virou-se de má vontade para mim. Escolhi o primeiro prato que vi na ementa.

— Hum... Quero o *ravioli* de cogumelos.

— E o senhor? — perguntou ela, virando-se novamente para ele com um sorriso no rosto.

— Eu não quero nada — afirmou ele.

Claro que não queria.

— Se mudar de ideias, avise-me.

O sorriso delico-doce continuava no mesmo lugar, mas ele não estava a olhar para ela, pelo que se foi embora descontente.

— Bebe — ordenou ele.

Sorvi o meu refrigerante de modo obediente e, em seguida, bebi mais avidamente, surpreendida com a sede que sentia. Apercebi-me de que o consumira até ao fim quando ele empurrou o seu copo na minha direcção.

— Obrigada — murmurei por entre dentes, estando ainda sequiosa.

A sensação de frio que derivava do refrigerante gelado estava a difundir-se pelo meu peito e eu arrepiei-me.

— Tens frio?

— É só da Coca-Cola — expliquei, sentindo outro arrepio.

— Não tens um casaco?

O seu tom de voz era recriminador.

— Tenho.

Olhei para o banco vazio a meu lado.

— Oh! Deixei-o no carro da Jessica — constatei.

Edward estava a despir o casaco. De repente, apercebi-me de que não reparara uma única vez nas roupas que ele vestia — não só nesta noite, mas nunca. Simplesmente não conseguia tirar os olhos do seu semblante. Obriguei-me a olhar agora, concentrando-me. Estava a tirar um casaco de pele bege-claro; por baixo, tinha uma camisola de gola alta cor de marfim. Assentava-lhe confortavelmente, realçando-lhe o peito musculado.

Deu-me o casaco, interrompendo o meu olhar amoroso.

– Obrigada! – exclamei, com os braços a deslizarem pelas mangas do seu casaco.

Estava frio – como o meu quando pegava nele de manhã, na entrada repleta de correntes de ar, onde estava pendurado. Senti outro arrepio. Exalava um odor fantástico. Inspirei, tentando identificar a deliciosa fragrância. Não cheirava a água-de-colónia. As mangas eram demasiado compridas; arregacei-as de modo a libertar as mãos.

– Essa cor azul condiz maravilhosamente com a tua pele – disse ele, observando-me.

Fiquei surpreendida; baixei o olhar, ruborizando, como é evidente. Empurrou o cesto do pão na minha direcção.

– A sério, não vou entrar em estado de choque – protestei.

– Mas devias; a uma pessoa *normal* era isso que aconteceria. Nem sequer pareces abalada.

Ele parecia inquieto. Olhava-me fixamente nos olhos e eu consegui ver quão claros os seus estavam, mais claros do que alguma vez os vira, do tom dourado dos caramelos de manteiga.

– Sinto-me muito protegida na tua companhia – confessei, ficando novamente hipnotizada e sendo outra vez induzida a dizer a verdade.

A minha afirmação desagradou-lhe; a sua testa de alabastro enrugou-se. Abanou a cabeça, franzindo o sobrolho.

– Isto é mais complicado do que eu imaginara – murmurou para consigo mesmo.

Peguei num gressino e comecei a mordiscar a respectiva extremidade, analisando a sua expressão facial. Perguntei-me quando seria o momento indicado para começar a interrogá-lo.

– Normalmente, estás mais bem-disposto quando os teus olhos estão assim claros – comentei, tentando distraí-lo do pensamento que o fizera franzir o sobrolho e ficar melancólico.

Fitou-me, estupefacto.

— O quê?

— Estás sempre mais rabugento quando os teus olhos estão negros; nessa altura, já sei o que esperar — prossegui. — Tenho uma teoria a esse respeito.

Os seus olhos semicerraram-se.

— Mais teorias?

— Sim.

Eu mastigava um pequeno pedaço de pão, tentando parecer indiferente.

— Gostaria que, desta vez, fosses mais criativa... ou continuas a inspirar-te nos livros de banda desenhada?

O seu ténue sorriso era escarnecedor; os seus olhos continuavam tensos.

— Bem, não, não me baseei num livro de banda desenhada, mas também não a elaborei sozinha — confessei.

— E então? — incitou-me.

No entanto, nesse momento, a empregada de mesa contornou a divisória a passos largos, trazendo a minha comida. Apercebi-me de que estávamos inconscientemente inclinados na direcção um do outro, por cima da mesa, pois ambos nos endireitámos quando ela se aproximou. Ela colocou o prato à minha frente — tinha um aspecto bastante apetitoso — e virou-se rapidamente para Edward.

— Mudou de ideias? — perguntou ela. — Não quer que lhe traga nada?

Eu podia estar a imaginar o duplo significado das suas palavras.

— Não, obrigado, mas convinha que trouxesse mais refrigerante.

Ele fez um gesto com a mão longa e branca na direcção dos copos vazios que se encontravam diante de mim.

— Com certeza.

Ela retirou os copos vazios e afastou-se.

— O que estavas a dizer? — perguntou.

— Digo-te no carro. Se...

Detive-me.

— Há condições?

Ele levantou a sobrancelha, falando num tom de voz sinistro.

— Tenho, de facto, algumas questões a colocar, evidentemente.

— Evidentemente.

A empregada voltou com mais duas Coca-Colas. Desta vez, pousou-as na mesa sem proferir uma única palavra e voltou a ir-se embora.

Sorvi um trago.

— Bem, continua — instigou, ainda com uma voz ríspida.

Comecei pela menos exigente. Ou assim pensava eu.

— Porque estás em Port Angeles?

Baixou o olhar, unindo lentamente as suas mãos grandes sobre a mesa. O seu olhar incidiu sobre mim por baixo das suas pestanas, com o indício de um sorriso pretensioso a surgir-lhe no rosto.

— A seguinte.

— Mas esta é a mais fácil — protestei.

— A seguinte — repetiu.

Baixei o olhar, frustrada. Desenrolei o guardanapo que envolvia os meus talheres, peguei no garfo e espetei cuidadosamente um pedaço de *ravioli*. Coloquei-o na boca lentamente, ainda com o olhar baixo, mastigando enquanto pensava. Os cogumelos eram bons. Engoli e sorvi outro trago de Coca-Cola antes de levantar o olhar.

— Então, muito bem — lancei-lhe um olhar feroz e prossegui lentamente. — Digamos, hipoteticamente, como é evidente, que... alguém... podia adivinhar os pensamentos das pessoas, ler a mente, tu sabes... com algumas excepções.

— Com apenas *uma* excepção — corrigiu ele — hipoteticamente.

— Muito bem, que seja, então, uma excepção — estava radiante por verificar que ele iria cooperar, mas tentei mostrar indiferença. – Como é que isso funciona? Quais são as limitações? Como é que... essa pessoa... encontraria outra exactamente no momento certo? Como poderia ele saber que ela estava em apuros?

Perguntei-me se as minhas perguntas intrincadas chegavam sequer a ter nexo.

– Hipoteticamente? – interrogou ele.

– Claro.

– Bem, se... essa pessoa...

– Chamemos-lhe «Joe» – sugeri.

Ele esboçou um sorriso enviesado.

– Joe, então. Se o Joe estivesse a prestar atenção, o sentido de oportunidade não teria de ser assim tão exacto.

Ele abanou a cabeça, revirando os olhos.

– Só *tu* poderias arranjar sarilhos numa cidade assim tão pequena. Terias arrasado as estatísticas referentes à taxa de criminalidade da cidade por uma década, sabes.

– Estávamos a referir-nos a um caso hipotético – relembrei-lhe friamente.

Ele riu-se de mim, com um olhar caloroso.

– Pois estávamos – concordou. – Chamamos-te «Jane»?

– Como é que sabias? – perguntei, incapaz de refrear a minha impetuosidade.

Apercebi-me de que estava novamente inclinada na direcção dele. Ele parecia estar a vacilar, dividido por algum dilema interior. Os seus olhos fixaram-se nos meus e deduzi que ele estava, naquele preciso momento, a tomar a decisão de simplesmente me contar ou não a verdade.

– Sabes que podes confiar em mim – murmurei.

Estendi a mão, sem pensar, para tocar as suas, que estavam unidas, mas ele afastou-as sumariamente e eu retirei a minha.

– Não sei se ainda tenho alternativa – disse ele com um tom de voz quase sussurrante. – Estava enganado, tu és muito mais observadora do que eu julgava.

– Pensava que tinhas sempre razão.

— Costumava ter — abanou a cabeça. — Também me enganei a teu respeito acerca de outro aspecto. Tu não atrais acidentes, esta definição não é suficientemente abrangente. Tu atrais *sarilhos*. Se houver alguma situação de perigo num raio de quinze quilómetros, acabará invariavelmente por te envolver.

— E tu inseres-te nessa categoria? — conjecturei.

O seu rosto tornou-se frio, inexpressivo.

— Inequivocamente.

Voltei a estender a mão por cima da mesa — ignorando-o quando ele se retraiu um pouco uma vez mais — para tocar timidamente as costas da sua mão com as pontas dos meus dedos. A sua pele estava fria e dura, como uma pedra.

— Obrigada — a minha voz estava fervorosa de gratidão. — Já é a segunda vez.

O seu rosto amoleceu.

— Não vamos experimentar a terceira, de acordo?

Olhei-o mal-humorada, mas acenei com a cabeça. Retirou a mão da minha, colocando as duas mãos debaixo da mesa, mas inclinou-se na minha direcção.

— Segui-te até Port Angeles — confessou, falando num ímpeto. — Nunca tentei manter viva uma pessoa em especial, e é muito mais problemático do que eu imaginara, mas, provavelmente, é por essa pessoa seres tu. As pessoas normais parecem conseguir chegar ao fim do dia sem tantas catástrofes.

Deteve-se. Perguntei-me se deveria ficar incomodada com o facto de ele andar a seguir-me; em vez disso, fui invadida por uma estranha sensação de prazer. Ele olhava-me fixamente, talvez perguntando-se por que motivo os meus lábios esboçavam um trejeito que progredia para um sorriso involuntário.

— Já te ocorreu a ideia de que talvez tivesse chegado a minha vez naquela primeira ocasião, com a carrinha, e tu tens estado a interferir no destino? — especulei, perdendo-me em devaneios.

— Não foi essa a primeira vez — disse ele, sendo difícil ouvir a sua voz; eu fitava-o com assombro, mas ele tinha o olhar baixo. — A tua vez chegou quando te conheci.

Senti um acesso de medo ao escutar as suas palavras e recordei bruscamente o olhar furioso que ele me lançara naquele dia... mas a avassaladora sensação de segurança que eu sentia na sua presença aquietou-me. Quando ele ergueu o olhar para decifrar o meu, não havia nele qualquer vestígio de medo.

— Lembras-te? — perguntou, com o seu semblante solene de anjo.

— Lembro — estava calma.

— E, no entanto, aqui estás tu sentada.

Havia um laivo de incredulidade na sua voz; levantou uma sobrancelha.

— Sim, aqui estou eu sentada... por tua causa — detive-me. — Porque, de alguma forma, tu sabias como encontrar-me hoje... — incitei-o a explicar.

Ele apertou os lábios, fitando-me com os olhos semicerrados, tomando uma nova decisão. O seu olhar incidiu subitamente sobre o meu prato e, em seguida, sobre mim.

— Tu comes e eu falo — negociou.

Peguei rapidamente noutra garfada de *ravioli* e levei-a à boca, mastigando com pressa.

— É mais difícil do que deveria ser, localizar-te. Normalmente, consigo encontrar uma pessoa com muita facilidade quando já auscultei a sua mente antes.

Ele olhou-me com ansiedade e apercebi-me de que paralisara. Obriguei-me a mim mesma a engolir e, em seguida, espetei outro pedaço de *ravioli* e abocanhei-o.

— Andava a vigiar a Jessica, sem grandes cuidados — como já referi, só tu poderias arranjar sarilhos em Port Angeles — e, a princípio, não reparei que partiras sozinha. Então, quando me apercebi de que já não estavas com elas, fui à tua procura à livraria que eu vira na cabeça dela. Percebi que não tinhas entrado e te deslocavas para Sul... e sabia que terias de voltar para trás em breve. Assim, estava apenas à tua espera, perscrutando aleatoriamente os pensamentos das pessoas que passavam na rua — para ver se alguém reparara em ti, de modo a poder saber onde estavas. Não tinha motivos para estar preocupado... mas estava estranhamente ansioso...

Estava perdido nos seus pensamentos, fixando o olhar além de mim, vendo coisas que eu não podia imaginar.

— Comecei a andar às voltas, ainda... à escuta. O Sol estava finalmente a pôr-se e eu prestes a sair do carro e a seguir-te a pé. Então... — ele parou, cerrando os dentes numa fúria repentina. Esforçou-se por se acalmar.

— Então o quê? — sussurrei.

Ele continuou a olhar fixamente por cima da minha cabeça.

— Ouvi o que eles estavam a pensar — resmungou, com o seu lábio superior a retrair-se ligeiramente por cima dos dentes. — Vi o teu rosto na mente dele.

Subitamente, inclinou-se para a frente, com um cotovelo a surgir sobre a mesa e a mão a tapar-lhe os olhos. O movimento foi tão ágil que me assustou.

— Foi muito... difícil para mim... não imaginas quanto... simplesmente levar-te dali e deixá-los... vivos — a sua voz era abafada pelo seu braço. — Podia ter-te deixado ir com a Jessica e a Angela, mas receava que, se me deixasses sozinho, eu fosse à procura deles — confessou num sussurro.

Eu permanecia silenciosamente sentada, aturdida, com as ideias a surgirem-me incoerentemente. As minhas mãos estavam unidas no meu colo e eu encostava-me sem energia às costas do assento. Ele ainda segurava o rosto com a mão e estava imóvel como se tivesse sido esculpido na pedra à qual se assemelhava a sua pele.

Finalmente, ergueu o olhar, com os seus olhos a procurarem os meus, pejados das suas próprias perguntas.

— Estás pronta para ir para casa? — interrogou.

— Estou pronta para me ir embora — reformulei, excessivamente grata por ainda podermos desfrutar, juntos, da hora que demorava a viagem até casa. Não estava preparada para me despedir dele.

A empregada de mesa apareceu como se tivesse sido chamada ou estivesse a observar-nos.

— Está tudo bem? — perguntou ela a Edward.

— Já pode trazer-nos a conta, obrigado.

A voz dele estava serena, mais ríspida, reflectindo ainda a tensão da nossa conversa. Tal facto pareceu perturbar o espírito da empregada. Ele levantou o olhar, esperando.

— C... com certeza — tartamudeou ela. — Aqui tem.

Retirou uma pequena pasta de pele do bolso da frente do avental preto e entregou-lha.

Ele já tinha uma nota na mão. Colocou-a no interior da pasta e devolveu-lha.

— Não é necessário dar-me o troco.

Sorriu. Levantou-se e eu pus-me de pé de forma desajeitada. Ela sorriu-lhe novamente de modo convidativo.

— Tenha uma boa noite.

Ele não desviou sequer o olhar de mim enquanto lhe agradecia. Eu reprimi um sorriso.

Caminhou muito próximo de mim enquanto nos dirigíamos para a porta, tendo ainda o cuidado de não me tocar. Lembrei-me do que Jessica dissera a respeito da sua relação com Mike, de como estavam quase a chegar à fase do beijo. Suspirei. Edward pareceu ouvir-me e baixou curiosamente o olhar. Olhei para o passeio, grata pelo facto de, aparentemente, ele não ser capaz de adivinhar os meus pensamentos.

Abriu a porta do lado do passageiro, segurando-a enquanto eu entrava e fechando-a suavemente quando eu já me encontrava no interior do automóvel. Observei-o enquanto contornou a frente do carro, espantada, uma vez mais, com a sua graciosidade. Provavelmente, já devia estar habituada a isso — mas não estava. Tinha a impressão de que Edward não era o género de pessoa a quem as outras se habituavam.

Assim que entrou no carro, ligou o motor e pôs o aquecimento no máximo. A temperatura baixara significativamente e eu calculei que o bom tempo chegara ao fim. O casaco dele, porém, mantinha-me quente e eu aspirava o seu perfume quando pensava que ele não poderia ver-me a fazê-lo.

Edward saiu do estacionamento, avançando por entre o tráfego, aparentemente sem um olhar, virando de repente para trás para seguir em direcção à estrada nacional.

— Agora — disse ele de forma sugestiva — é a tua vez.

Capítulo Nove

TEORIA

— Posso fazer apenas mais uma pergunta? — pedi enquanto ele acelerava excessivamente ao percorrer a rua sossegada. Não parecia estar a prestar nenhuma atenção à estrada.

Suspirei.

— Só uma — acedeu, com os lábios cerrados a formarem uma linha cautelosa.

— Bem... disseste que sabias que eu não entrara na livraria e que me dirigira para Sul. Estava apenas a interrogar-me como é que sabias isso.

Desviou o olhar, deliberando.

— Pensei que já tínhamos superado todas as atitudes evasivas — resmunguei.

Ele quase sorriu.

— Então, muito bem. Segui o teu cheiro.

Olhou para a estrada, concedendo-me tempo para me recompor. Não me ocorria uma réplica aceitável para aquela afirmação, mas arquivei-a cuidadosamente para análise futura. Tentei voltar a concentrar-me. Não estava preparada para deixá-lo terminar, agora que estava finalmente a explicar os factos.

— E, então, não respondeste a uma das minhas primeiras perguntas... — empatei.

Ele olhou-me com um ar reprovador.

— Qual?

— Como é que funciona a questão da adivinhação do pensamento? Consegues adivinhar os pensamentos de qualquer pessoa, em qualquer lugar? Como é que consegues? O resto da tua família também pode...?

Senti-me tola ao pedir esclarecimentos acerca de um faz-de-
-conta.

— Isso é mais do que uma pergunta — salientou ele.

Limitei-me a entrelaçar os dedos e a olhá-lo fixamente,
aguardando uma resposta.

— Não, só eu é que posso. E não consigo auscultar qualquer
pessoa, em qualquer lugar. Tenho de estar relativamente próximo. Quanto mais conhecida é a... «voz» de uma pessoa, maior é
a distância a que consigo auscultá-la, mas, mesmo assim, a não
mais do que a alguns quilómetros — deteve-se pensativamente.
— Assemelha-se um pouco a estar num enorme salão cheio de
pessoas, com toda a gente a falar ao mesmo tempo. É apenas
um murmúrio, um burburinho de vozes ao fundo. Até me concentrar numa única voz e, então, o que essa pessoa estiver a
pensar torna-se claro para mim. Durante a maior parte do tempo, desligo-me simplesmente de tudo isso, é muito perturbador.
E, depois, é mais fácil parecer *normal* — franziu o sobrolho ao
pronunciar a palavra — quando não estou acidentalmente a responder aos pensamentos de alguém em vez de responder às suas
palavras.

— Por que motivo julgas que não consegues auscultar-me? —
perguntei com curiosidade.

Fitou-me com olhos enigmáticos.

— Não sei — murmurou. — O meu único palpite é que talvez
a tua mente não funcione da mesma forma que a das restantes
pessoas, como se os teus pensamentos estivessem na frequência
AM e eu só conseguisse sintonizar em FM.

Lançou-me um sorriso rasgado, subitamente divertido.

— A minha mente não funciona convenientemente? Sou uma
aberração?

Tais palavras incomodavam-me mais do que deviam, provavelmente devido ao facto de a sua especulação ter tocado no
ponto sensível. Eu sempre tivera essa suspeita e envergonhava-
-me que a mesma fosse confirmada.

— Ouço vozes dentro da minha cabeça e tu é que estás

preocupada com a possibilidade de seres uma aberração — riu-se. — Não te preocupes; trata-se apenas de uma teoria... — o seu semblante cerrou-se —, o que nos leva novamente a ti.

Suspirei. Por onde havia de começar?

— Não superámos já todas as evasivas? — relembrou-me suavemente.

Desviei o olhar do rosto dele pela primeira vez, tentando encontrar as palavras certas. Reparei, por acaso, no velocímetro.

— Valha-me Deus! — gritei. — Abranda!

— O que é que se passa? — inquiriu ele sobressaltado, mas o carro não desacelerou.

— Vais a cento e sessenta quilómetros por hora!

Eu continuava a gritar. Lancei um olhar de pânico pelo vidro, mas estava demasiado escuro para conseguir ver grande coisa. A estrada só era visível na longa mancha de claridade azulada projectada pelos faróis. A floresta que se estendia de ambos os lados da estrada assemelhava-se a um muro negro — tão sólido como uma parede de aço se nós saíssemos da estrada àquela velocidade.

— Descontrai-te, Bella.

Revirou os olhos, continuando sem abrandar.

— Estás a tentar fazer com que ambos morramos? — interroguei.

— Não vamos bater.

Tentei modular a voz.

— Porque estás com tanta pressa?

— Conduzo sempre desta forma.

Virou-se para me sorrir de través.

— Não tires os olhos da estrada!

— Nunca me envolvi num acidente, Bella; nunca fui sequer multado — esboçou um sorriso largo e bateu com a mão na testa. — Detector de radar incorporado.

— Muito engraçado! — exclamei, irritada. — O Charlie é polícia, lembras-te? Fui educada para obedecer às regras de trânsito. Além disso, se nos transformares numa rosquilha de marca Volvo a envolver o tronco de uma árvore, podes provavelmente sair ileso.

— Provavelmente — concordou com uma breve e vigorosa

gargalhada. — Mas tu não — suspirou e eu vi, com alívio, o ponteiro a baixar gradualmente para os cento e vinte quilómetros por hora. — Satisfeita?

— Quase.

— Detesto conduzir devagar — murmurou ele por entre dentes.

— Isto é devagar?

— Já chega de comentários sobre a minha condução — disse ele com brusquidão. — Ainda estou à espera de ouvir a tua mais recente teoria.

Mordi o lábio. Ele olhou-me de cima, com olhos cor de mel subitamente ternos.

— Eu não me rio — prometeu.

— Receio mais que fiques zangado comigo.

— É assim tão má?

— Sim, bastante.

Ele aguardou. Eu olhava para as minhas mãos, de modo a não poder ver a expressão estampada no seu rosto.

— Continua.

A sua voz estava calma.

— Não sei por onde começar — reconheci.

— Porque não começas pelo princípio... disseste que não a elaboraste sozinha.

— Pois não.

— O que é que a desencadeou? Um livro? Um filme? — sondou.

— Não, foi o dia de sábado, na praia.

Arrisquei um olhar de relance para o seu rosto. Ele parecia intrigado.

— Encontrei um velho amigo de família, o Jacob Black — prossegui. — O pai dele e o Charlie são amigos desde que eu era bebé.

Ele continuava com um ar confuso.

— O pai dele é um dos anciãos Quileutes — eu observava-o cuidadosamente. A sua expressão de confusão manteve-se inalterada. — Fomos dar uma volta — omiti todas as minhas maquinações da história — e ele contou-me algumas lendas antigas, tentando assustar-me, creio eu. Contou-me uma... — hesitei.

— Continua — disse ele.

— Sobre vampiros.

Apercebi-me de que estava a sussurrar. Não conseguia agora olhá-lo no rosto, mas vi os nós dos seus dedos a contraírem-se compulsivamente no volante.

— E pensaste imediatamente em mim?

Continuava calmo.

— Não. Ele... mencionou a tua família.

Calou-se, olhando fixamente para a estrada. Fiquei subitamente preocupada, preocupada com a segurança de Jacob.

— Ele pensava apenas que se tratava de uma superstição tola — disse eu rapidamente. — Não esperava que eu retirasse daí algumas ilações.

Tal não pareceu ser suficiente; tinha de confessar.

— A culpa foi minha; obriguei-o a contar-me.

— Porquê?

— A Lauren disse algo a teu respeito, estava a tentar provocar-me, e um rapaz mais velho da tribo referiu que a tua família não ia à reserva, só que parecia que as suas palavras tinham um segundo sentido. Assim, fiz por ficar a sós com o Jacob e levei-o a fazer-me essas revelações — admiti, baixando a cabeça.

Ele assustou-me ao rir-se. Lancei-lhe um olhar irado. Estava a rir-se, mas os seus olhos estavam ferozes, fixando-se no que se encontrava à sua frente.

— Como é que o levaste a fazê-lo? — perguntou.

— Tentei namoriscá-lo... foi mais eficaz do que eu pensava.

A incredulidade enrubesceu-me ao lembrar-me.

— Gostava de ter assistido — soltou um sinistro riso abafado. — E acusaste-me *a mim* de deslumbrar as pessoas. Pobre Jacob Black!

Corei e olhei, pelo vidro do meu lado, para a noite.

— O que fizeste então? — perguntou um momento depois.

— Fiz algumas pesquisas na Internet.

— E isso convenceu-te?

O seu tom de voz revelava um escasso interesse, mas as suas mãos seguravam firmemente o volante.

— Não. Nada se encaixava. A maior parte da informação era bastante disparatada. Então... — detive-me.

— O quê?

— Cheguei à conclusão de que não tinha importância — sussurrei.

— Não tinha *importância*?

O seu tom de voz fez-me erguer o olhar — conseguira finalmente penetrar na sua máscara cuidadosamente composta. O rosto transmitia incredulidade, com apenas um laivo da raiva que eu temera.

— Não — disse brandamente. — Não me interessa o que tu és.

Uma ponta de escárnio e de dureza introduziu-se na sua voz.

— Não te importas que eu seja um monstro? Que eu não seja *humano*?

— Não.

Ficou calado, fixando de novo o olhar em frente. O seu rosto estava frio e austero.

— Estás zangado — disse eu, suspirando. — Não devia ter-te dito nada.

— Não! — exclamou, mas o seu tom de voz estava tão duro como o seu rosto. — Prefiro saber o que pensas, mesmo que o que penses seja de loucos.

— Então, estou enganada outra vez? — desafiei-o.

— Não era a isso que eu me referia. «Não tem importância»! — citou, rangendo os dentes.

— Tenho razão? — exclamei com voz ofegante.

— Isso tem alguma *importância*?

Respirei fundo.

— Nem por isso — detive-me. — Mas estou com curiosidade — a minha voz, pelo menos, estava calma.

Ele ficou subitamente resignado.

— Sentes curiosidade em relação a quê?

— Quantos anos tens?

— Dezassete — respondeu prontamente.

— E há quanto tempo tens dezassete anos?

Os seus lábios contorceram-se enquanto ele olhava para a estrada.

— Há algum — confessou por fim.

— Muito bem.

Sorri, satisfeita pelo facto de ele ainda estar a ser sincero comigo. Olhou-me com cautela, quase como fizera antes, quando estava preocupado com a possibilidade de eu entrar em estado de choque. Esbocei um sorriso mais rasgado, como forma de incentivo, e ele franziu o sobrolho.

— Não te rias... mas como é que podes andar na rua durante o dia?

Riu-se na mesma.

— Mito.

— Ser queimado pelo Sol?

— Mito.

— Dormir em caixões?

— Mito — hesitou por um momento e um tom peculiar introduziu-se na sua voz. — Não consigo dormir.

Levei alguns instantes a assimilar tal informação.

— De todo?

— Nunca — disse ele, com a voz quase inaudível.

Virou-se para me olhar com uma expressão de melancolia. Os olhos dourados pousaram-se nos meus e eu perdi a linha de raciocínio. Fitei-o até ele desviar o olhar.

— Ainda não me colocaste a questão mais importante.

A sua voz estava agora ríspida e, quando voltou a olhar-me, os seus olhos estavam frios.

Pisquei os olhos, ainda aturdida.

— Qual?

— Não estás interessada no meu regime alimentar? — perguntou sarcasticamente.

— Ah! — murmurei — isso.

— Pois, isso — a sua voz estava soturna. — Não queres saber se eu bebo sangue?

Eu retraí-me.

— Bem, o Jacob mencionou algo a esse respeito.

— O que é que o Jacob mencionou? — perguntou com uma voz monótona.

— Mencionou que vocês não... caçavam pessoas. Mencionou que a tua família não devia ser perigosa porque só caçava animais.

— Disse que nós não éramos perigosos?

A sua voz transmitia um profundo cepticismo.

— Não propriamente. Disse que não *deviam* ser perigosos, mas os Quileutes continuavam a não querer que vocês pisassem nas suas terras, não vá o Diabo tecê-las.

Ele olhava em frente, mas eu não consegui perceber se estava a prestar atenção à estrada ou não.

— Então, ele tinha razão? A respeito de vocês não caçarem pessoas?

Tentei manter a voz o mais normal possível.

— Os Quileutes têm uma memória de longo alcance — sussurrou ele.

Interpretei as suas palavras como sendo uma confirmação.

— Mas não deixes que isso te torne complacente — advertiu--me. — Eles agem acertadamente ao manterem a distância em relação a nós. Continuamos a ser perigosos.

— Não compreendo.

— Nós tentamos — explicou lentamente. — Costumamos ser muito bons naquilo que fazemos. Por vezes, cometemos erros. Eu, por exemplo, ao permitir-me ficar a sós contigo.

— Isto é um erro?

Detectei a tristeza patente na minha voz, mas não sabia se o mesmo acontecia com ele.

— Um erro muito perigoso — murmurou ele.

Ambos ficámos, então, calados. Observei as luzes dos faróis a retorcerem-se com as curvas da estrada. Estas sucediam-se com demasiada rapidez; tal não parecia real, assemelhando-se, sim, a um jogo de vídeo. Estava ciente de que o tempo passava demasiado depressa, como a estrada negra debaixo de nós, e receava medonhamente não voltar a ter outra oportunidade para estar sozinha com ele daquela forma — abertamente, sem muros a dividir-nos pela primeira vez. As palavras dele indiciavam um fim e eu repeli tal ideia. Não podia desperdiçar um só minuto do tempo de que dispunha na companhia dele.

— Conta-me mais coisas — pedi desesperadamente, não me importando com o que ele dissesse, apenas para voltar a ouvir a sua voz.

Olhou-me rapidamente, espantado com a mudança no meu tom de voz.

— O que queres saber mais?

— Diz-me porque é que caças animais em vez de pessoas — sugeri, com a voz ainda marcada por um tom de desespero. Apercebi-me de que os meus olhos estavam húmidos e debati-me contra a dor que tentava acabrunhar-me.

— Eu não *quero* ser um monstro.

Falava com um tom de voz muito grave.

— Mas os animais não são suficientes?

Ele deteve-se.

— Não posso ter a certeza, como é evidente, mas compará-lo-ia a uma alimentação à base de tofu e leite de soja; consideramo-nos vegetarianos. É uma pequena piada só entre nós. Não sacia completamente a fome — ou, melhor, a sede —, mas mantém-nos suficientemente fortes para conseguirmos resistir. A maior parte do tempo.

O seu tom de voz tornou-se ominoso.

— Umas vezes é mais difícil do que outras.

— Está a ser muito difícil para ti agora? — perguntei.

Ele suspirou.

— Está.

— Mas, agora, não tens fome — disse de modo confiante, afirmando, não perguntando.

— Porque pensas isso?

— Por causa dos teus olhos. Eu disse-te que tinha uma teoria. Reparei que as pessoas, principalmente os homens, ficam mais rabugentas quando têm fome.

Soltou um riso abafado.

— És observadora, não és?

Não respondi; ouvi apenas o som do seu riso, fixando-o na memória.

— Foste caçar no passado fim-de-semana, com o Emmett? — perguntei quando o silêncio voltou a instalar-se.

— Fui — deteve-se por um instante, como se estivesse a decidir se haveria ou não de dizer algo. — Não queria partir, mas era necessário. É um pouco mais fácil estar perto de ti quando não estou sedento.

— Porque é que não querias partir?

— Fico... ansioso... quando estou longe de ti — disse, com um olhar afável, mas intenso, parecendo estar a fazer com que os meus ossos amolecessem. — Não estava a brincar quando te pedi que tentasses não cair ao mar nem ser atropelada na passada quinta-feira. Passei todo o fim-de-semana com o espírito inquieto, preocupado contigo, e, depois do que aconteceu esta noite, estou surpreendido por teres conseguido escapar ilesa a um fim-de-semana inteiro — abanou a cabeça e, em seguida, pareceu lembrar-se de algo. — Bem, não totalmente ilesa.

— O quê?

— As tuas mãos — relembrou-me.

Olhei para as palmas das minhas mãos, para os arranhões quase sarados que marcavam a base das mesmas. Nada escapava aos seus olhos.

— Caí! — exclamei, suspirando.

— Foi o que eu pensei — os seus lábios esboçaram um trejeito nos cantos. — Suponho que, tratando-se de ti, poderia ter sido muito pior, e essa possibilidade atormentou-me durante todo o tempo que passei fora. Foram três dias muito longos. Irritei o Emmett a sério.

Sorriu-me com um ar de arrependimento.

— Três dias? Não regressaram hoje?

— Não, regressámos no domingo.

— Então, porque é que nenhum de vós estava na escola?

Sentia-me frustrada, quase zangada ao pensar na tamanha decepção que sofrera devido à ausência dele.

— Bem, perguntaste-me se o Sol me magoava e não magoa, mas não posso expor-me à luz solar — pelo menos, em lugares onde alguém possa ver-me.

— Porquê?

— Um dia destes, mostro-te — prometeu.

Reflecti sobre as suas palavras por um momento.

— Podias ter-me telefonado — resolvi dizer.

Ele ficou perplexo.

— Mas eu sabia que estavas a salvo.

— Mas *eu* não sabia onde *tu* estavas. Eu — hesitei, baixando o olhar.

— O quê?

A sua voz aveludada era irresistível.

— Não gostei. De não te ver. Também me faz ficar ansiosa.

Ruborizei por estar a dizer isto em voz alta. Ele ficou calado. Olhei de relance, apreensiva, e vi que ele tinha uma expressão de dor estampada no rosto.

— Ah — lamentou-se calmamente. — Isto está errado.

Não consegui compreender a sua réplica.

— O que é que eu disse?

— Não vês, Bella? Fazer-me infeliz a mim mesmo é uma coisa, mas outra coisa completamente diferente é o facto de tu estares tão envolvida — virou os olhos subitamente angustiados para a estrada, com as palavras a fluírem demasiado depressa para que eu as compreendesse. — Não quero ouvir-te dizer que te sentes assim — falava em voz baixa, mas com insistência. As suas palavras trespassavam-me. — Está errado. Não é seguro. Eu sou perigoso, Bella, por favor, compreende isso.

— Não.

Esforçava-me arduamente por não parecer uma criança amuada.

— Estou a falar a sério — resmungou.

— Eu também. Já te disse que não me interessa o que tu és.

Já é demasiado tarde.

A sua voz precipitou-se, grave e ríspida.

— Nunca digas isso.

Mordi o lábio e fiquei contente por ele não poder saber quanto aquilo me magoava. Fixei o olhar na estrada. Já devíamos estar perto. Ele conduzia com demasiada velocidade.

— Em que estás a pensar? — perguntou-me, com a voz ainda rude.

Abanei apenas a cabeça, não sabendo ao certo se conseguiria falar. Sentia o seu olhar pregado em mim, mas continuei a olhar em frente.

— Estás a chorar?

Parecia estarrecido. Não me apercebera de que a humidade que me inundava os olhos transbordara. Apressei-me a passar a mão pela face e, de facto, ali se encontravam lágrimas traiçoeiras.

— Não! — exclamei, mas a voz falhou-me.

Vi-o tentar alcançar-me, de forma hesitante, com a mão direita, mas, de repente, deteve-se e voltou a pousá-la lentamente no volante.

— Desculpa.

A sua voz queimava de arrependimento. Eu sabia que ele não estava a desculpar-se apenas pelas palavras que me tinham transtornado.

A escuridão passava por nós em silêncio.

— Diz-me uma coisa — pediu após um instante, esforçando-se por falar com um tom de voz mais brando.

— Sim?

— Em que é que estavas a pensar esta noite, mesmo antes de eu contornar a esquina? Não consegui perceber a expressão estampada no teu rosto e não parecias assim tão assustada, mas parecias, sim, estar a concentrar-te profundamente em algo.

— Estava a tentar lembrar-me de como incapacitar um agressor — tu sabes, autodefesa. Ia esmurrar-lhe o nariz e enfiar-lho no cérebro. Lembrei-me do homem de cabelo escuro com um acesso de ódio.

— Ias lutar com eles? — perguntou transtornado com o facto. — Não pensaste em fugir?

— Caio muitas vezes quando corro — confessei.

— E em gritar?

— Estava a chegar a essa parte.

Ele abanou a cabeça.

— Tinhas razão — estou decididamente a lutar contra o destino ao tentar manter-te viva.

Suspirei. Estávamos a abrandar, a entrar nos limites de Forks. Demorara menos de dez minutos.

— Vemo-nos amanhã? — perguntei.

— Vemos, também tenho um trabalho a entregar — sorriu. — Guardo-te um lugar ao almoço.

Depois de tudo aquilo por que passáramos nesta noite, era disparatada a forma como aquela pequena promessa me provocou palpitações no coração e fez com que eu ficasse incapaz de falar.

Estávamos em frente da casa de Charlie. As luzes estavam acesas, a minha *pick-up* no seu devido lugar, tudo absolutamente normal. Era como se acordasse de um sonho. Ele parou o carro, mas eu não me mexi.

— *Prometes* estar lá amanhã?

— Prometo.

Pensei nestas palavras por um momento e, em seguida, acenei com a cabeça. Despi o casaco dele, sentindo o seu cheiro uma última vez.

— Podes ficar com ele — não tens casaco para vestir amanhã — relembrou-me.

Voltei a estender-lho.

— Não quero ter de dar explicações ao Charlie.

— Ah, pois! — esboçou um sorriso largo.

Hesitei, com a mão no manípulo da porta, tentando prolongar o momento.

— Bella?! — exclamou num tom de voz diferente, sério, mas hesitante.

— Sim? — tornei a virar-me para ele com demasiada ansiedade.

— Prometes-me uma coisa?

— Prometo — disse eu, arrependendo-me imediatamente do meu assentimento incondicional. E se ele me pedisse para me manter afastada dele? Não conseguiria cumprir tal promessa.

— Não entres no bosque sozinha.

Olhei-o confusa.

— Porquê?

Ele franziu o sobrolho e os seus olhos estavam cerrados enquanto ele lançava o olhar além de mim, pelo vidro.

— Nem sempre sou a criatura mais perigosa que por ali deambula. Fiquemos por aqui.

Estremeci ligeiramente perante a súbita soturnidade patente na sua voz, mas fiquei aliviada. Esta, pelo menos, era uma promessa fácil de honrar.

— Como queiras.

— Até amanhã! — exclamou ele com um suspiro e eu soube que ele queria que eu saísse naquele momento.

— Até amanhã, então.

Abri a porta com relutância.

— Bella?

Virei-me e ele estava inclinado na minha direcção, com o rosto pálido e sublime a apenas alguns centímetros de distância do meu. O meu coração parou de bater.

— Dorme bem — disse.

Senti a respiração dele na minha cara, atordoando-me. Exalava o mesmo cheiro soberbo que se mantinha no seu casaco, mas de uma forma mais concentrada. Pisquei os olhos, completamente aturdida. Ele afastou-se.

Não consegui mexer-me enquanto as minhas ideias, de algum modo, não se clarificaram. Então, saí desajeitadamente do carro, tendo de me apoiar no chassis. Pensei tê-lo ouvido soltar um riso abafado, mas o som fora demasiado discreto para que eu pudesse ter a certeza.

Esperou até que eu, aos tropeções, chegasse à porta da frente e, em seguida, ouvi o motor do seu carro a embalar calmamente.

Voltei-me para ver o automóvel prateado desaparecer ao contornar a esquina. Apercebi-me de que estava muito frio.

Alcancei a chave mecanicamente, abri a porta e entrei. Charlie chamou-me da sala de estar.

— Bella?

— Sim, pai, sou eu.

Fui até lá para vê-lo. Estava a assistir a um jogo de basebol.

— Chegaste cedo.

— Cheguei?

Estava surpreendida.

— Ainda nem são oito horas — informou-me. — As meninas divertiram-se?

— Sim, foi muito divertido — a minha cabeça girava enquanto fazia um esforço de memória para conseguir lembrar-me da saída que eu planeara só com raparigas. — Ambas encontraram vestidos.

— Estás bem?

— Estou apenas cansada. Caminhei muito.

— Bem, talvez devesses ir deitar-te — parecia preocupado.

Perguntei-me como estaria a minha cara.

— Vou só telefonar à Jessica primeiro.

— Não estiveste mesmo agora com ela? — perguntou, surpreendido.

— Estive — mas deixei o casaco no carro dela. Quero certificar-me de que ela o leva amanhã.

— Bem, deixa-a primeiro chegar a casa.

— Certo — concordei.

Fui para a cozinha, deixei-me cair, exausta, numa cadeira. Agora, sentia-me realmente tonta. Perguntei-me se sempre iria entrar em estado de choque. «Controla-te», disse para comigo mesma.

De repente, o telefonou tocou, sobressaltando-me. Arranquei o auscultador do gancho.

— Está lá! — exclamei de forma ofegante.

— Bella?

— Olá, Jess, ia mesmo agora telefonar-te.

— Conseguiste chegar a casa?

A sua voz transmitia alívio... e surpresa.

— Sim. Deixei o casaco no teu carro, podias levar-mo amanhã?

— Claro. Mas conta-me o que aconteceu! — exigiu ela.

— Hum, amanhã, na aula de Trigonometria, está bem?

Ela depressa percebeu.

— Ah, o teu pai está aí?

— Sim, é isso mesmo.

— Muito bem, falamos amanhã, então. Adeus!

Eu detectava impaciência na voz dela.

— Adeus, Jess.

Subi as escadas vagarosamente, com um pesado torpor a toldar-me o espírito. Preparei-me para me deitar sem prestar atenção ao que estava a fazer. Só quando estava no duche — com a água demasiado quente a queimar-me a pele — é que me apercebi de que estava enregelada. Tremi violentamente durante vários minutos até que o jacto de água fumegante relaxou os meus músculos rígidos. Então, permaneci de pé, no duche, demasiado cansada para me mover, até que a água quente começou a faltar.

Saí aos tropeções, envolvendo-me cuidadosamente numa toalha, tentando manter o calor da água no corpo, de modo a que os dolorosos arrepios não voltassem. Vesti agilmente a roupa de dormir e deitei-me sob a colcha, enroscando-me como uma bola, abraçando-me a mim mesma para me manter quente. Alguns pequenos tremores perpassaram-me.

A minha cabeça ainda rodopiava vertiginosamente, repleta de imagens que eu não conseguia compreender e de algumas que eu me esforçava por recalcar. A princípio, nada parecia claro, mas, à medida que o meu estado se aproximava mais da inconsciência, algumas certezas tornaram-se evidentes.

Em três pontos, eu estava absolutamente segura. Em primeiro lugar, Edward era um vampiro. Em segundo lugar, uma parte dele — e eu não sabia qual era o poder dessa parte — ansiava pelo meu sangue. Por fim, em terceiro lugar, eu estava incondicional e irrevogavelmente apaixonada por ele.

Capítulo Dez

Interrogações

Foi muito difícil, de manhã, argumentar com a parte de mim que aceitava a noite anterior como um sonho. A lógica não estava a meu favor, nem o senso comum. Agarrei-me ao que não poderia ter imaginado — como o cheiro dele. Tinha a certeza de que nunca poderia ter sonhado semelhante coisa a partir do nada.

Do lado de fora da minha janela, o tempo estava sombrio e enevoado, algo absolutamente perfeito. Ele não tinha qualquer motivo para se ausentar da escola nesse dia. Vesti roupas pesadas, lembrando-me de que não tinha casaco. Outra prova de que a minha recordação era real.

Quando desci, Charlie já saíra — estava mais atrasada do que pensara. Engoli uma barra de *muesli* em três dentadas, empurrei-a com leite bebido directamente do pacote e, em seguida, precipitei-me porta fora. Com alguma sorte, a chuva aguentar-se-ia até eu conseguir encontrar Jessica.

Havia muito nevoeiro, e o ar quase se tornava fumarento de tão cerrado que era. Sentia o frio glacial da neblina ao depositar-se na pele do meu rosto e do meu pescoço. Mal podia esperar por ligar o aquecimento da *pick-up*. O nevoeiro era de tal forma denso que eu já avançara alguns metros ao longo da entrada quando me apercebi de que um automóvel se encontrava imerso nele: um automóvel prateado. Senti um baque no coração, que titubeou e, depois, recomeçou a bater de forma muito mais acelerada.

Não vi de onde ele viera, mas, de repente, ali estava, abrindo-me a porta para eu entrar.

— Queres ir comigo hoje? — perguntou, achando graça à expressão estampada no meu rosto depois de me ter apanhado desprevenida uma vez mais.

Havia um tom de incerteza na sua voz. Estava, de facto, a dar-me a escolher — eu era livre de recusar e, por um lado, ele esperava que eu o fizesse. Era uma esperança vã.

— Quero, obrigada — disse eu, tentando manter a voz calma.

Ao entrar no carro quente, reparei que o seu casaco casta-nho-amarelado estava suspenso no apoio para a cabeça do lugar do passageiro. A porta fechou-se depois de eu ter entrado e, mais depressa do que deveria ser possível, já ele se encontrava sentado a meu lado, a ligar a ignição.

— Trouxe o casaco para ti. Não queria que ficasses doente.

A sua voz transmitia cautela. Notei que ele não trazia nenhum casaco vestido, mas apenas uma camisola de malha cinzento--clara de mangas compridas com decote em V. Uma vez mais, o tecido ajustava-se ao seu peito perfeitamente musculado. Era um tributo colossal ao seu rosto o facto de este manter os meus olhos afastados do seu corpo.

— Não sou assim tão delicada — afirmei, mas puxei o casaco para o meu colo, enfiando os braços nas mangas demasiado compridas, curiosa por ver se o odor era, de facto, tão agradá-vel como eu me lembrava. Era mais.

— Ai não? — contestou ele, falando num tom de voz tão baixo que eu não sabia ao certo se pretendia que o ouvisse.

Percorremos as ruas envoltas em nevoeiro, sempre com de-masiada velocidade, sentindo-nos pouco à vontade. Eu, pelo menos, sentia-me assim. Na noite anterior, derrubaramos todos os muros que nos separavam... quase todos. Não sabia se, nes-te dia, continuaríamos a ser francos um com o outro. Este fac-to deixou-me sem saber o que dizer. Esperei que ele falasse.

Virou-se e sorriu-me pretensiosamente.

— Então, hoje não tens duas dezenas de perguntas para me fazer?

— As minhas perguntas incomodam-te? — interroguei, aliviada.

— Não tanto como as tuas reacções — parecia estar a gracejar, mas eu não tinha a certeza disso.

Franzi o sobrolho.

— Eu reajo mal?

— Não, o problema é esse. Encaras tudo com tanta frieza... não é natural. Faz com que me interrogue sobre o que estás realmente a pensar.

— Eu digo-te sempre o que realmente penso.

— És selectiva — acusou-me.

— Não muito.

— O suficiente para dar comigo em doido.

— Tu não queres ouvir o que penso — balbuciei, quase sussurrando.

Assim que proferi tais palavras, arrependi-me de o ter feito. A dor patente na minha voz era extremamente ténue; só me restava esperar que ele não a tivesse detectado.

Ele não retorquiu e eu perguntei-me se tinha estragado o ambiente. O rosto dele estava indecifrável ao entrarmos no parque de estacionamento da escola. Algo me veio tardiamente ao espírito.

— Onde está o resto da tua família? — perguntei bem contente por estar sozinha com ele, mas lembrando-me de que o seu carro costumava andar cheio.

— Veio no carro da Rosalie — encolheu os ombros ao estacionar ao lado de um reluzente descapotável vermelho com a capota colocada. — É ostentoso, não é?

— Hum, ena — pronunciei baixinho. — Se ela tem *aquela* bomba, porque se desloca no teu carro?

— Como já disse, é ostentoso. Nós *tentamos* passar despercebidos.

— Não conseguem — ri-me e abanei a cabeça ao sairmos do carro. Já não estava atrasada; a sua condução de loucos fizera com que eu chegasse à escola com bastante tempo de antecedência. — Porque é que Rosalie resolveu vir hoje a conduzir se dá mais nas vistas?

— Ainda não tinhas reparado? Agora, estou a quebrar *todas* as regras.

Juntou-se a mim em frente do carro, permanecendo a meu lado, bastante próximo, enquanto nos dirigíamos para o recinto da escola. Eu queria encurtar essa pequena distância, estender a mão e tocar-lhe, mas receava que ele não desejasse que eu o fizesse.

— Porque é que têm carros como aquele? — perguntei-me em voz alta. — Se estão à procura de privacidade?

— É uma forma de satisfazermos uma das nossas vontades — confessou com um sorriso endiabrado. — Todos nós gostamos de conduzir com velocidade.

— Já era de calcular — murmurei por entre dentes.

Abrigada sob a aba do telhado da cantina, Jessica esperava, com os olhos prestes a saltarem das órbitas. Por cima do seu braço — graças a Deus —, estava o meu casaco.

— Olá, Jessica! — exclamei quando estávamos a escassos metros de distância. — Obrigada por te teres lembrado.

Entregou-me o casaco sem falar.

— Bom dia, Jessica — disse Edward educadamente.

Não tinha propriamente culpa de que a sua voz fosse de tal modo irresistível, nem do efeito que os seus olhos eram capazes de exercer.

— Aah... viva! — desviou o olhar na minha direcção, tentando colocar as ideias em ordem. — Suponho que nos vemos na aula de Trigonometria.

Lançou-me um olhar expressivo e eu reprimi um suspiro. Que iria dizer-lhe?

— Sim, vemo-nos lá.

Afastou-se, parando duas vezes para nos espreitar por cima do ombro.

— Que vais dizer-lhe? — murmurou Edward.

— Eh, pensei que não conseguias adivinhar os meus pensamentos! — exclamei.

— E não consigo — retorquiu ele, sobressaltado; então, a compreensão iluminou-lhe os olhos. — No entanto, consigo adivinhar os dela, ela vai estar à espera para te atacar de surpresa na aula.

Lamentei-me enquanto despia o casaco dele e lho entregava, trocando-o pelo meu. Ele dobrou-o e colocou-o por cima do braço.

— Então, que vais dizer-lhe?

— Que tal dares-me uma ajudinha? — pedi. — Que quer ela saber?

Ele abanou a cabeça, esboçando um sorriso perverso.

— Isso não é justo.

— Não, o facto de tu não partilhares o que sabes, isso é que não é justo.

Ponderou por um momento enquanto caminhávamos. Parámos à entrada da sala onde eu iria assistir à minha primeira aula.

— Ela quer saber se nós andamos a namorar às escondidas. E quer saber o que sentes por mim — acabou por dizer.

— Ai, ai. O que devo dizer?

Tentei manter um ar muito inocente. As pessoas passavam por nós a caminho da aula, provavelmente olhando fixamente, mas eu mal notava a sua presença.

— Hum — deteve-se para apanhar uma madeixa desgarrada do meu cabelo que estava a escapar-se da trança junto do meu pescoço e devolveu-a ao seu devido lugar. O meu coração disparou hiperactivamente. — Suponho que podias responder afirmativamente à primeira questão... se não te importares, é mais fácil do que dar qualquer outra explicação.

— Não me importo — declarei com uma voz débil.

— E quanto à outra questão... bem, ficarei à escuta para eu próprio ouvir a resposta.

Um dos lados da sua boca fez um trejeito, esboçando o meu sorriso assimétrico preferido. Não consegui recuperar o fôlego a tempo de retorquir àquela observação. Ele virou-se e afastou-se.

— Vemo-nos ao almoço! — exclamou por cima do ombro.

Três pessoas que entravam na sala pararam para me olhar.

Apressei-me a entrar na sala de aula, corada e irritada. Ele era tão batoteiro. Agora, eu estava ainda mais preocupada em relação àquilo que iria dizer a Jessica. Sentei-me no meu lugar habitual, pousando violentamente a mala exasperada.

— Bom dia, Bella — disse Mike do lugar a meu lado; ergui o olhar e vi uma expressão estranha, quase de resignação, estampada no seu rosto. — Como correu o passeio a Port Angeles?

— Correu... — não havia uma forma sincera de resumir aqueles acontecimentos. — Optimamente — concluí de forma medíocre.

— A Jessica comprou um vestido mesmo giro.

— Ela comentou algo a respeito da noite de segunda-feira? — perguntou ele, com os olhos a iluminarem-se.

Sorri perante a mudança de rumo que a conversa tomara.

— Disse que se divertiu mesmo muito — assegurei-lhe.

— Ai disse! — exclamou com impaciência.

— Muito claramente.

O professor Mason impôs, então, a ordem na sala, pedindo-nos para entregarmos os nossos trabalhos. As aulas de Inglês e de Administração Pública passaram sem que nada ficasse retido na minha memória, enquanto me preocupava com a forma como haveria de explicar os factos a Jessica e me afligia a possibilidade de Edward estar realmente a ouvir o que eu diria por intermédio dos pensamentos de Jessica. Quão inconveniente podia ser a sua pequena faculdade — quando não estava a salvar-me a vida.

O nevoeiro quase se dissipara ao final do segundo tempo, mas o dia continuava sombrio devido às nuvens ameaçadoras que pairavam pesadamente a baixa altitude. Sorri para o céu.

Edward tinha razão, como é evidente. Quando entrei na sala de Trigonometria, Jessica estava sentada na fila do fundo, quase saltando do seu lugar com tanta agitação. Fui, com relutância, sentar-me a seu lado, tentando convencer-me de que seria melhor despachar o assunto o mais rapidamente possível.

— Conta-me tudo! — exigiu antes de eu me sentar.

— O que queres saber? — perguntei, procurando não me comprometer.

— O que aconteceu na noite passada?

— Ele pagou-me o jantar e, depois, levou-me a casa.

Ela fitou-me com uma expressão rígida de cepticismo.

— Como é que chegaste a casa tão depressa?

— Ele conduz como um louco. Foi apavorante.

Esperei que ele tivesse ouvido aquelas minhas palavras.

— Foi um encontro amoroso? Disseste-lhe para se encontrar contigo lá?

Não pensara nisso.

— Não — fiquei *muito* espantada ao vê-lo lá.

Os lábios dela franziram-se com a desilusão perante a sinceridade transparente patente na minha voz.

— Mas ele foi buscar-te para te trazer à escola hoje? — indagou.

— Foi, isso também me espantou. Ele reparou que eu não tinha casaco na noite passada — expliquei.

— Então, vão sair novamente?

— Ele ofereceu-se para me levar a Seattle no sábado, por pensar que a minha *pick-up* não está apta para fazer tal viagem. Isso conta?

— Conta — disse ela, acenando com a cabeça.

— Bem, então, vamos.

— E-na! — enfatizou a interjeição ao pronunciá-la por sílabas. — O Edward Cullen.

— Eu sei — concordei.

A interjeição «ena» não chegava sequer a fazer jus à realidade.

— Espera! — levantou as mãos subitamente, virando as palmas na minha direcção, como se estivesse a parar o trânsito. — Ele beijou-te?

— Não — balbuciei. — A nossa relação não é nada assim.

Ela pareceu ficar desiludida. De certeza que eu também.

— Achas que no sábado...? — ergueu a sobrancelha.

— Tenho muitas dúvidas.

O descontentamento patente na minha voz foi mediocremente dissimulado.

— De que é que vocês falaram? — insistiu com um sussurro, de modo a obter mais informação.

A aula já começara, mas o professor Varner não estava a prestar muita atenção e nós não éramos as únicas que ainda conversavam.

— Não sei, Jess. De muita coisa — sussurrei-lhe também. — Falámos um pouco sobre a dissertação de Inglês, muito, muito pouco. Penso que ele a mencionou de passagem.

— Por favor, Bella — implorou. — Dá-me alguns pormenores.

– Bem... está bem, vou dar-te um. Devias ter visto a empregada de mesa a namoriscá-lo... foi de mais. Mas ele não lhe prestou nenhuma atenção.

Ele que interpretasse aquelas minhas palavras como entendesse.

– Esse é um bom sinal – disse ela, acenando com a cabeça. – Ela era bonita?

– Muito, e devia ter dezanove ou vinte anos.

– Ainda melhor. Ele deve gostar de ti.

– *Julgo* que sim, mas é difícil dizer. É sempre tão reservado – comentei suspirando para que ele ficasse a saber o que eu pensava.

– Não sei como tens coragem para ficar a sós com ele – murmurou Jessica.

– Porquê?

Fiquei escandalizada, mas ela não compreendeu a minha reacção.

– Ele é tão... intimidador. Eu não saberia o que lhe dizer.

Ela fez um ar relutante, lembrando-se provavelmente daquela manhã ou da noite anterior, quando ele utilizara a força avassaladora dos seus olhos sobre ela.

– De facto, tenho alguns problemas de incoerência quando estou perto dele – reconheci.

– Oh, bem, ele é incrivelmente lindo.

Jessica encolheu os ombros como se este facto compensasse quaisquer defeitos e, na sua cartilha, provavelmente compensava.

– Ele é muito mais do que isso.

– A sério? O quê, por exemplo?

Preferia não ter insistido naquela questão. Quase tanto como esperava que ele estivesse a brincar quando disse que ficaria à escuta.

– Não consigo explicar adequadamente... mas ele é ainda mais incrível *por trás* do rosto.

O vampiro que queria ser bom, que corria de um lado para o outro a salvar a vida às pessoas de modo a não ser um monstro... Fixei o olhar na parte da frente da sala.

– Isso é *possível*?! – exclamou ela, soltando risinhos.

Ignorei-a, tentando parecer que estava a prestar atenção ao

professor Varner.

— Então, gostas dele?

Ela não queria desistir.

— Sim — respondi concisamente.

— Quero dizer, gostas dele *a sério?* — insistiu.

— Sim — repeti, ruborizando.

Esperei que aquele pormenor não ficasse registado nos pensamentos dela.

As respostas monossilábicas já tinham sido suficientemente esclarecedoras.

— A que *ponto* gostas dele?

— Gosto demasiado — respondi-lhe, sussurrando. — Mais do que ele gosta de mim, mas não vejo como evitá-lo.

Suspirei, com um rubor contínuo. Então, felizmente, o professor Varner chamou Jessica para que respondesse a uma pergunta.

Ela não teve oportunidade para puxar novamente o assunto durante a aula e, assim que a campainha tocou, assumi uma postura evasiva.

— Na aula de Inglês, o Mike perguntou-me se tu comentaras algo a respeito da noite de segunda-feira — comuniquei-lhe.

— Estás a brincar! O que é que respondeste? — disse ela, de forma ofegante, tendo sido completamente desviada dos seus intuitos.

— Disse-lhe que tu referiras que te divertiras muito, ele pareceu satisfeito.

— Diz-me exactamente quais foram as palavras dele e o que lhe respondeste!

Passámos o resto da caminhada a analisar estruturas sintácticas em pormenor e a maior parte da aula de Espanhol numa descrição minuciosa das expressões faciais de Mike. Não teria suportado que o assunto se prolongasse durante tanto tempo se não me preocupasse o facto de a conversa poder voltar-se para mim.

Então, a campainha tocou para a pausa do almoço. Ao saltar do lugar, enfiando com rudeza os livros na mala, o meu ar animado deve ter dado algo a entender a Jessica.

— Hoje, não vais sentar-te à nossa mesa, pois não? — deitou--se a adivinhar.

— Não me *parece*.

Não podia estar certa de que ele não voltasse a desaparecer inoportunamente.

No entanto, à entrada da sala onde decorreu a nossa aula de Espanhol, encostado à parede — parecendo mais um deus grego do que deveria ser permitido a alguém —, Edward esperava-me. Jessica olhou, revirou os olhos e foi-se embora.

— Vemo-nos mais logo, Bella.

A sua voz estava carregada de implicações. Talvez tivesse de desligar a campainha do telefone.

— Olá!

A voz dele transmitia divertimento e irritação ao mesmo tempo. Era óbvio que estivera a escutar.

— Viva!

Não me ocorreu mais nada que pudesse dizer e ele não falou — esperando a sua hora, depreendi —, tratando-se, portanto, de uma caminhada silenciosa até à cantina. Caminhar com Edward por entre a grande afluência de pessoas à hora de almoço asse-melhou-se bastante ao meu primeiro dia de aulas naquela esco-la; todos olhavam.

Ele seguiu à frente, em direcção à fila, continuando sem fa-lar, ainda que os seus olhos voltassem a incidir continuamente sobre o meu rosto, com um ar especulativo. Afigurava-se-me que a irritação prevalecia sobre o divertimento em termos da emoção no seu semblante. Eu mexia nervosamente no fecho de correr do meu casaco.

Dirigiu-se ao balcão e encheu um tabuleiro de comida.

— O que estás a fazer? — protestei. — Não vais levar tudo is-so para mim?

Ele abanou a cabeça, avançando para pagar a comida.

— Metade é para mim, como é evidente.

Ergueu uma sobrancelha.

Seguiu novamente à minha frente, em direcção ao mesmo lugar

onde nos sentáramos da outra vez. Da extremidade oposta da longa mesa, um grupo de estudantes de um nível mais avançado lançou-nos um olhar pasmado quando nos sentámos um em frente do outro. Edward parecia não dar importância.

— Tira o que desejares — disse ele, empurrando o tabuleiro na minha direcção.

— Estou curiosa — afirmei ao pegar numa maçã, revolvendo-a nas minhas mãos. — O que farias se alguém te desafiasse a ingerir comida?

— Estás sempre curiosa.

Fez uma careta, abanando a cabeça. Lançou-me um olhar irritado, fixando-o no meu enquanto retirava a fatia de piza do tabuleiro e, de modo intencional, deu uma dentada, mastigou rapidamente e, em seguida, engoliu. Observei-o, de olhos arregalados.

— Se alguém te desafiasse a comer terra, podias fazê-lo, não podias? — perguntou condescendentemente.

Torci o nariz.

— Já comi... num encontro — confessei. — Não foi assim tão mau.

Ele riu-se.

— Suponho que não estou surpreendido.

Por cima do meu ombro, algo pareceu chamar a atenção dele.

— A Jessica está a analisar tudo o que eu faço... há-de facultar-te a sua interpretação mais logo.

Empurrou o resto da piza na minha direcção. A referência a Jessica fez com que um laivo da anterior irritação voltasse a manifestar-se nos traços do seu rosto.

Pousei a maçã e dei uma dentada na piza, desviando o olhar, sabendo que ele estava prestes a principiar.

— Com que então a empregada de mesa era bonita? — perguntou ele com indiferença.

— Não reparaste mesmo?

— Não. Não estava a prestar atenção. Tinha muito em que pensar.

— Pobre rapariga!

Podia, agora, dar-me ao luxo de ser generosa.

— Algo que disseste à Jessica... bem, incomoda-me.

Recusava-se a ser distraído. A sua voz estava rouca e fitou-me com olhos inquietos.

— Não me admira que tenhas ouvido algo que não te agradou. Sabes o que se diz das pessoas que escutam as conversas alheias — lembrei-lhe.

— Eu avisei-te de que estaria à escuta.

— E eu avisei-te de que não querias saber tudo o que eu pensava.

— Pois avisaste — concordou, mas a sua voz continuava áspera. — No entanto, não estás bem certa. Eu quero, de facto, saber o que estás a pensar... tudo. Só gostaria... que não pensasses algumas coisas.

Lancei-lhe um olhar carregado.

— Grande diferença.

— Mas não é propriamente essa a questão neste momento.

— Então, qual é?

Estávamos, agora, inclinados na direcção um do outro sobre a mesa. Ele tinha as mãos unidas debaixo do queixo; inclinei-me para a frente, com a mão direita em concha à volta do pescoço. Tinha de manter presente no meu espírito que nos encontrávamos num refeitório a abarrotar de gente, provavelmente com muitos olhos curiosos pousados em nós. Era demasiado fácil deixar-me embrenhar no nosso enleio.

— Crês verdadeiramente que gostas mais de mim do que eu de ti? — murmurou ele, aproximando-se mais à medida que falava, com os seus olhos dourado-escuros a trespassar-me.

Tentei lembrar-me de como se expirava. Tive de desviar o olhar para me recordar.

— Estás a fazê-lo novamente — disse por entre dentes.

Os olhos dele arregalaram-se de admiração.

— O quê?

— A deslumbrar-me — confessei, tentando concentrar-me ao voltar a olhar para ele.

— Ah! — franziu o sobrolho.

— A culpa não é tua — afirmei, suspirando. — Não consegues evitar.

— Vais responder à pergunta?

Baixei o olhar.

— Sim.

— Referes-te a responder à pergunta ou ao facto de realmente pensares assim? — estava novamente irritado.

— Sim, penso mesmo assim.

Mantive o olhar pregado na mesa, com os meus olhos a seguirem o motivo dos falsos veios de madeira impressos no laminado. O silêncio arrastou-se. Recusei-me teimosamente a ser a primeira a quebrá-lo desta vez, debatendo-me com ardor contra a tentação de espreitar o seu rosto.

Ele acabou por falar, com uma voz suave como veludo.

— Estás enganada.

Olhei-o de relance e vi que os seus olhos estavam ternos.

— Não podes saber isso — discordei num sussurro.

Abanei a cabeça em dúvida, apesar de o meu coração ter palpitado ao ouvir as suas palavras e de eu desejar ardentemente acreditar nelas.

— O que te leva a pensar assim?

Os seus olhos cristalinos cor de topázio eram penetrantes, tentando em vão, presumi eu, arrancar a verdade directamente da minha mente.

Retribuí-lhe o olhar, esforçando-me por manter o pensamento lúcido apesar do seu rosto, para encontrar uma forma de me explicar. Enquanto procurava as palavras adequadas, via-o a ficar impaciente; sentindo-se frustrado com o meu silêncio, começou a olhar-me com um ar carregado. Tirei a mão do pescoço e coloquei um dedo no ar.

— Deixa-me pensar — insisti.

A expressão estampada no seu rosto tornou-se menos carregada, visto que ficou satisfeito por saber que eu tencionava responder-lhe. Deixei cair a mão sobre a mesa, movendo a esquerda de modo a que as palmas de ambas ficassem unidas. Olhei fixamente para as minhas mãos, entrelaçando e desentrelaçando os dedos, até que finalmente me pronunciei.

— Bem, além do óbvio, por vezes... — hesitei. — Não posso ter a certeza, pois não consigo adivinhar pensamentos, mas, por vezes, parece que estás a tentar despedir-te quando estás a dizer outra coisa.

Foi o melhor que consegui fazer: sintetizar a sensação de angústia que as suas palavras, por vezes, suscitavam em mim.

— És muito perspicaz — sussurrou; e eis que a angústia me assolou novamente, surgindo quando ele confirmou o meu receio. — É, porém, exactamente por isso que estás enganada — começou a explicar, mas, de repente, os seus olhos semicerraram-se. — A que te referes quando falas do «óbvio»?

— Bem, olha para mim — disse eu, desnecessariamente, visto que ele já estava a fitar-me. — Sou absolutamente vulgar, bem, à excepção de todos os aspectos negativos, como as experiências de morte iminente e o facto de ser tão desastrada que quase chego a ser inválida. Agora, olha para ti — fiz um gesto com a mão na direcção dele e de toda a sua desconcertante perfeição.

A sua testa enrugou-se em sinal de cólera por um momento e, em seguida, alisou-se à medida que os seus olhos se revelaram sabedores.

— Sabes, não tens uma imagem muito clara de ti mesma. Admito que estás absolutamente certa quanto aos aspectos negativos — disse ele, soltando sinistramente um riso abafado — mas não ouviste o que cada humano do sexo masculino pensou no teu primeiro dia de aulas.

Pisquei os olhos, atónita.

— Não acredito... — resmunguei para comigo mesma.

— Confia em mim só desta vez, és o contrário de vulgar.

O meu embaraço era muito mais intenso do que o meu deleite perante o olhar com que ele ficou ao proferir tais palavras. Apressei-me a relembrar-lhe o meu argumento inicial.

— Mas eu não vou despedir-me de ti — salientei.

— Será que não vês? É isso que prova que eu tenho razão. Os meus sentimentos são mais fortes, pois, se eu consigo fazê-lo — abanou a cabeça, parecendo debater-se contra tal ideia — se partir for a atitude correcta a tomar, magoar-me-ei a mim mesmo para evitar magoar-te, para manter-te a salvo.

Lancei-lhe um olhar furioso.

— E tu julgas que eu não faria o mesmo?

— Jamais terias de tomar tal decisão.

De repente, o seu humor imprevisível voltou a alterar-se; um sorriso malicioso e arrebatador recompôs os traços do seu rosto.

— É claro que manter-te a salvo começa a revelar-se uma ocupação a tempo inteiro que requer a minha presença constante.

— Ninguém tentou livrar-se de mim hoje — lembrei-lhe, grata pelo tema de conversa mais ligeiro.

Não queria que ele voltasse a falar em despedidas. Se fosse necessário, suponho que podia colocar-me a mim própria propositadamente em perigo de modo a mantê-lo por perto... Bani este pensamento antes que os seus rápidos olhos o decifrassem no meu rosto. Tal ideia iria decididamente colocar-me em dificuldades.

— Por enquanto — acrescentou ele.

— Por enquanto — concordei; teria argumentado, mas agora desejava que ele estivesse à espera de desgraças.

— Tenho outra pergunta para te fazer.

O seu rosto continuava ainda marcado pela indiferença.

— Diz.

— Precisas mesmo de ir a Seattle no próximo fim-de-semana ou tal não passou de um pretexto para evitares recusar os convites de todos os teus admiradores?

Fiz um esgar ao lembrar-me.

— Sabes, ainda não te perdoei por causa do Tyler — adverti-o. — Foi por tua culpa que ele se iludiu, pensando que eu vou ao baile com ele.

— Oh, ele teria arranjado uma oportunidade para te convidar sem a minha ajuda, eu só queria mesmo ver a tua cara — disse, rindo por entre dentes.

Eu teria ficado mais zangada se o seu riso não fosse tão fascinante.

— Se eu te tivesse convidado, tu ter-me-ias rejeitado? — perguntou, rindo ainda para consigo mesmo.

— Provavelmente, não — confessei. — Mas teria cancelado o compromisso mais tarde, inventando uma doença ou uma entorse num tornozelo.

Ele ficou abismado.

— Porque farias isso?

Abanei a cabeça com tristeza.

— Suponho que nunca me viste na aula de Educação Física, mas pensei que compreenderias.

— Estás a referir-te ao facto de não conseguires percorrer uma área plana e estável sem encontrar algo em que tropeçar?

— É claro.

— Isso não constituiria um problema — disse ele, muito confiante. — Tudo tem a ver com a forma como a dança é conduzida — apercebeu-se de que eu estava prestes a protestar e antecipou--se. — Mas nunca chegaste a contar-me... estás decidida a ir a Seattle ou importas-te que nós façamos algo diferente?

Desde que a parte do «nós» se mantivesse, nada mais me interessava.

— Estou aberta a outras opções — cedi. — Mas tenho um favor a pedir-te.

Ele pareceu cauteloso, tal como acontecia sempre que eu fazia uma pergunta que tudo deixava em aberto.

— Qual?

— Posso conduzir?

Franziu o sobrolho.

— Porquê?

— Bem, principalmente porque, quando disse ao Charlie que ia a Seattle, ele perguntou-me especificamente se ia sozinha e, na altura, ia. Se ele voltasse a perguntar, eu, provavelmente, não mentiria, mas não me parece que ele o *faça* e o facto de deixar a minha *pick-up* em casa só contribuiria para que o assunto viesse à baila desnecessariamente. Além disso, também porque a maneira como conduzes me assusta.

Ele revirou os olhos.

— De todas as coisas em mim que podiam assustar-te, preocupas-te com a minha maneira de conduzir.

Abanou a cabeça de descontentamento, mas, de repente, o seu olhar voltou a ficar sério.

— Não queres contar ao teu pai que vais passar o dia comigo?

Havia uma conotação na sua pergunta que eu não compreendi.

— Tratando-se do Charlie, quanto menos souber, melhor — tinha a certeza disso. — Já agora, aonde vamos?

— O tempo estará agradável, portanto, evitarei aparecer em público... e tu podes ficar comigo, se assim desejares.

Uma vez mais, deixou a decisão nas minhas mãos.

— E mostras-me aquilo a que te referias, a respeito do Sol? — perguntei, entusiasmada com a ideia de desvendar mais uma incógnita.

— Mostro — sorriu e, em seguida, deteve-se. — Mas, se não quiseres ficar... a sós comigo, continuo a preferir que não vás a Seattle sozinha. Tremo só de pensar nos sarilhos que poderias arranjar numa cidade daquele tamanho.

Fiquei ofendida.

— Phoenix é três vezes maior do que Seattle, apenas em termos populacionais. A nível de dimensão geográfica...

— Mas, pelos vistos... — interrompeu-me — ainda não tinhas dado o teu melhor quando lá estavas. Assim, preferia que ficasses perto de mim.

Os seus olhos voltaram a mostrar-se ardentes daquela forma irresistível.

Não podia argumentar, nem com os olhos, nem com a motivação, e, de qualquer modo, tratava-se de um ponto discutível.

— Por acaso, não me importo de ficar a sós contigo.

— Eu sei — suspirou, matutando. — Mas devias informar o Charlie.

— Por que carga de água haveria de fazer isso?

Os olhos dele ficaram subitamente irritados.

— Para me dares um pequeno incentivo para te trazer de volta.

Engasguei-me, mas, após um momento de reflexão, tive a certeza.

— Acho que correrei esse risco.

Expirou irritado e desviou o olhar.

— Vamos conversar sobre outra coisa — sugeri.

— Queres conversar sobre o quê? — perguntou, ainda aborrecido.

Olhei em nosso redor, certificando-me de que estávamos bem fora do alcance dos ouvidos de todos. Ao lançar o olhar pela sala, supreendi o da irmã dele, Alice, que me olhava fixamente. Os restantes olhavam para Edward. Desviei logo o olhar na direcção dele e fiz-lhe a primeira pergunta que me veio à cabeça.

— Porque foste àquele lugar chamado Goat Rocks no fim-de-semana passado? Foste caçar? O Charlie disse que não era um bom sítio para passear, devido aos ursos.

Fitou-me como se me estivesse a escapar algo demasiado óbvio.

— Ursos? — proferi de forma ofegante, enquanto ele esboçou um sorriso pretensioso. — Sabes, não estamos na época dos ursos — acrescentei com severidade, para disfarçar o meu abalo.

— Se leres com atenção, as leis só abrangem a caça com armas — informou-me.

Ele observou a minha cara com satisfação enquanto eu assimilava aquela informação.

— Ursos? — repeti com dificuldade.

— O urso-pardo é o preferido do Emmett. — A voz dele estava ainda desprovida de constrangimentos, mas os olhos examinavam a minha reacção. Tentei recompor-me.

— Hum! — exclamei, dando outra dentada na piza como pretexto para baixar o olhar. Mastiguei lentamente e, em seguida, sorvi um grande trago de Coca-Cola sem levantar os olhos.

— Então — disse após um momento, cruzando o meu olhar

com o dele, agora ansioso — qual é o teu preferido?

Ergueu uma sobrancelha e os cantos da boca viraram-se-lhe para baixo em sinal de reprovação.

— O puma.

— Ah! — exclamei num tom educadamente desinteressado, procurando o meu refrigerante.

— Como é evidente — afirmou e, então, o seu tom de voz reflectiu o meu —, temos ter o cuidado de não causar impacto no ambiente com a caça imprudente. Tentamos concentrar-nos em áreas com um excesso de predadores, distanciando-nos no terreno tanto quanto necessário. Aqui, existe sempre uma grande abundância de veados e alces e estes servem, mas que gozo dá caçá-los?

Sorriu de modo provocador.

— Sim, de facto — murmurei ao dar outra dentada na piza.

— O início da Primavera é a época de caça ao urso preferido do Emmett — estão mesmo a sair da hibernação e, por conseguinte, estão mais irritáveis.

Sorriu ao lembrar-se de alguma piada.

— Não há nada mais divertido do que um urso-pardo irritado — concordei, acenando com a cabeça.

Soltou um riso algo reprimido, abanando a cabeça.

— Por favor, diz-me o que estás pensar.

— Estou a tentar imaginar, mas não consigo — admiti. — Como é que caçam um urso sem armas?

— Oh, nós temos armas — ele exibiu os seus dentes brilhantes num breve e ameaçador sorriso. Reprimi um arrepio antes que este me denunciasse. — Só que não são do tipo daquelas que se levam em consideração quando se redigem as leis da caça. Se já assististe ao ataque de um urso na televisão, devias conseguir visualizar a caçada do Emmett.

Não consegui evitar novo arrepio que me percorreu a coluna vertebral. Dei uma espreitadela ao lado oposto da cantina, em busca de Emmett, ficando grata por ele não estar a olhar na minha direcção. As espessas massas musculares que lhe envolviam os braços e o tronco eram agora, de alguma forma, ainda mais ameaçadoras.

Edward viu para onde eu estava a olhar e soltou um riso abafado. Fitei-o, desalentada.

— Também te assemelhas a um urso? — perguntei em voz baixa.

— Assemelho-me mais ao leão ou, pelo menos, é isso que me dizem — disse ele, de ânimo leve. — Talvez as nossas preferências sejam indicativas.

Tentei sorrir.

— Talvez — repeti. A minha cabeça estava repleta de imagens opostas que eu não conseguia amalgamar. — Trata-se de algo a que eu poderei assistir?

— Claro que não!

O rosto dele ficou ainda mais branco do que o habitual e os seus olhos ficaram subitamente furiosos. Recostei-me, espantada e — ainda que jamais lho confessasse — assustada com a sua reacção. Ele também se recostou, cruzando os braços.

— É algo demasiado assustador para mim? — perguntei quando consegui voltar a controlar a voz.

— Se o problema fosse esse, levava-te hoje mesmo a fazê-lo — afirmou, com uma voz incisiva. — Tu *precisas* de uma dose saudável de medo. Nada te seria tão benéfico.

— Então, porquê? — insisti, tentando ignorar o seu ar zangado.

Olhou-me furioso durante um longo instante.

— A resposta a essa pergunta fica para depois — acabou por dizer, pôs-se de pé num pequeno movimento. — Vamos chegar atrasados.

Olhei em volta, ficando sobressaltada ao ver que ele tinha razão e que a cantina estava quase vazia. Quando estava com ele, o tempo e o espaço eram uma confusão de tal modo desordenada que eu perdia por completo a noção de ambos. Levantei-me de um salto, pegando na minha mala que se encontrava pendurada nas costas da cadeira.

— Fica, então, para depois — concordei, não me esqueceria.

Capítulo Onze

COMPLICAÇÕES

Todos nos observaram enquanto caminhámos juntos em direcção à nossa bancada do laboratório. Reparei que ele já não posicionava a cadeira de forma a sentar-se tão longe de mim; e sentava-se a meu lado de modo bastante próximo, com os nossos braços quase a tocarem-se.

O professor Banner entrou, então, de costas na sala — que magnífico sentido de oportunidade ele tinha —, puxando uma estrutura de metal sobre rodas que sustentava um televisor e um videogravador ultrapassados e de aspecto pesado. Era dia de filme, quase se vislumbrava um clima de elevação na aula.

O professor Banner introduziu a cassete no relutante videogravador e dirigiu-se à parede para apagar as luzes.

Então, quando a sala ficou às escuras, tomei de repente profunda consciência de que Edward estava sentado a menos de vinte centímetros de distância de mim. Fiquei aturdida com a inesperada electricidade que me perpassou, admirada com a possibilidade de me tornar *mais* sabedora a seu respeito do que já era. Um louco impulso no sentido de estender a mão e tocá-lo, de acariciar o seu rosto perfeito uma única vez na escuridão, quase me esmagou. Cruzei os braços firmemente junto ao peito, com as mãos a fecharem-se, de punhos cerrados. Estava a perder o juízo.

O genérico de abertura iniciou-se, iluminando a sala de forma simbólica. Os meus olhos, de modo próprio, tremularam na direcção dele. Sorri timidamente ao aperceber-me de que a sua postura era idêntica à minha: desde os punhos cerrados debaixo dos braços aos olhos a espreitarem-me de lado. Ele retribuiu-me com um sorriso largo, com os olhos, de algum modo, a conseguirem mostrar-se ardentes, mesmo na escuridão. Desviei o olhar antes que a minha respiração começasse a ficar ofegante. Era absolutamente ridículo que eu me sentisse tonta.

Aquela hora pareceu muito longa. Não consegui concentrar-me no filme, não sabia sequer de que é que tratava. Tentei em vão descontrair-me, mas a corrente eléctrica que parecia ter origem algures no corpo dele nunca cedeu. De vez em quando, permitia a mim mesma um rápido olhar na sua direcção, mas também ele nunca parecia descontrair-se. A avassaladora ânsia de lhe tocar também se recusava a esmorecer e eu, por prevenção, apertei os punhos contra as costelas até os dedos me doerem devido ao esforço.

Soltei um suspiro de alívio quando o professor Banner voltou a acender as luzes no final da aula e estiquei os braços, flectindo os dedos rígidos. Edward soltou um riso abafado a meu lado.

— Bem, foi interessante — murmurou ele.

A sua voz estava sombria e os olhos cautelosos.

— Hum! — foi tudo o que consegui dizer em resposta.

— Vamos? — perguntou, erguendo-se logo.

Quase soltei um lamento. Estava na hora da aula de Educação Física. Levantei-me com cuidado, preocupada com a possibilidade de o meu equilíbrio ter sido afectado pela nova e estranha intensidade que existia entre nós.

Acompanhou-me à aula seguinte em silêncio e deteve-se junto à porta; virei-me para me despedir. O seu rosto assustou-me. Estava com uma expressão abatida, quase de sofrimento, e tão ferozmente bela que a dor provocada pela vontade de lhe tocar me assomou de forma tão intensa como antes. A minha despedida ficou presa na garganta.

Levantou a mão, hesitante, com um conflito a assolar os seus olhos, e, então, acariciou rapidamente a maçã do meu rosto em toda a sua extensão com as pontas dos dedos. A sua pele estava gelada como sempre, mas o seu toque queimou.

Deu meia volta sem proferir uma só palavra e afastou-se de mim a passos largos.

Entrei no ginásio, atordoada e com passo vacilante. Deixei-me ir até ao balneário, mudando de roupa num estado semelhante a transe, apenas vagamente consciente de que havia outras pessoas ao meu redor. Só caí inteiramente na realidade quando me entregaram uma raqueta. Esta não era pesada, mas parecia estar pouco segura na minha mão. Conseguia ver alguns dos alunos da turma a olharem-me furtivamente. O treinador Clapp mandou-nos formar equipas de dois elementos.

Graças a Deus, alguns vestígios do cavalheirismo de Mike ainda subsistiam; colocou-se a meu lado.

— Queres formar uma equipa?

— Obrigada, Mike. Sabes que não tens de fazer isto —, afirmei, fazendo um esgar como quem pede desculpa.

— Não te preocupes, eu não te atrapalho.

Esboçou um sorriso rasgado. Às vezes, era tão fácil gostar do Mike.

A aula não decorreu sem percalços. Consegui, sem saber como, bater na minha própria cabeça com a raqueta e atingir Mike no ombro com o mesmo movimento. Passei o resto da hora de aula no canto ao fundo do campo, segurando prudentemente a raqueta atrás das costas. Apesar de estar em desvantagem por minha causa, Mike teve um desempenho bastante bom: venceu três jogos em quatro sem qualquer ajuda. Deu-me uma imerecida palmada na mão quando o treinador finalmente apitou, dando a aula por terminada.

— Então — disse ele enquanto saímos do campo.

— Então, o quê?

— Tu e o Cullen, hã? — perguntou ele, com um tom de voz revoltado.

O meu anterior sentimento de afecto desvaneceu-se.

— Isso não te diz respeito, Mike — avisei-o, condenando, no meu íntimo, Jessica às profundezas ardentes do Hades.

— Não me agrada — murmurou, mesmo assim, por entre dentes.

— Não tem de te agradar — disse eu com brusquidão.

— Ele olha-te como... como se fosses algo de comer — continuou, ignorando-me.

Reprimi a histeria que ameaçava explodir, mas um risinho abafado conseguiu escapulir-se apesar dos meus esforços. Ele fitou-me com um ar zangado. Eu acenei e escapei-me para o balneário.

Vesti-me depressa, com um nervosismo mais do que intenso a agitar-me descontroladamente as paredes do estômago, sendo a minha discussão com Mike já uma lembrança remota. Perguntava-me se Edward estaria à minha espera ou se eu deveria encontrar-me com ele junto do seu automóvel. E se a sua família lá estivesse? Senti uma onda de verdadeiro pavor. Será que eles sabiam que eu sabia? Será que eu devia saber que eles sabiam que eu sabia ou não?

Quando saí do ginásio, acabara, de certo modo, por resolver ir directamente para casa, a pé, sem sequer olhar na direcção do parque de estacionamento, mas as minhas inquietações foram desnecessárias. Edward encontrava-se à minha espera, encostando-se de forma descontraída à parte lateral do ginásio, com o seu rosto deslumbrante agora sereno. Enquanto caminhava para junto dele, senti uma singular sensação de libertação.

— Olá! — saudei, esboçando um enorme sorriso.

— Olá! — o sorriso com que ele me retribuiu era resplandecente. — Como correu a aula de Educação Física?

O meu rosto ficou um pouquinho mais desanimado.

— Correu bem — menti.

— Deveras?

Não estava convencido. Os seus olhos focaram um ponto ligeiramente distanciado, observando algo por cima do meu ombro e semicerrando-se. Olhei de relance para trás e vi as costas de Mike à medida que este se afastava.

— O que foi? — interroguei.

Os olhos dele voltaram a fixar-se nos meus, ainda tensos.

— O Newton está a irritar-me.

— Não estiveste a escutar novamente?

Eu estava aterrada. Todos os resquícios da minha repentina

boa disposição desapareceram.

— Como está a tua cabeça? — perguntou inocentemente.

— És incrível!

Voltei-me, caminhando sem grande determinação na direcção do parque de estacionamento, embora, nesta altura, ainda não tivesse excluído a hipótese de regressar a casa a pé.

Ele acompanhou-me sem dificuldade.

— Foste tu que referiste que eu nunca te vira na aula de Educação Física... fiquei curioso.

Não parecia arrependido, pelo que eu o ignorei.

Caminhámos em silêncio — um silêncio furioso e constrangido da minha parte — até ao carro dele. Mas eu tive de parar a alguns passos de distância, um grande número de pessoas, só rapazes, cercavam-no. Então, apercebi-me de que não estavam a cercar o Volvo, estando, na verdade, reunidos em torno do descapotável vermelho de Rosalie, com inequívoca cobiça espelhada nos olhos. Nenhum deles ergueu sequer o olhar quando Edward se esgueirou por entre eles para abrir a porta do seu carro. Entrei rapidamente para o lado do passageiro, tendo também passado despercebida.

— Ostentoso — murmurou por entre dentes.

— De que carro se trata? — perguntei.

— É um M3.

— Não falo o dialecto "automobilês".

— É um BMW.

Revirou os olhos, sem olhar para mim, tentando recuar sem atropelar os adeptos de automóveis.

Acenei com a cabeça, daquela marca já ouvira falar.

— Ainda estás zangada? — perguntou ele enquanto fazia com cuidado a manobra de saída do estacionamento.

— Sem dúvida.

Suspirou.

— Perdoas-me se eu te pedir desculpa?

— Talvez... se o fizeres com sentimento. E também se prometeres não repetir a façanha — insisti.

De repente, os seus olhos revelaram sagacidade.

— E se eu o fizer com sentimento e, além disso, concordar em deixar-te conduzir no sábado? — disse, regateando as minhas condições.

Analisei a proposta e cheguei à conclusão de que seria, provavelmente, a melhor que conseguiria obter.

— Combinado — concordei.

— Então, lamento muito ter-te aborrecido — os seus olhos brilharam de sinceridade por um prolongado momento, provocando grandes estragos no ritmo do meu coração e, em seguida, tornaram-se gracejadores. — E estarei à porta de tua casa no sábado de manhã, bem cedo.

— Hum, no que se refere à questão do Charlie, não ajuda muito que um Volvo seja inexplicavelmente abandonado na entrada.

O seu sorriso era agora condescendente.

— Não tencionava ir de carro.

— Como é que... — interrompeu-me.

— Não te preocupes. Eu lá estarei, sem carro.

Não insisti mais. Tinha uma pergunta mais premente a fazer.

— Já é depois? — perguntei de modo expressivo.

Ele franziu o sobrolho.

— Suponho que já é depois.

Mantive uma expressão educada enquanto aguardava.

Ele parou o carro. Eu ergui o olhar, surpreendida — era evidente que já chegáramos a casa de Charlie, estando parados atrás da *pick-up*. Era mais fácil andar de carro com ele quando eu só olhava depois de a viagem ter terminado. Quando voltei a fitá-lo, ele fixava-me, analisando-me.

— E tu ainda queres saber porque é que não podes ver-me caçar?

Tinha um ar solene, mas pareceu-me ter visto um laivo de humor bem no fundo dos seus olhos.

— Bem — esclareci — estava sobretudo a interrogar-me a respeito da tua reacção.

— Amedrontei-te?

Sim, havia ali, decididamente, uma ponta de humor.

— Não — menti.

Ele não acreditou.

— Peço desculpa por te ter assustado — insistiu ele com um ligeiro sorriso, mas, de repente, todos os sinais de provocação desapareceram. — Deveu-se apenas à mera ideia de tu estares presente... enquanto eu caçava.

Cerrou os maxilares.

— Seria mau?

Ele falou por entre os dentes cerrados.

— Muito.

— Porque...?

Respirou fundo e fixou o olhar, através do vidro, nas densas e ondulantes nuvens que pareciam pesar sobre nós, quase ao alcance da nossa mão.

— Quando nós caçamos — falava devagar, com relutância — entregamo-nos aos nossos sentidos... regemo-nos menos pela nossa cabeça. Sobretudo ao sentido do olfacto. Se estivesses perto de mim quando eu perdesse o controlo dessa forma...

Abanou a cabeça, com o olhar ainda taciturnamente fixo nas nuvens carregadas.

Mantive a expressão do meu rosto firmemente sob controlo, esperando que o ágil movimento dos seus olhos avaliasse a minha reacção, que depressa se seguiria. O meu semblante nada revelou.

No entanto, os nossos olhares mantiveram-se fixos um no outro e o silêncio intensificou-se, e alterou-se. Laivos da electricidade que eu sentira nessa mesma tarde começaram a impregnar o ambiente à medida que ele me fixava implacavelmente nos olhos. Só quando a minha cabeça começou a andar à roda é que me apercebi de que não estava a respirar. Quando inspirei de modo irregular, quebrando a quietude, ele fechou os olhos.

— Bella, penso que devias entrar agora.

A sua voz grave estava enrouquecida e o seu olhar incidia sobre as nuvens.

Abri a porta e a corrente de ar árctico que irrompeu pelo interior do carro ajudou-me a desanuviar a cabeça. Receando poder tropeçar no estado entontecido em que me encontrava, saí cuidadosamente do automóvel e fechei a porta sem olhar para trás. O ruído do vidro eléctrico a abrir-se fez-me virar.

— Bella! — chamou-me, com a voz mais regular. Inclinou-se na direcção do vidro aberto com um leve sorriso nos lábios.

— Sim?

— Amanhã é a minha vez — declarou.

— A tua vez de quê?

Esboçou um sorriso mais rasgado, exibindo os seus dentes cintilantes.

— De fazer as perguntas.

Então, partiu, com o carro a acelerar pela rua abaixo e a desaparecer ao contornar a esquina antes que eu conseguisse sequer colocar as minhas ideias em ordem. Sorri ao encaminhar-me para casa. Era notório que ele tencionava estar comigo no dia seguinte, ainda que não passasse disso.

Nessa noite, Edward protagonizou os meus sonhos, como de costume. No entanto, o ambiente da minha inconsciência alterara-se. Vibrava com a mesma electricidade que carregara a tarde e eu revirava-me na cama agitadamente, acordando com frequência. Só de madrugada acabei por cair no sono, exausta, sem sonhar.

Quando acordei, ainda estava cansada, mas também irritável. Vesti a camisola de gola alta castanha e as inevitáveis calças de ganga, suspirando enquanto fantasiava com camisolas de alças fininhas e calções. O pequeno-almoço foi a habitual ocorrência tranquila que já esperava. Charlie estrelou ovos para ele; eu comi a minha taça de cereais. Perguntei-me se ele se esquecera do que sucederia naquele sábado. Respondeu à pergunta que eu não chegara a exprimir verbalmente ao levantar-se para levar o prato para o lava-louça.

— Acerca do próximo sábado... — principiou, atravessando a cozinha e abrindo a torneira.

Eu retraí-me.

— Sim, pai?

— Ainda estás decidida a ir a Seattle? — perguntou.

— Era essa a ideia.

Fiz um esgar, esperando que ele não abordasse o assunto para que eu não tivesse de elaborar cuidadosas meias verdades.

Colocou um pouco de detergente para a louça no prato dele e espalhou-o em círculos com a escova.

— E tens a certeza de que não consegues regressar a tempo de ir ao baile?

— Eu não vou ao baile, pai.

Lancei-lhe um olhar irritado.

— Ninguém te convidou? — perguntou, tentando disfarçar a sua preocupação ao concentrar-se em enxaguar o prato.

Desviei-me do campo minado.

— São as raparigas que escolhem os pares.

— Ah! — franziu o sobrolho enquanto secava o seu prato.

Eu compreendia-o. Deve ser difícil ser pai, vivendo com o receio de que a filha conheça um rapaz de quem goste, mas tendo também de se preocupar com a possibilidade de tal não acontecer. Pensei como seria pavoroso, se Charlie tivesse uma vaga ideia daquilo de que eu gostava.

Em seguida, Charlie saiu, despedindo-se com um aceno, e eu dirigi-me ao andar superior para escovar os dentes e reunir os meus livros. Quando ouvi o carro de rádio-patrulha a afastar-se, consegui apenas esperar alguns segundos até ir espreitar pela janela. O automóvel prateado já lá estava, esperando no lugar de Charlie na entrada. Precipitei-me pelas escadas abaixo e porta fora, perguntando-me por quanto tempo é que aquela rotina se prolongaria. Eu queria que nunca acabasse.

Ele estava à espera no carro, não parecendo estar a olhar quando eu bati a porta depois de ter saído, sem me preocupar em fechá-la à chave. Caminhei até ao carro, detendo-me timidamente antes de abrir a porta e entrar. Ele estava a sorrir, descontraído — e, como sempre, perfeito e belo a um nível excruciante.

— Bom dia! — a sua voz era suave como seda. — Como te sentes hoje?

Os seus olhos deambulavam pelo meu rosto, como se a sua pergunta fosse algo mais do que uma mera cortesia.

— Sinto-me bem, obrigada.

Sentia-me sempre bem — muito mais do que bem — quando estava junto dele.

O seu olhar demorou-se sobre as minhas olheiras.

— Pareces cansada.

— Não consegui dormir — confessei, passando automaticamente o cabelo por cima do ombro, de modo a proporcionar-me algum resguardo.

— Eu também não — gracejou ao ligar a ignição. Começava a habituar-me ao reduzido ruído produzido pelo motor. Tinha a certeza de que o roncar da minha *pick-up* me assustaria quando voltasse a conduzi-la.

Ri-me.

— Acho que tens razão. Suponho que dormi um pouco mais do que tu.

— Eu apostaria em como dormiste.

— Então, que fizeste na noite passada? — perguntei.

Soltou um riso abafado.

— Nem penses. Hoje é o meu dia de fazer perguntas.

— Ah, é verdade. Que queres saber?

A minha testa enrugou-se. Não conseguia imaginar nada a meu respeito que pudesse interessar-lhe.

— Qual é a tua cor preferida? — interrogou, com o rosto grave.

Revirei os olhos.

— Varia de dia para dia.

— Qual é a tua cor preferida hoje? — continuava com um ar solene.

— Talvez o castanho.

Tinha tendência para me vestir de acordo com o meu estado de espírito.

Ele resfolegou, abandonando a expressão de seriedade.

— O castanho? — perguntou com cepticismo.

— Claro. O castanho é quente. Sinto *falta* do castanho. Aqui, tudo o que deve ser castanho, os troncos das árvores, as rochas, a terra, está coberto de substâncias verdes, moles e húmidas — lamentei-me.

Ele parecia fascinado com o meu pequeno discurso empolado. Reflectiu por um momento, fitando-me nos olhos.

— Tens razão — concluiu, outra vez sério. — O castanho é quente.

Tentou alcançar-me rapidamente, mas, de certo modo, ainda com hesitação, para me pôr o cabelo atrás do ombro.

Já estávamos na escola. Tornou a virar-se para mim enquanto estacionava.

— Que tipo de música está no teu leitor de CD neste preciso momento? — perguntou, com o rosto carregado como se tivesse acabado de pedir a confissão de um homicídio.

Apercebi-me de que não chegara a retirar o CD que Phil me oferecera. Quando disse o nome do grupo, ele sorriu de través, com um olhar estranho. Abriu um compartimento debaixo do leitor de CD do carro e dali retirou um dos cerca de trinta CDs que estavam atulhados naquele espaço exíguo, entregando-mo.

— Debussy para isto? — levantou uma sobrancelha.

Era o mesmo CD. Examinei o conhecido motivo da capa, mantendo os olhos baixos.

Isto arrastou-se durante todo do dia. Enquanto me acompanhava até à aula de Inglês, quando foi encontrar-se comigo depois da aula de Espanhol, durante toda a hora de almoço, interrogou-me sem piedade acerca de todos os pormenores insignificantes da minha existência. Filmes de que eu gostava e que detestava, os escassos lugares onde eu estivera e os inúmeros lugares aonde eu queria ir e livros — livros sem fim.

Não me lembrava da última vez que falara tanto. Bastantes vezes, sentia-me inibida, certa de que devia estar a entediá-lo, mas a absoluta atenção que o seu rosto transmitia e a sua interminável sucessão de perguntas obrigavam-me a prosseguir.

Na sua maioria, as questões que ele colocava eram fáceis, havendo apenas algumas delas que desencadeavam os meus fáceis rubores. No entanto, quando corava, este facto ocasionava toda uma nova sequência de perguntas.

Quando me perguntou, por exemplo, qual era a minha pedra preciosa preferida, deixei irreflectidamente escapar que era o topázio. Ele estivera a lançar-me perguntas com uma tal rapidez que eu tinha a sensação de que estava a ser submetida a um daqueles exames psiquiátricos em que temos de responder com a primeira palavra que nos vem à cabeça. Estava certa de que ele teria continuado a seguir qualquer que fosse a lista mental por que se regia, se não fosse por eu ruborizar. O meu rosto enrubesceu porque, até há muito pouco tempo, a minha pedra preciosa preferida era a granada. Era impossível, enquanto fixava os seus olhos cor de topázio, não perceber do motivo da mudança e, naturalmente, ele não sossegaria até que eu confessasse por que motivo ficara envergonhada.

— Diz-me — acabou por ordenar, depois de a persuasão ter falhado, apenas porque eu mantinha o olhar prudentemente afastado do seu rosto.

— É a cor com que os teus olhos estão hoje — suspirei, capitulando, olhando fixamente para as minhas mãos enquanto mexia numa mecha do meu cabelo. — Suponho que, se me fizesses essa pergunta daqui a duas semanas, eu responderia ónix.

Facultara mais informação do que o necessário na minha involuntária sinceridade e preocupou-me a possibilidade de isso suscitar a estranha raiva que se manifestava sempre que eu cometia um deslize e revelava de modo demasiado claro quão obcecada estava.

No entanto, o seu silêncio foi muito breve.

— Que tipo de flores preferes? — disparou.

Suspirei de alívio e continuei com a psicanálise.

A aula de Biologia foi novamente uma complicação. Edward prosseguira com o seu interrogatório até o professor Banner entrar na sala, arrastando de novo o móvel dos aparelhos audiovisuais.

Quando o professor se aproximava do interruptor, reparei que Edward afastou ligeiramente a sua cadeira da minha. Não adiantou. Assim que a sala ficou às escuras, verificou-se a mesma descarga eléctrica, a mesma ânsia desassossegada pelo toque, do dia anterior.

Inclinei-me para a frente, sobre a mesa, pousando o queixo nos braços cruzados, com os dedos escondidos a agarrarem a borda da mesa enquanto me esforçava por ignorar o insensato desejo que me inquietava. Não olhava para ele, receando que, se ele estivesse a olhar para mim, esse facto apenas contribuísse para que o meu autocontrolo fosse ainda mais difícil. Tentei realmente assistir ao filme, mas, no final da hora que durava a aula, não fazia a menor ideia do que acabara de ver. Voltei a suspirar de alívio quando o professor Banner acendeu as luzes, olhando, por fim, de relance para Edward; ele fitava-me com um olhar ambíguo.

Levantou-se em silêncio e, em seguida, manteve-se imóvel, à minha espera. Caminhámos até ao ginásio em silêncio, como no dia anterior, e, tal como no dia anterior, ele tocou-me no rosto sem proferir uma só palavra – desta vez, com as costas da sua mão fria, acariciando-me uma vez, de uma das têmporas ao maxilar – antes de dar meia volta e se afastar.

A aula de Educação Física passou depressa, comigo a assistir à exibição a solo de Mike na prática do badminton. Nesse dia, ele não falou, em resposta à minha expressão vazia ou por estar ainda zangado devido à nossa questiúncula do dia anterior. Algures, num recanto da minha mente, sentia-me mal quanto a isso, mas não conseguia concentrar-me nele.

Apressei-me, depois, a mudar de roupa, sentindo-me pouco à vontade, pois sabia que, quanto mais me despachasse, mais depressa estaria com Edward. Tal pressão tornava-me ainda mais desastrada do que o habitual, mas acabei por conseguir sair, experimentando a mesma sensação de libertação quando o vi ali espécado; automaticamente um largo sorriso rasgou-se no meu rosto. Ele reagiu com outro sorriso antes de se lançar em mais uma inquirição.

No entanto, as suas perguntas eram agora diferentes, não sendo de tão fácil resposta. Queria saber sob que aspectos eu sentia a falta de casa, insistindo em descrições de tudo aquilo que não conhecia. Permanecemos sentados diante da casa de Charlie durante várias horas, enquanto o céu escurecia e a chuva caía à nossa volta num súbito dilúvio.

Tentei descrever coisas impossíveis, tais como o odor do creosoto — amargo, ligeiramente resinoso, mas, ainda assim, agradável —, o canto estridente e intenso das cigarras em Julho, a penugenta aridez das árvores, a própria dimensão do céu, estendendo-se em tons azuis e brancos em toda a sua dimensão, quase nada interrompido pelas montanhas pouco elevadas cobertas de rocha vulcânica roxa. O mais difícil de explicar era por que motivo tal se me afigurava como sendo tão belo — justificar uma beleza que não dependia da esparsa e espinhosa vegetação que parecia, muitas vezes, estar meio morta, uma beleza que tinha mais a ver com a forma exposta da terra, com as bacias pouco profundas dos vales entre os montes escarpados e a forma como se agarravam ao Sol. Dei por mim a gesticular enquanto tentava descrever-lhe tudo isto.

As suas perguntas calmas e inquisidoras levavam-me a falar de forma livre e contínua, esquecendo-me, sob a claridade esbatida da tempestade, de ficar envergonhada por estar a monopolizar a conversa. Finalmente, quando acabara de descrever com minúcia o meu quarto atulhado, ele deteve-se em vez de retorquir com mais uma pergunta.

— Já acabaste? — perguntei com alívio.

— Nem por sombras, mas o teu pai vai chegar a casa daqui a pouco.

— O Charlie! — lembrei-me subitamente da sua existência e suspirei. Olhei para o céu escurecido pela chuva, mas este nada deixava entrever. — Já é muito tarde? — perguntei-me em voz alta ao olhar para o relógio.

Fiquei surpreendida com as horas; Charlie devia estar a caminho de casa naquele momento.

— Está na hora do crepúsculo — murmurou Edward, olhando o horizonte a Ocidente, obscurecido como estava devido às nuvens.

A sua voz soava pensativa, como se o seu espírito estivesse longe dali. Fitei-o enquanto ele lançava o olhar pelo pára-brisas sem nada ver.

Estava ainda a fitá-lo quando os seus olhos, de repente, voltaram a fixar-se nos meus.

— É a altura mais segura do dia para nós — disse ele, respondendo à pergunta tacitamente formulada nos meus olhos. — A altura mais tranquila, mas, de certo modo, também a mais triste... o fim de mais um dia, o regresso da noite. A escuridão é tão previsível, não achas? — sorriu melancolicamente.

— Eu gosto da noite. Sem o anoitecer, nunca veríamos as estrelas — franzi o sobrolho. — Não que aqui se vejam muito bem.

Ele riu-se e, de repente, o ambiente ficou menos pesado.

— O Charlie chega dentro de alguns minutos. Portanto, a não ser que queiras dizer-lhe que vais estar comigo no sábado... — levantou uma sobrancelha.

— Obrigada, mas não — peguei nos meus livros, apercebendo-me de que estava com o corpo rígido por ter estado sentada durante tanto tempo. — Então, amanhã é a minha vez?

— Claro que não! — o seu rosto estava provocadoramente indignado. — Eu disse-te que ainda não tinha acabado, não disse?

— Que mais tens para perguntar?

— Ficas a saber amanhã.

Estendeu a mão para me abrir a porta e a sua repentina proximidade pôs-me o coração a palpitar freneticamente.

A mão, porém, paralisou-se no manípulo.

— Isto não é nada bom — afirmou por entre dentes.

— O que foi?

Fiquei espantada ao ver que os seus maxilares estavam cerrados e os olhos perturbados.

Olhou-me por um breve instante.

– Outra complicação – disse de forma sorumbática.

Abriu a porta num movimento ágil e, em seguida, afastou-se rapidamente de mim, quase retraindo-se.

O clarão provocado por luzes de faróis que se precipitava através da chuva chamou-me a atenção quando um automóvel escuro parou junto da borda do passeio a escassos metros de distância de nós, virado na nossa direcção.

– O Charlie encontra-se ao virar da esquina – advertiu, olhando fixamente, através do aguaceiro, para o outro veículo.

Saí imediatamente do carro, num salto, apesar da minha confusão e curiosidade. A chuva era mais sonora ao ricochetear no meu casaco.

Tentei distinguir com clareza as figuras no banco dianteiro do outro carro, mas estava demasiado escuro. Conseguia ver Edward iluminado pela luz ofuscante projectada pelos faróis do carro recentemente aparecido; ainda olhava em frente, fixando algo ou alguém que eu não conseguia ver. A expressão estampada no seu rosto era uma estranha mescla de frustração e provocação.

Então, ele embalou o motor e os pneus chiaram no piso molhado. Em escassos segundos, o Volvo deixou de estar ao alcance da minha vista.

– Eh, Bella – exclamou uma conhecida voz rouca do lado do condutor do pequeno carro preto.

– Jacob? – perguntei, olhando de soslaio através da chuva.

Nesse preciso momento, o carro de rádio-patrulha de Charlie contornou a esquina, com as luzes a incidirem sobre os ocupantes do automóvel que se encontrava diante de mim.

Jacob já estava a sair do carro, sendo o seu largo sorriso visível mesmo na escuridão. No lugar do passageiro, encontrava-se um homem muito mais velho, um homem entroncado com um rosto difícil de esquecer, um rosto que transbordava, com as faces apoiadas nos ombros e rugas a percorrerem a pele castanho-avermelhada como num velho casaco de couro. Tinha também uns olhos surpreendentemente familiares, uns olhos negros que pareciam, ao mesmo tempo, demasiado jovens e demasiado idosos para o rosto largo em que estavam implantados. Tratava--se de Billy Black, o pai de Jacob. Conheci-o imediatamente, apesar de, no período superior a cinco anos que decorrera desde que o vira pela última vez, eu ter conseguido esquecer o seu nome, quando Charlie falara dele no meu primeiro dia naquela cidade. Olhava-me fixamente, examinando-me o rosto, pelo que lhe sorri. Os seus olhos estavam arregalados, como se estivesse escandalizado ou receoso, e as suas largas narinas abertas. O meu sorriso desvaneceu-se.

Outra complicação, dissera Edward.

Billy continuava a fitar-me com um olhar intenso e ansioso. No íntimo, eu lamentava-me. Será que Billy reconhecera Edward com tanta facilidade? Seria possível que ele realmente acreditasse nas inverosímeis lendas de que o filho escarnecera?

A resposta estava claramente espelhada nos olhos de Billy. Sim. Sim, era possível.

Capítulo Doze

EQUILÍBRIO

— Billy! — exclamou Charlie assim que saiu do carro.

Virei-me na direcção da casa, fazendo sinal a Jacob enquanto me esquivava para debaixo do alpendre. Ouvi Charlie a cumprimentá-los sonoramente atrás de mim.

— Vou fingir que não te vi atrás do volante, Jake — disse de modo reprovador.

— Na reserva, é-nos concedida licença para conduzir precocemente — afirmou Jacob enquanto eu destrancava a porta e acendia a luz do alpendre.

— Claro que é — retorquiu Charlie, rindo-se.

— Tenho de me deslocar de alguma forma.

Reconheci facilmente a voz ressonante de Billy, apesar dos anos passados. O som fez-me sentir mais nova, uma criança.

Entrei, deixando a porta aberta, acendi as luzes antes de pendurar o casaco. Depois, mantive-me de pé junto da porta, observando com ansiedade enquanto Charlie e Jacob ajudavam Billy a sair do carro e a sentar-se na sua cadeira de rodas.

Recuei de modo a desimpedir o caminho quando os três se precipitaram para dentro de casa, sacudindo a água da chuva.

— Mas que surpresa! — disse Charlie.

— Há quanto tempo! — retorquiu Billy. — Espero que não tenhamos aparecido em má altura.

Os seus olhos escuros voltaram a incidir sobre mim, com uma expressão indecifrável.

— Não, a altura é óptima. Espero que possam ficar para assistir ao jogo.

Jacob esboçou um sorriso rasgado.

— Acho que a intenção é essa, o nosso televisor avariou na semana passada.

Billy mostrou um ar de desagrado ao filho.

— E, como é evidente, o Jacob estava ansioso por voltar a ver a Bella — acrescentou.

Jacob lançou-lhe um olhar irritado e curvou a cabeça, enquanto eu me debatia com uma onda de remorsos. Talvez tivesse sido demasiado convincente na praia.

— Têm fome? — perguntei, virando-me na direcção da cozinha.

Estava ansiosa por me furtar ao olhar inquisidor de Billy.

— Não, comemos antes de vir — respondeu Jacob.

— E o Charlie? — interroguei por cima do ombro, enquanto me escapava ao contornar a quina da parede.

— Claro que sim — replicou, com a sua voz a deslocar-se na direcção da sala de estar e do televisor.

Conseguia ouvir a cadeira de Billy a segui-lo.

As sandes de queijo gratinado estavam na frigideira e eu cortava um tomate às rodelas quando senti a presença de alguém atrás de mim.

— Então, como estão as coisas? — perguntou Jacob.

— Bastante bem! — sorri. Era difícil resistir ao entusiasmo dele. — E contigo? Terminaste o teu carro?

— Não — franziu o sobrolho. — Ainda preciso de peças. Pedimos aquele emprestado.

Apontou com o polegar na direcção do jardim da frente.

— Lamento. Não vi nenhum... como é que se chamava aquilo de que andavas à procura?

— Cilindro principal — esboçou um sorriso largo. — Há algo de errado com a *pick-up*? — acrescentou de repente.

— Não.

— Ah. Só me admirei por não estares a conduzi-la.

Fixei o olhar na frigideira, puxando uma sanduíche pela extremidade para verificar a parte inferior.

— Um amigo deu-me uma boleia.

— Num belo carro — a voz de Jacob exprimia admiração. —

Mas não reconheci o condutor. Pensei que conhecia a maioria dos miúdos daqui.

Acenei com a cabeça, de modo a evitar comprometer-me, mantendo os olhos baixos enquanto virava as sandes.

— O meu pai parecia conhecê-lo de algum lado.

— Jacob, podias passar-me alguns pratos? Estão no armário por cima do lava-louça.

— Claro.

Foi buscar os pratos em silêncio. Esperei que não insistisse mais no assunto.

— Então, de quem se tratava? — perguntou, pousando dois pratos no balcão a meu lado.

Suspirei, derrotada.

— Do Edward Cullen.

Para meu espanto, ele riu-se. Olhei-o de relance. Parecia um pouco constrangido.

— Suponho, então, que isso explica tudo — disse ele. Perguntei-me porque é que o meu pai estava a agir de maneira tão estranha.

— É verdade — fiz um falso ar de inocente. — Ele não gosta dos Cullen.

— Velho supersticioso — murmurou Jacob por entre dentes.

— Achas que ele diz alguma coisa ao Charlie?

Não consegui evitar a pergunta, com as palavras a saírem num débil ímpeto.

Jacob fitou-me por um momento e não consegui decifrar a expressão dos seus olhos escuros.

— Duvido — acabou por responder. — Julgo que o Charlie o repreendeu de forma bastante severa da última vez. Desde então, pouco falaram, aquilo que está a suceder esta noite é uma espécie de reunião, creio eu. Penso que ele não voltará a abordar o assunto.

— Ah! — exclamei, tentando parecer indiferente.

Fiquei na sala de estar depois de ter levado a comida a Charlie, fingindo assistir ao jogo enquanto Jacob tagarelava comigo.

Eu estava, na verdade, a ouvir a conversa dos homens, procurando qualquer indício de que Billy estivesse prestes a denunciar-me, tentando pensar em maneiras de o deter se ele principiasse.

Foi uma longa noite. Tinha imensos trabalhos de casa que estava a deixar por fazer, mas receava deixar Billy a sós com Charlie. Finalmente, o jogo terminou.

— Tu e os teus amigos vão voltar à praia em breve? — perguntou Jacob enquanto empurrava a cadeira de rodas do pai de modo a transpor a saliência da soleira da porta.

— Não sei ao certo — respondi, procurando não me comprometer.

— Foi divertido, Charlie — afirmou Billy.

— Aparece no próximo jogo — incitou Charlie.

— Claro, claro — disse Billy. — Cá estaremos. Tenham uma boa noite! — os seus olhos desviaram-se para os meus e o seu sorriso desapareceu. — Tem cuidado contigo, Bella — acrescentou com seriedade.

— Obrigada — murmurei por entre dentes, desviando o olhar.

Dirigi-me às escadas enquanto Charlie acenava da entrada.

— Espera, Bella! — exclamou.

Eu retraí-me. Será que Billy comentara algo antes de eu ter ido fazer-lhes companhia para a sala?

Charlie estava, porém, descontraído, esboçando um sorriso largo na sequência da visita inesperada.

— Não tive oportunidade de conversar contigo esta noite. Como foi o teu dia?

— Foi bom — hesitei com um pé no primeiro degrau, rebuscando na memória pormenores que podia partilhar com segurança. — A minha equipa de badminton venceu os quatro jogos.

— Ena, eu não sabia que tu jogavas badminton.

— Bem, na verdade, não jogo, mas o meu colega é muito bom — admiti.

— Quem é ele? — perguntou em sinal de interesse.

— Hum... o Mike Newton — revelei-lhe com relutância.

— Ah, pois... referiste que eras amiga do miúdo dos Newton! — animou-se. — Bela família! — reflectiu por um instante. — Porque não o convidaste para o baile do próximo fim-de-semana?

— Pai! — resmunguei. — De certo modo, ele namora a minha amiga Jessica. Além disso, o pai sabe que eu não sei dançar.

— Ah, pois — murmurou. Em seguida, sorriu-me como quem pede desculpa. — Então, suponho que seja bom que vás para fora no sábado... Combinei ir pescar com a malta da esquadra. O tempo deve estar bastante quente. No entanto, se quisesses protelar a tua viagem até que alguém pudesse ir contigo, eu ficaria em casa. Eu sei que te deixo aqui sozinha demasiadas vezes.

— Pai, está a sair-se muito bem — sorri, esperando que o meu alívio não se notasse. — Nunca me importei de estar sozinha, sou demasiado parecida consigo.

Pisquei-lhe o olho e ele esboçou o seu sorriso de olhos enrugados.

Dormi melhor nessa noite, estando demasiado cansada para voltar a sonhar. Quando despertei para a manhã de luminosidade cinzento-pérola, a minha disposição era de beatitude. O tenso serão na companhia de Billy e Jacob parecia, agora, bastante inofensivo; decidi esquecê-lo por completo. Dei por mim a assobiar enquanto prendia, atrás, a parte da frente do cabelo num gancho e, depois, novamente quando descia as escadas, saltitando. Charlie reparou.

— Esta manhã, estás animada — comentou durante o pequeno-almoço.

Encolhi os ombros,

— É sexta-feira.

Apressei-me de modo a estar pronta para sair assim que Charlie se fosse embora. Tinha a minha mala preparada, os sapatos calçados, os dentes escovados, mas, apesar de me ter precipitado para a porta assim que tive a certeza de que Charlie já estava fora do campo visual, Edward foi mais célere. Estava à espera no seu carro reluzente, com os vidros abertos e o motor desligado.

Desta vez, não hesitei, entrando rapidamente para o lugar do passageiro, de modo a ver o seu rosto o mais depressa possível. Ele lançou-me um sorriso enviesado, suspendendo-me a respiração e o bater do coração. Não conseguia imaginar como é que um anjo poderia ser mais sublime. Não havia nada nele que pudesse ser alvo de aperfeiçoamentos.

— Dormiste bem? — interrogou.

Perguntei-me se ele teria uma vaga ideia de como a sua voz era cativante.

— Dormi. Como foi a tua noite?

— Agradável.

O seu sorriso era de divertimento; senti-me como se não tivesse percebido uma piada íntima.

— Posso perguntar-te o que fizeste? — interroguei.

— Não — esboçou um sorriso rasgado. — O dia de hoje ainda *me* pertence.

Neste dia, queria obter informação a respeito de pessoas: queria saber mais acerca de Renée, dos seus passatempos, do que fazíamos no tempo livre que passávamos juntas e, depois, da única avó que eu conhecera, dos meus escassos amigos da escola — envergonhando-me ao pedir-me para lhe falar de rapazes com quem eu namorara. Fiquei aliviada por nunca ter, de facto, namorado ninguém, pelo que aquela conversa, em particular, não se prolongaria demasiado. Pareceu ficar surpreendido, tal como Jessica e Angela, com a minha falta de um passado romântico.

— Então, nunca conheceste ninguém que desejasses? — perguntou num tom de voz sério que me levou a interrogar-me sobre aquilo em que ele estaria a pensar.

Fui renitentemente sincera.

— Em Phoenix, não.

Os seus lábios apertaram-se um contra o outro, formando uma linha firme.

Nesta altura, encontrávamo-nos na cantina. O dia passara a

correr na indefinição que rapidamente se tornara rotina. Tirei proveito do seu breve silêncio para dar uma dentada no meu pãozinho.

— Devia ter-te deixado vir sozinha hoje — comunicou-me a propósito de nada em especial enquanto eu mastigava.

— Porquê? — interroguei.

— Vou-me embora com a Alice depois do almoço.

— Ah! — pisquei os olhos, confusa e desiludida. — Não faz mal, não é longe para ir a pé.

Franziu-me o sobrolho com impaciência.

— Não te vou deixar ir a pé para casa. Vamos buscar a tua *pick-up* e deixar-ta aqui.

— Não tenho a chave comigo — suspirei. — Não me importo mesmo de ir a pé.

Aquilo que me importava era o facto de perder o tempo que passaria com ele.

Ele abanou a cabeça.

— A tua *pick-up* estará aqui e a chave estará na ignição — a não ser que receies que alguém a roube.

Riu-se só de pensar nisso.

— Está bem — assenti, franzindo os lábios.

Tinha quase a certeza de que a minha chave estava no bolso de um par de calças de ganga que eu vestira na quarta-feira, debaixo de um monte de roupa na lavandaria. Mesmo que ele forçasse a entrada em minha casa ou fizesse o que quer que fosse, jamais a encontraria. Pareceu aperceber-se do desafio implícito no meu consentimento. Sorriu pretensiosamente, excessivamente confiante.

— Então, aonde vais? — perguntei da forma mais descontraída que consegui.

— Vou caçar — respondeu soturnamente. — Já que vou estar sozinho contigo amanhã, vou tomar o máximo de precauções.

— O seu rosto ficou taciturno... e suplicante. — Podes sempre cancelar a viagem, sabes.

Baixei o olhar, receando o poder persuasivo dos seus olhos.

Recusei-me a ser convencida a temê-lo, por mais real que o perigo fosse. *Não importa*, repeti na minha cabeça.

— Não — sussurrei, voltando a olhar o seu rosto de relance. — Não posso.

— Talvez tenhas razão — murmurou sorumbaticamente.

A cor dos seus olhos parecia escurecer enquanto eu os observava. Mudei de assunto.

— A que horas nos encontramos amanhã? — perguntei, já deprimida com a ideia de ele se ir embora agora.

— Depende... é sábado. Não queres dormir até mais tarde? — sugeriu.

— Não — respondi com demasiada prontidão.

Ele reprimiu um sorriso.

— Então, à hora de sempre — decidiu. — O Charlie estará lá?

— Não, amanhã vai pescar.

Sorri de alegria ao lembrar-me de como tudo se resolvera de forma conveniente.

A voz dele tornou-se incisiva.

— E, se tu não voltares para casa, o que é que ele pensará?

— Não faço a menor ideia — respondi friamente. — Ele sabe que eu tencionava lavar a roupa. Talvez pense que caí dentro da máquina de lavar.

Lançou-me um olhar mal-humorado e eu retribuí-lho. A sua raiva era muito mais impressionante do que a minha.

— O que vão caçar esta noite? — perguntei quando tive a certeza de que perdera a prova do olhar ameaçador.

— O que encontrarmos no parque. Não vamos para muito longe.

Parecia estupefacto com a minha referência descontraída às suas secretas realidades.

— Porque vais com a Alice? — indaguei.

— A Alice é quem me dá mais... apoio — franziu o sobrolho enquanto falava.

— E os outros? — perguntei timidamente. — Qual é a atitude deles?

A sua testa franziu-se por um breve momento.

— De incredulidade, na maior parte dos casos.

Espreitou rapidamente para trás de mim, para onde se encontrava a sua família. Eles estavam sentados, olhando em diversas direcções, exactamente da mesma forma que da primeira vez que eu os vira, só que, agora, eram quatro; o seu lindo irmão de cabelo cor de bronze estava sentado à minha frente, com os seus olhos dourados perturbados.

— Não gostam de mim — deitei-me a adivinhar.

— Não é isso — discordou, mas os seus olhos eram demasiado inocentes. — Não compreendem porque não posso deixar-te em paz.

Fiz um esgar.

— Eu, por acaso, também não.

Edward abanou a cabeça lentamente, revirando os olhos na direcção do tecto antes de os voltar a fixar nos meus.

— Já te disse, não tens, de todo, uma imagem muito clara de ti mesma. És diferente de todas as pessoas que já conheci. Fascinas-me.

Lancei-lhe um olhar furioso, certa de que, agora, estava a provocar-me.

Sorriu como se tivesse decifrado a minha expressão.

— Dispondo das vantagens de que eu disponho — murmurou, tocando discretamente na testa — compreendo, de uma forma superior à média, a natureza humana. As pessoas são previsíveis. Mas tu... tu nunca fazes aquilo de que eu estou à espera. Apanhas-me sempre de surpresa.

Desviei o olhar, procurando novamente a sua família, constrangida e descontente. As palavras dele faziam com que eu me sentisse uma experiência científica. Queria rir-me de mim por ter esperado algo diferente.

— Isso é bastante fácil de explicar — continuou.

Senti os olhos dele pousados no meu rosto, mas ainda não podia fitá-lo, receando que se apercebesse do desgosto espelhado nos meus olhos.

— Mas existe algo mais... e não é assim tão fácil de verbalizar...

Eu ainda fixava os Cullen quando ele falou. De repente, Rosalie, a sua irmã loura e deslumbrante, virou-se e olhou para mim. Não, não olhou para mim — fulminou-me com os olhos escuros e frios. Eu queria desviar o olhar, mas o dela manteve-o preso até que Edward se deteve a meio de uma frase e emitiu um som de cólera muito baixinho. Era quase um cicio.

Rosalie virou a cabeça e fiquei aliviada por estar livre. Voltei a olhar para Edward e sabia que ele conseguia ver o medo e a confusão que me arregalavam os olhos.

O seu semblante estava tenso enquanto explicava.

— Sinto muito pelo aconteceu. Ela está apenas preocupada. Sabes... não é perigoso só para mim se, depois de passar tanto tempo contigo tão publicamente... — baixou o olhar.

— Se?

— Se isto acabar... mal.

Baixou a cabeça e apoiou-a nas mãos, tal como fizera naquela noite em Port Angeles. A sua angústia era evidente; ansiava por consolá-lo, mas não sabia como fazê-lo. A minha mão estendeu-se involuntariamente na direcção dele; contudo, depressa a deixei cair sobre a mesa, receando que o meu toque só piorasse a situação. Apercebi-me lentamente de que aquelas palavras deviam atemorizar-me. Esperei que tal temor surgisse, mas só parecia sentir uma dor provocada pelo sofrimento dele.

Sentia também frustração, frustração por Rosalie ter interrompido o que quer que fosse que ele estava prestes a dizer. Não sabia como abordar novamente o assunto. Ele continuava com a cabeça apoiada nas mãos.

Tentei falar com uma voz normal.

— E tens de ir embora agora?

— Tenho — levantou o rosto, ficou sério por um momento e, em seguida, a sua disposição alterou-se e ele sorriu. — É melhor assim. Ainda temos de suportar quinze minutos daquele maldito filme na aula de Biologia... acho que não aguentaria mais.

Estremeci. Alice, com o seu cabelo curto de um tom carregado num halo de desalinho espetado em torno do seu rosto sublime com traços próprios de gnomo, encontrava-se subitamente de pé atrás do ombro dele. A sua constituição delicada era esbelta, graciosa mesmo em absoluta imobilidade.

Cumprimentou-a sem desviar os olhos de mim.

— Alice.

— Edward — retorquiu ela, sendo a sua voz aguda de soprano quase tão sedutora como a dele.

— Alice, esta é a Bella. Bella, esta é a Alice — apresentou-nos, gesticulando de modo descontraído com a mão, com um sorriso enviesado estampado no rosto.

— Olá, Bella! — os seus olhos brilhantes cor de obsidiana eram indecifráveis, mas o seu sorriso era amável. — É bom conhecer-te finalmente.

Edward lançou-lhe um olhar misterioso.

— Olá, Alice — murmurei acanhadamente.

— Estás pronto? — perguntou-lhe ela.

A voz dele estava distante.

— Quase. Encontramo-nos no carro.

Ela foi-se embora sem proferir nenhuma outra palavra; o seu andar era tão fluido, tão sinuoso, que eu senti uma lancinante pontada de inveja.

— Deverei dizer «diverte-te» ou esta não é a expressão adequada? — perguntei, virando-me para ele.

— Não. A expressão «diverte-te» aplica-se tanto como qualquer outra — esboçou um sorriso rasgado.

— Então, diverte-te.

Esforcei-me por parecer sincera. Evidentemente, não o enganei.

— Vou tentar — continuava a sorrir. — E tu, por favor, tenta ficar bem.

— Ficar bem em Forks, que desafio!

— Para ti é, de facto, um desafio — cerrou o maxilar. — Promete.

— Prometo ficar bem — assegurei-lhe. — Vou cuidar da roupa esta noite. Deve ser uma actividade repleta de perigos.

— Não caias para dentro da máquina de lavar — troçou.

— Farei o meu melhor.

Então, ele pôs-se de pé e eu também.

— Até amanhã! — suspirei.

— Parece-te muito tempo, não é? — reflectiu.

Eu acenei sorumbaticamente com a cabeça.

— De manhã, lá estarei — garantiu, esboçando o seu sorriso de través.

Estendeu a mão, ao longo da mesa, para me tocar no rosto, acariciando-me suavemente a maçã do rosto uma vez mais. Em seguida, deu meia volta e afastou-se. O meu olhar seguiu-o até ter desaparecido.

Sentia-me mesmo tentada a fazer gazeta durante o resto do dia, pelo menos, à aula de Educação Física, mas um instinto de aviso levou-me a não o fazer. Eu sabia que, se desaparecesse naquele momento, Mike e os restantes depreenderiam que eu estava com Edward e este estava preocupado com o tempo que nós passáramos juntos em público... no caso de algo correr mal. Recusei deter-me nesta última ideia, concentrando-me, em vez disso, em tornar tudo mais seguro para ele.

Sabia intuitivamente — e sentia que o mesmo acontecia com ele — que o dia seguinte seria fulcral. A nossa relação não podia continuar a equilibrar-se, como se equilibrava, no fio da navalha. Cairíamos para um lado ou para o outro, dependendo apenas da decisão ou dos instintos dele. A minha decisão estava tomada, mesmo antes de eu ter conscientemente feito a minha escolha, estando empenhada em levá-la a cabo. Isto porque, para mim, não havia nada mais aterrador, mais excruciante do que a ideia de lhe virar costas. Era impossível.

Fui para a aula, sentindo que cumpria o meu dever. Não podia dizer com sinceridade o que acontecera na aula de Biologia, pois a minha mente estava demasiado abstraída com o dia seguinte. Na aula de Educação Física, Mike já me falava novamente. Desejou que eu me divertisse em Seattle.

Expliquei-lhe que cancelara a viagem por estar preocupada

com a minha *pick-up.*

— Vais ao baile com o Cullen? — perguntou ele, subitamente amuado.

— Não, não vou sequer ao baile.

— Então, o que vais fazer? — interrogou, demasiado interessado.

A minha vontade natural era dizer-lhe que não metesse o nariz onde não era chamado. Em vez disso, menti.

— Vou lavar a roupa e, depois, tenho de estudar para o teste de Trigonometria ou ainda vou reprovar.

— O Cullen vai ajudar-te a estudar?

— O *Edward* — frisei — não vai ajudar-me a estudar. Foi passar o fim-de-semana algures para fora.

Verifiquei, com surpresa, que proferia tais mentiras com maior naturalidade do que o habitual.

— Ah! — animou-se. — Sabes, mesmo assim, podias vir ao baile com o nosso grupo, seria porreiro. Todos dançaríamos contigo — garantiu.

A imagem mental da cara de Jessica levou-me a retorquir num tom mais incisivo do que o necessário.

— Eu *não* vou ao baile, Mike, está bem?

— Pronto — amuou novamente. — Estava só a fazer-te uma proposta.

Quando o dia de aulas terminou, dirigi-me ao parque de estacionamento sem entusiasmo. Não me apetecia nada ir a pé para casa, mas não via como ele poderia ter ido buscar a minha *pick-up.* Mas, depois, começava a acreditar que, para ele, nada era impossível. Esta última intuição revelou estar correcta, a minha *pick-up* encontrava-se no mesmo lugar em que ele estacionara o seu Volvo naquela manhã. Abanei a cabeça, incrédula, ao abrir a porta destrancada e ver a chave na ignição.

Havia um pedaço de papel branco no meu banco. Entrei e fechei a porta antes de o desdobrar. Duas palavras estavam escritas na sua caligrafia elegante «Fica bem.»

O som da *pick-up* a roncar assustou-me. Ri-me de mim.

Quando cheguei a casa, o trinco da porta estava fechado e a lingueta da fechadura aberta, tal como eu os deixara de manhã. Quando entrei, dirigi-me imediatamente à lavandaria. Também esta parecia estar tal como eu a deixara. Remexi na roupa em busca das minhas calças de ganga e, depois de as ter encontrado, verifiquei os bolsos. Vazios. Afinal, talvez eu sempre tivesse pendurado a chave no seu lugar, pensei, abanando a cabeça.

Seguindo o mesmo instinto que me levara a mentir a Mike, telefonei a Jessica com o pretexto de lhe desejar boa sorte para o baile. Quando ela exprimiu o mesmo desejo relativamente ao dia que eu iria passar na companhia de Edward, informei-a de que tal compromisso fora cancelado. Ficou mais decepcionada do que, para uma mera espectadora, era realmente necessário. Depois disso, apressei-me a despedir-me.

Charlie tinha o espírito ausente durante o jantar, preocupado com algo relacionado com o seu trabalho, calculei, ou talvez com um jogo de basquetebol. Por outro lado, podia estar simplesmente a saborear a lasanha — era difícil saber, quando se tratava de Charlie.

— Sabes, pai... — principiei, interrompendo o seu devaneio.

— O que foi, Bell?

— Acho que tens razão quanto a Seattle. Acho que vou esperar até que Jessica ou outra pessoa possa ir comigo.

— Ah! — exclamou, surpreendido. — Ah!, está bem. Então, queres que eu fique em casa?

— Não pai, não alteres os teus planos. Tenho um milhão de coisas para fazer... trabalhos de casa, roupa para lavar... Preciso de ir à biblioteca e à mercearia. Passarei todo o dia a entrar e a sair de casa... Vai e diverte-te.

— Tens a certeza?

— Absoluta, pai. Além disso, o congelador está a ficar perigosamente desprovido de peixe, estamos reduzidos a uma provisão para dois, talvez três anos.

— É fácil viver contigo, Bella — sorriu.

— Eu poderia dizer o mesmo de ti — afirmei, rindo.

O meu riso não tinha som, mas ele não pareceu reparar nesse facto. Senti-me tão culpada por estar a enganá-lo que quase segui o conselho de Edward, dizendo onde estaria. Quase.

Depois do jantar, dobrei roupa e coloquei uma nova carga na máquina de secar. Infelizmente, tratava-se do tipo de tarefa que só ocupa as mãos. O meu espírito dispunha de demasiado tempo livre e estava a ficar fora de controlo. Eu oscilava entre um sentimento de expectativa tão intenso que quase chegava a ser doloroso e um medo insidioso que afectava a minha determinação. Tentava manter presente no espírito que fizera a minha escolha e não voltaria atrás. Retirei o bilhete dele do bolso muito mais vezes do que o necessário para assimilar as duas pequenas palavras que ele escrevera. Quer que eu fique bem, repeti para comigo uma e outra vez. Eu agarrar-me-ia apenas à crença de que, no final, tal desejo sobrepor-se-ia aos restantes. Qual era, afinal, a minha outra opção, excluí-lo da minha vida? Intolerável. Além disso, desde que eu fora para Forks, parecia realmente que a minha vida girava *em torno* dele.

No entanto, uma vozinha no fundo da minha mente inquietava-se, perguntando-se se seria muito doloroso... se aquela situação acabasse mal.

Fiquei aliviada quando ficou suficientemente tarde para eu me ir deitar. Sabia que estava demasiado tensa para dormir e, por conseguinte, fiz o que nunca fizera antes. Tomei deliberadamente um medicamento para dormir, do género que me deixava inconsciente durante umas boas oito horas. Em geral, estranharia este tipo de comportamento em mim, mas o dia seguinte já seria bem complicado sem que eu, além de tudo o mais, estivesse débil de espírito devido à privação de sono. Enquanto esperava que os fármacos fizessem efeito, sequei o cabelo lavado até ficar impecavelmente liso e procurei nas minhas roupas o que vestir no dia seguinte.

Com tudo a postos, deitei-me finalmente na cama. Sentia-me irrequieta, não conseguia parar de me contorcer. Levantei-me e esquadrinhei a caixa de sapatos que continha os meus

CDs até encontrar uma compilação de nocturnos de Chopin. Pu-la a tocar muito baixinho e, em seguida, voltei a deitar-me, concentrando-me em relaxar partes específicas do corpo. Algures a meio desse exercício, os comprimidos para dormir fizeram efeito e caí de bom grado na inconsciência.

Acordei cedo, tendo dormido profundamente e sem sonhar graças aos fármacos a que recorrera de modo gratuito. Apesar de me sentir repousada, voltei à mesma agitação frenética da noite anterior. Vesti-me à pressa, compondo a gola no pescoço, remexendo a camisola castanho-amarelada até assentar convenientemente sobre as minhas calças de ganga. Dei uma rápida olhadela para o exterior, através da janela, verificando que Charlie já saíra. Uma fina camada de nuvens velava o céu. Não pareciam muito persistentes.

Tomei o pequeno-almoço sem saborear a comida, apressando-me a lavar a louça quando terminei. Espreitei uma vez mais pela janela, mas nada se alterara. Acabara de escovar os dentes e dirigia-me novamente para o piso de baixo quando alguém bateu discretamente à porta, fazendo com que o meu coração desatasse a palpitar.

Precipitei-me para a porta e tive alguma dificuldade em abrir o fecho, mas acabei por conseguir abrir a porta e ali estava ele. Toda a agitação deu lugar à calma assim que olhei para o rosto dele. Soltei um suspiro de alívio. Os medos do dia anterior pareciam extremamente disparatados com a sua presença.

A princípio, não sorria, o seu semblante estava carregado. No entanto, em seguida, a expressão do seu rosto iluminou-se enquanto me examinava, e riu-se.

— Bom dia! — soltou um riso abafado.

— O que se passa?

Olhei para baixo de modo a certificar-me de que não me esquecera de nada importante, como os sapatos ou as calças.

— Estamos vestidos a condizer — riu-se novamente.

Apercebi-me de que ele envergava uma comprida camisola castanho-amarelada clara com uma gola branca a aparecer por baixo e calças de ganga azul. Ri-me com ele, dissimulando um laivo de pena, porque é que ele tinha de parecer um manequim de *passerelle* quando eu não conseguia que o mesmo acontecesse comigo?

Fechei a porta ao sair, enquanto ele se dirigia para a *pick-up*. Esperou junto à porta do lado do passageiro com uma expressão de martírio que era fácil de compreender.

— Fizemos um acordo — relembrei-lhe com grande satisfação, sentando-me no lugar do condutor e esticando-me para destrancar a porta dele.

— Para onde vamos? — perguntei.

— Coloca o cinto de segurança. Já estou nervoso.

Lancei-lhe um olhar de desagrado enquanto lhe obedecia.

— Para onde vamos? — repeti com um suspiro.

— Segue pela estrada 101, em direcção a Norte — ordenou.

Era surpreendentemente difícil concentrar-me na estrada enquanto sentia o olhar dele fixo no meu rosto. Compensei este facto conduzindo com mais cautela do que o habitual ao atravessar a cidade adormecida.

— Tencionavas sair de Forks antes do anoitecer?

— Esta *pick-up* tem idade para ser o carro do teu avô, mostra algum respeito — retorqui.

Depressa saímos dos limites da cidade, apesar do derrotismo dele.

Densa vegetação rasteira e troncos envoltos num manto verde tomaram o lugar dos relvados e das casas.

— Vira à direita na 110 — orientou-me precisamente quando eu estava prestes a pedir-lhe que o fizesse.

Obedeci em silêncio.

— Agora, seguimos em frente até que o piso alcatroado chegue ao fim.

Conseguia detectar um sorriso na voz dele, mas receava demasiado despistar-me para olhar para ele e confirmar.

– E o que há aí, no ponto em que o piso alcatroado termina? – indaguei.

– Um trilho.

– Vamos fazer uma caminhada? – perguntei, preocupada.

Graças a Deus, eu calçara sapatos de ténis.

– Há algum problema?

A forma como ele falara dava a entender que esperava que houvesse.

– Não.

Tentei fazer com que a mentira parecesse convincente, mas, se ele pensava que a minha *pick-up* era lenta...

– Não te preocupes. São apenas cerca de oito quilómetros e nós não temos pressa.

Oito quilómetros. Não repliquei, de modo a que ele não ouvisse a minha voz a sucumbir ao pânico. Oito quilómetros de raízes traiçoeiras e pedras soltas a tentarem torcer-me os tornozelos, se não mesmo a incapacitar-me. Iria ser humilhante.

Seguimos em silêncio durante alguns momentos, enquanto eu pensava no horror que se aproximava.

– Em que estás a pensar? – perguntou ele impacientemente após alguns instantes.

Voltei a mentir.

– Estou apenas a perguntar-me aonde iremos.

– Trata-se de um lugar aonde eu gosto de ir quando o tempo está agradável.

Ambos olhámos pelos vidros, na direcção das nuvens que se dissipavam, depois de ele falar.

– O Charlie referiu que hoje estaria calor.

– E chegaste a dizer ao Charlie o que estavas a arquitectar? – perguntou ele.

– Não.

– Mas a Jessica pensa que nós vamos juntos a Seattle?

Tal ideia parecia alegrá-lo.

– Não, eu disse-lhe que tu tinhas cancelado o nosso compromisso, o que é verdade.

— Ninguém sabe que tu estás comigo? — perguntou, agora colericamente.

— Depende... Deduzo que contaste à Alice?

— Isso ajuda muito, Bella — disse ele com brusquidão.

Fingi não ter ouvido aquelas palavras.

— Forks deprimiu-te assim tanto que fez com que tivesses tendências suicidas? — interrogou quando eu o ignorei.

— Disseste que podia criar-te dificuldades... o facto de aparecermos juntos em público — lembrei-lhe.

— Então, estás preocupada com as dificuldades que isso pode criar-me a *mim*, se *tu* não voltares para *casa*? — a voz dele continuava a denotar cólera, assim como um sarcasmo mordaz.

Acenei com a cabeça, não tirando os olhos da estrada.

Ele murmurou algo por entre dentes, falando tão rapidamente que não consegui compreendê-lo.

Permanecemos calados durante o resto da viagem de automóvel. Conseguia sentir as ondas de reprovação enfurecida a emanarem dele e não me ocorria nada que pudesse dizer.

Então, a estrada chegou ao fim, constringindo-se num acanhado trilho pedonal assinalado com uma pequena placa de madeira. Estacionei na estreita berma e saí da *pick-up*, receosa por ele estar zangado comigo e eu não ter a condução como pretexto para não olhar para ele. Agora, estava calor, mais calor do que jamais estivera em Forks desde o dia em que eu chegara, estando o tempo quase mormacento sob as nuvens. Despi a camisola e atei-a à cintura, contente por ter vestido a camisa leve e sem mangas — sobretudo tendo em consideração que me esperava uma caminhada de oito quilómetros.

Ouvi a porta dele a bater e olhei, vendo que também ele despira a sua camisola. Estava de costas para mim, virado para a floresta inviolada que se estendia ao lado da *pick-up*.

— Por aqui! — exclamou, olhando-me de relance, por cima do ombro, com um ar ainda aborrecido. Começou a embrenhar-se na floresta sombria.

— E o trilho?

O pânico era notório na minha voz quando me apressei a contornar a *pick-up* de modo a alcançá-lo.

— Eu disse que existia um trilho no final da estrada, não que iríamos enveredar por ele.

— Não há trilho? — perguntei desesperadamente.

— Eu não deixo que te percas.

Então, ele virou-se, com um sorriso trocista, e eu reprimi um arquejo. A sua camisa branca não tinha mangas e ele usava-a desabotoada, pelo que a suave pele branca do pescoço se estendia ininterruptamente sobre os contornos marmóreos do seu peito, já não sendo a sua perfeita musculatura apenas insinuada por trás de roupas que a ocultavam. Ele era demasiado perfeito, apercebi-me com uma trespassante estocada de desespero. Não era possível que aquela criatura divina estivesse predestinada a ficar comigo.

Ele olhava-me fixamente, desconcertado com o meu ar de tormento.

— Queres ir para casa? — perguntou calmamente, com uma dor diferente da minha a impregnar-lhe a voz.

— Não.

Avancei até estar bem próxima dele, desejosa de não perder um só segundo da sua companhia.

— O que se passa? — quis saber, com uma voz afável.

— Não sou muito boa a fazer longas caminhadas — respondi monotonamente. — Terás de ser muito paciente.

— Eu consigo ser paciente, se fizer um grande esforço.

Sorriu, fixando o seu olhar no meu, numa tentativa de me ajudar a superar o súbito e inexplicado desânimo.

Tentei retribuir-lhe o sorriso, mas não fui convincente. Ele perscrutava o meu rosto.

— Eu levo-te a casa — prometeu.

Não consegui perceber se a promessa era incondicional ou dependia de uma partida imediata. Eu sabia que ele julgava que era o medo que me transtornava e fiquei grata por ser a única pessoa cuja mente ele não conseguia auscultar.

— Se queres que eu desbrave caminho ao longo de oito quilómetros em plena selva antes do pôr do Sol, é melhor começares
a andar à minha frente — disse com azedume.

Ele franziu-me o sobrolho, esforçando-se por compreender o
tom da minha voz e a expressão do meu rosto.

Desistiu após um momento e indicou o caminho em direcção
ao interior da floresta.

Não foi tão difícil como eu temera. O caminho era, na maior
parte, plano e ele afastava os fetos húmidos e as teias de musgo para que eu passasse. Quando a vereda recta nos fazia passar por cima de árvores caídas ou pedregulhos, ele ajudava-me,
segurando-me pelo cotovelo e, em seguida, soltando-me imediatamente quando o obstáculo já fora transposto. O seu toque
frio na minha pele nunca deixou de fazer com que o meu coração batesse de forma irregular. Por duas vezes, quando isso
aconteceu, vi uma expressão no rosto dele que me levou a ter a
certeza de que, de alguma forma, ele conseguia ouvi-lo.

Tentei manter os olhos afastados da sua perfeição tanto
quanto possível, mas sucumbia frequentemente. De cada vez, a
sua beleza trespassava-me, inundando-me de tristeza.

Durante a maior parte do percurso, caminhámos em silêncio.
De vez em quando, ele fazia, aleatoriamente, uma pergunta que
não chegara a fazer nos dois anteriores dias de interrogatório.
Colocou questões acerca dos meus aniversários, dos meus professores da escola primária, dos animais de estimação que tivera durante a minha infância — e tive de confessar que, depois de
ter deixado morrer três peixes consecutivamente, desistira de tal
empreitada. Ele riu-se, de um modo mais sonoro do que eu estava habituada — com ecos semelhantes ao repicar de sinos a
ser-nos devolvido dos bosques vazios.

Levei quase toda a manhã a fazer tal caminhada, mas ele
nunca revelou qualquer sinal de impaciência. A floresta alastra-
va-se em nosso redor num labirinto ilimitado de árvores antigas
e comecei a ficar nervosa com a possibilidade de nunca mais vol-
tarmos a encontrar a saída. Ele estava perfeitamente tranquilo,

à vontade no dédalo verde, parecendo nunca ter quaisquer dúvidas quanto à nossa orientação.

Após várias horas, a luz que se infiltrava através da abóbada formada pela copa das árvores transformou-se, com o sombrio tom verde-azeitona a converter-se num jade mais luminoso. O dia ficara soalheiro, tal como ele previra. Comecei, pela primeira vez desde que entráramos no bosque, a sentir um frémito de entusiasmo, que rapidamente se transformou em impaciência.

— Já chegámos? — provoquei-o, fingindo um olhar carregado.

— Quase — sorriu perante a minha mudança de humor. — Vês a claridade ali à frente?

Olhei com atenção para o interior da floresta cerrada.

— Hum, devia ver?

Ele esboçou um sorriso pretensioso.

— Talvez ainda esteja um pouco fora de alcance para os *teus* olhos.

— Está na altura de consultar o optometrista — disse por entre dentes.

O seu sorriso tornou-se mais vincado.

No entanto, após termos percorrido mais cem metros, já conseguia ver um clarão nas árvores, mais adiante, uma luz que era amarela em vez de verde. Acelerei a marcha, com a minha ansiedade a aumentar a cada passo que dava. Ele deixava-me, agora, caminhar à frente, seguindo-me silenciosamente.

Cheguei à beira da mancha de luz e atravessei a última orla de fetos para deparar com o sítio mais encantador que eu jamais vira. O prado era pequeno, perfeitamente redondo e repleto de flores silvestres — de uma suave cor violeta, amarela e branca. Algures por perto, eu conseguia ouvir a música borbulhante de um ribeiro. O Sol encontrava-se exactamente por cima, preenchendo o círculo com uma bruma de claridade untuosa. Avancei lentamente, assombrada, por entre a erva macia, flores ondulantes e ar quente e dourado. Dei meia volta, querendo partilhar aquilo com ele, mas ele não se encontrava já atrás de mim. Girei em torno de mim mesma, procurando-o com uma súbita inquietação.

Acabei por localizá-lo, ainda sob a densa sombra da abóbada florestal, à beira da depressão no terreno, observando-me com olhos cautelosos. Só então me lembrei daquilo que a beleza do prado me afastara do pensamento — o enigma da relação de Edward com o Sol, que ele me prometera esclarecer nesse dia.

Dei um passo novamente na direcção dele, estando os meus olhos iluminados de curiosidade. Os olhos dele estavam desconfiados, relutantes. Sorri de forma encorajadora e fiz-lhe um sinal com a mão, dando outro passo na sua direcção. Ele levantou uma das mãos em sinal de aviso e eu hesitei, balançando para trás.

Edward pareceu respirar profundamente e, em seguida, avançou em direcção à intensa claridade do Sol do meio-dia.

Capítulo Treze

Confissões

Edward, sob a luz do Sol, era estarrecedor. Não me conseguia habituar, apesar de ter passado toda a tarde a olhá-lo fixamente. A sua pele, branca apesar do vago rubor provocado pela caçada do dia anterior, brilhava na verdadeira acepção do termo, como se milhares de ínfimos diamantes estivessem incrustados à superfície. Ele permaneceu estendido e absolutamente imóvel sobre a erva, com a camisa aberta sobre o seu peito escultural e incandescente e os cintilantes braços desnudos. As suas reluzentes e pálidas pálpebras cor de alfazema estavam fechadas, ainda que, evidentemente, ele não estivesse a dormir. Uma estátua perfeita, esculpida em alguma pedra desconhecida, polida como mármore, resplandecente como cristal.

De vez em quando, os seus lábios mexiam-se tão rapidamente que pareciam estar a tremer, mas, quando lhe perguntei, ele disse-me que estava a cantar para ele; fazia-o em voz demasiado baixa para que eu conseguisse ouvir.

Eu também desfrutei do Sol, ainda que o ar não estivesse suficientemente seco para o meu gosto. Também teria gostado de me deitar, como ele fizera, e deixar o Sol aquecer-me o rosto, mas permaneci recurvada, com o queixo apoiado nos joelhos, não querendo tirar os olhos de cima dele. O vento era suave; emaranhava-me o cabelo e soprava a erva que se agitava em torno da sua figura imóvel.

O prado, que, a princípio, se me afigurou como sendo imensamente espectacular, empalideceu quando comparado com a magnificência dele.

Com hesitação, sempre receosa, mesmo naquele momento, em que ele podia desaparecer como uma miragem, sendo demasiado belo para ser real... com hesitação, estendi um dedo e acariciei as costas da sua mão tremeluzente onde esta se encontrava ao meu alcance. Fiquei novamente maravilhada com a perfeita textura, suave como cetim, fria como pedra. Quando voltei a erguer o olhar, os olhos dele estavam abertos, observando-me. Estavam, neste dia, da cor de caramelos de manteiga, mais claros, mais calorosos, na sequência da caçada. O seu rápido sorriso virou para cima os cantos dos seus lábios perfeitos.

— Não te assusto? — perguntou jocosamente, mas eu detectei uma curiosidade genuína na sua voz suave.

— Não mais do que o habitual.

O seu sorriso rasgou-se ainda mais, os seus dentes resplandeciam ao Sol.

Aproximei-me um pouco mais, estendi, desta vez, toda a minha mão para seguir os contornos do seu antebraço com as pontas dos meus dedos. Vi que tremiam e sabia que esse facto não escaparia à sua atenção.

— Importas-te? — perguntei, pois ele voltara a fechar os olhos.

— Não — respondeu, sem abrir os olhos. — Não consegues imaginar a sensação que isso provoca em mim.

Suspirou.

Arrastei levemente a mão pelos músculos perfeitos do seu braço, segui o ténue padrão das suas veias azuladas na dobra da parte interior do seu cotovelo. Com a outra mão, tentei alcançar a dele para virá-la. Apercebendo-se do que eu desejava fazer, virou a palma da mão para cima num daqueles seus movimentos extraordinariamente rápidos e desconcertantes. Assustou-me, os meus dedos ficaram paralisados sobre o seu braço por um breve instante.

— Desculpa — murmurou. Levantei o olhar a tempo de ver os seus olhos dourados fecharem-se novamente. — É demasiado fácil ser eu próprio quando estou contigo.

Levantei-lhe a mão, colocando-a em diferentes posições enquanto via o Sol a reluzir na palma da mesma. Aproximei-a mais do meu rosto, tentando ver as facetas ocultas da pele dele.

— Diz-me o que estás a pensar — sussurrou. Olhei para ver

que os seus olhos estavam a observar-me, subitamente atentos.
— Ainda me é tão estranho o facto de não o saber.

— Sabes, todos nós nos sentimos sempre assim.

— A vida é difícil — será que o laivo de arrependimento no tom da sua voz foi fruto da minha imaginação? — Mas não me disseste.

— *Estava* a pensar que gostaria de saber em que é que tu estavas a pensar... — hesitei.

— E?

— Estava a pensar que gostaria de poder acreditar que tu és real e de não ter medo.

— Eu não quero que tenhas medo.

A sua voz era apenas um suave murmúrio. Ouvi aquilo que ele não podia dizer de forma sincera: que eu não precisava de ter medo, que nada havia a temer.

— Bem, não era propriamente a esse tipo de medo que eu me referia, ainda que seja, sem dúvida, algo digno de reflexão.

Tão depressa que eu nem me apercebi do seu movimento, já ele se encontrava meio sentado, apoiado no braço direito, com a palma da mão esquerda ainda entre as minhas. O seu rosto angélico encontrava-se apenas a alguns centímetros de distância do meu. Eu poderia, deveria, ter-me retraído perante a sua inesperada proximidade, mas não consegui movimentar-me. Os seus olhos dourados hipnotizavam-me.

— Então, de que tens medo? — sussurrou com determinação.

Não consegui responder. Tal como acontecera apenas uma vez, senti o cheiro do seu hálito fresco na minha cara. Doce e delicioso, o odor fez-me crescer água na boca. Era algo absolutamente único. De modo instintivo e impensado, aproximei-me mais, aspirando.

De repente, ele desapareceu, arrancando a mão das minhas. No tempo que os meus olhos demoraram a focar, já ele se encontrava a sessenta metros de distância, estando, de pé, na orla do pequeno prado, sob a sombra cerrada de um enorme abeto. Ele fitou-me, com os olhos escuros nas sombras e uma expressão indecifrável.

Eu sentia o sofrimento e o abalo expressos no meu rosto. Sentia uma dor pungente nas minhas mãos vazias.

— Sinto... muito... Edward — sussurrei.

Sabia que conseguia ouvir-me.

— Dá-me um momento! — exclamou, apenas suficientemente alto para que os meus ouvidos menos sensíveis conseguissem alcançar.

Permaneci sentada e muito quieta.

Passados dez longos segundos, voltou para trás, lentamente para o seu passo. Deteve-se, ainda a alguns metros de distância, e deixou-se cair graciosamente sobre o solo, cruzando as pernas. Os seus olhos nunca deixaram os meus. Respirou profundamente duas vezes e, em seguida, sorriu como se apresentasse um pedido de desculpas.

— Lamento imenso — hesitou. — Compreenderias o que eu queria dizer se afirmasse ser apenas humano?

Acenei uma vez com a cabeça, não sendo propriamente capaz de sorrir na sequência da sua piada. A adrenalina pulsava nas minhas veias à medida que a percepção do perigo se entranhava. O seu olfacto conseguia percepcionar esse facto a partir do local onde estava sentado. O seu sorriso tornou-se trocista.

— Sou o melhor predador do mundo, não sou? Tudo em mim te cativa: a minha voz, o meu rosto, até o meu *cheiro*. Como se eu precisasse disso!

Inesperadamente, ele colocou-se de pé, afastando-se, saindo imediatamente do meu campo visual, apenas para aparecer debaixo da mesma árvore de antes, tendo dado a volta ao prado numa fracção de segundo.

— Como se tu conseguisses correr mais do que eu.

Riu-se de modo amargo.

Levantou uma mão e, com um estalo ensurdecedor, arrancou sem esforço um ramo com sessenta centímetros de espessura do tronco do abeto. Equilibrou-o naquela mão durante um momento e, em seguida, arremessou-o com uma velocidade extraordinária, despedaçando-o contra outra árvore enorme, a qual abanou e tremeu ao sofrer tal golpe.

De repente, voltara a estar diante de mim, especado a sessenta centímetros de distância, estático como uma pedra.

— Como se pudesses afugentar-me — disse suavemente.

Permaneci sentada sem me mover, mais intimidada por ele do que alguma vez estivera. Nunca o vira tão liberto daquela fachada cuidadosamente mantida. Ele nunca fora menos humano, nem mais belo. Com rosto pálido e olhos arregalados, mantinha--me sentada como se fosse uma ave na mira de uma serpente.

Os seus olhos encantadores pareciam brilhar de impetuoso entusiasmo. Então, à medida que os segundos passaram, turvaram-se. O seu semblante foi envolvido por uma máscara de antiga tristeza.

— Não tenhas medo — murmurou, com um involuntário tom sedutor na voz aveludada. — Eu prometo...

Hesitou.

— Eu *juro* que não vou magoar-te.

Parecia mais preocupado em convencer-se a si próprio do que a mim.

— Não tenhas medo — sussurrou, enquanto se aproximava, com uma exagerada lentidão.

Sentou-se sinuosamente, com movimentos propositadamente vagarosos, até os nossos rostos se encontrarem ao mesmo nível, a apenas trinta centímetros de distância um do outro.

— Por favor, perdoa-me — disse com delicadeza. — Eu *consigo* controlar-me. Apanhaste-me desprevenido, mas, agora, vou comportar-me o melhor possível.

Esperou, mas eu ainda não conseguia falar.

— Hoje, sinceramente, não estou sedento.

Piscou o olho.

Daquelas palavras, eu tinha de me rir, ainda que o som do meu riso fosse débil e ofegante.

— Estás bem? — perguntou-me com ternura, estendendo a mão marmórea de modo lento e cuidadoso para voltar a pousá--la na minha.

Olhei para a sua mão fria e suave e, depois, para os seus

olhos. Estavam meigos, arrependidos. Tornei a olhar para a sua mão e, então, voltei deliberadamente a seguir as respectivas linhas com a ponta do meu dedo. Ergui o olhar e sorri a medo.

O sorriso que me retribuiu foi deslumbrante.

— Então, em que ponto estávamos, antes de eu me ter comportado com tanta indelicadeza? — perguntou nas suaves cadências de um século anterior.

— Sinceramente, não me lembro.

Sorriu, mas o seu rosto estava envergonhado.

— Acho que estávamos a conversar acerca do motivo por que sentias medo, além do óbvio.

— Ah, pois.

— Então?

Baixei o olhar e fixei a sua mão, passando-lhe os dedos ao acaso pela suave e iridescente palma. Os segundos passavam.

— Quão facilmente fico frustrado! — suspirou.

Olhei-o nos olhos, compreendendo de repente que aquela situação era tão nova para ele como para mim. Por mais anos de imperscrutável experiência que ele tivesse, também lhe era difícil. Retirei coragem de tal ideia.

— Sentia medo... porque, bem, por motivos óbvios, não posso ficar contigo. E tenho medo de querer estar contigo muito mais do que deveria.

Olhava para as suas mãos enquanto falava. Era-me difícil exprimir tais sentimentos em voz alta.

— Pois — concordou lentamente. — Esse é, de facto, um motivo para ter medo. Querer estar comigo. Não é propriamente para teu benefício.

— Eu sei. Suponho que podia *tentar* não desejar isso, mas acho que não iria resultar.

— Quem me dera poder ajudar-te. Sinceramente.

Não restavam dúvidas quanto à franqueza dos seus olhos cristalinos.

— Devia ter partido há muito tempo. Devia partir agora, mas não sei se consigo.

— Não quero que partas — balbuciei pateticamente olhando outra vez para baixo.

— E é mesmo por isso que eu devia fazê-lo. Mas não te preocupes. Sou por natureza uma criatura egoísta. Anseio demasiado pela tua companhia para conseguir fazer o que devia.

— Fico contente por isso.

— Não fiques!

Retirou a mão, desta vez com mais delicadeza, a sua voz estava mais áspera do que o habitual. Ríspida para ele, mas, mesmo assim, mais bela do que qualquer voz humana. Era difícil acompanhá-lo — as suas repentinas mudanças de humor deixavam-me sempre um passo atrás, aturdida.

— Não é só pela tua companhia que eu anseio! Nunca te esqueças *disso*. Nunca te esqueças de que represento um perigo maior para ti do que para qualquer outra pessoa.

Deteve-se e eu olhei, vendo-o a fixar o interior da floresta sem, porém, nada ver.

Reflecti por um momento.

— Acho que não compreendo bem o que queres dizer; pelo menos, essa última parte — declarei.

Voltou a olhar para mim e sorriu com malícia, tendo o seu humor sofrido uma nova alteração.

— Como hei-de explicar? — meditou. — E sem te assustar... hum.

De forma aparentemente espontânea, pousou de novo a mão na minha. Eu segurei-a com firmeza entre as minhas mãos. Ele olhou-as.

— É espantosamente agradável, o calor.

Suspirou.

Demorou um momento a colocar as ideias em ordem.

— Sabes que todos gostam de sabores diferentes, não é? — principiou. — Algumas pessoas adoram gelado de chocolate, outras preferem de morango.

Acenei com a cabeça.

— Desculpa a analogia com a comida, mas não me ocorreu outra forma de explicar.

Sorri. Ele retribuiu-me o sorriso com um ar arrependido.

— Sabes, cada pessoa tem um cheiro diferente, uma essência diferente. Se fechasses um alcoólico numa sala cheia de cerveja velha, ele bebê-la-ia de bom grado. No entanto, podia resistir, se desejasse fazê-lo, se fosse um alcoólico em recuperação. Agora, digamos que se colocava, nessa sala, um copo de brandy de cem anos, o melhor e mais raro conhaque e que se preenchia a sala com o seu aroma quente. Como é que achas que ele se comportaria nessa situação?

Ficámos sentados em silêncio, olhando-nos nos olhos, tentando adivinhar os pensamentos um do outro.

Foi ele o primeiro a quebrar o silêncio.

— Talvez essa não seja a comparação adequada. Talvez fosse demasiado rejeitar o brandy. Eu deveria, porventura, ter feito do nosso alcoólico um viciado em heroína.

— Então, o que estás a querer dizer é que eu sou o teu tipo de heroína? — gracejei, tentando aliviar o ambiente.

Ele esboçou um rápido sorriso, parecendo agradecer o meu esforço.

— Pois, és *exactamente* o meu tipo de heroína.

— Acontece com muita frequência? — perguntei.

Ele lançou o olhar pela copa das árvores, pensando na sua resposta.

— Conversei com os meus irmãos a esse respeito.

Continuava com o olhar fixo no horizonte.

— Para o Jasper, todos vocês são praticamente iguais. É o membro mais recente da nossa família. Para ele, a própria abstinência é um grande esforço. Ainda não teve tempo para se tornar sensível às diferenças em termos de cheiro, de sabor.

Olhou subitamente na minha direcção, com um ar de quem pede desculpa.

— Desculpa — disse.

— Não me importo. Por favor, não te preocupes com a possibilidade de me ofenderes, assustares ou o que quer que seja. É esse o teu modo de pensar. Eu consigo compreender ou, pelo menos, tentar. Explica simplesmente da forma que conseguires.

Respirou fundo e fixou o olhar no céu.

— Então, o Jasper não sabia ao certo se já se cruzara com alguém que fosse tão... — hesitou, procurando a palavra certa — *cativante* como tu és para mim, o que me leva a pensar que tal não aconteceu. O Emmett já é mais experiente nestas andanças, por assim dizer, e percebeu aquilo a que eu me referia. Disse que lhe aconteceu duas vezes, tendo uma delas sido mais intensa do que a outra.

— E a ti?

— Nunca.

A palavra pairou ali por um momento na brisa cálida.

— O que é que o Emmett fez? — perguntei para quebrar o silêncio.

Fiz a pergunta errada. O rosto tornou-se-lhe sombrio e o punho cerrou-se na minha mão. Desviou o olhar. Eu esperei, mas ele não ia responder.

— Acho que já sei — acabei por dizer.

Ergueu o olhar, a expressão estampada no seu rosto era de melancolia, de súplica.

— Até o mais forte dentre nós sucumbe à tentação, não é?

— O que estás a pedir? A minha autorização?

O meu tom de voz era mais incisivo do que eu pretendia. Tentei suavizá-lo, conseguia imaginar o quanto lhe custava ser sincero.

— Quero dizer, não há, então, esperança?

Quão calmamente eu conseguia debater a minha própria morte!

— Não, não!

Ficou imediatamente contrito.

— É claro que há esperança! Quero dizer, é claro que eu não...

Deixou a frase suspensa. Os seus olhos ardiam ao incidirem sobre os meus.

— Connosco, é diferente. Em relação ao Emmett... tratava-se apenas de estranhos com quem ele se cruzou por acaso. Já foi há muito tempo e ele não era tão... experimentado, tão cuidadoso como é agora.

Calou-se e observou-me com atenção enquanto eu reflectia sobre tudo aquilo.

— Então, se nos tivéssemos encontrado... ah, num beco escuro ou algo parecido...

As minhas palavras perderam intensidade.

— Tive de recorrer a todas as minhas forças para não saltar no meio daquela aula cheia de crianças e... — parou de repente, desviando o olhar. — Quando passaste por mim, eu podia ter arruinado tudo o que o Carlisle construiu para nós, naquele preciso momento e naquele mesmo lugar. Se eu não tivesse reprimido a minha sede ao longo dos últimos, bem, demasiados anos, não teria sido capaz de o evitar.

Deteve-se, olhando para as árvores com um ar carregado.

Olhou-me de relance de modo soturno, estando ambos a recordar.

— Deves ter pensado que eu estava possesso.

— Não conseguia perceber porquê. Como podias odiar-me tão depressa...

— Para mim, era como se tu fosses uma espécie de demónio, convocado directamente do meu inferno pessoal para me desgraçar. O perfume que emanava da tua pele... Pensei que iria enlouquecer-me naquele primeiro dia. Só durante aquela hora, pensei numa centena de maneiras diferentes de te atrair para fora da sala comigo, de te apanhar sozinha. E repeli-as todas, pensando na minha família, no que lhe faria. Tinha de fugir, de desaparecer antes que conseguisse proferir as palavras que te levariam a seguir-me...

Então, olhou para a minha expressão de assombro enquanto eu tentava assimilar as suas amargas recordações. Os seus olhos dourados queimavam debaixo das pestanas, hipnóticos e mortíferos.

— Terias ido comigo — garantiu.

Tentei falar calmamente.

— Sem dúvida.

Franziu o sobrolho ao fitar as minhas mãos, libertando-me da força do seu olhar.

— Então, quando tentava reorganizar o meu horário numa descabida tentativa de te evitar, lá estavas tu, naquela exígua salinha aconchegante. O odor era de perder a cabeça. Estive mesmo à beira de me apossar de ti nessa altura. Estava apenas presente um outro frágil ser humano, do qual podia tratar com *tanta* facilidade.

Arrepiei-me debaixo do Sol quente, visualizando de novo as minhas recordações através da perspectiva dele. Pobre menina Cope, arrepiei-me perante a percepção de quão perto eu estivera de ser inadvertidamente responsável pela morte dela.

— Mas resisti. Não sei como. Obriguei-me a mim próprio a *não* esperar por ti, a *não* te seguir a partir da escola. No exterior, quando já não conseguia sentir o teu cheiro, era mais fácil pensar com lucidez, tomar a decisão acertada. Deixei os outros perto de casa, tinha demasiada vergonha de lhes dizer quão fraco eu era. Eles só sabiam que havia algo de muito errado, e, depois, fui ter imediatamente com o Carlisle, ao hospital, para lhe comunicar que ia partir.

Eu olhava-o fixamente, espantada.

— Troquei de carro com ele. O dele tinha o depósito atestado e eu não queria fazer paragens. Não me atrevi a ir a casa, a encarar a Esme. Ela não me teria deixado ir embora sem antes fazer uma cena. Teria tentado convencer-me de que não era necessário... Na manhã seguinte, já me encontrava no Alasca.

Parecia envergonhado, como se estivesse a confessar uma grande cobardia.

— Passei lá dois dias, com alguns velhos conhecidos... mas sentia saudades de casa. Detestava saber que aborrecera a Esme e todos os restantes, a minha família adoptiva. Ao respirar o ar puro das montanhas, era difícil crer que tu eras tão irresistível. Convenci-me a mim mesmo de que fugir era um sinal de fraqueza. Já lidara com a tentação, não desta magnitude, nem nada que se parecesse, mas eu era forte. Quem eras tu, uma rapariguinha insignificante – esboçou subitamente um sorriso largo –, para me afugentares do lugar onde eu queria estar? Assim, voltei...

Fixou o olhar no vazio. Eu não conseguia falar.

– Tomei precauções, caçando, alimentando-me mais do que o habitual, antes de voltar a ver-te. Estava convicto de que era suficientemente forte para conseguir tratar-te como a qualquer outro ser humano. Encarava a questão com arrogância. O facto de eu não conseguir simplesmente adivinhar os teus pensamentos, de modo a saber qual era a tua reacção em relação a mim, constituía sem dúvida uma complicação. Não estava habituado a ter de recorrer a medidas tão tortuosas, ouvindo as tuas palavras na mente da Jessica... A mente dela não é muito original e era fastidioso ter de descer a esse nível. E, depois, não podia saber se as tuas palavras exprimiam fielmente o que te ia na alma. Tudo isso era extremamente irritante.

Franziu o sobrolho ao lembrar-se.

– Queria que esquecesses o meu comportamento naquele primeiro dia, se possível, e, por isso, tentei falar contigo como falaria com qualquer outra pessoa. Na verdade, estava ansioso, esperando decifrar alguns dos teus pensamentos, mas tu eras demasiado interessante e dei por mim enredado nas expressões do teu rosto... e, de vez em quando, agitavas o ar com a tua mão ou com o teu cabelo e o odor voltava a atordoar-me... E, claro, quase morreste esmagada, em seguida, diante dos meus olhos. Mais tarde, inventei uma desculpa perfeitamente aceitável para o facto de ter tomado uma atitude naquele momento: é que, se não te tivesse salvado, o teu sangue teria sido derramado ali, à minha frente, e creio que não teria conseguido evitar revelar quem nós somos. No entanto, tal desculpa só me ocorreu depois. Na altura, só conseguia pensar: «Ela, não».

Fechou os olhos, absorto na sua angustiada confissão. Eu escutava, mais ansiosa do que racional. O senso comum dizia-me que devia estar aterrorizada. Em vez disso, estava aliviada por finalmente compreender e inundada de compaixão pelo sofrimento dele, precisamente agora que confessava a sua ânsia de me ceifar a vida.

Por fim, consegui falar, apesar de a minha voz estar fraca.

— E no hospital?

Os seus olhos incidiram rapidamente sobre os meus.

— Fiquei estarrecido. Não conseguia acreditar que, afinal, nos colocara em perigo, me colocara à tua mercê, justamente à tua mercê. Como se precisasse de outro motivo para te matar.

Ambos estremecemos quando aquela palavra lhe escapou.

— Mas a situação exerceu o efeito inverso — continuou rapidamente. — Discuti com a Rosalie, o Emmett e o Jasper quando insinuaram que o momento chegara... Foi a discussão mais acesa que alguma vez tivéramos. O Carlisle colocou-se do meu lado, tal como a Alice.

Não sei por que motivo, fez um esgar quando pronunciou o nome dela.

— A Esme disse-me para fazer o que fosse necessário para poder ficar.

Abanou a cabeça de modo indulgente.

— Durante todo o dia seguinte, auscultei a mente de todas as pessoas com quem falavas, ficando profundamente surpreendido por verificar que cumprias a palavra. Não te compreendia mesmo nada, mas sabia que não podia envolver-me mais contigo. Esforcei-me ao máximo por me manter tão afastado de ti quanto possível. E, todos os dias, o perfume da tua pele, do teu hálito, do teu cabelo... afectava-me tanto como no primeiro dia.

Os seus olhos pousaram nos meus e estavam surpreendentemente ternos.

— E, por tudo isso — prosseguiu — seria mais fácil para mim se eu nos *tivesse*, de facto, denunciado a todos naquele primeiro momento do que se, aqui e agora, sem quaisquer testemunhas nem nada que me possa travar, eu te magoasse.

Eu era suficientemente humana para ter de perguntar:

— Porquê?

— Isabella.

Proferiu o meu nome completo e, depois, mexeu-me no cabelo com a mão que tinha livre. Um choque perpassou-me o corpo quando ele me tocou por casualidade.

— Bella, eu não conseguiria viver comigo mesmo se alguma vez te magoasse. Não sabes como isso me tem atormentado.

Baixou o olhar, envergonhado.

— Só a ideia de te ver quieta, branca, fria... para nunca mais ver o rubor das tuas faces coradas, para nunca mais ver aquele rasgo de intuição nos teus olhos quando não te deixas enganar pelos meus fingimentos... seria insuportável.

Ergueu os seus sublimes e angustiados olhos para os fixar nos meus.

— Agora, és a coisa mais importante para mim. A coisa mais importante para mim desde sempre.

A minha cabeça girava com a rápida mudança de rumo que a nossa conversa sofrera. Depois do alegre tema do meu falecimento iminente, estávamos, de repente, a declarar-nos. Ele esperou e, apesar de eu ter baixado o olhar para examinar as nossas mãos, que se interpunham entre nós, sabia que os seus olhos dourados estavam pousados em mim.

— Já sabes, com certeza, o que eu sinto — acabei por dizer. — Estou aqui... o que, numa tradução aproximada, significa que preferia morrer a ficar longe de ti — franzi o sobrolho. — Sou uma idiota.

— És uma idiota — concordou ele com uma gargalhada.

Os nossos olhares cruzaram-se e eu ri-me também. Rimo-nos em conjunto da idiotice e da mera impossibilidade de um tal momento.

— E, assim, o leão se apaixonou pelo cordeiro — murmurou ele.

Desviei o olhar, escondendo os olhos ao emocionar-me com aquela palavra.

— Que cordeiro parvo! — suspirei.

— Que leão doentio e masoquista!

Ele olhou fixamente para o interior da umbrosa floresta durante um longo momento e eu perguntei-me aonde os seus pensamentos o haviam levado.

— Porque é que...? — principiei e, depois, detive-me, não sabendo ao certo como continuar.

Ele olhou-me e sorriu. A luz do Sol reflectia no seu rosto, nos seus dentes.

— Sim?

— Diz-me porque é que fugias de mim antes.

O seu sorriso desvaneceu-se.

— Tu sabes bem porquê.

— Não, quero dizer, o que eu fiz de errado *exactamente*? Sabes, terei de estar atenta, logo, é melhor começar a aprender aquilo que não devo fazer. Com isto, por exemplo — acariciei-lhe as costas da mão —, parece não haver problema.

Sorriu novamente.

— Não fizeste nada de errado, Bella. A culpa foi minha.

— Mas eu quero contribuir, se puder, para que isto não se torne mais difícil para ti.

— Bem...

Ele meditou por um momento.

— O problema era apenas a tua proximidade. A maioria dos humanos afasta-se instintivamente de nós, é repelida pela nossa natureza diferente... Não esperava que te aproximasses tanto. E o cheiro do teu *pescoço*.

Ele parou de repente, procurando ver se me perturbara.

— Então, muito bem — disse eu, de modo irreverente, tentando aliviar o ambiente que ficara tenso. Escondi o queixo. — Nada de expor o pescoço.

Resultou: ele riu-se.

— Não, na verdade, deveu-se mais à surpresa do que a qualquer outro factor.

Ele levantou a mão que tinha livre e pousou-a com suavidade no meu pescoço, de lado. Permaneci sentada, muito quieta, sendo a frieza do seu toque um aviso natural, um aviso que me transmitia a ideia de que deveria estar apavorada. Mas não havia qualquer sentimento de medo no meu âmago. Havia, no entanto, outros sentimentos...

— Vês? — disse ele. — Não há problema nenhum.

O meu fluxo sanguíneo estava extremamente acelerado e desejei poder abrandá-lo, sentindo que aquele facto devia tornar tudo muito mais difícil — o batimento da minha pulsação nas veias. Decerto, ele conseguia ouvi-lo.

— O rubor das tuas faces é encantador — murmurou.

Libertou delicadamente a outra mão. As minhas caíram sem energia sobre o meu colo. Acariciou-me suavemente a face e, em seguida, segurou o meu rosto entre as suas mãos marmóreas.

— Fica muito quieta — sussurrou, como se eu já não estivesse paralisada.

Devagarinho, sem nunca afastar os seus olhos dos meus, inclinou-se na minha direcção. Então, de repente, mas com muita delicadeza, encostou a face fria à cavidade na base do meu pescoço. Quase não conseguia movimentar-me, mesmo que desejasse fazê-lo. Ouvi o som da sua respiração regular, vendo os efeitos do Sol e do vento ao incidirem sobre o seu cabelo cor de bronze, o qual era mais humano do que qualquer outra parte do seu corpo.

Com propositada lentidão, as suas mãos deslizaram ao longo do meu pescoço, uma de cada lado. Arrepiei-me e ouvi-o a recuperar o fôlego, mas as suas mãos não se detiveram à medida que avançavam suavemente para os meus ombros e, de repente, pararam.

O seu rosto virou-se para o lado, com o nariz a passar levemente sobre a minha clavícula. Imobilizou-se com a parte lateral do rosto ternamente encostada ao meu peito.

Ouvia o meu coração.

— Ah! — suspirou.

Não sei durante quanto tempo ali permanecemos sentados, sem nos movermos. Poderão ter passado várias horas. A minha pulsação acabou por se aquietar, mas ele não se voltou a mexer nem a falar enquanto me abraçava. Eu sabia que, a qualquer momento, aquela situação poderia tornar-se superior às suas forças e a minha vida chegaria ao fim, tão rapidamente que eu podia nem dar por isso. E não conseguia incutir medo em mim própria. Não conseguia pensar em nada, além do facto de ele estar a tocar-me.

Então, demasiado cedo, ele soltou-me.

Os seus olhos estavam serenos.

— Não voltará a ser tão difícil — afirmou com satisfação.

— Foi muito difícil para ti?

— Não foi, de modo nenhum, tão mau como imaginei que seria. E para ti?

— Não, não foi mau... para mim.

Ele sorriu devido à modulação da minha voz.

— Sabes bem a que me refiro.

Sorri.

— Repara.

Pegou na minha mão e encostou-a à sua face.

— Sentes como está quente?

A sua pele normalmente gelada estava, de facto, quase quente, mas mal notei, pois estava a tocar o seu rosto, algo com que sonhara constantemente desde o primeiro dia em que o vira.

— Não te mexas — sussurrei.

Ninguém conseguia ficar quieto como Edward. Fechou os olhos e ficou imóvel como uma pedra, uma escultura sob a minha mão.

Movi-me ainda mais lentamente do que ele, tendo o cuidado de não fazer nenhum movimento inesperado. Acariciei-lhe a face, afaguei-lhe a pálpebra, a sombra roxa na cavidade por baixo do olho, os lábios perfeitos. Os lábios separaram-se sob a minha mão e eu conseguia sentir o seu hálito fresco nas pontas dos meus dedos. Queria aproximar-me, aspirar o seu cheiro. Assim, baixei a mão e afastei-me, não querendo levá-lo a ir longe de mais.

Ele abriu os olhos e estes estavam ávidos. Não de modo a atemorizar-me, mas sim a fazer com que os músculos do meu estômago se contraíssem e o sangue corresse, de novo, desenfreadamente nas minhas veias.

— Quem me dera — sussurrou ele —, quem me dera que conseguisses sentir a... complexidade... a confusão... que eu sinto. Isso conseguirias compreender.

Elevou a mão até ao meu cabelo e, em seguida, acariciou-me cuidadosamente o rosto.

— Explica-me — murmurei.

— Acho que não consigo. Por um lado, já te falei da fome, da sede, do que a criatura deplorável que eu sou sente por ti. E julgo que consegues compreender isso, até certo ponto. No entanto — esboçou um meio sorriso —, como não és viciada em nenhuma substância ilícita, não deves conseguir entender completamente.

— Mas...

Os seus dedos tocaram levemente os meus lábios, fazendo-me arrepiar novamente.

— Existem outros apetites. Apetites que nem sequer compreendo, que me são estranhos.

— Posso compreender *isso* melhor do que pensas.

— Não estou habituado a sentir-me tão humano. É sempre assim?

— Para mim? — detive-me. — Não, nunca. Nunca antes disto.

Segurou as minhas mãos entre as suas. Pareciam tão débeis, tendo em conta a sua força férrea.

— Não sei como hei-de estar perto de ti — reconheceu. — Não sei se consigo.

Inclinei-me para a frente muito devagar, prevenindo-o com os meus olhos. Encostei a face ao seu peito pétreo.

Conseguia ouvir-lhe a respiração e nada mais.

— Isto basta — suspirei, fechando os olhos.

Num gesto muito humano, envolveu-me com o braço e enterrou o rosto no meu cabelo.

— Sais-te melhor nisto do que julgas — observei.

— Eu tenho instintos humanos, podem estar escondidos bem cá no fundo, mas existem.

Permanecemos assim sentados durante um outro momento incomensurável. Perguntei-me se ele estaria tão avesso a mover-se como eu, mas conseguia ver que a luz começava a extinguir-se, com as sombras da floresta a começarem a alcançar-nos, e suspirei.

— Tens de ir.

— Pensei que não conseguias adivinhar os meus pensamentos — acusei.

— Começam a ficar mais transparentes.

Conseguia detectar um sorriso na sua voz.

Ele segurou-me nos ombros e eu olhei-o no rosto.

— Posso mostrar-te uma coisa? — perguntou, com um súbito entusiasmo a trazer-lhe um brilho ao olhar.

— Mostrar-me o quê?

— Vou mostrar-te como *eu* me desloco na floresta.

Viu a expressão estampada no meu rosto.

— Não te preocupes, estarás absolutamente a salvo e chegaremos junto da tua *pick-up* muito mais depressa.

A sua boca esboçou um trejeito, formando aquele sorriso enviesado, tão belo que o meu coração quase parou.

— Vais transformar-te num morcego? — perguntei cautelosamente.

Ele riu-se do modo mais sonoro que alguma vez ouvira.

— Como se eu nunca tivesse ouvido *essa*!

— É verdade, tenho a certeza de que deves ouvir isso constantemente.

— Anda lá, cobardezinha, sobe para as minhas costas.

Esperei para ver se ele estava a brincar, mas, pelos vistos, falava a sério. Sorriu ao aperceber-se da minha hesitação e estendeu-me a mão. O meu coração reagiu, ainda que ele não conseguisse adivinhar os meus pensamentos, a minha pulsação denunciava-me sempre. Então, colocou-me às cavalitas, com muito pouco esforço da minha parte além de, quando já lá estava, fincar as pernas e os braços em torno dele tão firmemente que sufocaria uma pessoa normal. Era como segurar-me a uma pedra.

— Sou um pouco mais pesada do que a tua mochila normal — adverti.

— Ah! — desdenhou.

Quase consegui ouvir os seus olhos a revirarem-se. Nunca o vira tão animado.

Assustou-me, pegando de repente na minha mão, encostando a palma ao seu rosto e inspirando profundamente.

— Torna-se cada vez mais fácil — disse por entre dentes.

Então, começou a correr.

Se alguma vez receara a morte na presença dele, tal em nada se comparava ao que eu sentia naquele momento.

Ele deslocou-se através da escura e densa vegetação rasteira da floresta como uma bala, como um fantasma. Não havia qualquer ruído, qualquer prova de que os seus pés tocavam no chão.

A sua respiração nunca se alterou, nunca indiciou qualquer esforço, mas as árvores passavam por nós a uma velocidade vertiginosa, sempre sem nos acertarem por uma questão de centímetros.

Estava demasiado apavorada para fechar os olhos, embora a aragem mais fresca soprasse no meu rosto e os fizesse arder. Senti-me como se, estupidamente, tivesse colocado a cabeça de fora da janela de um avião em pleno voo e, pela primeira vez na vida, senti as tonturas e o mal-estar provocados pelo enjoo do movimento.

De repente, terminara. Caminháramos durante horas naquela manhã até chegarmos ao prado de Edward e, agora, numa questão de minutos, estávamos junto da *pick-up*.

— Emocionante, não é?

Falava com um tom de voz alto, entusiasmado.

Ficou imóvel, esperando que eu descesse. Tentei, mas os músculos não me obedeciam. Os braços e as pernas ficaram presos à volta dele, enquanto a cabeça girava de modo incómodo.

— Bella? — perguntou, já ansioso.

— Acho que preciso de me deitar — disse de modo ofegante.

— Oh, desculpa.

Ficou à minha espera, mas eu continuava a não conseguir mover-me.

— Acho que preciso de ajuda — reconheci.

Ele riu-se discretamente e, com delicadeza, soltou o meu abraço estrangulador em torno do seu pescoço. Não havia nada que resistisse à força férrea das suas mãos. Em seguida, puxou-me para que ficasse de frente para ele, segurando-me ao colo como se fosse uma criança pequena. Suportou-me por um momento e, em seguida, pousou-me nos tenros fetos.

— Como te sentes? — interrogou.

Não conseguia saber ao certo como me sentia quando a minha cabeça girava tão freneticamente.

— Tonta, acho eu.

— Põe a cabeça entre os joelhos.

Tentei seguir o seu conselho e surtiu algum efeito. Inspirei e expirei lentamente, mantendo a cabeça muito quieta. Senti-o a sentar-se a meu lado. O tempo passou e acabei por achar que já conseguia levantar a cabeça. Sentia um zunido cavernoso nos meus ouvidos.

— Acho que não foi a melhor das ideias — reflectiu.

Tentei ser optimista, mas a minha voz estava fraca.

— Não, foi muito interessante.

— Ah! Estás tão branca como um fantasma, não, estás tão branca como *eu*!

— Julgo que devia ter fechado os olhos.

— Lembra-te disso na próxima vez.

— Na próxima vez! — gemi.

Ele riu-se, ainda com uma disposição exultante.

— Exibicionista — murmurei por entre dentes.

— Abre os olhos, Bella — disse ele calmamente.

Estava mesmo ali, com o rosto bem próximo do meu. A sua beleza toldava-me as ideias, era demasiado, um excesso a que eu não conseguia habituar-me.

— Estava a pensar, enquanto corria...

Deteve-se.

— Em não embater nas árvores, espero eu.

— Bella tonta — soltou um riso abafado. — Correr faz parte da minha natureza, não é coisa em que eu tenha de pensar.

— Exibicionista — murmurei novamente.

Ele sorriu.

— Não — prosseguiu. — Estava a pensar que havia algo que eu queria experimentar.

Então, tomou o meu rosto nas suas mãos.

Eu não conseguia respirar.

Ele hesitou, mas não da maneira normal, da maneira humana.

Não da maneira como um homem hesitaria antes de beijar uma mulher, para sondar a sua reacção, para ver como seria recebido. Talvez hesitasse para prolongar o momento, aquele momento ideal de expectativa, por vezes melhor do que o próprio beijo.

Edward hesitou para se pôr à prova, para ver se era seguro, para se certificar de que ainda controlava a sua necessidade.

Então, os seus frios lábios marmóreos encostaram-se muito suavemente aos meus.

Aquilo para que nenhum de nós estava preparado foi a minha reacção.

O sangue fervia sob a minha pele, queimava nos meus lábios. Eu respirava num frenético arquejo. Os meus dedos entrelaçaram-se nos seus cabelos, prendendo-o a mim. Os meus lábios separaram-se enquanto eu aspirava o seu perfume estonteante. Imediatamente, senti-o transformar-se numa pedra sem reacção debaixo dos meus lábios. As suas mãos, delicadamente, mas com uma força irresistível, afastaram o meu rosto. Abri os olhos e vi o seu ar de cautela.

— Ups — sussurrei.

— Isso é dizer pouco.

Os seus olhos apresentavam-se selvagens, o maxilar cerrado numa intensa coibição. Todavia, ele não descurou da sua perfeita dicção. Segurou o meu rosto a apenas alguns centímetros do seu. Ofuscava-me.

— Será que devo...?

Tentei libertar-me, dar-lhe algum espaço.

As suas mãos recusaram deixar que me deslocasse um só centímetro.

— Não, é tolerável. Aguarda um momento, por favor.

A sua voz era gentil, controlada.

Mantive os olhos pousados nos dele, observei enquanto o entusiasmo neles reflectido se desvaneceu e aplacou.

Em seguida, esboçou um sorriso surpreendentemente endiabrado.

— Pronto — disse ele, manifestamente satisfeito consigo mesmo.

— Tolerável? — perguntei.

Ele riu-se sonoramente.

— Sou mais forte do que pensava. É bom saber.

— Quem me dera poder dizer o mesmo. Desculpa.

— Afinal, *és* apenas humana.

— Obrigadíssima! — exclamei, com uma voz cáustica.

Colocou-se de pé num dos seus movimentos ágeis e quase invisivelmente rápidos. Estendeu-me a mão num gesto inesperado. Eu estava muito habituada ao nosso critério de cautelosa ausência de contacto. Peguei na sua mão gelada, precisando de apoio mais do que julgava. O meu equilíbrio ainda não se restabelecera.

— Ainda te sentes fraca devido à corrida? Ou foi a perícia do meu beijo?

Quão descontraído, quão humano ele parecia enquanto se ria agora, com o seu rosto seráfico sereno. Era um Edward diferente daquele que eu conhecera e eu sentia-me ainda mais perdida de amores por ele. Estar agora separada dele provocaria em mim dor física.

— Não sei ao certo, ainda estou tonta — consegui responder. — Acho que se deve um pouco a ambos os factores.

— Talvez devesses deixar-me conduzir.

— Estás louco? — protestei.

— Conduzo melhor do que tu no teu melhor dia — gracejou. — Os teus reflexos são muito mais lentos.

— Tenho a certeza de que isso é verdade, mas acho que os meus nervos e a minha *pick-up* não aguentariam.

— Um pouco de confiança, por favor, Bella.

Tinha a mão no bolso, fechada firmemente em torno da chave.

Franzi os lábios, ponderei e, depois, abanei a cabeça e esbocei um sorriso tenso.

— Não. Nem pensar.

Ele levantou a sobrancelha, incrédulo.

Comecei a avançar, desviando-me dele e dirigindo-me para o lado do condutor. Ele podia ter-me deixado passar se eu não tivesse cambaleado ligeiramente. E, daí, talvez não o tivesse feito.

— Bella, nesta altura, já fiz consideráveis esforços pessoais para te manter viva. Não vou deixar que te sentes ao volante de um veículo quando não consegues sequer andar como deve ser. Além disso, os amigos não deixam que os amigos conduzam embriagados — referiu com um riso abafado, formando o seu braço um laço inelutável à volta da minha cintura. Eu conseguia sentir o perfume insuportavelmente doce que emanava do seu peito.

— Embriagados? — reclamei.

— Estás inebriada com a minha própria presença.

Esboçava mais uma vez aquele sorriso pretensioso e trocista.

— Não posso contestar isso — suspirei.

Não havia volta a dar-lhe; não conseguia resistir-lhe. Ergui a chave bem alto e deixei-a cair, vendo a mão dele precipitar-se como um raio para a apanhar sem produzir qualquer ruído.

— Vai com calma, a minha *pick-up* é um veículo da terceira idade.

— Muito sensato — aprovou.

— E tu? Não ficas minimamente afectado? — perguntei, aborrecida. — Com a minha presença?

Uma vez mais, os traços inconstantes do seu rosto transformaram-se, com a sua expressão a tornar-se afável, calorosa. A princípio, não respondeu, inclinou simplesmente o rosto na direcção do meu e passou levemente os lábios ao longo do meu maxilar, desde a orelha até ao queixo, para a frente e para trás. Eu tremi.

— Seja como for — acabou por murmurar —, os meus reflexos são melhores.

Capítulo Catorze

O Domínio da Mente sobre a Matéria

Eu tinha de reconhecer que, quando mantinha uma velocidade aceitável, ele conduzia bem. Como tantas outras coisas, parecia não requerer qualquer esforço da sua parte. Mal olhava para a estrada, porém, os pneus nunca se afastavam mais de um centímetro do meio da faixa de rodagem. Conduzia só com uma mão, segurando, com a outra, a minha no banco. Por vezes, fixava o olhar no sol-poente e, outras vezes, olhava na minha direcção, fitando o meu rosto, o meu cabelo a agitar-se ao sabor do vento para fora da janela, as nossas mãos unidas.

Sintonizara o rádio numa estação de êxitos antigos e acompanhou a letra de uma música que eu nunca ouvira. Sabia cada frase da letra.

— Gostas de música dos anos cinquenta? — perguntei.

— A música dos anos cinquenta era boa. Muito melhor do que a dos anos sessenta ou setenta, uf!

Estremeceu.

— Os anos oitenta foram toleráveis.

— Alguma vez me vais dizer que idade tens? — perguntei, com alguma hesitação, não querendo perturbar a sua alegre disposição.

— Tem muita importância?

O seu sorriso, para meu alívio, não se ensombrou.

— Não, mas continuo a sentir curiosidade... — fiz um esgar. — Não há nada como um enigma por resolver para nos manter acordados à noite.

— Pergunto-me se irá perturbar-te — reflectiu.

Fixou o olhar no Sol, os minutos passaram.

— Experimenta — acabei por dizer.

Suspirou e, em seguida, olhou-me nos olhos, parecendo esquecer a estrada por completo durante alguns instantes. O que quer que neles tenha visto deve tê-lo incentivado. Olhou para o Sol — a luz da esfera poente reflectia na pele dele em lampejos de tom rubro — e falou:

— Nasci em Chicago, em 1901.

Fez uma pausa e olhou-me pelo canto do olho. O meu rosto estava cuidadosamente impávido, aguardando com paciência a restante informação. Ele esboçou um pequeno sorriso e prosseguiu:

— O Carlisle encontrou-me num hospital no Verão de 1918. Eu tinha dezassete anos e estava a morrer com a gripe espanhola.

Ouviu-me inspirar, embora tal fosse quase inaudível aos meus próprios ouvidos. Olhou-me nos olhos.

— Não me lembro muito bem; já foi há muito tempo e as recordações humanas desvanecem-se.

Ficou absorto nos seus pensamentos antes de continuar:

— Mas recordo-me da sensação que me invadiu quando o Carlisle me salvou. Não é uma coisa fácil, algo que se poderia esquecer.

— E os teus pais?

— Já tinham morrido, padecendo da mesma doença. Eu estava sozinho. Foi por isso que ele me escolheu. No meio de todo o caos provocado pela epidemia, nunca ninguém se aperceberia de que eu desaparecera.

— Como é que ele... te salvou?

Demorou alguns instantes a responder. Parecia escolher as palavras com cuidado.

— Foi difícil. Não há muitos de nós que tenham o comedimento necessário para cometer tal acto, mas o Carlisle sempre foi o mais humano, o mais compassivo dentre nós... Creio que não seria possível encontrar alguém como ele em toda a história — deteve-se. — Para mim, foi apenas muitíssimo doloroso.

Pelo modo como ele colocara os lábios, eu percebi que ele recusaria continuar a falar sobre aquele assunto. Refreei a curiosidade, ainda que esta estivesse bem acesa. Havia muitas coisas sobre as quais eu precisava de reflectir no que se referia àquela questão em concreto, coisas que só agora começavam a vir-me à ideia. A sua mente ágil já apreendera, sem dúvida, todos os aspectos que me escapavam.

A sua voz suave interrompeu os meus pensamentos.

— Ele agiu movido pela solidão. É normalmente essa a razão por trás da escolha. Eu fui o primeiro a pertencer à família de Carlisle, embora ele tenha encontrado a Esme pouco tempo depois. Ela caiu de um penhasco. Levaram-na directamente para a morgue do hospital, mas, de alguma forma, o seu coração ainda batia.

— Então, as pessoas têm de estar às portas da morte para se tornarem...

Nós nunca proferíamos aquela palavra e eu não conseguia formulá-la agora.

— Não, só o Carlisle é que age dessa forma. Ele nunca faria isso a alguém que tivesse outra opção.

O respeito patente na sua voz era profundo, sempre que falava da sua figura paterna.

— No entanto, segundo ele — prosseguiu —, é mais fácil se o sangue estiver fraco.

Olhou para a estrada, agora imersa na escuridão, e eu senti novamente que o assunto estava a ser encerrado.

— E quanto ao Emmett e à Rosalie?

— A seguir o Carlisle integrou a Rosalie na nossa família. Só muito mais tarde percebi que ele esperava que ela fosse para mim o que a Esme era para ele; tinha muito cuidado com o que pensava quando estava perto de mim.

Revirou os olhos.

— Mas ela nunca foi mais do que uma irmã. Só dois anos depois é que encontrou o Emmett. Estava a caçar (na altura, estávamos na Appalachia) e deparou com um urso que estava prestes a matá-lo. Levou-o até ao Carlisle, tendo percorrido mais de cento e sessenta quilómetros, receando não ser capaz de ser ela a fazê-lo.

Só agora começo a imaginar quão difícil aquela viagem deve ter sido para ela.

Lançou um olhar penetrante na minha direcção e ergueu as nossas mãos, ainda unidas, para acariciar a minha face com as costas da sua mão.

— Mas ela conseguiu — incitei, desviando o olhar da insuportável beleza dos seus olhos.

— Conseguiu — murmurou ele. — Viu algo no rosto dele que lhe deu forças suficientes e, desde então, estão juntos. Por vezes, vivem separados de nós, como marido e mulher, mas, quanto mais jovens fingirmos ser, mais tempo podemos ficar num dado lugar. Forks parecia perfeita e, assim, todos nos matriculámos no liceu.

Riu-se.

— Suponho que teremos de ir ao casamento deles dentro de alguns anos; *outra vez.*

— E a Alice e o Jasper?

— A Alice e o Jasper são duas criaturas muito raras. Ambos desenvolveram uma consciência, como nós lhe chamamos, sem qualquer orientação externa. O Jasper pertencia a outra... família, um tipo de família muito diferente. Ficou deprimido e partiu sozinho. A Alice encontrou-o. Tal como eu, ela tem certos dons que fogem à norma da nossa espécie.

— A sério? — interrompi, fascinada. — Mas tu disseste que eras o único que conseguia auscultar os pensamentos das outras pessoas.

— É verdade. Ela sabe outras coisas. Tem visões, visões de possíveis acontecimentos, mas é algo muito subjectivo. O futuro não está gravado numa pedra. As coisas mudam.

O seu maxilar cerrou-se quando fez tal afirmação e os seus olhos precipitaram-se para o meu rosto, afastando-se com tanta rapidez que eu não sabia ao certo se teria sido imaginação minha.

— Que género de visões tem ela?

— Visionou o Jasper e soube que ele a procurava antes de

ele mesmo o saber. Visionou o Carlisle e a nossa família, tendo ambos partido à nossa procura. Tem uma maior sensibilidade em relação a não-humanos. Sabe sempre, por exemplo, quando outro grupo da nossa espécie está a aproximar-se e os problemas que poderá levantar.

— Existem muitos... da vossa espécie?

Fiquei surpreendida.

— Quantos poderiam infiltrar-se no nosso seio sem serem detectados?

— Não, não muitos. Mas a maioria não se estabelece em qualquer lugar. Só aqueles que são como nós, que desistiram de caçar pessoas — um olhar furtivo na minha direcção —, podem coexistir com humanos durante qualquer período de tempo. Ainda só encontrámos uma família como a nossa, numa pequena aldeia do Alasca. Coabitámos durante algum tempo, mas éramos tantos que começámos a dar demasiado nas vistas. Aqueles que, como nós, vivem... de um modo diferente tendem a reunir-se em grupos.

— E os outros?

— São essencialmente nómadas. Já todos nós vivemos dessa forma em determinadas alturas. Torna-se deveras entediante. No entanto, de vez em quando, cruzamo-nos com os outros, pois a maior parte de nós prefere o Norte.

— Por que motivo?

Já estávamos parados diante de minha casa e ele desligara o motor da *pick-up*. Imperava o silêncio e a escuridão, não havia lua. A luz do alpendre estava apagada, pelo que eu sabia que o meu pai ainda não chegara a casa.

— Tinhas os olhos abertos esta tarde? — gracejou. — Julgas que eu poderia descer a rua, sob a luz do Sol, sem provocar acidentes no trânsito? Há uma razão para termos escolhido a Península Olímpica, um dos lugares do mundo onde o Sol brilha menos. É agradável poder sair durante o dia. Não acreditarias em como podemos ficar fartos da noite em oitenta e tal anos.

— Então, é essa a origem das lendas?

— Provavelmente.

— E a Alice veio de outra família, como o Jasper?

— Não, e isso é, de facto, um mistério. Alice não tem qualquer lembrança da sua vida humana e não sabe quem a criou. Despertou sozinha. Quem quer que a tenha transformado, abandonou-a e nenhum de nós percebe porquê ou como é que o poderia ter feito. Se ela não possuísse aquele outro sentido, se não tivesse visionado o Jasper e o Carlisle e sabido que, um dia, se tornaria uma de nós, ter-se-ia, provavelmente, transformado numa absoluta selvagem.

Havia tanto que assimilar, tantas perguntas que eu ainda queria fazer, mas, para meu grande embaraço, o meu estômago roncou. Estivera tão intrigada que nem notara que tinha fome. Apercebia-me agora de que estava faminta.

— Desculpa, estou a impedir-te de ires jantar.

— Eu estou bem, a sério.

— Nunca passei muito tempo perto de alguém que se alimenta de comida. Esqueço-me.

— Eu quero ficar contigo.

Era mais fácil exprimir, na escuridão, a minha irremediável obsessão por ele sabendo, enquanto falava, como a minha voz me atraiçoaria.

— Posso entrar? — perguntou.

— Gostarias de o fazer?

Não conseguia visualizar aquela imagem, aquela criatura divina sentada na cadeira gasta da cozinha do meu pai.

— Gostaria, se não houver problema.

Ouvi a porta fechar-se em silêncio e, quase em simultâneo, ele estava junto à minha, do lado de fora, abrindo-a para que eu saísse.

— Muito humano — felicitei-o.

— Está, sem dúvida, a ressurgir.

Caminhou a meu lado pela noite, tão silenciosamente que eu tinha de espreitá-lo constantemente para me certificar de que ele ainda ali estava. Na escuridão, ele parecia muito mais normal. Ainda pálido e com uma beleza de sonho, mas já não a fantástica criatura cintilante que se revelara durante a nossa tarde iluminada pelo Sol.

Chegou à porta antes de mim e abriu-ma. Eu detive-me a meio caminho da ombreira da porta.

— A porta estava destrancada?

— Não, utilizei a chave que se encontrava debaixo do beiral.

Entrei, acendi a luz do alpendre e voltei-me para olhá-lo com as sobrancelhas erguidas. Tinha a certeza de que nunca usara aquela chave à frente dele.

— Estava curioso em relação a ti.

— Andaste a espiar-me?

No entanto, não consegui infundir na minha voz o devido tom de indignação. Sentia-me lisonjeada.

Ele não se mostrava arrependido.

— O que mais há para se fazer à noite?

Não insisti mais no assunto naquele momento e percorri o corredor até à cozinha. Ele estava lá, diante de mim, não tendo precisado de guia. Sentou-se precisamente na cadeira onde eu tentara imaginá-lo. A sua beleza iluminou a cozinha. Decorreu um instante até eu conseguir desviar o olhar.

Concentrei-me em preparar o jantar, retirando a lasanha da noite anterior do frigorífico, colocando um quadrado num prato e aquecendo-o no microondas. Girou, preenchendo a cozinha com o odor do tomate e dos orégãos. Não tirei os olhos de cima do prato enquanto falava.

— Com que frequência? — perguntei com indiferença.

— Hã?

Parecia que o distraíra de outra linha de raciocínio.

Eu continuava a não me voltar.

— Com que frequência vinhas aqui?

— Venho aqui quase todas as noites.

Eu virei-me rapidamente, estupefacta.

— Porquê?

— És interessante quando dormes — proferiu de modo objectivo.

— Falas.

— Não! — exclamei ofegante, com um calor a inundar-me o rosto até à linha do cabelo.

Agarrei-me ao balcão da cozinha para me apoiar. Eu sabia, evidentemente, que falava durante o sono, a minha mãe troçava de mim a esse respeito. No entanto, pensei que era algo com que não tinha de me preocupar ali.

A expressão dele alterou-se imediatamente, mostrando-se desgostoso.

— Estás muito zangada comigo?

— Depende!

Sentia-me como se me tivessem tirado o fôlego e o meu tom de voz reflectia esse facto.

Ele esperou.

— De quê? — insistiu.

— Daquilo que ouviste! — lamentei-me.

Logo a seguir, silencioso, ele encontrava-se a meu lado, tomando cuidadosamente as minhas mãos nas suas.

— Não fiques aborrecida! — pediu.

Baixou o rosto ao nível dos meus olhos, fitando-os. Fiquei envergonhada, tentei desviar o olhar.

— Sentes saudades da tua mãe — sussurrou. — Preocupas-te com ela. E, quando chove, o som faz-te ficar inquieta. Costumavas falar muito da tua casa, mas agora falas menos frequentemente. Certa vez, disseste: «É demasiado *verde*».

Riu-se suavemente, esperando não me ofender mais, o que eu conseguia perceber.

— Mais alguma coisa? — interroguei.

Ele sabia aonde eu queria chegar.

— Disseste o meu nome — admitiu.

Eu soltei um suspiro de derrota.

— Muitas vezes?

— O que queres dizer, ao certo, com «muitas vezes»?

— Oh, não!

Baixei a cabeça.

Ele puxou-me contra o seu peito, suavemente e com naturalidade.

— Não fiques constrangida — sussurrou-me ao ouvido. — Se eu pudesse sonhar, seria contigo. E não tenho vergonha disso.

Então, ambos ouvimos um ruído de pneus na entrada ladrilhada e vimos luzes de faróis a precipitarem-se pelas janelas da frente da casa, ao longo do corredor, até chegarem até nós. Eu contraí-me nos braços dele.

— O teu pai deve saber que eu estou aqui? — perguntou ele.

— Não sei bem...

Tentei pensar rapidamente.

— Então, fica para outra altura...

E fiquei sozinha.

— Edward! — exclamei.

Ouvi um fantasmal riso abafado e, depois, nada mais.

A chave do meu pai rodou na fechadura da porta.

— Bella? — chamou.

Este facto já me incomodara; quem haveria de ser? De repente, não parecia assim tão descabido.

— Estou aqui.

Esperava que ele não detectasse o laivo de histeria na minha voz. Retirei o meu jantar do microondas e sentei-me à mesa enquanto ele entrava. Os seus passos pareciam muito ruidosos depois do dia que passara com Edward.

— Podes preparar-me um pouco disso? Estou estafado.

Pisou a zona dos calcanhares das botas para descalçá-las, apoiando-se nas costas da cadeira de Edward.

Levei a minha comida comigo, ingerindo-a enquanto preparava o jantar dele. Queimou-me a língua. Enchi dois copos de leite enquanto a lasanha dele estava a aquecer e traguei o meu para refrescar a boca. Quando pousei o copo, notei que o leite se agitava e que a minha mão estava a tremer. Ele sentou-se na cadeira e o contraste entre ele e o anterior ocupante era cómico.

— Obrigado — disse ele quando coloquei a sua comida sobre a mesa.

— Como foi o teu dia? — perguntei.

Tais palavras foram proferidas à pressa, estava morta por me escapar para o quarto.

— Foi bom. Os peixes estavam a morder o isco... E o teu? Conseguiste fazer tudo aquilo que pretendias?

— Nem por isso; o dia estava demasiado agradável para ficar dentro de casa.

Abocanhei outra grande garfada.

— Foi, de facto, um belo dia — concordou.

«Isso é dizer muito pouco», pensei para comigo.

Tendo engolido a última garfada de lasanha, peguei no copo e bebi apressadamente o resto do leite.

Charlie surpreendeu-me ao mostrar-se observador.

— Estás com pressa.

— Pois, estou cansada. Vou deitar-me cedo.

— Pareces algo nervosa — comentou.

Porquê? Mas porque é que aquela tinha de ser a noite em que ele resolvera prestar atenção?

— Pareço?

Nada mais consegui dizer em resposta. Lavei rapidamente a louça e pousei-a num pano para secar.

— É sábado — devaneou.

Eu não retorqui.

— Não tens planos para esta noite? — perguntou subitamente.

— Não, pai, quero apenas dormir um pouco.

— Nenhum dos rapazes da cidade faz o teu género, é?

Estava desconfiado, mas tentava abordar o assunto de forma subtil.

— Não, ainda nenhum dos rapazes me chamou a atenção.

Tive o cuidado de não dar demasiada ênfase à palavra *rapazes* na minha demanda no sentido de responder a Charlie com a verdade.

— Pensei que talvez aquele Mike Newton... dissesse que ele era amável.

— Ele é *só* um amigo, pai.

— Bem, seja como for, és demasiado boa para todos eles. Espera até ingressares na faculdade para começares à procura.

O sonho de qualquer pai: que a sua filha saia de casa antes de as hormonas começarem a exercer os seus efeitos.

— Parece-me uma boa ideia — concordei ao subir as escadas.

— Boa noite, querida! — exclamou à medida que eu me afastava.

Estaria, sem dúvida, cuidadosamente à escuta durante todo o serão, esperando que eu tentasse esgueirar-me.

— Até amanhã, pai.

Até à meia-noite, quando entrares sorrateiramente no meu quarto para me controlares.

Esforcei-me por fazer com que as minhas passadas parecessem lentas e cansadas à medida que subia as escadas para me dirigir ao meu quarto. Fechei a porta, fazendo barulho suficiente para que ele pudesse ouvir, e, em seguida, corri em bicos de pés até à janela. Abri-a e inclinei-me, imergindo na noite. Os meus olhos perscrutaram a escuridão, as sombras impenetráveis das árvores.

— Edward? — sussurrei, sentindo-me idiota.

Discreta e risonha a resposta surgiu de trás de mim:

— Sim?

Eu virei-me rapidamente, com uma mão a precipitar-se para o meu pescoço com a surpresa.

Ele estava estendido na minha cama, com um enorme sorriso nos lábios, as mãos atrás da cabeça e os pés a balouçarem-se, suspensos, na extremidade: a imagem viva do à vontade.

— Oh! — exclamei, deixando-me cair de modo vacilante no chão.

— Desculpa.

Apertou os lábios, tentando dissimular o seu divertimento.

— Dá-me só um minuto para o meu coração recomeçar a bater.

Sentou-se lentamente, de modo a não voltar a sobressaltar-me. Em seguida, inclinou-se para a frente e estendeu os longos braços para pegar em mim, pela parte superior dos meus braços, como se eu fosse uma criança pequena. Sentou-me na cama, a seu lado.

— Porque é que não te sentas aqui comigo? — sugeriu, pousando a mão fria na minha. — Como é que está esse coração?

— Diz-me tu, estou certa de que consegues ouvi-lo melhor do que eu.

Senti o seu riso silencioso abanar a cama.

Ficámos ali sentados, em silêncio, por um momento, ouvindo o meu batimento cardíaco a abrandar. Reflecti sobre o facto de ter Edward no meu quarto, com o meu pai em casa.

— Posso ser humana durante um instante? — perguntei.

— Com certeza.

Fez um gesto com a mão, dizendo-me para prosseguir.

— Quieto! — exclamei, tentando parecer severa.

— Sim, senhora.

Então, fingiu ter-se transformado numa estátua à beira da minha cama.

Levantei-me de um salto, apanhando o pijama do chão e pegando na minha bolsa de produtos de higiene pessoal, que se encontrava em cima da secretária. Deixei a luz apagada e saí de mansinho, fechando a porta.

Conseguia ouvir o som da televisão propagar-se pelas escadas acima. Bati ruidosamente com a porta da casa de banho para que Charlie não subisse para me incomodar.

Tencionava apressar-me. Escovei os dentes com energia, tentando ser meticulosa e célere, eliminando todos os vestígios de lasanha. No entanto, a água quente do duche não podia ser apressada. Relaxou os músculos das minhas costas, acalmou-me a pulsação. O cheiro familiar do meu champô fez-me sentir a mesma pessoa daquela manhã. Tentei não pensar em Edward, sentado no meu quarto, à espera, pois, nesse caso, teria de recomeçar o processo calmante. Por fim, já não podia adiar mais. Fechei a torneira, limpando-me rapidamente e apressando-me de novo. Vesti a camisola de mangas curtas, repleta de buracos, e as calças de fato de treino cinzentas. Já era demasiado tarde para lamentar não ter trazido o pijama de seda Victoria's Secret que a minha mãe me oferecera há dois aniversários, cujas etiquetas eu ainda não retirara e que se encontrava guardado em alguma gaveta lá de casa.

Friccionei novamente a toalha no cabelo e, em seguida, escovei-o. Atirei a toalha para o cesto da roupa suja e guardei a escova e a pasta de dentes na bolsa. Depois, precipitei-me pelas escadas abaixo para que Charlie visse que eu vestira o pijama e tinha o cabelo molhado.

— Boa noite, pai.

— Boa noite, Bella.

Pareceu, de facto, espantado com a minha aparência. Talvez isso o impedisse de me controlar naquela noite.

Subi as escadas, galgando dois degraus de cada vez, tentando não fazer muito barulho, e precipitei-me para o quarto, fechando bem a porta depois de ter entrado.

Edward não se deslocara uma fracção de centímetro: uma escultura de Adónis em cima da minha colcha desbotada. Sorri e os lábios dele contraíram-se, com a estátua a ganhar vida.

Os seus olhos avaliaram-me, reparando no cabelo húmido e na camisola esburacada. Ele ergueu uma sobrancelha.

— Que giro.

Fiz um esgar.

— Não, fica-te bem.

— Obrigada — sussurrei.

Voltei para junto dele, sentando-me de pernas cruzadas a seu lado. Olhei para as estrias do chão de madeira.

— Para que foi tudo isso?

— O Charlie pensa que vou sair às escondidas.

— Ah!

Reflectiu sobre as minhas palavras.

— Porquê?

Como se não conseguisse conhecer a mente de Charlie muito mais claramente do que eu podia conjecturar.

— Pelos vistos, pareço estar um pouco entusiasmada de mais.

Ele ergueu-me o queixo, examinando o meu rosto.

— Na verdade, pareces estar um tanto animada.

Inclinou o seu rosto lentamente na direcção do meu, encostando a sua face fria à minha pele. Manteve-se absolutamente imóvel.

— Mmmmmm... — sussurrou.

Foi muito difícil, enquanto ele me tocava, formular uma pergunta coerente. Demorei um momento de concentração dispersa para principiar.

— Parece ser... muito mais fácil para ti, agora, estar perto de mim.

— É isso que te parece? — murmurou, com o nariz a deslizar até à curva do meu maxilar. Senti a mão dele, mais leve do que a asa de uma mariposa, afastar o meu cabelo, de modo a que os seus lábios pudessem tocar a cavidade debaixo da minha orelha.

— Muitíssimo mais fácil — disse eu, tentando expirar.

— Hum.

— Então, estava a perguntar-me... — principiei novamente, mas os seus dedos acariciavam-me lentamente a clavícula e eu perdi a linha de raciocínio.

— Sim? — murmurou.

— A que se deve isso? — a minha voz tremia, causando-me embaraço. — Que achas?

Senti o tremor da sua respiração no meu pescoço enquanto ele se ria.

— A mente domina a matéria.

Recuei. Quando me mexi, ele ficou paralisado e eu deixei de ouvir o som da sua respiração.

Entreolhámo-nos cautelosamente por um momento e, então, enquanto o seu maxilar cerrado se descontraiu aos poucos, a sua expressão tornou-se perplexa.

— Fiz algo errado?

— Não, pelo contrário. Estás a dar comigo em doida — expliquei.

Reflectiu sobre as minhas palavras durante breves instantes e, quando falou, pareceu satisfeito.

— A sério?

Um sorriso triunfante iluminou-lhe lentamente o rosto.

— Desejas uma salva de palmas? — perguntei sarcástica.

Ele esboçou um largo sorriso.

— Estou apenas agradavelmente surpreendido — esclareceu. — Ao longo dos últimos cem anos — a sua voz era provocadora — nunca imaginei nada disto. Não acreditava poder encontrar alguém com quem eu quisesse ficar... de uma forma diferente dos meus irmãos e irmãs. E, depois, descobrir, embora tudo seja novo para mim, que sou bom nisso... em estar contigo.

— Tu és bom em tudo — salientei.

Ele encolheu os ombros, assentindo nisso, e ambos nos rimos muito baixinho.

— Mas como é que pode ser tão fácil agora? — insisti. — Esta tarde...

— Não é *fácil* — suspirou. — Mas, esta tarde, eu ainda estava... indeciso. Peço-te desculpa pelo que aconteceu; o meu comportamento foi imperdoável.

— Imperdoável, não — discordei.

— Obrigado — sorriu. — Sabes — continuou, baixando agora o olhar —, não sabia ao certo se era suficientemente forte... — pegou numa das minhas mãos e encostou-a levemente ao seu rosto — e, enquanto havia aquela possibilidade de eu ser... subjugado... — aspirou o perfume do meu pulso —, estava... susceptível. Até eu me mentalizar de que *era* suficientemente forte, de que não havia mesmo nenhuma possibilidade de eu ir... de eu alguma vez conseguir...

Nunca o vira debater-se tão intensamente em busca de palavras. Era algo tão... humano.

— Então, já não existe qualquer possibilidade?

— A mente domina a matéria — repetiu, sorrindo, com os dentes resplandecentes mesmo na escuridão.

— Ena, foi fácil — disse eu.

Inclinou a cabeça para trás e riu-se, tão baixinho como num sussurro, mas ainda com exuberância.

— Fácil para *ti!* — corrigiu, tocando no meu nariz com a ponta do dedo.

De repente, o seu semblante ficou sério.

— Estou a tentar — sussurrou, com dor patente na voz. — Se se tornar... demasiado, estou bastante seguro de que serei capaz de partir.

Lancei-lhe um olhar irritado. Não me agradava que ele falasse em partir.

— E, amanhã, vai ser mais difícil — continuou. — Tive o teu cheiro na minha cabeça durante todo o dia e fiquei espantosamente dessensibilizado. Se ficar longe de ti, seja por que período de tempo for, terei de começar do princípio, ainda que não propriamente do nada, julgo eu.

— Então, não te vás embora — retorqui, incapaz de esconder a ânsia na minha voz.

— Isso calha-me bem — replicou, com o seu rosto a descontrair-se, esboçando um terno sorriso. — Traz as algemas; sou o teu prisioneiro.

No entanto, foram as suas longas mãos que manietaram os *meus* pulsos enquanto ele falava. Soltou a sua gargalhada silenciosa e melódica. Nesta noite, rira-se mais do que durante todo o tempo que eu já passara com ele.

— Pareces mais... optimista do que o habitual — observei. — Nunca te vi assim antes.

— Não é assim que deve ser? — sorriu. — A glória do primeiro amor e tudo isso. A diferença que existe entre ler a respeito de algo, vê-lo nos filmes e vivê-lo é incrível, não é?

— É muito diferente — concordei. — É mais vivo do que eu imaginara.

— Por exemplo — as suas palavras fluíam agora com maior rapidez e eu tinha de me concentrar para conseguir compreender tudo o que ele dizia —, o sentimento do ciúme. Já li a esse respeito uma centena de milhar de vezes, vi actores representarem-no num milhar de peças e filmes diferentes. Cria ter compreendido esse sentimento bastante claramente, mas fiquei muito abalado...

Fez um esgar.

— Recordas-te do dia em que o Mike te convidou para o baile?

Acenei com a cabeça, embora me lembrasse daquele dia por um motivo diferente:

— O dia em que voltaste a falar comigo.

— Fiquei surpreendido com o acesso de despeito, quase de fúria, que senti. A princípio, não identifiquei tal sentimento. Sentia-me mais exasperado do que o costume por não conseguir saber o que estavas a pensar, por que motivo recusaras o convite dele. Tê-lo-ias feito simplesmente pelo bem da tua amiga? Haveria mais alguém? Eu sabia que não tinha nenhum direito de me importar em qualquer dos casos. *Tentei* não me importar. Então, a fila começou a formar-se — soltou um riso abafado.

Carreguei o sobrolho na escuridão.

— Esperei, ansioso, além do razoável, por ouvir o que lhes responderias, observar as tuas expressões. Não conseguia negar o alívio que sentia ao ver o aborrecimento estampado no teu rosto. Mas não podia ter a certeza. Essa foi a primeira noite em que vim aqui. Debati-me durante toda a noite, ao observar-te enquanto dormias, com o hiato entre aquilo que sabia ser *correcto*, moral, ético e aquilo que eu *queria*. Sabia que, se continuasse a ignorar-te como deveria fazer ou partisse para uma ausência de alguns anos, até tu te ires embora, tu acabarias, um dia, por dar uma resposta afirmativa ao Mike ou a alguém como ele. Esse facto enfureceu-me. Então — sussurrou —, enquanto dormias, disseste o meu nome. Falaste com tanta clareza que, a princípio, pensei que tivesses acordado. Mas reviraste-te na cama com inquietação, balbuciaste o meu nome uma vez mais e suspiraste. O sentimento que me assolou nesse momento foi perturbador, desconcertante. E eu soube que não podia continuar a ignorar-te.

Ficou calado durante um momento, porventura ouvindo o batimento subitamente irregular do meu coração.

— Mas o ciúme... é algo estranho. Muito mais intenso do que eu poderia ter imaginado. E irracional! Agora mesmo, quando o Charlie te interrogou acerca daquele desprezível Mike Newton...

Abanou a cabeça furiosamente.

— Devia ter calculado que estavas a ouvir — resmunguei.

— É evidente.

— Mas *isso* fez-te mesmo ficar com ciúmes?

— Sou um novato nestas andanças. Estás a ressuscitar o humano que há em mim e tudo parece mais intenso por ser recente.

— Mas, sinceramente — trocei —, para isso te incomodar, depois de eu ter ouvido que a Rosalie (a Rosalie, que é a beleza em pessoa) estava destinada a ser tua... Com Emmett ou sem Emmett, como é que eu posso competir com isso?

— Não existe nenhuma competição.

Os seus dentes cintilaram. Colocou as minhas mãos unidas nas suas costas, segurando-me contra o seu peito. Mantive-me tão quieta quanto consegui, respirando mesmo com cautela.

— Eu *sei* que não existe nenhuma competição — murmurei para a sua pele fria. — É esse o problema.

— É claro que a Rosalie é linda, à sua maneira, mas, mesmo que não fosse como uma irmã para mim, mesmo que o lugar do Emmett não fosse ao lado dela, ela nunca exerceria um décimo, não, um centésimo da atracção que tu exerces sobre mim.

Ele estava agora sério, pensativo.

— Durante mais de noventa anos, movimentei-me entre os da minha espécie e da tua... sempre julgando que era um ser pleno, sem perceber aquilo que procurava e sem encontrar nada, pois tu ainda não nasceras.

— Não me parece muito justo — sussurrei, com o meu rosto ainda apoiado no seu peito, ouvindo-o inspirar e expirar. — Não tive de esperar nada. Porque é que hei-de safar-me tão facilmente?

— Tens razão — concordou, divertido. — Devia, sem dúvida, tornar isto mais difícil para ti.

Libertou uma das mãos, soltando o meu pulso apenas para o unir cuidadosamente à sua outra mão. Passou a mão pelo meu cabelo molhado, desde o cimo da minha cabeça até à minha cintura.

— Tens apenas de arriscar a tua vida a cada segundo que passas comigo, o que, seguramente, não é muito. Tens apenas de voltar as costas à natureza, à humanidade... mas que importância é que isso tem?

— Muito pouca, não me sinto privada de nada.

— Por enquanto.

A sua voz estava, de repente, marcada pela antiga dor.

Tentei recuar, olhar-lhe no rosto, mas a sua mão segurava os meus pulsos com uma força inquebrantável.

— Que é que... — comecei a perguntar, quando o seu corpo ficou alerta.

Eu paralisei, mas, subitamente, ele libertou-me as mãos e desapareceu. Por pouco não caí com a cara no chão.

— Deita-te! — exclamou.

Não conseguia perceber de onde ele falava, na escuridão.

Coloquei-me debaixo da colcha, enroscando-me de lado, da forma como costumava dormir. Ouvi a porta a abrir-se e Charlie espreitou para se assegurar de que eu estava onde deveria estar. Mantive uma respiração regular, exagerando o movimento.

Decorreu um longo minuto. Fiquei à escuta, não sabendo ao certo se ouvira a porta a fechar-se. Depois, o braço frio de Edward envolveu-me, debaixo dos cobertores, estando os seus lábios junto ao meu ouvido.

— És uma péssima actriz; eu diria que, para ti, enveredar por essa carreira está fora de questão.

— Bolas! — resmunguei.

O meu coração disparava no peito.

Ele cantarolou uma melodia que eu não reconheci; parecia uma canção de embalar.

Deteve-se.

— Queres que cante até adormeceres?

— Pois sim — ri-me. — Como se eu conseguisse dormir contigo aqui.

— Fazes isso constantemente — relembrou-me.

— Mas eu não *sabia* que estavas aqui — retorqui com frieza.

— Então, se não queres dormir... — insinuou, ignorando o meu tom de voz.

A minha respiração ficou suspensa.

— Se não quero dormir...?

Soltou um riso abafado.

— Nesse caso, o que queres fazer?

A princípio, não consegui responder.

— Não sei bem — acabei por dizer.

— Quando decidires, avisa-me.

Conseguia sentir o seu hálito fresco no meu pescoço, o nariz a passar levemente pelo meu maxilar, aspirando.

— Pensei que ficaras dessensibilizado.

— O facto de estar a abster-me do vinho não implica que não consiga apreciar o seu aroma — sussurrou. — Tens um cheiro muito floral, a alfazema... ou frésia — observou. — Faz crescer água na boca.

— Pois, para mim, um dia não é dia sem que *alguém* me diga quão comestível o meu cheiro me torna.

Ele soltou um riso abafado e, em seguida, suspirou.

— Já decidi o que quero fazer — disse-lhe. — Quero saber mais sobre ti.

— Pergunta-me o que quiseres.

Analisei todas as questões que tinha a colocar em busca da mais essencial.

— Porque é que o fazes? — perguntei. — Ainda não consigo compreender como é que consegues esforçar-te tanto por resistir àquilo que tu... és. Por favor, não me interpretes mal; é evidente que eu fico satisfeita por o fazeres. Só não vejo por que motivo é que te dás a esse trabalho.

Ele hesitou antes de responder.

— Essa é uma boa pergunta e tu não és a primeira a fazê-la. Também os outros (a maioria dos que pertencem à nossa espécie, que está bastante satisfeita com a nossa sorte) se interrogam acerca do nosso modo de vida. Mas, sabes, o mero facto de nos ter sido... dada uma certa capacidade... não implica que não possamos optar por ascender a um plano mais elevado, conquistar os limites de um destino que nenhum de nós quis. Tentar conservar a humanidade essencial que conseguirmos.

Eu permanecia estática, imobilizada num silêncio de assombro.

— Adormeceste? — sussurrou ele após alguns minutos.

— Não.

— É só em relação a isso que sentes curiosidade?

Eu revirei os olhos.

— Não propriamente.

— O que mais desejas saber?

— Por que motivo consegues adivinhar os pensamentos? Porquê só tu? E a Alice, que prevê o futuro... Porque é que isso acontece?

Senti-o encolher os ombros na escuridão.

— Não sabemos ao certo. O Carlisle tem uma teoria... Acredita que todos nós trazemos connosco algo dos nossos traços humanos mais marcantes para esta vida, onde estes se intensificam; como, por exemplo, as nossas mentes e os nossos sentidos. Ele julga que eu já devia ser muito sensível aos pensamentos daqueles que me rodeavam e que a Alice possuía algum poder de clarividência, onde quer que ela se encontrasse.

— Que é que ele e os outros trouxeram para a actual vida?

— O Carlisle trouxe a sua compaixão. A Esme trouxe a sua capacidade de amar apaixonadamente. O Emmett trouxe a sua força, a Rosalie a sua... tenacidade, que também se poderia chamar teimosia — soltou um riso abafado. — O Jasper é muito interessante. Ele era bastante carismático na sua primeira vida, capaz de influenciar aqueles que o rodeavam no sentido de verem as coisas à sua maneira. Agora, é capaz de manipular as emoções daqueles que o rodeiam; por exemplo, acalmar uma sala repleta de pessoas enfurecidas ou, pelo contrário, animar uma multidão letárgica. É um dom extremamente subtil.

Reflecti sobre as características que ele descrevia, tentando assimilá-las. Ele esperou pacientemente enquanto eu pensava.

— Então, como é que tudo começou? Quero dizer, o Carlisle transformou-te. Logo, alguém o deve ter transformando e por aí adiante...

— Bem, qual foi a vossa origem? A evolução? A criação? Não podemos ter evoluído da mesma forma que as outras espécies, como presa e predador? Ou, então, se não acreditares que todo este mundo poderia apenas ter-se formado espontaneamente, o que, mesmo para mim, é difícil de aceitar, será assim tão difícil acreditar que a mesma força que criou o delicado peixe-anjo juntamente com o tubarão, a foca-bebé e a baleia-assassina, poderia criar as nossas duas espécies em conjunto?

— Deixa-me ver se entendi: eu sou a foca-bebé, certo?

— Certo.

Ele riu-se e algo tocou os meus cabelos, teriam sido os seus lábios?

Eu queria virar-me na direcção dele, para ver se eram mesmo os seus lábios que estavam a ser pressionados contra o meu cabelo, mas tinha de me portar bem, não queria tornar aquilo ainda mais difícil para ele.

— Estás pronta para dormir? — perguntou ele, interrompendo o breve silêncio. — Ou tens mais perguntas a fazer?

— Só um milhão ou dois.

— Temos o dia de amanhã, o seguinte e o outro... — relembrou-me.

Eu sorri, ficando eufórica só de pensar nisso.

— Tens a certeza de que não vais desaparecer de manhã? — queria que este ponto ficasse assente. — Afinal, és um ser mítico.

— Eu não te abandonarei.

A sua voz tinha o cunho de uma promessa.

— Então, só mais uma, esta noite...

Enrubesci. A escuridão não ajudava muito, estou certa de que ele sentiu o súbito calor sob a minha pele.

— De que se trata?

— Não, esquece. Mudei de ideias.

— Bella, podes perguntar-me o que quiseres.

Eu não repliquei e ele lamentou-se:

— Eu estou sempre a pensar que o facto de não conseguir adivinhar os teus pensamentos se tornará menos frustrante, mas só *piora* a cada dia que passa.

— Ainda bem que não consegues adivinhar os meus pensamentos. Já é suficientemente mau que escutes o que digo enquanto durmo.

— Por favor? — a sua voz era tão persuasiva, tão impossível de resistir...

Abanei a cabeça.

— Se não me disseres, partirei apenas do princípio de que se trata de algo muito pior do que realmente é — ameaçou sombriamente. — Por favor! — exclamou, com aquele tom de voz suplicante.

— Bem — principiei, contente por ele não poder ver o meu rosto.

— Sim?

— Referiste que a Rosalie e o Emmett vão casar em breve... Esse... casamento... é semelhante ao dos humanos?

Ele riu-se, agora com seriedade, compreendendo.

— Era *aí* que querias chegar?

Eu remexia-me, incapaz de responder.

— Sim, suponho que é praticamente idêntico — disse ele. — Já te disse que a maioria dos desejos humanos estão presentes, escondendo-se apenas por trás de desejos mais intensos.

— Ah.

Nada mais consegui dizer.

— Havia alguma intenção por trás da tua curiosidade?

— Bem, de facto, eu interroguei-me... acerca de nós... um dia...

Ele ficou imediatamente sério, o que percebi através da súbita imobilidade do seu corpo. Também eu paralisei, reagindo automaticamente.

— Acho que... isso... não seria possível no nosso caso.

— Por ser demasiado difícil para ti, se nós estivéssemos assim tão... próximos?

— Isso constitui, sem dúvida, um problema, mas não era nisso que eu estava a pensar. É só que tu és tão delicada, tão frágil. Tenho de ter cuidado com os meus actos a cada momento que passamos juntos, de modo a não te magoar. Podia matar-te com bastante facilidade, Bella, apenas por acaso.

A sua voz transformara-se apenas num suave murmúrio. Deslocou a palma gélida da sua mão para pousá-la na minha face.

— Se eu fosse demasiado precipitado... se, por um segundo, não prestasse atenção suficiente, podia estender a mão, pretendendo tocar o teu rosto, e esmagar-te o crânio por engano. Não tens noção de quão incrivelmente *quebradiça* és. Nunca, nunca posso dar-me ao luxo de perder qualquer tipo de controlo quando estou contigo.

Esperou que eu retorquisse, ficando ansioso quando não o fiz.

— Estás assustada? — perguntou.

Aguardei um instante até responder, de modo a que as minhas palavras correspondessem à verdade.

— Não, estou bem.

Ele pareceu ponderar durante um momento.

— Agora, estou curioso — declarou, novamente com uma voz branda. — Tu já...? — deixou a frase por terminar de modo sugestivo.

— É claro que não — ruborizei. — Já te disse que nunca me senti assim em relação a ninguém, nem nada que se parecesse.

— Eu sei. Só que conheço os pensamentos das outras pessoas e sei que o amor e a luxúria nem sempre mantêm a mesma companhia.

— Para mim, mantêm. Pelo menos, agora que existem para mim — suspirei.

— Ainda bem. Pelo menos isso temos em comum — disse, parecendo satisfeito.

— Os teus instintos humanos... — principiei, enquanto ele esperava. — Bem, consideras-me minimamente atraente *nesse* aspecto?

Ele riu-se e despenteou-me ligeiramente o cabelo quase seco.

— Posso não ser humano, mas sou homem — assegurou-me.

Bocejei involuntariamente.

— Já respondi às tuas perguntas, agora, devias dormir — insistiu.

— Não sei bem se consigo.

— Queres que me vá embora?

— Não! — exclamei num tom de voz demasiado elevado.

Ele riu-se e, depois, começou a cantarolar a mesma canção de embalar que me era desconhecida. A voz de um arcanjo a soar suavemente ao meu ouvido.

Estando mais cansada do que pensara, exausta na sequência do longo dia que fora marcado por uma tensão mental e emocional como eu jamais sentira, adormeci nos seus braços frios.

Capítulo Quinze

Os Cullen

A claridade ensombrada de mais um dia nublado acabou por me acordar. Coloquei o braço diante dos olhos, estando ensonada e encandeada. Algo, um sonho a tentar ser lembrado, debatia-se por irromper pela minha consciência. Gemi e virei-me de lado, esperando que o sono viesse novamente. Então, o dia anterior voltou a inundar o meu consciente.

— Oh!

Sentei-me tão depressa que a minha cabeça começou a andar à roda.

— O teu cabelo parece uma meda de feno... mas agrada-me.

A sua voz serena era projectada da cadeira de baloiço que se encontrava ao canto.

— Edward! Ficaste!

Eu rejubilei e, irreflectidamente, atravessei o quarto e lancei-me no seu colo. No instante em que os meus pensamentos alcançaram os meus actos, paralisei, profundamente espantada com o meu próprio entusiasmo desenfreado. Fixei o olhar nele, receando ter pisado o risco errado.

No entanto, ele riu-se.

— É evidente — retorquiu, surpreendido, mas parecendo satisfeito com a minha reacção.

Passava as mãos pelas minhas costas.

Pousei cautelosamente a cabeça no ombro dele, aspirando o cheiro da sua pele.

— Estava certa de que fora um sonho.

— Não és assim tão criativa — escarneceu.

— O Charlie! — lembrei-me, pondo-me irreflectidamente de pé, dando um salto e dirigindo-me à porta.

— Saiu há uma hora, depois de ter voltado a ligar os cabos da tua bateria, permite-me acrescentar. Tenho de reconhecer que fiquei desiludido. Seria mesmo necessário só isso para te travar, se estivesses decidida a ir?

Ponderei enquanto estava de pé, desejando voltar para junto dele, mas receando ter o hálito de quem acaba de acordar.

— Não costumas estar tão confusa de manhã — comentou.

Abriu os braços para que eu voltasse para junto dele. Um convite quase irresistível.

— Preciso de outro momento humano — confessei.

— Eu espero.

Dei um salto até à casa de banho, com as minhas emoções irreconhecíveis. Não me reconhecia, nem por dentro, nem por fora. O rosto no espelho era praticamente o de uma estranha: olhos demasiado brilhantes, febris manchas rubras a tingir-me as maçãs do rosto. Depois de ter escovado os dentes, dediquei-me a tentar esticar o caótico emaranhado do meu cabelo. Lavei o rosto com água fria e tentei respirar normalmente, sem êxito digno de nota. Voltei para o quarto quase em passo de corrida.

O facto de ele estar ali, com os braços ainda à minha espera, parecia um milagre. Estendeu-mos e o meu coração começou a bater de modo irregular.

— Bem-vinda — murmurou, tomando-me nos seus braços.

Balançou-me de um lado para o outro durante alguns instantes em silêncio, até eu ter reparado que as suas roupas eram outras e o seu cabelo estava macio.

— Saíste? — perguntei, em tom acusador, tocando no colarinho da sua camisa lavada.

— Dificilmente podia sair com as mesmas roupas com que entrei. O que iriam os vizinhos pensar?

Fiz beicinho.

— Estavas a dormir profundamente. Não perdi nada. — Os seus olhos cintilaram. — Já falaras antes.

Lamentei-me.

— O que é que ouviste?

Os seus olhos dourados tornaram-se muito afáveis.

— Disseste que me amavas.

— Já sabias isso — relembrei-lhe, afastando a cabeça.

— Mas foi igualmente agradável ouvir.

Escondi o rosto no seu ombro.

— Amo-te — sussurrei.

— Agora, és a minha vida — retorquiu simplesmente.

Não havia nada mais a dizer naquele momento. Ele balançou-nos para a frente e para trás à medida que o quarto foi ficando mais iluminado.

— Está na hora do pequeno-almoço — acabou por dizer, de modo descontraído, decerto para provar que se lembrava de todas as minhas fraquezas humanas.

Assim, agarrei o meu pescoço com ambas as mãos e fixei-o com os olhos arregalados. O sobressalto ficou estampado no seu rosto.

— Estava a brincar! — exclamei, soltando um riso reprimido. — E disseste tu que eu não sabia representar!

Ele franziu o sobrolho de indignação.

— Não teve graça.

— Teve muita graça e tu sabes.

Examinei, porém, os seus olhos dourados cuidadosamente, de modo a certificar-me de que estava perdoada. Pelos vistos, estava.

— Queres que reformule a frase? — perguntou. — Está na hora do pequeno-almoço da humana.

— Ah, está bem.

Atirou-me para o seu ombro pétreo, delicadamente, mas com uma agilidade que me cortou a respiração. Protestei enquanto me levava facilmente pelas escadas abaixo, mas ele ignorou-me. Sentou-me delicadamente, na posição correcta, numa cadeira.

A cozinha estava luminosa, alegre, parecendo absorver a minha disposição.

— Que há para o pequeno-almoço? — perguntei prazenteiramente, o que o deixou desorientado por um instante.

— Ah, não sei bem. O que gostarias de tomar?

A sua fronte marmórea franziu-se.

Esbocei um largo sorriso, levantando-me de um salto.

— Não faz mal, eu arranjo-me bastante bem sozinha. Observa-me enquanto caço.

Encontrei uma taça e um pacote de cereais. Conseguia sentir os seus olhos pousados em mim enquanto verti o leite e peguei numa colher. Coloquei a minha comida sobre a mesa e, em seguida, detive-me.

— Queres que te prepare algo? — perguntei, não desejando ser indelicada.

Ele revirou os olhos.

— Limita-te a comer, Bella.

Sentei-me à mesa, observando-o enquanto levei uma colherada à boca. Ele olhava-me fixamente, analisando cada movimento meu. Fiquei inibida. Engoli a comida que mastigava para falar, de modo a distraí-lo.

— O que temos marcado na agenda para hoje? — perguntei.

— Hum.

Observei-o enquanto formulava cuidadosamente a sua resposta.

— Que dirias quanto a conhecer a minha família?

Engasguei-me.

— Agora, já tens medo?

Parecia esperançoso.

— Já — confessei.

Como poderia negá-lo? Ele conseguia vê-lo nos meus olhos.

— Não te preocupes — esboçou um sorriso pretensioso. — Eu protejo-te.

— Eu não tenho medo *deles* — expliquei. — Tenho medo de que eles não... gostem de mim. Não vão ficar, bem, admirados por levares alguém... como eu... a casa para conhecê-los? Eles sabem que eu conheço a verdade a respeito deles?

— Oh, eles já sabem tudo. Ontem, já tinham feito apostas, sabes — sorriu, mas a sua voz estava ríspida —, a respeito de eu te trazer ou não de volta, ainda que não consiga imaginar o motivo por que ninguém se atreveu a apostar contra a Alice. De qualquer modo, nós não temos segredos no seio da família. Não é propriamente exequível, com a minha capacidade de adivinhar os pensamentos, o dom da Alice de prever o futuro e tudo isso.

— E o Jasper a fazer-vos sentir animados e inebriados para desembucharem tudo, não te esqueças.

— Prestaste atenção — esboçou um sorriso de aprovação.

— Tenho fama de o fazer de vez em quando.

Fiz um esgar.

— Então, a Alice previu a minha chegada?

A sua reacção foi estranha.

— Foi mais ou menos isso — disse pouco à vontade, voltando-se de costas para que eu não conseguisse ver-lhe os olhos.

Eu fitei-o com curiosidade.

— Isso é alguma coisa que preste? — perguntou, virando-se, de repente, para mim outra vez e olhando para o meu pequeno-almoço com uma expressão de troça estampada no rosto. — Para ser sincero, não parece muito apetitoso.

— Bem, não é nenhum urso-pardo irascível... — murmurei, ignorando-o quando me fitou com um ar zangado.

Ainda me perguntava porque é que ele reagira daquela maneira quando mencionei Alice. Apressei-me a comer os cereais, especulando.

Ele encontrava-se de pé, no meio da cozinha, novamente tal qual a estátua de Adónis, olhando de modo absorto pela janela das traseiras.

Depois, os seus olhos voltaram a incidir sobre mim e ele esboçou o seu sorriso de partir o coração.

— E, na minha opinião, tu também devias apresentar-me ao teu pai.

— Ele já te conhece — relembrei-lhe.

— Como teu namorado, quero eu dizer.

Fitei-o com desconfiança.

— Porquê?

— Não é costume? — perguntou inocentemente.

— Não sei — confessei.

A minha experiência em termos de namoros proporcionava-me poucos pontos de referência pelos quais pudesse reger-me. Não que quaisquer regras normais de namoro se aplicassem ao nosso caso.

— Sabes, não é necessário. Eu não espero que tu... Quero dizer, não tens de fingir por minha causa.

O seu sorriso expressava paciência.

— Não estou a fingir.

Empurrei os restos dos cereais pelo rebordo da taça, mordendo o lábio.

— Vais contar ao Charlie que eu sou o rapaz que namora contigo ou não? — interrogou.

— É isso que és?

Reprimi o meu retraimento interior só de pensar em Edward, Charlie e a palavra *namorado* na mesma sala ao mesmo tempo.

— Tenho de admitir que se trata de uma interpretação livre da palavra «rapaz».

— Na verdade, tinha a impressão de que eras algo mais — confessei, olhando para a mesa.

— Bem, não sei se necessitamos de lhe fornecer todos os pormenores macabros.

Estendeu a mão por cima da mesa para me erguer o queixo com um dedo frio e delicado.

— Mas ele vai precisar de uma explicação para o facto de estar constantemente presente. Não quero que o chefe Swan interponha uma providência cautelar contra mim.

— Estarás mesmo? — perguntei, subitamente ansiosa. — Estarás mesmo aqui?

— Enquanto tu me quiseres — assegurou-me.

— Eu hei-de querer-te sempre — avisei-o. — Eternamente.

Ele contornou lentamente a mesa e, detendo-se a alguns centímetros de distância, estendeu a mão para tocar a minha face com as pontas dos dedos. A sua expressão estava impenetrável.

— Isso entristece-te? — interroguei.

Ele não respondeu. Fixou os meus olhos durante um período de tempo incomensurável.

— Já terminaste? — acabou por perguntar.

Levantei-me de um salto.

— Já.

— Vai vestir-te, eu espero aqui.

Foi difícil escolher o que vestir. Duvidava de que existissem alguns livros de etiqueta que especificassem que roupas usar quando o nosso namorado-vampiro nos leva a sua casa para conhecermos a sua família de vampiros. Foi um alívio pensar na palavra para comigo mesma. Eu sabia que me coibia intencionalmente de o fazer.

Acabei por optar pela minha única saia, comprida, de cor caqui, mas informal. Enverguei a blusa azul-escura que ele elogiara certa vez. Uma rápida olhadela ao espelho fez-me perceber que o meu cabelo estava completamente impossível, pelo que o apanhei num rabo-de-cavalo.

— Pronto.

Desci as escadas aos pulos.

— Estou decente.

Estava à minha espera ao fundo das escadas, mais perto do que eu pensara, e saltei para junto dele. Apoiou-me, devolvendo-me o equilíbrio e segurando-me a uma cuidadosa distância durante alguns instantes antes de, de repente, me puxar para mais perto de si.

— Estás mais uma vez enganada — murmurou-me ao ouvido.

— Estás absolutamente indecente. Ninguém devia ter uma aparência tão tentadora, não é justo.

— Tentadora em que aspecto? — perguntei. — Posso trocar de roupa...

Ele suspirou, abanando a cabeça.

— És *tão* absurda.

Encostou delicadamente os lábios frios à minha testa e a sala

começou a andar à roda. O cheiro do seu hálito impossibilitava-
-me o raciocínio.

— Queres que te explique em que aspecto estás a tentar-me?
— perguntou.

Tratava-se claramente de uma pergunta retórica. Os seus dedos
percorreram-me lentamente a coluna vertebral, com a respiração a
incidir mais rapidamente sobre a minha pele. As minhas mãos
apoiavam-se, sem energia, no seu peito e senti-me zonza. Ele inclinou, devagarinho, a cabeça e os seus lábios frios tocaram os
meus pela segunda vez, com muito cuidado, separando-os ligeiramente.

Então, sucumbi.

— Bella? — a sua voz estava inquieta ao agarrar-me para me
manter de pé.

— Tu... fizeste-me... desmaiar — acusei-o, sentindo-me tonta.

— O que hei-de fazer contigo? — resmungou, exasperado. —
Ontem, beijei-te e atacaste-me! Hoje, perdes os sentidos!

Ri debilmente, deixando que os seus braços me sustentassem
enquanto a minha cabeça girava.

— Afinal, não sou bom em tudo — suspirou.

— O problema reside aí.

Continuava a sentir-me tonta.

— És demasiado bom. Extraordinariamente bom.

— Sentes-te enjoada? — perguntou. Já me vira assim antes.

— Não, não foi, de todo, o mesmo tipo de desfalecimento.
Não sei o que aconteceu.

Abanei a cabeça como quem pede desculpa.

— Acho que me esqueci de respirar.

— Não posso levar-te a parte nenhuma nesse estado.

— Eu estou bem — insisti. — Seja como for, a tua família vai
pensar que eu sou louca, logo, que diferença faz?

Ele avaliou a minha expressão por um momento.

— Adoro a forma como essa cor condiz com a tua pele — referiu inesperadamente.

Eu corei de prazer e desviei o olhar.

— Escuta, estou a esforçar-me imenso por não pensar naquilo que estou prestes a fazer, por isso, podemos ir já embora? — perguntei.

— E estás preocupada, não por ires conhecer uma casa cheia de vampiros, mas por pensares que esses vampiros não irão aceitar-te, correcto?

— É isso mesmo — respondi imediatamente, disfarçando a minha surpresa perante o emprego descontraído da palavra por parte dele.

Ele abanou a cabeça.

— És incrível.

Apercebi-me, enquanto ele conduzia para fora da zona principal da cidade, de que não fazia a menor ideia onde ele morava. Atravessámos a ponte sobre o rio Calawah, com a estrada a serpentear em direcção a Norte e as casas a passarem rapidamente por nós, sendo cada vez maiores e mais espaçadas entre si. De repente, já passáramos todas as casas e atravessávamos uma floresta brumosa. Eu tentava decidir se deveria perguntar ou ser paciente quando ele virou bruscamente para uma estrada por alcatroar. Não estava assinalada, mal sendo visível entre os fetos. A floresta avançava de ambos os lados, deixando a estrada que se estendia à nossa frente apenas discernível ao longo de alguns metros ao contorcer-se, qual serpente, à volta das árvores antigas.

Então, alguns quilómetros depois, os bosques tornaram-se menos densos e estávamos subitamente num pequeno prado ou seria, na verdade, um campo relvado? No entanto, a obscuridade da floresta não abrandou, pois havia seis cedros primevos que lançavam sombra sobre cerca de meio hectare com o longo alcance dos seus ramos. Estendiam essa sombra protectora até às paredes da casa que se erguia entre eles, tornando obsoleto o alpendre que circundava o rés-do-chão.

Não sei o que esperara, mas não era, decididamente, aquilo. A casa era intemporal, airosa e tinha, provavelmente, cem anos. Estava pintada de um suave e esmorecido tom de branco, tinha três andares de altura, era rectangular e bem proporcionada. As portas e as janelas faziam parte da estrutura original ou, então, eram uma imitação perfeita. A minha *pick-up* era a única viatura à vista. Conseguia ouvir o rio por perto, escondido na escuridão da floresta.

— Ena.

— Gostas? — sorriu.

— Tem... um certo encanto.

Puxou a extremidade do meu rabo-de-cavalo e soltou um riso abafado.

— Estás preparada? — perguntou, abrindo-me a porta.

— Nem um pouco, vamos.

Tentei rir, mas o riso parecia ficar preso na minha garganta. Passei a mão pelo cabelo com nervosismo.

— Estás linda!

Pegou na minha mão com à vontade, sem pensar.

Caminhámos ao longo da sombra carregada até ao alpendre. Eu sabia que ele conseguia sentir a minha tensão, o seu polegar desenhava círculos tranquilizadores nas costas da minha mão.

Abriu-me a porta.

O interior era ainda mais surpreendente, menos previsível do que o exterior. Extremamente luminoso, amplo e espaçoso. Inicialmente, deviam ser várias divisões, mas as paredes tinham sido suprimidas da maior parte do rés-do-chão de modo a criar um espaço amplo. A parede das traseiras, virada para Sul, fora integralmente substituída por vidro e, para lá da sombra dos cedros, o campo relvado estendia-se, de forma despojada, até ao largo rio. Uma maciça escadaria curva dominava o lado ocidental da sala. As paredes, o tecto de vigas elevadas, os soalhos e os grossos tapetes eram tingidos de variados tons de branco.

À espera para nos cumprimentar, mesmo à esquerda da porta, numa parte elevada do piso junto a um espectacular piano de cauda, estavam os pais de Edward.

Eu já vira, é claro, o Dr. Cullen, mas não consegui evitar ficar novamente impressionada com a sua juventude, com a sua afrontosa perfeição. A seu lado, depreendi que estava Esme, o único membro da família que eu nunca vira. Tinha os mesmos traços belos e pálidos de todos os restantes. Havia algo no seu rosto em forma de coração, nas ondas dos seus cabelos macios da cor do caramelo, que me fazia lembrar as ingénuas da era do cinema mudo. Era pequena, esguia, mas menos angular, com formas mais torneadas do que os outros. Ambos envergavam trajes informais, de cores que combinavam com o interior da casa. Esboçaram um sorriso de boas-vindas, mas não fizeram qualquer movimento no sentido de se aproximarem de nós. Supus que tentavam não me assustar.

— Carlisle, Esme — a voz de Edward quebrou o breve silêncio —, apresento-vos a Bella.

— És muito bem-vinda, Bella.

O andar de Carlisle era calculado, cuidadoso, à medida que se aproximava de mim. Ergueu a mão com hesitação e eu avancei para lha apertar.

— É um prazer voltar a vê-lo, Dr. Cullen.

— Por favor, trata-me por Carlisle.

— Carlisle.

Dirigi-lhe um sorriso rasgado, com a minha súbita confiança a surpreender-me. Sentia o alívio de Edward a meu lado.

Esme sorriu e avançou também, estendendo a mão na direcção da minha. O seu aperto de mão frio e pétreo foi exactamente como eu esperava.

— É um imenso prazer conhecer-te — afirmou com sinceridade.

— Obrigada. Também estou feliz por conhecê-la.

E, de facto, estava. Foi como conhecer uma personagem de conto de fadas — a Branca de Neve, em carne e osso.

— Onde estão a Alice e o Jasper? — perguntou Edward, mas ninguém respondeu, visto que eles acabavam de aparecer no cimo da larga escadaria.

— Olá, Edward! — exclamou Alice com entusiasmo.

Desceu as escadas a correr, uma visão de cabelos negros e pele branca, parando súbita e graciosamente diante de mim. Carlisle e Esme lançaram-lhe olhares admoestadores, mas a sua atitude agradou-me. Era natural, para ela, pelo menos.

— Olá, Bella! — disse Alice, dando um salto para a frente para me beijar na face.

Se Carlisle e Esme pareciam cautelosos anteriormente, agora pareciam estupefactos. Também havia surpresa nos meus olhos, mas eu estava igualmente muito satisfeita por ela parecer aceitar-me de forma tão plena. Fiquei sobressaltada ao sentir Edward contrair-se a meu lado. Olhei de relance para o seu rosto, mas a sua expressão era indecifrável.

— É verdade que cheiras bem, nunca reparara — comentou ela, para meu grande constrangimento.

Mais ninguém sabia ao certo o que dizer e, de repente, chegou Jasper, alto e leonino. Uma sensação de bem-estar invadiu-me e, de repente, sentia-me à vontade, apesar do sítio onde me encontrava. Edward olhava fixamente para Jasper, erguendo uma sobrancelha, e eu lembrei-me das capacidades deste último.

— Olá, Bella — disse Jasper.

Manteve-se a uma certa distância, não fazendo menção de me apertar a mão. Era, porém, impossível sentirmo-nos pouco à vontade perto dele.

— Olá, Jasper.

Sorri-lhe timidamente e, depois, fiz o mesmo aos restantes.

— É um prazer conhecê-los a todos. Têm uma casa muito bonita — acrescentei num tom convencional.

— Obrigada — retorquiu Esme. — Estamos muito contentes por teres vindo.

Ela falava com sentimento e eu apercebi-me de que me achava corajosa.

Também me apercebi da ausência de Rosalie e de Emmett e lembrei-me da demasiado inocente resposta negativa de Edward, quando lhe perguntara se os outros não gostavam de mim.

A expressão de Carlisle distraiu-me desta linha de raciocínio, olhava intencionalmente para Edward com uma expressão intensa. Pelo canto do olho, vi Edward acenar uma vez com a cabeça.

Desviei o olhar, tentando ser educada. Voltei-me novamente na direcção do belo instrumento que se encontrava sobre o estrado junto da porta. Lembrei-me de repente da minha fantasia de infância, segundo a qual, se alguma vez ganhasse a lotaria, compraria um piano de cauda para a minha mãe. Ela não era realmente boa, tocando apenas para si mesma no nosso piano vertical, que fora comprado em segunda mão, mas eu adorava vê-la tocar. Ficava feliz, absorta. Nesses momentos, afigurava-se-me como sendo um ser novo e misterioso, alguém extrínseco à pessoa de «mãe» que eu tomava por certa. Ela inscrevera-me, evidentemente, em aulas de piano, mas, como a maioria das crianças, lamuriei-me até que me deixou desistir.

A Esme reparou no meu alheamento.

— Tocas? — perguntou, inclinando a cabeça na direcção do piano.

Abanei a cabeça.

— Nada. Mas é tão belo. É seu?

— Não — riu-se. — O Edward não te contou que era um amante de música?

— Não.

Olhei a sua expressão subitamente inocente com os olhos semicerrados.

— Creio que devia ter calculado.

Esme ergueu as suas delicadas sobrancelhas, confusa.

— O Edward consegue fazer tudo, não é? — comentei.

Jasper soltou um riso reprimido e Esme lançou a Edward um olhar reprovador.

— Espero que não tenhas andado a exibir-te, é uma falta de educação — censurou-o.

— Só um pouco — riu-se de modo espontâneo.

O rosto dela enterneceu-se ao ouvi-lo rir e ambos trocaram um breve olhar que eu não compreendi, embora o semblante de Esme quase parecesse presumido.

— Na verdade, tem sido demasiado modesto — corrigi.

— Bem, toca para ela — incitou Esme.

— Acabou de dizer que o exibicionismo é uma falta de educação — contrapôs ele.

— Todas as regras têm as suas excepções — retorquiu ela.

— Gostava de te ouvir tocar! — exclamei.

— Então, está decidido — disse Esme, empurrando-o, em seguida, na direcção do piano.

Ele arrastou-me atrás de si, sentando-me no banco a seu lado.

Lançou-me um olhar demorado e exasperado antes de se voltar para as teclas.

Depois, os seus dedos fluíram agilmente pelo marfim e a sala foi preenchida por uma composição tão complexa, tão exuberante, que era impossível acreditar que apenas um par de mãos tocava. Senti o meu queixo cair, a minha boca abrir-se de espanto e ouvi discretos risos abafados atrás de mim, provocados pela minha reacção.

Edward olhou-me com um ar descontraído, com a música ainda a afluir à nossa volta incessantemente, e piscou o olho.

— Gostas?

— Foste tu que a compuseste?! — exclamei com um arquejo, compreendendo.

Ele acenou com a cabeça.

— É a preferida da Esme.

Fechei os olhos, abanando a cabeça.

— O que se passa?

— Sinto-me mesmo insignificante.

A música abrandou, adoptando um ritmo mais suave, e, para minha surpresa, detectei a melodia da sua canção de embalar a insinuar-se na profusão de notas.

— Esta foi inspirada em ti — disse ele com doçura.

A música tornava-se cada vez mais insuportavelmente doce. Eu não conseguia falar.

— Eles gostam de ti, sabes — afirmou, em tom de conversa. — Sobretudo a Esme.

Olhei para trás, mas a enorme sala estava agora vazia.

— Aonde foram eles?

— Estão, muito subtilmente, a dar-nos alguma privacidade, suponho eu.

Suspirei.

— *Eles* gostam de mim, mas a Rosalie e o Emmett...

Deixei a frase por terminar, não sabendo ao certo como exprimir as minhas dúvidas.

Ele franziu o sobrolho.

— Não te preocupes com a Rosalie — disse ele, com os olhos arregalados e persuasivos. — Ela há-de vir a si.

Franzi os lábios cepticamente.

— E o Emmett?

— Bem, é verdade que ele pensa que *eu sou* maluco, mas não tem nada contra ti. Está a tentar levar a Rosalie à razão.

— O que é que a aborrece?

Não tinha a certeza de querer saber a resposta.

Ele suspirou profundamente.

— Rosalie é quem mais se debate... com aquilo que somos. É difícil para ela saber que existe alguém de fora que sabe a verdade. E tem um pouco de inveja.

— A *Rosalie* tem inveja de *mim*? — perguntei incredulamente.

Tentei imaginar um universo onde alguém tão deslumbrante como a Rosalie pudesse ter algum motivo para sentir inveja de alguém como eu.

— Tu és humana — encolheu os ombros. — Ela também gostava de ser.

— Ah — murmurei, ainda estupefacta. — Mas até o Jasper...

— A culpa disso é mesmo minha — declarou. — Eu disse-te que ele era o que experimentara o nosso modo de vida há menos tempo. Eu avisei-o no sentido de manter a distância.

Pensei no que motivara tal aviso e estremeci.

— E quanto à Esme e ao Carlisle? — apressei-me a continuar, de modo a evitar que ele reparasse.

— Estão felizes por me verem feliz. Na verdade, a Esme não se importava mesmo que tu tivesses um terceiro olho e pés providos de membrana interdigital. Durante todo este tempo, ela tem estado preocupada comigo, temendo que faltasse algo na essência da minha maneira de ser, que eu fosse demasiado jovem quando o Carlisle me transformara... Está extática. Sempre que eu te toco, ela quase sufoca de tanta satisfação.

— A Alice parece muito... entusiasmada.

— A Alice tem a sua própria maneira de ver as coisas — disse ele, por entre os lábios tensos.

— E tu não vais explicar isso, pois não?

Decorreu um momento de comunicação sem palavras entre nós. Ele percebeu que eu sabia que estava a omitir-me algo; eu percebi que ele nada ia revelar. Pelo menos, naquele instante.

— Então, o que é que o Carlisle estava a dizer-te há pouco?

As suas sobrancelhas uniram-se.

— Reparaste nisso, foi?

Encolhi os ombros.

— Naturalmente.

Olhou-me pensativamente durante alguns instantes antes de me responder.

— Queria dar-me uma novidade; não sabia se se tratava de algo que eu compartilharia contigo.

— E vais fazê-lo?

— Tenho de o fazer, pois vou ser um pouco... ditatorialmente protector durante os próximos dias, ou semanas, e não queria que pensasses que eu sou um tirano por natureza.

— O que se passa?

— Não se passa nada, ao certo. A Alice só prevê a chegada de alguns visitantes em breve. Sabem que nós estamos aqui e estão curiosos.

— Visitantes?

— Sim... bem, não são como nós, é claro; no que se refere aos seus hábitos de caça, quero eu dizer. Provavelmente, não entrarão sequer na cidade, mas não vou seguramente perder-te de vista enquanto eles não partirem.

Arrepiei-me.

— Finalmente, uma reacção racional! — murmurou. — Começava a pensar que não tinhas absolutamente nenhum sentido de autopreservação.

Não respondi a tal comentário, desviando o olhar, percorrendo novamente com os olhos a sala espaçosa.

O seu olhar seguiu o meu.

— Não é bem aquilo de que estavas à espera, pois não? — perguntou, com um tom de voz pretensioso.

— Não — reconheci.

— Nada de caixões, de caveiras empilhadas nos cantos; julgo que não temos sequer teias de aranha... Que decepção que isto deve ser para ti — prosseguiu de forma zombeteira.

Ignorei as suas provocações.

— É tão luminoso... tão amplo.

Já estava mais sério quando retorquiu.

— É o único lugar onde nunca temos de nos esconder.

A música que ele ainda tocava, a minha música, foi-se aproximando do fim, com os acordes finais a serem executados numa clave mais melancólica. A última nota pairou pungentemente no silêncio.

— Obrigada — murmurei.

Apercebi-me de que chorava. Apressei-me a limpar as lágrimas, envergonhada.

Ele tocou o canto do meu olho, detendo uma que me escapara. Levantou o dedo, examinando a gota de humidade pensativamente. Em seguida, tão rápido que eu não podia ter a certeza de que ele o fizera, levou o dedo à boca para sentir o seu sabor.

Lancei-lhe um olhar de interrogação e ele fitou-me também durante um longo momento antes de, por fim, sorrir.

— Queres conhecer o resto da casa?

— Nada de caixões? — procurei confirmar, com o sarcasmo patente na voz a não conseguir disfarçar a ligeira, mas genuína curiosidade que sentia.

Ele riu-se, pegando na minha mão e conduzindo-me para longe do piano.

— Nada de caixões — asseverou.

Subimos a escadaria maciça, com a minha mão a percorrer o corrimão suave como cetim. O longo corredor ao cimo das escadas estava revestido de uma madeira cor de mel, idêntica à do soalho.

— O quarto da Rosalie e do Emmett... O escritório do Carlisle... O quarto da Alice... — apontava à medida que passávamos pelas portas, com ele a guiar-me.

Ele teria continuado, mas eu fiquei absolutamente estática ao chegar ao fundo do corredor, olhando incredulamente para o ornato que estava pendurado na parede acima da minha cabeça. Edward soltou um riso abafado ao ver o meu ar de perplexidade.

— Podes rir-te — disse ele. — É, de facto, algo irónico.

Não me ri. A minha mão ergueu-se automaticamente, com um dedo esticado como se fosse tocar na grande cruz de madeira, cuja pátina escura contrastava com o tom mais claro da parede. No entanto, não lhe toquei, ainda que sentisse curiosidade em saber se a madeira envelhecida seria tão macia ao tacto como parecia.

— Deve ser muito antiga — conjecturei.

Ele encolheu os ombros.

— Data mais ou menos dos anos de 1630.

Desviei o olhar da cruz para fitá-lo.

— Porque é que mantêm isto aqui? — interroguei.

— Por nostalgia. Pertencia ao pai do Carlisle.

— Ele coleccionava antiguidades? — quis saber.

— Não. Foi ele próprio que a esculpiu. Costumava estar pendurada na parede por cima do púlpito do vicariato onde ele pregava.

Não sabia ao certo se o meu rosto denunciava a minha profunda surpresa, mas fixei novamente o olhar na simples e antiga cruz só para prevenir. Depressa fiz os cálculos mentais, a cruz tinha mais de trezentos e setenta anos. O silêncio prolongou-se enquanto eu me esforçava por assimilar o conceito de tão grande número de anos.

— Estás bem?

Ele parecia preocupado.

— Que idade tem o Carlisle? — perguntei calmamente, ignorando a sua pergunta e ainda olhando para cima.

— Acabou de comemorar o seu tricentésimo sexagésimo segundo aniversário — declarou Edward.

Voltei a olhar para ele, com uma infinidade de interrogações espelhadas nos olhos.

Ele observou-me com atenção enquanto falava:

— O Carlisle nasceu em Londres, nos anos de 1640, segundo ele crê. Na altura, o tempo não era assinalado com tanta exactidão, pelo menos no que se referia às pessoas comuns. Mas foi mesmo antes do regime de Cromwell.

Mantive uma expressão de calma, estando consciente de que ele me examinava enquanto eu o escutava. Era mais fácil se eu não tentasse acreditar.

— Era o único filho de um pastor anglicano. A mãe morreu durante o parto. O pai era um homem intolerante. Quando os Protestantes assumiram o poder, foi fervoroso na sua perseguição aos Católicos Romanos e aos seguidores de outras religiões. Também acreditava piamente na real existência do mal. Conduziu caças às bruxas, aos lobisomens... e aos vampiros.

Fiquei muito quieta ao ouvir tal palavra. Tenho a certeza de que ele reparou, mas continuou sem se deter.

— Queimaram muitas pessoas inocentes, as verdadeiras criaturas que ele buscava não eram, evidentemente, tão fáceis de apanhar. Quando o pastor envelheceu, incumbiu o seu obediente filho de realizar tais incursões. A princípio, o Carlisle foi uma decepção: não era célere a acusar, a ver demónios onde não existiam. No entanto, ele era persistente e mais esperto do que o pai. Descobriu, com efeito, um grupo de verdadeiros vampiros que vivia, escondido, nos esgotos da cidade, saindo apenas à noite para caçar. Naqueles tempos, em que os monstros não eram apenas mitos e lendas, era dessa forma que muitos viviam. As pessoas muniram-se, então, de forquilhas e archotes, é claro — o seu breve riso era agora mais sinistro — e ficaram à espera no local de onde o Carlisle vira os monstros saírem para a rua.

Um deles acabou por aparecer.

Falava em voz muito baixa e eu esforçava-me por apreender as suas palavras.

— Devia ser idoso e estar debilitado pela fome. O Carlisle ouviu-o a clamar em Latim pelos outros quando sentiu o cheiro da turba. Correu ao longo das ruas e o Carlisle, que tinha vinte e cinco anos e era muito veloz, comandava a perseguição. A criatura podia ter-lhes escapado facilmente, mas o Carlisle julga que ele estava demasiado esfaimado, pelo que se voltou e atacou. Caiu sobre o Carlisle em primeiro lugar, mas os outros estavam logo atrás e ele virou-se para se defender. Matou dois homens e fugiu com um terceiro, deixando o Carlisle a sangrar na rua.

Deteve-se. Eu sentia que ele estava a omitir algo, a esconder-me algo.

— O Carlisle sabia o que o pai faria. Os cadáveres seriam queimados, tudo aquilo que fora contaminado devia ser destruído. Agiu instintivamente para salvar a própria vida. Afastou-se do beco, arrastando-se, enquanto a turba seguia o demónio e a sua vítima. Escondeu-se numa cave e enterrou-se a si mesmo em batatas putrefactas, onde permaneceu durante três dias. Foi um milagre ter conseguido manter-se em silêncio e não ser descoberto. Então, já de outro lado, e ele percebeu aquilo em que se tornara.

Não sei ao certo o que o meu rosto revelava, mas, de repente, ele cessou.

— Como te sentes? — perguntou.

— Estou bem — assegurei-lhe.

Apesar de ter mordido o lábio com a hesitação, ele deve ter visto a curiosidade a iluminar-me os olhos.

Sorriu.

— Deduzo que tens mais algumas questões a colocar-me.

— Algumas.

O sorriso rasgou-se sobre os seus dentes brilhantes. Começou a percorrer novamente o corredor, no sentido inverso, puxando-me pela mão.

— Então, vem — incitou. — Eu mostro-te.

Capítulo Dezasseis

CARLISLE

Levou-me novamente até à divisão que me indicara como sendo o escritório de Carlisle. Deteve-se à entrada durante um instante.

— Entrem — convidou a voz de Carlisle.

Edward abriu a porta, revelando uma sala de tecto elevado com janelas altas, viradas para Oeste. As paredes estavam revestidas de novo, mas de uma madeira mais escura, nos pontos em que eram visíveis. A maior parte do espaço das paredes era preenchida por estantes altas que se erguiam consideravelmente acima da minha cabeça e sustentavam mais livros do que eu jamais vira fora de uma biblioteca.

Carlisle estava sentado a uma enorme secretária de mogno, numa cadeira de couro. Estava a acabar de colocar um marcador nas páginas do grosso volume que segurava. A sala correspondia à ideia que eu sempre fizera da configuração do gabinete de um reitor universitário, apenas Carlisle parecia demasiado jovem para se encaixar em tal papel.

— Em que posso ajudar-vos? — perguntou-nos amavelmente, levantando-se.

— Queria mostrar à Bella um pouco da nossa história — disse Edward. — Bem, na verdade, da sua história.

— Não tínhamos a intenção de o incomodar — pedi desculpa.

— Sem dúvida. Por onde vão começar?

— Pelo Cocheiro — respondeu Edward colocando levemente uma mão no meu ombro e fazendo-me rodar para olhar na direcção da porta pela qual acabávamos de entrar. Sempre que me tocava, mesmo da forma mais fortuita, o meu coração reagia audivelmente. Era mais embaraçoso na presença de Carlisle.

A parede para a qual estávamos agora virados era diferente das outras. Em vez de estantes com livros, esta parede estava repleta de quadros emoldurados de todos os tamanhos, sendo alguns de cores vibrantes e outros monocromos apagados. Procurei alguma lógica, algum motivo unificador que a colecção tivesse em comum, mas nada encontrei na minha apressada inspecção.

Edward puxou-me na direcção do extremo do lado esquerdo, colocando-me diante de uma pequena pintura a óleo, quadrada, numa simples moldura de madeira. Esta não sobressaía entre os quadros maiores e mais vivos; pintada em variados tons de sépia, representava uma cidade em miniatura cheia de telhados acentuadamente inclinados, com finas flechas a encimarem algumas torres destruidas. Um rio largo preenchia o primeiro plano, atravessado por uma ponte coberta de estruturas que pareciam minúsculas catedrais.

— Londres nos anos de 1650 — afirmou Edward.

— A Londres da minha juventude — acrescentou Carlisle, escassos metros atrás de nós.

Estremeci, não o ouvira aproximar-se. Edward apertou-me a mão.

— Não queres ser *tu* a contar a história? — perguntou Edward.

Torci-me um pouco para ver a reacção de Carlisle.

O seu olhar cruzou-se com o meu e ele sorriu.

— Fá-lo-ia — retorquiu —, mas, na verdade, estou a ficar um pouco atrasado. Telefonaram-me do hospital esta manhã, o Dr. Snow ficou de baixa. Além disso, conheces as histórias tão bem como eu — acrescentou, lançando agora um largo sorriso a Edward.

Era uma estranha combinação para assimilar: as preocupações quotidianas do médico da cidade introduzidas no meio de uma conversa acerca dos seus tempos de juventude na cidade de Londres do século XVII.

Era também desconcertante saber que ele falava em voz alta apenas por minha causa.

Depois de me dirigir outro sorriso caloroso, Carlisle abandonou a sala.

Olhei com atenção para o pequeno quadro onde figurava a terra natal de Carlisle durante um longo momento.

— Então, o que aconteceu? — acabei por perguntar, olhando para Edward, que me observava. — Quando é que ele se apercebeu do que lhe acontecera?

Voltou a olhar para as pinturas e eu procurei ver qual era a imagem que agora lhe prendia a atenção. Era uma paisagem mais vasta em apagadas cores de Outono: um prado vazio e ensombrado numa floresta, com um cume escarpado ao longe.

— Quando percebeu aquilo em que se tornara — disse Edward calmamente —, ficou revoltado. Tentou destruir-se a si mesmo, mas isso não é uma tarefa fácil.

— Como?

Não pretendia perguntá-lo em voz alta, mas a palavra irrompeu para meu profundo espanto.

— Saltou de sítios muito elevados — contou-me Edward, com a voz impassível. — Tentou afogar-se no mar... mas era principiante naquela nova vida e muito forte. É espantoso que tenha conseguido resistir... a alimentar-se... enquanto era ainda tão inexperiente. Nessa altura, o instinto é mais forte, apodera-se de tudo, mas ele sentia tamanha repulsa em relação a si que teve a força necessária para tentar morrer de fome.

— Isso é possível?

A minha voz estava fraca.

— Não, existem muito poucas formas de podermos ser mortos.

Abri a boca para perguntar, mas ele falou antes que eu pudesse fazê-lo.

— Então, começou a ter muita fome e acabou por ficar fraco. Mantinha-se o mais longe possível da população humana, reconhecendo que também a sua força de vontade estava a debilitar--se. Durante vários meses, vagueou durante a noite, procurando os lugares mais isolados, sentindo aversão por si mesmo. Certa noite, uma manada de gamos selvagens passou pelo seu esconderijo. Estava tão louco de sede que os atacou sem sequer pensar. As suas forças voltaram e ele apercebeu-se de que tinha uma alternativa para não ser o monstro vil que temia. Não comera carne de veado na sua vida passada? Ao longo dos meses que se seguiram, nasceu a sua nova filosofia. Ele podia existir sem ser um demónio. Reencontrou-se. Começou a empregar melhor o tempo. Sempre fora inteligente, ávido de aprender. Agora, tinha um tempo ilimitado diante de si. Estudava à noite e fazia planos de dia. Nadou até França e...

— Ele *nadou* até França?

— As pessoas atravessam o Canal a nado a toda a hora, Bella — lembrou-me pacientemente.

— Suponho que seja verdade. Pareceu apenas curioso nesse contexto. Continua.

— Nadamos com muita facilidade...

— *Vocês* fazem tudo com muita facilidade — resmunguei.

Ele esperou, com uma expressão de divertimento estampada no rosto.

— Não voltarei a interromper-te. Prometo.

Soltou sombriamente um riso abafado e concluiu a frase:

— Porque, na prática, não precisamos de respirar.

— Vocês...

— Não, não, tu prometeste — riu-se, pousando levemente o seu dedo frio nos meus lábios. — Queres ouvir a história ou não?

— Não podes fazer-me revelações dessas e, depois, esperar que eu não diga nada — resmunguei contra o seu dedo.

Ele levantou a mão, movendo-a para pousá-la no meu pescoço. O ritmo acelerado do meu coração reagiu a esse movimento, mas eu insisti:

— Tu não tens de *respirar*? — interroguei.

— Não, não é necessário. Trata-se apenas de um hábito.

Encolheu os ombros.

— Quanto tempo aguentas... sem *respirar*?

— Indefinidamente, julgo eu; não sei. Torna-se um pouco incómodo, por ficar desprovido do sentido do olfacto.

— Um pouco incómodo... — repeti.

Não estava a prestar atenção à expressão do meu próprio rosto, mas algo o fez ficar sorumbático. A mão caiu-lhe para o lado e ele ficou muito quieto, com os olhos fixos no meu rosto. O silêncio prolongou-se. As suas feições ficaram imóveis como pedra.

— Que é isso? — sussurrei, tocando o seu rosto paralisado, que se embrandeceu sob a minha mão.

Então, declarou com um suspiro:

— Continuo à espera de que aconteça.

— De que aconteça o quê?

— Eu sei que, a dada altura, algo que eu te disser ou que vires será a gota de água. Então, irás fugir de mim, gritando enquanto te afastas.

Antes de prosseguir, esboçou um ligeiro sorriso, mas os seus olhos estavam sérios.

— Não te travarei. Eu quero que isso aconteça, pois quero que fiques a salvo e, contudo, desejo ficar contigo. Os dois desejos são impossíveis de conciliar...

Deixou a frase por terminar, fixando o meu rosto. Esperando.

— Eu não vou fugir para parte nenhuma — garanti.

— Tu verás — disse ele, sorrindo novamente.

Franzi-lhe o sobrolho.

— Então, continua. O Carlisle estava a nadar em direcção a França.

Fez uma pausa, voltando à história que narrava. Reflexivamente, os seus olhos incidiram sobre outro quadro: o mais colorido de todos, o que tinha a moldura mais elaborada e o maior; tinha o dobro da largura da porta junto da qual se encontrava pendurado. A tela transbordava de figuras luminosas com vestidos rodopiantes, enrolando-se em longas colunas e ficando suspensas de varandas de mármore. Não conseguia determinar se representava a mitologia grega ou se se pretendia que as personagens que pairavam nas nuvens acima fossem bíblicas.

— O Carlisle nadou até França e continuou a percorrer a Europa, frequentando as universidades. À noite, estudava Música, Ciência, Medicina, tendo encontrado aqui a sua vocação, a sua penitência: salvar vidas humanas.

A sua expressão tornou-se respeitosa, quase reverente, após o que continuou:

— Não consigo descrever adequadamente a sua luta; foram necessários dois séculos de esforço supliciante para que Carlisle conseguisse aperfeiçoar o seu autodomínio. Agora, é imune ao odor do sangue humano e pode dedicar-se ao trabalho que adora sem sofrimento. Encontra muita paz lá no hospital...

Edward fixou o olhar no vazio durante um longo momento. De repente, pareceu lembrar-se dos seus intentos. Bateu com o dedo na enorme pintura que se encontrava à nossa frente e prosseguiu.

— Estudava em Itália quando descobriu lá os outros. Eram muito mais civilizados e instruídos do que os espectros dos esgotos de Londres.

Tocou num quarteto relativamente tranquilo de figuras pintadas na varanda mais elevada, que lançavam calmamente o olhar para o caos debaixo de si. Examinei o conjunto com atenção e percebi, com uma gargalhada de surpresa, que reconhecia o homem de cabelos dourados.

— Solimena inspirava-se muito nos amigos do Carlisle. Retratava-os frequentemente como deuses — Edward soltou um riso abafado — Aro, Marcus, Caius — disse, indicando os outros três, dos quais dois tinham cabelo negro e um branco como a neve — Mecenas nocturnos das artes.

— O que foi feito deles? — perguntei-me em voz alta, com a ponta do meu dedo a pairar a um centímetro de distância das figuras representadas na tela.

— Ainda lá estão — encolheu os ombros. — Tal como têm estado sabe-se lá há quantos milénios. O Carlisle ficou com eles apenas durante um breve período, só algumas décadas. Admirava imenso a sua civilidade, o seu requinte, mas eles insistiam em tentar curar a aversão que ele sentia em relação à «sua fonte natural de alimento», como lhe chamavam. Tentaram convencê-lo e ele tentou fazer-lhes o mesmo, mas em vão. Nessa altura, Carlisle resolveu experimentar o Novo Mundo. Sonhava encontrar outros como ele. Sentia-se muito sozinho, sabes. Não encontrou ninguém durante muito tempo, mas, como os monstros começavam a tornar-se meras tolices de contos de fadas, descobriu que podia interagir com humanos que de nada desconfiavam, como se fosse um deles. Começou a exercer Medicina, mas a companhia por que ansiava escapava-lhe; não podia correr o risco de criar laços de intimidade. Quando surgiu a epidemia da gripe, ele fazia os turnos da noite num hospital de Chicago. Já remoía uma ideia no seu espírito há vários anos e quase decidira agir: já que não conseguia encontrar um companheiro, criaria um. Não estava absolutamente certo da forma como se dera a sua própria transformação e, por isso, estava hesitante. Além disso, era avesso a tirar a vida a alguém da mesma forma que a sua lhe fora tirada. Foi nesse estado de espírito que me encontrou. Não havia quaisquer esperanças de que eu sobrevivesse; deixaram-me numa enfermaria com os moribundos. Ele cuidara dos meus pais e sabia que eu estava sozinho. Decidiu experimentar...

A sua voz, agora quase um sussurro, perdeu intensidade. Olhava sem nada ver pelas janelas viradas para Oeste. Perguntei-me que imagens preencheriam a sua mente naquele momento: as lembranças de Carlisle ou as suas? Esperei em silêncio.

Quando voltou a virar-se para mim, um doce sorriso de anjo iluminou-lhe o semblante.

— E, assim, chegámos ao fim — concluiu.

— Então, ficaste sempre com o Carlisle? — interroguei.

— Quase sempre.

Colocou levemente a mão na minha cintura e levou-me consigo ao passar a porta. Olhei para trás, para a parede repleta de quadros, perguntando-me se alguma vez chegaria a conhecer as outras histórias.

Edward nada mais disse enquanto percorríamos o corredor e, por conseguinte, eu perguntei:

— Quase?

Ele suspirou, parecendo relutante em responder.

— Bem, tive uma típica crise de adolescente rebelde, cerca de dez anos depois de ter... nascido... sido criado, o que quer que lhe queiras chamar. Não estava rendido ao seu modo de vida abstinente e levava-lhe a mal o facto de ele refrear o meu apetite. Assim, andei sozinho por uns tempos.

— A sério?

Eu estava mais intrigada do que assustada, como seria natural.

Ele percebeu. Apercebi-me vagamente de que nos dirigíamos para o lanço de escadas seguinte, mas não prestava muita atenção àquilo que me rodeava.

— Isso não te causa repulsa?

— Não.

— Porque não?

— Julgo... que parece razoável.

Soltou uma gargalhada, mais sonora do que as anteriores. Encontrávamo-nos agora ao cimo das escadas, noutro corredor revestido.

— A partir do meu novo nascimento — murmurou —, tive a vantagem de saber o que todos os que me rodeavam pensavam, tanto humanos como não-humanos. Foi por isso que levei dez anos a desafiar o Carlisle; eu conseguia detectar a sua absoluta sinceridade, compreender exactamente por que motivo ele cultivava aquele modo de vida. Decorreram apenas alguns anos até eu voltar para junto do Carlisle e me entregar de novo à sua visão. Eu pensava que estaria isento da... depressão... que acompanha uma consciência, pois eu conhecia os pensamentos da minha presa, podendo ignorar os inocentes e perseguir apenas os perversos. Se seguisse um assassino até um beco escuro onde ele perseguia uma rapariguinha... Se eu a salvasse, decerto não seria assim tão horrível.

Eu arrepiei-me, imaginando apenas demasiado claramente aquilo que ele descrevia: o beco à noite, a rapariga assustada, o homem sinistro atrás dela e Edward; Edward enquanto caçava, terrível e magnífico como um jovem deus, imparável. Teria ela, aquela rapariga, ficado agradecida ou mais assustada do que antes?

— Mas, à medida que o tempo passava, comecei a ver o monstro reflectido nos meus olhos. Não conseguia escapar à dívida de tantas vidas humanas ceifadas, por mais que tal se justificasse. Então, voltei para junto do Carlisle e da Esme. Receberam-me de volta como o filho pródigo. Foi mais do que eu merecia.

Paráramos diante da última porta do corredor.

— O meu quarto — informou-me, abrindo a porta e puxando-me para o interior.

O seu quarto estava virado para Sul, com uma janela do tamanho da parede, como a grande sala de baixo. Toda a parte das traseiras da casa devia ser envidraçada. Ele olhou para baixo, para o serpenteante rio Sol Duc, para lá da floresta intacta, na direcção da cordilheira das Montanhas Olímpicas. As montanhas estavam muito mais próximas do que eu teria crido.

A parede ocidental estava completamente coberta de prateleiras atrás de prateleiras com CDs. O quarto estava mais bem fornecido do que uma loja de música. No canto, encontrava-se um sistema de som com um aspecto sofisticado, do género daqueles que eu receava tocar pois tinha a certeza de que partiria algo. Não havia cama, mas apenas um largo e convidativo sofá de couro. O piso estava coberto com um grosso tapete dourado e, das paredes, pendia um tecido num tom ligeiramente mais escuro.

— Boa acústica? — tentei adivinhar.

Ele soltou um riso abafado e acenou com a cabeça.

Pegou num telecomando e ligou a aparelhagem. O som não estava muito alto, mas parecia que os calmos acordes de *jazz* estavam a ser tocados por uma banda que se encontrava no quarto connosco. Fui ver a sua espantosa colecção de música.

— Qual é o teu critério de organização? — perguntei, não conseguindo encontrar nexo nos títulos.

Ele não estava a prestar atenção.

— Hummm, o ano e, depois, dentro desse critério, o meu gosto pessoal — disse com o espírito ausente.

Eu voltei-me e ele olhava-me com um ar estranho.

— O que foi?

— Estava preparado para me sentir... aliviado quando tu soubesses tudo e eu não tivesse de ter segredos para ti, mas não esperava sentir mais do que isso. *Agrada-me.* Faz-me sentir... feliz.

Encolheu os ombros, sorrindo ligeiramente.

— Ainda bem — declarei, retribuindo-lhe o sorriso.

Preocupara-me a possibilidade de ele se arrepender de me contar tudo aquilo. Era bom saber que tal não era o caso.

Então, os seus olhos dissecaram o meu semblante, o sorriso esmoreceu e a testa franziu-se.

— Ainda estás à espera de que eu desate a correr aos gritos, não estás? — conjecturei.

Um ténue sorriso desenhou-se nos seus lábios e ele acenou com a cabeça.

— Detesto desiludir-te, mas não és mesmo tão assustador como pensas. Na verdade, eu não te considero minimamente assustador — menti com à vontade.

Ele deteve-se, levantando as sobrancelhas numa incredulidade flagrante. Em seguida, exibiu um sorriso largo e perverso.

— Na *verdade*, não devias realmente ter dito isso — soltou um riso abafado.

Rosnou, emitindo um som grave do fundo da garganta; os lábios enrolaram-se-lhe sobre os dentes perfeitos. O corpo modificou-se subitamente, meio agachado, retesado como um leão prestes a investir.

Afastei-me dele, lançando-lhe um olhar feroz.

— Não serias capaz.

Não o vi saltar na minha direcção, foi demasiado rápido. Só dei por mim a voar subitamente pelo ar e, depois, caímos sobre o sofá, levando-o a bater na parede. Durante todo este tempo, os seus braços formaram uma protectora jaula de ferro à minha volta, mal tendo sofrido um empurrão, mas ainda arquejava ao tentar endireitar-me.

Ele não iria permiti-lo. Enroscou-me como uma bola contra o seu peito, prendendo-me mais firmemente do que correntes de ferro. Lancei-lhe um olhar furioso, sobressaltada, mas ele parecia ter tudo controlado, estando o seu maxilar relaxado enquanto ele sorria e os seus olhos a brilhar apenas por divertimento.

— O que dizias? — resmungou jocosamente.

— Que és um monstro muitíssimo aterrador — afirmei, com o meu sarcasmo a ser um pouco afectado pela minha voz ofegante.

— Muito melhor — aprovou.

— Hum — debati-me. — Já posso levantar-me?

Ele limitou-se a rir.

— Podemos entrar? — perguntou uma voz suave vinda do corredor.

Debati-me para me libertar, mas Edward apenas corrigiu a minha posição para que eu ficasse, de certo modo, mais convencionalmente sentada no seu colo. Então, percebi que era Alice e, atrás dela, Jasper que estavam à porta. As minhas faces queimavam, mas Edward parecia estar à vontade.

— Entrem.

Edward ainda se ria discretamente.

Alice não pareceu ver nada de anormal no nosso abraço; caminhou — quase dançou, já que os seus movimentos eram tão graciosos — até ao centro do quarto, onde se sentou sinuosamente no chão. Jasper, todavia, deteve-se à porta, com ar um tudo-nada espantado. Olhou fixamente para o rosto de Edward e eu perguntei-me se ele estava a auscultar o ambiente com a sua invulgar sensibilidade.

— Parecia que a Bella ia ser o teu almoço e nós viemos ver se dividias — comunicou Alice.

Eu contraí-me por um instante, até perceber que Edward sorria ironicamente; não consegui perceber se tal se devia ao comentário dela ou à minha reacção.

— Lamento, creio que não tenho nada para dividir — retorquiu ele, com os braços a segurarem-me de forma ousadamente próxima.

— Na verdade — disse Jasper, não conseguindo evitar sorrir ao entrar no quarto —, a Alice afirmou que irá haver uma grande tempestade esta noite e o Emmett quer jogar à bola. Alinhas?

Todas as palavras eram bastante comuns, mas o contexto confundiu-me. Inferi, porém, que Alice era um pouco mais fiável do que o apresentador do boletim meteorológico.

Os olhos de Edward iluminaram-se, mas hesitou.

— É claro que deves levar a Bella — chilreou Alice.

Pensei ter visto Jasper lançar-lhe um rápido olhar.

— Queres ir? — perguntou-me Edward, entusiasmado, com uma expressão animada.

— Claro.

Não podia decepcionar tal rosto.

— Hum, aonde vamos?

— Temos de esperar pela trovoada para jogar à bola; verás porquê — garantiu.

— Vou precisar de um guarda-chuva?

Os três riram-se sonoramente.

— Vai? — perguntou Jasper a Alice.

— Não — respondeu categoricamente. — A tempestade vai abater-se sobre a cidade. Na clareira, o tempo deverá estar bastante seco.

— Então, óptimo.

O entusiasmo patente na voz de Jasper foi contagioso. Dei por mim ansiosa, em vez de ficar paralisada com medo.

— Vamos ver se o Carlisle quer ir.

Alice levantou-se e dirigiu-se à porta de uma maneira que despedaçaria o coração de uma bailarina.

— Como se tu não soubesses — gracejou Jasper.

Então, foram-se rapidamente embora. Depois de terem saído, Jasper conseguiu fechar a porta sem dar nas vistas.

— O que vamos jogar? — perguntei.

— Tu vais ficar a assistir — esclareceu Edward. — Nós vamos jogar basebol.

Revirei os olhos.

— Os vampiros gostam de basebol?

— É um passatempo americano — disse ele com uma solenidade simulada.

Capítulo Dezassete

O Jogo

Estava mesmo a começar a chuviscar quando Edward virou para a minha rua. Até àquele momento, eu não tinha quaisquer dúvidas de que ele ficaria comigo enquanto eu passava algumas horas de intervalo no mundo real.

Depois, vi o carro preto, um Ford desgastado pela acção do tempo, estacionado na entrada da casa de Charlie e ouvi Edward resmungar algo ininteligível num tom de voz baixo e ríspido.

Afastando-se da chuva sob o baixo alpendre da frente, Jacob Black erguia-se atrás da cadeira de rodas do pai. O rosto de Billy permaneceu impassível como pedra quando Edward estacionou a minha *pick-up* junto da borda do passeio. Jacob baixou o olhar, vexado.

A voz grave de Edward exprimia fúria.

— Isto já está a passar das marcas.

— Ele veio avisar o Charlie? — palpitei, mais horrorizada do que zangada.

Edward limitou-se a acenar com a cabeça, retribuindo o olhar fixo de Billy através da chuva com os olhos semicerrados.

Senti-me aliviada por Charlie ainda não ter chegado a casa.

— Deixa-me tratar disto — sugeri.

O olhar sombrio de Edward provocava em mim ansiedade.

Para meu espanto, ele assentiu.

— Deve ser melhor. Mas tem cuidado. A criança não faz a menor ideia.

Fiquei um pouco irritada ao ouvir a palavra *criança*.

— O Jacob não é assim tão mais novo do que eu — lembrei-lhe.

Então, ele olhou para mim, com a cólera a desvanecer-se de repente.

— Oh, eu sei — assegurou-me com um sorriso rasgado.

Eu suspirei e coloquei a mão no manípulo da porta.

— Leva-os para dentro — aconselhou —, para que eu me possa ir embora. Voltarei por volta do anoitecer.

— Queres levar a minha *pick-up*? — ofereci, perguntando-me, entretanto, como explicaria a Charlie a sua ausência.

Ele revirou os olhos.

— Eu conseguia *caminhar* mais depressa do que esta *pick-up* se desloca.

— Não tens de te ir embora — disse eu, melancolicamente.

Ele sorriu perante o meu ar sorumbático.

— Na verdade, tenho. Depois de te livrares deles — lançou um olhar sombrio na direcção dos Black —, ainda tens de preparar o Charlie para conhecer o teu namorado.

Esboçou um largo sorriso, exibindo todos os seus dentes.

Eu lamentei-me.

— Obrigadinha.

Ele esboçou aquele sorriso enviesado que eu adorava.

— Estarei de volta em breve — prometeu.

Voltou a olhar na direcção do alpendre e, em seguida, inclinou-se para me beijar depressa mesmo por baixo da aresta do meu maxilar. O meu coração disparou freneticamente e também eu olhei para o alpendre. O rosto de Billy já não estava impassível; com as mãos agarrava os braços da cadeira.

— *Em breve* — frisei ao abrir a porta e sair, ficando exposta à chuva.

Conseguia sentir os seus olhos pousados nas minhas costas enquanto me dirigia para o alpendre, debaixo dos leves chuviscos, quase em passo de corrida.

— Olá, Billy. Olá, Jacob — cumprimentei-os com o máximo de entusiasmo possível. — O Charlie saiu para passar todo o dia fora; espero que não estejam há muito tempo à espera.

— Não esperámos muito tempo — disse Billy num tom de voz preocupado. — Queria apenas trazer isto.

Apontou para um saco de papel pardo que se encontrava no seu colo.

— Obrigada! — exclamei, embora não fizesse a menor ideia do que poderia ser. — Porque não entram um instante para se secarem?

Fingi não reparar na sua intensa análise enquanto eu abria a porta e fiz-lhes sinal com a mão para que entrassem à minha frente.

— Eu levo isso — prontifiquei-me, virando-me para fechar a porta.

Permiti-me um último olhar para Edward. Ele esperava, absolutamente imóvel, com o olhar grave.

— É melhor que coloques isso no frigorífico — observou Billy ao entregar-me o pacote. — É um pouco do peixe frito caseiro do Harry Clearwater, o preferido do Charlie. O frigorífico mantém-no mais seco.

Encolheu os ombros.

— Obrigada — repeti, mas, desta vez, com sentimento. — Estava a ficar sem ideias para preparar peixe e ele deve trazer mais esta noite.

— Foi pescar outra vez? — perguntou Billy com um brilho subtil no olhar. — Foi para o lugar do costume? Talvez passe por lá para falar com ele.

— Não — apressei-me a mentir, com o rosto carregado. — Dirigia-se para algum sítio novo... mas não faço ideia onde fica.

Ele analisou a minha expressão alterada e ficou pensativo.

— Jake — disse ele, ainda a avaliar-me. — Porque não vais buscar aquela nova fotografia da Rebecca ao carro? Vou deixá-la também ao Charlie.

— Onde está? — perguntou Jacob, com uma voz taciturna.

Olhei-o de relance, mas ele tinha os olhos pregados no chão, de sobrolho franzido.

— Julgo tê-la visto no porta-bagagem — respondeu Billy. — Talvez tenhas de a procurar.

Jacob voltou a sair, baixando os ombros e a cabeça debaixo da chuva.

Eu e Billy ficámos de frente um para o outro, calados. Após alguns instantes, o silêncio começou a tornar-se constrangedor, pelo que me virei e me dirigi à cozinha. Conseguia ouvir o chiar das rodas molhadas da sua cadeira ao entrarem em contacto com o linóleo enquanto ele me seguia.

Enfiei o saco na sobrecarregada prateleira de cima do frigorífico e dei meia volta para confrontá-lo. O seu rosto profundamente enrugado era indecifrável.

— O Charlie ainda vai demorar.

O meu tom de voz era quase indelicado.

Ele acenou com a cabeça, assentindo, mas nada disse.

— Obrigada, mais uma vez, pelo peixe frito — insinuei.

Ele continuou a acenar com a cabeça. Suspirei e cruzei os braços.

Ele pareceu ter percebido que eu desistira da conversa de ocasião.

— Bella — exclamou e, depois, hesitou.

Eu esperei.

— Bella — repetiu —, o Charlie é um dos meus melhores amigos.

— Sim.

Pronunciava cada palavra cuidadosamente, com a sua voz troante.

— Reparei que tens andado com um dos Cullen.

— Sim — repeti secamente.

Os seus olhos semicerraram-se.

— Talvez não seja da minha conta, mas acho que não é muito boa ideia.

— Tem razão — concordei. — Não é, de facto, da sua conta.

Levantou as sobrancelhas cada vez mais grisalhas.

— Não deves saber disto, mas a família Cullen tem uma reputação desagradável na reserva.

— Por acaso, eu já sabia disso — informei-o, num tom de voz ríspido, o que o surpreendeu. — Mas essa reputação não pode ser merecida, pois não? Isto porque os Cullen nunca põem os pés na reserva, não é?

Notei que a minha referência, que não fora propriamente subtil, ao acordo que vinculava e protegia a sua tribo o fez deter-se bruscamente.

— É verdade — anuiu, com olhos cautelosos. — Pareces estar... bem informada a respeito dos Cullen. Mais informada do que eu esperava.

Olhei-o fixamente.

— Talvez até mais bem informada do que o Billy.

Franziu os lábios grossos ao reflectir sobre as minhas palavras.

— Talvez — admitiu, mas sempre de olho vivo. — O Charlie também está tão bem informado?

Encontrara o ponto fraco da minha armadura.

— O Charlie simpatiza muito com os Cullen — afirmei de modo vago.

Ele apercebeu-se claramente da minha evasiva. O seu semblante estava descontente, mas não surpreendido.

— Não é da minha conta — disse ele —, mas pode ser da do Charlie.

— Embora seja então da minha conta avaliar se esse facto é ou não da conta do Charlie, certo?

Perguntei-me se ele chegara sequer a compreender a minha confusa pergunta, enquanto me esforçava por não dizer nada de comprometedor, mas pareceu que assim era. Ponderou durante alguns momentos, enquanto a chuva fustigava o telhado, sendo este o único som que quebrava o silêncio.

— Sim — acabou por ceder. — Creio que também isso é da tua conta.

Suspirei de alívio.

— Obrigada, Billy.

— Pensa apenas naquilo que estás a fazer, Bella — exortou.

— Está bem — apressei-me a assentir.

Ele franziu o sobrolho.

— Aquilo que eu queria dizer era que não fizesses aquilo que estás a fazer.

Olhei-o nos olhos, repletos apenas de preocupação em relação a mim, e nada consegui dizer.

Nesse preciso momento, a porta da frente bateu ruidosamente e o som sobressaltou-me.

— Não há fotografia nenhuma naquele carro.

A voz queixosa de Jacob chegou até nós antes dele. Os seus ombros estavam manchados pela chuva e o seu cabelo pingava quando contornou a quina da parede.

— Hum — gemeu Billy, subitamente desprendido, fazendo rodar a cadeira para se virar para o filho. — Devo tê-la deixado em casa.

Jacob revirou os olhos com veemência.

— Fantástico.

— Bem, Bella, diz ao Charlie... — Billy deteve-se antes de prosseguir — que nós passámos por aqui, quero eu dizer.

— Fá-lo-ei — murmurei por entre dentes.

Jacob ficou admirado.

— Já vamos embora?

— O Charlie vai chegar tarde — explicou Billy ao passar por Jacob.

— Ah! — exclamou Jacob, parecendo desiludido. — Bem, suponho, então, que nos vemos depois, Bella.

— Claro — concordei.

— Tem cuidado contigo — preveniu-me Billy.

Não repliquei.

Jacob ajudou o pai a sair pela porta. Acenei por breves instantes, lançando um rápido olhar na direcção da minha *pick-up*, agora vazia, e, em seguida, fechei a porta antes de eles se terem ido embora.

Fiquei especada na entrada durante um momento, ouvindo o som do carro deles a recuar e a afastar-se. Permaneci onde estava, esperando que a irritação e a ansiedade se aplacassem. Quando a tensão finalmente se atenuou um pouco, dirigi-me ao andar de cima para trocar as minhas roupas de cerimónia.

Experimentei algumas peças de vestuário para a parte de cima, não sabendo ao certo o que esperar daquela noite. Ao concentrar-me naquilo que se avizinhava, o que acabara de acontecer tornava-se insignificante. Agora que já não estava sob a influência de Jasper e Edward, comecei a compensar o facto de não ter ficado apavorada anteriormente. Depressa desisti de escolher uma roupa, vestindo uma velha camisa de flanela e um par de calças de ganga, já que sabia que, de qualquer forma, passaria toda a noite enfiada na gabardina.

O telefone tocou e eu precipitei-me para o piso inferior para o atender. Havia apenas uma voz que eu queria ouvir; tudo o mais seria uma decepção. No entanto, eu sabia que, se ele desejasse falar comigo, provavelmente se limitaria a materializar-se no meu quarto.

— Está lá? — exclamei, sem fôlego.

— Bella? Sou eu — disse Jessica.

— Ah, olá, Jess — debati-me por um momento para regressar à realidade.

Parecia que tinham decorrido meses e não dias desde a última vez que falara com Jessica.

— Como foi o baile?

— Foi tão divertido! — declarou Jessica de forma muito efusiva.

Não precisando de mais incentivos, lançou-se num relato minucioso do que acontecera na noite anterior. Eu exclamava «hum» e «ah» nas alturas certas, mas não era fácil concentrar-me. Jessica, Mike, o baile, a escola, tudo parecia estranhamente irrelevante naquele momento. Os meus olhos incidiam sistematicamente sobre a janela, tentando avaliar a quantidade de luz por trás das nuvens carregadas.

— Ouviste o que eu disse, Bella? — perguntou Jess, irritada.

— Desculpa, o que disseste?

— Disse que o Mike me beijou! Acreditas?

— Isso é maravilhoso, Jess — afirmei.

— Então, o que é que *tu* fizeste ontem? — desafiou Jessica, parecendo ainda incomodada com a minha falta de atenção ou estando aborrecida por eu não lhe ter pedido pormenores.

— Na verdade, nada. Andei apenas lá por fora para desfrutar do Sol.

Ouvi o carro de Charlie na garagem.

— Chegaste a ter mais algumas notícias do Edward Cullen?

A porta da frente bateu e eu conseguia ouvir Charlie a fazer barulho debaixo das escadas, guardando os seus apetrechos.

— Hum.

Hesitei, já não sabendo ao certo qual era a história que tinha para contar.

— Olá, pequena! — exclamou Charlie ao entrar na cozinha.

Acenei-lhe.

Jess ouviu a sua voz.

— Ah, o teu pai está aí. Esquece, falamos amanhã. Vemo-nos na aula de Trigonometria.

— Até amanhã, Jess.

Desliguei o telefone.

— Olá, pai — disse eu, enquanto ele lavava as mãos no lava-louça. — Onde está o peixe?

— Coloquei-o no congelador.

— Vou buscar umas postas antes que congelem. O Billy veio cá esta tarde trazer um pouco do peixe frito do Harry Clearwater.

Esforcei-me por parecer entusiasmada.

— Ai sim?

Os olhos de Charlie iluminaram-se.

— É o meu preferido.

Charlie lavou-se enquanto eu preparei o jantar. Não decorreu muito tempo até nos sentarmos à mesa, a comer em silêncio. Charlie degustava a sua comida. Eu perguntava-me desesperadamente como haveria de cumprir a minha tarefa, tentando, a muito custo, pensar numa forma de abordar o assunto.

— O que fizeste esta tarde? — perguntou, interrompendo o meu devaneio.

— Bem, esta tarde, fiquei apenas aqui por casa...

Na verdade, apenas no fim da tarde. Tentei manter um tom de voz alegre, mas sentia um vazio no estômago.

— E esta manhã estive em casa dos Cullen.

Charlie deixou cair o garfo.

— Em casa do Dr. Cullen? — perguntou, atónito.

Fingi não ter reparado na sua reacção.

— Sim.

— O que foste lá fazer?

Não voltara a pegar no garfo.

— Bem, eu tenho, de certa forma, um encontro marcado com o Edward Cullen para esta noite e ele queria apresentar-me aos pais dele... pai?

Parecia que Charlie estava a sofrer um aneurisma.

— Pai, estás bem?

— Vais sair com o Edward Cullen? — vociferou.

Ai, ai.

— Pensei que gostavas dos Cullen.

— Ele é demasiado velho para ti — afirmou num tom de voz empolado.

— Ambos frequentamos o segundo ano do liceu — corrigi, embora ele estivesse mais certo do que imaginava.

— Espera... — deteve-se. — Qual é o Edwin?

— O *Edward* é o mais novo, o que tem o cabelo castanho-aver-melhado.

O lindo, o divinal...

— Oh, bem, assim... — fez um grande esforço — está melhor, acho eu. Não me agrada o ar daquele maior. Tenho a certeza de que é um bom rapaz e tudo isso, mas parece demasiado... maduro para ti. Esse Edwin é teu namorado?

— Ele chama-se *Edward*, pai.

— É?

— Mais ou menos, suponho eu.

— Na noite passada, disseste que não estavas interessada em nenhum dos rapazes da cidade.

No entanto, ele voltou a pegar no garfo e, por conseguinte, percebi que o pior já passara.

— Bem, o Edward não vive na cidade, pai.

Lançou-me um olhar de censura enquanto mastigava.

— E, seja como for — continuei —, a nossa relação ainda está, de certo modo, numa fase inicial, sabes. Não me envergonhes com todo o discurso sobre namorados, está bem?

— Quando é que ele vem cá a casa?

— Deve chegar dentro de alguns minutos.

— Aonde é que ele te vai levar?

Gemi sonoramente.

— Espero que agora expulses a Inquisição Espanhola do teu espírito. Vamos jogar basebol com a família dele.

O seu rosto contraiu-se e, depois, por fim, soltou um riso abafado.

— Tu, vais jogar basebol?

— Bem, provavelmente só devo ficar a assistir durante a maior parte do tempo.

— Deves gostar mesmo desse rapaz — observou com desconfiança.

Suspirei e revirei os olhos para esclarecê-lo.

Ouvi o roncar do motor de um carro a encostar à frente da casa. Levantei-me de um salto e comecei a lavar a louça.

— Deixa a louça, eu posso lavá-la esta noite. Apaparicas-me demasiado.

A campainha tocou e Charlie foi abrir a porta, caminhando de modo altivo. Eu seguia meio passo atrás dele.

Não me apercebera de como chovia violentamente lá fora. Edward encontrava-se no halo da luz do alpendre, parecendo um manequim masculino num anúncio a gabardinas.

— Entra, Edward.

Soltei um suspiro de alívio quando Charlie acertou no nome dele.

— Obrigado, chefe Swan — retorquiu Edward, num tom de voz respeitoso.

— Podes tratar-me por Charlie. Dá-me o teu casaco.

— Obrigado, senhor.

— Senta-te ali, Edward.

Eu fiz um esgar.

Edward sentou-se com agilidade na única cadeira, obrigando-me a sentar ao lado do chefe Swan no sofá. Apressei-me a lançar-lhe um olhar de desagrado. Ele piscou o olho nas costas de Charlie.

— Então, soube que vais levar a minha menina para assistir a um jogo de basebol!...

Só mesmo em Washington é que o facto de estar a chover a cântaros não influenciaria em nada a prática de desportos ao ar livre.

— Sim, senhor, é essa a ideia.

Não parecia surpreendido por eu ter contado a verdade ao meu pai, mas também podia ter estado a ouvir.

— Bem, mais poder para ti, creio eu.

Charlie riu-se e Edward fez-lhe companhia.

— Muito bem — disse, levantando-me. — Já chega de piadas à minha custa. Vamos embora.

Voltei à entrada e vesti o casaco. Eles seguiram-me.

— Não chegues muito tarde, Bell.

— Não se preocupe, Charlie. Eu trago-a a casa cedo — prometeu Edward.

— Cuida bem da minha menina, sim?

Eu lamentei-me, mas eles ignoraram-me.

— Ela estará a salvo comigo. Prometo.

Charlie não podia duvidar da sinceridade de Edward, pois esta ressoava em cada palavra.

Saí com um ar altivo. Ambos se riram e Edward seguiu-me.

Fiquei paralisada no alpendre. Ali, atrás da minha *pick-up*, estava um jipe monstruoso. Os seus pneus elevavam-se acima da minha cintura. Os faróis dianteiros e traseiros estavam providos de protecções de metal e havia quatro grandes holofotes presos à barra de protecção. A capota era de um tom vermelho reluzente.

Charlie soltou um assobio pouco sonoro.

— Ponham os cintos de segurança — pronunciou com dificuldade.

Edward seguiu-me até ao lado do passageiro e abriu a porta. Medi a distância até ao banco e preparei-me para saltar até lá. Ele suspirou e, em seguida, elevou-me com uma mão. Esperei que Charlie não tivesse reparado.

Enquanto ele contornou o jipe para se dirigir ao lado do condutor, a um passo normal e humano, tentei colocar o meu cinto de segurança, mas havia demasiadas fivelas.

— O que é tudo isto? — perguntei quando ele abriu a porta.

— É um arnês para trajectos todo-o-terreno.

— Ai, ai.

Tentei encontrar os encaixes certos para todas as fivelas, mas tal tarefa não estava a processar-se com muita celeridade. Ele suspirou novamente e esticou-se para me ajudar. Fiquei contente por a chuva ser demasiado intensa para conseguir ver Charlie nitidamente no alpendre, o que também implicava que ele não conseguia ver como as mãos de Edward se demoraram junto do meu pescoço e me acariciaram as clavículas. Desisti de tentar ajudá-lo e concentrei-me em evitar que a minha respiração se tornasse ofegante.

Edward rodou a chave na ignição e o motor roncou ao arrancar. Afastámo-nos da casa.

— Mas que... hum... *grande* jipe tu tens!

— Pertence ao Emmett. Não me pareceu que quisesses correr ao longo de todo o percurso.

— Onde é que vocês guardam esta coisa?

— Transformámos um dos anexos numa garagem.

— Não vais colocar o cinto de segurança?

Lançou-me um olhar incrédulo.

De repente, assimilei algo:

— Correr ao longo de *todo* o percurso? Queres dizer que ainda vamos correr ao longo de uma parte do percurso? — a minha voz subiu algumas oitavas de tom.

Ele esboçou um firme e largo sorriso.

— Tu não vais correr.

— Eu *vou* ficar enjoada.

— Mantém os olhos fechados; ficarás bem.

Mordi o lábio, debatendo-me com o pânico.

Ele inclinou-se para me beijar o cimo da cabeça e, em seguida, gemeu. Olhei para ele, confusa.

— Cheiras tão bem à chuva — explicou.

— De um ponto de vista positivo ou negativo? — perguntei cautelosamente.

Ele suspirou.

— De ambos, sempre de ambos.

Não sei como encontrou o caminho na escuridão e sob os aguaceiros, mas, de alguma forma, encontrou uma estrada secundária que não era propriamente uma estrada, mas mais um caminho de montanha. Durante longos momentos, manter uma conversa foi impossível, pois eu saltitava no banco como um martelo pneumático. Ele, porém, parecia apreciar a viagem, tendo sorrido imenso durante todo o trajecto.

Então, chegámos ao fim da estrada; as árvores formavam muralhas verdes em três lados do jipe. A chuva não passava de meros chuviscos, amainando a cada segundo que passava, com o céu a mostrar-se mais luminoso através das nuvens.

— Lamento, Bella. Temos de ir a pé a partir daqui.

— Sabes que mais? Eu espero aqui.

— O que foi feito de toda a tua coragem? Foste extraordinária esta manhã.

— Ainda não me esqueci da última vez.

Poderia ter sido apenas no dia anterior?

Num ápice, ele já estava no meu lado do carro. Começou a libertar-me do arnês.

— Eu trato disso; vai andando — protestei.

— Humm... — meditou depois de ter rapidamente concluído a tarefa. — Parece que terei de interferir na tua memória.

Antes que eu pudesse reagir, ele arrancou-me do jipe e assentou-me os pés no chão. Agora, mal pairava uma neblina; Alice teria razão.

— Interferir na minha memória? — perguntei nervosamente.

— Algo do género.

Ele observava-me atenta e cuidadosamente, mas, bem no fundo dos seus olhos, havia graça. Apoiou as mãos no jipe, de ambos os lados da minha cabeça, e inclinou-se para a frente, obrigando-me a encostar à porta. Aproximou-se ainda mais, colocando o rosto a escassos centímetros do meu. Eu não tinha por onde escapar.

— Agora — sussurrou, e só o seu cheiro me perturbou o raciocínio —, o que é que te preocupa ao certo?

— Bem, hum, embater numa árvore — disse, engasgando-me — e morrer. E, depois, ficar enjoada.

Conteve um sorriso. Em seguida, inclinou a cabeça e tocou suavemente com os lábios frios a cavidade na base do meu pescoço.

— Ainda estás preocupada? — murmurou contra a minha pele.

— Estou — respondi, esforçando-me por me concentrar. — Em relação a embater nas árvores e ficar enjoada.

O seu nariz traçou uma linha desde a pele do meu pescoço até à extremidade do meu queixo. A sua respiração fresca fazia-me cócegas na pele.

— E agora? — os seus lábios sussurravam contra o meu maxilar.

— Árvores — disse, com uma respiração ofegante. — Enjoo do movimento.

Levantou o rosto para me beijar as pálpebras.

— Bella, não pensas mesmo que eu embateria numa árvore, pois não?

— Não, mas eu poderia fazê-lo.

Não havia nenhuma confiança na minha voz. Ele pressentiu uma vitória fácil.

Beijou-me lentamente a face, parando mesmo ao canto da minha boca.

— Achas que eu deixaria que uma árvore te magoasse?

Os seus lábios mal roçavam o meu trémulo lábio inferior.

— Não — sussurrei.

Eu sabia que não havia uma segunda parte para a minha brilhante defesa, mas não podia propriamente voltar atrás.

— É que, sabes — disse ele, com os seus lábios separados a
unirem-se aos meus —, não há nada de que ter medo, pois não?

— Não — suspirei, desistindo.

Então, ele segurou o meu rosto com as mãos, quase violentamente, e beijou-me a sério, com os seus lábios obstinados a
moverem-se em contacto com os meus.

Não havia realmente desculpa para o meu comportamento.
Nesta altura, eu já estava mais esclarecida. Mesmo assim, parecia que não conseguia evitar reagir como da primeira vez. Em
vez de permanecerem prudentemente imóveis, os meus braços
estenderam-se para lhe envolverem o pescoço e eu estava subitamente unida à sua figura pétrea. Suspirei e os meus lábios en-
treabriram-se.

Ele recuou de modo vacilante, libertando-se do meu abraço
sem qualquer esforço.

— Raios, Bella! — exclamou bruscamente, de modo ofegante.
— Hás-de ser a minha morte. Juro que serás.

Inclinei-me, colocando as mãos sobre os joelhos para me apoiar.

— Tu és indestrutível — balbuciei, tentando recuperar o fôlego.

— Posso ter acreditado nisso antes de *te* conhecer. Agora, vamos sair daqui antes que eu faça algum tremendo disparate —
resmungou.

Atirou-me para as suas costas como já fizera antes e eu percebi o esforço suplementar que ele tinha de fazer para ser tão
delicado como era. Coloquei as minhas pernas à volta da sua
cintura e envolvi-lhe o pescoço num abraço sufocante.

— Não te esqueças de fechar os olhos — advertiu severamente.

Apressei-me a esconder o rosto na sua omoplata, debaixo do
meu próprio braço, e fechei bem os olhos.

Mal notava que estávamos em andamento. Conseguia senti-
-lo a deslizar debaixo de mim, mas podia estar a deambular por
um passeio, de tão suave que era o seu movimento. Senti-me
tentada a espreitar, só para ver se ele se precipitava pela floresta

como fizera antes, mas resisti a fazê-lo. Não valia aquelas horrorosas tonturas. Contentei-me em ouvi-lo a expirar e inspirar de modo regular.

Não tinha a certeza de termos parado até ele ter tentado alcançar-me e tocado o meu cabelo.

— Já acabou, Bella.

Ousei abrir os olhos e, de facto, estávamos parados. Libertei-lhe rigidamente o corpo do meu abraço asfixiante e deslizei até ao solo, aterrando com o traseiro.

— Oh! — exclamei ao cair no chão molhado.

Ele olhou-me com incredulidade, não sabendo ao certo se ainda estava demasiado zangado comigo para me achar engraçada, mas o meu ar desorientado fê-lo descontrolar-se e desatou a rir às gargalhadas.

Levantei-me, ignorando-o enquanto sacudia a lama e os fetos das costas do meu casaco, o que o fez rir ainda mais. Irritada, comecei a avançar para o interior da floresta.

Senti os seus braços à volta da minha cintura.

— Aonde vais, Bella?

— Assistir a um jogo de basebol. Já não pareces estar interessado em jogar, mas tenho a certeza de que os outros se divertirão sem ti.

— Vais na direcção errada.

Voltei-me sem olhar para ele e encaminhei-me no sentido oposto. Ele alcançou-me novamente.

— Não fiques zangada. Não consegui evitar. Devias ter visto a tua cara.

Soltou um riso abafado antes de conseguir contê-lo.

— Ah, tu és o único que pode ficar zangado? — perguntei, erguendo as sobrancelhas.

— Não estava zangado contigo.

— «Bella, hás-de ser a minha morte»? — citei com azedume.

— *Isso* foi apenas a constatação de um facto.

Tentei voltar-lhe as costas novamente, mas ele segurou-me com firmeza.

— Tu estavas zangado — insisti.

— Pois estava.

— Mas acabaste de dizer...

— Que não estava zangado *contigo*. Será que não vês, Bella? Ficou subitamente arrebatado, tendo desaparecido todos os sinais de jocosidade.

— Não compreendes?

— Não vejo o quê? — interroguei, confundida tanto com a sua repentina mudança de humor como com as suas palavras.

— Eu nunca fico irado contigo; como poderia? Sendo corajosa, confiante... calorosa como és.

— Então, porquê? — sussurrei, lembrando-me dos sombrios estados de espírito que o afastavam de mim e que eu sempre interpretara como uma frustração perfeitamente justificada, uma frustração relativamente à minha fraqueza, à minha lentidão, às minhas descontroladas reacções humanas...

Pousou com cuidado as mãos em ambos os lados do meu rosto.

— Enfureço-me a mim mesmo — disse suavemente. — Pela forma como pareço não evitar pôr-te em perigo. A minha própria existência coloca-te em risco. Por vezes, chego a odiar-me. Devia ser mais forte, devia ser capaz de...

Coloquei a mão sobre a sua boca.

— Não digas isso.

Pegou na minha mão, retirando-a de cima dos seus lábios, mas segurando-a junto ao rosto.

— Eu amo-te — declarou. — É uma fraca desculpa para aquilo que estou a fazer, mas não deixa de ser verdade.

Foi a primeira vez que ele disse que me amava com todas as letras. Talvez ele não se tivesse apercebido, mas eu sem dúvida que sim.

— Agora, por favor, tenta comportar-te bem — continuou e inclinou-se para afagar os meus lábios com os seus.

Eu mantive-me devidamente imóvel. Depois, suspirei.

— Prometeste ao chefe Swan que me levarias a casa cedo,

lembras-te? É melhor irmos andando.

— Sim, senhora.

Sorriu melancolicamente e libertou-me por completo, à excepção da minha mão. Conduziu-me ao longo de alguns metros, através dos fetos altos e húmidos e do musgo drapejante, contornando um maciço abeto-do-canadá, até chegarmos ao nosso destino, à orla de um enorme campo aberto no regaço dos cumes Olímpicos. Tinha o dobro do tamanho de qualquer estádio de basebol.

Conseguia ver que todos os outros estavam presentes; Esme, Emmett e Rosalie, sentados na saliência despida de uma rocha, eram os que estavam mais próximos de nós, talvez a cerca de cem metros de distância. Muito mais ao longe, conseguia avistar Jasper e Alice, distanciados, pelo menos, por quatrocentos metros, parecendo lançar algo para a frente e para trás, mas eu não cheguei a ver qualquer bola. Parecia que Carlisle estava a marcar bases, mas será que eles podiam ficar tão afastados?

Quando nos tornámos visíveis, os três que se encontravam sobre as rochas ergueram-se. Esme começou a avançar na nossa direcção. Emmett seguiu-se-lhe após um demorado olhar para as costas de Rosalie; esta levantara-se graciosamente e encaminhara-se a passos largos para o campo sem olhar uma única vez na nossa direcção. O meu estômago estremeceu em resposta a esta reacção.

— Foste tu quem ouvimos, Edward? — perguntou Esme ao aproximar-se.

— Parecia um urso a sufocar — esclareceu Emmett.

Lancei um sorriso hesitante a Esme.

— Era ele — disse-lhe.

— A Bella estava a ser engraçada sem ter tal intenção — explicou Edward, acertando as contas.

Alice abandonara a sua posição e corria, ou dançava na nossa direcção. Precipitou-se e parou fluidamente ao pé de nós.

— Está na hora — comunicou.

Assim que ela falou, um intenso trovejar abalou a floresta para lá do local onde nos encontrávamos e, em seguida, rumou para Oeste, em direcção à cidade.

— É arrepiante, não é? — disse Emmett com tranquila familiaridade, piscando-me o olho.

— Vamos.

Alice pegou na mão de Emmett e ambos se precipitaram em direcção ao campo descomunal, ela corria como uma gazela. Era quase tão gracioso como ela e igualmente veloz, mas Emmett nunca poderia ser comparado a uma gazela.

— Estás pronta para assistir a um jogo de bola? — perguntou Edward, com os olhos brilhantes e ávidos.

Tentei parecer adequadamente entusiasmada.

— Força, equipa!

Ele soltou um riso algo reprimido e, depois de me ter passado a mão pela cabeça e desgrenhado os cabelos, partiu atrás dos outros dois. A sua corrida era mais agressiva, assemelhando-se mais a uma chita do que a uma gazela, e depressa os ultrapassou. O seu vigor e graciosidade cortaram-me a respiração.

— Descemos? — perguntou Esme com a sua voz suave e melódica. Apercebi-me de que estava a fixá-lo, boquiaberta.

Apressei-me a recompor a expressão do meu rosto e acenei com a cabeça. Esme mantinha uma distância de escassos metros entre nós e eu perguntei-me se ela estava ainda a ser cuidadosa de modo a não me assustar. Manteve o seu andar ao ritmo do meu sem parecer impacientar-se com a velocidade.

— A Esme não joga com eles? — perguntei a medo.

— Não, prefiro arbitrar. Gosto de os obrigar a serem honestos — explicou ela.

— Então, eles gostam de fazer batota?

— Oh, sim! Devias ouvir as discussões que eles têm uns com os outros! Na verdade, espero que não ouças, pensarias que eles foram criados por uma alcateia.

— Parece a minha mãe a falar — ri-me, admirada.

Ela também se riu.

— Bem, eu considero-os meus filhos em quase todos os aspectos. Nunca consegui superar os meus instintos maternais. O Edward contou-te que eu perdi um filho?

— Não — murmurei, estupefacta, esforçando-me por compreender a que vida ela se referia.

— Pois perdi, o meu primeiro e único bebé. Morreu apenas alguns dias depois de ter nascido, o pobrezinho — suspirou. — Fiquei com o coração despedaçado. Foi por isso que saltei do penhasco, sabes — acrescentou com objectividade.

— O Edward mencionou apenas que a Esme caíra — gaguejei.

— Sempre um cavalheiro — sorriu. — O Edward foi o primeiro dos meus novos filhos. Sempre o encarei dessa forma, apesar de ser mais velho do que eu, pelo menos num aspecto.

Sorriu-me calorosamente.

— É por isso que estou tão feliz por ele te ter encontrado, querida.

O enternecimento parecia muito natural nos seus lábios.

— Ele foi um homem sem cara-metade durante muito tempo, custava-me vê-lo sozinho.

— Então, não se importa? — perguntei, de novo hesitante. — Que eu não seja... de todo a pessoa indicada para ele?

— Não — ficou pensativa. — És quem ele quer. Seja como for, há-de resultar — disse ela, ainda que a sua testa se enrugasse de preocupação.

Começou outro ribombar de trovão.

Então, Esme deteve-se. Pelos vistos, chegáramos ao limite do campo. Parecia que eles tinham formado equipas. Edward encontrava-se, ao longe, no lado esquerdo do campo, Carlisle estava entre a primeira e a segunda bases e Alice segurava a bola, posicionada no local que devia ser a elevação onde se colocava o lançador.

Emmett balançava uma barra de alumínio e esta assobiava pelo ar, sendo quase impossível determinar a origem de tal assobio. Esperei que ele se aproximasse da casa-base, mas, depois, quando ele se posicionou para bater a bola, percebi que ele já lá se encontrava — mais distante do lugar do lançador do que eu julgava ser possível. Jasper estava atrás dele, a vários metros de distância, tendo a função de apanhar as bolas para a equipa adversária. Evidentemente, nenhum deles tinha luvas.

— Muito bem! — exclamou Esme com uma voz límpida, que eu sabia que até Edward ouviria, apesar de estar tão longe. — Batedor a postos.

Alice endireitou-se, estando ilusoriamente imóvel. Parecia ter um estilo furtivo, ao invés de proceder a uma preparação para o lançamento com movimentos intimidantes. Segurou a bola com ambas as mãos junto à cintura e, depois, qual investida de uma cobra-capelo, a sua mão direita precipitou-se e a bola atingiu a mão de Jasper, emitindo um estalo.

— Foi ponto para o batedor? — sussurrei a Esme.

— Se não se acerta na bola, é ponto para o batedor — informou-me.

Jasper voltou a lançar a bola com violência para a mão expectante de Alice. Ela permitiu-se esboçar um breve sorriso e, depois, a sua mão disparou novamente.

Desta vez, o taco conseguiu, de alguma forma, balançar-se a tempo de atingir a bola invisível. O estalo provocado pelo impacto foi arrasador, atroador; ecoou pelas montanhas. Compreendi logo a necessidade da trovoada.

A bola projectou-se como um meteoro por cima do campo, voando bem para o âmago da floresta circundante.

— *Home run!* — murmurei.

— Espera — acautelou Esme, escutando atentamente, com uma mão erguida.

Emmett era uma névoa à volta das bases, com Carlisle a seguir no seu encalço. Apercebi-me de que Edward desaparecera.

— Fora! — gritou Esme com voz clara.

Fiquei a olhar, incrédula, quando Edward surgiu da orla das árvores, com a bola na mão levantada, sendo o seu rasgado sorriso visível até para mim.

— O Emmett é o que bate com mais força — explicou Esme —, mas o Edward é o que corre mais rápido.

A rotação prosseguiu diante dos meus olhos incrédulos. Era impossível acompanhar a velocidade a que a bola era arremessada, o ritmo a que os corpos deles se deslocavam pelo campo.

Descobri o outro motivo pelo qual eles esperavam por uma trovoada para jogarem, quando Jasper, tentando evitar a infalível capacidade de Edward de correr e apanhar a bola, atirou uma bola rasteira na direcção de Carlisle. Este precipitou-se para a bola e, depois, Jasper correu para a primeira base. Quando colidiram, o ruído provocado parecia advir do embate entre dois pedregulhos maciços em queda. Levantei-me de um salto, preocupada, mas, de uma maneira ou doutra, eles estavam incólumes.

— Salvo! — exclamou Esme num tom de voz calmo.

A equipa de Emmett ganhava por um ponto — Rosalie conseguiu percorrer as bases depois de ter seguido de perto e persistentemente um dos longos arremessos de Emmett — quando Edward apanhou a terceira bola fora. Correu para junto de mim, irradiando entusiasmo.

— O que te parece? — perguntou.

— Uma coisa é certa: nunca mais conseguirei assistir aos jogos do velho e enfadonho basebol da Liga Principal na íntegra.

— E até parece que antes o fazias com muita frequência — riu-se.

— Estou um pouco decepcionada — gracejei.

— Porquê? — perguntou ele, perplexo.

— Bem, seria agradável descobrir uma só coisa que não fizesses melhor do que qualquer pessoa.

Exibiu o seu especial sorriso enviesado, deixando-me sem fôlego.

— Chegou a minha vez — disse ele, dirigindo-se para a casa--base.

Jogava com inteligência, mantendo a bola baixa, fora do alcance da mão de Rosalie sempre a postos na zona do campo mais distante do batedor, ganhando duas bases num ápice, antes que Emmett conseguisse colocar a bola novamente em jogo.

Carlisle bateu uma bola para tão longe do campo — produzindo um estrondo que me feriu os tímpanos — que tanto ele como Edward conseguiram pontuar. Alice deu-lhes graciosas palmadas nas mãos.

A pontuação alterava-se constantemente, à medida que o jogo continuava, e eles troçavam uns dos outros, como quaisquer jogadores de rua, quando assumiam a liderança. De vez em quando, Esme chamava-os à atenção para que a ordem fosse restabelecida. A trovoada ribombava incessantemente, mas nós permanecemos secos, tal como Alice previra.

Carlisle assumira a posição de batedor, cabendo a Edward a tarefa de apanhar a bola, quando Alice, de repente, se sobressaltou sonoramente. Os meus olhos estavam pousados em Edward, como de costume, e vi a sua cabeça virar-se num ápice para olhar para ela. Os olhares de ambos cruzaram-se e, num instante, algo foi comunicado entre eles. Ele já se encontrava a meu lado antes de os restantes terem podido perguntar a Alice o que se passava.

— Alice?

A voz de Esme estava tensa.

— Não vi; não consegui perceber — sussurrou ela.

Nesta altura, já todos os outros estavam reunidos.

— O que foi, Alice? — perguntou Carlisle com a voz calma de autoridade.

— Eles viajam muito mais depressa do que eu pensava — disse ela. — Vejo que, anteriormente, tinha a perspectiva errada — murmurou.

Jasper inclinou-se na direcção dela, com uma postura protectora.

— O que mudou? — interrogou ele.

— Ouviram-nos a jogar e mudaram de rumo — respondeu, contrita, como se se sentisse responsável pelo que quer que fosse que a assustara.

Sete pares de rápidos olhos incidiram sobre o meu rosto e desviaram-se.

— Dentro de quanto tempo? — perguntou Carlisle, voltando-se para Edward.

Uma expressão de concentração intensa atravessou-lhe o rosto.

— Menos de cinco minutos. Estão a correr; querem jogar.

O seu semblante carregou-se.

— Consegues? — perguntou-lhe Carlisle, olhando novamente na minha direcção.

— Levando-a às costas, não — disse laconicamente. — Além disso, a última coisa de que precisamos é que eles sintam o cheiro e comecem a caçar.

— Quantos são? — perguntou Emmett a Alice.

— Três — respondeu ela, de forma lapidar.

— Três! — zombou. — Que venham.

As faixas de aço que eram os seus músculos flectiam-se ao longo dos seus braços maciços.

Durante uma fracção de segundos que pareceu muito mais demorada do que realmente fora, Carlisle deliberou. Só Emmett parecia impassível; os restantes fitavam o rosto de Carlisle com olhos ansiosos.

— Vamos apenas continuar o jogo — acabou Carlisle por decidir.

A sua voz estava serena e regular.

— Segundo a Alice, eles estão simplesmente curiosos.

Tudo isto foi dito num frenesim de palavras que durou apenas alguns segundos. Eu escutara com atenção e percebera a maior parte, ainda que não conseguisse ouvir o que Esme agora perguntava a Edward com uma vibração silenciosa dos lábios. Vi apenas o ligeiro abanar da cabeça dele e a expressão de alívio no rosto dela.

— A Esme fica a apanhar as bolas — disse ele. — Agora, arbitro eu.

Então, colocou-se à minha frente.

Os outros voltaram para o campo, perscrutando com cuidado a floresta sombria com olhos vigilantes. Alice e Esme pareciam concentrar-se na área que rodeava o local onde eu me encontrava.

— Solta o cabelo — exclamou Edward num tom de voz baixo e regular.

Retirei obedientemente o elástico dos cabelos e sacudi-os à minha volta.

Constatei o óbvio.

— Os outros vão chegar agora.

— Sim, fica muito quieta, mantém-te calada e não te afastes de mim, por favor.

Ele disfarçava bem a tensão na voz, mas eu conseguia detectá-la. Puxei o meu longo cabelo para a frente, emoldurando o rosto.

— Isso não adianta nada — disse Alice com suavidade. — Eu conseguia sentir o cheiro dela do outro lado do campo.

— Eu sei.

Um laivo de frustração marcava o tom de voz dele.

Carlisle encontrava-se de pé na casa-base e os outros foram participar no jogo sem empenho.

— Que é que a Esme te perguntou? — sussurrei.

Ele hesitou durante um instante antes de responder.

— Se eles estavam sedentos — murmurou, com relutância, por entre dentes.

Os segundos passavam; o jogo decorria agora com apatia. Ninguém ousava bater a bola com muita violência e Emmett, Rosalie e Jasper circulavam pela zona do campo mais próxima do batedor. De vez em quando, apesar do medo que me tolhia o cérebro, tinha consciência de que os olhos de Rosalie estavam pousados em mim. Eram inexpressivos, mas algo no trejeito da sua boca me levou a pensar que ela estava zangada.

Edward não prestava a mínima atenção ao jogo, com os olhos e a mente a percorrerem a floresta.

— Lamento, Bella — murmurou, furioso. — Foi uma imbecilidade, uma irresponsabilidade expor-te desta forma. Lamento imenso.

Ouvi a sua respiração suspender-se e os seus olhos fixaram-se na zona da direita do campo. Deu meio passo, posicionando-se estrategicamente entre mim e aquilo que se avizinhava.

Carlisle, Emmett e os outros viraram-se na mesma direcção, ouvindo sons de passagem demasiado imperceptíveis para os meus ouvidos.

Capítulo Dezoito

A Caçada

Surgiram, um a um, da orla da floresta, com uma distância de cerca de uma dezena de metros entre si. O primeiro elemento do sexo masculino a chegar à clareira recuou imediatamente, permitindo que o outro assumisse a dianteira, orientando-se em redor do homem alto e de cabelo escuro de uma maneira que revelava logo quem chefiava o bando. O terceiro indivíduo era uma mulher; àquela distância, só conseguia ver que o seu cabelo era de um assustador tom de vermelho.

Cerraram fileiras antes de continuarem a caminhar com cuidado na direcção da família de Edward, mostrando o respeito natural de uma trupe de predadores quando depara com um grupo maior e desconhecido da sua própria espécie.

À medida que se aproximavam, apercebi-me de como eram diferentes dos Cullen. Andar felino, porte que parecia estar constantemente à beira de um agachamento. Envergavam roupas e acessórios característicos de turistas que viajavam de mochila às costas: calças de ganga e camisas informais de botões de tecidos pesados e à prova de água. As roupas estavam, porém, gastas pelo uso e eles estavam descalços. Ambos os homens tinham o cabelo cortado rente, mas o brilhante cabelo avermelhado da mulher estava repleto de folhas e detritos dos bosques.

Os seus olhos atentos analisaram a postura mais educada e urbana de Carlisle, que, ladeado por Emmett e Jasper, avançou com prudência para ir ter com eles. Sem ter havido qualquer comunicação aparente entre eles, todos se endireitaram, assumindo uma postura erecta e mais descontraída.

O homem que seguia à frente era sem dúvida o mais bonito,

com pele cor de azeitona debaixo da característica palidez e cabelo reluzentemente preto. Era de estatura média; bastante musculado, evidentemente, mas nada que se comparasse ao físico de Emmett. Esboçou um sorriso tranquilo, exibindo um clarão de dentes brilhantes.

A mulher era mais bravia, com os olhos a oscilarem irrequietamente entre os homens que a encaravam e o grupo disperso que me rodeava e com os caóticos cabelos a agitarem-se na ligeira aragem que corria. A sua postura era distintamente felina. O segundo elemento masculino rondava com discrição atrás deles, sendo mais franzino do que o chefe, tinha o cabelo castanho-claro e os seus traços simétricos indefiníveis. Os olhos, ainda que se mantivessem completamente quietos, pareciam, de algum modo, ser os mais vigilantes.

Os olhos deles também eram diferentes. Não eram dourados nem negros como eu esperara, mas sim de um carregado tom grená sinistro e perturbador.

O homem moreno, ainda a sorrir, avançou na direcção de Carlisle.

— Pensámos ter ouvido um jogo — disse num tom de voz descontraído com um ligeiríssimo sotaque francês. — Chamo-me Laurent e eles são a Victoria e o James.

Gesticulou, apontando para os vampiros a seu lado.

— Eu chamo-me Carlisle e esta é a minha família. O Emmett e o Jasper, a Rosalie, a Esme e a Alice, o Edward e a Bella.

Apontou para nós em grupos, não chamando especial atenção para cada pessoa. Senti um sobressalto quando ele pronunciou o meu nome.

— Há lugar para mais alguns jogadores? — perguntou Laurent de modo sociável.

Carlisle respondeu num tom de voz amável, semelhante ao de Laurent:

— Por acaso, já estávamos a acabar, mas estaríamos certamente interessados em jogar noutra altura. Tencionam permanecer nesta zona durante muito tempo?

— Na verdade, rumávamos para Norte, mas sentimos curiosidade em saber quem estava nas proximidades. Não encontramos companhia há muito tempo.

— Pois, esta região costuma ser ocupada apenas por nós e um ou outro visitante de ocasião, como vós.

O ambiente tenso dera lentamente lugar a uma conversa descontraída; imaginei que Jasper estivesse a utilizar o seu dom peculiar para controlar a situação.

— Qual é a vossa área de caça? — inquiriu Laurent com descontracção.

Carlisle ignorou a dedução implícita na pergunta.

— Aqui a Cordilheira Olímpica, às vezes ao longo das Cordilheiras Coast. Temos uma residência fixa aqui perto. Existe outro domicílio fixo como o nosso em Denali.

Laurent balançou-se ligeiramente para trás.

— Fixo? Como é que conseguem isso?

Havia uma curiosidade sincera na sua voz.

— Porque não vêm connosco até nossa casa para podermos conversar confortavelmente? — convidou Carlisle. — É uma história bastante longa.

James e Victoria trocaram um olhar de surpresa ao ouvirem a palavra «casa», mas Laurent controlou melhor a sua expressão.

— Parece-me uma ideia muito interessante e bem-vinda.

O seu sorriso era amável.

— Andamos à caça desde Ontário e já há algum tempo que não temos oportunidade para nos lavarmos.

Os seus olhos percorreram com admiração a aparência requintada de Carlisle.

— Por favor, não se ofendam, mas agradecíamos que se abstivessem de caçar nesta área mais próxima. Como devem compreender, temos de evitar dar nas vistas — explicou Carlisle.

— Claro — Laurent acenou com a cabeça. — Não iremos seguramente invadir o vosso território. Seja como for, já comemos nos arredores de Seattle — riu-se.

Um calafrio percorreu-me a coluna vertebral.

— Indicamo-vos o caminho se quiserem fazer-nos companhia numa corrida; Emmett e Alice, podem ir com o Edward e a Bella buscar o jipe — acrescentou com descontracção.

Pareceram dar-se três acontecimentos em simultâneo enquanto Carlisle falava. O meu cabelo agitou-se na leve aragem, Edward contraiu-se e James, o segundo elemento masculino, virou a cabeça de repente, examinando-me, com as narinas a dilatarem-se-lhe.

Uma súbita rigidez pareceu abater-se sobre todos eles quando James deu um passo em frente e se agachou. Edward mostrou os dentes, agachando-se também de modo a colocar-se numa posição defensiva, soltando uma feroz rosnadela da garganta. Esta em nada se assemelhava aos sons alegres que eu o ouvira emitir naquela manhã; foi o ruído mais ameaçador que eu jamais ouvira e, desde o cimo da minha cabeça até aos calcanhares, o meu corpo foi perpassado por calafrios.

— O que é isto? — exclamou Laurent com uma franca surpresa.

Nem James, nem Edward moderaram as suas poses agressivas. James fez uma ligeira finta para o lado e, em resposta, Edward mudou de posição.

— Ela está connosco.

A firme tirada de Carlisle era dirigida a James. Laurent parecia sentir o meu cheiro menos intensamente do que James, mas a compreensão revelava-se agora no seu rosto.

— Trouxeram uma merenda? — perguntou com um ar incrédulo ao dar um passo involuntário em frente.

Edward rosnou ainda com mais ferocidade e rispidez, com o lábio a recolher-se bem acima dos seus cintilantes dentes expostos. Laurent recuou novamente.

— Eu já disse que ela está connosco — corrigiu Carlisle com uma voz incisiva.

— Mas ela é *humana* — protestou Laurent.

As suas palavras não eram, de modo nenhum, agressivas, mas apenas de estupefacção.

— Pois é.

A presença de Emmett ao lado de Carlisle destacava-se consideravelmente, tendo ele os olhos pousados em James. Este endireitou-se, deixando de estar agachado, mas os seus olhos nunca deixaram de estar fixos em mim, as narinas ainda bem abertas. Edward manteve-se retesado como um leão à minha frente.

Quando Laurent falou, o seu tom de voz foi tranquilizador; tentava acalmar a súbita hostilidade.

— Parece que temos muito a aprender uns com os outros.

— De facto.

A voz de Carlisle continuava serena.

— Ainda gostaríamos de aceitar o vosso convite.

Os olhos dele viraram-se na minha direcção e, depois, voltaram a fixar-se em Carlisle.

— E, como é evidente, não iremos fazer mal à rapariga humana. Tal como já referi, não caçaremos na vossa área.

James fitou Laurent com incredulidade e irritação e trocou outro breve olhar com Victoria, cujos olhos ainda oscilavam de rosto em rosto.

Carlisle avaliou a expressão franca de Laurent durante um momento antes de falar.

— Nós indicamo-vos o caminho. Jasper, Rosalie, Esme? — chamou.

Todos se concentraram, deixando-me fora do alcance da vista dos outros ao convergirem. Alice colocou-se imediatamente a meu lado e Emmett retirou-se lentamente, com os seus olhos fixos nos de James à medida que recuava na nossa direcção.

— Vamos, Bella.

Edward falava num tom de voz baixo e soturno.

Durante todo este tempo, eu ficara paralisada no mesmo sítio, apavorada ao ponto de ficar completamente imobilizada. Edward teve de me agarrar o cotovelo e puxá-lo com violência para interromper o meu transe. Alice e Emmett seguiam logo atrás de nós, escondendo-me. Eu caminhava aos tropeções, ao lado de Edward, ainda aturdida com o medo. Não conseguia perceber se o grupo principal já partira. A impaciência de Edward era quase palpável à medida que nos deslocávamos, a uma velocidade humana, para a orla da floresta.

Assim que nos embrenhámos nas árvores, Edward atirou-me para as suas costas sem interromper a caminhada a passos largos. Segurei-me com o máximo de firmeza que consegui quando ele arrancou, seguindo os outros logo atrás dele. Mantive a cabeça baixa, mas os meus olhos, arregalados com o pavor, recusavam fechar-se. Precipitaram-se pela floresta, agora negra, como espectros. A alegria de viver que, normalmente, parecia apossar-se de Edward quando corria, estava completamente ausente, tendo sido substituída por uma fúria que o consumia e o levava a deslocar-se ainda mais depressa. Mesmo levando-me às costas, os outros ficavam para trás.

Chegámos ao jipe num lapso de tempo incrivelmente curto e Edward mal abrandou ao atirar-me para o banco de trás.

— Coloca-lhe o arnês — ordenou a Emmett, que entrou para o jipe e se sentou a meu lado.

Alice já se encontrava no banco dianteiro e Edward ligava o motor. Este roncou ao arrancar e guinámos para trás, rodopiando, para ficarmos virados para a estrada tortuosa.

Edward resmungava algo demasiado rápido para eu conseguir compreender, mas soava bastante a uma torrente de impropérios.

Os solavancos que caracterizavam aquele percurso foram, desta vez, muito mais sentidos e a escuridão só o tornava ainda mais assustador. Tanto Emmett como Alice lançavam olhares furiosos pelos vidros laterais.

Chegámos à estrada principal e, apesar de a velocidade a que seguíamos ter aumentado, eu conseguia ver muito mais nitidamente para onde nos dirigíamos. Rumávamos para Sul, para longe de Forks.

— Aonde vamos? — interroguei.

Ninguém respondeu. Ninguém sequer olhou para mim.

— Raios, Edward! Para onde me levas?

— Temos de te levar para longe daqui, para muito longe, e já.

Não olhou para trás, mantendo os olhos atentos à estrada.

O velocímetro indicava cento e setenta quilómetros por hora.

— Volta para trás! Tens de me levar para casa! — gritei.

Debatia-me com o maldito arnês, puxando as correias com violência.

— Emmett — disse Edward, de modo soturno.

Então, Emmett segurou-me as mãos com a sua força de aço.

— Não! Edward! Não, não podes fazer isto.

— Tenho de o fazer, Bella. Agora, por favor, fica calada.

— Não fico! Tens de me levar de volta; o Charlie vai chamar o FBI! Não deixarão a tua família em paz, o Carlisle e a Esme! Terão de partir, de permanecer eternamente escondidos!

— Acalma-te, Bella — a sua voz estava fria. — Já passámos por isto antes.

— Mas, por minha causa, não hão-de passar! Não vão deitar tudo a perder por minha causa!

Debatia-me com violência, totalmente em vão.

— Edward, encosta.

Alice falou pela primeira vez.

Ele lançou-lhe um olhar duro e, em seguida, acelerou.

— Edward, vamos apenas conversar sobre isto.

— Tu não compreendes — bradou em sinal de frustração.

Nunca o ouvira falar tão alto. A sua voz era ensurdecedora no espaço exíguo do jipe. O ponteiro do velocímetro aproximou-se dos cento e oitenta e cinco quilómetros por hora.

— Ele é um batedor, Alice. Viste isso? É um batedor!

Senti que Emmett se contraía a meu lado e fiquei admirada com a sua reacção ao ouvir tal palavra. Significava algo mais para os três do que para mim. Eu queria compreender, mas não tive oportunidade para perguntar.

— Encosta, Edward.

A voz de Alice transmitia sensatez, mas havia nela um tom de autoridade que eu nunca ouvira antes.

O ponteiro do velocímetro ultrapassou os cento e noventa quilómetros por hora.

— Faz isso, Edward.

— Escuta-me, Alice. Eu vi os pensamentos dele. A perseguição de presas é a sua paixão, a sua obsessão, e ele deseja-a, Alice; a ela, especificamente. Vai dar início à caçada esta noite.

— Mas não sabe onde...

Ele interrompeu-a:

— Quanto tempo julgas que ele vai demorar a isolar o rasto
odorífero dela na cidade? O seu plano já estava definido antes
de as palavras saírem da boca do Laurent.

Arquejei, sabendo aonde o meu rasto odorífero conduziria.

— O Charlie! Não podes deixá-lo lá! Não podes abandoná-lo!
Eu batia violentamente contra o arnês.

— Ela tem razão — afirmou Alice.

O carro abrandou um pouco.

— Vamos só analisar as nossas opções por um instante — ali-
ciou Alice.

O carro abrandou novamente, de modo mais notório, e, de repente, parámos, ouvindo-se os pneus chiar, na berma da estrada.
Precipitei-me contra o arnês e, depois, fui outra vez lançada com
violência contra o banco.

— Não existem opções! — exclamou Edward, irritado.

— Eu não abandono o Charlie! — gritei.

— Cala-*te*, Bella.

— Temos de levá-la de volta — disse Emmett, por último.

— Não — retorquiu Edward peremptoriamente.

— Ele não é capaz de nos fazer frente, Edward. Não será capaz
de lhe tocar.

— Ele espera.

Emmett sorriu.

— Eu também posso esperar.

— Tu não viste; não compreendes. Quando ele se empenha
numa caçada, é inabalável. Teríamos de matá-lo.

Emmett não pareceu ficar transtornado com tal ideia.

— É uma opção.

— E a mulher. Está com ele. Se isto se transformar numa dis-
puta, o chefe também se lhes aliará.

— Nós somos em número suficiente para conseguirmos dar conta deles.

— Existe outra opção — disse Alice, tranquila.

Edward virou-se para ela, enfurecido, falando num tom de voz extremamente ríspido:

— Não — existe — nenhuma — outra — opção.

Tanto eu como Emmett o fitámos com um ar escandalizado, mas Alice não pareceu ficar surpreendida. O silêncio prolongou--se por um longo minuto, durante o qual Edward e Alice se olharam fixamente.

Eu quebrei-o.

— Será que alguém deseja conhecer o meu plano?

— Não — resmungou Edward.

Alice lançou-lhe um olhar feroz, exasperada.

— Escutem — supliquei. — Vocês levam-me de volta.

— Não — interrompeu ele.

Lancei-lhe um olhar furioso e prossegui:

— Vocês levam-me de volta. Eu digo ao meu pai que quero regressar a Phoenix e faço as malas. Em seguida, esperamos até que esse batedor esteja a vigiar-nos e fugimos. Ele seguir-nos-á e deixará o Charlie em paz. Assim, o Charlie não chamará o FBI para investigar a vossa família. Depois, podem levar-me para onde lhes apetecer.

Eles fitavam-me, estupefactos.

— Até nem é uma má ideia.

O espanto de Emmett era, decididamente, uma afronta.

— Pode resultar e, além disso, não podemos sem mais nem menos deixar o pai dela desprotegido. Tu sabes disso — disse Alice.

Todos olharam para Edward.

— É demasiado perigoso; não o quero num raio de cento e cinquenta quilómetros do local onde ela se encontra.

Emmett estava muitíssimo confiante.

— Edward, ele não consegue passar por nós.

Alice reflectiu por um momento.

— Não prevejo um ataque da parte dele. Irá esperar até que a deixemos sozinha.

— Não vai demorar muito tempo a perceber que isso não vai acontecer.

— Eu *exijo* que me levem a casa.

Tentei mostrar firmeza.

Edward encostou os dedos às têmporas e fechou bem os olhos.

— Por favor — disse eu, num tom de voz muito mais débil.

Ele não ergueu o olhar. Quando falou, a sua voz estava esgotada.

— Partes esta noite, quer o batedor veja, quer não. Dizes ao Charlie que não aguentas ficar mais um minuto em Forks. Conta-lhe qualquer história, desde que resulte. Emala as primeiras coisas que te vierem às mãos e, depois, entra na tua *pick-up*. Não me interessa o que ele te diga. Tens quinze minutos. Estás a ouvir-me? Quinze minutos a partir do momento em que passares a soleira da porta.

O jipe troou ao arrancar e ele inverteu a marcha, ouvindo-se os pneus a chiar. O ponteiro do velocímetro começou a avançar pelo mostrador.

— Emmett?! — exclamei, olhando de forma incisiva para as minhas mãos.

— Ah, desculpa.

Soltou-me.

Decorreram alguns minutos de silêncio, ouvindo-se apenas o roncar do motor. Depois, Edward falou novamente:

— Eis a forma como tudo se vai passar: quando chegarmos a casa, se o batedor não estiver lá, eu acompanho-a à porta. Então, ela dispõe de quinze minutos.

Olhou-me irado pelo espelho retrovisor.

— Emmett, vigias o exterior da casa. Alice, vais buscar a *pick-up*. Permanecerei no interior enquanto ela lá estiver. Depois de ela sair, vocês os dois podem levar o jipe para casa e avisar o Carlisle.

— Nem pensar — interrompeu Emmett. — Eu fico contigo.

— Pensa bem, Emmett. Não sei durante quanto tempo estarei ausente.

— Enquanto não soubermos até onde isto vai, fico contigo.

Edward suspirou.

— Se o batedor lá estiver — continuou, soturno —, seguimos em frente.

— Vamos conseguir chegar lá antes dele — disse Alice de modo confiante.

Edward pareceu aceitar as suas palavras. Qualquer que fosse o seu problema com Alice, não duvidava dela agora.

— O que fazemos ao jipe? — perguntou ela.

A voz dele tinha um laivo de rispidez.

— Tu vais conduzi-lo até casa.

— Não vou, não — disse ela, tranquila.

A ininteligível torrente de impropérios recomeçou.

— Não cabemos todos na minha *pick-up* — sussurrei.

Edward não pareceu ouvir-me.

— Acho que devias deixar-me ir sozinha — murmurei num tom de voz ainda mais baixo.

Ele já me ouviu.

— Bella, por favor, limita-te a fazer isto à minha maneira, só desta vez — disse ele, por entre os seus dentes cerrados.

— Escuta, o Charlie não é um idiota — protestei. — Se tu não estiveres na cidade amanhã, vai ficar desconfiado.

— Isso é irrelevante. Certificar-nos-emos de que ele fica em segurança e só isso é que importa.

— E quanto a esse batedor? Ele viu a forma como agiste esta noite. Vai pensar que estás comigo, estejas onde estiveres.

Emmett olhou-me, espantado de novo.

— Edward, escuta-a — exortou. — Creio que ela tem razão.

— Pois tem — concordou Alice.

— Não posso fazer isso.

A voz de Edward estava glacial.

— O Emmett também devia ficar — prossegui. — Ele ficou-lhe, decididamente, debaixo de olho.

— O quê?! — exclamou Emmett, virando-se contra mim.

— Será mais fácil teres uma oportunidade de o apanhar se ficares — concordou Alice.

Edward fitou-a com incredulidade.

— Achas que eu devo deixá-la ir sozinha?

— Claro que não — respondeu Alice. Eu e o Jasper levamo-la.

— Não posso fazer isso — repetiu Edward.

Desta vez, porém, havia um laivo de derrota na sua voz. A lógica começava a exercer nele os seus efeitos.

Tentei ser persuasiva.

— Permanece aqui durante uma semana... — vi a expressão do seu rosto no espelho e reformulei a frase — alguns dias. Deixa que o Charlie veja que não me raptaste e leva-o a encetar uma caça aos gambozinos. Certifica-te de que ele perdeu por completo o meu rasto. Depois, parte para te encontrares comigo. Segue por caminhos indirectos, é claro, e, então, o Jasper e a Alice poderão regressar a casa.

Conseguia vê-lo começar a encarar aquela possibilidade.

— Encontrar-me contigo onde?

— Em Phoenix. Como é evidente.

— Não. Ele ouvirá qual é o teu destino — disse ele de modo impaciente.

— E tu farás, obviamente, com que pareça tratar-se de um ardil. Ele saberá que nós sabemos que ele está à escuta. Nunca acreditará que eu irei mesmo para onde disser que vou.

— Ela é diabólica — afirmou Emmett, soltando um riso abafado.

— E se isso não resultar?

— Existem vários milhões de pessoas em Phoenix — informei-o.

— Não é assim tão difícil arranjar uma lista telefónica.

— Não vou para casa.

— Ai não? — perguntou ele, com um tom de perigo na voz.

— Já tenho idade suficiente para ter o meu próprio canto.

— Edward, nós estaremos com ela — relembrou-lhe Alice.

— Que é que *vocês* vão fazer em *Phoenix?* — perguntou-lhe ele de forma contundente.

— Vamos permanecer dentro de casa.

— Essa ideia até me agrada.

Emmett estava, sem dúvida, a pensar em encurralar James.

— Cala-te, Emmett.

— Escuta, se tentarmos apanhá-lo enquanto ela ainda estiver por perto, é muito mais provável que alguém se magoe; poderá ser ela ou, então, tu, tentando protegê-la... Mas, se estivermos sozinhos quando o fizermos... — deixou a frase por terminar, esboçando um sorriso brando.

Eu tinha razão.

O jipe avançava agora lentamente ao entrarmos na cidade. Apesar das minhas palavras destemidas, conseguia sentir os pêlos dos meus braços a eriçarem-se. Pensei em Charlie, sozinho em casa, e tentei ser corajosa.

— Bella — a voz de Edward estava muito meiga. Alice e Emmett olhavam pelos vidros. — Se deixares que algo te aconteça, seja o que for, eu responsabilizo-te. Compreendes isso?

— Compreendo — respondi com dificuldade.

Ele virou-se para Alice.

— O Jasper consegue dar conta disto?

— Confia um pouco nele, Edward. Vendo bem as coisas, ele tem-se saído muitíssimo bem.

— E *tu*, consegues dar conta disto? — perguntou ele.

Então, a pequena e graciosa Alice contraiu os lábios numa horrenda careta e soltou uma rosnadela gutural que me fez aninhar no banco, de tão aterrorizada que fiquei.

Edward sorriu-lhe.

— Mas guarda as tuas opiniões para ti — disse, de repente, por entre dentes.

Capítulo Dezanove

DESPEDIDAS

Charlie estava acordado, à minha espera. Todas as luzes da casa estavam acesas. Nada me ocorria ao tentar pensar numa forma de fazer com que ele me deixasse partir. Não ia ser uma situação agradável.

Edward encostou lentamente, ficando logo atrás da minha *pick-up*. Estavam os três em alerta, direitos como um fuso nos seus bancos, atentos a cada som proveniente dos bosques, penetrando cada sombra com o olhar, detectando cada odor, procurando algo que não se encaixasse. O motor parou e eu permaneci sentada, imóvel, enquanto eles continuavam à escuta.

— Ele não está aqui — afirmou Edward, de modo tenso. — Vamos.

Emmett alcançou-me para me ajudar a libertar-me do arnês.

— Não te preocupes, Bella — disse ele num tom de voz baixo, mas alegre — nós trataremos rapidamente de tudo aqui.

Senti lágrimas a inundarem-me os olhos ao fitar Emmett. Mal o conhecia, mas, de alguma forma, o facto de não saber quando voltaria a vê-lo depois desta noite era angustiante. Sabia que isto era apenas uma pequena amostra das despedidas a que teria de sobreviver na hora seguinte e tal ideia fez com que as lágrimas começassem a correr-me pelo rosto.

— Alice, Emmett. — Edward entoou tais palavras como sendo uma ordem.

Eles mergulharam em silêncio na escuridão, desaparecendo imediatamente. Edward abriu-me a porta, pegou-me na mão e, depois, envolveu-me de forma protectora com o braço. Conduziu-me a toda a velocidade em direcção à casa, com os olhos sempre a perscrutarem a noite.

— Quinze minutos — advertiu, segredando.

— Eu consigo fazer isto — funguei. As minhas lágrimas deram-
-me inspiração.

Parei no alpendre e segurei o rosto dele com as minhas mãos.
Olhei-o intensamente nos olhos.

— Amo-te — disse eu, num tom de voz baixo e fervoroso. —
Hei-de amar-te sempre, aconteça o que acontecer agora.

— Nada vai acontecer-te, Bella — afirmou ele com a mesma
intensidade.

— Limita-te a seguir o plano, está bem? Mantém-me o Charlie em segurança. Depois disto, ele não vai gostar muito de mim
e eu quero ter a oportunidade de, mais tarde, pedir desculpa.

— Entra, Bella, temos de nos apressar.

A voz dele transmitia urgência.

— Só mais uma coisa — sussurrei de modo arrebatado. — Não
ouças nem mais uma palavra que eu disser esta noite!

Ele estava inclinado na minha direcção, pelo que só tive de
me esticar e colocar em bicos de pés para lhe beijar os lábios espantados e imóveis com o máximo de força que conseguia. Em
seguida, virei-me e abri a porta com um pontapé.

— Vai-te embora, Edward! — berrei-lhe, precipitando-me para dentro de casa e batendo-lhe com a porta na cara ainda espantada.

— Bella?

Charlie estivera a andar de um lado para o outro na sala de
estar e já se encontrava de pé.

— Deixa-me em paz! — gritei-lhe enquanto as lágrimas me
corriam pelo rosto, fazendo-o já de modo inexorável. Subi as escadas a correr, em direcção ao meu quarto, fechando a porta de
forma abrupta e trancando-a. Precipitei-me para junto da minha
cama, atirando-me para o chão para ir buscar o meu saco. Estendi agilmente a mão por entre o colchão e o estrado para pegar
na velha meia atada que continha o meu dinheiro secreto.

Charlie batia à porta do meu quarto.

— Bella, estás bem? O que é que se passa?

Falava num tom de voz assustado.

— Vou para *casa* — vociferei, com a minha voz a embargar-se no momento ideal.

— Ele magoou-te?

O seu tom de voz começou a denotar cólera.

— Não! — gritei um pouco mais alto.

Virei-me para a minha cómoda e Edward já ali estava, retirando braçadas de roupa ao acaso, que, em seguida, me atirava.

— Ele acabou tudo contigo?

Charlie estava perplexo.

— Não! — bradei, com a respiração ligeiramente mais ofegante enquanto colocava tudo dentro do saco. Edward lançou-me o conteúdo de outra gaveta. O saco já estava bastante cheio.

— O que aconteceu, Bella? — gritou Charlie através da porta, batendo outra vez.

— *Eu* é que acabei tudo com *ele*! — respondi, também gritando, puxando o fecho de correr do meu saco. As hábeis mãos de Edward afastaram as minhas e fecharam-no suavemente. Colocou a alça com cautela por cima do meu braço.

— Estarei na *pick-up*, vai! — sussurrou ele, empurrando-me, em seguida, na direcção da porta. Lançou-se pela janela e desapareceu.

Destranquei a porta e passei por Charlie com brusquidão, debatendo-me com o meu saco pesado ao descer as escadas a correr.

— O que aconteceu? — bradou, mesmo atrás de mim. — Pensei que gostavas dele.

Conseguiu agarrar-me pelo cotovelo na cozinha. Embora ainda estivesse confuso, segurava-me com firmeza.

Fez-me dar meia volta para olhá-lo e eu vi no seu rosto que ele não tinha qualquer intenção de me deixar partir. Ocorreu-me apenas uma forma de conseguir escapar — magoá-lo tanto que me odiei a mim própria só por ter considerado tal hipótese. Não tinha, porém, tempo a perder e tinha de mantê-lo a salvo.

Olhei para o meu pai, brotando novas lágrimas dos olhos devido àquilo que estava prestes a fazer.

— Eu gosto mesmo dele e o problema é esse. Não posso continuar a fazer isto! Não posso assentar mais raízes aqui! Não quero acabar presa nesta cidade estúpida e enfadonha como a mãe! Não vou cometer o mesmo erro idiota que ela cometeu. Detesto este lugar; não posso ficar aqui nem mais um minuto!

A mão dele largou-me o braço como se eu o tivesse electrocutado. Voltei as costas ao seu semblante ferido e escandalizado e dirigi-me para a porta.

— Bells, não podes ir-te embora agora. É de noite — sussurrou ele atrás de mim.

Não me virei.

— Se ficar cansada, durmo na *pick-up.*

— Espera só mais uma semana — pediu, ainda transtornado. — A Renée já estará de volta nessa altura.

Tais palavras desorientaram-me por completo.

— O quê?

Charlie prosseguiu ansiosamente, quase balbuciando de alívio quando eu hesitei.

— Ela telefonou enquanto estiveste fora. Nem tudo está a correr bem na Florida e, se o Phil não assinar um contrato até ao final da semana, eles vão regressar ao Arizona. O treinador adjunto dos Sidewinders disse que talvez tivessem um lugar para outro defesa.

Abanei a cabeça, tentando pôr em ordem as minhas ideias agora confusas. Cada segundo que passava colocava Charlie em maior perigo.

— Eu tenho a chave — murmurei por entre dentes, rodando a maçaneta. Ele estava demasiado próximo, com uma mão estendida na minha direcção e o rosto aturdido. Não podia perder mais tempo a discutir com ele. Teria de magoá-lo ainda mais.

— Deixa-me ir embora, Charlie — disse, repetindo as últimas palavras que a minha mãe proferira ao sair por aquela mesma porta há tantos anos. Pronunciei-as com o máximo de raiva que consegui e abri a porta com brusquidão. — Não resultou, está bem? Eu *detesto* Forks!

As minhas palavras cruéis foram eficazes. Charlie ficou paralisado na soleira da porta, estupefacto, enquanto eu corria, mergulhando na noite. Tinha um imenso pavor do jardim vazio. Corri desalmadamente até à *pick-up*, visualizando uma sombra obscura atrás de mim. Atirei o saco para a caixa de carga e abri a porta com violência. A chave estava à espera na ignição.

— Telefono-lhe amanhã! — vociferei, desejando poder explicar-lhe tudo nessa altura, mas sabendo que nunca seria capaz de o fazer. Liguei o motor e arranquei ruidosamente.

Edward estendeu a mão para pegar na minha.

— Encosta! — exclamou quando a casa e Charlie desapareceram atrás de nós.

— Eu consigo conduzir — disse-lhe com as lágrimas a escorrerem-me pelas faces.

As suas longas mãos agarraram-me inesperadamente pela cintura e o seu pé afastou o meu do acelerador. Puxou-me, fazendo-me passar pelo seu colo, arrancando-me as mãos do volante, e, de repente, já estava no lugar do condutor. A *pick-up* não se desviou um só centímetro do seu percurso.

— Não conseguirias encontrar a casa — explicou.

De repente, surgiu um clarão de luzes atrás de nós. Olhei pelo vidro traseiro em sobressalto.

— É só a Alice — tranquilizou-me. Voltou a pegar na minha mão.

A imagem de Charlie à porta preenchia-me os pensamentos.

— O batedor?

— Ouviu a parte final da tua actuação — disse Edward soturnamente.

— O Charlie? — perguntei, apavorada.

— O batedor seguiu-nos. Vem agora a correr atrás de nós.

O meu corpo gelou.

— Conseguimos ser mais rápidos do que ele?

— Não — respondeu, acelerando enquanto falava. O motor da *pick-up* gemeu em sinal de protesto.

De repente, o meu plano já não parecia tão brilhante.

Estava a olhar fixamente para os faróis do carro de Alice quando a *pick-up* estremeceu e uma sombra obscura surgiu do lado de fora do vidro.

O meu grito horripilante prolongou-se por uma fracção de segundo antes de a mão de Edward me tapar a boca.

— É o Emmett!

Destapou-me a boca e colocou o braço em torno da minha cintura.

— Está tudo bem, Bella — garantiu. — Vais ficar em segurança.

Atravessámos a cidade tranquila a grande velocidade, em direcção à estrada do Norte.

— Não tinha percebido que a vida na cidade pequena ainda te aborrecia tanto — disse ele em tom de conversa, sabendo eu que ele estava a tentar distrair-me. — Parecia que estavas a adaptar-te relativamente bem, sobretudo nos últimos tempos. Talvez estivesse apenas a alimentar o meu ego ao pensar que estava a tornar a tua vida mais interessante.

— Eu não estava a ser simpática — confessei, ignorando a sua tentativa no sentido da distracção e fixando o olhar nos meus joelhos. — Foi o que a minha mãe disse quando o abandonou. Poder-se-ia dizer que eu recorri a um golpe baixo.

— Não te preocupes. Ele perdoa-te.

Esboçou um pequeno sorriso, ainda que este não se tivesse reflectido nos seus olhos.

Fitei-o com um ar desesperado e ele viu o puro pânico espelhado nos meus olhos.

— Bella, vai ficar tudo bem.

— Mas vai deixar de ficar quando eu já não estiver contigo — sussurrei.

— Estaremos outra vez juntos dentro de alguns dias — disse ele, cingindo o abraço, que me envolvia. — Não te esqueças de que a ideia foi tua.

— Foi a melhor ideia, é claro que foi minha.

O sorriso que ele esboçou em resposta foi soturno e desapareceu logo de seguida.

— Porque é que isto aconteceu? — perguntei, com a voz a falhar-me. — Porquê a mim?

Fixou o olhar sombrio na estrada que se estendia à frente.

— A culpa é minha; foi uma loucura da minha parte expor-te daquela forma.

A raiva patente na sua voz era dirigida ao seu íntimo.

— Não era isso que eu queria dizer — insisti. — Eu estava lá, grande coisa. Esse facto não pareceu incomodar os outros dois. Porque é que esse James decidiu matar-me? Existem pessoas por toda a parte, porquê eu?

Ele hesitou, pensando antes de falar.

— Eu consegui perscrutar bastante bem a sua mente esta noite — principiou em voz baixa. — Não sei bem se poderia ter feito algo para evitar isto, assim que ele te viu. Em parte, a culpa é tua — disse, num tom de voz perverso. — Se não exalasses um cheiro tão espantosamente apelativo, ele poderia não se ter dado a tal trabalho. Mas quando eu te defendi... bem, isso agravou ainda mais a situação. Não está habituado a ser contrariado, por mais insignificante que o alvo seja. Considera-se um caçador e nada mais. A sua existência resume-se à perseguição de presas e é só um desafio que ele deseja da vida. De repente, apresentámos-lhe um belo desafio: um numeroso clã de fortes lutadores que se dedica a proteger o único elemento vulnerável. Não acreditarias na euforia que agora o invade. Trata-se do seu jogo preferido e nós acabámos de o tornar no jogo mais emocionante de sempre.

O seu tom de voz estava repleto de repulsa.

Deteve-se por um momento.

— Mas, se eu não tivesse reagido, ele ter-te-ia matado naquele preciso momento — disse com uma frustração desesperada.

— Pensei... que os outros sentiam o meu cheiro de forma diferente... de ti — disse com hesitação.

— E sentem. Mas isso não implica que não continues a ser uma tentação para todos eles. Se *tivesses* cativado o batedor ou qualquer um deles do mesmo modo que me cativas a mim, isso teria levado a que se travasse um combate ali mesmo.

Estremeci.

— Agora, acho que não tenho outra hipótese senão matá-lo — murmurou por entre dentes. — O Carlisle não gostará nada disso.

Conseguia ouvir os pneus a atravessarem a ponte, embora não conseguisse ver o rio na escuridão. Sabia que estávamos a aproximar-nos. Agora, tinha de lho perguntar.

— Como é que se mata um vampiro?

Ele fitou-me com um olhar indecifrável e, num instante, a sua voz tornou-se ríspida.

— A única forma de a morte ser certa é esquartejando o corpo, queimando, em seguida, as partes.

— E os outros dois irão lutar a seu lado?

— A mulher irá. Não estou certo quanto ao Laurent. Não têm uma ligação muito forte. Ele só está com eles por conveniência. Ficou constrangido com a atitude de James no prado...

— Mas o James e a mulher... tentarão matar-te? — perguntei com um tom de voz brusco.

— Bella, não te *atrevas* a perder tempo a preocupares-te comigo. Deves preocupar-te apenas em manter-te a salvo e, por favor, por favor, em *tentar* não ser imprudente.

— Ele ainda está a seguir-nos?

— Está. Mas não atacará a casa. Esta noite, não.

Enveredou pelo caminho invisível, com Alice a seguir-nos.

Avançámos mesmo em direcção à casa. As luzes no interior eram intensas, mas pouco contribuíam para atenuar o negrume da floresta invasora. Emmett abriu-me a porta antes de a *pick--up* parar por completo, puxou-me do banco, apertou-me como uma bola de futebol contra o seu peito largo e conduziu-me até à porta em passo de corrida.

Irrompemos pela ampla sala branca, com Edward e Alice a ladearem-nos. Todos estavam presentes, já de pé por nos terem ouvido aproximar. Laurent estava entre eles. Conseguia ouvir baixas rosnadelas vindas do fundo da garganta de Emmett quando este me pousou no chão, ao lado de Edward.

— Ele está a seguir-nos — comunicou Edward, lançando um olhar ameaçador a Laurent.

O semblante de Laurent demonstrou descontentamento.

— Já temia isso.

Alice deslocou-se graciosamente para junto de Jasper e sussurrou-lhe ao ouvido, com os lábios a tremerem com a rapidez da sua fala silenciosa. Subiram as escadas com agilidade, lado a lado. Rosalie observou-os e, em seguida, colocou-se rapidamente ao lado de Emmett. Os seus belos olhos estavam repletos de energia e, quando incidiram involuntariamente sobre o meu rosto, de fúria.

— O que fará ele? — perguntou Carlisle a Laurent num tom de voz arrepiante.

— Lamento — respondeu. — Quando ali o seu rapaz a defendeu, receei que isso fosse provocá-lo.

— Pode detê-lo?

Laurent abanou a cabeça.

— Nada consegue deter o James quando enceta uma demanda.

— Nós detê-lo-emos — garantiu Emmett. Não havia dúvidas quanto ao significado das suas palavras.

— Não conseguem derrotá-lo. Nunca vi nada como ele nos meus trezentos anos de vida. É absolutamente letal. Foi por esse motivo que me juntei ao seu grupo.

«*O seu* grupo», pensei. «É claro. A demonstração de liderança na clareira fora apenas isso: uma demonstração.»

Laurent abanava a cabeça. Olhou para mim, perplexo, e, depois, de novo para Carlisle.

— Têm a certeza de que vale a pena?

O brado enfurecido de Edward preencheu a sala. Laurent recuou, encolhendo-se.

Carlisle lançou um olhar grave a Laurent.

— Receio que vá ter de fazer uma escolha.

Laurent compreendeu. Deliberou por um momento. Os seus olhos observaram cada rosto e, por fim, examinaram a luminosa sala.

— Sinto-me intrigado com o modo de vida que aqui criaram, mas não interferirei neste assunto. Não tenho inimizade por nenhum de vós, mas não farei frente ao James. Julgo que me encaminharei para Norte, para junto daquele clã de Denali — hesitou.

— Não subestimem o James. Ele possui uma mente brilhante e sentidos incomparavelmente apurados. Sente-se tão à vontade no mundo dos humanos como vocês parecem sentir-se e não vos enfrentará de modo frontal... Lamento o que se desencadeou aqui. Lamento sinceramente.

Fez uma vénia com a cabeça, mas eu vi-o lançar outro olhar de perplexidade na minha direcção.

— Vai em paz — retorquiu Carlisle com formalismo.

Laurent olhou novamente em seu redor e, em seguida, precipitou-se para a porta.

O silêncio imperou durante menos de um segundo.

— Está muito perto? — perguntou Carlisle, olhando para Edward.

Esme já se encontrava em movimento; a sua mão tocou num discreto teclado na parede e, com um gemido, gigantescos estores de metal começaram a cobrir a parede envidraçada. Eu fiquei boquiaberta.

— A cerca de cinco quilómetros para lá do rio, desloca-se em círculos para se encontrar com a mulher.

— Qual é o plano?

— Nós despistamo-lo e, em seguida, o Jasper e a Alice levam-na para Sul.

— E depois?

O tom de voz de Edward era mortal.

— Assim que a Bella estiver livre de perigo, caçamo-lo.

— Creio que não há outra hipótese — concordou Carlisle, com o semblante soturno.

Edward virou-se para Rosalie.

— Leva-a para cima e troquem de roupa — ordenou Edward.

Ela fitou-o com uma lívida incredulidade.

— Porque haveria de o fazer? — sibilou. — Que é que ela representa para mim? Além de uma ameaça, de um perigo que optaste por impor a todos nós?

Retraí-me perante o veneno patente na sua voz.

— Rose — murmurou Emmett, pousando a mão no ombro dela.

Ela sacudiu-a.

Eu, porém, observava Edward com atenção, conhecendo o seu temperamento, preocupada com a sua reacção.

Ele surpreendeu-me. Desviou o olhar de Rosalie como se ela não tivesse falado, como se não existisse.

— Esme? — perguntou calmamente.

— Com certeza — murmurou Esme.

Colocou-se a meu lado num piscar de olhos, pegando em mim, sem dificuldade, com os seus braços e precipitando-se pelas escadas acima antes que eu pudesse verbalizar o meu sobressalto.

— O que estamos nós a fazer? — interroguei de modo ofegante quando ela me pousou numa sala escura, algures ao longo do corredor do primeiro andar.

— A tentar confundir o cheiro. Não irá resultar durante muito tempo, mas poderá dar-te uma ajuda.

Eu ouvia as roupas dela a caírem no chão.

— Acho que as roupas não me servirão... — hesitei, mas, de súbito, as mãos dela estavam a puxar-me a camisa pela cabeça. Despi rapidamente as calças de ganga. Ela deu-me algo que parecia ser uma camisa. Debati-me para conseguir fazer passar os braços pelos orifícios certos. Quando terminei, ela deu-me as suas calças largas. Vesti-as bruscamente, mas não consegui libertar os pés; eram demasiado compridas. Ela dobrou as bainhas algumas vezes para que eu conseguisse pôr-me de pé. De alguma forma, ela já conseguira vestir as minhas roupas. Puxou-me de novo na direcção das escadas, onde se encontrava Alice, com um pequeno saco de couro numa mão. Cada uma delas agarrou-me por um cotovelo e ambas praticamente me carregaram ao descerem, apressadas, as escadas.

No piso de baixo, parecia que tudo fora resolvido durante a nossa ausência. Edward e Emmett estavam prontos para partir, tendo este último uma mochila aparentemente pesada ao ombro. Carlisle entregava algo pequeno a Esme. Voltou-se e entregou a Alice a mesma coisa — tratava-se de um minúsculo telemóvel prateado.

— A Esme e a Rosalie levam a tua *pick-up*, Bella — informou-me ele ao passar. Acenei com a cabeça, lançando um olhar cauteloso na direcção de Rosalie. Ela fitava Carlisle com uma expressão ofendida.

— Alice, Jasper levem o Mercedes. A tonalidade escura ser-vos-á útil no Sul.

Também eles acenaram com a cabeça.

— Nós levamos o jipe.

Fiquei espantada ao verificar que Carlisle tencionava acompanhar Edward. De repente, com um assomo de medo, apercebi-me de que eles formavam o grupo de caça.

— Alice — perguntou Carlisle — eles cairão no engodo?

Todos observaram Alice enquanto esta fechou os olhos e ficou incrivelmente imóvel.

Por fim, os seus olhos abriram-se.

— Ele seguir-vos-á. A mulher irá atrás da *pick-up*. Devemos conseguir partir depois disso.

A sua voz transmitia certeza.

— Vamos.

Carlisle começou a caminhar em direcção à cozinha.

Edward, porém, acercou-se logo de mim. Envolveu-me no seu abraço férreo, apertando-me contra si. Parecia ignorar a presença da sua família vigilante quando puxou o meu rosto para o seu, levantando-me os pés do chão. Durante o mais breve dos segundos, os seus lábios duros e gélidos encostaram-se aos meus. De repente, acabara. Ele pousou-me no chão, segurando-me ainda o rosto, com os seus magníficos olhos a fixarem com vivacidade os meus.

Os olhos dele ficaram vazios, curiosamente mortos, quando se afastou.

Então, partiram.

Ficámos ali especados, com os outros a desviarem o olhar de mim quando as lágrimas começaram a escorrer-me em silêncio pelo rosto.

O momento de silêncio arrastou-se e, de repente, o telefone

de Esme vibrou-lhe na mão, precipitando-se, em seguida, para o seu ouvido.

— Agora — disse ela.

Rosalie saiu pela porta da frente sem voltar a olhar-me, mas Esme tocou-me na face ao passar.

— Fica bem.

O seu sussurro continuou a pairar atrás delas ao esgueirarem-se pela porta. Ouvi a minha *pick-up* começar a trabalhar de forma atroadora e, depois, a afastar-se, com o ruído a desvanecer-se.

Jasper e Alice aguardaram. Pareceu que Alice já tinha o telefone ao ouvido antes de este zunir.

— O Edward disse que a mulher está a seguir no encalço da Esme. Vou buscar o carro.

Desapareceu por entre as sombras da mesma forma que Edward o fizera.

Eu e Jasper entreolhámo-nos. Ele permaneceu do lado oposto da entrada... sendo cuidadoso.

— Estás enganada, sabes — disse ele calmamente.

— O quê? — interroguei, arquejando.

— Eu consigo percepcionar aquilo que tu estás a sentir neste momento e tu mereces isto.

— Não mereço — balbuciei. — Se algo lhes acontecer, tudo terá sido em vão.

— Estás enganada — repetiu ele, sorrindo-me amavelmente.

Eu nada ouvi, mas, de repente, Alice entrou pela porta da frente e dirigiu-se a mim com os braços estendidos.

— Posso? — perguntou.

— És a primeira a pedir licença — sorri de través.

Içou-me nos seus braços magros com a mesma facilidade com que Emmett o fizera, amparando-me de forma protectora, e, depois, precipitámo-nos pela porta fora, deixando as luzes intensas para trás de nós.

Capítulo Vinte

Impaciência

Quando acordei, estava confusa. Os meus pensamentos eram nebulosos, ainda mergulhados em sonhos e pesadelos. Levei mais tempo do que deveria a perceber onde estava.

O quarto onde me encontrava era demasiado incaracterístico para pertencer a outro lugar que não um hotel. Os candeeiros de cabeceira, aparafusados às mesinhas, eram um franco indício, tal como os longos cortinados feitos do mesmo tecido que a colcha e as gravuras genéricas a aguarela.

Tentei recordar-me de como ali chegara, mas, a princípio, nada me veio à memória.

Lembrei-me do carro preto lustroso, cujos vidros eram mais escuros do que os de uma limusina. O motor era quase silencioso, embora tivéssemos percorrido as negras vias rápidas a mais do dobro da velocidade permitida.

Lembrei-me também de Alice, sentada a meu lado no banco traseiro de couro escuro. De alguma forma, durante a longa noite, a minha cabeça acabara por cair no seu pescoço granítico. A minha proximidade não parecia, de todo, incomodá-la e a sua pele fria e dura afigurou-se-me estranhamente reconfortante. A parte da frente da sua fina camisa de algodão ficou fria e húmida com as lágrimas que caíam dos meus olhos até que estes, vermelhos e doridos, secaram.

O sono escapara-me. Os meus olhos doridos insistiam em manter-se abertos, apesar de a noite ter finalmente terminado e o dia romper sobre um baixo cume algures na Califórnia. A pálida claridade, raiando o céu limpo, feria-me os olhos, mas eu não conseguia fechá-los, quando o fazia, as imagens que surgiam com demasiado realismo, quais diapositivos parados por trás das minhas pálpebras, eram insuportáveis. O ar abatido de Charlie; o rosnar brutal de Edward, expondo os dentes; o olhar contrariado de Rosalie; a atenta vigilância do batedor; o olhar vazio de Edward depois de me ter beijado pela última vez... Não suportava vê-los. Assim, debati-me contra o meu cansaço e o Sol elevou-se cada vez mais no céu.

Ainda estava acordada quando atravessámos uma garganta pouco funda entre montanhas e o Sol, atrás de nós, reflectia nos telhados do Vale do Sol. Não me restava emoção suficiente para ficar admirada por termos realizado uma viagem de três dias num só. Lançava um olhar vazio para a vastidão imensa e plana que se estendia diante de mim. Phoenix: as palmeiras, o emaranhado de asfalto, as linhas fortuitas das vias rápidas que se cruzam, as faixas verdes dos campos de golfe e as manchas azul-turquesa das piscinas, todos imersos num ténue nevoeiro e abraçados pelas cristas curtas e rochosas que não eram, de facto, suficientemente grandes para serem apelidadas de montanhas.

As sombras das palmeiras enviesadas ao longo da via rápida — definidas, mais aguçadas do que eu me recordava, mais pálidas do que deveriam ser. Nada podia esconder-se nestas sombras. A estrada aberta e luminosa parecia suficientemente favorável, mas não fui invadida por qualquer sensação de alívio, de regresso a casa.

— Qual é o caminho para o aeroporto, Bella? — perguntara Jasper, sobressaltando-me, ainda que se tivesse dirigido a mim num tom de voz bastante suave e que não transmitia preocupação. Além do ruído do carro, este foi o primeiro som a quebrar o silêncio da longa noite.

— Continua na I-10 — respondi automaticamente. — Passamos mesmo por lá.

O meu cérebro conseguira aos poucos superar a nébula provocada pela privação do sono.

— Vamos viajar de avião para algum lado? — perguntara eu a Alice.

— Não, mas, por via das dúvidas, é melhor ficarmos por perto.

Lembrava-me do momento em que enveredáramos pelo desvio que circundava o aeroporto internacional de Sky Harbor... mas não daquele em que o abandonáramos. Suponho que tenha sido nessa altura que eu adormeci.

No entanto, agora, ao tentar recuperar a memória, tinha uma vaga impressão de ter saído do carro — com o Sol a pôr-se no horizonte — com o meu braço sobre o ombro de Alice e o braço desta a envolver-me a cintura com firmeza, arrastando-me enquanto eu tropeçava ao percorrer as sombras quentes e secas.

Não tinha qualquer lembrança daquele quarto.

Olhei para o relógio digital que se encontrava na mesinha-de-cabeceira. Os números vermelhos alegavam que eram três horas, mas não davam nenhuma indicação relativamente ao facto de ser de dia ou de noite. Nenhuma nesga de luz se insinuava através das espessas cortinas, mas o quarto estava iluminado com a claridade produzida pelos candeeiros.

Levantei-me com rigidez e cambaleei até à janela, afastando os cortinados.

Lá fora, estava escuro. Eram, então, três horas da madrugada. O meu quarto tinha vista para uma parte deserta da via rápida e para o novo parque de estacionamento de longa duração do aeroporto. O facto de poder identificar a minha localização era ligeiramente reconfortante.

Olhei para mim própria. Ainda envergava as roupas de Esme e estas não me assentavam nada bem. Examinei o quarto, ficando satisfeita ao descobrir o meu saco em cima da cómoda baixa.

Ia buscar roupas novas quando alguém bateu levemente à porta, sobressaltando-me.

— Posso entrar? — perguntou Alice.

Respirei fundo.

— Com certeza.

Ela entrou e observou-me com atenção.

— Estás com ar de quem dormiria mais um pouco — disse.

Limitei-me a abanar a cabeça.

Deambulou até junto das cortinas e fechou-as com cuidado antes de se virar para mim.

— Não poderemos sair — informou-me.

— Está bem. — A minha voz estava rouca e falhou.

— Tens sede? — interrogou.

Encolhi os ombros.

— Estou bem. E tu?

— Nada que não tenha remédio — sorriu.

Encomendei alguma comida para ti; está na sala da frente. O Edward lembrou-me que tens de comer com muito mais frequência do que nós.

Eu fiquei logo mais alerta.

— Ele telefonou?

— Não — respondeu ela, vendo o meu rosto ficar desanimado. — Foi antes de partirmos.

Pegou-me na mão com cuidado e conduziu-me, pela porta, até à sala de estar da suite do hotel. Conseguia ouvir o burburinho de vozes provenientes da televisão. Jasper estava sentado, imóvel, à secretária do canto, com os seus olhos nas notícias sem qualquer rasgo de interesse.

Sentei-me no chão, junto à mesinha de centro, onde um tabuleiro de comida me esperava, e comecei a debicá-la sem reparar naquilo que estava a comer.

Alice empoleirou-se no braço do sofá e fixou o olhar vazio na televisão, tal como Jasper.

Comi sem pressa, observando-a e virando-me de vez em quando para olhar na direcção de Jasper. Comecei a perceber que eles estavam demasiado quietos. Nunca desviavam o olhar do ecrã, apesar de, naquele momento, estarem a ser exibidos anúncios publicitários. Afastei o tabuleiro, sentindo, de repente, um mal--estar no estômago. Alice olhou para mim.

— O que foi, Alice? — perguntei.

— Não foi nada.

Os seus olhos eram grandes, sinceros... e eu não acreditei neles.

— O que fazemos agora?

— Aguardamos o telefonema do Carlisle.

— E ele já devia ter telefonado?

Percebi que andava perto da verdade. Os olhos de Alice deixaram os meus para incidirem no telefone que se encontrava em cima do seu saco de couro e voltarem a fixar-se em mim.

— Que quer isso dizer? — a minha voz tremeu e eu esforcei-me por controlá-la. — O facto de ele ainda não ter telefonado?

— Quer apenas dizer que eles nada têm a comunicar-nos.

A sua voz, porém, estava demasiado regular e o ar tornou-se mais difícil de respirar.

Jasper, de repente, colocou-se ao lado de Alice, aproximando-se mais de mim do que o habitual.

— Bella — disse ele, num tom de voz tranquilizante que era de desconfiar. — Não tens nada com que te preocupar. Aqui, estás completamente a salvo.

— Eu sei disso.

— Então, porque é que estás assustada? — perguntou ele, confuso.

Podia percepcionar o teor das minhas emoções, mas não conseguia decifrar as razões por trás delas.

— Vocês ouviram o que o Laurent disse — a minha voz não passava de um sussurro, mas eu tinha a certeza de que eles conseguiam ouvir-me. — Ele disse que o James era letal. E se algo correr mal e eles se separarem? Se algo acontecer a algum deles, ao Carlisle, ao Emmett... ao Edward... — reprimi um soluço. — Se aquela mulher selvagem magoar a Esme... a minha voz começara a elevar-se, com um tom de histeria a começar a insinuar-se nela. — Como é que eu conseguiria viver comigo mesma sendo tudo culpa minha? Nenhum de vós devia estar a arriscar-se por mim...

— Bella, Bella, pára... — interrompeu-me, proferindo tais palavras com tanta rapidez que eram difíceis de compreender. — Estás a preocupar-te com os aspectos errados, Bella. Confia em mim no que a isto diz respeito: nenhum de nós está em perigo.

Tu já te encontras sob demasiada tensão, portanto, não piores isso com preocupações totalmente desnecessárias. Escuta-me! — ordenou, pois eu desviara o olhar. — A nossa família é forte. O nosso único medo é perder-te.

— Mas porque é que vocês...

Desta vez, foi Alice quem me interrompeu, tocando a minha face com os seus dedos frios.

— O Edward já está sozinho há quase um século. Agora, encontrou-te. Tu não consegues ver as mudanças que nós, que já estamos com ele há tanto tempo, vemos. Achas que algum de nós quer olhá-lo nos olhos nos próximos cem anos se ele te perder?

O meu sentimento de culpa atenuou-se lentamente ao olhar nos seus olhos negros, mas, mesmo enquanto a calma me invadia, eu sabia que não podia confiar nos meus sentimentos na presença de Jasper.

Foi um dia muito longo.

Permanecemos no quarto. Alice telefonou para a recepção e pediu-lhes que, por enquanto, não se preocupassem com os serviços de limpeza do nosso quarto. As janelas permaneceram fechadas e a televisão ligada, ainda que ninguém estivesse a assistir. Com intervalos regulares, era entregue comida para mim. O telefone prateado que se encontrava pousado na secretária parecia ficar maior à medida que as horas passavam.

Os meus acompanhantes lidavam melhor com a expectativa do que eu. Enquanto eu me inquietava e andava de um lado para o outro, eles ficavam cada vez mais quietos, assemelhando-se a duas estátuas cujos olhos me seguiam imperceptivelmente enquanto eu me movimentava. Entretinha-me a fixar a disposição do quarto na memória; o padrão listrado dos sofás: castanho--amarelado, cor de pêssego, creme, dourado mate e, depois, novamente castanho-amarelado. Por vezes, olhava fixamente para as gravuras abstractas, descobrindo aleatoriamente figuras nas formas, tal como descobria figuras nas nuvens quando era criança. Divisei os contornos de uma mão azul, de uma mulher a pentear o cabelo e de um gato a espreguiçar-se, mas, quando o círculo vermelho-pálido se transformou num olho arregalado, desviei o olhar.

Como a tarde se arrastava lentamente, voltei para a cama, apenas para ter algo que fazer. Esperei que, ficando sozinha no escuro, conseguisse entregar-me aos terríveis medos que pairavam no limiar da minha consciência, incapazes de se libertar sob a atenta vigilância de Jasper.

Alice, porém, seguiu-me discretamente, como se, por alguma coincidência, se tivesse fartado de estar na sala da frente ao mesmo tempo. Eu começava a questionar-me sobre que tipo de instruções, ao certo, Edward lhe dera. Estendi-me na cama, de través, e ela sentou-se, com as pernas dobradas, a meu lado. A princípio, ignorei-a, subitamente cansada o bastante para dormir. No entanto, volvidos alguns minutos, o pânico que se mantivera afastado na presença de Jasper começou a revelar-se. Então, desisti rapidamente da ideia de dormir, enroscando-me até formar uma bola, envolvendo as pernas com os braços.

— Alice?! — exclamei.

— Sim?

Mantive um tom de voz extremamente calmo.

— O que julgas que eles estão a fazer?

— O Carlisle queria conduzir o batedor o máximo possível para Norte, esperar que ele se aproximasse e, depois, dar meia volta e armar-lhe uma emboscada. A Esme e a Rosalie deviam dirigir-se para Oeste, desde que mantivessem a mulher no seu encalço. Se ela voltasse para trás, elas deveriam regressar a Forks e manter o teu pai debaixo de olho. Logo, se eles não podem telefonar, imagino que tudo esteja a correr bem. Isso significa que o batedor está bastante próximo e eles não querem que ele escute a conversa.

— E a Esme?

— Penso que ela deverá estar de regresso a Forks. Não telefonará se houver alguma possibilidade de a mulher escutar a conversa. Parece-me que todos estão apenas a ser muito cuidadosos.

— Achas mesmo que eles estão em segurança?

— Bella, quantas vezes tenho de te dizer que não existe qualquer perigo para nós?

— Mas dir-me-ias a verdade?

— Diria. Eu sempre te direi a verdade — a sua voz era sincera.

Reflecti por um momento e cheguei à conclusão de que ela falava a sério.

— Então, diz-me... como é que alguém se transforma em vampiro?

A minha pergunta apanhou-a desprevenida. Ficou calada. Virei-me na cama para olhar para ela e a expressão estampada no seu rosto parecia ambivalente.

— O Edward não quer que eu te revele isso — respondeu firmemente, mas tive a impressão de que ela não estava de acordo.

— Não é justo. Julgo que tenho o direito de saber.

— Eu sei.

Olhei-a, esperando.

Ela suspirou.

— Ele vai ficar *extremamente* zangado.

— Não é da sua conta. Isto é entre nós. Alice, como tua amiga, suplico-te.

E, agora, de alguma forma, éramos amigas — tal como, provavelmente, ela sempre soubera que seríamos.

Ela olhou-me com os seus olhos magníficos e sensatos... tomando uma decisão.

— Vou contar-te a mecânica do processo — acabou por dizer — mas eu, pessoalmente, não me recordo e nunca o desencadeei, nem assisti ao seu desencadeamento. Logo, mantém presente no teu espírito que só posso revelar-te a teoria.

Fiquei à espera.

— Enquanto predadores, dispomos de uma superabundância de armas no nosso arsenal físico, muitíssimas mais do que aquelas que são de facto necessárias. A força, a velocidade, os sentidos apurados, já para não falar daqueles dentre nós que, como eu, o Edward e o Jasper, possuem faculdades de percepção sensorial adicionais. Além disso, qual flor carnívora, somos fisicamente atraentes para a nossa presa.

Fiquei muito quieta, recordando a forma contundente como Edward me demonstrara o mesmo conceito no prado.

Ela esboçou um sorriso rasgado e ominoso.

— Possuímos outra arma bastante supérflua. Também somos venenosos — declarou, com os dentes a brilhar. — O veneno não é mortal, mas apenas incapacitante. Actua lentamente, propagando-se pela corrente sanguínea, de modo a que a nossa presa, uma vez mordida, sinta dores físicas de tal forma intensas que não consiga escapar-nos. Tal como referi, trata-se sobretudo de algo supérfluo. Se estivermos assim tão próximos, a presa não consegue escapar. É claro que existem sempre excepções. O Carlisle, por exemplo.

— Então... se se deixar que o veneno alastre — murmurei.

— A transformação leva alguns dias a consumar-se, dependendo da quantidade de veneno que se encontra na corrente sanguínea, da proximidade do coração a que o veneno foi introduzido. Enquanto o coração continuar a bater, o veneno alastra, curando, transformando o corpo à medida que o perpassa. Acaba por deixar de bater e a mutação é concluída, mas, durante todo esse tempo, a cada minuto que passa, a vítima deseja a morte.

Arrepiei-me.

— Como podes ver, não é agradável.

— O Edward disse que era algo muito difícil de fazer... Não consigo compreender muito bem — afirmei.

— De certa forma, assemelhamo-nos a tubarões. Quando provamos o sangue ou simplesmente sentimos o seu cheiro, torna-se muito difícil abstermo-nos de nos alimentarmos. Por vezes, impossível. Portanto, como vês, o facto de chegarmos, de facto, a morder alguém, provar o sangue, desencadearia o frenesim. É difícil em ambas as vertentes: por um lado, a sede de sangue e, por outro, as dores terríveis.

— Porque julgas que não te lembras?

— Não sei. Para os outros, a dor da transformação é a recordação mais intensa que possuem da sua vida humana. Eu não me lembro de nada que se refira à época em que era humana – o seu tom de voz era melancólico.

Ficámos deitadas em silêncio, absortas nas nossas meditações individuais.

Os segundos passaram e, de tão absorta nos meus pensamentos, quase esquecera a presença dela.

Então, de forma inesperada, Alice saltou da cama, colocando-se de pé com graciosidade. Levantei bruscamente a cabeça ao olhá-la, sobressaltada.

– Algo mudou – a sua voz transmitia urgência e ela já não se dirigia a mim.

Chegou à porta ao mesmo tempo que Jasper. Era notório que ele escutara a nossa conversa e a súbita exclamação de Alice. Pousou-lhe as mãos nos ombros e conduziu-a novamente até à cama, fazendo-a sentar-se à beira da mesma.

– O que vês? – perguntou de modo concentrado, fixando-lhe o olhar. Os olhos dele estavam focados em algo muito distante. Eu estava sentada perto dela, inclinando-me na sua direcção de modo a ouvir a sua voz baixa e rápida.

– Vejo uma sala; é comprida e existem espelhos por toda a parte. O chão é de madeira. Está nessa sala e está à espera. Há uma lista... uma lista dourada que atravessa os espelhos.

– Onde fica esse quarto?

– Não sei. Falta algo, uma outra decisão que ainda não foi tomada.

– Quanto tempo falta?

– Pouco. Ele estará na sala dos espelhos hoje ou talvez amanhã. Tudo está pendente. Está à espera de algo e, agora, encontra-se na escuridão.

A voz de Jasper estava calma, metódica, enquanto a interrogava de modo experiente.

– O que está ele a fazer?

– Está a ver televisão... não, está a assistir a um vídeo, às escuras, noutro lugar.

— Consegues ver onde ele está?

— Não, está demasiado escuro.

— E, quanto à sala dos espelhos, o que mais existe lá?

— Apenas os espelhos e o dourado. É uma faixa que percorre toda a sala. E há uma mesa preta com uma grande aparelhagem de som e um televisor. Aí, ele toca no videogravador, mas não fica a assistir como faz na sala escura. É nesta sala que ele espera.

Os seus olhos vaguearam e, depois, fixaram-se no rosto de Jasper.

— É só isso?

Ela acenou com a cabeça. Ambos se entreolharam, imóveis.

— O que significa isso?

Por um instante, nenhum deles respondeu e, depois, Jasper olhou para mim.

— Significa que os planos do batedor sofreram uma alteração, que ele tomou uma decisão que o levará ao quarto dos espelhos e ao quarto escuro.

— Mas nós não sabemos onde ficam essas salas?

— Não.

— Mas sabemos que ele não ficará nas montanhas a Norte de Washington, sendo perseguido. Há-de escapar-lhes.

A voz de Alice estava soturna.

— Devemos telefonar? — perguntei.

Eles trocaram um olhar sério e indeciso. Então, o telefone tocou.

Alice já se encontrava do outro lado do quarto antes de eu conseguir levantar a cabeça para olhar para o objecto.

Premiu um botão e segurou o telefone junto do ouvido, mas não foi a primeira a falar.

— Carlisle — sussurrou. Não parecia surpreendida nem aliviada, ao contrário de mim.

— Sim — disse ela, olhando-me de relance. Ficou a escutar durante um longo momento.

— Acabei de o ver — voltou a descrever a visão que tivera. — O que quer que seja que o tenha levado a embarcar naquele avião... conduzia-o àquelas salas — deteve-se. — Sim — disse Alice ao telefone e, em seguida, dirigiu-se a mim — Bella?

Estendeu a mão com o telefone na minha direcção. Precipitei-me para ele.

— Estou? — disse.

— Bella! — exclamou Edward.

— Oh, Edward! Estava tão preocupada.

— Bella — suspirou, frustrado. — Eu disse-te para não te preocupares com mais nada além de ti.

Era tão incrivelmente bom ouvir a sua voz. Senti a nuvem de desespero que pairava sobre mim aligeirar-se e afastar-se enquanto ele falava.

— Onde estão vocês?

— Estamos às portas de Vancouver. Bella, lamento, perdemo-lo. Ele parece desconfiar de nós, tem o cuidado de se manter afastado de nós o suficiente para eu não conseguir auscultar os seus pensamentos. Mas, agora, desapareceu. Parece que embarcou num avião. Julgamos que está de regresso a Forks para começar do princípio.

Eu ouvia Alice a pôr Jasper a par dos acontecimentos atrás de mim, com as suas palavras rápidas a amalgamarem-se umas nas outras, gerando um burburinho.

— Eu sei. A Alice viu que ele escapara.

— Mas não tens com que te preocupar, pois ele não encontrará nada que o conduza até ti. Tens apenas de permanecer onde estás e esperar até que voltemos a encontrá-lo.

— Eu fico bem. A Esme está com o Charlie?

— Está. A mulher esteve na cidade e foi a casa do Charlie, mas enquanto ele estava a trabalhar. Não se aproximou dele, portanto, não tenhas medo. Está em segurança sob a vigilância da Esme e da Rosalie.

— Que é que ela está a fazer?

— Deve estar a tentar reencontrar o rasto. Vasculhou toda a

cidade durante a noite. A Rosalie seguiu a pista dela pelo aeroporto, por todas as estradas que circundam a cidade, pela escola... anda a investigar, Bella, mas não há nada a encontrar.

— E tens a certeza de que o Charlie está em segurança?

— Tenho, a Esme não o perderá de vista. E, em breve, nós estaremos lá. Se o batedor se aproximar de Forks, nós apanhamo-lo.

— Tenho saudades tuas — sussurrei.

— Eu sei, Bella. Acredita que sei. É como se tivesses levado metade do meu ser contigo.

— Então, vem buscá-la — desafiei-o.

— Em breve, assim que me for possível. Antes disso, *farei* com que fiques em segurança.

A sua voz era dura.

— Amo-te — lembrei-lhe.

— Apesar de tudo aquilo que te fiz passar, serias capaz de acreditar que eu também te amo?

— Sim, por acaso, até sou.

— Voltarei para ti em breve.

— Ficarei à espera.

Assim que o telefone ficou mudo, a nuvem de desânimo começou a insinuar-se sobre mim novamente.

Virei-me para devolver o telefone a Alice, encontrando-a a ela e ao Jasper debruçados sobre a mesa em que Alice rabiscava num pedaço de papel do hotel. Inclinei-me sobre as costas do sofá, olhando por cima do ombro dela.

Ela desenhava um quarto: comprido, rectangular, com uma zona quadrada, mais estreita, ao fundo. As pranchas de madeira que compunham o soalho estendiam-se longitudinalmente pelo quarto. Ao longo das paredes, desenhavam-se linhas que denotavam os intervalos entre os espelhos e, depois, envolvendo as paredes, à altura da cintura, encontrava-se uma longa faixa. A faixa que, segundo Alice, era dourada.

— É um estúdio de *ballet* — disse eu, reconhecendo, subitamente, as formas que não me eram estranhas.

Eles olharam-me, espantados.

— Conheces esta sala?

A voz de Jasper parecia calma, mas havia nela algo implícito e que não consegui identificar. Alice inclinou a cabeça sobre o seu trabalho, com a mão a voar, agora, pela página e a forma de uma saída de emergência a revelar-se na parede do fundo, com uma aparelhagem e um televisor numa mesa baixa no canto direito, em frente.

— Assemelha-se a um lugar aonde eu costumava ir para ter aulas de dança, quando tinha oito ou nove anos. Tinha exactamente a mesma configuração — toquei no ponto da página onde a zona quadrada se destacava, estreitando a parte do fundo da sala. — Aí, situavam-se os lavabos; tinha-se acesso às portas através da outra pista de dança. Mas a aparelhagem ficava aqui; — apontei para o canto esquerdo — era mais antiga e não havia televisor. Havia uma janela na sala de espera; ver-se-ia a sala desta perspectiva se se olhasse através dela.

Alice e Jasper olhavam-me fixamente.

— Tens a certeza de que se trata da mesma sala? — perguntou Jasper, ainda calmo.

— Não, de forma nenhuma... suponho que todos os estúdios de dança sejam parecidos... os espelhos, a barra — arrastei o dedo ao longo da barra de *ballet* cravada nos espelhos. — Só a configuração é que me pareceu conhecida — toquei na porta, colocada no mesmo local daquela de que me recordava.

— Terias algum motivo para ir lá agora? — perguntou Alice, interrompendo o meu devaneio.

— Não, não vou lá há quase dez anos. Era uma péssima bailarina, nos recitais, posicionavam-me sempre atrás — confessei.

— Então, não há nenhuma forma de aquela sala ser relacionada contigo? — perguntou Alice atentamente.

— Não, acho que nem o proprietário é o mesmo. Tenho a certeza de que se trata de outro estúdio de dança, algures.

— Onde se situava o estúdio que frequentavas? — perguntou Jasper como se nada fosse, tentando parecer despreocupado.

— Situava-se logo ao dobrar da esquina da rua onde ficava a

casa da minha mãe. Costumava ir até lá a pé depois das aulas...
— respondi, com a minha voz a diminuir de intensidade. Não me
escapou o olhar que eles trocaram.

— Então, situa-se aqui em Phoenix? — a sua voz continuava
descontraída.

— Sim — sussurrei. — Na intersecção da rua 58 com a Cactus.
Todos ficámos sentados em silêncio, olhando fixamente para
o desenho.

— Alice, esse telefone é seguro?

— É — tranquilizou-me. — A localização do número remete-
ria apenas para Washington.

— Então, posso servir-me dele para telefonar à minha mãe.

— Pensei que ela estivesse na Florida.

— E está, mas regressará a casa em breve e não pode voltar
àquela casa enquanto... — a minha voz tremeu. Eu pensava em
algo que Edward dissera, a respeito da mulher ruiva em casa de
Charlie, na escola, onde estariam os documentos com os meus
dados.

— Como conseguirás contactá-la?

— Eles não têm um número fixo senão em casa. Ela ficou de
verificar as mensagens regularmente.

— Jasper?! — exclamou Alice.
Ele reflectiu sobre o assunto.

— Julgo que não será prejudicial sob nenhum aspecto; certifica-te, como é evidente, de que não dizes onde estás.

Peguei no telefone com ansiedade, marcando o número conhecido. Tocou quatro vezes e, depois, ouvi a voz jovial da minha mãe, dizendo-me para deixar uma mensagem.

— Mãe — disse depois do apito —, sou eu. Escuta, preciso que
faças uma coisa. É importante. Assim que receberes esta mensagem, telefona-me para este número — Alice já se encontrava a
meu lado, anotando-me o número na margem inferior do seu
esboço. Li-o cuidadosamente, por duas vezes. — Por favor, não
vás a lado nenhum até falares comigo. Não te preocupes, eu estou bem, mas tenho de falar contigo com urgência, por mais

tardiamente que ouças esta chamada, está bem? Gosto muito de ti, mãe. Adeus.

Fechei os olhos e rezei com todas as minhas forças para que nenhuma mudança de planos imprevista a fizesse voltar para casa antes de receber o meu recado.

Acomodei-me no sofá, debicando um prato de fruta que sobrara, prevendo uma longa noite. Pensei em telefonar a Charlie, mas não estava certa se ele já estaria em casa ou não. Concentrei-me nas notícias, ficando atenta a reportagens sobre a Florida ou sobre a pré-temporada — greves, furacões ou ataques terroristas —, qualquer coisa que pudesse fazê-los regressar a casa mais cedo.

A imortalidade deve conceder uma paciência infinita. Nem Jasper, nem Alice pareciam sentir necessidade de fazer o que quer que fosse. Durante alguns momentos, Alice delineou os vagos contornos da sala escura que aparecera na sua visão, esboçando tudo quanto conseguira ver através da luz projectada pela televisão. No entanto, quando terminou, sentou-se, olhando as paredes vazias com os seus olhos intemporais. Jasper também não parecia sentir-se impelido a andar de um lado para o outro, nem a espreitar através das cortinas ou a precipitar-se pela porta fora aos gritos, ao contrário do que acontecia comigo.

Devo ter adormecido no sofá, esperando que o telefone voltasse a tocar. O toque das mãos frias de Alice acordou-me por breves instantes quando ela me levou para a cama, mas depressa voltei a cair no sono.

Capítulo Vinte e Um

TELEFONEMA

Percebi que era novamente demasiado cedo quando acordei e tive consciência de que estava a inverter aos poucos o meu horário diurno e nocturno. Fiquei deitada na cama a ouvir as discretas vozes de Alice e de Jasper na divisão contígua. O facto de falarem suficientemente alto para eu os ouvir era estranho. Virei-me com prontidão na cama até os meus pés tocarem no chão e, depois, cambaleei até à sala de estar.

Segundo o relógio da televisão, passavam poucos minutos das duas horas da madrugada. Alice e Jasper estavam sentados lado a lado no sofá, estando ela a desenhar novamente, enquanto ele olhava por cima do ombro dela. Não ergueram o olhar quando eu entrei, estando demasiado absortos no trabalho de Alice.

Desloquei-me sem fazer barulho até junto de Jasper para dar uma espreitadela.

— Ela visionou mais alguma coisa? — perguntei discretamente a Jasper.

— Visionou. Algo o fez voltar à sala do videogravador, mas, agora, esta está iluminada.

Vi Alice desenhar uma sala quadrada com vigas escuras a atravessarem-lhe o tecto baixo. As paredes eram forradas a madeira, um pouco escuras de mais, ultrapassadas. O piso estava coberto por um tapete escuro com motivos decorativos. Havia uma grande janela na parede virada para Sul e uma passagem na parede ocidental que dava acesso à sala de estar. Um dos lados dessa entrada era de pedra — uma grande lareira de pedra castanho-amarelada que abrangia ambas as divisões. O televisor e o videogravador, o ponto central da sala a partir daquela perspectiva, assentavam num pequeno móvel de madeira no canto

Sudoeste da sala. Um velho sofá composto por módulos estava dobrado diante do televisor, tendo à sua frente uma mesinha de centro redonda.

— O telefone fica ali — sussurrei, apontando.

Dois pares de olhos eternos fixaram-se em mim.

— É a casa da minha mãe.

Alice já se levantara do sofá, segurando o telefone enquanto marcava um número. Eu olhei para o retrato preciso da sala de estar da casa da minha mãe. Quase sem se notar, Jasper aproximou-se mais de mim. Tocou-me levemente o ombro com a mão e este contacto físico pareceu intensificar a sua influência tranquilizadora. O pânico permaneceu tolhido, impreciso.

Os lábios de Alice tremiam com a velocidade das suas palavras, sendo quase inaudível o murmúrio impossível de decifrar. Não conseguia concentrar-me.

— Bella — disse Alice.

Eu olhei-a, entorpecida.

— Bella, o Edward vem buscar-te. Ele, o Emmett e o Carlisle vão levar-te para um sítio, para te esconder durante algum tempo.

— O Edward vem a caminho?

Tais palavras exerceram um efeito semelhante ao de um colete salva-vidas, mantendo-me a cabeça à tona de água.

— Vem. Vai apanhar o primeiro voo que partir de Seattle. Vamos ter com ele ao aeroporto e tu partirás com ele.

— Mas... a minha mãe... ele veio para cá à procura da minha mãe, Alice!

Apesar da influência de Jasper, a histeria revelou-se na minha voz.

— Eu e o Jasper ficaremos aqui até que ela esteja a salvo.

— Não há maneira de eu sair vitoriosa, Alice. Vocês não podem vigiar para sempre todas as pessoas que eu conheço. Não vês o que ele está a fazer? Não está, de todo, a seguir a minha pista. Irá encontrar alguém, irá magoar alguém de quem eu gosto... Alice, eu não posso...

— Nós vamos apanhá-lo, Bella — assegurou-me.

— E se vocês se magoarem, Alice? Achas que isso não me afecta? Achas que ele só consegue atingir-me se fizer mal à minha família humana?

Alice lançou um olhar expressivo a Jasper. Fui invadida por uma pesada e profunda onda de letargia e os meus olhos fecharam-se sem o meu consentimento. A minha mente debateu-se contra a tal nébula, apercebendo-se do que estava a acontecer. Abri os olhos com esforço e coloquei-me de pé, afastando-me da mão de Jasper.

— Não quero voltar a adormecer — protestei, furiosa.

Caminhei até ao meu quarto e fechei a porta, quase batendo com ela de verdade, de modo a poder ir-me abaixo em privado. Desta vez, Alice não me seguiu. Durante três horas e meia, olhei fixamente para a parede, enroscada sobre mim mesma, balouçando-me. A minha cabeça dava voltas, tentando arranjar uma maneira de sair deste pesadelo. Não havia fuga nem indulto possíveis. Via apenas um final provável a desenhar-se sombriamente no meu futuro. A única questão que se colocava era quantas pessoas sairiam magoadas até que eu lá chegasse.

O único consolo, a única esperança que me restava residia no facto de saber que veria Edward em breve. Se pudesse apenas voltar a ver o seu rosto, talvez fosse também capaz de achar a solução que agora me escapava.

Quando o telefone tocou, voltei para a sala da frente, um pouco envergonhada com o meu comportamento. Esperava não ter ofendido nenhum deles, que eles soubessem quão grata eu estava pelos sacrifícios que eles estavam a fazer por minha causa.

Alice falava tão depressa como sempre, mas o que chamou a minha atenção foi o facto de, pela primeira vez, Jasper estar ausente da sala. Olhei para o relógio — eram cinco e meia da madrugada.

— Estão precisamente a embarcar no avião — informou-me Alice. — Aterram às nove horas e quarenta e cinco minutos.

Só tinha de continuar a respirar durante mais algumas horas até que ele chegasse.

— Onde está o Jasper?

— Foi tratar da nossa saída do hotel.

— Vocês não ficam aqui?

— Não, vamos mudar-nos para um local mais próximo da casa da tua mãe.

O meu estômago contraiu-se com inquietação ao ouvir as palavras dela.

O telefone, porém, voltou a tocar, distraindo-me. Ela pareceu surpreendida, mas eu já estava a avançar, tentando alcançar o telefone, repleta de esperança.

— Estou?! — exclamou Alice. — Não, ela está mesmo aqui — estendeu-me a mão com o telefone e, movendo apenas os lábios, disse que era a minha mãe.

— Estou?

— Bella? Bella?

Era a voz da minha mãe, num tom familiar que eu ouvira milhares de vezes na minha infância, sempre que me aproximava demasiado da beira do passeio ou ela me perdia de vista num local apinhado de gente. Era o som do pânico.

Suspirei. Já esperava isto, embora tivesse tentado tornar a minha mensagem o menos alarmista possível, sem minorar o carácter urgente da mesma.

— Acalma-te, mãe — disse eu, no meu tom de voz mais tranquilizador, afastando-me aos poucos de Alice. Não sabia se conseguiria mentir de forma tão convincente com os olhos dela pousados em mim. — Está tudo bem, sim? Dá-me apenas um minuto que eu explico tudo. Prometo.

Detive-me, admirada por ela ainda não me ter interrompido.

— Mãe?

— Tem muito cuidado para não dizeres nada enquanto eu não te instruir nesse sentido.

A voz que eu ouvia agora era-me tão estranha como inesperada. Era uma voz masculina de tenor, uma voz comum, muito agradável. O género de voz de fundo que se ouvia em anúncios publicitários de automóveis de luxo. Falava com muita rapidez.

— Eu não preciso de magoar a tua mãe, portanto, faz o favor de agir exactamente conforme eu disser e ela ficará bem — deteve-se por um instante, enquanto eu escutava num estado de pavor mudo. — Muito bem — felicitou-me. — Agora, repete depois de mim e tenta parecer espontânea. Diz o seguinte: «Não, mãe, fica onde estás».

— Não, mãe, fica onde estás.

A minha voz quase não passava de um sussurro.

— Vejo que vai ser difícil — a voz estava divertida, ainda alegre e amável. — Porque não vais para outra divisão, de modo a que a tua cara não deite tudo a perder? Não existe motivo nenhum para que a tua mãe tenha de sofrer. Enquanto caminhas, diz o seguinte: «Mãe, por favor, escuta-me». Di-lo agora.

— Mãe, por favor, escuta-me — pediu a minha voz. Caminhei muito devagar até ao quarto, sentindo o olhar de preocupação de Alice pousado nas minhas costas. Fechei a porta depois de ter entrado, tentando pensar com lucidez, apesar do pavor que se apoderava do meu cérebro.

— Pronto, já estás sozinha? Responde apenas sim ou não.

— Sim.

— Mas, decerto, eles ainda conseguem ouvir-te.

— Sim.

— Muito bem; então — a voz bem-disposta manteve-se — diz: «Mãe, confia em mim».

— Mãe, confia em mim.

— Isto correu melhor do que eu esperava. Estava preparado para esperar, mas a tua mãe chegou mais cedo do que o previsto. Assim, torna-se mais fácil, não é? Vives momentos de menor expectativa, de menor ansiedade.

Esperei.

— Agora, quero que me escutes com muita atenção. Preciso que escapes aos teus amigos. Achas que consegues fazer isso? Responde sim ou não.

— Não.

— Lamento ouvir isso. Estava com esperança de que fosses

um pouco mais criativa. Achas que conseguirias escapar-lhes se a vida da tua mãe dependesse disso? Responde sim ou não.

De uma maneira ou de outra, devia haver uma solução. Lembrei-me de que íamos para o aeroporto. O aeroporto internacional de Sky Harbor: a abarrotar de gente, com uma disposição confusa...

— Sim.

— Assim está melhor. Estou certo de que não será fácil, mas, se eu tiver a mínima desconfiança de que estás acompanhada por alguém, bem, isso seria muito mau para a tua mãe — garantiu a voz amável. — Já deves saber o suficiente sobre nós para teres noção de quão depressa eu me aperceberia da tua tentativa de levar alguém contigo. E de quão pouco tempo eu precisaria para me encarregar da tua mãe se fosse esse o caso. Compreendes? Responde sim ou não.

— Sim — a minha voz embargou-se.

— Muito bem, Bella. Agora, eis o que tens de fazer: quero que vás a casa da tua mãe. Junto do telefone, estará um número. Telefona para esse número e eu dir-te-ei aonde deverás ir em seguida.

Eu já sabia aonde iria e onde isto terminaria, mas segui as suas instruções à risca.

— Consegues fazer isso? Responde sim ou não.

— Sim.

— Por favor, antes do meio-dia, Bella. Não tenho o dia todo — disse com delicadeza.

— Onde está o Phil? — perguntei.

— Ah, agora, tem cuidado, Bella. Espera até eu te pedir para falares, por favor.

Esperei.

— Agora, é importante que não levantes suspeitas entre os teus amigos quando voltares para junto deles. Diz-lhes que a tua mãe telefonou e que a dissuadiste de voltar a casa por enquanto. Agora, repete depois de mim: «Obrigada, mãe». Di-lo agora.

— Obrigada, mãe.

As lágrimas ameaçavam começar a cair. Tentei contê-las.

— Diz: «Gosto muito de ti, mãe; vemo-nos em breve». Di-lo agora.

— Gosto muito de ti, mãe — a minha voz estava rouca. — Vemo-nos em breve — prometi.

— Adeus, Bella. Espero ansiosamente por voltar a ver-te.

Desligou o telefone.

Mantive o telefone encostado ao ouvido. As minhas articulações estavam paralisadas com o pavor e eu não conseguia esticar os dedos para o largar.

Sabia que tinha de raciocinar, mas o som do pânico da minha mãe não me saía da cabeça. Os segundos passavam enquanto eu me esforçava por me controlar.

Muito lentamente, os meus pensamentos começaram a transpor a muralha de dor. Precisava de traçar um plano, pois, agora, tinha apenas uma opção: ir até à sala espelhada e morrer. Não tinha quaisquer garantias, nada para dar em troca da vida da minha mãe. Restava-me apenas esperar que James ficasse satisfeito com a sua vitória no jogo, que o facto de ter conseguido derrotar Edward fosse suficiente. O desespero apoderou-se de mim; não havia forma de negociar, nem nada que eu pudesse oferecer ou sonegar de modo a influenciá-lo, mas eu continuava a não ter alternativa. Tinha de tentar.

Reprimi o pavor tanto quanto me foi possível. A minha decisão estava tomada. Era escusado perder tempo a afligir-me ao pensar no desfecho daquela situação. Tinha de pensar com clareza, pois Alice e Jasper estavam à minha espera e escapar-lhes era algo absolutamente essencial, mas também absolutamente impossível.

De súbito, estava grata por Jasper ter saído. Se ele tivesse estado presente e percepcionado a minha angústia nos últimos cinco minutos, como conseguiria eu evitar que eles ficassem desconfiados? Abafei o pavor, a ansiedade, tentando reprimir tais sentimentos. Não podia dar-me agora ao luxo de os alimentar. Não sabia quando é que ele voltaria.

Concentrei-me na minha fuga. Esperava que o facto de conhecer bem os meandros do aeroporto virasse a situação a meu favor. Tinha, de alguma forma, de manter Alice afastada...

Eu sabia que Alice estava na divisão contígua à minha espera, curiosa, mas tinha de tratar de mais uma questão em privado, antes que Jasper voltasse.

Tinha de aceitar que não voltaria a ver Edward, que não teria sequer um derradeiro vislumbre do seu rosto para levar comigo para a sala dos espelhos. Ia magoá-lo e não podia despedir-me. Deixei que as ondas de tormento me inundassem, que levassem a melhor por alguns momentos. Depois, também as repeli e fui enfrentar Alice.

A única expressão que consegui colocar no rosto foi um ar apagado e vazio. Apercebi-me da sua preocupação e não esperei que ela fizesse qualquer pergunta. Tinha apenas um guião a seguir e, naquele momento, jamais conseguiria improvisar.

— A minha mãe estava preocupada. Queria voltar para casa. Mas está tudo bem, eu convenci-a a manter-se afastada.

A minha voz estava sem vida.

— Nós certificar-nos-emos de que ela fica bem, Bella, não te preocupes.

Voltei-lhe as costas. Não podia deixá-la ver-me o rosto.

Os meus olhos pousaram numa página em branco que fazia parte do papel de carta que se encontrava sobre a secretária. Dirigi-me a ela lentamente, com um plano a tomar forma na minha cabeça. Havia também um envelope, o que era útil.

— Alice — perguntei devagar, sem me virar, mantendo o tom de voz. — Se eu escrever uma carta para a minha mãe, entregas-lha? Quero dizer, deixas-lha em casa?

— Claro, Bella.

A sua voz era cautelosa. Ela via-me a rebentar pelas costuras. Eu *tinha* de controlar melhor as minhas emoções.

Fui novamente para o quarto e ajoelhei-me junto da mesinha-de-cabeceira para escrever.

«Edward» — escrevi. A minha mão tremia e as letras liam-se mal.

«Amo-te. Lamento imenso. Ele capturou a minha mãe e eu tenho de tentar. Sei que pode não resultar. Lamento muitíssimo. Não te zangues com a Alice e o Jasper. Será um milagre se eu conseguir escapar-lhes. Agradece-lhes por mim. Sobretudo à Alice.

Peço-te também, por favor, que não vás atrás dele. É isso que ele quer. Não suportarei se alguém se magoar por minha causa, sobretudo tu. Por favor. Este é o único pedido que posso fazer-te neste momento. Por mim.

Amo-te. Perdoa-me.

Bella.»

Dobrei a carta com cuidado e coloquei-a dentro do envelope. Ele acabaria por encontrá-la. Só esperava que ele conseguisse compreender e respeitasse a minha vontade só desta vez.

Em seguida, fechei o meu coração.

Capítulo Vinte e Dois

Jogar às Escondidas

Demorara muito menos tempo do que eu pensara — todo o pavor, o desespero, o despedaçar do meu coração. Os minutos passavam mais devagar do que o habitual. Jasper ainda não regressara quando voltei para junto de Alice. Receava estar na mesma sala que ela, a possibilidade de ela adivinhar... e esconder-me dela pelo mesmo motivo.

Pensava ter perdido por completo a capacidade de ficar surpreendida, sendo os meus pensamentos atormentados e instáveis, mas tal aconteceu quando vi Alice debruçada sobre a secretária, segurando-se à borda da mesma com ambas as mãos.

— Alice?

Não reagiu quando proferi o seu nome, mas a sua cabeça balouçava lentamente de um lado para o outro e vi-lhe o rosto. Os seus olhos estavam vazios, ofuscados... Pensei imediatamente na minha mãe. Já seria tarde de mais?

Apressei-me para junto dela, estendendo automaticamente a mão para tocar a dela.

— Alice! — vociferou Jasper de repente, aparecendo mesmo atrás dela, com as mãos a agarrarem as dela, fazendo-a largar a mesa. Do outro lado da sala, a porta fechou-se, produzindo um estalido pouco sonoro.

— O que foi? — perguntou.

Ela virou-me a cara, afundando-a no peito dele.

— A Bella! — exclamou.

— Estou aqui — retorqui.

A cabeça dela virou-se de repente, fixando os seus olhos nos meus, ainda com uma expressão estranhamente vazia. Apercebi-me de imediato de que não estava a falar comigo, mas sim a responder à pergunta de Jasper.

— O que é que viste? — disse eu, não havendo qualquer entoação interrogativa na minha voz indiferente e monocórdica.

Jasper lançou-me um olhar penetrante. Mantive uma expressão apática e esperei. Os olhos dele estavam confusos enquanto oscilavam entre o rosto de Alice e o meu, percepcionando o caos... pois eu já calculava o que Alice vira naquele momento.

Senti um ambiente tranquilo instalar-se à minha volta. Recebi-o de bom grado, utilizando-o para manter as minhas emoções disciplinadas, sob controlo.

Também Alice se recompôs.

— Nada de especial — acabou ela por responder, com uma voz extraordinariamente calma e convincente. — Apenas a mesma sala que vira antes.

Por fim, olhou-me, com um ar sereno e distante.

— Querias tomar o pequeno-almoço?

— Não, como qualquer coisa no aeroporto.

Também eu estava muito calma. Fui ao quarto de banho para tomar um duche. Quase como se Jasper me tivesse cedido a sua estranha capacidade sensorial adicional, eu sentia o profundo desespero, ainda que bem disfarçado, de Alice, ansiando que eu saísse da sala, para ficar a sós com Jasper. Assim, poderia dizer-lhe que estavam a fazer algo errado, que iriam fracassar...

Arranjei-me a preceito, concentrando-me em cada pequena tarefa. Soltei o cabelo, deixando-o rodopiar à minha volta, cobrindo-me o rosto. O sereno estado de espírito que Jasper me incutira apoderou-se de mim e ajudou-me a pensar com clareza. Ajudou-me a delinear um plano. Remexi no meu saco até encontrar a minha meia cheia de dinheiro. Esvaziei o seu conteúdo no bolso.

Estava ansiosa por chegar ao aeroporto e fiquei satisfeita quando partimos por volta das sete horas. Desta vez, sentei-me sozinha no banco traseiro do carro negro. Alice encostou-se à porta, de costas para esta e com o rosto virado para Jasper, mas, por trás dos óculos de sol, olhando na minha direcção de tantos em tantos segundos.

— Alice? — perguntei de modo indiferente.

Ela estava cautelosa.

— Sim?

— Como é que isso funciona? As visões que tens? — Olhei pelo vidro lateral e a minha voz parecia aborrecida. — O Edward disse que não era algo definitivo... que as coisas mudam.

Era mais difícil do que eu pensava proferir o nome dele. Deve ter sido esse facto que alertou Jasper, já que uma nova onda de serenidade inundou o carro.

— Sim, as coisas mudam... — murmurou ela.

«Esperemos que sim», pensei eu.

— Algumas coisas são mais certas do que outras... como o tempo. As pessoas são mais complexas. Só vejo o rumo que tomam enquanto o seguem. Quando mudam de ideias, tomando uma nova decisão, por mais insignificante que esta seja, todo o futuro se altera.

Acenei com a cabeça de forma pensativa.

— Então, só conseguiste ver o James em Phoenix quando ele decidiu vir para cá.

— Sim — assentiu, novamente cautelosa.

Também só me vira na sala dos espelhos com James quando tomei a decisão de ali me encontrar com ele. Tentei não pensar no que ela poderia ter visto além disto. Não queria que o meu pânico suscitasse em Jasper uma desconfiança ainda maior. De qualquer forma, na sequência da visão de Alice, já iriam vigiar--me com cuidados redobrados. Aquilo que eu tencionava fazer seria impossível.

Chegámos ao aeroporto. A sorte estava do meu lado ou, por outro lado, talvez as probabilidades estivessem apenas a meu favor. O avião de Edward ia aterrar no terminal quatro, o mais amplo e no qual a maioria dos aviões aterrava, não sendo, portanto, de espantar que o mesmo acontecesse com o dele. Tratava-se, porém, do terminal que me convinha: o maior e mais confuso. Além disso, existia uma porta no terceiro piso que podia constituir a única possibilidade de fuga.

Estacionámos no quarto piso do enorme parque de estacionamento. Eu indiquei o caminho, conhecendo melhor do que eles, pela primeira vez, o meu meio envolvente. Apanhámos o elevador até ao terceiro piso, onde os passageiros desembarcavam. Alice e Jasper ficaram durante bastante tempo a olhar para o monitor no qual constavam as partidas. Eu ouvi-os a debater os prós e os contras de uma viagem para Nova Iorque, Atlanta ou Chicago. Lugares que eu nunca conhecera e que nunca viria a conhecer.

Esperei pela minha oportunidade, impaciente, incapaz de parar de bater o pé. Sentámo-nos nas longas filas de cadeiras junto dos detectores de metais, com Jasper e Alice a fingirem observar as pessoas, mas, na verdade, a vigiarem-me. Ao mínimo movimento da minha parte, enquanto estava sentada na cadeira, seguia-se um rápido olhar pelo canto do olho de ambos. Não tinha hipóteses. Deveria fugir? Será que eles se atreveriam a deter-me fisicamente naquele local público? Ou limitar-se-iam a seguir-me?

Retirei o envelope em branco do bolso e coloquei-o em cima da mala de couro preto de Alice. Ela olhou-me.

— A minha carta — disse eu.

Ela acenou com a cabeça, guardando-o debaixo da aba de cima da mala. Ele encontrá-la-ia bastante depressa.

Os minutos passaram e o momento da chegada de Edward aproximou-se. Era espantosa a forma como cada célula do meu corpo parecia saber que ele estava a chegar, bastante antes da sua chegada, o que dificultou muito a minha tarefa. Dei por mim a tentar arranjar pretextos para ficar, para vê-lo primeiro e, depois, proceder à minha fuga, mas sabia que, para ter alguma hipótese de escapar, tal era impossível.

Alice ofereceu-se várias vezes para ir tomar o pequeno-almoço comigo, ao que eu respondia «mais tarde» e «ainda não».

Eu olhava fixamente para o monitor que anunciava as chegadas, vendo voo após voo chegar pontualmente. O voo proveniente de Seattle aproximava-se cada vez mais do topo do monitor.

Então, quando já me restavam apenas quarenta minutos para proceder à fuga, os números alteraram-se. O avião em que ele viajava ia chegar com dez minutos de antecedência. Eu não dispunha de mais tempo.

— Acho que vou comer agora — disse, apressada.

Alice pôs-se de pé.

— Eu vou contigo.

— Importas-te que seja o Jasper a vir? — perguntei. — Sinto-me um pouco...

Não terminei a frase. Os meus olhos estavam suficientemente expressivos para transmitir aquilo que eu não disse.

Jasper levantou-se. Alice tinha um olhar confuso, mas — constatei para meu alívio — não desconfiado. Devia estar a atribuir a alteração na sua visão a algum estratagema do batedor e não a uma traição da minha parte.

Jasper caminhou a meu lado em silêncio, com a mão pousada ao fundo das minhas costas, como se me guiasse. Fingi-me desinteressada nos primeiros cafés do aeroporto, com a cabeça a indagar aquilo que eu realmente procurava. Lá estavam eles, ao virar da esquina, fora da vista arguta de Alice: os lavabos femininos do terceiro piso.

— Importas-te? — perguntei a Jasper ao passarmos. — Demoro-me apenas um instante.

— Eu fico aqui — retorquiu.

Assim que a porta se fechou depois de eu ter entrado, comecei a correr. Lembrei-me da ocasião em que me perdera depois de ter estado nesta casa de banho, pois tinha duas saídas.

Depois de sair pela porta mais distante, bastava-me encetar uma pequena corrida para chegar aos elevadores e, se Jasper ficasse onde dissera que ficava, a sua vista nunca conseguiria alcançar-me. Não olhei para trás enquanto corria. Esta era a minha única hipótese e, mesmo que ele me visse, eu tinha de continuar.

As pessoas ficavam a olhar para mim, mas eu ignorava-as. Ao virar da esquina, os elevadores aguardavam e eu precipitei-me na sua direcção, interpondo a mão entre as portas prestes a fecharem-se de um elevador cheio que ia descer. Forcei a entrada, por entre os utentes irritados e certifiquei-me de que o botão correspondente ao primeiro piso fora premido. Já estava aceso e as portas fecharam-se.

Logo que a porta se abriu, lancei-me de novo numa corrida, ao som de murmúrios de descontentamento atrás de mim. Abrandei a marcha ao passar pelos seguranças que se encontravam junto dos tapetes rolantes que transportam as bagagens, para desatar a correr novamente ao divisar as portas de saída. Não havia forma de saber se Jasper já andava à minha procura. No caso de ele já andar a seguir o meu rasto odorífero, eu disporia apenas de escassos segundos. Precipitei-me pelas portas automáticas, quase esbarrando no vidro quando estas se abriram demasiado devagar.

Ao longo do passeio apinhado de gente, não havia um táxi à vista.

O meu tempo era escasso. Alice e Jasper estavam prestes a aperceber-se de que eu desaparecera ou, então, tal já acontecera. Encontrar-me-iam num piscar de olhos.

Um autocarro que assegurava continuamente o transporte do aeroporto para o hotel Hyatt e vice-versa estava prestes a fechar as portas alguns metros atrás de mim.

— Espere! — exclamei, a correr, fazendo sinais ao motorista.

— Este é o autocarro para o Hyatt — disse o motorista, confuso, ao abrir as portas.

— Sim — retorqui, arquejando — é para lá que eu vou. — Apressei-me a subir os degraus.

Olhou-me de soslaio, interrogando-se sobre o facto de eu não transportar bagagem, mas, depois, encolheu os ombros, não se importando a ponto de fazer perguntas.

A maioria dos lugares sentados estava vaga. Sentei-me o mais longe possível dos restantes passageiros e olhei pela janela, observando, em primeiro lugar, o passeio e, depois, o aeroporto a ficarem cada vez mais distantes. Não conseguia deixar de imaginar Edward à beira da estrada, especado no local onde o meu rasto era interrompido. Disse para comigo mesma que agora não podia chorar. Tinha ainda um longo caminho a percorrer.

A minha maré de sorte manteve-se. Em frente do Hyatt, um casal com um ar cansado retirava a última mala do porta-bagagens de um táxi. Precipitei-me para fora do autocarro e corri até ao táxi, entrando e sentando-me no lugar atrás do motorista. O casal cansado e o motorista do autocarro ficaram a olhar para mim.

Disse ao taxista espantado a morada da minha mãe.

— Preciso de lá chegar o mais rapidamente possível.

— Isso fica em Scottsdale — reclamou.

Atirei quatro notas de vinte dólares para cima do banco.

— Isso chega?

— Claro, miúda, não há problema.

Recostei-me no banco, cruzando os braços sobre o colo. A cidade conhecida começou a mover-se impetuosamente à minha volta, mas eu não olhei pelos vidros. Esforcei-me por manter o controlo. Estava decidida a não perder a calma nesta altura, agora que o meu plano fora concluído com sucesso. Era escusado entregar-me a um maior pavor, a uma maior ansiedade. O meu caminho estava traçado. Agora, só tinha de o seguir.

Assim, em vez de entrar em pânico, fechei os olhos e passei os vinte minutos de duração da viagem a fantasiar sobre o meu encontro com Edward.

Imaginei que ficara no aeroporto para me encontrar com Edward. Visualizei a forma como eu me colocaria em bicos de pés para conseguir ver o seu rosto o mais depressa possível. Quão rápida e graciosamente ele se movimentaria por entre as multidões que nos separavam. Depois, eu correria para encurtar aqueles derradeiros metros que se interpunham entre nós — irreflectida como sempre — e cairia nos seus braços marmóreos, finalmente a salvo.

Questionei-me sobre o nosso destino. Algures no Norte, de modo a que ele pudesse sair durante o dia, ou talvez um local extremamente isolado, para que ambos pudéssemos voltar a estender-nos ao Sol. Imaginei-o na praia, com a sua pele a cintilar como o mar. O período durante o qual tínhamos de permanecer escondidos era irrelevante. Ficar presa num quarto de hotel com ele seria uma espécie de paraíso. Tinha ainda tantas questões a colocar-lhe. Podia passar o resto da vida a conversar com ele, sem nunca dormir, sem nunca sair do seu lado.

Agora, conseguia ver o seu rosto com tanta nitidez... e quase ouvir a sua voz. E, apesar de todo o pavor e desespero, fui fugazmente feliz. Estava tão embrenhada nos meus devaneios de fuga à realidade que perdi a noção do tempo, o qual passava a correr.

— Eh, qual era o número?

A pergunta do taxista deu cabo da minha fantasia, fazendo com que os meus encantadores delírios perdessem toda a cor. O medo, lúgubre e difícil de suportar, esperava para preencher o vazio que esta deixara.

— Cinco mil, oitocentos e vinte e um.

A minha voz parecia abafada. O taxista olhou para mim, nervoso por pensar que eu iria ter um ataque ou algo do género.

— Então, cá estamos.

Estava ansioso por que eu saísse do carro, esperando, provavelmente, que eu não pedisse o troco.

— Obrigada — sussurrei.

Disse para comigo que não precisava de ter medo. A casa estava vazia. Tinha de me apressar, a minha mãe estava à minha espera, assustada, dependendo de mim.

Precipitei-me para a porta, estendendo automaticamente a mão para alcançar a chave que se encontrava debaixo do beiral. Abri a porta. O interior estava escuro, vazio, normal. Precipitei-me para o telefone, acendendo a luz da cozinha pelo caminho. Aí, no quadro branco, estava escrito um número de dez algarismos numa caligrafia pequena e cuidada. As minhas mãos atrapalhavam-se nos botões do telefone, enganando-se na marcação do número. Tinha de desligar e recomeçar. Desta vez, concentrei-me apenas nos botões, carregando, com cuidado, em cada um sequencialmente. Fui bem sucedida. Encostei o telefone ao ouvido com a mão trémula. Tocou uma só vez.

— Olá, Bella — respondeu aquela voz calma. — Foste muito rápida. Estou impressionado.

— A minha mãe está bem?

— Está óptima. Não te preocupes, Bella. Não tenho nenhuma razão de queixa dela. A não ser, como é evidente, que não tenhas vindo sozinha — disse, alegre e bem-disposto.

— Estou sozinha.

Nunca estivera tão só em toda a minha vida.

— Muito bem. Agora, conheces o estúdio de *ballet* que fica mesmo ao virar da esquina da rua de tua casa?

— Conheço. Sei como lá chegar.

— Bem, pronto, então, vemo-nos em breve.

Desliguei o telefone. Saí da sala, pela porta, para o calor abrasador.

Não tinha tempo para olhar para trás, para a minha casa, e não queria vê-la como ela estava naquele momento: vazia, um símbolo de medo em vez de refúgio. A última pessoa que percorrera aquelas divisões conhecidas era minha inimiga.

Pelo canto do olho, quase conseguia ver a minha mãe, de pé, à sombra de um grande eucalipto, onde eu brincava quando era pequena, ou ajoelhada junto da pequena parcela de terra que circundava a caixa do correio, o cemitério de todas as flores que ela tentara cultivar. As recordações eram mais agradáveis do que qualquer realidade a que eu assistisse neste dia, mas eu fugi-lhes em grande velocidade, em direcção à esquina, deixando tudo para trás de mim.

Sentia-me tão lenta, como se estivesse a correr sobre areia molhada — parecia que o betão não me sustentava cabalmente. Tropecei várias vezes, acabando por cair, apoiando-me nas mãos, que ficaram arranhadas na sequência do contacto com o passeio, e, depois, levantando-me de modo vacilante para voltar a precipitar-me para a frente. Mas, por fim, consegui chegar à esquina. Agora, só faltava percorrer mais uma rua; corri, com o suor a escorrer-me abundantemente pelo rosto, arquejando. O calor do Sol incidia sobre a minha pele, sendo a sua luz demasiado intensa ao reflectir no piso branco e encandear-me. Senti-me perigosamente exposta. Com mais intensidade do que julgava ser capaz, desejei estar nas protectoras florestas verdes de Forks... de casa.

Quando dobrei a última esquina, para enveredar pela rua Cactus, consegui avistar o estúdio, tendo este exactamente o aspecto de que eu me recordava. O parque de estacionamento em frente estava vazio e os estores verticais de todas as janelas estavam corridos. Já não conseguia correr — não conseguia respirar; o esforço e o medo tinham levado a melhor sobre mim. Pensei na minha mãe para manter os pés em movimento, um atrás do outro.

Ao aproximar-me, vi o letreiro colocado do lado de dentro da porta. Fora escrito à mão em papel rosa-choque; informava que o estúdio de dança estava fechado por ocasião das férias da Páscoa. Toquei no manípulo e puxei-o com cuidado. A porta estava destrancada. Esforcei-me por recuperar o fôlego e abri a porta.

O vestíbulo estava escuro, vazio e fresco, ouvindo-se o ruído produzido pelo aparelho de ar condicionado. As cadeiras moldadas em plástico estavam empilhadas ao longo das paredes e o tapete cheirava a champô. Eu conseguia ver que a pista de dança ocidental estava às escuras através da janela que dava para ela, a qual se encontrava aberta. A pista de dança oriental, a sala de maiores dimensões, estava iluminada, mas os estores da janela estavam fechados.

O pavor apoderou-se de mim de modo tão intenso que fiquei imobilizada, na verdadeira acepção da palavra. Não conseguia fazer com que os meus pés avançassem.

Então, a voz da minha mãe bradou:

— Bella? Bella?

Aquele mesmo tom de pânico histérico. Precipitei-me para a porta, na direcção de onde vinha o som da sua voz.

— Bella, assustaste-me! Não voltes a fazer-me isso! — prosseguiu a sua voz quando eu irrompi pela sala comprida e de tecto alto.

Olhei à minha volta, tentando descobrir de onde vinha a sua voz. Ouvi-a rir e avancei rapidamente na direcção do som.

Ali estava ela, no ecrã da televisão, passando-me a mão pela cabeça e desgrenhando-me o cabelo, aliviada. Era o Dia de Acção de Graças e eu tinha doze anos. Tínhamos ido visitar a minha avó à Califórnia, no último ano antes da sua morte. Certo dia, fomos à praia e eu inclinara-me demasiado à beira do molhe. Ela vira os meus pés a agitarem-se, tentando devolver-me o equilíbrio.

— Bella?! Bella?! — exclamara, receosa.

Depois, o ecrã da televisão ficou azul.

Virei-me lentamente. Ele estava de pé, muito quieto, junto da saída das traseiras, tão quieto que, a princípio, eu não reparara nele. Na sua mão, encontrava-se um comando à distância. Entreolhámo-nos durante um longo momento e, depois, ele sorriu.

Caminhou na minha direcção, aproximando-se bastante, e, depois, passou por mim para pousar o comando ao lado do videogravador. Virei-me com cuidado para observá-lo.

— Desculpa-me, Bella, mas não achas que é melhor que não tenha sido realmente necessário envolver a tua mãe nisto?

A sua voz era cortês, gentil.

De repente, percebi tudo. A minha mãe estava a salvo. Ainda se encontrava na Florida. Nunca recebera a minha mensagem. Nunca ficara apavorada com os olhos vermelho-escuros do rosto anomalamente pálido que se encontrava diante de mim. Estava a salvo.

— Acho — respondi, estando a minha voz repleta de alívio.

— Não pareces zangada por eu te ter enganado.

— E não estou.

O meu súbito júbilo deu-me coragem. Que importância tinha

agora? Em breve, chegaria o fim. Charlie e a minha mãe não sofreriam qualquer mal, não teriam de ter medo. Senti-me quase estonteada. Uma parte analítica da minha mente avisou-me de que eu estava perigosamente perto de sucumbir à tensão.

— Que estranho! Estás mesmo a falar a sério. — Os seus olhos escuros examinaram-me com interesse. A íris era quase negra, tendo apenas um laivo de vermelho-vivo no limite. Estavam sedentos.

— Faço esta concessão em relação ao vosso estranho grupo: vocês, os seres humanos, conseguem ser bastante interessantes. Suponho que percebo por que motivo é que o facto de te observar consegue ser tão cativante. É espantoso; alguns de vós não parecem ter a mínima noção do próprio interesse pessoal.

Ele encontrava-se a escassos metros de distância de mim, com os braços cruzados, fitando-me com um ar curioso. Não havia um ar de ameaça no seu rosto, nem na sua postura. Tinha uma aparência extremamente normal, não havendo nada de extraordinário no seu rosto nem no seu corpo. Apenas a pele branca e os olhos redondos a que tanto me habituara. Envergava uma camisa azul-clara de mangas compridas e calças de ganga azuis desbotadas.

— Suponho que vais dizer-me que o teu namorado te vingará? — perguntou, quase formulando um desejo, segundo me pareceu.

— Não, não me parece. Pelo menos, pedi-lhe para não o fazer.

— E qual foi a resposta dele?

— Não sei — era estranhamente fácil conversar com este educado caçador. — Deixei-lhe uma carta.

— Que romântico, uma última carta. E achas que ele a honrará?

A sua voz estava agora apenas um pouco mais ríspida, com um laivo de sarcasmo a perturbar o seu tom educado.

— Espero que sim.

— Humm. Bem, então, as nossas esperanças divergem. É que, sabes, tudo isto foi apenas um pouco fácil de mais, rápido de mais. Para ser absolutamente sincero, estou desiludido. Esperava um desafio muito maior. E, afinal, eu só precisava de um pouco de sorte.

Esperei em silêncio.

— Quando a Victoria não conseguiu apanhar o teu pai, pedi-lhe que obtivesse mais informações a teu respeito. Não tinha sentido percorrer todo o planeta atrás de ti quando podia esperar-te confortavelmente num lugar à minha escolha. Assim, depois de ter falado com a Victoria, decidi vir a Phoenix fazer uma visita à tua mãe. Ouvira-te dizer que ias para casa. A princípio, não me passou pela cabeça que estivesses a falar a sério, mas, depois, comecei a pensar. Os seres humanos conseguem ser muito previsíveis; gostam de estar num lugar conhecido, num lugar seguro. Além disso, não seria o estratagema perfeito? Ir para o último lugar onde deverias estar enquanto te escondes: o lugar onde disseras que estarias. Mas, como é evidente, eu não tinha a certeza, era apenas um palpite. Normalmente, tenho um pressentimento quanto à presa que persigo, um sexto sentido, se preferires. Ouvi a tua mensagem quando cheguei a casa da tua mãe, mas não podia, evidentemente, estar certo quanto ao local de onde telefonaras. Era muito útil ter o teu número de telefone, mas, tanto quanto eu sabia, tu podias até estar na Antárctida e o jogo não funcionaria se não estivesses por perto. Então, o teu namorado apanhou um avião com destino a Phoenix. A Victoria estava, naturalmente, a vigiá-los a meu pedido; num jogo com tantos jogadores, eu não podia trabalhar sozinho. E, assim, eles deram-me a informação que eu esperava — tu sempre estavas aqui. Sentia-me preparado; já visionara todos os teus encantadores vídeos caseiros. Depois, tudo se resumia simplesmente a conseguir iludir-te. Foi muito fácil, sabes; não foi propriamente uma tarefa à minha altura. Portanto, como vês, espero que estejas enganada quanto ao teu namorado. Chama-se Edward, não é?

Não respondi. A bravata começava a desvanecer-se. Pressenti que ele estava a chegar ao fim do seu discurso de regozijo. De qualquer forma, não era a mim que este se dirigia. Não havia qualquer glória em espancar-me, a mim, uma fraca humana.

— Importavas-te muito que eu deixasse uma cartinha minha ao teu Edward?

Recuou um passo e pegou numa câmara de vídeo digital do tamanho da palma de uma mão, cuidadosamente equilibrada em cima da aparelhagem de som. Uma pequena luz vermelha indicava que já estava a gravar. Ele regulou-a algumas vezes, ampliou o plano. Eu arregalava os olhos, apavorada.

— Lamento, mas acho simplesmente que ele não será capaz de resistir a perseguir-me depois de assistir a isto. E eu não quereria que ele perdesse alguma coisa. Como é evidente, foi tudo arquitectado para ele. Tu és uma mera humana que, por infelicidade, estava no lugar errado à hora errada e que, se me permites acrescentar, andava indiscutivelmente com a companhia errada.

Avançou na minha direcção, sorrindo.

— Antes de começarmos...

Senti uma espiral de náuseas no estômago enquanto ele falava. Isto era algo que eu não previra.

— Queria apenas dar uma lição, uma liçãozinha. A resposta estivera sempre bem visível e eu receava imenso que Edward se apercebesse desse facto e acabasse com o meu divertimento. Oh, aconteceu uma vez, há séculos. A única vez em que a minha presa me escapou. Sabes, o vampiro que gostava tão imbecilmente dessa vítima tomou a decisão que o teu Edward foi demasiado fraco para tomar. Quando o velho soube que eu andava atrás da sua amiguinha, levou-a do hospício onde ele trabalhava (jamais compreenderei a obsessão que vocês, seres humanos, suscitam em alguns vampiros) e, assim que a libertou, pô-la a salvo. A pobre criaturazinha nem sequer pareceu aperceber-se da dor. Estivera enfiada no buraco negro daquela cela durante tanto tempo. Cem anos antes, teria sido queimada na fogueira por ter aquelas visões. Na década de 1920, o método adoptado era o hospício e os tratamentos de choques eléctricos. Quando abriu os olhos, estando forte depois de ter acabado de ser rejuvenescida, foi como se nunca antes tivesse visto o Sol. O velho vampiro transformou-a num vampiro novo e poderoso e, então, não havia qualquer motivo para eu lhe tocar — suspirou. — Aniquilei o mais velho como forma de vingança.

— A Alice — murmurei, atónita.

— Sim, a tua amiguinha. *Fiquei*, de facto, espantado ao vê-la na clareira. Logo, suponho que o grupo deveria ser capaz de retirar algum consolo desta experiência. Eu fico contigo, mas eles ficam com ela. A única vítima que me escapou; trata-se, na verdade, de uma grande honra. E ela exalava um cheiro tão delicioso. Ainda lamento não ter chegado a provar... Ela cheirava ainda melhor do que tu. Desculpa; a minha intenção não é a de ser ofensivo. Tu tens um cheiro muito agradável. Algo floral...

Deu outro passo na minha direcção até estar a escassos centímetros de distância de mim. Pegou numa madeixa do meu cabelo e aspirou delicadamente o seu cheiro. Em seguida, largou os fios de cabelo, afagando-os para não ficarem desalinhados, e eu senti as pontas frias dos seus dedos no meu pescoço. Levantou a mão para me acariciar a face, rapidamente e uma só vez, com o polegar, com uma expressão de curiosidade estampada no rosto. Desejava ardentemente fugir, mas estava paralisada. Não conseguia sequer retrair-me.

— Não — murmurou para consigo mesmo ao baixar a mão —, não compreendo — suspirou. — Bem, suponho que devamos prosseguir. Depois, posso telefonar aos teus amigos e dizer-lhes onde podem encontrar-te, assim como à minha pequena missiva.

Agora, eu estava definitivamente doente. Conseguia ver nos seus olhos que a dor se avizinhava. Não lhe bastaria sair vitorioso, alimentar-se e partir. Não haveria o fim rápido com que eu contava. Os meus joelhos começaram a tremer e eu receei que fosse cair.

Ele recuou e começou a deslocar-se em círculo, de forma descontraída, como se tentasse obter o melhor ângulo de visão de uma estátua num museu. O seu rosto continuava com uma expressão acessível e amável enquanto decidia por onde começar.

Depois, baixou-se bruscamente num movimento para a frente, agachando-se de uma forma que eu reconheci, e o seu sorriso amável rasgou-se, dilatou-se de forma lenta, até deixar de ser um sorriso e se transformar numa contorção de dentes, expostos e brilhantes.

Foi mais forte do que eu: tentei fugir. Por mais inútil que eu sabia que seria, por mais fracos que os meus joelhos já estivessem, o pânico tomou conta de mim e eu precipitei-me para a saída de emergência.

Pôs-se à minha frente num ápice. Não vi se ele utilizara a mão ou o pé, pois foi um movimento demasiado rápido. Um golpe esmagador atingiu-me no peito; senti-me a voar para trás e, depois, ouvi o ruído produzido pelo embate da minha cabeça nos espelhos. O vidro cedeu, com alguns pedaços a quebrarem-se e a estilhaçarem-se no chão, a meu lado.

Estava demasiado aturdida para sentir dor. Ainda não conseguia respirar.

Ele caminhou devagar na minha direcção.

– Esse é um efeito bastante giro – disse, examinando o amontoado de vidro, com um tom de voz novamente amável. – Pareceu-me que esta sala seria visualmente dramática para o meu pequeno filme. Foi por esse motivo que escolhi este local para o nosso encontro. É perfeito, não é?

Ignorei-o, apoiando-me nas mãos e nos joelhos e rastejando em direcção à outra porta.

Ele pôs-se logo em cima de mim, com o seu pé a pisar-me a perna com força. Ouvi o estalo revoltante antes de o sentir, mas, depois, senti-o e não pude conter o meu grito de sofrimento. Contorci-me para conseguir alcançar a minha perna e ele estava especado em cima de mim, a sorrir.

– Gostarias de repensar o teu último pedido? – perguntou de modo amável. O seu dedo do pé tocou ao de leve a minha perna partida e eu ouvi um grito lancinante. Chocada, percebi que era meu.

— Não preferias que o Edward tentasse encontrar-me? — instigou-me.

— Não! — resmunguei. — Não, Edward, não faças...! — e, depois, algo embateu com força no meu rosto, atirando-me novamente para cima dos espelhos quebrados.

Além da dor na perna, senti o profundo golpe que o vidro abrira no meu couro cabeludo. Em seguida, a humidade cálida começou a propagar-se pelo meu cabelo com uma rapidez alarmante. Sentia-a a ensopar a minha camisa na zona do ombro e ouvia-a a pingar na madeira em baixo. O seu cheiro revoltou-me o estômago.

Apesar das náuseas e das tonturas, vi algo que me deu uma súbita e derradeira réstia de esperança. Os olhos dele, anteriormente apenas atentos, incendiavam-se agora com uma necessidade incontrolável. O sangue — um rubor que se alastrava pela minha camisa branca, formando rapidamente uma poça no chão — estava a deixá-lo louco de tanta sede. Quaisquer que fossem as suas intenções iniciais, ele não conseguiria prolongar aquela situação por muito mais tempo.

À medida que o fluxo de sangue que brotava da minha cabeça arrastava consigo os meus sentidos, eu só podia esperar que tudo acabasse depressa. Os meus olhos estavam a fechar-se.

Ouvi, como se viesse de debaixo de água, o derradeiro rosnar do caçador. Conseguia ver, através dos longos túneis em que os meus olhos se haviam transformado, o seu vulto negro avançar na minha direcção. Com o meu último esforço, a minha mão levantou-se por instinto para me proteger o rosto. Os meus olhos fecharam-se e eu deixei-me levar.

Capítulo Vinte e Três

O Anjo

Ao deixar-me levar, comecei a sonhar.

Onde flutuava, sob as águas escuras, ouvi o som mais venturoso que a minha mente podia evocar — tão belo e animador como sinistro. Era outro rosnar; um rugido mais profundo, mais selvático, que denotava fúria.

Fui trazida de volta, quase até à superfície, por uma dor lancinante que perpassou a minha mão erguida, mas não consegui encontrar o caminho de volta a ponto de conseguir abrir os olhos.

Então, soube que estava morta.

Isto porque, através das densas águas, ouvi a voz de um anjo a entoar o meu nome, chamando-me para o único paraíso que eu ambicionava.

— Oh, não, Bella, não! — clamava a voz do anjo, horrorizada.

Por trás desse som ansiado, havia outro ruído — um horrível tumulto que a minha mente repudiava. Um perverso rosnar grave, um estarrecedor som de arremetidas violentas e um estrídulo lamento, subitamente interrompido...

Tentei antes concentrar-me na voz do anjo.

— Bella, por favor! Bella, escuta-me, por favor. Por favor, Bella, por favor! — implorava.

Eu queria dizer «sim» ou pronunciar qualquer outra palavra, mas não conseguia encontrar os meus lábios.

— Carlisle! — chamou o anjo, com sofrimento patente na sua voz perfeita. — Bella, Bella, não. Oh, por favor, não, não!

E o anjo chorava sem derramar lágrimas, soltando soluços descontínuos.

O anjo não devia chorar; não estava certo. Tentei encontrá-lo, dizer-lhe que tudo estava bem, mas as águas eram muito profundas, pesando sobre mim, e eu não conseguia respirar.

Havia um ponto de pressão na minha cabeça. Doía-me. Depois, quando essa dor irrompeu das trevas para chegar até mim, surgiram outras dores, dores mais fortes. Gritei, arquejando, rasgando o escuro charco.

— Bella! — clamou o anjo.

— Ela perdeu algum sangue, mas o ferimento na cabeça não é profundo — informou-me uma voz calma. — Tem cuidado com a perna dela; está partida.

Um uivo de raiva estrangulou os lábios do anjo.

Senti uma cutilada lancinante de lado. Isto não podia ser o paraíso, pois não? Havia demasiada dor para tal.

— Assim como algumas costelas, creio eu — prosseguiu a metódica voz.

As dores lancinantes estavam, porém, a atenuar-se. Havia uma nova dor, uma dor escaldante na minha mão que suplantava tudo o resto.

Alguém estava a queimar-me.

— Edward — tentei dizer-lhe, mas a minha voz estava muito pesada e lenta. Nem eu conseguia perceber aquilo que dizia.

— Bella, vais ficar bem. Consegues ouvir-me, Bella? Eu amo-te.

— Edward — tentei outra vez.

A minha voz já estava um pouco mais compreensível.

— Sim, estou aqui.

— Dói — lamentei-me.

— Eu sei, Bella, eu sei.

E, depois, longe de mim, perguntou, angustiado:

— Não podes fazer nada?

— Passa-me a minha mala, por favor... Sustém a respiração, Bella; isso será uma ajuda — garantiu Carlisle.

— Alice? — gemi.

— Ela está aqui; sabia onde encontrar-te.

— Dói-me a mão — tentei dizer-lhe.

— Eu sei, Bella. O Carlisle vai dar-te algo; deixará de doer.

— A minha mão está a arder! — gritei, derrotando finalmente

o que restava das trevas, com os meus olhos a abrirem-se. Não conseguia ver-lhe o rosto, havendo algo escuro e quente a turvar-me a vista. Porque é que eles não conseguiam ver o fogo e extingui-lo?

A voz dele estava assustada.

— Bella?

— O fogo! Alguém que apague o fogo! — gritei enquanto este me queimava.

— Carlisle! A mão dela!

— Ele mordeu-a.

A voz de Carlisle já não estava calma, mas sim aterrada.

Ouvi Edward recuperar o fôlego, horrorizado.

— Edward, tens de o fazer.

Era a voz de Alice, a soar bem perto da minha cabeça. Dedos frios roçaram a humidade nos meus olhos.

— Não! — bradou ele.

— Alice — gemi.

— Pode haver uma hipótese — disse Carlisle.

— O quê? — interrogou Edward.

— Vê se consegues sugar o veneno; a ferida está razoavelmente limpa.

Quando Carlisle falou, senti uma maior pressão sobre a cabeça, algo que me tocava e puxava o couro cabeludo. A dor que tal provocava fundia-se na que derivava do ardor.

— Isso resultará? — a voz de Alice estava tensa.

— Não sei — respondeu Carlisle. — Mas temos de nos apressar.

— Carlisle, eu... — hesitou Edward. — Não sei se consigo fazer isso.

A sua linda voz estava novamente marcada pela aflição.

— Seja como for, a decisão é tua, Edward. Não posso ajudar-te. Tenho de estancar já esta hemorragia se fores extrair sangue da mão dela.

Contorci-me sob o domínio do ígneo suplício, fazendo este movimento com que a dor na minha perna se intensificasse de modo atroz.

— Edward! — gritei.

Apercebi-me de que os meus olhos estavam de novo fechados. Abri-os, querendo a todo o custo ver o rosto dele. E vi. Finalmente, conseguia ver o seu rosto perfeito, fitando-me, desfigurado por uma máscara de indecisão e sofrimento.

— Alice, arranja-me algo para lhe apertar a perna! — Carlisle estava curvado sobre mim, cuidando-me da cabeça. — Edward, tens de o fazer agora, senão será tarde de mais.

O rosto de Edward estava abatido. Observei o seu olhar quando a dúvida deu subitamente lugar a uma intensa determinação. Os maxilares contraíram-se-lhe. Senti os seus dedos fortes e frios na minha mão escaldante, imobilizando-a. Em seguida, inclinou a cabeça sobre ela e encostou os seus lábios frios à minha pele.

A princípio, a dor agravou-se. Gritei e agitei-me violentamente contra as mãos frias que me subjugavam. Ouvi a voz de Alice, tentando acalmar-me. Algo pesado prendia a minha perna ao chão e Carlisle prendia a minha cabeça no seu abraço pétreo.

Depois, aos poucos, o meu estremecimento serenou à medida que a minha mão foi ficando cada vez mais dormente. O fogo estava a aplacar-se, reduzindo-se a um foco cada vez mais pequeno.

Senti os meus sentidos a abandonarem-me à medida que a dor se atenuava. Receava cair novamente nas águas negras e perdê-lo na escuridão.

— Edward — tentei dizer, mas não conseguia ouvir a minha voz. Eles, porém, conseguiam ouvir-me.

— Ele está mesmo aqui, Bella.

— Fica, Edward, fica comigo...

— Eu fico. — A sua voz transmitia cansaço, mas também, de certa forma, triunfo.

Sorri de contentamento. O ardor desaparecera, sendo as restantes dores entorpecidas por uma sonolência que começava a apoderar-se do meu corpo.

— Já saiu todo? — perguntou Carlisle, algures de muito longe.

— De acordo com o sabor, o sangue dela parece estar limpo

— disse Edward, tranquilo. — Consigo sentir o gosto da morfina.

— Bella?! — exclamou Carlisle, chamando-me.

Tentei responder.

— Mmmmm?

— O ardor já desapareceu?

— Sim — suspirei. — Obrigada, Edward.

— Amo-te — retorquiu.

— Eu sei — murmurei, extremamente cansada.

Ouvi o meu som preferido dentre todos os do mundo: o discreto riso de Edward, débil com o alívio que o assomava.

— Bella?! — exclamou Carlisle uma vez mais.

Franzi o sobrolho; queria dormir.

— O que foi?

— Onde está a tua mãe?

— Na Florida — suspirei. — Ele enganou-me, Edward. Viu as nossas gravações.

O sentimento de indignação patente na minha voz era deploravelmente ténue.

No entanto, tais palavras reavivaram-me a memória.

— Alice — tentei abrir os olhos. — Alice, a gravação... Ele conhecia-te, Alice; sabia de onde vinhas — queria falar com um tom de urgência, mas a minha voz estava fraca. — Cheira-me a gasolina — acrescentei, admirada, apesar da nébula que me toldava os pensamentos.

— Está na hora de a levarmos daqui — disse Carlisle.

— Não, quero dormir — reclamei.

— Podes dormir, querida, eu levo-te ao colo — tranquilizou-me Edward.

Então, ele tomou-me nos seus braços, ficando eu aninhada contra o seu peito — flutuando, sem qualquer resquício de dor.

— Agora, dorme, Bella.

Foram estas as últimas palavras que ouvi.

Capítulo Vinte e Quatro

Um Impasse

Os meus olhos abriram-se para me deparar com uma luz branca e intensa. Encontrava-me num quarto que me era desconhecido, um quarto branco. A parede ao meu lado estava coberta por longos estores verticais; por cima da minha cabeça, as luzes ofuscantes encandeavam-me. Estava deitada, com as costas ligeiramente levantadas, numa cama dura e assimétrica — uma cama com grades. As almofadas eram achatadas e tinham uma superfície irregular. Um som irritante, semelhante a um apito, era produzido algures por perto. Esperei que esse facto significasse que eu ainda estava viva. A morte não devia ser tão desconfortável.

As minhas mãos estavam completamente envoltas em tubos transparentes e havia algo colado ao meu rosto, debaixo do meu nariz. Levantei a mão para o arrancar.

— Nem penses.

Simultaneamente, a minha mão foi agarrada por uns dedos frios.

— Edward? — virei a cabeça um pouco e vi que o seu rosto deslumbrante se encontrava a escassos centímetros do meu, apoiando o queixo à beira da minha almofada. Apercebi-me novamente de que estava viva, desta vez com gratidão e júbilo. — Oh, Edward, lamento imenso!

— Chiu! — fez-me calar. — Agora, está tudo bem.

— O que aconteceu?

Não conseguia lembrar-me com clareza e a minha mente insurgia-se contra mim quando eu tentava recordar-me.

— Quase chegava tarde de mais. Podia ter chegado tarde de mais — sussurrou ele, com um tom de voz atormentado.

— Fui tão estúpida, Edward. Pensei que ele apanhara a minha mãe.

— Ele enganou-nos a todos.

— Tenho de telefonar ao Charlie e à minha mãe — percebi, apesar da nébula que me toldava os pensamentos.

— A Alice telefonou-lhes. A Renée está aqui, ou melhor, aqui, no hospital. Foi comer alguma coisa.

— Ela está aqui?

Tentei sentar-me, mas a minha cabeça começou a girar a um ritmo mais acelerado e a mão dele empurrou-me delicadamente para cima das almofadas.

— Ela estará de volta daqui a pouco — garantiu ele. — E tu tens de ficar quieta.

— Mas o que é que lhe disseste? — perguntei, em pânico. Não me interessava minimamente ser acalmada. A minha mãe estava ali e *eu* estava a recuperar do ataque de um vampiro. — Como é que lhe justificaste o facto de eu estar aqui?

— Caíste de dois lanços de escadas e atravessaste uma janela — disse, fazendo uma breve pausa. — Tens de reconhecer que poderia acontecer.

Suspirei e senti dor. Olhei para o corpo, por baixo do lençol, observando o enorme inchaço que era a minha perna.

— O meu estado é muito grave? — perguntei.

— Tens uma perna fracturada, quatro costelas partidas, algumas fissuras no crânio, hematomas que cobrem cada centímetro da tua pele e perdeste muito sangue. Foste submetida a algumas transfusões. Não gostei; ficaste com um cheiro completamente diferente durante algum tempo.

— Deve ter sido uma mudança agradável para ti.

— Não, eu gosto do *teu* cheiro.

— Como é que fizeste aquilo? — perguntei com calma.

Ele soube imediatamente a que é que eu me referia.

— Não sei bem. — Desviou o olhar dos meus olhos inquiridores, levantando a minha mão envolta em gaze da cama e segurando-a delicadamente com a sua, tendo o cuidado de não causar interferências no fio que me ligava a um dos monitores.

Esperei pacientemente pelo resto.

Ele suspirou sem corresponder ao meu olhar.

— Era impossível... parar — sussurrou. — Impossível. Mas eu parei — finalmente, ergueu o olhar, esboçando um meio sorriso. — *Devo* mesmo amar-te.

— Não achas que tenho um sabor tão agradável como o meu cheiro? — sorri em resposta, o que me fez doer a cara.

— Mais agradável ainda; mais agradável do que imaginara.

— Desculpa — pedi.

Os seus olhos elevaram-se até ao tecto.

— De todas as coisas por que poderias pedir desculpa...

— Porque é que deveria pedir desculpa?

— Por quase me teres privado de ti para sempre.

— Desculpa — pedi novamente.

— Eu sei porque o fizeste — disse com voz reconfortante. — Mas, como é evidente, não deixa de ter sido irracional. Devias ter esperado por mim, devias ter-me dito.

— Não me terias deixado ir.

— Pois não — concordou num tom taciturno —, não teria.

Algumas lembranças desagradáveis começavam a assomar--me à memória. Estremeci e, depois, retraí-me.

Ele ficou imediatamente ansioso.

— Bella, o que se passa?

— O que é que aconteceu ao James?

— Depois de eu o ter afastado de ti, o Emmett e o Jasper encarregaram-se dele.

Havia um intenso tom de remorso na sua voz.

Estas suas palavras confundiram-me.

— Não vi lá o Emmett nem o Jasper.

— Tiveram de abandonar a sala... havia muito sangue.

— Mas tu ficaste.

— Sim, fiquei.

— Tal como a Alice e o Carlisle... — disse, espantada.

— Eles também gostam muito de ti, sabes.

Um lampejo de imagens dolorosas que se reportavam à última vez em que eu vira Alice fez-me lembrar algo.

— A Alice viu a gravação? — perguntei com ansiedade.

— Viu.

Um novo som carregou-lhe a voz, um tom de puro ódio.

— Ela estivera sempre na escuridão. Era por esse motivo que não se lembrava.

— Eu sei. Agora, ela já compreende.

O seu tom de voz mantinha-se regular, mas o seu rosto estava negro de fúria.

Tentei alcançar-lhe o rosto com a minha mão livre, mas algo me deteve. Olhei para baixo e vi o cateter a contrariar os movimentos da minha mão.

— Ai — retraí-me.

— O que foi? — perguntou ele, com ansiedade, estando distraído, mas nem tanto. A lugubridade não lhe abandonou o olhar por completo.

— Agulhas — expliquei, desviando o olhar da que estava espetada na minha mão. Concentrei a atenção numa telha recurvada do tecto e tentei respirar fundo, apesar da dor que sentia nas costelas.

— Com medo de uma agulha — murmurou ele para consigo mesmo, muito baixinho, abanando a cabeça. — Oh, quando se trata de um vampiro sádico, decidido a torturá-la até à morte, com certeza, não há problema, vai a correr ter com ele. Já um cateter, pelo contrário...

Revirei os olhos. Fiquei satisfeita por descobrir que esta reacção, pelo menos, era isenta de dor. Decidi mudar de assunto.

— Porque é que *tu* estás aqui? — perguntei.

Ele fitou-me, com os olhos a reflectirem, a princípio, confusão e, depois, mágoa. As sobrancelhas uniram-se quando ele franziu o sobrolho.

— Queres que eu me vá embora?

— Não! — protestei imediatamente, horrorizada com tal ideia. — Não, quero dizer, a que é que a minha mãe pensa que se deve a tua presença aqui? Tenho de fazer com que a minha história bata certo antes de ela voltar.

— Ah! — exclamou ele, com a testa a alisar-se e a retomar o

seu aspecto marmóreo. — Vim a Phoenix para tentar incutir-te algum juízo, para te convencer a regressares a Forks — acrescentou ele; e os seus grandes olhos eram tão francos e sinceros que eu própria quase cheguei a acreditar nele. — Tu acedeste a falar comigo e foste de carro até ao hotel onde eu estava hospedado, na companhia do Carlisle e da Alice; como é evidente, eu estava cá sob vigilância paternal — acrescentou virtuosamente —, mas tu tropeçaste nas escadas quando te dirigias ao meu quarto e... bem, o resto já sabes. Não precisas, porém, de te lembrar de quaisquer pormenores; tens uma óptima justificação para estares um pouco confusa quanto aos aspectos mais minuciosos.

Reflecti, por um momento, sobre as suas palavras.

— Essa história tem algumas falhas, como, por exemplo, o facto de não haver vidros partidos.

— Não propriamente — retorquiu. — A Alice divertiu-se um pouco de mais a forjar provas. Tudo foi tratado de modo muito convincente; provavelmente, até poderias processar o hotel se assim desejasses. Não tens nada com que te preocupar — garantiu, acariciando-me a face com o mais leve dos toques. — Agora, a única coisa que tens a fazer é restabelecer-te.

Não estava tão alienada pela dor nem pelo estado de confusão provocado pela medicação a ponto de não reagir ao toque dele. O apito emitido pelo monitor subia e descia irregularmente de tom; agora, ele não era o único a ouvir o mau comportamento do meu coração.

«Isto vai ser embaraçoso», murmurei para com os meus botões.

Ele soltou um riso abafado e o seu olhar tornou-se especulativo.

— Humm, pergunto-me se... — disse ele.

Inclinou-se devagarinho na minha direcção e o apito acelerou desenfreadamente até os seus lábios tocarem os meus, mas, quando tal aconteceu, ainda que com a mais suave das pressões, o apito cessou por completo.

Recuou bruscamente, com a sua expressão de ansiedade a

transformar-se em alívio quando o monitor indicou que o meu coração recomeçara a bater.

— Parece que vou ter de ser ainda mais cauteloso contigo do que o habitual — franziu o sobrolho.

— Ainda não tinha acabado de te beijar — reclamei. — Não me obrigues a ir até aí.

Ele esboçou um largo sorriso e curvou-se para encostar ao de leve os seus lábios aos meus. O monitor ficou descontrolado.

No entanto, de repente, os seus lábios ficaram tensos e ele afastou-se.

— Creio que estou a ouvir a tua mãe — disse ele, sorrindo novamente.

— Não me deixes — clamei, com uma onda de pânico irracional a inundar-me.

Não podia deixá-lo ir embora, poderia desaparecer outra vez.

Ele detectou o pavor nos meus olhos por um breve instante.

— Não deixo — prometeu solenemente e, depois sorriu. — Vou dormir uma sesta.

Levantou-se da cadeira de plástico rígido ao meu lado e sentou-se na poltrona reclinável de couro sintético azul-turquesa aos pés da minha cama, inclinando-a completamente para trás e fechando os olhos. Ficou absolutamente imóvel.

— Não te esqueças de respirar — sussurrei de modo sarcástico. Ele respirou fundo, mantendo os olhos fechados.

Eu já conseguia ouvir a minha mãe. Ela falava com alguém, talvez uma enfermeira, parecendo cansada e perturbada. Eu queria saltar da cama e correr até ela, acalmá-la, garantir-lhe que tudo estava bem, mas não estava, de modo nenhum, em condições de saltar, pelo que esperei com ansiedade.

A porta entreabriu-se e ela espreitou com cautela.

— Mãe — sussurrei, com a minha voz repleta de amor e alívio.

Reparou na figura imóvel de Edward na poltrona reclinável e avançou em bicos de pés até à cabeceira da minha cama.

— Ele nunca se vai embora, pois não? — balbuciou para consigo mesma.

— Mãe, estou tão contente por ver-te!

Ela curvou-se para me abraçar com carinho e eu senti lágrimas tépidas a escorrerem-me pelas faces.

— Bella, estava tão preocupada!

— Desculpa, mãe. Mas não faz mal, agora está tudo bem — reconfortei-a.

— Só estou contente por, finalmente, ver os teus olhos abertos.

Sentou-se à beira da minha cama.

De repente, apercebi-me de que não fazia ideia que *dia* era.

— Durante quanto tempo é que estiveram fechados?

— Hoje é sexta-feira, querida; estiveste inconsciente durante algum tempo.

— Sexta-feira?

Fiquei escandalizada. Tentei lembrar-me de que dia era quando... Não quis, todavia, pensar nisso.

— Tiveram de te manter sob o efeito de sedativos durante algum tempo, querida; tens muitas lesões.

— Eu sei.

Conseguia senti-las.

— Tiveste sorte em o Dr. Cullen estar aqui. Ele é um homem tão simpático... mas é muito jovem. E parece mais um manequim do que um médico...

— Conheceu o Carlisle?

— E a Alice, a irmã do Edward. É uma rapariga encantadora.

— Pois é — concordei com toda a sinceridade.

Ela olhou por cima do ombro, na direcção de Edward, que estava deitado na poltrona com os olhos fechados.

— Não me disseste que tinhas tão grandes amigos em Forks.

Encolhi-me e, depois, gemi.

— O que é que te dói? — perguntou com ansiedade, voltando-se de novo para mim.

Os olhos de Edward precipitaram-se para o meu rosto.

— Está tudo bem — assegurei-lhes. — Só tenho de me lembrar de não me mexer.

Ele continuou a fingir que dormia.

Aproveitei a distracção momentânea da minha mãe para evitar que a conversa voltasse a incidir sobre o meu comportamento nada cândido.

— Onde está o Phil? — apressei-me a perguntar.

— Na Florida. Oh, Bella, não imaginas! Mesmo quando estávamos prestes a partir, recebemos a melhor das novidades!

— O Phil assinou um contrato? — deitei-me a adivinhar.

— Assinou! Como é que adivinhaste? Para jogar nos Suns, acreditas?

— Isso é formidável, mãe — disse com o máximo de entusiasmo que consegui, embora não tivesse grande noção do que tal significava.

— E tu vais adorar Jacksonville — afirmou enquanto eu a fitava com um olhar vago. — Fiquei um pouco preocupada quando o Phil começou a falar de Akron, com a neve e tudo isso, pois tu sabes o quanto eu detesto o frio, mas Jacksonville...! Está sempre Sol e a humidade, de facto, não é assim *tão* má. Encontrámos uma casa giríssima, amarela, com madeiras de limpos brancas, um alpendre que parece retirado de um filme antigo e um carvalho enorme. Fica apenas a alguns minutos do mar e tu terás uma casa de banho privativa...

— Mãe, espera! — interrompi-a; Edward continuava com os olhos fechados, mas parecia demasiado tenso para passar por adormecido. — De que é que estás a falar? Eu não vou para a Florida. Eu vivo em Forks.

— Mas já não precisas de viver, tontinha! — riu-se. — Agora, o Phil poderá estar muito mais presente... Conversámos longamente sobre isso e o que eu vou fazer é alternar quando ele jogar fora de casa: metade das vezes fico contigo e a outra metade vou com ele.

— Mãe — hesitei, pensando na melhor forma de lidar diplomaticamente com aquela questão. — Eu *quero* viver em Forks. Já me adaptei à escola e tenho algumas amigas... — ela, porém, voltou a olhar na direcção de Edward quando eu lhe relembrei que tinha amigos, pelo que tentei enveredar por outro caminho.

— Além disso, o Charlie precisa de mim. Está completamente sozinho lá em cima e não sabe, de todo, cozinhar.

— Queres ficar em Forks? — perguntou ela, confusa. Tal ideia era, para ela, inconcebível. Então, o seu olhar voltou a fixar-se em Edward. — Porquê?

— Já te disse: por causa da escola, do Charlie. Au!

Eu encolhera os ombros. Não fora uma boa ideia.

As mãos dela agitavam-se impotentes sobre mim, tentando encontrar um sítio onde pudessem acariciar-me sem me magoar. Remediou-se com a minha testa, que não estava ligada.

— Bella, querida, tu detestas Forks — relembrou-me.

— Não é assim tão mau.

Franziu o sobrolho e o seu olhar oscilou entre mim e Edward, desta vez de forma claramente intencional.

— É por causa deste rapaz? — sussurrou ela.

Abri a boca, preparando-me para mentir, mas os olhos dela examinavam o meu rosto e eu sabia que ela não se deixaria enganar.

— Em parte — admiti. Não havia necessidade de confessar quão grande era essa parte. — Então, tiveste oportunidade de falar com o Edward? — perguntei.

— Tive — hesitou, olhando para a figura perfeitamente imóvel de Edward. — E quero conversar contigo a esse respeito.

Ai, ai.

— Que tem? — perguntei.

— Acho que aquele rapaz está apaixonado por ti — declarou, em tom de acusação, mantendo a voz baixa.

— Eu também acho — confidenciei.

— E que é que tu sentes em relação a ele? — perguntou, disfarçando bastante mal a imensa curiosidade patente na sua voz.

Suspirei, desviando o olhar. Por mais que gostasse da minha mãe, esta era uma conversa que não queria ter com ela.

— Estou bastante louca por ele.

Pronto. Parecia algo que uma adolescente que namorava pela primeira vez diria.

— Bem, ele *parece* ser muito simpático e, meu Deus, é incrivelmente bem-parecido, mas tu és tão nova, Bella...

A sua voz estava insegura; tanto quanto eu me lembrava, esta era a primeira vez, desde que eu tinha oito anos de idade, que ela tentava falar minimamente como uma autoridade parental. Reconheci o tom de voz razoável, mas firme, de conversas que já tivéramos a respeito de homens.

— Eu sei, mãe. Não te preocupes com isso. É só uma paixoneta — tranquilizei-a.

— É isso mesmo — concordou, dando-se facilmente por satisfeita.

Em seguida, suspirou e olhou por cima do ombro, com um ar de culpa, para o grande relógio redondo que se encontrava na parede.

— Tens de te ir embora?

Ela mordeu o lábio.

— O Phil ficou de telefonar daqui a pouco... Eu não sabia que ias acordar...

— Não há problema, mãe — tentei atenuar o tom de alívio patente na minha voz, de modo a não ferir os seus sentimentos.

— Eu não fico sozinha.

— Eu não demoro. Tenho dormido aqui, sabes — comunicou, orgulhosa de si própria.

— Oh, mãe, não precisas de fazer isso! Podes dormir em casa; eu não darei por isso.

O turbilhão de analgésicos no meu cérebro ainda me dificultava a concentração, embora, aparentemente, eu tivesse dormido durante vários dias.

— Estava demasiado nervosa — confessou com timidez. — Tem-se verificado alguma actividade criminosa na vizinhança e eu não gosto de estar lá sozinha.

— Actividade criminosa? — perguntei, alarmada.

— Alguém forçou a entrada naquele estúdio de dança ao virar da esquina da rua de nossa casa e incendiou-o por completo. Não resta absolutamente nada! E deixaram um carro roubado mesmo em frente. Recordas-te de quando dançavas lá, querida?

— Recordo — senti um arrepio e encolhi-me.

— Se precisares de mim, eu posso ficar, fofinha.

— Não, mãe, eu fico bem. O Edward fica comigo.

A sua expressão deu a entender que poderia ser esse o motivo pelo qual ela queria ficar.

— Eu volto esta noite.

Parecia tanto um aviso como uma promessa e, ao dizê-lo, voltou a olhar de relance para Edward.

— Gosto muito de ti, mãe.

— Eu também gosto muito de ti, Bella. Tenta ter mais cuidado quando andas, querida; não quero perder-te.

Os olhos de Edward permaneceram fechados, mas um largo sorriso rasgou-lhe subitamente o rosto.

Então, uma enfermeira entrou a toda a pressa no quarto para verificar todos os meus tubos e fios. A minha mãe beijou-me a testa, acariciou-me a mão envolta em gaze e foi-se embora.

A enfermeira estava a conferir o registo em papel do meu monitor cardíaco.

— Sentes-te ansiosa, querida? O teu ritmo cardíaco acelerou ali um pouco.

— Eu estou bem — assegurei-lhe.

— Vou informar a tua enfermeira responsável de que já acordaste. Ela virá observar-te dentro de alguns instantes.

Assim que ela fechou a porta, Edward já se encontrava a meu lado.

— Roubaste um carro? — ergui as sobrancelhas.

Ele sorriu, não mostrando sinais de arrependimento.

— Era um bom carro, muito veloz.

— Como foi a sesta? — perguntei.

— Interessante. — Os seus olhos semicerraram-se.

— O que foi?

Ele baixou os olhos ao responder.

— Estou admirado. Pensei que a Florida... e a tua mãe... bem, pensei que seria isso que quererias.

Eu olhei-o fixamente, sem compreender.

— Mas, na Florida, tu ficarias dentro de casa durante todo o dia. Só poderias sair à noite, tal qual um verdadeiro vampiro.

Ele quase sorriu, mas não chegou propriamente a fazê-lo e, depois, o seu rosto ficou grave.

— Eu ficaria em Forks, Bella. Ou em algum sítio semelhante — explicou. — Em algum sítio onde já não pudesse magoar-te.

A princípio, não apreendi o que ele me dizia. Continuei a fitá-lo com um olhar vazio à medida que as palavras, uma a uma, se encaixavam na minha mente como um sinistro quebra-cabeças. Mal me apercebi do som do meu coração a acelerar, mas, quando a minha respiração ficou ofegante, fiquei, de facto, consciente da dor lancinante nas minhas costelas em protesto.

Ele nada disse; observou o meu rosto com ponderação à medida que a dor, que nada tinha a ver com ossos fracturados, uma dor que era infinitamente mais insuportável, ameaçava esmagar-me.

Então, uma outra enfermeira entrou de modo decidido no quarto. Edward ficou imóvel como uma pedra enquanto ela examinou a minha expressão com um olhar experiente antes de se voltar para os monitores.

— Está na hora de te serem administrados mais analgésicos, querida? — perguntou com amabilidade, dando leves pancadinhas na fonte de alimentação do cateter.

— Não, não — balbuciei, tentando não revelar sofrimento na voz. — Não preciso de nada.

Não podia dar-me ao luxo de fechar os olhos nesse momento.

— Não precisas de te armar em corajosa, querida. É melhor que não fiques muito agitada; precisas de repousar.

Ela aguardou, mas eu limitei-me a abanar a cabeça.

— Muito bem — suspirou. — Carrega no botão de chamada quando quiseres.

Lançou a Edward um olhar severo e, antes de sair, voltou a olhar, com ansiedade, na direcção das máquinas.

As mãos frias dele estavam pousadas no meu rosto; eu fitava-o com um olhar intenso.

— Pronto, Bella, acalma-te.

— Não me deixes — implorei com uma voz entrecortada.

— Não deixo — prometeu. — Agora, descansa antes que eu chame a enfermeira para te medicar.

O ritmo do meu coração, porém, não abrandava.

— Bella — acariciou-me o rosto com ansiedade. — Eu não saio daqui. Estarei aqui enquanto precisares de mim.

— Juras que não me deixas? — sussurrei.

Tentei, pelo menos, controlar os arquejos. As minhas costelas latejavam.

Ele colocou uma mão em cada uma das minhas faces e aproximou o seu rosto do meu. Os seus olhos estavam arregalados e sérios.

— Juro.

O cheiro do seu hálito era tranquilizador. Parecia aliviar a dor que eu sentia ao respirar. Continuou com o seu olhar fixo no meu à medida que o meu corpo se descontraía aos poucos e o apito retomava um ritmo normal. Os seus olhos estavam escuros, com uma tonalidade mais próxima do negro do que do dourado neste dia.

— Estás melhor? — perguntou.

— Estou — respondi com cautela.

Ele abanou a cabeça e murmurou algo ininteligível. Pensei ter ouvido a palavra «exagero».

— Porque é que disseste isso? — sussurrei, tentando evitar que a minha voz tremesse. — Estás farto de teres de estar constantemente a salvar-me? *Queres* que eu me vá embora?

— Não, eu não quero ficar sem ti, Bella, é claro que não. Sê racional. E também não tenho qualquer problema em salvar-te; se não fosse pelo facto de ser eu quem te coloca em perigo... de ser eu o motivo pelo qual tu estás aqui.

— Sim, o motivo és tu — franzi o sobrolho. — És tu o motivo pelo qual eu estou aqui, *viva*.

— Por pouco — disse num tom de voz que não passava de um sussurro. — Coberta de gaze e gesso e quase sem conseguires mexer-te.

– Eu não me referia à minha mais recente experiência de morte iminente – disse eu, começando a ficar irritada. – Estava a pensar nas outras; tens muitas à escolha. Se não fosses tu, eu estaria a apodrecer no cemitério de Forks.

Ele estremeceu ao ouvir as minhas palavras, mas o seu olhar não deixou de se mostrar perturbado.

– Mas essa não é a pior parte – continuou a sussurrar. Agia como se eu não me tivesse pronunciado. – O pior não foi o facto de te ver ali no chão... prostrada e ferida – a sua voz estava abafada. – De pensar que chegara tarde de mais. Nem sequer de te ouvir gritar de dor, todas essas recordações que me acompanharão por toda a eternidade. Não, o pior de tudo foi sentir... saber que podia não parar. Acreditar que seria eu próprio a matar-te.

– Mas não mataste.

– Podia tê-lo feito. Com tanta facilidade.

Eu sabia que tinha de permanecer calma... mas ele estava a tentar convencer-se a si próprio a abandonar-me e o pânico agitava-se nos meus pulmões, tentando sair.

– Promete-me – sussurrei.

– O quê?

– Tu bem sabes o quê.

Agora, eu começava a ficar zangada. Ele estava tão obstinadamente decidido a insistir no lado negativo.

Detectou a mudança no meu tom de voz. Os seus olhos cerraram-se.

– Não pareço ser suficientemente forte para me manter afastado de ti, portanto, suponho que conseguirás o que queres... quer isso te leve à morte ou não – acrescentou com rudeza.

– Óptimo.

No entanto, ele não prometera, um facto que não me passara despercebido. Mal conseguia conter o pânico; já não me restavam forças para controlar a raiva.

– Disseste-me como paraste... agora, quero saber porquê – exigi.

– Porquê? – repetiu com cuidado.

— *Por que motivo* o fizeste. Por que é que não deixaste simplesmente que o veneno se alastrasse? Agora, eu seria exactamente como tu.

Os olhos de Edward pareceram ficar muito espantados e eu lembrei-me de que se tratava de algo que ele nunca quisera que eu soubesse. Alice devia ter ficado abstraída com aquilo que descobrira acerca de si própria... ou, então, fora muito cuidadosa em relação aos seus pensamentos quando se encontrava perto dele; era evidente que ele não fazia ideia de que ela me pusera a par da mecânica das conversões vampíricas. Ficou admirado e enfurecido. As narinas dilataram-se-lhe e a sua boca parecia ter sido esculpida em pedra.

Não ia responder e esse facto era claro.

— Eu sou a primeira a admitir que não tenho qualquer experiência no que se refere a relacionamentos amorosos — disse eu —, mas parece simplesmente lógico... que um homem e uma mulher tenham de estar, de certa forma, em pé de igualdade... ou seja, um deles não pode, por exemplo, andar sempre a aparecer para salvar o outro. Têm de se salvar mútua e *igualmente*.

Ele cruzou os braços junto da minha cama e pousou o queixo nos mesmos. A expressão estampada no seu rosto era de serenidade, de raiva controlada. Chegara, evidentemente, à conclusão de que não estava zangado comigo. Eu esperava ter oportunidade para prevenir Alice antes que ele a encontrasse.

— Tu salvaste-me — disse ele com tranquilidade.

— Não posso ser sempre a Lois Lane — insisti. — Também quero ser o Super-Homem.

— Não sabes o que estás a pedir-me.

A sua voz era suave e os seus olhos fixavam atentamente o rebordo da fronha da almofada.

— Creio que sei.

— Bella, *não* sabes. Eu tive quase noventa anos para pensar nisto e ainda não tenho a certeza.

— Gostavas que o Carlisle não te tivesse salvado?

— Não, não gostava. — Deteve-se antes de prosseguir. — Mas

a minha vida chegara ao fim. Não estava a abdicar de nada.

— Tu és a minha vida. És a única coisa que me custaria perder.

Eu estava a apanhar-lhe o jeito. Era fácil admitir o quanto eu precisava dele.

Ele, porém, estava muito calmo. Decidido.

— Não consigo fazê-lo, Bella. Não te farei isso.

— Porque não? — a minha voz arranhava e as palavras não saíram tão sonoras como eu tencionava. — Não me digas que é demasiado difícil! Depois do que aconteceu hoje, ou melhor, suponho que há alguns dias... seja como for, depois disso, não devia ser nada.

Lançou-me um olhar cheio de indignação.

— E a dor? — perguntou com sarcasmo.

Eu empalideci. Foi mais forte do que eu, mas tentei evitar que a minha expressão demonstrasse quão vivamente me lembrava de tal sensação... o ardor nas minhas veias.

— Isso é um problema meu — disse-lhe. — Eu aguento.

— É possível levar a coragem até ao ponto em que se torna insanidade.

— Isso não constitui um problema. Três dias. Grande coisa.

Edward fez um novo esgar quando as minhas palavras o fizeram lembrar de que eu estava mais informada do que ele jamais quisera que eu estivesse. Vi-o conter a fúria e vi os seus olhos ficarem com um ar inquiridor.

— E o Charlie? — perguntou sem muitas palavras. — E a Renée?

Decorreram alguns minutos de silêncio enquanto eu procurava responder à sua pergunta. Abri a boca, mas não proferi qualquer som. Voltei a fechá-la. Ele esperou e a sua expressão tornou-se triunfante, pois sabia que eu não tinha uma resposta concreta a dar.

— Escuta, isso também não constitui qualquer problema — acabei por dizer por entre dentes; a minha voz era tão pouco convincente como sempre que eu mentia. — A Renée sempre fez as opções que mais lhe convinham; ela quereria que eu fizesse o mesmo. E o Charlie é resistente, está habituado a estar sozinho. Não posso cuidar deles eternamente. Tenho a minha própria vida para viver.

— Pois tens — disse ele com brusquidão. — E eu não lhe porei termo.

— Se estás à espera que eu esteja no meu leito de morte, tenho uma novidade para te dar: acabei de lá estar!

— Vais recuperar — relembrou-me.

Respirei fundo para me acalmar, ignorando o espasmo de dor que tal desencadeou. Olhei-o bem nos olhos e ele retribuiu-me o olhar. Não havia uma expressão de cedência no seu rosto.

— Não — disse devagar. — Não vou.

A testa franziu-se-lhe.

— É claro que vais. Podes ficar com uma cicatriz ou duas...

— Estás enganado — insisti. — Eu vou morrer.

— Francamente, Bella! — desabafou, ansioso. — Sairás daqui dentro de alguns dias. Duas semanas, quando muito.

Lancei-lhe um olhar de irritação.

— Posso não morrer agora... mas vou morrer algum dia. A cada minuto que passa, esse momento está mais próximo. E vou *envelhecer.*

Franziu o sobrolho ao apreender aquilo que eu dizia, pressionando os seus longos dedos contra as têmporas e fechando os olhos.

— É assim que tudo se processa. Que tudo deve processar-se. Que se teria processado se eu não existisse — e eu não *devia existir.*

Bufei. Ele abriu os olhos, admirado.

— Isso é uma estupidez. É como abordar alguém que acabou de ganhar a lotaria, tirar-lhe o dinheiro e dizer: «Olhe, vamos deixar que tudo volte a ser como deveria ser. É melhor assim». E eu não aceito isso.

— Não sou propriamente um prémio da lotaria — resmungou.

— Tens razão. És muito melhor.

Ele revirou os olhos e cerrou os lábios.

— Bella, não quero continuar com esta conversa. Recuso-me a condenar-te a uma noite eterna e ponto final.

— Se pensas que ficamos por aqui, não me conheces muito bem — avisei-o. — Não és o único vampiro que eu conheço.

Os seus olhos voltaram a ficar negros.

— A Alice não se atreveria.

Então, por um instante, ele fez um ar tão assustador que não pude senão acreditar nele; não conseguia imaginar alguém tão corajoso que estivesse disposto a enfrentá-lo.

— A Alice já viu que isso vai acontecer, não foi? — conjecturei. — É por isso que tudo o que ela diz te perturba. Ela sabe que eu vou ser como vocês... um dia.

— Ela está enganada. Também viu que tu morrerias, mas isso não aconteceu.

— Nunca *me* verás apostar contra a Alice.

Entreolhámo-nos durante um longo momento. O silêncio imperava, quebrado apenas pelo ruído das máquinas, pelo apito, pelo gotejar, pelo tiquetaque do grande relógio de parede. Por fim, a sua expressão tornou-se menos dura.

— Então, como é que nós ficamos? — indaguei.

Ele soltou um riso abafado, algo forçado.

— Creio que se chama *impasse*.

Suspirei.

— Au! — murmurei por entre dentes.

— Como é que te sentes? — perguntou ele, fixando o botão para chamar a enfermeira.

— Eu estou bem — menti.

— Não acredito em ti — disse ele delicadamente.

— Não vou voltar a adormecer.

— Precisas de repousar. Esta discussão não te faz bem.

— Então, cede — sugeri.

— Boa tentativa. — Estendeu a mão para alcançar o botão.

— Não!

Ele ignorou-me.

— Sim? — ouviu-se gritar no altifalante que se encontrava na parede.

— Acho que estamos preparados para a administração de

mais analgésicos — disse ele com calma, ignorando a minha expressão de fúria.

— Vou chamar a enfermeira! — a voz dele parecia muito aborrecida.

— Eu não os tomo — asseverei.

Olhou para o saco de líquidos suspenso ao lado da minha cama.

— Acho que não vão pedir-te que ingiras nada.

O meu ritmo cardíaco começou a acelerar. Ele detectou medo no meu olhar e suspirou em sinal de frustração.

— Bella, tu estás a sofrer. Precisas de repousar para poderes curar-te. Porque é que estás a ser tão difícil? Eles já não vão espetar-te mais agulhas.

— Eu não tenho medo das agulhas — balbuciei. — Tenho medo de fechar os olhos.

Então, ele esboçou o seu sorriso enviesado e segurou o meu rosto com as mãos.

— Eu já te disse que não saio daqui. Não tenhas medo. Enquanto isso te fizer feliz, estarei aqui.

Eu retribuí-lhe o sorriso, ignorando a dor que sentia nas faces.

— Tens consciência de que te referes à eternidade?

— Oh, tu hás-de superar isso; não passa de uma paixoneta.

Abanei a cabeça, incrédula, o que me fez ficar tonta.

— Fiquei admirada quando a Renée engoliu essa; pensei que tu fosses mais perspicaz.

— É esse o lado belo de se ser humano — disse ele. — As coisas mudam.

Os meus olhos semicerraram-se.

— É melhor esperares sentado.

Ele ria-se quando a enfermeira entrou, brandindo uma seringa.

— Com licença — disse ela a Edward com brusquidão.

Ele levantou-se e atravessou o pequeno quarto, encostando-se à parede, ao fundo. Cruzou os braços e esperou. Eu mantive os olhos pregados nele, estando ainda apreensiva. Ele retribuía-me o olhar calmamente.

— Aqui tens, querida! — a enfermeira sorriu ao injectar o

medicamento no meu tubo. — Agora, sentir-te-ás melhor.

— Obrigada — balbuciei, sem qualquer entusiasmo. O medicamento não demorou muito tempo a actuar. Senti a sonolência a fluir pela minha corrente sanguínea quase de imediato.

— Isso deve bastar — disse ela por entre dentes quando as minhas pestanas começavam a pesar.

Ela deve ter saído do quarto, pois algo suave e frio tocou o meu rosto.

— Fica. — Tal palavra foi proferida de forma pouco clara.

— Eu fico — prometeu ele. A sua voz era bela, tal e qual como uma canção de embalar. — Tal como já disse, enquanto isso te fizer feliz... enquanto for o melhor para ti.

Tentei abanar a cabeça, mas estava demasiado pesada.

— N' é a mesma coisa — balbuciei.

Ele riu-se.

— Não te preocupes com isso agora, Bella. Podes discutir comigo quando acordares.

Creio que sorri.

— 'Tá bem.

Sentia os seus lábios na minha orelha.

— Amo-te — sussurrou.

— Eu também.

— Eu sei — riu-se com serenidade.

Virei a cabeça um pouco... procurando. Ele sabia o que eu pretendia. Os seus lábios tocaram os meus com suavidade.

— Obrigada — suspirei.

— Sempre às ordens.

O meu espírito já não estava, de todo, presente, mas eu debatia-me, ainda que debilmente, contra o torpor. Havia apenas mais uma coisa que eu queria dizer-lhe:

— Edward? — esforcei-me por pronunciar o seu nome com clareza.

— Sim?

— Eu aposto na Alice — balbuciei.

Então, a noite envolveu-me.

Epílogo

UMA OCASIÃO ESPECIAL

Edward ajudou-me a entrar no carro, tendo muito cuidado com os feixes de seda e *chiffon*, com as flores que acabara de prender nos meus caracóis penteados a preceito e com o meu volumoso gesso. Ignorava o trejeito da minha boca que revelava a minha irritação.

Depois de me ter acomodado, entrou para o lugar do condutor e seguiu outra vez pela estrada longa e estreita.

— Até que ponto exactamente vais contar-me o que se passa? — perguntei de modo rabugento. Eu detestava mesmo surpresas. E ele sabia disso.

— Admira-me muito que ainda não tenhas percebido.

Lançou um sorriso trocista na minha direcção, cortando-me a respiração. Será que alguma vez me habituaria à sua perfeição?

— Eu já referi que estás com óptimo aspecto, pois já? — confirmei.

— Já — sorriu de novo. Nunca o vira vestido de preto e, em contraste com a sua pele clara, a sua beleza era absolutamente surreal. Isso eu não podia negar, ainda que o facto de ele envergar um *smoking* me pusesse muito nervosa.

Não me punha, porém, tão nervosa como o vestido ou o sapato. Apenas um sapato, pois o meu outro pé estava ainda solidamente revestido de gesso. O salto de agulha, porém, preso apenas por fitas de cetim, não iria, com certeza, ajudar-me enquanto tentava andar de um lado para o outro, coxeando.

— Eu vou deixar de ir a tua casa se a Alice e a Esme me tratarem como a Barbie Porquinho-da-Índia sempre que eu lá for — reclamei. Nada de bom poderia advir dos nossos trajes formais e disso eu tinha a certeza. A não ser que... mas eu receava verbalizar as minhas suspeitas, mesmo na minha cabeça.

Fui, então, distraída pelo som de um telefone a tocar. Edward retirou o telemóvel de um bolso do interior do casaco, olhando por breves instantes para a identificação de quem estava a telefonar antes de atender.

— Olá, Charlie — disse com cautela.

— Charlie? — entrei em pânico.

Eu sofrera algumas sequelas da provação por que passara havia já mais de dois meses, uma das quais era o facto de eu ser, agora, hipersensível quanto às pessoas de quem gostava. O meu papel e o de Renée tinham-se invertido, pelo menos, no que se referia à comunicação; se ela não desse notícias diárias através de correio electrónico, eu não descansava enquanto não lhe telefonasse. Eu sabia que tal era desnecessário; ela era muito feliz em Jacksonville.

E, todos os dias, quando Charlie saía para o trabalho, eu despedia-me com muito mais ansiedade do que o necessário.

A cautela patente na voz de Edward tinha outra origem. Charlie mostrara-se... difícil desde o meu regresso a Forks. Ele compartimentara a minha má experiência em duas reacções bem definidas. Em relação a Carlisle, estava quase veneradoramente grato. Por outro lado, estava obstinadamente convencido de que Edward estava em falta — pois, se não fosse por ele, eu não teria, para começar, saído de casa — e este último estava longe de discordar dele. Nos dias de hoje, eu tinha regras que não existiam antes: horas para recolher... e para receber visitas.

Edward olhava, agora, para mim, detectando preocupação na minha voz. O seu semblante estava calmo, o que atenuou a minha súbita e irracional ansiedade. Os seus olhos, porém, estavam afectados por um sofrimento peculiar. Ele compreendia a minha reacção e considerava-se responsável por todas as alterações que se tinham processado em mim.

Algo que Charlie estava a dizer distraiu Edward destes pensamentos sombrios. Os seus olhos arregalaram-se de incredulidade, o que provocou em mim outro tremular de medo, até que um largo sorriso lhe iluminou o rosto.

— Está a brincar! — riu-se.

— O que foi? — perguntei, agora curiosa.

Ele ignorou-me.

— E se me deixasse falar com ele? — sugeriu Edward com uma satisfação evidente. Aguardou alguns segundos. — Olá, Tyler; fala o Edward Cullen.

A sua voz era amável, à primeira vista. Eu sabia muito bem detectar o brando laivo de ameaça. O que fazia Tyler em minha casa? A terrível verdade começou a tornar-se compreensível para mim. Olhei para o elegante vestido azul-escuro que Alice me obrigara a vestir.

— Lamento que tenha havido algum tipo de falha de comunicação, mas a Bella não está disponível esta noite — a voz de Edward alterou-se e o tom de ameaça nela patente tornou-se, num instante, muito mais evidente à medida que ele prosseguia. — Para ser completamente sincero, ela não estará disponível para ninguém, excepto para mim, durante toda a noite. Sem ofensa. E lamento quanto à tua noite.

Edward não parecia lamentar minimamente. Em seguida, desligou o telefone, com um enorme sorriso afectado no rosto.

O meu rosto e o meu pescoço enrubesceram de cólera. Sentia as lágrimas provocadas pela raiva a começarem a inundar-me os olhos.

Ele olhou-me, surpreendido.

— Achas que a última parte foi um pouco excessiva? Não tencionava ofender-te.

Eu ignorei as suas palavras.

— Vais levar-me ao *baile de finalistas*! — gritei, furiosa.

Era, agora, embaraçosamente óbvio. Se tivesse estado com um pouco de atenção, tenho a certeza de que teria reparado na data afixada nos cartazes que enfeitavam os edifícios da escola. No entanto, nunca me passara pela cabeça que ele estava a pensar em sujeitar-me a tal coisa. Será que não me conhecia minimamente?

Ele não esperava uma reacção tão intensa da minha parte e isso era claro. Apertou os lábios e os olhos semicerraram-se-lhe.

— Não sejas difícil, Bella.

Olhei bruscamente pelo vidro; já estávamos a meio do caminho para a escola.

— Porque é que estás a fazer-me isto? — perguntei, horrorizada.

— Sinceramente, Bella, o que é que pensavas que íamos fazer? — apontou para o seu *smoking*.

Fiquei estarrecida. Em primeiro lugar, porque não constatara o óbvio, mas também pelo facto de as minhas vagas suspeitas — esperanças, na verdade — que eu formulara durante todo o dia, enquanto Alice e Esme tentavam transformar-me num modelo de beleza, estarem tão longe da verdade. As minhas esperanças algo receosas pareciam agora despropositadas de todo.

Eu calculara que se avizinhava algum tipo de ocasião especial. Mas o *baile de finalistas!* Era a última coisa que me passaria pela cabeça.

As lágrimas de raiva escorriam-me pelas faces. Lembrei-me com consternação de que, atipicamente, usava rímel. Apressei-me a limpar a zona debaixo dos olhos para evitar ficar esborratada. A minha mão estava imaculada quando a afastei; talvez Alice soubesse que eu precisaria de maquilhagem à prova de água.

— Isto é completamente ridículo. Porque é que estás a chorar? — interrogou, frustrado.

— Porque estou *furiosa*!

— Bella. — Ele fez incidir toda a intensidade do seu olhar ardente sobre mim.

— O que foi? — murmurei por entre dentes, imediatamente abstraída.

— Faz-me a vontade — insistiu.

Os seus olhos estavam a abrandar toda a minha fúria. Era impossível discutir com ele quando fazia batota desta forma. Eu rendi-me de má vontade.

— Tudo bem — amuei, incapaz de o olhar com um ar tão irritado quanto desejava. — Irei sem oferecer resistência. Mas tu vais ver — adverti —, há já muito tempo que o azar não me bate à porta. Provavelmente, ainda hei-de partir a outra perna. Olha bem para este sapato! É uma armadilha mortal! — estendi a perna sã para corroborar as minhas afirmações.

— Hummm! — fixou o olhar na minha perna durante mais tempo do que o necessário. — Lembra-me de agradecer isso à Alice esta noite.

— A Alice vai lá estar?

Esse facto consolou-me um pouco.

— Com o Jasper, o Emmett... e a Rosalie — confessou.

A sensação de consolo desvaneceu-se. Não houvera progressos quanto a Rosalie, ainda que eu estivesse de bastante boas relações com o seu marido ocasional. Emmett achava-me divertidíssima. Rosalie agia como se eu não existisse. Enquanto abanava a cabeça para afastar os meus pensamentos do rumo que tinham tomado, cogitei outra possibilidade.

— O Charlie está metido nisto? — perguntei, subitamente desconfiada.

— É evidente — sorriu e, depois, soltou um riso abafado. — Mas, pelos vistos, o Tyler não estava.

Rangi os dentes. A forma como Tyler conseguia ser tão alheado da realidade transcendia-me. Na escola, onde Charlie não podia intrometer-se, eu e Edward éramos inseparáveis — exceptuando aqueles raros dias de Sol.

Já nos encontrávamos na escola; o descapotável vermelho de Rosalie destacava-se no parque de estacionamento. Neste dia, as nuvens eram ténues, com alguns raios de Sol a escaparem por entre elas ao longe, a Ocidente.

Ele saiu e contornou o carro para me abrir a porta. Estendeu a mão.

Permaneci teimosamente sentada no meu lugar, com os braços cruzados. Senti uma secreta pontinha de regozijo; o parque de estacionamento estava repleto de pessoas em trajes formais: testemunhas. Ele não podia tirar-me do carro à força como poderia fazer se estivéssemos sozinhos.

Suspirou.

– Quando alguém quer matar-te, tens a coragem de um leão. Já quando alguém fala em dançar... – abanou a cabeça.

Engasguei-me. Dançar.

– Bella, não deixarei que nada te magoe; nem mesmo tu própria. Não me afastarei de ti um único instante, prometo.

Pensei nas suas palavras e, de repente, senti-me muito melhor. Ele viu isso no meu rosto.

– Pronto, vá – disse com brandura –, não será assim tão mau.

Curvou-se e envolveu-me a cintura com um dos seus braços. Peguei-lhe na outra mão e deixei-o tirar-me do carro.

Manteve o braço a envolver-me com firmeza, apoiando-me enquanto eu coxeava em direcção à escola.

Em Phoenix, os bailes de finalistas realizavam-se nos salões de baile dos hotéis. Este baile iria, é evidente, decorrer no ginásio. Era provavelmente a única sala da cidade com dimensões suficientes para acolher um baile. Quando entrámos, soltei uns risinhos. Havia mesmo arcos formados por balões e grinaldas retorcidas de papel crepe pastel a enfeitar as paredes.

– Isto parece um filme de terror prestes a acontecer – disse, reprimindo o riso.

– Bem – murmurou ele por entre dentes à medida que nos aproximávamos da mesa dos bilhetes; suportava quase todo o meu peso, mas eu tinha ainda de arrastar e balançar os pés para a frente – estão presentes vampiros em número *mais* do que suficiente.

Olhei para a pista de dança; formara-se um grande hiato no centro da pista, onde dois casais rodopiavam com graciosidade. Os restantes dançarinos comprimiam-se nos extremos da sala, de modo a darem-lhes espaço – ninguém queria contrastar com tamanho esplendor. Emmett e Jasper estavam intimidantes e impecáveis nos seus *smokings* clássicos. Alice notabilizava-se no seu vestido de cetim negro com recortes geométricos que expunham grandes triângulos da sua pele branca como neve. Rosalie, por seu turno, estava... bem, igual a si própria. Estava incrível.

O seu vestido vermelho-vivo deixava-lhe as costas destapadas e ficava-lhe justo até à barriga das pernas, a partir de onde alargava para formar uma cauda franzida, e caracterizava-se por um decote que se prolongava até à cintura. Senti pena de todas as raparigas que se encontravam na sala, inclusivamente de mim própria.

— Queres que eu tranque as portas para que vocês possam chacinar a incauta cidade? — sussurrei num tom de conspiração.

— E onde é que tu te encaixas nesse esquema? — perguntou, lançando-me um olhar irritado.

— Oh, eu estou do lado dos vampiros, como é evidente.

Ele sorriu com relutância.

— Tudo para te esquivares a dançar.

— Tudo.

Comprou os nossos bilhetes e, em seguida, virou-me na direcção da pista de dança. Encolhi-me contra o seu braço e arrastei os pés.

— Tenho a noite toda — avisou.

Acabou por me puxar até ao local onde a sua família revoluteava com elegância — ainda que de uma forma completamente desajustada à época e à música actuais. Eu assistia, horrorizada.

— Edward — a minha garganta estava tão seca que só consegui sussurrar. — Eu, *sinceramente*, não sei dançar!

Sentia o pânico a borbulhar.

— Não te preocupes, tonta — retorquiu ele, também a sussurrar. — Eu sei.

Pôs os meus braços à volta do seu pescoço e elevou-me para colocar os pés debaixo dos meus.

De repente, também nós estávamos a rodopiar.

— Sinto-me como se tivesse cinco anos — ri-me depois de alguns minutos a dançar a valsa sem me esforçar minimamente.

— Não pareces ter cinco anos — murmurou ele, puxando-me para si por um instante, o que fez com que os meus pés ficassem, por breves momentos, a trinta centímetros do chão.

O olhar de Alice cruzou-se com o meu quando estávamos a

dar uma volta e sorriu, incentivando-me; eu retribuí-lhe o sorriso. Fiquei espantada por constatar que estava, de facto, a divertir-me... um pouco.

— Pronto, está bem, isto até nem é mau de todo — reconheci.

Edward, todavia, fixava o olhar na direcção das portas e o seu rosto estava zangado.

— O que foi? — perguntei-me em voz alta.

O meu olhar seguiu o seu, estando eu desorientada com o rodopiar mas, por fim, vi o que o incomodava. Jacob Black, não de *smoking*, mas com uma camisa branca de mangas compridas e de gravata, com o cabelo puxado para trás e apanhado no seu habitual rabo-de-cavalo, estava a atravessar a pista na nossa direcção.

Após o choque inicial do reconhecimento, não consegui senão sentir pena de Jacob. Ele estava nitidamente pouco à vontade — avassaladoramente pouco à vontade. Quando os seus olhos se cruzaram com os meus, o seu rosto parecia pedir desculpa.

Edward rosnou muito discretamente.

— *Comporta-te*! — sibilei.

A sua voz era cáustica:

— Ele quer conversar contigo.

Então, Jacob chegou junto de nós, sendo o constrangimento e o ar de quem pede desculpa ainda mais evidentes no seu rosto.

— Viva, Bella, tinha esperança de que estivesses aqui.

O modo como Jacob falava levava a crer que ele tinha esperança de que acontecesse exactamente o contrário, mas o seu sorriso era tão caloroso como sempre.

— Olá, Jacob — retribuí-lhe o sorriso. — Novidades?

— Posso interromper-vos? — perguntou com hesitação, olhando para Edward pela primeira vez. Fiquei surpreendida ao reparar que Jacob não tinha de levantar o olhar. Devia ter crescido cerca de quinze centímetros desde a última vez que o tinha visto.

O rosto de Edward estava calmo, com uma expressão vazia. A sua única reacção foi pousar-me cuidadosamente no chão e recuar um passo.

— Obrigado! — disse Jacob amavelmente.

Edward limitou-se a acenar com a cabeça, lançando-me um olhar expressivo antes de se afastar.

Jacob colocou as mãos na minha cintura e eu estiquei os braços para pousar as mãos nos seus ombros.

— Ena, Jacob, quanto é que medes?

Ele ficou todo cheio de si.

— Um metro e oitenta e nove centímetros.

Não estávamos a dançar de verdade, pois a minha perna impossibilitava tal tarefa. Em vez disso, balançávamo-nos desajeitadamente de um lado para o outro sem mexermos os pés. Era melhor assim; o recente salto que ele dera em termos de altura deixara-o com um aspecto esgalgado e descoordenado e, provavelmente, não era melhor dançarino do que eu.

— Então, como é que vieste aqui parar esta noite? — perguntei sem genuína curiosidade. Tendo em consideração a reacção de Edward, fazia uma ideia.

— Acreditas que o meu pai me pagou vinte dólares para vir ao teu baile de finalistas? — confessou, um tanto envergonhado.

— Sim, acredito — murmurei por entre dentes. — Bem, espero que, pelo menos, estejas a divertir-te. Viste algo que te agrade? — gracejei, olhando na direcção de um grupo de raparigas perfiladas junto da parede como compotas pastel.

— Vi — admitiu. — Mas já tem par.

Ele baixou o olhar, cruzando-se este com o meu, que se mostrava curioso, apenas por um instante; em seguida, ambos desviámos o olhar, constrangidos.

— A propósito, estás muito bonita — acrescentou, um pouco tímido.

— Hum, obrigada. Então, porque é que o Billy te pagou para vires aqui? — perguntei, embora soubesse a resposta.

Jacob não pareceu ficar grato pela mudança de assunto; desviou o olhar, estando mais uma vez pouco à vontade.

— Disse que era um lugar «seguro» para falar contigo. Juro que o velho está a perder o juízo.

Ele riu-se e eu acompanhei-o debilmente...

— Seja como for, ele afirmou que, se eu te dissesse algo, me arranjaria aquele cilindro principal de que necessito — confessou com um sorriso acanhado.

— Então, diz-me. Quero que termines o teu carro.

Retribuí-lhe o sorriso. Pelo menos, Jacob não acreditava em nada daquilo, o que facilitava um pouco a situação. Encostado à parede, Edward observava o meu rosto, estando o seu inexpressivo. Vi uma aluna do décimo ano, que envergava um vestido cor-de-rosa, a fitá-lo com tímida especulação, mas ele parecia alheio à presença dela.

Jacob desviou de novo o olhar, envergonhado.

— Não te zangues, está bem?

— Eu não me zangarei contigo de modo nenhum, Jacob — assegurei-lhe. — Nem sequer me zangarei com o Billy. Diz apenas aquilo que tens a dizer.

— Bem... Isto é uma tolice pegada; desculpa, Bella. Ele quer que termines tudo com o teu namorado. Disse-me para te pedir «por favor».

Abanou a cabeça em sinal de descontentamento.

— Ele continua a ser supersticioso, não é?

— É... Ficou algo escandalizado quando te magoaste em Phoenix. Não acreditava... — Jacob deixou a frase inacabada, constrangido.

Os meus olhos semicerraram-se.

— Eu caí.

— Bem sei — apressou-se Jacob a dizer.

— Ele pensa que o Edward teve algo a ver com o facto de eu me ter magoado.

Não se tratava de uma pergunta e, apesar da minha promessa, eu estava zangada.

Jacob evitava olhar-me nos olhos. Já nem sequer nos preocupávamos em balançar ao ritmo da música, apesar de as mãos dele ainda me segurarem pela cintura e as minhas lhe envolverem o pescoço.

— Olha, Jacob, eu sei que o Billy provavelmente não acreditará nisto, mas, só para que saibas — agora, ele olhava-me, reagindo à inaudita honestidade patente na minha voz —, o Edward salvou-me, de facto, a vida. Se não fosse o Edward e o pai dele, eu estaria morta.

— Eu sei — declarou, mas parecia que as minhas palavras sinceras o tinham afectado bastante. Talvez conseguisse, pelo menos, convencer Billy daquele facto.

— Ei, lamento que tenhas tido de chegar a isto, Jacob — desculpei-me. — De qualquer maneira, obterás as tuas peças, certo?

— Sim — murmurou por entre dentes. Parecia ainda pouco à vontade... perturbado.

— Há mais? — perguntei, incrédula.

— Esquece — balbuciou —, eu arranjo um emprego e guardo o dinheiro para mim.

Eu fitei-o com um ar irritado até o seu olhar se cruzar com o meu.

— Desembucha lá, Jacob.

— É tão mau.

— Não me importo. Diz-me — insisti.

— Está bem... mas, credo, isto soa mesmo mal — disse, abanando a cabeça. — Ele pediu-me para te dizer, não, para te *avisar* de que (e o plural foi empregue por ele, não por mim) — afastou uma das mãos da minha cintura, levantou-a e desenhou pequenas aspas no ar — «estaremos atentos». — Ficou cautelosamente à espera da minha reacção, fitando-me.

Parecia algo retirado de um filme de máfia. Ri-me.

— Lamento que tenhas tido de fazer isto, Jake — ri-me de um modo algo reprimido.

— Não me importo assim tanto — esboçou um largo sorriso de alívio. Os seus olhos examinavam-me ao percorrerem rapidamente o meu vestido. — Então, digo-lhe que não meta o nariz onde não é chamado? — perguntou com confiança.

— Não — suspirei. — Diz-lhe que eu lhe agradeci. Sei que as suas intenções são boas.

A música terminou e eu baixei os braços.

As mãos dele hesitaram na minha cintura e olhou para a minha perna lesionada.

— Queres dançar outra vez? Ou posso ajudar-te a ir a algum sítio?

Edward respondeu por mim:

— Não é necessário, Jacob. A partir de agora, é comigo.

Jacob estremeceu e fitou Edward, que se encontrava mesmo ao nosso lado, com os olhos arregalados.

— Ei, não vi que estavas aí — balbuciou. — Suponho que nos vemos por aí, Bella.

Recuou, acenando com pouco entusiasmo.

Eu sorri.

— Sim, vemo-nos depois.

— Desculpa — disse novamente, antes de se voltar para a porta.

Os braços de Edward envolveram-me quando a música seguinte começou a tocar. Esta tinha um ritmo um pouco acelerado para ser romanticamente dançada a dois, mas esse facto não parecia preocupá-lo. Encostei a cabeça ao peito dele, contente.

— Já te sentes melhor? — gracejei.

— Nem por isso — respondeu de modo conciso.

— Não fiques zangado com o Billy — suspirei. — Ele só se preocupa comigo por atenção ao Charlie. Não é nada pessoal.

— Não estou zangado com o Billy — corrigiu com uma voz entrecortada. — Mas o filho dele está a irritar-me.

Recuei para olhar para ele. O seu semblante estava muito sério.

— Porquê?

— Antes de mais, porque me obrigou a quebrar a minha promessa.

Eu fitei-o, confusa.

Ele esboçou um ligeiro sorriso.

— Prometi que não me afastaria de ti esta noite — explicou.

— Ah. Bem, eu perdoo-te.

— Obrigado, mas há algo mais — Edward franziu o sobrolho.

Esperei pacientemente.

— Ele disse que estavas *bonita* — acabou por prosseguir, com o seu sobrolho a ficar ainda mais carregado. — Isso é praticamente um insulto, tendo em conta a tua aparência neste momento. Estás muito mais do que linda.

Eu ri-me.

— A tua análise poderá ser um pouco tendenciosa.

— Não me parece que seja isso. Além disso, tenho uma visão excelente.

Estávamos novamente a rodopiar, com os meus pés em cima dos dele enquanto ele me apertava contra si.

— Então, vais explicar o que motivou tudo isto? — perguntei. Ele olhou-me, confuso, e eu lancei um olhar expressivo na direcção do papel de crepe.

Ele reflectiu por um momento e, depois, mudou de direcção, fazendo-me girar por entre a multidão até à porta das traseiras do ginásio. Vi de relance Jessica e Mike a dançarem, fixando-me com curiosidade. Jessica acenou e eu sorri-lhe por breves instantes. Também Angela estava presente, parecendo muito feliz nos braços do pequeno Ben Cheney; não desviava os olhos dos dele, que ficavam à distância de uma cabeça abaixo dos dela. Lee e Samantha, Lauren, que nos lançava um olhar irado, com Conner; sabia o nome de cada rosto que passava por mim, deslocando-se em espiral. De repente, estávamos ao ar livre, sob a luz fria e esbatida de um pôr do Sol moribundo.

Assim que ficámos sozinhos, ele pegou em mim e, comigo ao colo, atravessou o recinto escuro até chegar ao banco que ficava à sombra dos medronheiros. Aí se sentou, mantendo-me aninhada contra o peito. A Lua estava quase ao alto, visível através das nuvens diáfanas e o rosto dele resplandecia, pálido, sob a luz branca. A sua boca estava dura e os seus olhos perturbados.

— O objectivo? — dei-lhe a deixa.

Ele ignorou-me, olhando fixamente para a Lua.

— O crepúsculo outra vez — sussurrou. — Mais um final. Por mais perfeito que o dia seja, tem sempre de acabar.

— Nem tudo tem de acabar — murmurei por entre dentes, imediatamente tensa.

Ele suspirou.

— Trouxe-te ao baile — disse ele devagar, respondendo, por fim, à minha pergunta — porque não quero que percas nada. Não quero que a minha presença te prive de nada, se eu puder evitá-lo. Quero que sejas *humana*. Quero que a tua vida continue como teria continuado se eu tivesse morrido em mil novecentos e dezoito, como devia ter acontecido.

Estremeci ao ouvir as suas palavras e, depois, abanei a cabeça, furiosa.

— Em que estranha dimensão paralela é que eu teria, *alguma vez*, ido ao baile de finalistas de livre vontade? Se tu não fosses mil vezes mais forte do que eu, eu nunca te teria deixado levar isto avante impunemente.

Ele sorriu por breves instantes, mas tal sorriso não lhe afectou o olhar.

— Não foi assim tão mau; tu própria o disseste.

— Porque eu estava contigo.

Ficámos calados por um momento; ele olhava fixamente para a Lua e eu para ele. Gostaria que houvesse uma forma de explicar o quão desinteressada eu estava numa vida humana normal.

— Dizes-me uma coisa? — perguntou ele, olhando-me com um ligeiro sorriso nos lábios.

— Não digo sempre?

— Promete-me apenas que me dirás — insistiu, esboçando um sorriso rasgado.

Eu soube que iria arrepender-me disto quase de seguida.

— Está bem.

— Pareceste sinceramente surpreendida quando deduziste que eu ia trazer-te aqui — principiou.

— E *fiquei*! — exclamei.

— Precisamente — concordou. — Mas deves ter tido alguma outra teoria... Estou curioso; porque é que *julgavas* que eu estava a fazer com que te aperaltasses?

Sim, arrependimento imediato. Franzi os lábios, hesitando.

— Não quero dizer-te.

— Prometeste — protestou ele.

— Eu sei.

— Qual é o problema?

Eu sabia que ele pensava que era o mero constrangimento que me inibia.

— Acho que vai enfurecer-te; ou entristecer-te.

As sobrancelhas uniram-se-lhe sobre os olhos enquanto ele ponderava sobre as minhas palavras.

— Continuo a querer saber. Por favor?

Suspirei. Ele ficou à espera.

— Bem... Parti do princípio de que era de algum tipo de... ocasião especial. Mas não me ocorreu que se tratasse de algum banal evento humano... o baile de finalistas! — escarneci.

— Humano? — perguntou num tom monocórdico. Destacou a palavra-chave.

Olhei para o meu vestido, mexendo com inquietação numa tira desgarrada de *chiffon*. Ele esperou em silêncio.

— Pronto — confessei num ímpeto. — Eu estava com esperança de que tivesses mudado de ideias... de que, afinal, fosses transformar-*me*.

Uma dúzia de emoções revelaram-se no seu rosto. Eu reconheci algumas delas: raiva... sofrimento... Depois, porém, ele pareceu recompor-se e a sua expressão tornou-se divertida.

— Pensaste que isso seria motivo para fato de cerimónia, foi? — gracejou, tocando na lapela do casaco do seu *smoking*.

Lancei-lhe um olhar irritado para disfarçar o meu constrangimento.

— Não sei como é que estas coisas funcionam. A mim, pelo menos, afigura-se como sendo mais racional do que o baile de finalistas. — Ele continuava a esboçar um largo sorriso irónico. — Não tem graça — disse eu.

— Pois não, tens razão, não tem graça — concordou, com o seu sorriso a apagar-se. — Mas eu prefiro encarar isso como uma piada a acreditar que estás a falar a sério.

— Mas eu estou a falar a sério.

Ele suspirou profundamente.

— Eu sei. E estás mesmo assim tão desejosa?

O sofrimento voltara ao seu olhar. Mordi o lábio e acenei com a cabeça.

— Estás tão pronta para que chegue o fim — murmurou, quase para si mesmo — pois isso será o crepúsculo da tua vida, ainda que esta mal tenha começado. Estás pronta a abdicar de tudo.

— Não é o fim, é o princípio — discordei em voz baixa.

— Eu não mereço isso — disse ele, tristemente.

— Lembras-te de me teres dito que eu não tinha uma imagem muito clara de mim mesma? — perguntei, erguendo as sobrancelhas. — É evidente que sofres da mesma cegueira.

— Eu sei o que sou.

Suspirei.

No entanto, o seu inconstante estado de espírito alterou-se diante de mim. Ele franziu os lábios e os seus olhos estavam inquiridores. Examinou o meu rosto durante um longo momento.

— Então, sentes-te preparada neste instante? — perguntou.

— Hum — engasguei-me. — Sim?

Ele sorriu e inclinou lentamente a cabeça até os seus lábios frios roçarem a minha pele, mesmo abaixo da curva do meu maxilar.

— Neste preciso instante? — sussurrou, com a sua fresca respiração a incidir no meu pescoço. Arrepiei-me involuntariamente.

— Sim — sussurrei, de modo a não dar azo a que a minha voz se embargasse.

Se ele pensava que, da minha parte, tudo não passava de uma fanfarronada, iria sofrer uma desilusão. Eu já tomara tal decisão e tinha a certeza de que era a mais acertada. Não importava que o corpo estivesse rígido como uma tábua, que os meus punhos estivessem cerrados, que a minha respiração estivesse irregular...

Soltou um riso abafado e misterioso, afastando-se em seguida. O seu semblante parecia, de facto, desiludido.

— Não podes realmente acreditar que eu cederia tão facilmente — disse ele, com um laivo de amargura no seu tom de voz trocista.

— Uma rapariga pode sonhar.

As suas sobrancelhas ergueram-se.

— É isso que sonhas? Ser um monstro?

— Não propriamente — respondi, franzindo o sobrolho perante a sua escolha de palavras. Monstro, pois sim. — Sonho sobretudo ficar contigo para sempre.

A sua expressão mudou, enternecida e entristecida pela dor subtil patente na minha voz.

— Bella. — Os seus dedos percorreram ao de leve o contorno dos meus lábios. — Eu ficarei contigo; isso não basta?

Sorri sob as pontas dos seus dedos.

— Por enquanto, basta.

Ele franziu o sobrolho perante a minha tenacidade. Nesta noite, ninguém iria render-se. Ele expirou, o que soou praticamente como um rugido.

Eu toquei-lhe o rosto.

— Escuta — disse eu. — Eu amo-te mais do que tudo o resto no mundo junto. Isso não basta?

— Sim, basta — respondeu, sorrindo. — Basta para toda a eternidade.

Então, inclinou-se para encostar, uma vez mais, os seus lábios frios ao meu pescoço.